나혼자 끝내는 新 토익

FINAL 실전 모의고사

LC+RC

문제집 + 해설집

5회

나혼자 끝내는 新토익
FINAL 실전 모의고사 LC+RC

지은이 제이드 김 · 김선희
펴낸이 임상진
펴낸곳 (주)넥서스

초판 1쇄 발행 2018년 5월 30일
초판 4쇄 발행 2022년 7월 15일

출판신고 1992년 4월 3일 제311-2002-2호
10880 경기도 파주시 지목로 5
Tel (02)330-5500 Fax (02)330-5555

ISBN 979-11-6165-320-4 13740

가격은 뒤표지에 있습니다.
잘못 만들어진 책은 구입처에서 바꾸어 드립니다.

www.nexusbook.com

나혼자 끝내는 新 토익

FINAL 실전 모의고사

제이드 김 · 김선희 지음

LC+RC

문제집 + 해설집

5회

넥서스

PREFACE

토익은 누구나 목표 점수를 받을 수 있는 시험이지만, 아무나 단기간에 원하는 점수를 만들 수 있는 시험은 아닙니다. 토익 시험은 전문가가 제시하는 전략과 수험생의 확실한 의지가 만났을 때 가장 빠르게 목표 점수를 달성할 수 있습니다. 현장에서 강의를 해 오면서 수강생들의 오답 유형을 취합, 분석하였으며, 그 결과 고득점 달성의 발목을 잡는 유형의 문제들을 엄선할 수 있었습니다.

이 교재는 그중에서도 단기간에 고득점 진입을 위해 꼭 필요한 문제 유형들로 구성하였으며, 대화가 길어지고 선택지에 함정이 많아 더욱 어려워진 최근 토익 시험의 출제 경향을 반영하는 데 중점을 두고 기획하였습니다. 또한 가능한 한 실제 시험과 같은 난이도, 같은 구조를 가진 지문과 문제들을 제공함으로써 최적의 실전 연습을 할 수 있도록 구성하였습니다. 토익 고득점은 여러분의 최종 목표가 아니라 각자의 목표 달성을 위한 필요조건일 뿐입니다. 이 책을 통해 수험생들의 단기 목표 달성이 이루어지기를 응원합니다.

감사함을 전하고 싶은 이 순간에도 고마운 마음이 새로이 솟아오르는 가족에게 감사 드립니다.

저자 제이드 김

2016년 5월 신토익이 처음 시행된 이후 토익커들의 고민이 더욱 깊어진 것 같습니다. 신토익 RC에 등장하는 PART 6의 문장 삽입 문제 유형이나 PART 7의 삼중지문 등은 토익 시험이 요령과 요행에 기반을 둔 학습이 아니라 조금 더 깊이 있는 실력을 갖춰야만 원하는 점수를 얻을 수 있는 시험으로 바뀐 것을 보여 주는 좋은 예입니다.

토익을 준비하는 학습 방법은 일반 영어 공부를 하는 방법과 다를 수밖에 없습니다. 객관적인 수치의 점수가 곧 결과로 나오는 시험 과목이기 때문입니다. 원하는 점수를 얻기 위해 무엇보다 가장 중요한 것은 토익 시험의 최신 경향과 문제 유형을 파악하는 것입니다. 이 교재에서는 이 부분을 잘 반영하기 위해 많은 노력을 기울였습니다. 시험과 가장 유사한 수준의 난이도와 문제 유형으로 토익을 준비하시는 분들에게 큰 도움이 될 것이라고 확신합니다.

끝으로 늘 큰 딸을 응원해 주시고 믿어 주시는 부모님께 항상 사랑하고 존경한다고 전하고 싶습니다.

저자 김선희

CONTENTS

FEATURES

신토익을 완벽 반영한

실전 모의고사 5회

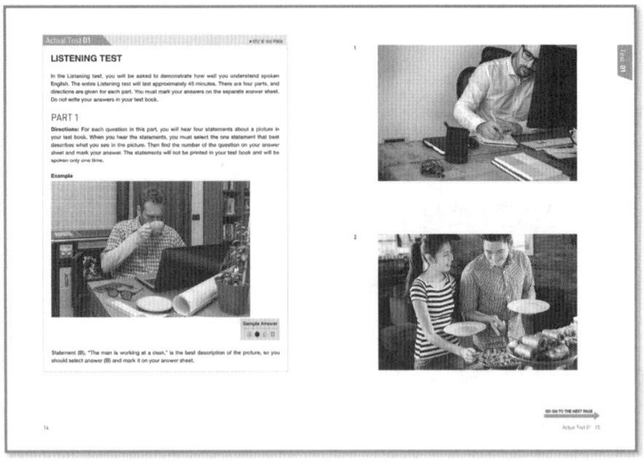

신토익 최신 출제 경향을 반영한 모의고사로 실전을 완벽 대비할 수 있습니다. LC와 RC를 한 권으로 구성한 실전 5회분으로 정기 토익 시험을 대비해서 실제 시험 환경과 같이 최종 마무리를 할 수 있습니다.

저자의 노하우가 담긴 쉽고 자세한

정답 및 해설

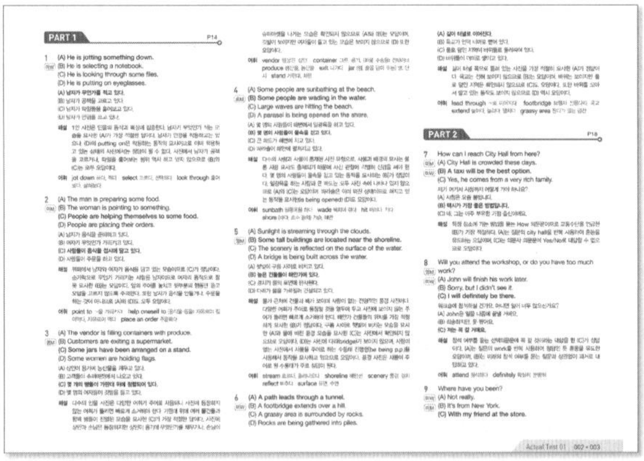

따로 구매할 필요 없이 해설집을 한 권에 담아 정답 및 해설을 확인하며 복습할 수 있습니다. 정답 및 오답의 이유, 패러프레이징을 수록하였고, 정답 키워드가 되는 부분을 표시하여 쉽게 정답을 찾고 이해할 수 있도록 구성하였습니다.

혼자서도 토익을 끝낼 수 있는 **막강 부가자료**

(1) **실전용 · 복습용 · 고사장 버전** & **영국 · 호주식 발음** MP3
실전용, 복습용 MP3 외에 실제 고사장 소음이 들어간 버전까지 제공하므로 실제 시험 환경과 가장 유사하게 대비할 수 있습니다. 추가적으로 영국, 호주식 발음을 완벽하게 대비하기 위한 PART 4 녹음 버전을 제공합니다.

(2) **모바일 단어장**
본 도서에 수록된 어휘 중에서 중요한 어휘를 언제 어디서든 복습할 수 있도록 모바일 단어장을 제공합니다.

(3) **온라인 받아쓰기**
Listening 받아쓰기 프로그램을 통해 청취력뿐만 아니라 영어 실력을 향상시킬 수 있습니다.

(4) **어휘 리스트 & 테스트**
본문에 수록된 어휘 중에서도 특히 중요한 빈출 어휘 리스트와 이를 학습할 수 있는 온라인 테스트지를 제공합니다.
www.nexusbook.com

MP3 바로 듣기
정답 자동 채점
모바일 단어장
받아쓰기 테스트

혼공족들을 위한 막강 부가자료
www.nexusbook.com

3가지 버전 MP3 | 영국·호주식 발음 MP3 | 모바일 단어장 | 온라인 받아쓰기 | 어휘 리스트 & 테스트

쉽고 빠른 MP3 이용법 **콜롬북스 APP**

(1) 구글 플레이, 앱스토어에서 "콜롬북스" 어플 설치
(아래 QR코드 이용 또는 "콜롬북스"라고 검색해서 설치 가능)

(2) 넥서스 또는 도서명으로 검색

(3) 실전용, 복습용, 고사장 버전의 3종 MP3 다운로드

신토익 핵심 정보

2016년 5월 29일 정기시험부터 현재의 영어 사용 환경을 반영한 신(新)토익이 시행되었습니다. 전체 문항 수와 시험 시간은 동일하지만 각 파트별로 문항 수는 변화가 있으며 그동안 출제되지 않았던 그래프와 문자 메시지, 채팅, 삼중 지문 등 새로운 지문 유형과 문제가 출제됩니다.

신토익 시험의 구성

구성	Part	Part별 내용	문항수	시간	배점
Listening Comprehension	1	사진 묘사	6	45분	495점
	2	질의 응답	25		
	3	짧은 대화	39		
	4	설명문	30		
Reading Comprehension	5	단문 공란 채우기	30	75분	495점
	6	장문 공란 채우기	16		
	7	단일 지문	29		
		이중 지문	10		
		삼중 지문	15		
Total	7 Parts		200문제	120분	990점

신토익 이후 달라진 부분

Part 1 문항 10개에서 6개로 감소
Part 2 문항 30개에서 25개로 감소
Part 3 문항 30개에서 39개로 증가, 〈3인 대화〉, 〈5턴 이상의 대화〉, 〈의도 파악, 시각 정보 연계 문제〉 추가
Part 4 문항 30개로 기존과 동일, 〈의도 파악 문제〉, 〈시각 정보 연계 문제〉 추가
Part 5 문항 40개에서 30개로 감소
Part 6 문항 12개에서 16개로 증가, 〈알맞은 문장 고르기〉 추가
Part 7 문항 48개에서 54개로 증가, 〈문자 메시지 · 온라인 채팅 지문〉, 〈의도 파악, 문장 삽입 문제〉, 〈삼중 지문〉 추가

신토익 핵심 정보

Part 3	화자의 의도 파악 문제	2~3문항	대화문에서 화자가 한 말의 의도를 묻는 유형
	시각 정보 연계 문제	2~3문항	대화문과 시각 정보(도표, 그래픽 등)간 연관 관계를 파악하는 유형
	3인 대화	대화 지문 1~2개	일부 대화문에서 세 명 이상의 화자가 등장함
	5턴 이상의 대화		주고 받는 대화가 5턴 이상으로 늘어난 대화 유형
Part 4	화자의 의도 파악 문제	2~3문항	담화문에서 화자가 한 말의 의도를 묻는 유형
	시각 정보 연계 문제	2~3문항	담화문과 시각 정보(도표, 그래픽 등)간 연관 관계를 파악하는 유형
Part 6	알맞은 문장 고르기	4문항 (지문당 1문항)	• 지문의 흐름상 빈칸에 들어갈 알맞은 문장 고르기 • 선택지가 모두 문장으로 제시되며 문맥 파악이 필수
Part 7	문장 삽입 문제	2문항 (지문당 1문항)	주어진 문장을 삽입할 수 있는 적절한 위치 고르기
	문자 메시지 · 온라인 채팅	각각 지문 1개	2명이 대화하는 문자 메시지, 다수가 참여하는 온라인 채팅
	의도 파악 문제	2문항 (지문당 1문항)	• 화자가 말한 말의 의도를 묻는 문제 • 문자 메시지, 온라인 채팅 지문에서 출제
	삼중 지문	지문 3개	세 개의 연계 지문에 대한 이해도를 묻는 문제

나혼토 학습 스케줄

초급 수험자 기본서로 공부는 했지만 아직 700점 넘기가 힘들어요.

기본서로 공부를 했다고는 하지만 아직 실전 연습이 부족할 수도 있습니다. 실제 토익 시험을 보면서 시간이 부족한 경우가 많은데 이는 평소에 실전처럼 시간을 기록하며 연습을 하는 것이 중요합니다. 또한 어휘 실력이 부족한 시기이므로 온라인으로 제공되는 어휘테스트도 활용해 보세요. (www.nexusbook.com에서 어휘리스트/테스트 제공)

1일차	2일차	3일차	4일차	5일차	6일차
Actual Test 1 문제 풀이 & 정답 확인	Actual Test 1 LC 해설 확인 & 받아쓰기	Actual Test 1 RC 해설 확인 & 어휘 복습	Actual Test 2 문제 풀이 & 정답 확인	Actual Test 2 LC 해설 확인 & 받아쓰기	Actual Test 2 RC 해설 확인 & 어휘 복습
7일차	**8일차**	**9일차**	**10일차**	**11일차**	**12일차**
Actual Test 3 문제 풀이 & 정답 확인	Actual Test 3 LC 해설 확인 & 받아쓰기	Actual Test 3 RC 해설 확인 & 어휘 복습	Actual Test 4 문제 풀이 & 정답 확인	Actual Test 4 LC 해설 확인 & 받아쓰기	Actual Test 4 RC 해설 확인 & 어휘 복습
13일차	**14일차**	**15일차**			
Actual Test 5 문제 풀이 & 정답 확인	Actual Test 5 LC 해설 확인 & 받아쓰기	Actual Test 5 RC 해설 확인 & 어휘 복습			

중급 수험자 감을 잡은 거 같은데 800점 전후로 왔다갔다 해요.

토익 공부도 좀 해보고 토익 시험도 2~3번 봤지만 여전히 점수가 잘 오르지 않는 경우입니다. LC는 실전 연습도 중요하지만 받아쓰기를 통해 다시 한번 복습해 보는 것이 좋습니다. RC는 각 파트별로 권장 풀이 시간에 맞춰 풀어보면서 취약한 부분이 어디인지 점검해 보세요.

1일차	2일차	3일차	4일차	5일차	6일차
Actual Test 1 문제 풀이	Actual Test 1 정답 및 해설 확인	Actual Test 2 문제 풀이	Actual Test 2 정답 및 해설 확인	Actual Test 3 문제 풀이	Actual Test 3 정답 및 해설 확인
7일차	**8일차**	**9일차**	**10일차**		
Actual Test 4 문제 풀이	Actual Test 4 정답 및 해설 확인	Actual Test 5 문제 풀이	Actual Test 5 정답 및 해설 확인		

고급 수험자 900점 이상을 목표로 하고 있지만 쉽지 않아요.

가끔은 정말 시험을 잘 봤다고 생각하지만 예상치 못한 곳에서 틀리는 문제가 있는 경우입니다. 한 번 틀렸던 문제들은 다시 틀리는 경우가 많으므로 꼭 다시 점검해 보세요.

1일차	2일차	3일차	4일차	5일차
Actual Test 1 & 해설	Actual Test 2 & 해설	Actual Test 3 & 해설	Actual Test 4 & 해설	Actual Test 5 & 해설

나혼토 실력 점검

테스트가 끝난 후 각 테스트별로 점검해 보세요. 테스트별로 맞은 개수를 확인하며 실력이 향상됨을 체크해 보세요.

정답 확인 전

	테스트 날짜	시험 소요 시간	체감 난이도
Actual Test 01			상 중 하
Actual Test 02			상 중 하
Actual Test 03			상 중 하
Actual Test 04			상 중 하
Actual Test 05			상 중 하

정답 확인 후

	맞힌 개수	환산 점수	총점
Actual Test 01	LC:		점
	RC:		
Actual Test 02	LC:		점
	RC:		
Actual Test 03	LC:		점
	RC:		
Actual Test 04	LC:		점
	RC:		
Actual Test 05	LC:		점
	RC:		

* 환산 점수는 222페이지에 있는 환산 점수표를 이용해 주세요.

잠깐!! 시작 전 **꼭** 확인하세요!

- 실제 시험과 같이 책상을 정리하고 마음의 준비를 하세요.
- 핸드폰은 잠깐 끄고 대신 아날로그 시계를 활용해 보세요.
- 제한 시간은 120분입니다. 제한 시간을 꼭 지켜주세요.
- 어렵다고 넘어가지 마세요. 가능하면 차례대로 풀어 보세요.

Actual Test

01

시작 시간 :

종료 시간 :

LISTENING TEST

In the Listening test, you will be asked to demonstrate how well you understand spoken English. The entire Listening test will last approximately 45 minutes. There are four parts, and directions are given for each part. You must mark your answers on the separate answer sheet. Do not write your answers in your test book.

PART 1

Directions: For each question in this part, you will hear four statements about a picture in your test book. When you hear the statements, you must select the one statement that best describes what you see in the picture. Then find the number of the question on your answer sheet and mark your answer. The statements will not be printed in your test book and will be spoken only one time.

Example

Sample Answer

Ⓐ ● Ⓒ Ⓓ

Statement (B), "The man is working at a desk," is the best description of the picture, so you should select answer (B) and mark it on your answer sheet.

1

2

GO ON TO THE NEXT PAGE

3

4

5

6

GO ON TO THE NEXT PAGE

▶정답 및 해설 P003

PART 2

Directions: You will hear a question or statement and three responses spoken in English. They will not be printed in your test book and will be spoken only one time. Select the best response to the question or statement and mark the letter (A), (B), or (C) on your answer sheet.

7 Mark your answer on your answer sheet.

8 Mark your answer on your answer sheet.

9 Mark your answer on your answer sheet.

10 Mark your answer on your answer sheet.

11 Mark your answer on your answer sheet.

12 Mark your answer on your answer sheet.

13 Mark your answer on your answer sheet.

14 Mark your answer on your answer sheet.

15 Mark your answer on your answer sheet.

16 Mark your answer on your answer sheet.

17 Mark your answer on your answer sheet.

18 Mark your answer on your answer sheet.

19 Mark your answer on your answer sheet.

20 Mark your answer on your answer sheet.

21 Mark your answer on your answer sheet.

22 Mark your answer on your answer sheet.

23 Mark your answer on your answer sheet.

24 Mark your answer on your answer sheet.

25 Mark your answer on your answer sheet.

26 Mark your answer on your answer sheet.

27 Mark your answer on your answer sheet.

28 Mark your answer on your answer sheet.

29 Mark your answer on your answer sheet.

30 Mark your answer on your answer sheet.

31 Mark your answer on your answer sheet.

PART 3

Directions: You will hear some conversations between two or more people. You will be asked to answer three questions about what the speakers say in each conversation. Select the best response to each question and mark the letter (A), (B), (C), or (D) on your answer sheet. The conversations will not be printed in your test book and will be spoken only one time.

32 What most likely is Business Circle?
(A) A trade conference
(B) A Wed site
(C) A magazine
(D) A radio program

33 What is the current status of the trade agreement?
(A) It has gone through.
(B) It is being discussed.
(C) It has been suspended.
(D) It will soon expire.

34 What does the man suggest doing?
(A) Preparing an alternative proposal
(B) Monitoring the situation closely
(C) Advertising job opportunities
(D) Analyzing the negative result

---

35 What are the speakers mainly talking about?
(A) The advancement of a coworker
(B) The retirement of a manager
(C) A recent business agreement
(D) The relocation of a headquarters

36 What type of company do the speakers most likely work for?
(A) A legal office
(B) A marketing firm
(C) A travel agency
(D) A medical firm

37 What does the man suggest?
(A) Leading a workshop
(B) Holding a farewell event
(C) Checking a report
(D) Asking for more information

38 Why is the woman calling?
(A) To announce a plan
(B) To offer an apology
(C) To request some supplies
(D) To pass along a complaint

39 In which department does Chris probably work?
(A) Housekeeping
(B) Reception
(C) Maintenance
(D) Security

40 What will the woman probably do next?
(A) Make some repairs
(B) Speak to a guest
(C) Call a hardware store
(D) Clean a guest's suite

---

41 Why does Peter want to go to a restaurant?
(A) To meet some clients
(B) To arrange an event
(C) To pick up an order
(D) To book a place

42 What does the woman mean when she says, "You'll make it"?
(A) She expects a coworker will attend a gathering.
(B) She knows who will prepare a meal.
(C) She thinks a colleague has enough time.
(D) She believes an evaluation will go well.

43 What do the men imply about the neighborhood?
(A) It has some nice restaurants.
(B) It is inconvenient.
(C) It is growing rapidly.
(D) It was featured in a magazine.

GO ON TO THE NEXT PAGE

44 Who most likely are the speakers?

(A) Potential clients
(B) Car dealers
(C) Product designers
(D) Advertising executives

45 What problems are the speakers discussing?

(A) Sales figures are unimpressive.
(B) Advertising is becoming more expensive.
(C) Customer satisfaction is low.
(D) Production is behind schedule.

46 What does the woman suggest?

(A) Reading customer feedback
(B) Reviewing an instruction manual
(C) Reducing prices
(D) Calling a client meeting

---

47 Who most likely is the man?

(A) A receptionist
(B) A new recruit
(C) A store clerk
(D) A security officer

48 Why does the man visit the woman?

(A) To get a refund
(B) To have an interview
(C) To apply for a card
(D) To pay for items

49 What will the man probably do next?

(A) Send an application form
(B) Have his photo taken
(C) Talk to a colleague
(D) Complete the document

50 What are the speakers mainly discussing?

(A) A research budget
(B) A consumer campaign
(C) A managerial promotion
(D) A marketing survey

51 What do the men suggest?

(A) Emphasizing particular points
(B) Shortening a form
(C) Conducting longer interviews
(D) Extending a deadline

52 What does the woman decide to do?

(A) Make a few revisions to a document
(B) Find a way to satisfy customers
(C) Alter the schedule for a meeting
(D) Relay some feedback

---

53 What does the woman ask the man to do?

(A) Review her work
(C) Draft a report
(D) Release some records
(D) Update a Web site

54 What kind of organization do the speakers work for?

(A) A marketing company
(B) A banking firm
(C) A newspaper
(D) A software company

55 What does the woman mean when she says, "who can blame them"?

(A) Customers did not cause the problem.
(B) Customers are likely to make some complaints.
(C) Customers' confusion was expected.
(D) Customers' behavior is understandable.

56 What best describes the speakers' jobs?
(A) They are medical staff.
(B) They are cashiers.
(C) They are office employees.
(D) They are restaurant servers.

57 What does Heather ask the other two people to do?
(A) Assign her different hours
(B) Have breakfast with her
(C) Go on a camping trip with her
(D) Fill in for her at work

58 What does Olivia imply?
(A) She cannot accommodate the request.
(B) She'll be off that day.
(C) Heather should return the favor.
(D) Heather should change her appointment.

---

59 Why does the woman ask for advice?
(A) To replace a current service
(B) To purchase a computer
(C) To provide a new device
(D) To design a Web site

60 Why does the woman say, "That's the bottom line"?
(A) She wants the long-term plan.
(B) She wants a cheap price.
(C) She uses Internet frequently.
(D) She wants fast online access.

61 What is the woman advised to do?
(A) Transfer to an overseas branch
(B) Get some feedback
(C) Compare options on the Internet
(D) Read some product instructions

Model	Price ($)
Modern 765 (Black and White)	1,530
Solusi 300 (Color)	1,720
Primark 200 (Black and White)	1,940
Allthatprint 500 (color)	2,250

62 According to the man, what has the advertising department requested?
(A) A client list
(B) A customer code
(C) An office device
(D) An e-mail address

63 Who most likely is Mr. Warren?
(A) A client
(B) A supplier
(C) A manufacturer
(D) A supervisor

64 Look at the graphic. How much will the company most likely pay for the order?
(A) $1,530
(B) $1,720
(C) $1,940
(D) $2,250

GO ON TO THE NEXT PAGE

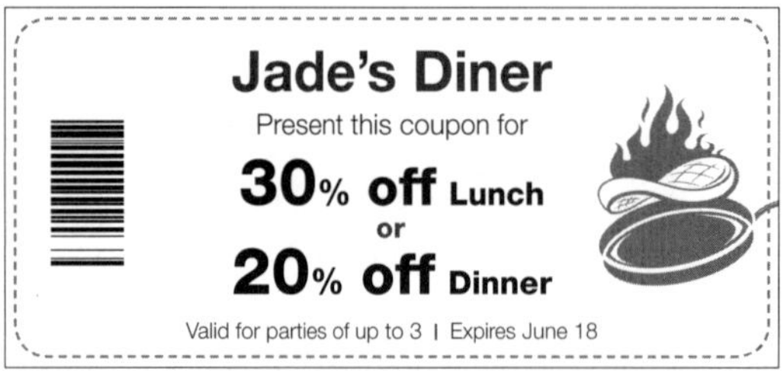

Jade's Diner
Present this coupon for
30% off Lunch
or
20% off Dinner
Valid for parties of up to 3 | Expires June 18

65 What does the man indicate about the woman?

(A) She ordered a dessert.
(B) She is a regular customer.
(C) She owns a business.
(D) She works near the restaurant.

66 Look at the graphic. How much of a discount will the woman receive?

(A) 5%
(B) 10%
(C) 20%
(D) 30%

67 What does the man say he will do?

(A) Speak to a manager
(B) Accept a credit card
(C) Make a calculation
(D) Fax an invoice

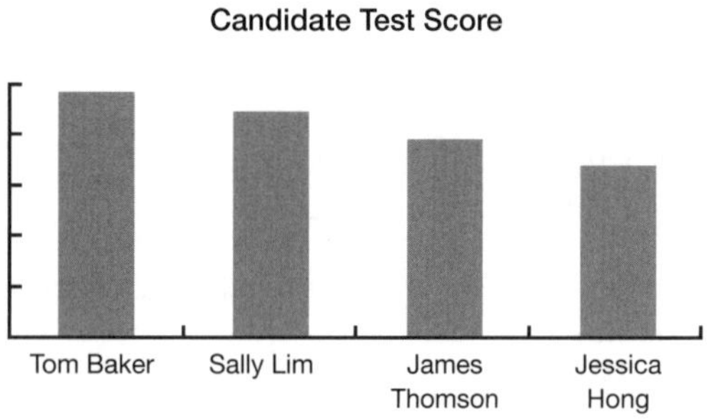

68 How was the job opening probably advertised?

(A) In a trade journal
(B) On some posters
(C) In a newspaper
(D) On a Web site

69 What does the man offer to do?

(A) Reply to an organization
(B) Screen résumés from applicants
(C) Write a job description
(D) Extend a deadline for a project

70 Look at the graphic. Who does the woman say gave the most impressive interview?

(A) Tom Baker
(B) Sally Lim
(C) James Thomson
(D) Jessica Hong

▶정답 및 해설 P014

PART 4

Directions: You will hear some talks given by a single speaker. You will be asked to answer three questions about what the speaker says in each talk. Select the best response to each question and mark the letter (A), (B), (C), or (D) on your answer sheet. The talks will not be printed in your test book and will be spoken only one time.

71 What is being advertised?
(A) A tour agency
(B) A hotel chain
(C) A catering service
(D) An airline company

72 According to the advertisement, what advantage does the business offer?
(A) Easy access
(B) Courteous service
(C) Corporate rates
(D) Membership bonuses

73 What will happen in August?
(A) A facility will be expanded.
(B) A discount will be offered.
(C) A Web site will be upgraded.
(D) A selection will be widened.

74 Why has the fight been delayed?
(A) The runway is busy.
(B) The plane has a mechanical problem.
(C) The fog prevented the plane from departing.
(D) Boarding took a long time.

75 What time will the flight depart?
(A) 5:00 P.M.
(B) 5:30 P.M.
(C) 6:00 P.M.
(D) 6:30 P.M.

76 What does the speaker suggest the listeners do?
(A) Relax in the lounge
(B) Take a look at some reading materials
(C) Fill out a form
(D) Revise their schedule

77 Why has the speaker called Mr. Aston?
(A) To ask for some personal information
(B) To solicit his participation
(C) To arrange an interview
(D) To finalize a job offer

78 What did Jennifer Ward do?
(A) She was Mr. Aston's supervisor.
(B) She recommended Mr. Aston.
(C) She is organizing the seminar.
(D) She founded Dantos Incorporated.

79 According to the speaker, what should Mr. Aston do next?
(A) Contact General Consulting
(B) Register for the seminar
(C) Return Ms. Rodriguez's call
(D) Submit the document

80 Who most likely is the speaker?
(A) An author
(B) A food critic
(C) A charity founder
(D) A restaurant manager

81 What has the speaker's organization created?
(A) A documentary film
(B) A complimentary publication
(C) A fundraising competition
(D) A nutrition workshop

82 According to the speaker, what will happen next month?
(A) A new product will be developed.
(B) An event venue will change.
(C) A new branch will open.
(D) A project will be expanded.

GO ON TO THE NEXT PAGE

83 What is true of the weather today?
(A) It is expected to warm up later.
(B) Heavy snowfall is forecast.
(C) It hit a record low temperature.
(D) Heavy rain is expected.

84 What potential hazard does the speaker mention?
(A) Loss of power
(B) Lack of fuel
(C) Shortage of supplies
(D) Health issues

85 What suggestion does the speaker make?
(A) Listeners should stay home.
(B) Listeners should exercise regularly.
(C) People should drive carefully.
(D) People should purchase supplies.

---

86 Who is the speaker addressing?
(A) University instructors
(B) Newly hired employees
(C) Potential clients
(D) Survey participants

87 According to the speaker, what will Mr. Ambrose do today?
(A) Conduct a series of interviews
(B) Show a video presentation
(C) Introduce the company founder
(D) Distribute guidebooks

88 What does the speaker mean when she says, "make sure to report back to me"?
(A) She is eager to see some results.
(B) She requires feedback from all attendees.
(C) She wants to give further information.
(D) She works as a department supervisor.

89 What is the report mainly about?
(A) The renovation of a town center
(B) The construction of a new facility
(C) The introduction of a new product
(D) The relocation of a stadium

90 What is an advantage of the plan?
(A) It will accommodate more people.
(B) It will reduce expenses.
(C) It will generate more income.
(D) It will improve delivery times.

91 Who is Ian Douglas?
(A) A factory manager
(B) A local land owner
(C) A company spokesperson
(D) A real estate agent

---

92 Why is the speaker calling?
(A) A change in schedule
(B) An equipment malfunction
(C) A policy proposal
(D) A revision to a manual

93 Why does the speaker say, "That will shut down the system"?
(A) To upgrade a system
(B) To change a suggestion
(C) To explain a process
(D) To make a complaint

94 What does the speaker offer to do?
(A) Email a document
(B) Issue a refund
(C) Install a system
(D) Deliver a new unit

Reservation Slip
See Dinosaurs at Whiterose!

Name of child: *Alex Hunt*

Parent of child: *Susan Hunt*

Age of child: *Six*

Your visit will take place at *1:30 P.M.*
Thank you and enjoy your shopping!

95 What is mentioned about the childcare center?

(A) It is on the second floor.
(B) It is exclusive to members.
(C) Children over 7 are not allowed.
(D) Children may stay for a day.

96 What can be found on the second floor?

(A) A reservation form
(B) A special event
(C) A childcare center
(D) An information desk

97 Look at the graphic. By when should Susan arrive at the special event?

(A) 1:20
(B) 1:25
(C) 1:30
(D) 1:35

Christchurch Tour – Day One		
Time	Location	Activity
09:00-10:30	Waitomo Caves	Morning walk
11:00-12:00	Central Square	Shopping
12:00-14:00	Victoria Park	Afternoon picnic
14:00-17:00	Bay of Islands	Boat ride

98 Who most likely is Phil Goff?

(A) A civil engineer
(B) A famous celebrity
(C) A local politician
(D) A renowned architect

99 According to the speaker, what is the purpose of the trip to Mission Bay?

(A) To ride bicycles
(B) To photograph wildlife
(C) To shop for souvenirs
(D) To visit a castle

100 Look at the graphic. Where will listeners probably go next?

(A) Waitomo Caves
(B) Central Square
(C) Victoria Park
(D) Bay of Islands

This is the end of the Listening test. Turn to Part 5 in your test book.

GO ON TO THE NEXT PAGE

READING TEST

In the Reading test, you will read a variety of texts and answer several different types of reading comprehension questions. The entire Reading test will last 75 minutes. There are three parts, and directions are given for each part. You are encouraged to answer as many questions as possible within the time allowed.

You must mark your answers on the separate answer sheet. Do not write your answers in your test book.

PART 5

Directions: A word or phrase is missing in each of the sentences below. Four answer choices are given below each sentence. Select the best answer to complete the sentence. Then mark the letter (A), (B), (C), or (D) on your answer sheet.

101 Brooks Bookstore can ship an order to your home, business, ------- local post office within 24 hours.

(A) but
(B) that
(C) or
(D) as

102 The use of high-quality yet ------- raw materials led to a cost reduction for Mr. Walton's factory.

(A) inexpensive
(B) unhappy
(C) incomplete
(D) undecided

103 Jason Flowers is always ------- to deliver nice decorations to your special events.

(A) ready
(B) skillful
(C) complete
(D) delicious

104 Kate Vausden was nominated as Best New Artist ------- her elaborate painting now on display at Lindsey Gallery.

(A) about
(B) for
(C) when
(D) since

105 If you want to take advantage of this month's sale, you must do so quickly as ------- ends next week.

(A) it
(B) he
(C) they
(D) your

106 The ------- of video materials to publication can help companies produce promotional merchandise.

(A) content
(B) addition
(C) pictures
(D) advances

107 Opponents of the city's mayor ------- the claim that she has revived the regional economy.

(A) propose
(B) rely
(C) extend
(D) reject

108 We, Sisco Designs, create a ------- of images that express an individual style suitable for your needs.

(A) frequency
(B) length
(C) shortage
(D) series

109 At Isaac Shoe Store, most customized shoes can be made ------- 2 business days.

(A) since
(B) to
(C) at
(D) within

110 Mr. Sanders is not checking his voice mail -------, so you can expect a delay in his response.

(A) scarcely
(B) similarly
(C) frequently
(D) partially

111 To avoid traffic congestion, the ------- of downtown Pleasant Valley requires extensive planning.

(A) restore
(B) restorative
(C) restored
(D) restoration

112 The School Outreach Program honors students ------- volunteer their time to help Twin City.

(A) for
(B) who
(C) those
(D) as

113 The evaluation report will be completed ------- after technicians inspect the lab equipment.

(A) when
(B) only
(C) still
(D) most

114 The construction of the Grunburg Building ------- because of modifications in the original floor plans.

(A) postponed
(B) has been postponed
(C) will postpone
(D) postponing

115 All passengers are advised to check baggage claim tags to verify that retrieved bags are in fact -------.

(A) they
(B) them
(C) theirs
(D) themselves

116 Customers of Charleston Bank can easily transfer funds from one account to -------.

(A) another
(B) either
(C) one
(D) it

117 Henry Bonaducci's proposal was approved in a ------- short time because of its feasibility.

(A) surprised
(B) surprise
(C) surprisingly
(D) surprising

118 Built in 1885, the St. Petersburg Cathedral has been preserved for its historical -------.

(A) signify
(B) significant
(C) significance
(D) significantly

119 After the ------- improvements have been implemented, the production process should run more efficiently.

(A) suggest
(B) suggested
(C) suggesting
(D) suggests

120 Clients should provide both an e-mail address and a telephone number in order to be notified of the most current status of any ------- orders.

(A) dependent
(B) representative
(C) practical
(D) pending

GO ON TO THE NEXT PAGE

121 RT Technology Services will use its training center in Austin ------- preregistered attendees number more than 350.

(A) if
(B) that
(C) either
(D) despite

122 New customers of Ortega Hardware Store ------- receive a 10 percent discount on their first order.

(A) customarily
(B) perfectly
(C) repeatedly
(D) obediently

123 McAfee Manufacturing is known as a company that makes uniquely ------- tools for the construction industry.

(A) precise
(B) precision
(C) precisely
(D) preciseness

124 Ms. Hogan, the director of personnel ------- the company's revised manual for recruiting interns at tomorrow's meeting.

(A) had been addressing
(B) is addressing
(C) will be addressed
(D) should be addressed

125 ------- slow the high-speed printer may be, it is still making copies that are adequate for our purposes.

(A) Rather
(B) Seldom
(C) Thoroughly
(D) However

126 Since the Wisconsin Daily is now available digitally, subscribers can read articles one day ------- the general public.

(A) between
(B) during
(C) ahead of
(D) away from

127 If the lamp had been damaged during shipment, the company ------- to send Mr. Oakley a replacement.

(A) would have offered
(B) has offered
(C) is being offered
(D) would have been offered

128 ------- you have submitted all the required documents for your grant proposal, the decision committee will be convened for evaluation.

(A) Then
(B) Next
(C) Once
(D) Always

129 Store managers will not ------- approve time off for employees during the peak season.

(A) generalization
(B) generalize
(C) generally
(D) general

130 The decision about company relocation will be ------- until the special meeting scheduled for next month.

(A) deferred
(B) resolved
(C) organized
(D) agreed

PART 6

Directions: Read the texts that follow. A word, phrase, or sentence is missing in parts of each text. Four answer choices for each question are given below the text. Select the best answer to complete the text. Then mark the letter (A), (B), (C), or (D) on your answer sheet.

Questions 131-134 refer to the following press release.

For Immediate Release

February 2 — P. H. Manning announces the appointment of Sean Renault as Chief Financial Officer, replacing Sandy Connelly who retired in January.

Prior to ------- **131.** P. H. Manning, Mr. Renault worked at KUB Systems. While there, he served in various accounting and treasury roles, including the role of Chief Financial Officer. He ------- **132.** his career in the audit division of Adams Financial Group.

"Mr. Renault's experience and leadership will be invaluable as we enter our next phase of growth," said Marco Colombo, P. H. Manning's Chief Executive Officer.

Ms. Connelly, the ------- **133.** Chief Financial Officer, worked at P. H. Manning for seventeen years. -------. **134.**

131 (A) joining
(B) founding
(C) promoting
(D) completing

132 (A) to begin
(B) begins
(C) began
(D) will begin

133 (A) nearest
(B) former
(C) alternate
(D) potential

134 (A) The accounting team is still hiring new people.
(B) All of our staff members will start work as of tomorrow.
(C) We have made a lot of effort to promote her to CEO.
(D) She will remain as an advisor to the board of directors.

GO ON TO THE NEXT PAGE

Questions 135-138 refer to the following e-mail.

To: Publishing Department Staff
From: Hans Shuler
Date: February 18
Subject: New Copy Machine

Dear colleagues:

Yesterday a new copy machine was installed in the resource room to replace the one that had ------- **135.** broken down. ------- **136.** It is an industrial-grade model, so we expect that it will serve us well for several years.

To ensure that the copier remains in working order, keep small objects ------- **137.** paper clips and staples away from the paper feeder.

You may have questions while learning how to operate the new copier. If so, you can ------- **138.** the manual located in the cabinet next to the copier.

Regards,

Hans

135 (A) repeats
(B) repetition
(C) repeated
(D) repeatedly

136 (A) We trust that the new one will be more reliable.
(B) There are several types of copy machines available at the store.
(C) Please let us know what time you would like to set up an appointment.
(D) We can give you an accurate estimate later.

137 (A) as well
(B) such as
(C) of these
(D) sort of

138 (A) consult
(B) discard
(C) approve
(D) revise

Questions 139-142 refer to the following article.

February 28 — After two years of construction, the largest hotel in Milwaukee history is almost ready to open. The Mendota Hotel, on the banks of the Cherish River, will have 1,200 rooms for visitors. It will have two conference rooms for groups of up to 300 people. -------. (139.) The project is among downtown area hotels currently -------. (140.) According to Sanjay Singh, president of Milwaukee Hotel & Lodging Association, these new developments are a -------. (141.) "We've had a massive influx of visitors over the past few years," said Mr. Singh. "-------, (142.) almost all the hotels in the city are completely full. Clearly, additional hotel rooms are needed."

139 (A) It is unclear whether it will be open to accept reservations or not.
(B) Building renovations will begin next year as originally scheduled.
(C) The first guests will soon arrive as part of a medical technology conference.
(D) There is a speculation that several companies will bid on the project.

140 (A) to construct
(B) are constructing
(C) were constructed
(D) being constructed

141 (A) necessity
(B) nuisance
(C) risk
(D) bargain

142 (A) Likewise
(B) Otherwise
(C) Additionally
(D) Consequently

GO ON TO THE NEXT PAGE

Questions 143-146 refer to the following flyer.

Attention, artists and craftspeople!

------- (**143.**) If so, you are encouraged to apply for a chance to display your artwork at the Bloomberg County Art Fair on May 17.

Applications are available online at www.bloombergfair.org and will be reviewed by several professors from the art department of our local college. Together with your completed application document, please upload ------- (**144.**) of your work. The images will aid the judges in their review process.

The application deadline is February 15, and the judges' decisions will be made by March 30. ------- (**145.**) applicants will have use of a 5 x 5 meter display booth and will be expected to participate ------- (**146.**) the entire day of the fair.

143 (A) If it is possible, we would like to send an invitation to your home to survey the event.
(B) Are you interested in a unique opportunity to showcase your talent in our area?
(C) As a loyal customer, you qualify for extended coverage of six years.
(D) You can see other types of artwork on our Web site.

144 (A) descriptions
(B) photographs
(C) requirements
(D) developments

145 (A) Inviting
(B) Invites
(C) Invitation
(D) Invited

146 (A) in
(B) to
(C) through
(D) toward

PART 7

Directions: In this part you will read a selection of texts, such as magazine and newspaper articles, e-mails, and instant messages. Each text or set of texts is followed by several questions. Select the best answer for each question and mark the letter (A), (B), (C), or (D) on your answer sheet.

Questions 147-148 refer to the following advertisement.

FANCY SKI RESORT
WEEKEND SPECIAL

Fancy Ski Resort is the perfect place for your family or group next weekend vacation.

Spend three nights in a one-bedroom condominium or suite for as low as $240 per person. Our lodgings are conveniently located two miles from scenic Mount Lyon and include an indoor swimming pool, sauna, and ice skating rink. A shuttle service operates between our lodgings and Mount Lyon every half hour from 5 A.M. to 8 P.M.

The Weekend Special price includes two days of skiing on Mount Lyon. This offer is valid from November 11 to February 20, excluding weekdays and holidays. For more information, visit www.skifancy.com.

147 How can customers get to Mount Lyon from their lodgings?
(A) By walking
(B) By driving
(C) By taking a taxi
(D) By taking a shuttle bus

148 What facility is NOT included at the lodgings?
(A) A sauna
(B) A swimming pool
(C) A ski rental service
(D) An ice skating rink

GO ON TO THE NEXT PAGE

Questions 149-150 refer to the following information.

ALTON CITY PARKING GARAGE

Please present this ticket with your payment to the attendant when you return to pick up your vehicle.

Date: *7 March*

Time: *9:15 A.M.*

The attendant can accept only cash and credit card payments.

* Monthly rates are available. Save up to 20%!

To obtain details, call 028-555-3421, or visit our Web site at altoncitygarage.co.uk.

149 How do customers pay for parking?

(A) By depositing money in a parking meter
(B) By paying a fee to an attendant
(C) By using a prepaid parking card
(D) By submitting a payment online

150 Why are customers invited to call the telephone number on the ticket?

(A) To request an alternative payment method
(B) To reserve a parking spot for the day
(C) To give feedback about an attendant
(D) To get more information about parking fees

Questions 151-153 refer to the following advertisement.

Attention!

The Capricorn Library Volunteer Association presents its Used Book Sale for four days only from November 3 through 6. You can browse thousands of books, most in excellent condition! There is something of interest for readers of all ages.

Thursday: Preview Sale
6 P.M. – 9 P.M.
$5 admission fee

Friday: General Sale
6 P.M. – 9 P.M.

Saturday: General Sale
9 A.M. – 3 P.M.

Sunday: Clearance Sale
11 A.M. – 2 P.M.
All books 20% off

Proceeds will benefit the building of an addition to the Capricorn Library.

Location: Capricorn Community Center, Main Event Hall, 15 Harper Street

If you have any questions, contact Leslie Ling, president of the Capricorn Library Volunteer Association at 555-0173

Please note that we are no longer accepting donations of books for the sale.

151 Where will the event take place?
(A) At a community center
(B) At a local bookstore
(C) At Ms. Ling's residence
(D) At the Capricorn Library

152 What is stated about Thursday's sales?
(A) Profits from the event will go to a charity.
(B) An entrance fee will be charged.
(C) Cash is the only method of payment accepted.
(D) It will run during the whole day.

153 What is NOT suggested about the books being sold?
(A) Some of them are suitable for young children.
(B) Many of them are in good condition.
(C) All of them were donated by library members.
(D) They will be sold at a reduced price on Sunday.

GO ON TO THE NEXT PAGE

Questions 154-155 refer to the following text message chain.

Douglas Carter **(10:05 A.M.)**
I just got a call from unit B at Carolina Apartments. The tenants would like to move out at the end of July, but their lease doesn't expire until 31 October.

Mia Sanders **(10:06 A.M.)**
Well, the contract says that tenants who leave before the lease expires must pay a penalty. But sometimes the owners of the property will waive the fee if they think they can get new tenants right away. What about calling the owner and seeing if they'll make an exception?

Douglas Carter **(10:07 A.M.)**
I think I can give it a try. I am going to let the owner know that we have many people who are waiting to rent the place.

Mia Sanders **(10:08 A.M.)**
Yes, Carolina Apartments is quite popular among local residents. It shouldn't be difficult to find tenants.

Douglas Carter **(10:10 A.M.)**
I'll talk to you soon.

Send

154 What do the tenants want to do?

(A) Purchase an apartment
(B) Rent a different apartment nearby
(C) Renovate a dining area
(D) Finish a contract early

155 At 10:07 A.M., what does Mr. Carter most likely mean when he writes, "I think I can give it a try"?

(A) He thinks that the rent is too high.
(B) He plans to ask the tenants to stay longer.
(C) He will contact the property owners.
(D) He is willing to pay a penalty.

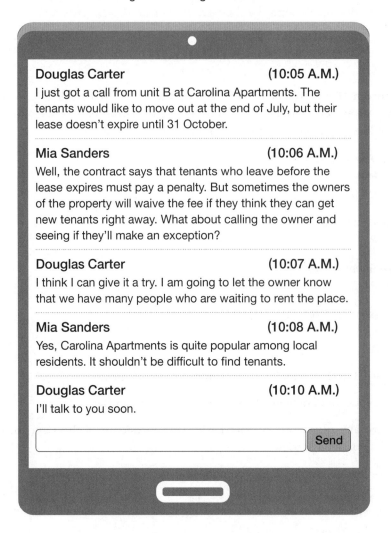

Questions 156-157 refer to the following notice.

NOTICE

The ticketing machine in the Garland waiting area near Platform 5 has been removed for repairs. We hope to have a new machine in place by Monday, April 14. Until then, railroad passengers may use the machine in the Midvale waiting area near Platform 7 or see one of the ticketing clerks at the counter in the Main Lobby next to the Information Booth. We apologize for the inconvenience. Passengers are reminded that they can save 10 to 20 percent and avoid lines at ticketing machines by purchasing weekly or monthly passes. Passes are only available online at www.fasttrackservice.com.

156 Where is the notice most likely posted?

(A) In a movie theater
(B) In a rental car agency
(C) In a train station
(D) In an airport

157 What is suggested about the ticketing machines?

(A) They do not sell weekly and monthly passes.
(B) They are for credit card customers only.
(C) They provide tickets that are discounted 10 to 20 percent.
(D) They have not yet been installed in Platform 7.

GO ON TO THE NEXT PAGE

Questions 158-160 refer to the following letter.

From: Carrie Fenway
To: Harper Randolph
Subject: Keeping on a discussion
Date: December 22

Dear Harper:

It was great to see you at the company's regional managers retreat last week. I wanted to follow up on the discussion we had about your office's upcoming move. The Bristol office's move last year taught me a lot about managing relocation, and I wanted to pass on what I learned to you. –[1]–.

First, I know you are still deciding on whether to close the office for a few days or to keep your office open as usual by moving gradually. I would recommend remaining open if possible. –[2]–. The Bristol office remained open and moved gradually over a period of two weeks, which made the move quite easy. Of course, maintaining the normal work schedule during that time was difficult because some employees had relocated to the new office while their team members remained at the old office. –[3]–. If you choose this approach, I would suggest moving all members of a team at the same time to minimize confusion.

Second, remember that relocation is time-consuming for everyone. Be clear in delivering the message to your employees that you will not be expecting to take on normal workloads during the move. –[4]–. Taking this step ahead of time, as the Bristol office did, greatly improves workflow and reduces stress.

I'll give you a call later this week to talk more about these issues.

Sincerely,

Carrie Fenway
President, Situation Consulting

158 Why is Ms. Fenway writing to Mr. Randolph?

(A) To offer advice
(B) To request a document
(C) To suggest a new project
(D) To appeal a decision

159 What did Ms. Fenway think was the error?

(A) Not closing the office early for a renovation
(B) Not keeping teams of employees together
(C) Not giving employees some time off during the move
(D) Not discussing a new policy with each employee individually

160 In which of the positions marked [1], [2], [3], and [4] does the following sentence best belong?

"Instead, talk in detail with each employee about reducing his or her workload during the relocation period."

(A) [1]
(B) [2]
(C) [3]
(D) [4]

Questions 161-163 refer to the following information on a Web page.

http://www.lowell.edu

FACULTY PROFILE

Edinburgh Campus

Direction | Home | Contact Us | Faculty

Dr. Margaret Pullman
Business Management
Pullman@lowell.edu

Dr. Margaret Pullman graduated from Arlington University in Manchester with dual degrees in Business and history. She embarked on her career as an educator when, as a graduate student in Duncan University in Liverpool, she tutored students in introductory Business courses. After receiving her doctorate in business management from Duncan University, she joined the business faculty at Lowell University's Edinburgh Campus. She is the author of *How Businesses Succeed* (forthcoming from Lowell University Press). She is also a member of the Great Lake Businesses Council. Currently on leave from Lowell University, Dr. Pullman is conducting a series of international business seminars at the Global Business Affairs Institute in London.

161 What is the purpose of the information?
(A) To announce dates for a business seminar
(B) To publicize facts about an employee
(C) To encourage business owners to buy a book
(D) To provide details about a job applicant

162 Where did Professor Pullman begin her teaching career?
(A) In Liverpool
(B) In Edinburgh
(C) In Manchester
(D) In London

163 What is indicated about Professor Pullman?
(A) She is currently teaching history at a university.
(B) She applied to be a member of a business council.
(C) She is working temporarily in London.
(D) She runs her own business throughout the world.

GO ON TO THE NEXT PAGE

Questions 164-167 refer the following advertisement.

Meyers Complex

Enjoy the scenic beauty of Mendota Bay from the newly renovated Meyers Complex. Formerly a sewing factory, the building has been completely updated to combine modern conveniences and technology with features representative of buildings from the early 1900s. Two years ago Gerund Remodeling Inc., the award-winning architecture firm based in Chicago, undertook the project to convert Fargo's sewing factory to both commercial and residential units. Next month's opening reception will mark the completion of the renovation.

Meyers Complex offers 240 apartments, many of which overlook Fargo Harbor, and 4,500 square meters of commercial space for offices and retail stores. In addition to its sweeping views, it offers beautifully landscaped gardens along the harbor. This appealing, multi-use facility is situated in a prime location. Meyers Complex is just a block away from Fargo's Maple Street, lined with boutique shops, art galleries and restaurants. It also sits at the end of the 23-kilometer Chanda Bay Bicycle Path, which was created from an old railroad line and connects Fargo to Alton City. There are several other well-maintained bicycle trails in the area. To the south, Jacksonville, with all of its attractions, is an easy 30-minute drive away.

To inquire about commercial or residential space, please contact Meyers Complex Property Management at 301-555-3241 or send an e-mail to rentalinfo@meyerscomplex.com. Floor plans for apartments vary. Commercial space can be customized. For more details, visit our Web site, www.meyerscomplex.com.

164 What is the purpose of the advertisement?
- (A) To announce a recently approved project
- (B) To promote an architectural awards event
- (C) To publicize new office and residential space
- (D) To explain a reason for the delay of the opening

165 What is mentioned about Gerund Remodeling Inc.?
- (A) It is a family-owned business.
- (B) It has been recognized for its work.
- (C) It specializes in commercial properties.
- (D) It is known for its unique sewing techniques.

166 What is NOT stated about Meyers Complex?
- (A) It will open next month.
- (B) It is right next to a subway station.
- (C) It is not far from a shopping district.
- (D) It is close to bicycle trails.

167 The word "prime" in paragraph 2, line 4, is closest in meaning to
- (A) central
- (B) heavy
- (C) leading
- (D) supreme

Questions 168-171 refer to the following online chat discussion.

Rebecca Walton [4:17 P.M.]	Thanks for attending the regional manager meeting earlier this afternoon. Are there any further questions?
Kelly Stevens [4:18 P.M.]	Juan and I are unclear about how the new sales districts affect existing customers. Do the new districts apply only to new customers?
Rebecca Walton [4:20 P.M.]	No, the new districts apply to both new and existing customers.
Kelly Stevens [4:21 P.M.]	So, does that mean I will no longer get incentives from current customers like Perot Publishing?
Rebecca Walton [4:22 P.M.]	Right. All existing clients in District 5 go to Juan.
Juan Rubble [4:23 P.M.]	But what if I agree to let Kelly keep Perot Publishing?
Rebecca Walton [4:25 P.M.]	Perot Publishing is a big client.
Juan Rubble [4:26 P.M.]	Yes, but I'd rather not interrupt a productive relationship. Perot Publishing is not that important to me.
Rebecca Walton [4:27 P.M.]	I don't see it as interrupting, necessarily. However, if you say so, Juan, I might be able to make an exception if our district manager approves it.
Kelly Stevens [4:28 P.M.]	Can I talk to the client in person?
Rebecca Walton [4:30 P.M.]	I don't think that's appropriate.
Kelly Stevens [4:31 P.M.]	I understand.
Juan Rubble [4:32 P.M.]	OK, we'll wait to hear back from you.

Send

168 Who most likely is Ms. Walton?
(A) A bookstore owner
(B) A sales manager
(C) A travel agent
(D) An author

169 What is suggested about Ms. Stevens?
(A) She has a good relationship with Perot Publishing.
(B) She'd like to transfer to an office in District 5.
(C) She is very satisfied with the new district assignment.
(D) She was not at the meeting in the morning.

170 At 4:25, what does Ms. Walton most likely mean when she writes, "Perot Publishing is a big client"?
(A) She doubts Mr. Rubble can meet Perot Publishing's needs.
(B) She believes Mr. Rubble is confused.
(C) She wants Mr. Rubble to visit District 5.
(D) She thinks Mr. Rubble's idea is surprising.

171 What will most likely happen next?
(A) Ms. Stevens will review the new map of sales districts.
(B) Ms. Stevens will meet with her client.
(C) Ms. Walton will contact the colleague.
(D) Mr. Rubble will accept a job offer from Perot Publishing.

GO ON TO THE NEXT PAGE

Questions 172-175 refer to the following article.

The McClellan Theater is one of Dublin's most treasured historic landmarks and needs to be preserved. The building, constructed almost two centuries ago on Dublin's Central Square, features many striking and unique attributes. –[1]–. The ornate plasterwork of its facade is a magnificent example of architecture of the period in which it was constructed. The walls of the lobby are covered by beautiful murals featuring many famous actors who have performed there over the years, including Wendy Ramsey and Madeline Estes. The theater is not only an architectural gem but also a highly valued entertainment venue for area residents, and it supports the local economy by attracting tourists to the area. –[2]–.

Due to the building's deterioration in recent years, it no longer attracts large theater productions and musical acts. Ensuring the theater's continued use would require extensive restoration. –[3]–. Over the next six months, this committee composed of city residents, local business owners and civic leaders will finalize the restoration plans and raise the capital necessary to complete the project. The committee will also be working to locate corporate and community sponsorships throughout Dublin. –[4]–.

For residents interested in following the restoration efforts, the committee will hold public information sessions on the first Tuesday of each month in the community room of the Dublin Public Library. Detailed plans for the project and information about making a donation to the effort are available at www.restoretheMcClellantheater.com.

172 What is the article mainly about?

(A) The award received by a town for its architecture
(B) The results of an election for a committee
(C) Information about an upcoming city project
(D) The dates of a theater's performance schedule

173 What is implied about the McClellan Theater?

(A) It is the largest building in Dublin.
(B) It offers discounted tickets to Dublin residents.
(C) It is no longer open to the public.
(D) It once attracted large crowds.

174 According to the article, how can people learn more about the changes at the McClellan Theater?

(A) By submitting a request to the city government
(B) By attending monthly meetings
(C) By speaking to Ms. Ramsey in person
(D) By singing up for a monthly newsletter

175 In which of the positions marked [1], [2], [3], and [4] does the following sentence best belong?

"For this reason, the McClellan Theater Restoration Committee was formed last month with an ambitious plan for restoring the theater."

(A) [1]
(B) [2]
(C) [3]
(D) [4]

GO ON TO THE NEXT PAGE

Questions 176-180 refer to the following article and form.

April 4

The National Association of Plastic Workers (NAPW) will hold its annual conference in Sydney from June 6 to 8. Once again, it will be held at the Stone Conference Center in Sydney's business district. Stan Keating, NAPW President, says that the organization will return to the venue because of its convenient location and the amenities it offers. Says Stan, "The conference center is state-of-the-art, and the staff members are extremely knowledgeable and helpful."

This year's theme is "Emerging Technologies in Plastic Fabrication and Molding." The keynote address on June will be given by Colleen Allen, CEO of Plastigic Innovators, Inc. In addition to Ms. Allen's speech, during the three-day event there will be twenty presentations and a closing address by Mr. Keating.

To register for the conference, visit the NAPW web site (www.napw.com/conference). The cost of the conference is $85 for NAPW members and $120 for nonmembers. Students, please contact your institution for discount information; the NAPW maintains pricing agreements with a number of universities and technical colleges. Hotel reservations can be made through the Web site as well. Attendees can choose from six area hotels at various price ranges. The NAPW is offering a free shuttle service to and from the participating hotels and conference site.

Mastuki Manufacturing
Expense reimbursement form

Employee name: *Rodney Kruger*
Payroll ID#: *129856*
Manager/supervisor name: *Michelle Robertson*
Purpose: *National Association of Plastic Workers Conference*

Itemized expenses:
Conference fee: $85.00
Bus fare: (round-trip Melbourne/Sydney) $43.34
Accommodation: (1 night at Jefferson Inn on June 6) $126.78

Total: *$255.12*

Attach receipts for all expenses. Allow two to three weeks for processing.

Employee signature: *R. Kruger*
Manager/supervisor signature: *M. Robertson*

Submitted for payment: *June 12*

176 What is stated about the Stone Conference Center?

(A) It is close to the airport.
(B) Its staff is very competent.
(C) It offers a discount on meeting rooms.
(D) It has recently undergone renovation.

177 Who is Ms. Allen?

(A) A guest speaker
(B) A conference organizer
(C) Mr. Kruger's manager
(D) The president of the NAPW

178 What does the article suggest about student discounts?

(A) They are given only to graduate students.
(B) They are provided to students working as interns.
(C) They are available through certain schools.
(D) They are available to international students.

179 What can be found on the NAPW Web site?

(A) A shuttle schedule
(B) A list of hotels
(C) A map of the conference center
(D) A description of the presentations

180 What can be inferred about Mr. Kruger?

(A) He did not listen to the closing speech.
(B) He was reimbursed on June 12 for expenses.
(C) He drove his car to the NAPW conference.
(D) He is not a member of the NAPW.

GO ON TO THE NEXT PAGE

Questions 181-185 refer to the following e-mails.

From: customerservice@lowndeselectronics.com
To: meredithclose@mail.com
Date: October 4
Subject: Order # 98345

Dear Ms. Close:

Thank you for your purchase of a Power Shot X12 Digital Camera for a total of $899. Your new digital camera with wide-angle optical zoom lens will come fully equipped with an additional battery pack and a battery charger. As a special bonus for spending over $700, you will also receive a complimentary carrying case with a special neck strap.

Your purchase is scheduled for delivery on October 15, but please be aware that you are eligible for our express shipping offer. For only $7.50, you can receive your purchase 5 days earlier, on October 10. In order to receive this upgrade offer, you must reply on or before October 6, after which the offer will expire.

Thank you again for shopping with Lowndes Electronics.

Sincerely,

Jeremy Harris
Customer Service

From: meredithclose@mail.com
To: customerservice@lowndeselectronics.com
Date: October 6
Subject: Re: Order #98345

Dear Mr. Harris:

Please upgrade my shipping to the express option and charge my account accordingly.

Additionally, I will be moving within the next two weeks and would like the items shipped to my office. The correct address is specified in the "bill to" section on my order form. Please disregard the "ship to" information that I entered in the form where I placed my initial order by fax.

Thank you.
Meredith Close

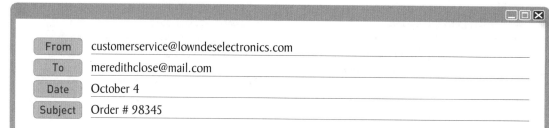

181 Why does Mr. Harris write the e-mail?

(A) To inform a customer of an error
(B) To issue an invitation
(C) To apologize for a shipping delay
(D) To present a limited-time offer

182 According to the first e-mail, why will Ms. Close receive a free item?

(A) She opened a business account.
(B) She made a purchase before October 6.
(C) She spent over a stated amount.
(D) She is a returning customer.

183 What can be inferred about Ms. Close?

(A) She would prefer to upgrade the digital camera.
(B) She is moving to an overseas location.
(C) She would like to cancel two items.
(D) She wants the shipment sent to a different address.

184 When will Ms. Close most likely receive her order?

(A) On October 5
(B) On October 6
(C) On October 10
(D) On October 15

185 In the second e-mail, the word "entered" in paragraph 2, line 4, is closest in meaning to

(A) went into
(B) typed
(C) started
(D) thought about

Questions 186-190 refer to the following memo, notice, and letter.

From	Thomas Reilly
To	All students
Date	February 26

Welcome to Stein College Residence.

We would like to welcome freshmen and returning students to our residence. We hope that this year will be as good if not better than the last. We have made some renovations to the building that we think you will really enjoy, including a new lounge with four pool tables, and a brand-new dartboard. This lounge will be open from 10 A.M. until 11 P.M. and will be supported by a café that offers a wide range of beverages and snacks for your pleasure.

For all of us to have a fun and safe year, it is important to set up some ground rules for your behavior. It is very important to note that breaking three rules can result in suspension of privileges, eviction from the residence, and possibly expulsion from school. In addition, you are responsible for the action of any guest that you bring into the residence. This means that upon entry and exit, any guest that you wish to stay with you MUST sign in and out. The maximum number of guests per person is two.

For further details of the residence rules and by-laws of the residence, refer to the notice on the bulletin board in the lobby.

Stein College Residence Rules

1. Drinking in the common spaces – for example, outside of your room – is prohibited.
2. Illegal drugs of any kind are banned.
3. Violence of any kind is prohibited.
4. Damage to the property is not tolerated.
5. Smoking inside the building is not allowed.
6. Noise in the hallways after 10 P.M. is prohibited.

We hope that these main rules will help everyone have a safe and educational year at Stein College.

If you have any questions, please ask the Resident Tutor, Thomas Reilly, in Room 102.

May 1

Dear Mr. Smith:

This letter is being sent to formally notify you that you are being summoned to the residence committee meeting this Friday, May 6. The actions of your guests on the night of April 21 were not in line with our rules, and you, as stated in the memo, are responsible.

Allegedly, your guests were involved in drinking and fighting in the hallway of the 12th floor at 1 o'clock in the morning. Upon arrival of the resident tutor, they were disrespectful and began shoving him around. This is completely unacceptable and requires us to take action. You will have to attend this meeting on the 11th floor of Johnson Hall with the Residence Board of Directors and committee. They will decide your ultimate fate.

Sincerely,

Vanessa Burkowitz
Residence Manager

186 Why was the memo sent?

(A) To ask the students to complete the form
(B) To remind the students to follow the rules
(C) To remind the students to attend the committee meeting
(D) To tell the students how to get into the residence

187 In the memo, the word "suspension" in paragraph 2, line 2, is closest in meaning to

(A) delay
(B) interruption
(C) trial
(D) difficulty

188 What is most likely the purpose of the letter?

(A) To announce the closure of the residence
(B) To suggest moving out of the residence
(C) To invite Mr. Smith to a community event
(D) To call Mr. Smith to a committee meeting

189 What is indicated about Mr. Smith's guests?

(A) They were approached by Thomas Reilly.
(B) They broke ground rules 3 and 5.
(C) They had visited the residence before April 21.
(D) They were supposed to leave the residence before 9.

190 What can be inferred about the meeting on Friday?

(A) Whether Mr. Smith can stay in the residence will be determined.
(B) It is open to all Stein college students.
(C) It is regularly scheduled to be held on Fridays.
(D) Mr. Smith will attend the meeting to select the board members.

GO ON TO THE NEXT PAGE

Questions 191-195 refer to the following Web page, flyer, and e-mail.

http://www.communityboard.com/housing

Name: Donovan Swayze

Date: January 23

I accepted a new position in Kensington and need to relocate near the downtown area before my start date on May 15. I'm seeking a simple, clean, one-bedroom rental or larger, depending on the price. A relaxing location with outdoor seating for entertaining friends or family would be a plus. I do have a car, but I'd appreciate having good access to public transportation. I have a budget of around £1,200 monthly to cover all housing costs, including utilities.

RELAX AT YOUR OWN PLACE IN KENSINGTON

Be the first to rent this two-bedroom apartment upon completion of extensive renovation. This property will be move-in ready on May 1. It will feature a clean modern look, new floors throughout, and all new appliances. It is situated downtown, and students are welcome as it is less than 10 minutes by bus to Trinity University from the City Transportation office. Cats and small dogs are potentially permitted but with conditions, so please inquire. £1,200 also pays for water, sewer, garbage pick-ups, and general upkeep of the property. The electricity and natural gas will be the responsibility of the tenant. A one-time security deposit equal to one month's rent should be paid upon signing the rental agreement.

If you are interested, please email us at nancyphan@kensingtonpalace.com.

To: Nancy Phan
From: Donovan Swayze
Date: January 24
Subject: Apartment

Dear Ms. Phan:

I happened to see your rental advertisement flyer. From the description, it sounds as if it may be just what I've been looking for. I'm eager to look over the apartment, and I am going to be in Kensington all this week for work. My last day in town will be Sunday, January 30. If the place suits me, I'd want to move in the same day that it's expected to be available. The timing would be perfect! I hope to hear from you soon.

Thank you.
Donovan Swayze

191 For what reason is Mr. Swayze relocating?
(A) To launch his own business
(B) To return to his hometown
(C) To work in a new place
(D) To begin his retirement

192 What aspect of the property does NOT match Mr. Swayze's preferences?
(A) The location
(B) The utility costs
(C) The size
(D) The available date

193 Why does Ms. Phan mention that she will need additional information?
(A) For needed changes to the décor
(B) For a tenant who does not pay a security deposit
(C) For remodeling of the apartment
(D) For someone who wants to keep a pet

194 What is the purpose of the e-mail?
(A) To agree to the terms of the contract
(B) To change the details of a residential advertisement
(C) To inquire about the features of the apartment
(D) To make an arrangement to view the property

195 When does Mr. Swayze want to start living in the residence?
(A) January 24
(B) January 30
(C) May 1
(D) May 15

GO ON TO THE NEXT PAGE

Questions 196-200 refer to the following e-mails and newsletter.

E-Mail Message

From: Elise Manning <emanning@ml.com>
To: Sandra McGowan, Easy Travel <easytravel@gm.com>
Subject: Cycling tours
Date: May 23
Attach: photo (scan #1)

Hi, Sandra.

Well, I'm ready to travel with you again to Andalucía. This time, I want to try one of your cycling tours if you plan on offering them. I'd love to have another look at Almeria Falls from a bike, but I am a beginning cyclist and am not ready for any tough tours. I would also like to take the train rather than the plane back to Valencia this year. Honestly, though, I'm not up to that long journey from Huelva! Would there be any suitable tours for me to join this summer?

I look forward to hearing from you.

Elise

P.S. I've enclosed an updated photo for my Andalucía travel visa, just so you have it on file when I apply for a tour.

From	Sandra McGowan, Easy Travel <easytravel@gm.com>
To	Elise Manning <emanning@ml.com>
Subject	Re: Cycling tours
Date	May 24

Hi, Elise.

Thank you for the inquiry and update. As chance would have it, our business partners in Andalucía have just given us permission to run more cycling tours this summer. I am sending our summer newsletter by mail at no charge this time, so you'll get it within 3 business days. Have a look at it. I'm sure you'll find a tour you'll like.

Hope to see you again this summer.

Sandra

EASY TRAVEL NEWSLETTER **new cycling tour opportunities in Andalucía!**

After celebrating our 20th anniversary at the Amalia Hotel during last week's National Day tour, EASY TRAVEL secured the rights to once again become the world's only tour company to offer cycling tours in the remote Andalucía area. Our tours are a good value at 1,100 Euros and include all meals, plane/train transport to/from Valencia, and use of mountain bikes. Note that we can now accommodate vegetarian dietary requests.

DATES AND ITINERARIES

TOUR A
July 3-8
Cadiz – Darya – Lenza – Slakotov – Cadiz
Level of difficulty: easy (exit Andalucía by plane only from Cadiz)

TOUR B
July 3-8
Cadiz – Darya – Lenza – Almeria Falls – Cadiz
Level of difficulty: challenging (exit Andalucía by plane or train from Cadiz)

TOUR C
July 3-8
Cadiz – Darya – Almeria Falls – Huelva
Level of difficulty: moderate (exit Andalucía by train from Huelva)

TOUR D
July 3-8
Cadiz – Darya – Almeria Falls – Cadiz
Level of difficulty: easy (exit Andalucía by plane or train from Cadiz)

NOTE: All of our tours rated "easy" and "moderate" offer a combination of light cycling and vehicle transport. If you are a keen cyclist, you should take a tour rated "challenging."

196 What is the purpose of the first e-mail?
(A) To schedule a meeting
(B) To request some information
(C) To make hotel reservations
(D) To announce a change in plans

197 Which has Ms. Manning attached with her e-mail?
(A) A project proposal
(B) A photo for visa
(C) A travel itinerary
(D) A tour application form

198 What is NOT mentioned about EASY TRAVEL?
(A) It runs a chain of hotels.
(B) It has been operating for 20 years.
(C) It has exclusive rights to some tours.
(D) It provides riding equipment on some of its tours.

199 Which tour plan is Ms. Manning most likely choose to join?
(A) Tour A
(B) Tour B
(C) Tour C
(D) Tour D

200 What can be implied about Ms. Manning?
(A) She has visited Huelva before.
(B) She likes to travel in winter.
(C) She works as a real estate agent.
(D) She does not subscribe to the Easy Travel newsletter.

Stop! This is the end of the test. If you finish before time is called, you may go back to Parts 5, 6, and 7 and check your work.

잠깐!! 시작 전 **꼭** 확인하세요!

- 실제 시험과 같이 책상을 정리하고 마음의 준비를 하세요.
- 핸드폰은 잠깐 끄고 대신 아날로그 시계를 활용해 보세요.
- 제한 시간은 120분입니다. 제한 시간을 꼭 지켜주세요.
- 어렵다고 넘어가지 마세요. 가능하면 차례대로 풀어 보세요.

Actual Test

02

시작 시간 :

종료 시간 :

LISTENING TEST

In the Listening test, you will be asked to demonstrate how well you understand spoken English. The entire Listening test will last approximately 45 minutes. There are four parts, and directions are given for each part. You must mark your answers on the separate answer sheet. Do not write your answers in your test book.

PART 1

Directions: For each question in this part, you will hear four statements about a picture in your test book. When you hear the statements, you must select the one statement that best describes what you see in the picture. Then find the number of the question on your answer sheet and mark your answer. The statements will not be printed in your test book and will be spoken only one time.

Example

Sample Answer

Ⓐ ● Ⓒ Ⓓ

Statement (B), "The man is working at a desk," is the best description of the picture, so you should select answer (B) and mark it on your answer sheet.

1

2

GO ON TO THE NEXT PAGE

3

4

5

6

GO ON TO THE NEXT PAGE

▶정답 및 해설 P035

PART 2

Directions: You will hear a question or statement and three responses spoken in English. They will not be printed in your test book and will be spoken only one time. Select the best response to the question or statement and mark the letter (A), (B), or (C) on your answer sheet.

7 Mark your answer on your answer sheet.

8 Mark your answer on your answer sheet.

9 Mark your answer on your answer sheet.

10 Mark your answer on your answer sheet.

11 Mark your answer on your answer sheet.

12 Mark your answer on your answer sheet.

13 Mark your answer on your answer sheet.

14 Mark your answer on your answer sheet.

15 Mark your answer on your answer sheet.

16 Mark your answer on your answer sheet.

17 Mark your answer on your answer sheet.

18 Mark your answer on your answer sheet.

19 Mark your answer on your answer sheet.

20 Mark your answer on your answer sheet.

21 Mark your answer on your answer sheet.

22 Mark your answer on your answer sheet.

23 Mark your answer on your answer sheet.

24 Mark your answer on your answer sheet.

25 Mark your answer on your answer sheet.

26 Mark your answer on your answer sheet.

27 Mark your answer on your answer sheet.

28 Mark your answer on your answer sheet.

29 Mark your answer on your answer sheet.

30 Mark your answer on your answer sheet.

31 Mark your answer on your answer sheet.

▶정답 및 해설 P038

PART 3

Directions: You will hear some conversations between two or more people. You will be asked to answer three questions about what the speakers say in each conversation. Select the best response to each question and mark the letter (A), (B), (C), or (D) on your answer sheet. The conversations will not be printed in your test book and will be spoken only one time.

32 Who is the woman talking to?
(A) A graphic designer
(B) A patron
(C) A sales clerk
(D) An interior decorator

33 What does the man expect to happen by the end of this week?
(A) An order will be placed.
(B) A range of new patterns will be designed.
(C) Some supplies will run out.
(D) Additional merchandise will be delivered.

34 What will the woman probably do next?
(A) Visit a different store
(B) Make a purchase
(C) Call a regular customer
(D) Look at color samples

---

35 Where do the speakers probably work?
(A) At a manufacturing company
(B) At a hockey field
(C) At a department store
(D) At a storage facility

36 According to the man, what did a representative ask to do?
(A) Increase an order
(B) Delay a shipment
(C) Revise a design
(D) Reschedule a visit

37 What does the woman want the man to do?
(A) Draft another design
(B) Arrange a meeting
(C) Send some information
(D) Change a plan

38 Who most likely is Ms. Kammerick?
(A) An actor
(B) A writer
(C) A producer
(D) A critic

39 What does Mr. Simon say about London?
(A) He will meet a publisher there.
(B) He went to university there.
(C) He recently moved there.
(D) He used to work there.

40 What problem does Ms. Kammerick mention?
(A) The cost of living is too high.
(B) Her schedule is full.
(C) The theater is fully booked.
(D) She cannot meet a deadline.

---

41 What did the man ask the woman to do in his e-mail?
(A) Confirm the length of a presentation
(B) Provide some feedback on his work
(C) Offer some presentation materials
(D) Contact the board of directors

42 What does the woman suggest?
(A) Contacting a coworker
(B) Increasing a budget
(C) Adding a visual aid
(D) Shortening a document

43 What does the woman mean when she says, "I'll leave that to you"?
(A) She plans to give an item to the man.
(B) She does not intend to stay for much longer.
(C) She will not accompany the man.
(D) She will allow the man to make a decision.

GO ON TO THE NEXT PAGE

44 What are the speakers concerned about?

(A) Defective items
(B) Wrong orders
(C) Lack of staff
(D) Rising expenses

45 What does the man suggest?

(A) Changing a supplier
(B) Checking the order form
(C) Reporting to a manager
(D) Discussing a problem

46 What does the woman decide to do?

(A) Cancel orders
(B) Work overtime
(C) Get some price quotes
(D) Help her coworker

---

47 What is the problem?

(A) The store is under construction.
(B) Only a few items are available.
(C) Some equipment is not working.
(D) A sale has just ended.

48 Why does the man say, "That's probably the case"?

(A) He agrees with the woman.
(B) He is searching in a display case.
(C) He hopes the weather will clear up.
(D) He is offering his idea.

49 Why does the man request the woman's personal information?

(A) To give her details of another location
(B) To tell her about upcoming sale
(C) To offer a membership discount
(D) To notify her when more stock arrives

50 What is the man nervous about?

(A) Making a public speech
(B) Showing his work
(C) Entering a competition
(D) Leading a discussion

51 What does the man say about his work?

(A) It is made from recycled material.
(B) It is being sold at an auction.
(C) It consists mainly of paintings.
(D) It has recently won an award.

52 What does the man suggest the women do?

(A) Collaborate on a design
(B) Support an artist
(C) Attend an exhibition
(D) Cast a vote online

---

53 What type of business does the man work for?

(A) A tour service
(B) A film production company
(C) A radio station
(D) An airline company

54 What has the man recently done?

(A) Written a book
(B) Attended an international seminar
(C) Returned for a trip abroad
(D) Started his own business

55 Who does the man say he talked with?

(A) Volunteer aid workers
(B) Government officials
(C) Many poor people
(D) Newspaper journalists

56 What activity are the speakers participating in?

(A) Driving to the post office
(B) Operating some office equipment
(C) Placing an order of supplies
(D) Preparing parcels to mail

57 At what time does the conversation most likely take place?

(A) 2:00
(B) 3:00
(C) 4:00
(D) 5:00

58 What does the woman mean when she says, "Let's get on with it, then"?

(A) Everyone should work faster.
(B) The labels are all ready.
(C) There is plenty of time left.
(D) They need to leave right now.

---

59 What is the conversation mainly about?

(A) Preparation for an award ceremony
(B) Plans for an event
(C) The cost of supplies
(D) Directions to a venue

60 What does the man say about the previous year's event?

(A) It had enough space.
(B) It was hard to get to.
(C) It was expensive to rent.
(D) It had free parking.

61 What is indicated about the tickets?

(A) They are quite expensive.
(B) They have already sold out.
(C) The prices are lower than before.
(D) They are selling well.

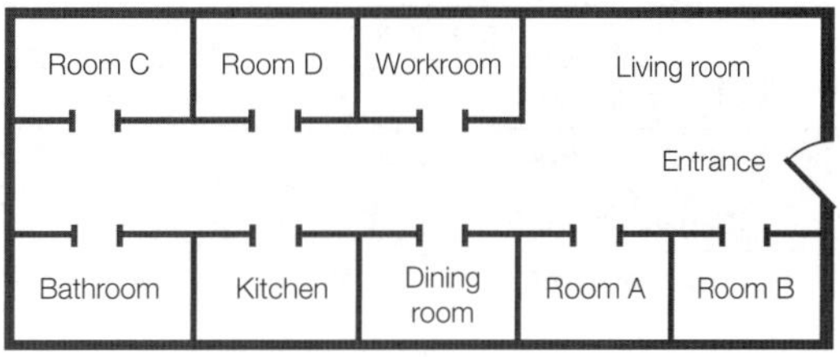

62 Who most likely is the man?

(A) A plumber
(B) An electrician
(C) A real estate agent
(D) A builder

63 Look at the graphic. Where does the woman say she would like to put the bathroom?

(A) Room A
(B) Room B
(C) Room C
(D) Room D

64 What does the man say about the project?

(A) It will take a long time.
(B) It requires a lot of travel.
(C) It will be started next week.
(D) It will be cheap to complete.

GO ON TO THE NEXT PAGE

SCHEDULE	
Tuesday, October 6	Financial Reports Due
Wednesday, October 7	Plant Inspection
Thursday, October 8	Plant Inspection
Friday, October 9	New Item Introduction

65 What is the main topic of the conversation?

(A) A guest speaker
(B) A sporting competition
(C) A welcome event
(D) A local festival

66 Look at the graphic. When most likely will the event be held?

(A) On Tuesday
(B) On Wednesday
(C) On Thursday
(D) On Friday

67 What does the woman say she will do?

(A) Attend a conference
(B) Book a venue
(C) Prepare an inspection
(D) Reserve a hotel room

Name: Joyce Hahn
Patient# 002875

Date:	Wednesday 9/13
Examination	$ 40.00
2x Gum Treatment	$ 200.00
2x Dental Filling	$ 260.00
Toothpaste	$ 10.00
Balance Due	$510.00

68 Look at the graphic. Which charge on the bill is incorrect?

(A) $10
(B) $40
(C) $200
(D) $260

69 What does the man say about the clinic?

(A) It changed its phone number.
(B) It installed a new program.
(C) It hired new staff members.
(D) It purchased new equipment.

70 What does the man say he will do?

(A) Upgrade a system
(B) Issue a refund
(C) Update software
(D) Send another statement

PART 4

Directions: You will hear some talks given by a single speaker. You will be asked to answer three questions about what the speaker says in each talk. Select the best response to each question and mark the letter (A), (B), (C), or (D) on your answer sheet. The talks will not be printed in your test book and will be spoken only one time.

71 Where does the announcement take place?
(A) In a train station
(B) At an airport
(C) On an express train
(D) At an express bus terminal

72 Why is the announcement being made?
(A) To provide information on destinations
(B) To explain a schedule change
(C) To ask passengers to start boarding
(D) To apologize for a delay

73 What are listeners asked to do?
(A) Proceed to a different platform
(B) Present their documents
(C) Wait for more instructions
(D) Confirm they are in the correct place

---

74 What is being celebrated?
(A) An opening of a new branch
(B) A business anniversary
(C) A retirement ceremony
(D) A special award

75 What is the restaurant planning to do on Friday?
(A) Extend its hours of operation
(B) Offer musical entertainment
(C) Provide complimentary meals
(D) Discount certain items

76 What does the speaker say about the restaurant?
(A) It uses local produce.
(B) It hired a renowned chef.
(C) It has multiple locations.
(D) It is under new ownership.

77 Where is the talk probably taking place?
(A) At an electronics store
(B) In a research center
(C) In a conference room
(D) At a construction site

78 Who most likely are the listeners?
(A) New employees
(B) Company investors
(C) Store patrons
(D) Factory workers

79 What does the speaker mean when he says, "let's get started"?
(A) A tour is about to begin.
(B) Some delivery is ready to be shipped.
(C) Listeners should go back to work immediately.
(D) Listeners should fill out some forms.

---

80 What type of organization recorded this message?
(A) A radio station
(B) A transportation service
(C) The National Weather Service
(D) A local school

81 What does the speaker say about Florence?
(A) Its roads have been repaved.
(B) It will experience a snowstorm.
(C) Its schools will all be closed.
(D) It is the largest city in the region.

82 What are listeners asked to do?
(A) Attend the afternoon classes
(B) Check for updated information
(C) Design a new Web site
(D) Listen to an upcoming broadcast

GO ON TO THE NEXT PAGE

83 What is the purpose of the talk?

(A) To introduce a new employee
(B) To reschedule a farewell party
(C) To explain about new policy
(D) To announce the resignation of an employee

84 What has Mr. Lansing recently done?

(A) Accepted a promotion
(B) Created an advertisement
(C) Submitted a report
(D) Attended a seminar

85 What will the speaker probably do next?

(A) Join a conference
(B) Talk to a supervisor
(C) Receive an electronic mail
(D) Send detailed information

89 Who is the intended audience for this talk?

(A) Golfers
(B) Caddies
(C) Teachers
(D) Volunteers

90 What is mentioned about the tournament?

(A) It is a national competition.
(B) It will last three days.
(C) It is an annual event.
(D) It will be rescheduled.

91 What is one instruction given to the listeners?

(A) Speak loudly during play
(B) Stay off the greens
(C) Ask questions to the athletes
(D) Check out the schedule

---

86 What is mentioned about the property?

(A) It's newly renovated.
(B) It is for up to 15 persons.
(C) It offers on-site parking.
(D) It is close to the station.

87 According to the message, what feature is Mr. Gupta looking for?

(A) A fully furnished office
(B) A convenient location
(C) Modern equipment
(D) Adequate parking

88 Why does the speaker recommend viewing the building as soon as possible?

(A) It will rent out quickly.
(B) Its price will go up soon.
(C) It will be renovated shortly.
(D) It will be advertised on TV.

92 What is the report mainly about?

(A) A planned closure of a facility
(B) An acquisition of two companies
(C) A new line of product
(D) A company's expanded operation

93 Who is Jack Wentworth?

(A) A company spokesperson
(B) A corporate executive
(C) A broadcast reporter
(D) A news reader

94 What does the speaker mean when he says, "That would make perfect sense"?

(A) United Textiles is an international company.
(B) Any local government would favor such a plan.
(C) Textile sales are strong in the local area.
(D) United Textiles is famous in the region.

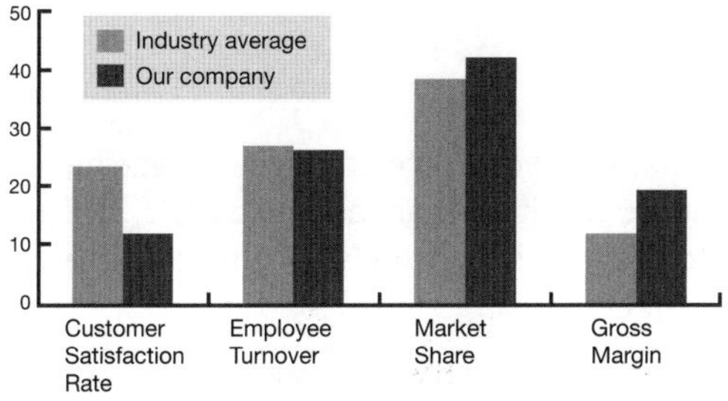

Alice Spring Regional Weather Report		
Day	Skies	Temperature
Tuesday	Sunny	Hot
Wednesday	Sunny	Warm
Thursday	Sunny	Warm
Friday	Cloudy	Cool

95 Why does the speaker thank the listeners?
(A) They formed a committee.
(B) They finished a quarterly report.
(C) They distributed a notice.
(D) They gathered quickly.

96 Look at the graphic. What area does the board of directors most want to improve?
(A) Customer satisfaction rate
(B) Employee turnover
(C) Market share
(D) Gross margin

97 What will Ms. Gallagher have to do?
(A) Use a different facility
(B) Create a document
(C) Report a current issue
(D) Contact a manager

98 According to the speaker, what is the park known for?
(A) Impressive rock formations
(B) Native species
(C) Exotic flowers
(D) High numbers of visitors

99 Look at the graphic. When does the talk probably take place?
(A) On Tuesday
(B) On Wednesday
(C) On Thursday
(D) On Friday

100 What does the speaker advise listeners to do?
(A) Take a lot of photographs
(B) Draw some pictures
(C) Wear sunglasses
(D) Stay on the hiking trail

This is the end of the Listening test. Turn to Part 5 in your test book.

GO ON TO THE NEXT PAGE

READING TEST

In the Reading test, you will read a variety of texts and answer several different types of reading comprehension questions. The entire Reading test will last 75 minutes. There are three parts, and directions are given for each part. You are encouraged to answer as many questions as possible within the time allowed.

You must mark your answers on the separate answer sheet. Do not write your answers in your test book.

PART 5

Directions: A word or phrase is missing in each of the sentences below. Four answer choices are given below each sentence. Select the best answer to complete the sentence. Then mark the letter (A), (B), (C), or (D) on your answer sheet.

101 Bergeson's began as a small retail store, but ------- transitioned into a large wholesaler.

(A) quickly
(B) well
(C) quite
(D) highly

102 The open-access database can be used to search ------- job opportunities at Jefferson Electronics.

(A) for
(B) up
(C) as
(D) to

103 It is ------- that managers be made aware of a shortage of supplies when it occurs.

(A) sudden
(B) actual
(C) eventful
(D) critical

104 Most of the employees at the company have work experience, but only a handful of ------- can see the future importance of current trends.

(A) we
(B) us
(C) our
(D) ourselves

105 Please read through ------- page of the contract carefully before signing on the final page.

(A) all
(B) each
(C) whole
(D) complete

106 A ------- shopping bag is a necessary item for someone who does not like the ordinary plastic bags from the grocery store.

(A) rigorous
(B) comparable
(C) durable
(D) vigorous

107 The judges for this year's debate competition include ------- from a broadcasting station.

(A) represents
(B) representatives
(C) represented
(D) represent

108 The filters of your Total Water Purifier must ------- at least once a month to keep the appliance functioning properly.

(A) be cleaned
(B) cleaning
(C) have cleaned
(D) clean

109 Mr. O'Neil ------- his speech when he realized that he hadn't printed out the draft.

(A) achieved
(B) improvised
(C) commanded
(D) officiated

110 Varner Bank works ------- with customers to establish long-term partnerships.

(A) nearly
(B) recently
(C) closely
(D) newly

111 The updated safety analysis report is limited to site supervisors ------- the Russell Software System.

(A) within
(B) until
(C) during
(D) since

112 ------- needs to be highlighted is the area of agriculture and natural resources.

(A) What
(B) Which
(C) Whichever
(D) Whose

113 San Remo Lemonade maintained ------- sales all year around though promoted as a summertime drink.

(A) final
(B) correct
(C) steady
(D) seasoned

114 Morrison Electronics is acquiring Yearwood Tech. for ------- $35 million in stocks and cash.

(A) approximates
(B) approximation
(C) approximately
(D) approximate

115 The building may be accessed only by personnel ------- have attended the employee orientation.

(A) must
(B) since
(C) who
(D) some

116 New technologies have ------- Poland Cell Tech. to expand its network and explore sales opportunities.

(A) emerged
(B) improved
(C) introduced
(D) enabled

117 Mr. Long repaired the fax machine ------- last Friday because the maintenance department was short on staff.

(A) his
(B) his own
(C) himself
(D) him

118 You can have fun at our indoor waterpark all through the year, ------- of the season.

(A) regardless
(B) regarded
(C) regarding
(D) regard

119 A panel may begin to review the entries ------- the deadline for submitting designs has passed.

(A) how
(B) nor
(C) whether
(D) now that

120 For results to be convincing, the temperature and humidity in the laboratory must remain ------- the same throughout the experiment.

(A) exacted
(B) exactness
(C) exact
(D) exactly

GO ON TO THE NEXT PAGE

121 ------- Ms. Motohashi missed her train, she was fortunately still on time for the awards ceremony.

(A) Though
(B) Despite
(C) As if
(D) Just as

122 Karl Byquist at Gordon Architecture, a British Company, is the ------- of this year's Master Architects Award.

(A) receiving
(B) received
(C) recipient
(D) receipt

123 Results of the two audit findings report ------- the director's expectations.

(A) surpassed
(B) surpassing
(C) to surpass
(D) having surpassed

124 If you have not visited the Valley Restaurant recently, you may be ------- to see how the interior has changed.

(A) pleasing
(B) pleased
(C) please
(D) pleaser

125 A nine-mile ------- of Fosberg Road between Norview Road and Harriot Avenue will be resurfaced in September.

(A) journey
(B) duration
(C) stretch
(D) instance

126 Article submissions to Journal Explore Nature must not exceed 2,000 words, ------- references.

(A) exclude
(B) excluding
(C) exclusive
(D) exclusion

127 Registration for the community programs will start with residents, ------- are students.

(A) inasmuch as
(B) the reason being
(C) because of them
(D) most of whom

128 The board meeting ended so ------- that few members had an opportunity to comment on the proposed road construction project.

(A) abruptly
(B) broadly
(C) practically
(D) obviously

129 Because of her lack of experience, Ms. Abraham was ------- to volunteer for the astronaut training.

(A) reluctance
(B) more reluctantly
(C) reluctance
(D) reluctant

130 In order to make an official purchase agreement, a manager must submit ------- from at least three qualified experts.

(A) combinations
(B) appointments
(C) estimates
(D) comprises

PART 6

Directions: Read the texts that follow. A word, phrase, or sentence is missing in parts of each text. Four answer choices for each question are given below the text. Select the best answer to complete the text. Then mark the letter (A), (B), (C), or (D) on your answer sheet.

Questions 131-134 refer to the following memo.

To: All staff

The Light Cloud Airlines' board of directors is pleased to announce that board chair Mathew Mavens has been appointed the new interim president of the foundation ------- **131.** the departure of Roberto Rinaldi. ------- **132.** We also wish him the best in his future endeavors. In the meantime, the committee for the new permanent president has been formed. Mr. Mavens will resume his duty as board chair ------- **133.** the new president of the organization is chosen.

If you have any questions or concerns, please feel free to contact me while we ------- **134.** the transition in leadership.

Thank you.
Rajiv Shrestha
Communication Director

131 (A) following
(B) follow
(C) follows
(D) followed

132 (A) I am happy to inform you that we have found the product he is looking for and have placed an order.
(B) I forgot to tell you that I would not be able to make it to the meeting because I have to meet some board members.
(C) Let me know if there's anything I can do for you to make the hiring process run smoothly.
(D) The board and staff greatly appreciate Mr. Rinaldi's commitment to our mission over the past seven years.

133 (A) so
(B) when
(C) because
(D) although

134 (A) question
(B) reconsider
(C) undergo
(D) avoid

GO ON TO THE NEXT PAGE

Questions 135-138 refer to the following announcement.

Qualified candidates are now being considered for the position of lead web designer at Gibson Ltd.

A well-known advertising firm, Gibson Ltd. provides businesses with the innovative technical resources that are -------(135.) of dramatically increasing a company's presence on the Internet. As demand for this unique service continues to grow, so does the number of Gibson Ltd.'s -------(136.). In fact, new offices have recently opened as far away as Berlin, Tokyo, and Abu Dhabi.

As a member of Gibson Ltd.'s production division, the new lead Web designer -------(137.) the efforts of a team responsible for developing and maintaining client Web sites. -------(138.).

135 (A) capably
(B) capabilities
(C) capability
(D) capable

136 (A) locations
(B) instructions
(C) reports
(D) schedules

137 (A) had overseen
(B) will oversee
(C) was overseen
(D) has been overseeing

138 (A) Thank you for your e-mail and for sharing the positive feedback from your clients.
(B) A full job description and other information for applicants are available at www.gibson.com/jobs.
(C) It has been a great pleasure working with you and the entire Gibson staff.
(D) If our work doesn't meet your standards, we will honor our guarantee.

Questions 139-142 refer to the following article.

November 29 — Jake's Restaurant on Sheboygan Street recently submitted an application for an entertainment permit. If -------, the permit will enable the restaurant to host live musical performances nightly.
139.

The restaurant is located in what is primarily a residential area, and some neighbors are concerned that they will be exposed to loud music ------- a regular basis. Others don't think that it will be a major -------, "We won't have a problem," said resident Beth Martinez.
140. **141.**

-------. However, the decision ultimately lies with the staff in the city licensing office.
142.

139 (A) approved
(B) approving
(C) approves
(D) approval

140 (A) at
(B) on
(C) from
(D) among

141 (A) investment
(B) issue
(C) deadline
(D) act

142 (A) Residents may still contact the town council to voice their concerns.
(B) We are looking for some volunteers to help perform at the restaurant.
(C) To make the transition go faster, please remove your personal items.
(D) This is one of the changes the management plans to implement.

GO ON TO THE NEXT PAGE

Questions 143-146 refer to the following e-mail.

To: Fred Jaspers <fjaspers@westfordmarketing.com>
From: Winnie Price <WPrice@lapimaelectronics.com>
Date: April 8
Subject: New Marketing Campaign
Attachment: Electronics

Hello, Fred.

Lapima Electronic Store will receive its summer inventory shortly. -------**143.**, I would like to begin another print and online advertisement campaign to promote our new products.

I would like to feature Mason's new home appliance line, which is made from 100 percent recycled materials. Lapima Electronic Store is -------**144.** of only two local retailers to offer this line, so we want it -------**145.** in our ads. -------**146.**. You may use these images at will.

Thank you.
Winnie Price
Vice President of Sales, Lapima Electronic Store

143 (A) Accordingly
(B) Likewise
(C) Moreover
(D) Nevertheless

144 (A) some
(B) both
(C) one
(D) other

145 (A) emphasis
(B) emphasizes
(C) emphasized
(D) emphasizing

146 (A) I would like to know what is going on with the order.
(B) I just wanted to remind you that we're meeting before the ceremony.
(C) I ordered a heater from your online store last Friday.
(D) I have attached some photos of the electronics for you.

PART 7

Directions: In this part you will read a selection of texts, such as magazine and newspaper articles, e-mails, and instant messages. Each text or set of texts is followed by several questions. Select the best answer for each question and mark the letter (A), (B), (C), or (D) on your answer sheet.

Questions 147-148 refer to the following text message.

Hello, Ms. Finkel.

It's Jeff from Pleasantville Realty Company. Glad you liked the office space.

I was wrong about the move-in date. It's not July 1 but June 1. The lease still needs your signature. Please come by my office as soon as possible.

Send

147 What is the purpose of the message?

(A) To purchase an apartment
(B) To introduce a moving company
(C) To give directions to an office
(D) To correct some information

148 What is Ms. Finkel asked to do?

(A) Sign a document
(B) Mail a package
(C) Make a donation
(D) Pay some fees

GO ON TO THE NEXT PAGE

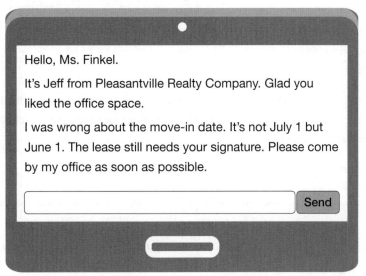

Questions 149-150 refer to the following Web page.

http://www.sanremowellbeingfoundation.com

San Remo Well-being Foundation is pleased to announce that we are now accepting applicants for our annual grants. Each year, we provide four grants to projects throughout the world that are committed to improving the health and well-being of a community.

The award amounts are detailed below.

◇ First place £2,000
◇ Second place £1,500
◇ Third place £1,000
◇ Fourth place £500

Only not-for-profit entities are eligible for our grants; for-profit businesses are ineligible. Previous years' winners include an adult swim program, a lunch program for schoolchildren, and a series of pet care workshops.

Click this link to download grant application forms.

149 What is the purpose of the Web page?

(A) To solicit a government grant
(B) To announce the winner of a sports event
(C) To encourage participation in an event
(D) To remind people that a new school has opened

150 What have San Remo Well-being grants been used for in the past?

(A) Educating people on how to take care of pets
(B) Organizing singing contests for children
(C) Purchasing medical equipment for community hospitals
(D) Holding an international conference on health

Questions 151-152 refer to the following text message chain.

Carol Lewis (2:29 P.M.)
Hi, Anthony. Do you have a minute? I want to talk with you about the inventory issue.

Anthony Ribisi (2:30 P.M.)
Sure, go ahead.

Carol Lewis (2:31 P.M.)
According to the database, we only have one box of printer paper left. Should I order more?

Anthony Ribisi (2:32 P.M.)
No need. We've switched to a new supplier. We are going to start carrying a less expensive brand. While you were out last week, I ordered 25 boxes of the new product. They are not in yet.

Carol Lewis (2:33 P.M.)
Thanks for taking care of that!

Send

151 At 2:30 P.M., what does Mr. Ribisi most likely mean when he writes, "go ahead"?

(A) He has time to answer Ms. Lewis' questions.
(B) He did what Ms. Lewis requested.
(C) He agrees to meet with Ms. Lewis.
(D) He gave Ms. Lewis permission to work on a project.

152 What is mentioned about Ms. Lewis?

(A) She created a new database.
(B) She received a delivery today.
(C) She placed an order last week.
(D) She recently took some time off.

GO ON TO THE NEXT PAGE

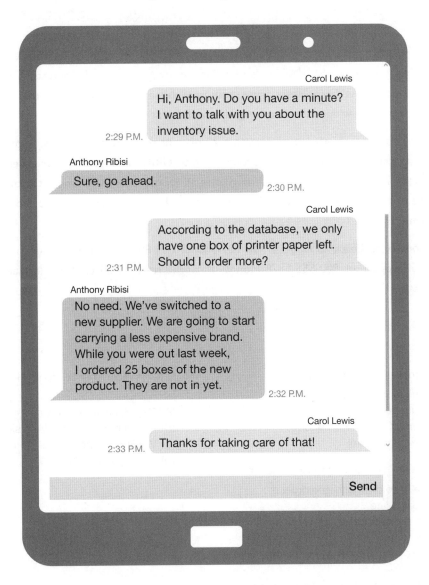

Questions 153-155 refer to the following information.

Thank you for purchasing a brand-new Cosmos 7 cell phone. An additional battery pack is included in your purchase. All kinds of cellphone accessories can be purchased directly from Cosmos at our online store, www.cosmoscellphone.com. We guarantee that you will receive your order within seven working days or the order is free of charge.

As a preferred customer, you will receive a 20 percent discount off your first purchase of cellphone accessories. Simply type in promo code BHURRY when placing your order. If you would rather purchase accessories through a retail location, our cellphone accessories are available at all leading electronics stores. Please note that most retailers do not honor our corporate discount.

Questions or feedback about your new cell phone? Call 800-555-9876 24 hours a day for technical support, or 800-555-9878 Monday through Friday 7 A.M to 8 P.M. for sales and accounts.

153 For whom was the notice written?
(A) Technical support professionals
(B) Product designers
(C) Owners of new mobile phones
(D) Research workers

154 What can be inferred from the information?
(A) There is no charge for the order if delivery is late.
(B) Sales representatives are available at all times.
(C) The product is under warranty for a full year.
(D) Technicians will return calls as soon as possible.

155 What is recommended to receive a discount?
(A) Calling customer service
(B) Entering a word on a Web site
(C) Visiting any electronics store
(D) Mailing in a coupon

Questions 156-157 refer to the following notice.

Easton's Books is pleased to host a public reading by writer Annette Lyons on Wednesday, August 12, from 3 P.M. to 5 P.M. A two-time winner of the prestigious Reily Award for best science fiction, Ms. Lyons will read excerpts from *Behind the Doors*. This fiction book, the fifth and final installment in her *Kingdoms of the Unknown* series, has topped the best-selling lists and earned enthusiastic praise from book reviewers. Don't miss an opportunity to hear one of the most popular SF authors of the last decade read from her latest work.

Tickets are $5 and can be purchased at Easton's Books, 27 Grey Lane, Memphis, or by calling the store's customer service line at 080-555-4834.

156 Who is Ms. Lyons?

(A) A librarian at a famous university
(B) The owner of Easton's Books
(C) A literary critic from a publishing company
(D) The author of a popular book

157 What is mentioned about *Behind the Doors*?

(A) It was written over a ten-year period.
(B) It received an important award.
(C) It is the last book in a series.
(D) It sold more than half a million copies.

GO ON TO THE NEXT PAGE

Questions 158-160 refer to the following article.

New Take Off for Edgerton

Vernon City, September 2 – Revised plans for the Edgerton International Airport were presented to the Vernon City Transportation Board by Nina Grant, the project's chief engineer, on August 30. –[1]–.

Plans for the new airport, to be located just west of Vernon City, were first approved three years ago. However, a study commissioned by the Transportation Board last year concluded that the number of passengers traveling by air to the region is expected to increase substantially within the next few years. –[2]–. This is largely a result of the decision by Marcus Hotel Ltd. to open a large beach resort about twenty kilometers north of Vernon City. –[3]–.

Proposed changes include lengthening the runways to accommodate the large-capacity planes, expanding the passenger waiting areas, and adding shopping areas to the passenger terminal. –[4]–.

Board chairperson Jenny Mason noted that the board is likely to approve the revised plans within the month, which will allow the first of four construction phases for the airport to begin in January as originally scheduled.

158 What is the reason for the meeting of Ms. Grant and board members?

(A) To request that research be conducted
(B) To announce an appointment of her company's new president
(C) To keep them updated about design plans
(D) To explain why construction work will start later than expected

159 What is suggested about the Edgerton International Airport?

(A) It will be able to accommodate large-capacity planes.
(B) It will be located to the north of Vernon City.
(C) It will have three passenger terminals.
(D) It will have the largest shipping area of any airport in the region.

160 In which of the positions marked [1], [2], [3], and [4] does the following sentence best belong?

"Plans for the design of the airport cargo terminal, already on track to be the largest in the region, remain unchanged."

(A) [1]
(B) [2]
(C) [3]
(D) [4]

Questions 161-164 refer to the following letter.

Whitfield Grocery

July 1

Dear Customer:

Exciting changes are happening at Whitfield Grocery! We hope you will visit us later this month and see the improvements we are making in order to enhance your shopping experience.

As you may know, we have been undergoing a significant renovation that is adding about 8,000 square meters to our store. Beginning on July 10, our produce section will be nearly twice as big, which will allow us to offer a variety of fruits and vegetables and allow you to move around the store with ease. We are also expanding our bakery section to provide you with freshly baked bread.

We will be celebrating the renovations on Saturday, July 20. There will be cooking demonstrations and free food tastings. In addition, we will start opening on Saturdays at 6 A.M. instead of 7 A.M.

To encourage you to visit the new Whitfield Grocery, we have enclosed discount coupons. The coupons are good until July 31. You will also find a calendar indicating special sale days.

Sincerely,

Ann O'Connor
Store manager

161 What is the purpose of the letter?
(A) To publicize the completion of a store renovation
(B) To advertise custom-made baking goods
(C) To announce a change in a store's ownership
(D) To promote a new store location

162 What is NOT mentioned in this letter?
(A) A wider selection of products
(B) Increased floor space
(C) Extended hours of operation
(D) Additional cashiers

163 What is included in the letter?
(A) A questionnaire
(B) A schedule of events
(C) A list of products
(D) A product sample

164 In the letter, the word "good" in paragraph 4, line 2, is closest in meaning to
(A) enough
(B) valid
(C) kind
(D) efficient

GO ON TO THE NEXT PAGE

Questions 165-167 refer to the following memo.

MEMO

To: Clarion Market Project Team Members
From: Marijus Fitzgerald
Date: September 4
Subject: Project Results

First, I would like to thank everyone for their hard work with the Clarion Outdoor Market held over the weekend at Jefferson Park. The event was a success overall, raising a large amount of proceeds for the medical center like we had hoped, and will definitely be continued. Nevertheless, we will need to improve a few areas before conducting the second installment of the event the month after next.

The main concern is inclement weather. As many of you noticed, despite the rain on Sunday, we still had a large turnout of guests, which was fantastic. Sadly, we had not prepared for this, and received a number of complaints from both merchants and customers about not having protective coverings on the booths. I have discussed this with staff at the park, and they are willing to provide us with several large tents for future markets.

On another note, we may also want to consider eliminating the registration fee, since some of the merchants complained about a lack of sales. Instead, we could consider collecting a percentage of what they earn in transactions. I would like for everyone to propose another suggestion to alleviate this problem, or perhaps methods that could be used to implement this idea without making the process unnecessarily difficult. If you have any ideas, please send them to Adam Mosley, the outdoor market coordinator.

Marijus Fitzgerald
Director, Clarion Market Project

165 What can be inferred about the Market Project?

(A) It has only been held one time.
(B) It takes place once a month.
(C) It was canceled due to weather.
(D) It will be changing locations.

166 What did the customers complain about?

(A) The expensive registration fee
(B) The lack of protection from rain
(C) The small number of merchants
(D) The low amount of product variety

167 What does Mr. Fitzgerald ask the members of the project to do?

(A) Organize a new event
(B) Contact park officials
(C) Submit some suggestions
(D) Speak with the merchants

Questions 168-171 refer to the following article.

THIS MONTH'S HIGHLIGHT

Susie Murray, who plans to step down as chief accountant in May, has served Harrison Accounting Firm in many capacities for 32 years. –[1]–. The president of the firm, Mario Vinchenso, said, "It's rare to find anyone who has the range of experience at Harrison that Susie has."

Ms. Murray began her career in accounting as a temporary receptionist at Miller Creek Accounting in Milwaukee. –[2]–. She was then hired as a full-time receptionist at Harrison's Norfolk branch. After two years of answering telephones and directing customers' calls, Ms. Murray was hired as a manager at Harrison Accounting's Richmond branch, and in less than a year was promoted to head manager.

–[3]–. Ms. Murray's promotions did not end there, however. She recounted, "I enjoyed working with numbers and wanted to move into the accounting department. My manager at the Richmond branch, Galen Broadbent, gave me advice on how I could achieve my goal. On Galen's recommendation, I decided to pursue an accounting degree at Whitney College in Norfolk, just as Galen had done some years before. –[4]–. By applying for a student loan and continuing to work as a part-time employer, I was able to complete the accounting program in five years."

Once she had received her degree from Whitney College, Ms. Murray joined the accounting department at Harrison Accounting's headquarters. Three years later, she was appointed assistant to Chief Accountant Jeanne Archer, and when Ms. Archer transferred to the commercial accounting division, Ms. Murray was chosen to fill the position. "Just think about that," Ms. Murray said, "I started out handling telephone calls, and I ended up as chief accountant at the firm's headquarters."

168 What is the article mainly about?

(A) An announcement of a result from a customer survey
(B) A variety of open positions at a bank
(C) A reason for holding special training programs
(D) A profile of an employee at an accounting firm

169 What is indicated about Mr. Broadbent?

(A) He is a part-time worker at Harrison.
(B) He was interviewed for the article.
(C) He studied accounting.
(D) He has experience as a professor.

170 What is suggested about Harrison Accounting?

(A) Its headquarters are in Richmond.
(B) It has a commercial accounting division.
(C) Its employees can receive a discount on college tuition.
(D) It recently merged with Miller Creek Accounting.

171 In which of the positions marked [1], [2], [3], and [4] does the following sentence best belong?

"She found the work to be very rewarding and, when her contract ended, began searching for a permanent position in the industry."

(A) [1]
(B) [2]
(C) [3]
(D) [4]

GO ON TO THE NEXT PAGE

Questions 172-175 refer to the following online chat discussion.

Sheila Paxton

Sheila Paxton [10:13 A.M.]	I invited Rob Housewell as one of the guest speakers for our workshop on Friday.
Emily Miller [10:14 A.M.]	That's great! He even won a prestigious Paddington Award for his book, *Attractions and Consumers*. I admire the depth of his insight into our field.
Martin Richards [10:15 A.M.]	Yeah, I know. I heard he is also a great speaker.
Sheila Paxton [10:25 A.M.]	I believe he can inspire our employees to make more creative and appealing advertisements. By the way, I think it would be nice for all of us to take him out to someplace fun while he is in town.
Emily Miller [10:26 A.M.]	If the weather stays nice, maybe we can do something outdoors.
Martin Richards [10:28 A.M.]	What time do you have in mind?
Sheila Paxton [10:29 A.M.]	Well, Professor Housewell told me he has plans for Friday afternoon. He is going to meet with a publisher about the book he is working on.
Emily Miller [10:30 A.M.]	Then we should plan something we can do in the evening.
Martin Richards [10:32 A.M.]	How about dinner at the Thai Restaurant right next to Mendota Lake?
Emily Miller [10:33 A.M.]	Yes! They have great live music on weekend nights.
Martin Richards [10:34 A.M.]	They also have good quality food, and this place also has a great view of the city. Mr. Housewell definitely will love that restaurant.
Sheila Paxton [10:35 A.M.]	I bet! Thank you, guys. When specific schedules come out, I'll let you know.

Send

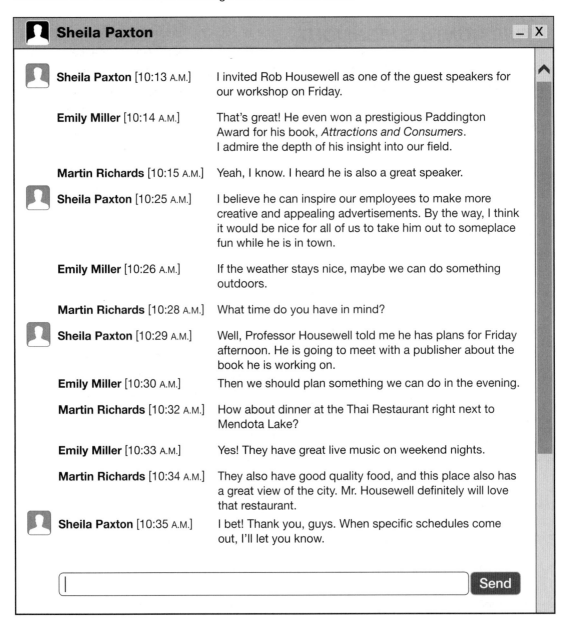

172 At what kind of company do the writers most likely work?

(A) An advertising firm
(B) An accounting office
(C) A publishing company
(D) A catering service

173 What can be inferred about Mr. Housewell?

(A) He teaches management at a local university.
(B) He has written several award-winning books.
(C) He has a meeting and a speech on the same day.
(D) He has met with all of the writers before.

174 What is suggested about the Thai Restaurant?

(A) It is located on the top floor of a building.
(B) It is a waterfront restaurant.
(C) It has music performances every night.
(D) It is open for dinner by reservation only.

175 At 10:35 A.M., what does Ms. Paxton mean when she writes, "I bet"?

(A) She thinks the restaurant is fully booked on Friday.
(B) She is confident that Mr. Housewell will like the place.
(C) She will contact Mr. Housewell in person.
(D) She needs to be in a hurry to organize a workshop.

GO ON TO THE NEXT PAGE

Questions 176-180 refer to the following memo and form.

To	All staff
From	Cathy Pinkerton, Vice President of Operations
Date	October 2
Re	Equipment Refresh

Please be reminded that it is again time to place orders for office equipment. Company policy states that standard equipment, such as computers, telephones and fax machines, is eligible for replacement after five years. To replace an item that is any newer, it must be determined that the cost of repair exceeds the cost of replacement. The staff in Purchasing Department will be happy to assist you in researching these costs.

Please use the attached form to list equipment requests. Photocopies of this form may be made as needed. All requests must have the signature of your department manager indicating his or her approval. Note that the Purchasing Department will return the form to its sender if any information is omitted. Make sure that a serial number or ID number appears for the items listed. Forward the completed form to Frank Wong, Purchasing Department, Building C, by October 14. Requests received after that date will be considered in the following quarter.

Thank you for your consideration.

CONNOR CHEMICALS
OFFICE EQUIPMENT ORDER FORM

Employee Name: Martin Jacobs
Title and Department: Quality Control Inspector, Production Department

Equipment Description	Serial Number	Age (years)
Photo Jet Printer	8 HDQ5	5
Computer Monitor		7
Power Cable	PH-3 AL	4

Approved by Daniel Donaldson

Date October 15

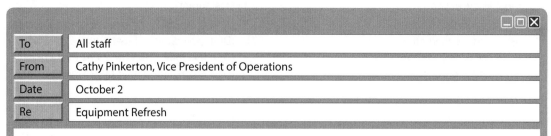

176 Why is the memo being sent?

(A) To notify staff about a budget reduction for office equipment
(B) To describe how the cost of office equipment is calculated
(C) To explain the process of new office equipment requests
(D) To revise the manual for the office equipment setup

177 What is mentioned about the forms?

(A) They are reviewed by the operation department once every five years.
(B) They should include the signature of department managers for submission.
(C) They must be submitted to the purchasing office by October 15.
(D) They have been issued in a variety of formats.

178 What is suggested about the power cable?

(A) Its purchase price is less than the repair costs.
(B) Its production was discontinued last year.
(C) It comes with an extended warranty.
(D) It is not compatible with the company's computers.

179 What staff position does Mr. Donaldson most likely hold?

(A) Purchasing director
(B) Repair technician
(C) Production manager
(D) Administrative assistant

180 Why would Mr. Jacobs most likely have the form returned to him?

(A) Because he submitted a photocopy of the form
(B) Because he left out some necessary information
(C) Because he listed equipment for his personal use
(D) Because he needed to obtain Ms. Pinkerton's signature

GO ON TO THE NEXT PAGE

Questions 181-185 refer to the following Web page and e-mail.

www.tartanairlines.com

Tartan Airlines | New Services and Special Offers | Reservations | Tartan Airlines Plus Program

Tartan Airlines is proud to offer new services from the Nashik Airport to the following destinations.

Kolkata - September 5
Agra - September 20
Chennai - September 15
Mumbai - September 25

Book a flight now and save money! Members of the Tartan Airlines frequent-flyers program, Tartan Airlines Plus, who book a flight for one of the above inaugural flights, will receive a 25% discount.

Click on Reservations to book a flight now.

Restrictions and other Reminders

** This offer is valid for one-way or round-way travel for flights originating from the Nashik Airport only on the dates specified above.

** Frequent Flyers can receive a 25% discount by using the Tartan Airlines Plus Membership number when reserving their flights.

** Tartan Airlines is no longer issuing paper tickets. Upon purchasing their tickets, passengers receive e-mails confirming their reservations. This includes an 8-digit confirmation number. Please, keep this number handy to speed your check-in process; passengers are asked to enter it at one of the self-check-in stations.

** In order to offer the lowest possible airfares, Tartan Airlines no longer offers free newspapers, magazines, or headsets and no food or snacks are served during flights. Each passenger is entitled to one complimentary beverage; beverage choices include fruit juice, coffee, tea or water.

e-mail

From: amcgosh200@dfmailer.com
To: customerservice@tartanairlines.ca
Date: July 29
Subject: Inaugural flight offer

To whom it may concern:

On July 8, I booked a seat on Tartan Airlines' first flight to Chennai from Nashik Airport. According to your Web site, Tartan Airlines Plus Club members are entitled to a 25% discount on this flight. I entered my frequent-flyer number when booking the seat, but my credit card statement shows that I was charged the full fare. I'd appreciate it if you could address this issue as soon as possible.

Sincerely,

Alice McGosh

181 What is NOT mentioned about Tartan Airlines?

(A) It is offering service to four new destinations.
(B) It charges customers a penalty of $25 to change itinerary.
(C) It has stopped providing customers with paper tickets.
(D) It currently provides one soft drink at no charge during flights.

182 According to the information, what must customers do to receive the advertised discount?

(A) Supply their frequent-flyer program number
(B) Make a reservation at least two weeks in advance
(C) Apply for membership in the frequent-flyer program
(D) Purchase tickets to any two of the featured destinations

183 Why did Ms. McGosh send the e-mail?

(A) To complain about delays she experienced on a recent trip
(B) To make a change to her departure date
(C) To ask for a replacement confirmation number
(D) To report a billing mistake with her reservation

184 When is Ms. McGosh scheduled to depart?

(A) On September 5
(B) On September 15
(C) On September 20
(D) On September 25

185 In the e-mail, the word "address" in paragraph 1, line 4, is closest in meaning to

(A) speak
(B) remark
(C) deal with
(D) write

GO ON TO THE NEXT PAGE

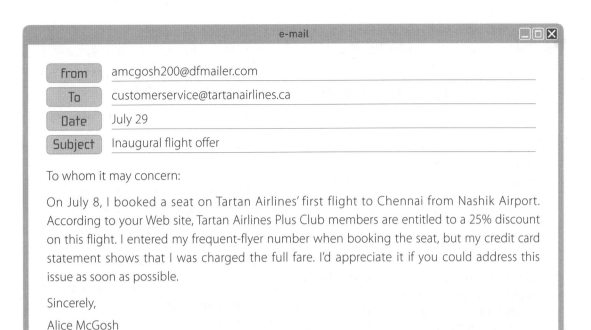

Questions 186-190 refer to the following article, advertisement, and Web page.

Vancouver (March 10)

Regina Regency Resorts Get Bigger

The Seattle-based Regina Hotel Group has acquired Orchid Inc., a small but exclusive locally owned hotel chain. With the addition of the Orchid properties, Regina now operates 11 hotels in the Vancouver area with more than 800 guest rooms.

Prior to the acquisition, Regina had been best known for its Regina Travel Suites, smaller hotels designed with business travelers in mind. Orchid's four properties include the luxurious Grand Hall Hotel, built in 1924, and the Hotel Olivia, a high-end hotel that opened just last year.

The Orchid Hotels are a very welcome addition to the Regina Brand, said Regina spokesperson Douglas Wong. Orchid has a solid reputation in Vancouver, and with accommodations that appeal especially to tourists, they are a perfect complement to Regina's existing hotels.

Regina loyalty-club members can now earn points when they stay at any of the former Orchid Hotels.

Your Home in Vancouver City Center

Visiting Vancouver? Want to be in the heart of the city? Choose Regina Hotel. Our hotel family now includes the popular Orchid Hotels. Below are a few of our most popular hotels in the downtown area.

■ Moon Hotel

From complimentary wireless Internet service to deluxe bed, large-screen TVs and an indoor swimming pool. This hotel has something for everyone. Great for families!

■ Hotel Fantastic Plaza

"Fantastic" does not begin to describe this hotel! Enjoy our newly refurbished luxurious guest rooms, fine dining at our recently remodeled restaurant, and convenient access to theaters, shopping and sightseeing.

■ Hotel South

With free transportation to the airport and a fully equipped business center, this is the perfect hotel for business travelers. It features conference rooms and complimentary wireless Internet service. This hotel makes it easy to work while traveling.

■ Cozy Inn

An old-fashioned inn with modern conveniences such as microwaves and hair dryers in every room. With its charming decor, tasty complimentary breakfast, and proximity to public transportation, this is a wonderful place to stay during your Vancouver holiday.

Or choose one of our many other hotels in the Vancouver region. When you choose Regina, you choose the best!

http://vancouverdays.com/review

RESTAURANTS | HOTELS | ATTRACTIONS | TRANSPORTATION

I really enjoyed my recent stay at the Hotel Fantastic Plaza. My room was comfortable and well furnished, and all my meals at the hotel restaurant were expertly prepared. The hotel staff provided outstanding service as well. I only wish there had been a shuttle service. I had a difficult time getting a taxi to the airport, and it was expensive. Aside from that minor inconvenience, I enjoyed my stay very much.

Shirley Rogers
London

186 What is the article mainly about?
(A) New trends in the hotel industry
(B) The results of a committee election
(C) The merger of two businesses
(D) Announcement of a new construction site

187 What can be inferred about Regina Regency Resorts?
(A) It is relocating its headquarters.
(B) It has discontinued its membership program.
(C) It specializes in luxury hotels.
(D) It attempts to draw a wider variety of customers.

188 What is indicated about the hotels in the advertisement?
(A) They all have swimming pools.
(B) They were first built in 1920.
(C) They are centrally located in downtown.
(D) They offer discounts to business travelers.

189 In the advertisement, the word "proximity" in paragraph 5, line 2, is closest in meaning to
(A) subsequence
(B) approximation
(C) nearness
(D) possibility

190 What is mentioned about the hotel in which Ms. Rogers has stayed?
(A) It is not far from the shopping place.
(B) Its restaurant recently hired a new chef.
(C) It is wheelchair-accessible.
(D) It offers free admission to the hotel facilities.

GO ON TO THE NEXT PAGE

Questions 191-195 refer to the following notice, schedule, and e-mail.

International Auto Trade Fair

This year's International Auto Trade Fair will be held at the MXFM Convention Center in Detroit from August 6th through 13th, and we will have some of the hottest cars and trucks you've ever seen – all under one roof! More sneak peeks, more new production models, and more concept vehicles than ever before. This year only, Cervi Automotive will be showcasing all of its vehicles from director Meredith Grazinski's blockbuster movie *Before the Sun Goes Down*. Stars of that movie, Peter Wiseman and Alicia Michel, will be on hand on August 11th and 12th to demonstrate some of the vehicles' super effects.

La Siesta

NINTH INTERNATIONAL AUTO TRADE FAIR IN DETROIT

- **Public Show Dates**

Friday, August 6th through Friday, August 13th
11:00 A.M. – 10:30 P.M. (Sunday: 10:00 A.M. – 7:30 P.M.)

- **Special Public Sneak Preview**

Friday, August 6th: 11:00 A.M. – 10:30 P.M.

- **Official Opening Day**

Saturday, August 7th
Festivities begin at 9:00 A.M.
The showroom floor opens at 11:00 A.M.

- **Press Preview**

Wednesday, August 11th & Thursday, August 12th
Media credentials required

- **Dealer Preview**

Thursday, August 12th from 4:00 P.M. – 10:00 P.M. (by invitation only)
Credentials required

From	Lenox Stewart
To	Themba Iherjirka
Date	August 1
Subject	Auto Trade Fair Updates

Dear Themba,

I am sorry I couldn't meet with you yesterday. I was busy meeting representatives from the various automakers that will be participating in this year's show. Today, I am meeting with the publicist from Zen Motors at one of its dealerships in the area.

There are a few things I need to talk to you about. The first is that Ms. Michel will not be able to attend the show because of scheduling conflicts with another film she's making. Her agent, Charles Levingston, called yesterday to inform me.

Another problem, and one that could potentially have a more damaging effect, is something that Ms. Woodward in admissions brought to my attention. Apparently all orders for advance tickets were supposed to be accompanied by a certificate that would be good for discounts at area hotels. Unfortunately, only about a third of the people who bought advance tickets received these certificates in time. Ms. Woodward wants to know if we can work out a system where we give the certificates to the people when they arrive for the show, to be retroactively applied to their hotel bills. I like this idea, but let me know what you think.

Sincerely,

Lenox Stewart
Public Relations Manager

191 What is the purpose of the notice?

(A) To explain the details of a new policy
(B) To promote an upcoming event
(C) To advertise a new line of products
(D) To raise money for an organization

192 What is mentioned about the event?

(A) Registration is required to attend.
(B) People can attend before the official opening.
(C) Invitations have been sent to only the media.
(D) A local industry will be hosting it.

193 Who is allowed to attend the Dealer Preview?

(A) All certified dealers
(B) All press officials
(C) Anyone who has paid for advance tickets
(D) People who are invited to come

194 What does Ms. Woodward suggest doing?

(A) Issuing certificates at the convention center
(B) Mailing out letters of apology
(C) Contacting each customer as soon as possible
(D) Waiting to see if there are any complaints

195 Who will probably attend the event on August 12?

(A) Mr. Granzinski
(B) Mr. Wiseman
(C) Ms. Michel
(D) Mr. Levingston

GO ON TO THE NEXT PAGE

Questions 196-200 refer to the following advertisement and e-mails.

Reporter Wanted

Daily Indiana, a leading publishing company, is seeking a reporter to join our team at our location in downtown Bloomington. The successful candidate will have previous experience as a reporter, preferably in a high-profile publishing company. Responsibilities include reading opinions from subscribers, contacting correspondents, processing mail, and other clerical work. This part-time position is 20 hours a week including evening and Saturday hours, which are paid at our overtime rate. Interested individuals should send résumés to hr@dailyindiana.ca.

E-Mail Message

To: hr@dailyindiana.ca
From: lstein@gmail.com
Date: August 8
Subject: Reporter position
Attachment: Stein_résumé; Stein_samples

Dear Human Resources,

I'm writing to express my interest in the reporter position. Though I'm a professional photographer, I have four years of experience working in office settings. While in art school, I worked for three years as an editor at a university newspaper. I also worked in a mailroom of a large corporation. In addition, I'm proficient at several software programs that can be used in editing articles.

Currently, I work as a reporter and photographer at a magazine. Since I only work three mornings a week, I want additional work to fill out my schedule. Though this would be my first job in a newspaper company, I'm willing to learn new skills, and the skills I have would be an asset to you. I'm sending my résumé and my sample work when I worked as an editor in a university newspaper. They demonstrate my writing and interview skills. I look forward to hearing from you and appreciate your consideration.

Sincerely,
Lucy Stein

To	Job Interview Members
From	Fred Jaspers
Date	August 13
Subject	Recruiting reporter position

Hello, everyone.

Our final interview will take place tomorrow at 9:30 A.M. We will be interviewing Ms. Stein. Please read the materials that she submitted so that the information is fresh in your mind during the interview. I know that some of you are concerned about her qualifications, but she could be easily trained to do routine office tasks. In my opinion, she offers much more. In fact, the materials she submitted demonstrate a creativity that could really spice up our marketing materials. If you would like to discuss anything before the interview, please contact me.

Fred

196 According to the advertisement, what is a duty of the reporter position?

(A) Reviewing feedback
(B) Scheduling board meetings
(C) Writing editorials
(D) Calling subscribers

197 What aspect of the position is likely the most appealing to Ms. Stein?

(A) The newspaper's reputation
(B) The downtown location
(C) The job responsibilities
(D) The work schedule

198 What is indicated about Ms. Stein?

(A) She is currently writing for a newspaper company.
(B) She will enroll as an art student.
(C) She has never worked for a newspaper before.
(D) She will relocate to Bloomington.

199 What is the purpose of the second e-mail?

(A) To encourage more interviewers to participate in the board
(B) To ask the job interview members to review some materials
(C) To remind staff members that an interview has been canceled
(D) To inform new employers about an orientation session

200 What does Mr. Jaspers think makes Ms. Stein a good candidate for the position?

(A) Her experience as an editor
(B) Her availability for extended work hours
(C) Her expertise in dealing with clients
(D) Her skills as a computer programmer

Stop! This is the end of the test. If you finish before time is called, you may go back to Parts 5, 6, and 7 and check your work.

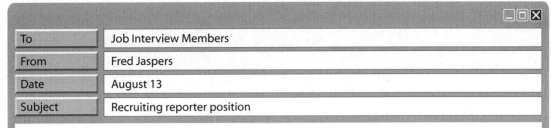

잠깐!! 시작 전 **꼭** 확인하세요!

- 실제 시험과 같이 책상을 정리하고 마음의 준비를 하세요.
- 핸드폰은 잠깐 끄고 대신 아날로그 시계를 활용해 보세요.
- 제한 시간은 120분입니다. 제한 시간을 꼭 지켜주세요.
- 어렵다고 넘어가지 마세요. 가능하면 차례대로 풀어 보세요.

Actual Test

03

시작 시간 :

종료 시간 :

LISTENING TEST

In the Listening test, you will be asked to demonstrate how well you understand spoken English. The entire Listening test will last approximately 45 minutes. There are four parts, and directions are given for each part. You must mark your answers on the separate answer sheet. Do not write your answers in your test book.

PART 1

Directions: For each question in this part, you will hear four statements about a picture in your test book. When you hear the statements, you must select the one statement that best describes what you see in the picture. Then find the number of the question on your answer sheet and mark your answer. The statements will not be printed in your test book and will be spoken only one time.

Example

Sample Answer

Ⓐ ● Ⓒ Ⓓ

Statement (B), "The man is working at a desk," is the best description of the picture, so you should select answer (B) and mark it on your answer sheet.

1

2

Test 03

GO ON TO THE NEXT PAGE

3

4

5

6

GO ON TO THE NEXT PAGE

PART 2

Directions: You will hear a question or statement and three responses spoken in English. They will not be printed in your test book and will be spoken only one time. Select the best response to the question or statement and mark the letter (A), (B), or (C) on your answer sheet.

7 Mark your answer on your answer sheet.

8 Mark your answer on your answer sheet.

9 Mark your answer on your answer sheet.

10 Mark your answer on your answer sheet.

11 Mark your answer on your answer sheet.

12 Mark your answer on your answer sheet.

13 Mark your answer on your answer sheet.

14 Mark your answer on your answer sheet.

15 Mark your answer on your answer sheet.

16 Mark your answer on your answer sheet.

17 Mark your answer on your answer sheet.

18 Mark your answer on your answer sheet.

19 Mark your answer on your answer sheet.

20 Mark your answer on your answer sheet.

21 Mark your answer on your answer sheet.

22 Mark your answer on your answer sheet.

23 Mark your answer on your answer sheet.

24 Mark your answer on your answer sheet.

25 Mark your answer on your answer sheet.

26 Mark your answer on your answer sheet.

27 Mark your answer on your answer sheet.

28 Mark your answer on your answer sheet.

29 Mark your answer on your answer sheet.

30 Mark your answer on your answer sheet.

31 Mark your answer on your answer sheet.

▶정답 및 해설 P068

PART 3

Directions: You will hear some conversations between two or more people. You will be asked to answer three questions about what the speakers say in each conversation. Select the best response to each question and mark the letter (A), (B), (C), or (D) on your answer sheet. The conversations will not be printed in your test book and will be spoken only one time.

32 What item does the man ask about?
(A) A color printer
(B) A copy machine
(C) A laptop
(D) A scanner

33 What does the woman say will happen next month?
(A) New equipment will be purchased.
(B) She will resign from her company.
(C) A new model will be released.
(D) Her work location will change.

34 What does the woman offer to do for the man?
(A) Remain after work
(B) Discount a price
(C) Speak with a seller
(D) Arrange a delivery

---

35 What is the purpose of the man's call?
(A) To request a discount
(B) To make a payment
(C) To inquire about a bill
(D) To open an account

36 What type of business is the man calling?
(A) A bank
(B) An Internet service provider
(C) An electric company
(D) An insurance company

37 What does the woman offer to do?
(A) Give a discount
(B) Fix some device
(C) Provide new service
(D) Return a payment

38 What does the woman say about the employee from Mitchell Cleaning?
(A) He was late for the meeting.
(B) He offered a persuasive deal.
(C) He left a product pamphlet.
(D) He will stop by the next day.

39 What does Oscar say about the company's current cleaning service?
(A) It is highly dependable.
(B) It charges less money.
(C) It has an international reputation.
(D) It offers a discount.

40 What does the woman suggest?
(A) Keeping the current service
(B) Negotiating better service
(C) Postponing a decision
(D) Searching for a different service

---

41 Who most likely is the man talking to?
(A) A tour conductor
(B) A secretary
(C) A manager
(D) A taxi driver

42 What will the man do next Monday?
(A) Tour the city
(B) Attend a convention
(C) Meet his friend
(D) See a client

43 How long will the man be away?
(A) About three days
(B) About a week
(C) More than two weeks
(D) More than a month

GO ON TO THE NEXT PAGE

44 What most likely did the man do last week?

(A) He emailed a document.
(B) He sent a floor plan.
(C) He changed the schedule.
(D) He analyzed the sales data.

45 What does the woman mean when she says, "There is just one thing that worries me"?

(A) The budget may not be sufficient.
(B) Information could have been missing.
(C) The layout might need adjusting.
(D) There may be a shortage of staff.

46 What does the man say he will do?

(A) Send the woman the modified document
(B) Call the woman later in the day
(C) Give the woman his feedback
(D) Visit the woman's office

---

47 Who most likely are the speakers?

(A) Company executives
(B) Business consultants
(C) New interns
(D) Seminar organizers

48 What does the man want to know about the workshops?

(A) The dates
(B) The registration fees
(C) The levels
(D) The attendees

49 What does the woman tell the man to do?

(A) Apply for the position
(B) Organize the event
(C) Speak to a manager
(D) Contact the person in charge

50 What will the speakers' company do in Europe during the fall?

(A) Conclude a research study
(B) Launch a product line
(C) Construct a new facility
(D) Open a new branch

51 Why does the woman say, "That's great. Congratulations"?

(A) The man was promoted to an executive position.
(B) The man finished a project ahead of schedule.
(C) The man enrolled in a well-known university.
(D) The man was given an important assignment.

52 According to the man, what will a former coworker help him do?

(A) Locate a residence
(B) Arrange transportation
(C) Prepare for a course
(D) Make professional contacts

---

53 Where does the conversation most likely take place?

(A) At a bus stop
(B) On a plane
(C) At an airport
(D) At a city center

54 What will the woman probably do next?

(A) Take a shuttle bus
(B) Purchase a ticket
(C) Exchange money
(D) Take a taxi

55 How many shuttle buses run per hour?

(A) One
(B) Two
(C) Three
(D) Four

56 What does Angela suggest doing?

(A) Remodeling the office
(B) Repainting a sign
(C) Selecting colors
(D) Buying more paint

57 What will most likely happen tomorrow?

(A) Angela will use the paint.
(B) Nathan will throw away the materials.
(C) Ms. Morris will install the shelves.
(D) They will go to the head office.

58 What does the man say he will do?

(A) Consult with his colleague
(B) Hire a professional
(C) Attend a workshop
(D) Renovate a staff lounge

---

59 What are the speakers mainly talking about?

(A) A missing flight
(B) A lost item
(C) A delayed flight
(D) A rude passenger

60 What does the woman mean when she says, "I'll start looking into it"?

(A) She will start an investigation.
(B) She will check out some information.
(C) She will book a flight.
(D) She will contact a colleague.

61 What does the woman ask the man to give her?

(A) Some traveler's checks
(B) His boarding pass
(C) His passport
(D) Some documents

The Triumph Building Directory

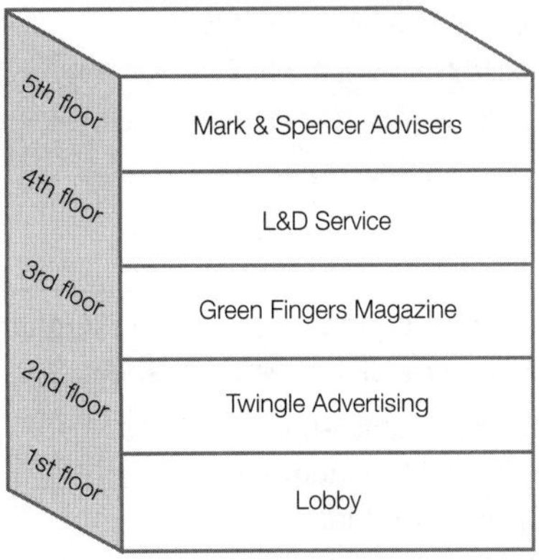

62 What kind of company has moved out of the building?

(A) An accounting company
(B) A legal office
(C) An advertising agency
(D) A publishing company

63 Look at the graphic. At what company do the speakers most likely work?

(A) Mark & Spencer Advisers
(B) L&D Service
(C) Green Fingers Magazine
(D) Tingle Advertising

64 What does the man suggest?

(A) Reviewing a document
(B) Planning an event
(C) Visiting a friend
(D) Hiring a lawyer

Test 03

GO ON TO THE NEXT PAGE

Management & Marketing Conference Presentations in July
Dr. Edward Williamson, Risk Management
Dr. Raymond Gomez, Time Management
Dr. Hillary Palin, Decision Making
Dr. Jina Hong, Group Working

65 Look at the graphic. Which presentation is the man most interested in seeing?

(A) Risk Management
(B) Time Management
(C) Decision Making
(D) Group Working

66 What does the woman advise the man to do?

(A) Arrive at the venue early
(B) Make a reservation
(C) Contact a presenter
(D) Create a credit card

67 According to the woman, what can the man do at the Web site?

(A) Sign up for the conference
(B) Access research data
(C) Check out the schedule
(D) Confirm the credit card number

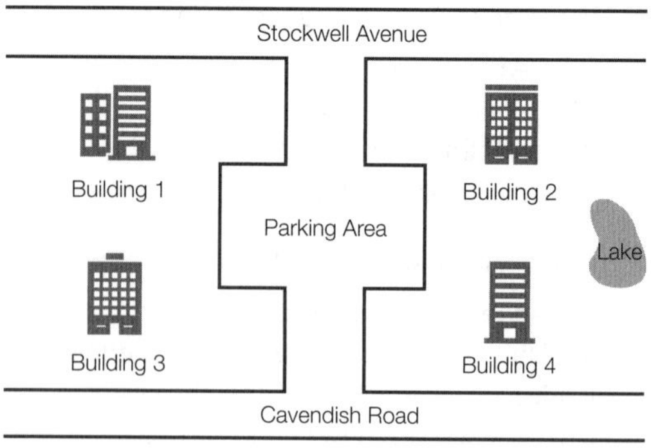

68 What does the man say is a near-term goal of the company?

(A) Reducing expenses
(B) Producing more energy
(C) Opening a new branch
(D) Completing a project

69 What does the woman say is ideal?

(A) The amount of sunlight
(B) Weather condition
(C) The worksite
(D) The work hours

70 Look at the graphic. Where will the installation be done?

(A) On building 1
(B) On building 2
(C) On building 3
(D) On building 4

PART 4

Directions: You will hear some talks given by a single speaker. You will be asked to answer three questions about what the speaker says in each talk. Select the best response to each question and mark the letter (A), (B), (C), or (D) on your answer sheet. The talks will not be printed in your test book and will be spoken only one time.

71 What is the purpose of the talk?
(A) To prepare for a meeting
(B) To vote on a proposal
(C) To change a presenter
(D) To appoint a project manager

72 What does the speaker suggest?
(A) Arriving ahead of time
(B) Postponing a meeting date
(C) Making a presentation
(D) Cutting a budget

73 Where are listeners asked to meet tomorrow morning?
(A) At a café
(B) In a parking lot
(C) At the park
(D) In a seminar room

---

74 Who most likely are the listeners?
(A) Office workers
(B) Computer technicians
(C) Packaging designers
(D) Factory workers

75 What is an advantage of the new machine?
(A) It uses less power.
(B) It requires fewer operators.
(C) It performs more quickly.
(D) It is easier to maintain.

76 According to the speaker, what will Ms. Miller do next?
(A) Distribute some documents
(B) Contact another department
(C) Give a demonstration
(D) Install some equipment

77 What kind of business is Ms. Holton calling?
(A) An architectural firm
(B) An art gallery
(C) An event agency
(D) A real estate agency

78 What does the speaker mean when she says, "that'll be all"?
(A) She thinks the event will finish soon.
(B) She has completed preparations.
(C) She bought new equipment.
(D) She has found what she was looking for.

79 What does Ms. Holton say she will do next week?
(A) Sign a contract
(B) Contact a manager
(C) Visit a client
(D) Revise an estimate

---

80 What is main topic of this report?
(A) The results of a sports match
(B) The completion of roadwork
(C) The expansion of a stadium
(D) The construction of a tennis court

81 According to the report, what caused the delay?
(A) Insufficient funding
(B) A legal dispute
(C) A supply shortage
(D) Inclement weather

82 What does the speaker say about the Wimbledon Tennis Tournament?
(A) It will attract many people to the area.
(B) It will not start on schedule.
(C) It is causing some traffic detours.
(D) It is held on a regular basis.

GO ON TO THE NEXT PAGE

83 What will the listener most likely do on Friday morning?

(A) View product samples
(B) Reserve a place
(C) Make a phone call
(D) Create a window display

84 Why is the speaker calling?

(A) To report an error
(B) To reschedule an appointment
(C) To give a reminder
(D) To make a sale

85 What does the speaker mean when he says, "I've really got to hand it to you"?

(A) He wants to give an item to the listener.
(B) He needs to rearrange the window display.
(C) He wants to offer the listener help.
(D) He thinks the listener deserves praise.

---

86 What type of information does Developing Yourself probably focus on?

(A) Developing new products
(B) Fashion trends
(C) Technological innovations
(D) Career advice

87 According to the broadcast, what has Sarah Parker done?

(A) She published a book.
(B) She ran a school.
(C) She took an online course.
(D) She owned a company.

88 What will Ms. Parker do at the end of the show?

(A) Take calls from listeners
(B) Introduce another guest
(C) Attend the educational training
(D) Make a questionnaire

89 What is the purpose of the talk?

(A) To announce a new policy
(B) To introduce a new employee
(C) To plan a company event
(D) To inform about a business hour

90 What does the speaker mean when she says, "So, we're lucky"?

(A) The company has received the media attention.
(B) Brian Price has accepted the job offer.
(C) Glen Keys will join the company.
(D) The company has been highly ranked in the industry.

91 What will most likely happen next?

(A) The employees will introduce themselves.
(B) There will be a discussion session.
(C) The staff will submit the forms.
(D) Mr. Price will speak about the company's future.

---

92 Why is the speaker calling?

(A) To congratulate on the success
(B) To complete the sales report
(C) To decline an invitation
(D) To confirm a meeting agenda

93 What does the speaker mean when he says, "A lot has to be done over and over again"?

(A) He bought several computers.
(B) He lost some of his work.
(C) He attended a variety of workshops.
(D) He needed to call a manager repeatedly.

94 According to the speaker, what did a department manager ask for?

(A) A deadline extension
(B) A personal visit
(C) Modification of information
(D) Completion of a questionnaire

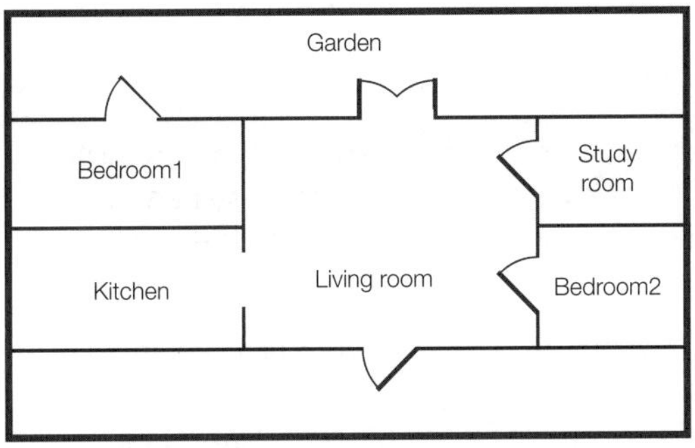

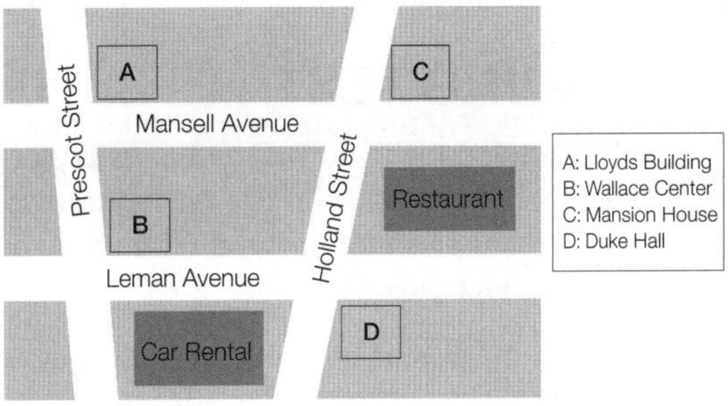

95 What type of business do the listeners probably work for?
(A) A furniture dealer
(B) An interior design agency
(C) A cleaning service
(D) A moving company

96 Look at the graphic. Where should the green boxes be placed?
(A) Bedroom 1
(B) Bedroom 2
(C) The study room
(D) The living room

97 What does the speaker say Ms. Clarkson will do?
(A) Leave the entrance open
(B) Unpack some boxes
(C) Clean up the new home
(D) Lock up some valuable items

98 What kind of event is going to be held?
(A) A product launch
(B) A business gathering
(C) A sales workshop
(D) A special dinner

99 Look at the graphic. Which venue does the speaker recommend?
(A) Lloyds Building
(B) Wallace Center
(C) Mansion House
(D) Duke Hall

100 How can the listeners contact the speaker?
(A) By text message
(B) By electronic mail
(C) By fax
(D) By extension phone

This is the end of the Listening test. Turn to Part 5 in your test book.

GO ON TO THE NEXT PAGE

READING TEST

In the Reading test, you will read a variety of texts and answer several different types of reading comprehension questions. The entire Reading test will last 75 minutes. There are three parts, and directions are given for each part. You are encouraged to answer as many questions as possible within the time allowed.

You must mark your answers on the separate answer sheet. Do not write your answers in your test book.

PART 5

Directions: A word or phrase is missing in each of the sentences below. Four answer choices are given below each sentence. Select the best answer to complete the sentence. Then mark the letter (A), (B), (C), or (D) on your answer sheet.

101 ------- new dental office will occupy the third floor of the new building on Mason Street.

(A) We
(B) Our
(C) Ours
(D) Us

102 Bus passengers ------- bicycles are responsible for securing them appropriately.

(A) with
(B) over
(C) of
(D) from

103 The advance deposit is ------- refundable as long as the rental car is returned without damage.

(A) full
(B) fully
(C) fuller
(D) fullest

104 ------ has worked harder than Lisa Stanley to market New Skin's new line of hair treatment products.

(A) Whoever
(B) Nothing
(C) Nobody
(D) Any

105 The ------- of the construction project was covered by a generous donation from some local entrepreneurs.

(A) currency
(B) benefit
(C) account
(D) cost

106 Please remember to double-check the spelling of Mr. Prichard's name when ------- the document.

(A) revising
(B) revises
(C) revised
(D) revise

107 Recruiting interns is a ------- solution to filling entry-level positions eventually at Cypher Bank.

(A) talented
(B) various
(C) willing
(D) sensible

108 Delegates visited the mayor to ask ------- developers will preserve the work of ancient artisans.

(A) although
(B) since
(C) whether
(D) both

109 Workers now send in travel requests electronically ------- submitting a paper form.

(A) instead of
(B) because of
(C) through
(D) which

110 Tenants who are ------- in renewing their lease should follow the process outlined on the Lakeview Apartments Web site.

(A) interest
(B) interests
(C) interested
(D) interesting

111 Juan Reyes, the newest employee of the Manheim Film Production, ------- worked in London for eight years.

(A) consequently
(B) always
(C) still
(D) previously

112 ------- Ms. Jenkins wrote her thesis on housing markets, she knew how to make profitable property investments.

(A) Either
(B) Rather
(C) Unless
(D) Because

113 At the Board meeting, it was mentioned that there is a slight ------- that the Carmichael Arts Center will be closed.

(A) possible
(B) possibility
(C) possibly
(D) possibilities

114 ------ receiving the prestigious Evangeline Award, Ms. Mehta made a point of thanking her long-time colleagues.

(A) Onto
(B) Unlike
(C) About
(D) Upon

115 Because the rates for the Wellington Hotel were very high, Logisoft Inc. will hold a workshop ------- this year.

(A) seldom
(B) recently
(C) somewhat
(D) elsewhere

116 Dr. Di Scala indicates that important shopping trends become ------- with the use of data analysis.

(A) predict
(B) prediction
(C) predictable
(D) predictably

117 ------- to Braxton Drive will be limited to one side of the street after the road work begins next month.

(A) Access
(B) Accesses
(C) Accessible
(D) Accessing

118 Professor Hillsman's ------- for teaching at Malkin College remains still strong at the age of 65.

(A) enthusiasm
(B) assortment
(C) likeness
(D) inclusion

119 To be eligible for the Jessie's Electronics discount, you must submit the coupon ------- in the mail.

(A) has sent
(B) have to send
(C) that was sent
(D) for sending

120 With the rainy season, Faye's Bicycle Rentals will most likely have ------- customers this month.

(A) neither
(B) every
(C) fewer
(D) higher

GO ON TO THE NEXT PAGE

121 ------- all interview processes have been completed, the top three candidates for the advertising director position will be contacted.

(A) Compared to
(B) As soon as
(C) So that
(D) Not only

122 ------- the assigned speaking time not work for you, please let Ms. Everett know, so she can rearrange the presentation schedule.

(A) Whenever
(B) Anywhere
(C) As well as
(D) Should

123 The hiring committee will ------- an offer of employment to Dwan Willis next Monday.

(A) extend
(B) assign
(C) displace
(D) commit

124 If you lose your identification card, the security manager will deactivate it and issue -------.

(A) other
(B) other one
(C) one another
(D) another

125 City inspectors will evaluate every office on 5th floor next week ------- determine how to best reduce energy usage.

(A) even if
(B) in order to
(C) after all
(D) given that

126 To select its Audit Committee members, Blake Techline Ltd. ------- employees who are ready for a challenge.

(A) seeking
(B) is seeking
(C) are sought
(D) have been sought

127 Ms. Perone provided an explanation of recent changes to keep the funding arrangement process as ------- as possible.

(A) interested
(B) forceful
(C) transparent
(D) remarkable

128 The workplace safety at Glaxton-Jenner Company is something ------- will never be compromised.

(A) where
(B) that
(C) when
(D) then

129 Relevant documents are ------- delivered to the lawyer's office by our secretary from the Legal Department.

(A) timely
(B) identifiably
(C) highly
(D) typically

130 Technicians will inspect the historic Karen Marx Building next week to ------- the building is still architecturally sound.

(A) ensure
(B) measure
(C) modify
(D) accept

PART 6

Directions: Read the texts that follow. A word, phrase, or sentence is missing in parts of each text. Four answer choices for each question are given below the text. Select the best answer to complete the text. Then mark the letter (A), (B), (C), or (D) on your answer sheet.

Questions 131-134 refer to the following memo.

From: Jin Li Zhang
To: All staff
Date: April 10
Subject: Natalie Albright

As some of you know, Natalie Albright, our head landscaper, will soon be leaving our company.

She has -------**131.** a position in residential construction industry. Natalie has been interested in that field for some time. -------**132.**. Even so, we are -------**133.** sorry to see her go.

Natalie's last day with us is Friday, 25, April. At 2:30 P.M., on that day, we have a farewell gathering in company cafeteria -------**134.** her ten year service with us. We look forward to seeing you all.

Marry Rogers
Facilities Director

131 (A) advertised
(B) supported
(C) accepted
(D) indicated

132 (A) Her new job is more in line with her ultimate goal of becoming construction engineer.
(B) Managers meetings will move from 10 A.M. to 2 P.M. starting next Monday.
(C) The human resources director will explain health insurance offered by the company.
(D) Employees are required to arrive at work at least five minutes before 9 A.M. every day.

133 (A) very
(B) rather
(C) too
(D) such

134 (A) has recognized
(B) is recognizing
(C) would recognize
(D) to recognize

Questions 135-138 refer to the following brochure excerpt.

-------. Sponsored by the Bronxville Visitors Bureau, each tour is led ------- a knowledgeable guide and features an unique area of town.
135. **136.**

The most popular focuses on Cyrus Square are the town's theater -------.
137.

In addition to three playhouses and two music halls, Cyrus Square includes an opera house and several historic hotels that represent a range of architectural styles. The tour lasts approximately two hours and ------- with a delicious meal at the Waterfront Café, one of Bronxville's best known dining establishments.
138.

To register for the Cyrus Square tour or learn about the other tours, call the Bronxville Visitor Bureau at 555-0114.

135 (A) Customers waited in line for six hours to purchase new guide books and city maps.
(B) Explore the town of Bronxville through one of our four regularly scheduled walking tours.
(C) The city gallery will feature relics about the Tang Dynasty in its spring exhibit.
(D) We think it's a great idea that will generate more revenue from the sale of food and beverages.

136 (A) for
(B) by
(C) during
(D) behind

137 (A) actors
(B) programs
(C) district
(D) school

138 (A) exits
(B) orders
(C) reserves
(D) concludes

Questions 139-142 refer to the following memo.

From: Gabrielle Rothschild, Building Manager
To: All employees
Date: Thursday, August 9
Re: Construction work

As you are -------, renovations to our office building will begin on Monday, August 13, and continue until the end of the day on Friday, August 17. As a result, you may experience some -------.
139. / 140.

-------. Employees who regularly use this elevator should take the stairs or use the elevator on the south side of the building.
141.

-------, the entrance on the northwest side of the building facing Ali Avenue will be closed on Tuesday through Thursday. All other entrances to the building will be open as usual during this time.
142.

139 (A) helpful
(B) aware
(C) informing
(D) famous

140 (A) inconvenience
(B) assignment
(C) addition
(D) interference

141 (A) Noise levels must be kept at a minimum at all times.
(B) Please dispose of garbage in the proper receptacles.
(C) The north-side elevator will be out of service for the entire week.
(D) Employees are forbidden from entering private area designated for CEO.

142 (A) However
(B) Instead
(C) Previously
(D) Also

Test 03

Questions 143-146 refer to the following news article.

July 1 – Beginning in September, the South Central School District will rely ------- (143.) on Chester Educational Publishing Group for health-related learning and teaching materials. ------- (144.).

As of July 30, the school board ------- (145.) its contracts with the other two vendors. This decision was based on a survey of teachers and school nurses, who attested to the superior quality of Chester's products. ------- (146.) the cost of Chester's textbooks is high, its workbooks, models, and teacher's guides are less expensive than those of its competitors, helping to keep overall expenditures within budget.

143 (A) formally
(B) periodically
(C) initially
(D) solely

144 (A) Thank you for your cooperation in abiding by all the teaching rules.
(B) Users of the Web site will be able to download the files for teaching.
(C) Chester also work closely with teachers to provide bilingual assistance if necessary.
(D) Historically, Chester was one of three preferred vendors for such content.

145 (A) was discontinuing
(B) is discontinued
(C) will discontinue
(D) would have discontinued

146 (A) Even though
(B) Unless
(C) Because
(D) As soon as

PART 7

Directions: In this part you will read a selection of texts, such as magazine and newspaper articles, e-mails, and instant messages. Each text or set of texts is followed by several questions. Select the best answer for each question and mark the letter (A), (B), (C), or (D) on your answer sheet.

Questions 147-148 refer to the following tag.

JUNG & JO APPAREL

MEDIUM

100% wool

Wash by hand or by machine on gentle cycle with similar colors.
Wash in cold water only.
Machine dry on coolest setting.

Please note that variations in color are an intended feature of this fabric.
With repeated washing, texture also may alter further.

Made in Italy

147 According to the tag, how should the item be care for?

(A) By washing it at a low temperature
(B) By drying it for a specific time
(C) By soaking it in warm water
(D) By wiping it with a damp cloth

148 What is stated about the item?

(A) It was made by hand.
(B) It will shrink after washing.
(C) It may change in texture.
(D) It was produced in France.

GO ON TO THE NEXT PAGE

Questions 149-150 refer to the following advertisement.

Major Technical Institute

Are you considering returning to school? Education can be an important part of your career path, and Major Tech. is pleased to offer a variety of continuing-education courses for the busy professional. In addition to our regular daytime course offerings, we now offer classes online that conveniently fit into anyone's schedules.

Choose from many training programs, including computer networking, food preparation, and medical technology. Consult our Web site www.majortech.edu for a complete list of courses available.

For detailed information regarding our certification programs, please contact admission at 090-555-7890 or send an e-mail to info@majortech.edu.

149 According to the advertisement, what is a recent development at Major Tech.?

(A) Courses over Internet
(B) Free consultation for graduates
(C) A revised admission policy
(D) Brand-new computers and monitors

150 What is NOT stated as a way to learn more about Major Tech.?

(A) Making a phone call
(B) Sending an e-mail
(C) Visiting the Web site
(D) Going to the campus

Questions 151-153 refer to the following Web page.

http://fantasticspain.com

Fantastic Spain Travels

HOME | DESTINATIONS | **REVIEW** | CONTACT

Recently, a colleague and I were on business in Madrid and had a free day for sightseeing. On advice from the clerk at the front desk of our hotel, we booked a tour of the royal palace through Fantastic Spain Travels (FST). It was my colleague's first chance to see this attraction and my second. The first time I visited, though, I was with a large group. I felt very rushed and was not able to really appreciate the palace or take as many photos as I would have liked. This time, I was happy to book a pricier private excursion, led by guide Juan Dominguez.

In contrast to my last tour, which did not include transportation, Mr. Dominguez took us to the palace by car. We could tell that Mr. Dominguez's historical knowledge was extensive. Since my colleague and I were his only clients, we were able to ask a lot of questions and took our time.

I was pleased that the entrance fees were covered by the excursion price, and that FST obtained our tickets in advance, so that we would not have to wait in line when we arrived. Lunch at a delicious local restaurant was provided, so we didn't even have to spend time looking for a good place to eat.

This tour is a great value and much more worth the price.

Jane Weatherly (Calcutta, Australia)

151 Who introduced FST to Ms. Weatherly?

(A) A travel agent
(B) A business associate
(C) A hotel employee
(D) A local friend

152 What was NOT covered in the price of tour?

(A) A souvenir photograph
(B) A meal
(C) Transportation
(D) Admission charges

153 What is suggested about Ms. Weatherly?

(A) She travels often for business.
(B) She is Mr. Dominguez's colleague.
(C) She has visited Madrid before.
(D) She is interested in Spanish history.

GO ON TO THE NEXT PAGE

Questions 154-155 refer to the following text message chain.

Martina Androva
I'm sorry to bother you after work, but I've got some questions I forgot to ask before going on my trip.
7:55 P.M.

Antonio Fuentez
It's okay. How can I help you?
7:57 P.M.

Martina Androva
I just got to Auto World Rentals, and they are asking about insurance. Since I am new to the company, I don't know our policy on this. Is it required?
7:59 P.M.

Antonio Fuentez
We are absolutely required to purchase insurance before driving the car off the lot.
8:01 P.M.

Martina Androva
Can I use the company credit card or my personal card?
8:03 A.M.

Antonio Fuentez
Company card is easier, but be sure to keep your receipt.
8:05 P.M.

Martina Androva
They offer e-receipts, so keeping track of receipts should be easy.
8:07 A.M.

Send

154 At 7:57 P.M., what does Mr. Fuentez mean when he writes, "It's okay"?

(A) Ms. Androva can submit proof of purchase electronically.
(B) Information on company travel is easy for Ms. Androva to obtain.
(C) He suggests that Ms. Androva not purchase insurance.
(D) He is willing to answer Ms. Androva's questions.

155 What is indicated about Ms. Androva?

(A) She has applied for a credit card.
(B) She is recently hired at the company.
(C) She would like a refund for travel expenses.
(D) She needs transportation to an airport.

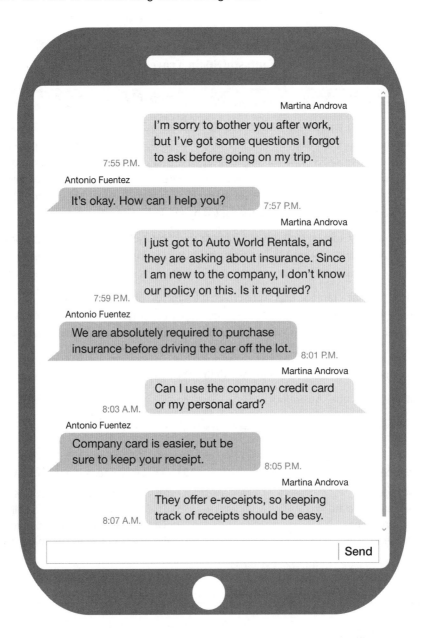

Questions 156-157 refer to the following notice.

Ranger Carpet Store

2389 Market Street

Laramie, WY 39877

902-555-0145 www.rangercarpet.ca

Don't miss out our special event on October 2!

As one of our best customers, you are invited to a special event marketing the introduction of Comfortzone, a new line of carpets featuring a revolutionary new carpet fiber. Factory tests show that Comfortzone carpets trap up to 25 percent less dirt and last longer than comparably priced carpets. And if you purchase a Comfortzone carpet at our store on October 2, you can save up to 40 percent off the regular price. Simply bring this notice to our store on October 2 and show it to a store employee to gain admission to the Comfortzone show room. We look forward to seeing you!

156 What is indicated about Comfortzone carpets?

(A) They come in a variety of colors.
(B) They are produced with a special new material.
(C) They last 40% longer than more expensive carpets.
(D) They can be delivered complimentarily.

157 How can a customer quality for a discount on a Comforzone carpet?

(A) By ordering the carpet online
(B) By participating in a store event
(C) By presenting a document
(D) By completing a customer survey

GO ON TO THE NEXT PAGE

Questions 158-160 refer to the following article.

May 10 – Media Tree, the company that contributed to artwork for the popular *Look at Others* billboard campaign, has been nominated for the prestigious Malta Award, which has been recognizing innovation in published artwork and illustration for 40 years. Selected from almost 2,000 entrants, Media Tree is the first Taipei-based illustration studio to be nominated for the artwork. –[1]–. All of this year's Malta Award winners will be announced on June 15 during a ceremony in London.

"We are very excited about this nomination, which is a testament to the high level of skill, expertise, and creativity of our staff," said Melinda Bonner, founder and CEO of the company.

–[2]–. The Malta Award judges, a group of twelve leading art executives from museums and galleries across the globe, noted that Media Tree was nominated based on the diversity, quality, and sophistication of its portfolio of art. "We illustrate everything from magazines and children's literature to cosmetics and food packaging," noted Ms. Bonner, "and we work closely with our clients to ensure the end product exceeds their expectations."

–[3]–. Since the names of the nominees were released, the studio has seen a large increase in the number of requests for its services. "There is no way we can meet the growing demand unless we hire more illustrators and project managers. Of course, that's exactly what we are going to do now," said Ms. Bonner.

More information about Media Tree can be found at www.mediatree.co.in. Details about the Malta Award are at www.maltaaward.org. –[4]–.

158 What is suggested about the Malta Award?

(A) It was established by a single individual.
(B) It has been awarded to advertising companies before.
(C) It gives cash prizes to its recipients.
(D) It was first awarded forty years ago.

159 According to the article, what does Ms. Bonner plan to do?

(A) Recruit new employees
(B) Open a second branch
(C) Decrease the publicity budget
(D) Attend a ceremony in Taipei

160 In which of the positions marked [1], [2], [3], and [4] does the following sentence best belong?

"Apart from the honor, the nomination has produced publicity and increased business for Media Tree."

(A) [1]
(B) [2]
(C) [3]
(D) [4]

Questions 161-164 refer to the following report.

PERFECT HEALTH AND FITNESS CENTER

Notes from the Board Meeting

■ **Financial**

Last year ended with a surplus of £3,100. This year's budget is estimated to have a surplus of £6,291.

■ **Membership/Retention**

This year is starting off strong in terms of membership numbers. January's New Year's Bash brought in 176 new members.

Not including the New Year's Bash, Fitness Center memberships were up 8% in January. In an effort to continue increasing membership, we are implementing a free one-week trial period.

Total membership is up from January last year, reflecting new membership sales as well as an increased percentage of renewing members. Membership usage has increased, which has caused some concern especially in the facilities located near office parks. We will need to address parking and locker availability in the near future.

161 What is stated about the coming year's budget?

(A) It is estimated to have a surplus.
(B) Several programs will need to be cut.
(C) Membership sales account for 60% of the budget.
(D) It is balanced for the first time in five years.

162 What is Perfect Health and Fitness Center offering?

(A) Free fitness tests
(B) A week-long trial period
(C) Three free training sessions
(D) One-time payment for individual classes

163 What will Perfect Health and Fitness Center need to address in the future?

(A) Extending the center's operating hours
(B) Adding more fitness classes and equipment
(C) Opening new centers closer to downtown
(D) Making more storage space available at centers

164 The word "reflecting" in paragraph 4, line 1, is closest in meaning to

(A) showing
(B) concerning
(C) returning
(D) wondering

GO ON TO THE NEXT PAGE

Questions 165-167 refer to the following memo.

A Memo from the Editor

This November issue of *Cuisine in New Orleans* marks the magazine's first anniversary. Just one year ago, we distributed our first issue, and since then we have become one of the area's most widely read magazines on regional cooking. Our circulation recently reached 50,000, and the number continues to climb. Local food enthusiasts have praised our publication, and at last month's New Orleans Food Fest we became the proud recipient of an award for best new culinary magazine. As editor-in-chief, I would like to share my appreciation for our hardworking staff, our contributors, our advertisers, and our expanding community of readers, all of whom have played an important part in our success.

Colin Green

165 What is the purpose of the memo?

(A) To express gratitude
(B) To extend an offer
(C) To introduce a contributor
(D) To send an invitation

166 What is mentioned about *Cuisine in New Orleans*?

(A) It is seeking additional writers.
(B) It will soon be distributed internationally.
(C) It is growing in popularity.
(D) It has increased its advertising rates.

167 Why does Mr. Green mention the New Orleans Food Fest?

(A) To give a cooking demonstration there
(B) To recruit staff members to volunteer there
(C) To indicate that the magazine sponsored the event
(D) To note that the magazine was honored at the event

Questions 168-171 refer to the following online chat discussion.

Lydia Johnson [11:30 A.M.]	Marie and I are grabbing a bite to eat for lunch around 12:30. Anyone wants to join us?
Joanie Lockhart [11:31 A.M.]	Maybe. I still have some work to do on the mid-year report. Where are you planning to go?
Lydia Johnson [11:32 A.M.]	We're thinking of trying the new Thai restaurant on Rexington Road. It's called Erawan Hit.
John Randolph [11:33 A.M.]	You're out of luck. That place closed a few days ago.
Lydia Johnson [11:34 A.M.]	Sorry to hear about that. People said great things about it.
John Randolph [11:36 A.M.]	How about Kaosan Road around the corner? They always have a special menu on Fridays.
Lydia Johnson [11:37 A.M.]	That would be great. Do you guys want to go Kaosan Road?
Joanie Lockhart [11:38 A.M.]	OK. But I won't be able to get there until about one.
Marie Cantanzaro [11:39 A.M.]	Sounds good to me. Joanie, I just sent you the updated figures for the report.

Send

168 What are the people discussing?

(A) The place to hold an award ceremony
(B) The best restaurant in the area
(C) Today's special at Erawan Hit
(D) The place for lunch

169 What information does Mr. Randolph provide about Erawan Hit?

(A) It has a good reputation for seafood.
(B) It usually closes on Sundays.
(C) It offers food at a low price.
(D) It does not operate any more.

170 At 11:34 A.M., why most likely does Ms. Johnson write, "Sorry to hear about that"?

(A) She wanted to try a new place.
(B) Mr. Randolph cannot complete a project.
(C) A restaurant is too small for everyone.
(D) She has a scheduling conflict.

171 What does Ms. Lockhart decide to do?

(A) Browse nearby restaurants
(B) Change her work shift tomorrow
(C) Have lunch with her colleagues
(D) Ask Ms. Johnson to get some sandwiches

GO ON TO THE NEXT PAGE

Questions 172-175 refer to the following letter.

IOFF

International Office Furnishing Foundation
40 Block Road
Bloomington, IN 01398

May 4

Risa Daniels
Taylor Office Furniture
14 Pine Street
Belleville, IL 80214

Dear Ms. Daniels,

On behalf of the IOFF board, I thank you for your early registration for the IOFF trade show in Bloomington this summer. We are confident that this year's event will be our best ever. Not only are we moving to a more spacious venue but the keynote speaker for the convention will be renowned furniture designer Lisa DeNoble.

As always, IOFF wishes to provide an enjoyable atmosphere where the top furniture designers can exhibit their works and develop professional relationships with high-end retailers throughout Bloomington. –[1]–. To accommodate a growing number of exhibitors, this year's event will be held at the Lafayette Convention Center. The center has over 70,000 square meters for exhibition and meeting spaces, and is located only minutes from Bloomington's central commercial area with easy access to restaurants, shops, and theatres. –[2]–. To help you prepare for participation in the convention, please read carefully the enclosed brochure.

One of our goals is to facilitate your installation in the exhibition hall. –[3]–. Please note the time and dates for exhibitor check in, set up, teardown for the trade show. IOFF volunteers will process on-site registration, check in registered exhibitors and hand out name badges at the registration desk outside Hall A, starting at noon, Sunday, August 24. Hall A and Hall B will be open on that day for installation from noon to 7 P.M. Teardown will be on Thursday, August 28 from 1 P.M. to 6 P.M. IOFF volunteers will be available to assist you on both days for set up and teardown.

The convention brochure has a complete event calendar and a map of the Convention Center including designated unloading areas. –[4]–. If you have questions beyond the scope of this letter and brochure, our special support staff are on site to help you with any matters. Just call us at 033-555-0011.

We are really honored to be having you at our convention and wish the event to be the most successful one.

Sincerely,

John Ellsworth
Senior Event Manager

172 According to the letter, what is a new feature of the IOFF convention?

(A) It will include entertainment performances.
(B) It will start at an earlier time.
(C) It will provide a wider range of events.
(D) It will take place at a bigger venue.

173 What is indicated about the Convention Center?

(A) The building was recently renovated.
(B) It is near Bloomington's business district.
(C) It has the latest technological equipment.
(D) The building includes restaurants and shops.

174 What is NOT mentioned as one of the ways IOFF volunteers will help at the convention?

(A) Registering participants
(B) Handing out badges
(C) Assisting with exhibits
(D) Answering phones

175 In which of the positions marked [1], [2], [3], and [4] does the following sentence best belong?

"A list of frequently asked questions with responses are also included."

(A) [1]
(B) [2]
(C) [3]
(D) [4]

Test 03

GO ON TO THE NEXT PAGE

Questions 176-180 refer to the following announcement and notice.

May 1st

Aberman Books Announces New Young Authors Titles

***Don't Look Back in Anger* by Gabr Alfarsi**
With a storm brewing off the coast and a newcomer in town, this gripping mystery set in a lighthouse is full of surprising twists. This is also the first of the enchanting series.

***The Visigoths the Western Goths* by Kenneth Ling**
In this anthology of essays, world traveler Kenneth Ling recounts his expeditions to the Iberian Peninsula in a way that reads like delightful fiction. Includes a classroom discussion guide.

***All the Way Up* by Ricardo Gomez**
No one knows what to expect when the queen of Geizan disappears and her young daughter inherits the throne. This humorous look at royal life is comedy writing at its best.

***Sit Next to Me* by Joseph Gustaferro**
A group of acquaintances vacationing in a quiet, seaside town learn about each other's past. This tale, from the winner of the Lennox Fiction Prize, deftly analyzes the power of friendship.

For immediate release contact:
Grover Misra at (212) 555-0130

Upcoming Events in Woodward Bookstore

Saturday, July 12

Woodward Bookstore (455 Mason Avenue) will host a panel discussion moderated by Sanjay Dellegrio, associate editor of Writing & Publishing Magazine. Authors Gabr Alfarsi, Kenneth Ling, Ricardo Gomez whose first books were released by Aberman Books earlier this year, will speak about how they became published authors. They'll answer questions and give advice to those hoping to do the same. A book signing will take place after the event. Call (212) 555-0187 for more information.

176 What do all of the books in the announcement have in common?

(A) They are all mystery books.
(B) They are being published at the same time.
(C) They are intended for young adults.
(D) They are written by young writers.

177 In the announcement, the word "recounts" in paragraph 3, line 1, is closest in meaning to

(A) describes
(B) calculates
(C) estimates
(D) returns

178 What is the topic of the July 12 event?

(A) How bookstores can attract customers
(B) How aspiring writers can get published
(C) How to become a magazine editor
(D) How to write lesson plans for a class

179 What will Mr. Dellegrio do at the event?

(A) Sign a book for fans
(B) Give teaching advice
(C) Lead a group discussion
(D) Serve refreshments

180 What book will NOT be signed by its author at the event?

(A) *Don't Look Back in Anger*
(B) *The Visigoths the Western Goths*
(C) *All the Way Up*
(D) *Sit Next to Me*

GO ON TO THE NEXT PAGE

Questions 181-185 refer to following e-mails.

To	Keith Blanchett
From	Sam Brewer
Subject	The Audit Schedule
Date	June 10

Dear Mr. Blanchett:

Thank you for contracting with Environment Safe. We are proud to be your choice for corporate environmental standards certification of your company and look forward to working with you.

As we discussed, the audit will determine whether your company is in compliance with government regulations regarding clean air, clean water, and waste disposal. It will cover four main categories: general practices, the quality of discharged air, the quality of discharged water, and waste removal and recycling. Ratings for each category will be included in the report along with an overall rating of your business. We will perform separate audits and ratings for your manufacturing facility, warehouse and shipping center.

As you know, the audit period lasts two weeks and must occur when all operations are running normally. On your enrollment application, you requested that the audit occur during the last two weeks of August. This time frame works well for us. Unless I hear from you otherwise, I will assume that this is the best time to schedule environmental assessment of your company. Please contact me at your convenience to go over the details of how to prepare for the audit.

Thank you,

Sam Brewer
Public Relations Manager
Environment Safe

To	Keith Blanchett
From	Tom McKnight
Subject	Schedule for 3rd quarter
Date	June 12
Attachment	schedule.pdf

Dear Keith,

I have attached the current draft of the company schedule for July, August and September. Please note that the warehouse staff will most likely need to work additional hours during these months depending on the Roberts Plumbing orders. We expect the orders to come in by the end of this week, at which point we should be able to finalize the schedule. All other existing orders have been finalized and entered into the schedule.

At our last meeting, you mentioned that we might add to the schedule. I have entered the July safety training sessions on it already, but could you let me know what else I should add? I'd like to send the schedule to the regional managers by the beginning of next week.

Tom

181 According to the first e-mail, what service does Environment Safe provide?

(A) Hiring of manufacturing and warehousing staff
(B) Preparing financial reports for companies
(C) Recycling of paper and other materials
(D) Rating companies' compliance with government rules

182 According to the second e-mail, what will likely happen next month in the warehouse?

(A) Some employees will be working extra hours.
(B) Some advanced equipment will be serviced.
(C) Waste materials will be collected for reprocessing.
(D) The revised company policy will be posted.

183 What does Mr. McKnight hope to do by the end of this week?

(A) Evaluate Environment Safe's offer
(B) Complete the company's calendar
(C) Begin an environmental standards assessment
(D) Order supplies from Roberts Plumbing

184 In the second e-mail, the word "note" in paragraph 1, line 2 is closest in meaning to

(A) write down
(B) pick up
(C) take out
(D) bear in mind

185 What will Mr. Blanchett probably say in his response to the second e-mail?

(A) Manufacturing facilities must prepare for increased business.
(B) An audit of the company must be added to the calendar.
(C) A safety training session must be arranged for September.
(D) The method for updating the calendar must be revised.

GO ON TO THE NEXT PAGE

Questions 186-190 refer to the following advertisement, e-mail, and text message.

CRESTPORT DANCE ACADEMY

Crestport Dance Academy is pleased to announce its next season of performances. From modern dance and hip-hop to classical ballet — come and see all that we have to offer! You can purchase tickets for the entire season or for single performances. Season ticket subscribers also receive 50 percent off same-day ticket purchases.

January 18 - 22
- The Shelburne Group comes with hip-hop music.

February 7
- Catelynn Martin performs her award-winning dance.

February 15-21
- The Strauss Trio puts on an amazing ballet performance.

February 22-27
- Zachary Keaton dances while accompanied by live piano.

To: Tara Craft
From: Jeanne Harris
Cc: Ben Springer
Subject: Your Visit to Belle Systems
Date: December 29

Dear Ms. Craft:

On behalf of Belle Systems, I would like to let you know how much we are looking forward to adopting the document maintaining project you will teach us about on February 21 and 22. I reserved a room, laptop, projector, and microphone as you requested. Please let me know if you need further assistance with your presentation.

Our department head, Ben Springer, has made a special plan to express our gratitude and make your visit more enjoyable. He has planned dinner with you at an acclaimed local restaurant on the first evening of your visit, followed by an outing to a dance performance offered by Crestport Dance Academy.

Sincerely,

Jeanne Harris
Marketing Manager
Belle Systems

To: Jeanne Harris
From: Ben Springer
Received: 8:33 A.M.

I just heard from Ms. Craft. Her connecting flight has been delayed. She has confirmed her new arrival time and we will still be able to hold the meetings today. Ms. Craft requested that the entertainment be moved to tomorrow, so we aren't rushed. If I order the tickets myself tomorrow rather than today we can receive a substantial discount. Would you reschedule the taxi service to and from the airport? I will postpone the dinner reservation.

Send

186 What is suggested about Crestport Dance Academy?

(A) It has been in operation over the past 20 years.
(B) It is now recruiting dance instructors.
(C) It showcases different styles of dance.
(D) It offers dance lessons to the public.

187 What is the purpose of the e-mail?

(A) To provide details about the schedule
(B) To explain improvements in equipment
(C) To give information to a potential client
(D) To suggest a new date for a meeting

188 What performance was Ms. Craft originally scheduled to attend?

(A) The Shelburne Group
(B) Catelynn Martin
(C) The Strauss Trio
(D) Zachary Keaton

189 According to the text message, what does Mr. Springer ask Ms. Harris to do?

(A) Reserve a meeting room
(B) Prepare dinner
(C) Rearrange transportation
(D) Cancel a performance

190 What can be inferred about Mr. Springer?

(A) He has not confirmed Ms. Craft's schedule yet.
(B) He is not sure whether Ms. Craft will like the performance.
(C) He will soon be able to get a credit for the old tickets.
(D) He has a subscription to Crestport Dance Academy.

GO ON TO THE NEXT PAGE

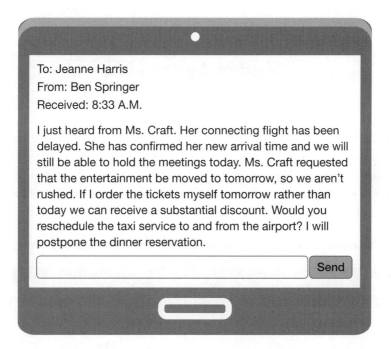

Questions 191-195 refer to the following advertisement, Web page and review.

Zentron Systems Inc.

At Zentron Systems Inc., our product testers' opinions are a key part of our market research work. We are one of the best-known research centers in the city, and we are now expanding our staff and product testers to meet higher demand. We help companies develop new and innovative products — from food to toys to electronics. We also follow rigorous quality standards. By becoming a product tester for Zentron Systems Inc., you can earn cash and even great prizes. Just click www.zentronsystems.org/tester and refer to our "Rewards program."

http://www.zentronsystems.org/tester/register

HOW TO BECOME A PRODUCT TESTER

THE FIRST STAGE

Complete our "new tester" registration form (click here), and then create a password that you will use every time you log on from this Web site. This registration places you on a list of available product testers.

THE SECOND STAGE

As product tests arise, you will be informed via phone or e-mail. Some people get called more than others; it all depends. However, we do not call any of our registered testers more than once a month.

THE THIRD STAGE

When you have expressed interest in a product test, our recruitment specialist will ask you some questions about your product preferences to see if you are a good match for the research study.

THE FOURTH STAGE

When chosen for a product test, the recruitment specialist will inform you how much it pays. Most tests take about 1 hour and pay $30 to $40 cash.

REWARDS PROGRAM

All product testers who register with us for the first time will automatically be entered into a random drawing to win $100 or a brand-new digital camera. No entry form is required. Current product testers who refer a friend to Zentron Systems Inc. will receive $25 when that person completes his/her first study. For more information on the program, click here.

http://www.zentronsystems.org/tester/register

Date: October 29th
Sandra Stable

Being a tester at Zentron Systems Inc.

I joined Zentron Systems Inc. as a product tester last year, and since then I've gotten paid to try beverages, soda, and much more. Registering is easy — you simply complete an online application and make a password — and the tests are fun and interesting. I usually get paid $40 cash for just one hour of testing each time I visit, but they call a lot! I received 5 to 6 calls a week during a month when I was out of the country, and my voicemail was full. It's a good way to earn money, but they do ask a number of questions about what products you like. That's part of the qualifying process for tests.

To participate as a product tester, just sign up here: www.zentronsystems.org.

I recommend joining! The testing facility, in Napa Valley, is near a city bus stop and there is also plenty of free parking in the lot in front of the building.

191 How most likely would a new registrant win $100 from Zentron Systems Inc.?
(A) By conducting a customer survey
(B) By doing two product tests
(C) By completing an entry form
(D) By being selected randomly

192 The word "refer" in paragraph 5, in line 3 of the Web page, is closest in meaning to
(A) address
(B) guide
(C) promise
(D) transport

193 What can be inferred about Ms. Stable?
(A) She used to be a recruiter for Zentron Systems Inc.
(B) She heard about Zentron Systems Inc. from a friend.
(C) She has tested various drinks in the past.
(D) She does not usually qualify for product tests.

194 Based on the review, which part of the Web page is most likely not accurate?
(A) The first stage
(B) The second stage
(C) The third stage
(D) The fourth stage

195 What is NOT mentioned about Zentron Systems Inc.?
(A) They are conveniently located in a city.
(B) They have free parking available.
(C) They give cash payments to product testers.
(D) They visit you in person with the product.

GO ON TO THE NEXT PAGE

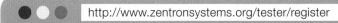

Questions 196-200 refer to the following e-mail, schedule, and news article.

To	Terzo Ventimiglia
From	Augustine Liu
Date	June 25
Subject	Events for Summer Interns
Attachment	Event Schedule

Hello, Terzo.

I have been asked to plan the summer events for our interns. Because there are far fewer interns in the research department than in product development, I want to invite your interns to join ours for some weekend and evening activities we will be offering. The experience will be very meaningful, and they will feel that being an intern gives them a chance to develop first-hand experience by participating in the events.

I'd like to introduce a new recreational opportunity I read about in the online edition of the Brandington Daily News. Here's the link to the article with information about the location of this year's new event: www.brandingtondailynews.com/mtduncan.

I am excited about the event, but I have some concerns and value any input you can offer me. Please let me know what you have in your mind for the events. Thank you in advance for any advice you can offer. Attached is this year's schedule.

Warm regards,

Augustine Liu
Product Development Manager

SUMMER CAMP SCHEDULE

July 6	Agricultural Fair at the Corners Farms in East Pleasantville
July 28	Day at the Topenski Amusement Park
August 14	Movie Night featuring Great Skies
September 10	Outdoor Hiking Day Trip

Please note that this year's schedule of activities is slightly different from that of previous years.

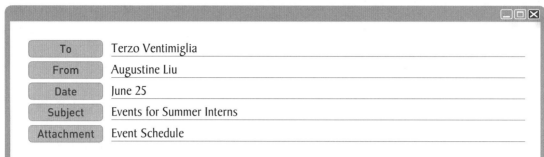

Brandington Daily News

Improved Trails on Mount Duncan to Open Next Week

June 23 – Park officials announced on Friday that three new hiking trails will be open to the public on July 1. Construction began on the trails last autumn. Work on the trails, which had been suspended from December through March due to winter weather, has been ongoing throughout April and May. The new trails are designed for beginners and will not require participants to have any experience and expertise.

Park and Recreation Director Nancy Phan said she is "thrilled" by the new opportunities the trails offer for recreation in the area. "Mount Duncan has always been a beloved local landmark," Ms. Phan said, "but it was previously accessible only to experienced hikers. Now, everyone in our community will be able to enjoy it." Ms. Phan added that she hopes the trails will increase tourism and create future business opportunities by providing a desirable location for corporate excursions and families on vacation.

196 What is the main purpose of the e-mail?
(A) To request feedback from a coworker
(B) To inquire about organizing a workshop
(C) To correct an event schedule
(D) To cancel a product demonstration

197 What does Ms. Liu suggest in the e-mail?
(A) Increasing the number of interns hired in the Research Department
(B) Planning a joint summer camp between two departments
(C) Decreasing the number of social gatherings to save money
(D) Appointing one of the interns to organize the event

198 What date does Ms. Liu suggest for this year's new activity?
(A) July 6
(B) July 28
(C) August 14
(D) September 10

199 What was the reason for construction being halted?
(A) Weather conditions
(B) Budgetary considerations
(C) A delay in obtaining city permits
(D) A lack of experienced workers

200 What can be suggested about Mount Duncan?
(A) Several sports competitions are scheduled to take place.
(B) Experienced hikers now enjoy the challenge to climb there.
(C) It becomes easily accessible to the general public.
(D) Its construction has been completed ahead of schedule.

Stop! This is the end of the test. If you finish before time is called, you may go back to Parts 5, 6, and 7 and check your work.

잠깐!! 시작 전 **꼭** 확인하세요!

- 실제 시험과 같이 책상을 정리하고 마음의 준비를 하세요.
- 핸드폰은 잠깐 끄고 대신 아날로그 시계를 활용해 보세요.
- 제한 시간은 120분입니다. 제한 시간을 꼭 지켜주세요.
- 어렵다고 넘어가지 마세요. 가능하면 차례대로 풀어 보세요.

Actual Test

04

시작 시간 :

종료 시간 :

LISTENING TEST

In the Listening test, you will be asked to demonstrate how well you understand spoken English. The entire Listening test will last approximately 45 minutes. There are four parts, and directions are given for each part. You must mark your answers on the separate answer sheet. Do not write your answers in your test book.

PART 1

Directions: For each question in this part, you will hear four statements about a picture in your test book. When you hear the statements, you must select the one statement that best describes what you see in the picture. Then find the number of the question on your answer sheet and mark your answer. The statements will not be printed in your test book and will be spoken only one time.

Example

Sample Answer

Ⓐ ● Ⓒ Ⓓ

Statement (B), "The man is working at a desk," is the best description of the picture, so you should select answer (B) and mark it on your answer sheet.

1

2

GO ON TO THE NEXT PAGE

3

4

5

6

GO ON TO THE NEXT PAGE

▶정답 및 해설 P095

PART 2

Directions: You will hear a question or statement and three responses spoken in English. They will not be printed in your test book and will be spoken only one time. Select the best response to the question or statement and mark the letter (A), (B), or (C) on your answer sheet.

7 Mark your answer on your answer sheet.

8 Mark your answer on your answer sheet.

9 Mark your answer on your answer sheet.

10 Mark your answer on your answer sheet.

11 Mark your answer on your answer sheet.

12 Mark your answer on your answer sheet.

13 Mark your answer on your answer sheet.

14 Mark your answer on your answer sheet.

15 Mark your answer on your answer sheet.

16 Mark your answer on your answer sheet.

17 Mark your answer on your answer sheet.

18 Mark your answer on your answer sheet.

19 Mark your answer on your answer sheet.

20 Mark your answer on your answer sheet.

21 Mark your answer on your answer sheet.

22 Mark your answer on your answer sheet.

23 Mark your answer on your answer sheet.

24 Mark your answer on your answer sheet.

25 Mark your answer on your answer sheet.

26 Mark your answer on your answer sheet.

27 Mark your answer on your answer sheet.

28 Mark your answer on your answer sheet.

29 Mark your answer on your answer sheet.

30 Mark your answer on your answer sheet.

31 Mark your answer on your answer sheet.

▶정답 및 해설 P098

PART 3

Directions: You will hear some conversations between two or more people. You will be asked to answer three questions about what the speakers say in each conversation. Select the best response to each question and mark the letter (A), (B), (C), or (D) on your answer sheet. The conversations will not be printed in your test book and will be spoken only one time.

32 Who most likely is the woman?
(A) An instructor
(B) A customer
(C) A personal assistant
(D) A delivery person

33 According to the man, what is the problem?
(A) A manager is not available.
(B) A list of customers is incomplete.
(C) A document has been misplaced.
(D) A meeting was postponed.

34 What will the woman do next?
(A) Contact the relevant person
(B) Check the customer list
(C) Search the Internet
(D) Provide an e-mail address

---

35 What does the woman complain about?
(A) A water leakage
(B) A broken electrical wire
(C) A cracked bathtub
(D) A locked door

36 What floor is the woman staying on?
(A) The second floor
(B) The fourth floor
(C) The sixth floor
(D) The eighth floor

37 What does the woman ask the man to do?
(A) Give her a wake-up call
(B) Bring her some refreshments
(C) Assist her with the luggage
(D) Pick up her laundry

38 What is the woman calling to discuss?
(A) An open position
(B) A university program
(C) A marketing proposal
(D) A fashion magazine

39 What does the man tell the woman?
(A) He is out of town.
(B) He is on another line.
(C) He has a flexible plan.
(D) He is in a hurry.

40 What does the woman want the man to review?
(A) A detailed résumé
(B) A job description
(C) A business report
(D) A magazine article

---

41 Why is the man impressed with the library?
(A) The membership fee is free.
(B) The library is open all year round.
(C) The library's selection is broad.
(D) The library is open until late.

42 How many books can the man borrow if he has a regular card?
(A) 5 books
(B) 10 books
(C) 15 books
(D) 20 books

43 What does the woman say is special about the library card?
(A) It requires no payment.
(B) It can be used indefinitely.
(C) It expires every 10 months.
(D) It can be replaced with an ID card.

GO ON TO THE NEXT PAGE

44 What are the speakers discussing?

(A) The number of participants
(B) A registration fee
(C) Enrollment in a course
(D) The process of a survey

45 What information does the woman give the man?

(A) A location of a brasserie
(B) Details of the delivery
(C) An updated number of guests
(D) A name of managing director

46 What does the man ask the woman about?

(A) If the woman has spoken with the managing director
(B) Whether food will be delivered
(C) Whether the woman has gotten any messages
(D) If the woman contacted a guest

---

47 What are the speakers concerned about?

(A) The size of the workforce
(B) New regulations
(C) The newspaper subscription
(D) The store location

48 What does the woman offer to do?

(A) Contact an executive
(B) Place an order
(C) Speak with a customer
(D) Give a raise

49 Why will Frank contact Steve?

(A) To correct an error
(B) To set up a meeting
(C) To create an advertisement
(D) To conduct an interview

50 What is the man asked to do?

(A) Provide a new password
(B) Help writing an e-mail
(C) Assist with getting online
(D) Analyze some data

51 What was the issue?

(A) The computer was broken.
(B) The password had been changed.
(C) The e-mail address was wrong.
(D) The connection was wrong.

52 Why does the woman say, "So that's all!"?

(A) She found an e-mail address.
(B) She understood the problem.
(C) She fixed the laptop.
(D) She had to restart the computer.

---

53 What work will be finished by Wednesday?

(A) Wall painting
(B) A floor plan
(C) Electrical construction
(D) A promotional campaign

54 What does the man say about the painting?

(A) The cost is reasonable.
(B) The work takes a long time.
(C) The painters delayed the schedule.
(D) The work will commence next Tuesday.

55 How does the woman say she will find more tenants?

(A) By passing out leaflets
(B) By designing a new Web site
(C) By advertising in a newspaper
(D) By talking to other tenants

56 Which city does the man probably work in?
(A) Bangkok
(B) Boston
(C) San Diego
(D) Los Angeles

57 Why can't the man leave on Thursday?
(A) He has other plans.
(B) He can't afford the price.
(C) He doesn't like a layover.
(D) He would arrive too late.

58 What decision does the man make?
(A) To postpone his workshop
(B) To pay for first class
(C) To depart on Tuesday
(D) To arrive on Friday

---

59 What is the purpose of the man's call?
(A) To reschedule a visit
(B) To change his physician
(C) To get a prescription
(D) To make an appointment

60 What does the woman mean when she says, "the next day is Saturday"?
(A) Dr. Leon usually works on weekends.
(B) The office is closed on weekends.
(C) Saturday is available for a reservation.
(D) Mr. Johnson is fully booked on Saturday.

61 On what day will the man visit the office?
(A) Tuesday
(B) Thursday
(C) Friday
(D) Saturday

Harvey Nichols Department Store
Clothing Department
€10.00 OFF
Any piece of clothing priced over €50
Expires Oct 19

62 What does the woman ask the man about?
(A) The hours of operation
(B) The price of a certain item
(C) The duration of a sale
(D) The location of a section

63 Where does the man suggest the woman go?
(A) To a staff lounge
(B) To a fitting room
(C) To a service desk
(D) To the main entrance

64 Look at the graphic. How much would the woman have to pay for the skirt?
(A) €50
(B) €60
(C) €70
(D) €80

GO ON TO THE NEXT PAGE

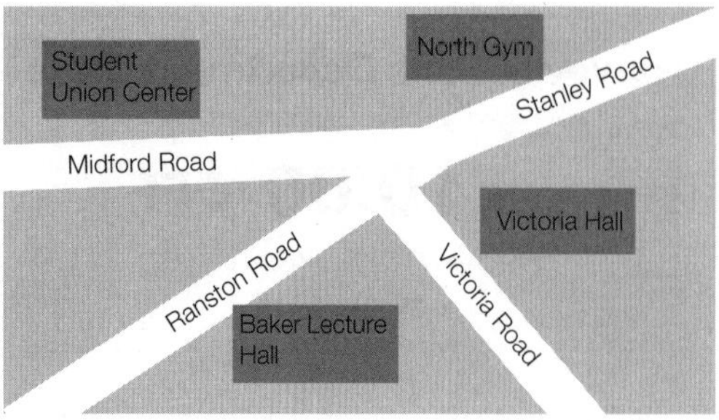

65 What does the man ask the woman to do?

(A) Take a map
(B) Make an appointment
(C) Arrange a tour
(D) Apply for a position

66 What most likely is the problem?

(A) An interview has been postponed.
(B) Some people do not like a tour.
(C) A guide is not available.
(D) There will not be another meeting.

67 Look at the graphic. Which building is under construction today?

(A) North Gym
(B) Student Union Center
(C) Baker Lecture Hall
(D) Victoria Hall

Items for repair		
Item	Quantity	Time
Fax machines	2	1:00 P.M.
Photocopiers	2	2:00 P.M.
Scanners	3	3:00 P.M.
Color printers	4	4:30 P.M.

68 Who most likely is Mr. Rodriguez?

(A) A client
(B) An accountant
(C) An assistant
(D) A supervisor

69 What does the man say he has already done?

(A) Sent some tools
(B) Brought items for repair
(C) Purchased new equipment
(D) Contacted a manager

70 Look at the graphic. What items will be repaired first?

(A) Fax machines
(B) Photocopiers
(C) Scanners
(D) Color printers

▶정답 및 해설 P107

PART 4

Directions: You will hear some talks given by a single speaker. You will be asked to answer three questions about what the speaker says in each talk. Select the best response to each question and mark the letter (A), (B), (C), or (D) on your answer sheet. The talks will not be printed in your test book and will be spoken only one time.

71 What is the purpose of today's session?
(A) To evaluate staff performance
(B) To conduct an interview
(C) To gather opinions
(D) To explain a company regulation

72 According to the speaker, how has the new device been improved?
(A) It performs more easily.
(B) It is light-weight.
(C) It is faster to use.
(D) It is a cost-effective product.

73 What will the listeners probably do next?
(A) Ask questions
(B) View package designs
(C) Create the advertisement
(D) Call a client's office

---

74 What is the purpose of the speech?
(A) To request funding
(B) To report research findings
(C) To accept an award
(D) To welcome guests

75 Where is the speech probably taking place?
(A) At a university
(B) At a firm's auditorium
(C) At a city's arena
(D) At a town center

76 What does the speaker mean when she says, "They are certainly in a class of their own"?
(A) Some of the researchers are excluded.
(B) Several of the colleagues are exceptional.
(C) Some of the instructors teach only one class.
(D) Several students contributed their ideas.

77 What type of business is being advertised?
(A) A beauty clinic
(B) A cosmetic company
(C) A stationery store
(D) A fitness center

78 What will happen tomorrow?
(A) A new product will be launched.
(B) A special offer will end.
(C) A consultation will begin.
(D) New premises will open.

79 What is offered at a 30 percent discount?
(A) A consultation
(B) Any treatment
(C) A training session
(D) All products

---

80 What is being reported?
(A) A stock offering
(B) A retirement event
(C) A construction project
(D) A business take-over

81 What did Glen Lunar do three months ago?
(A) He founded a new company.
(B) He opened a new store.
(C) He retired from his career.
(D) He launched a new line of products.

82 What does the speaker mean when he says, "Mr. Lunar supported the move"?
(A) Mr. Lunar approved of a decision.
(B) Mr. Lunar wanted to relocate the headquarters.
(C) Mr. Lunar provided financial assistance.
(D) Mr. Lunar rejected the offer.

GO ON TO THE NEXT PAGE

83 Who most likely are the listeners?

(A) Department heads
(B) Fitness instructors
(C) Marketing representatives
(D) Factory workers

84 What will happen next week?

(A) The company will move to a new building.
(B) Some employees will be recruited.
(C) The budget will be shortened.
(D) New tasks will be assigned.

85 What are some listeners requested to do?

(A) Contact their supervisors
(B) Put in extra hours
(C) Submit their report
(D) Assign a task

---

86 Who is the announcement intended for?

(A) Restaurant servers
(B) Hotel employees
(A) Married couples
(D) Overseas tourists

87 According to the speaker, what is contained in the folder?

(A) An employee ID card
(B) A floor plan
(C) An employee manual
(D) A wage slip

88 What does the speaker ask listeners to do next?

(A) Evaluate staff members
(B) Take a short break
(C) Work in groups
(D) Complete a questionnaire

89 What type of company does the speaker probably work for?

(A) A moving company
(B) A real estate agency
(C) An appliance dealer
(D) A cleaning service

90 What does the speaker offer to do tomorrow?

(A) Dispose of old equipment
(B) Repair a product
(C) Give a brochure
(D) Call before his arrival

91 What does the speaker imply when he says, "Don't worry about it"?

(A) His staff will not damage anything.
(B) His team will take care of a task.
(C) He will be able to sell the furniture.
(D) He will get an estimate.

---

92 What is the problem?

(A) Some cereal cartons have wrong information.
(B) Some products have been mislabeled.
(C) Some cereal cartons are not full.
(D) Some products are of poor quality.

93 What is mentioned about the packing equipment?

(A) It is no longer malfunctioning.
(B) It will be replaced next month.
(C) It had been repaired before the incident.
(D) It will be inspected regularly.

94 What will customers who return cartons receive?

(A) A new box of cereal
(B) A refund
(C) A complimentary gift
(D) A discount coupon

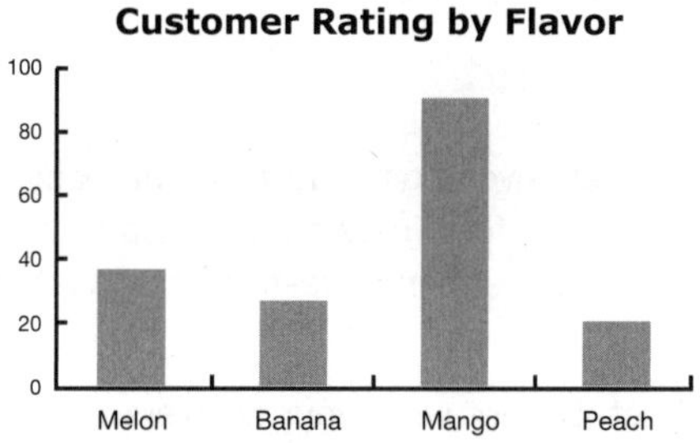

95 What does the speaker's company produce?

(A) Canned fruit
(B) Milk
(C) Bottled drinks
(D) Ice cream

96 According to the speaker, what did the company do last week?

(A) Conducted product trials
(B) Added a new facility
(C) Reduced a product price
(D) Launched an advertising campaign

97 Look at the graphic. Where most likely is the result of this graph relevant?

(A) California
(B) Florida
(C) Texas
(D) Colorado

The Future Conference Center		
Friday, June 18		
Hall Name	**Event**	**Time**
Apollo Hall	Employee Workshop	6:00 P.M. – 9:00 P.M.
Dominion Hall	Product Launching event	7:30 P.M. – 10:00 P.M.
Empire Hall	Retirement Party	6:30 P.M. – 9:30 P.M.
Warner Hall	Award Ceremony	8:00 P.M. – 11:00 P.M.

98 Why is the speaker delivering this speech?

(A) To introduce a celebrity
(B) To celebrate a company's anniversary
(C) To introduce a new employee
(D) To recognize an employee's service

99 What kind of services does M&T provide?

(A) Landscaping
(B) Product development
(C) Accounting
(D) Retail management

100 Look at the graphic. Where is the event taking place?

(A) Apollo Hal
(B) Dominion Hall
(C) Empire Hall
(D) Warner Hall

This is the end of the Listening test. Turn to Part 5 in your test book.

GO ON TO THE NEXT PAGE

READING TEST

In the Reading test, you will read a variety of texts and answer several different types of reading comprehension questions. The entire Reading test will last 75 minutes. There are three parts, and directions are given for each part. You are encouraged to answer as many questions as possible within the time allowed.

You must mark your answers on the separate answer sheet. Do not write your answers in your test book.

PART 5

Directions: A word or phrase is missing in each of the sentences below. Four answer choices are given below each sentence. Select the best answer to complete the sentence. Then mark the letter (A), (B), (C), or (D) on your answer sheet.

101 The owner of Casper Airline announced that ------- is negotiating a deal with Super Jet to buy new airplanes.

(A) him
(B) he
(C) his
(D) himself

102 ------- the last ten years, Madison City's population has grown by about 30 percent.

(A) As
(B) Again
(C) During
(D) Below

103 ------- to all the facilities is included with your stay at the Grand Plaza Hotel.

(A) Access
(B) Accessed
(C) Accessing
(D) Accessible

104 Ms. Chalmers will help with the final draft, so it is not necessary to do all the editing by -------.

(A) yours
(B) your
(C) you
(D) yourself

105 Because humidity can ------- iron, the climate in materials storage units must be controlled.

(A) damage
(B) damaging
(C) damaged
(D) damages

106 Mr. Bukowski is reviewing the training manual to see if updates -------.

(A) have need
(B) needing
(C) are needed
(D) to be needed

107 After working in France for ten years, Georgina Garcia has ------- to Madrid to plan the opening of a fancy restaurant.

(A) visited
(B) returned
(C) occurred
(D) related

108 The city council approved the bill to increase funding of its road improvement -------.

(A) statement
(B) permission
(C) ability
(D) project

109 After interviewing Mr. Finch personally, the company president ------- the committee's decision to hire him as Vice President.

(A) confirmed
(B) designed
(C) hosted
(D) created

110 Once the most recent update is installed, the tablet's platform will ------- longer support this software.

(A) not
(B) none
(C) no
(D) nowhere

111 Each sales team must ------- the result of its annual sales report by the end of the month.

(A) provide
(B) match
(C) reach
(D) earn

112 South Central School's district managers are retired executives with a ------- of expertise across a wide range of industries.

(A) fame
(B) height
(C) labor
(D) wealth

113 The first step of airport construction will be building a runway capable of ------- midsize commercial airplanes.

(A) handling
(B) handler
(C) handles
(D) handle

114 Sonja Pakov is one of the most popular musical artists in South America, ------- only the Wright Band in record sales.

(A) toward
(B) except
(C) among
(D) behind

115 Operating instructions are posted above the copy machine so that you can ------- refer to them.

(A) consequently
(B) standardly
(C) namely
(D) easily

116 The team's contributions to Narumi Skincare's marketing plan were very ------- acknowledged.

(A) favor
(B) favorably
(C) favorable
(D) favored

117 The figures we received last week ------- need to be entered into the digital database.

(A) lately
(B) evenly
(C) ever
(D) still

118 Contract holders may terminate their contract at any time, ------- notification is given in writing at least 14 days in advance.

(A) along with
(B) according to
(C) provided that
(D) regardless of

119 Choosing the best solution to elimination of computer viruses is rarely simple, ------- it is important to seek expert advice.

(A) why
(B) then
(C) nor
(D) so

120 Samuel Jenkins' original manuscript was published last year after Sylvon Publishing Company obtained his family's -------.

(A) permission
(B) suggestion
(C) comparison
(D) registration

GO ON TO THE NEXT PAGE

121 Mr. Lai's draft of Sientech Industries' new mission statement expresses the company's goals -------.

(A) precise
(B) more precise
(C) preciseness
(D) precisely

122 Yoon Station, provider of premium television content, welcomes ------- ideas for improving our services.

(A) specifics
(B) specifies
(C) specific
(D) specify

123 Jarman Food Company has attributed its recent popularity with consumers to changes in its recipes ------- its new packaging.

(A) as for
(B) even so
(C) rather than
(D) after all

124 The assembly line will continue to run unless a problem requires ------- attention.

(A) bright
(B) fluent
(C) gentle
(D) urgent

125 As the lease agreement with Charat Properties is set ------- soon, the available office space can be advertised.

(A) expired
(B) to expire
(C) will have expired
(D) expiring

126 Any furniture purchased at Green Company throughout November will be delivered ------- five business days.

(A) since
(B) between
(C) within
(D) above

127 Chung & Cho auto shop requires mechanics to contact a supervisor ------- if they notice any signs of wear on edges of belt.

(A) very few
(B) finally
(C) somewhat
(D) right away

128 ------- First Carey Bank's parking area is now open to the public, a section has been reserved only for the bank's VIP customers.

(A) While
(B) When
(C) But
(D) For

129 The contract for the Ricci Complex project will be awarded to ------- construction firm submits the most energy-efficient design.

(A) which
(B) whatever
(C) each
(D) those

130 Both Mr. Cresson's payment history and the amount ------- on his loan will be considered in his application for refinancing.

(A) interested
(B) owed
(C) joined
(D) occupied

PART 6

Directions: Read the texts that follow. A word, phrase, or sentence is missing in parts of each text. Four answer choices for each question are given below the text. Select the best answer to complete the text. Then mark the letter (A), (B), (C), or (D) on your answer sheet.

Questions 131-134 refer to the following e-mail.

To: jhewittt@mailday.co.uk
From: customerservice@powerprotection.com
Date: October 10
Subject: Product Review

Dear Ms. Hewitt:

Thank you for your recent -------(**131.**). We hope you are enjoying your Power Protection software. In the unlikely event that you -------(**132.**) any problems, please call customer service at 034-555-3746. Our technicians are ready to help 24 hours a day.

If you are happy with your product, please consider writing an online review by visiting www.powerprotection.com/yourvoice. -------(**133.**). They inform -------(**134.**) customers and help us grow our business so we can expand our line of high-quality software.

131 (A) production
(B) purchase
(C) application
(D) research

132 (A) experience
(B) experiencing
(C) should have experienced
(D) were experienced

133 (A) I just want to remind you about our monthly volunteer project.
(B) Our promotion just started when we offered discounts on all appliances.
(C) Construction will begin in about three months as scheduled.
(D) Such reviews are appreciated in several ways.

134 (A) selective
(B) required
(C) potential
(D) beneficial

GO ON TO THE NEXT PAGE

Questions 135-138 refer to the following e-mail.

From: Jane Fisherman
To: All staff
Date: May 1
Subject: New branding guidelines
Attachment: Document.pdf

----
135. to this e-mail is an abbreviated version of our corporate branding guidelines, including information on a new logo, font, and color palette. These guidelines, which are now -------
136., have also been posted on our internal employee Web site.

We are still working on revising the print and electronic publicity to reflect these new standards. -------
137.. A complete form reflecting the changes -------
138..

Please let me know if you have any problems or concerns.

135 (A) Attach
(B) Attached
(C) Attaching
(D) Attaches

136 (A) out of date
(B) in effect
(C) beside the point
(D) on purpose

137 (A) I'm pleased to inform you that our application for a grant was approved.
(B) Please talk to your manager to join the program.
(C) We hope to have the process finished by the end of this month.
(D) We're going to renovate one of our branches for a modern appearance.

138 (A) to distribute
(B) had distributed
(C) was distributing
(D) will be distributed

Questions 139-142 refer to the following information.

IMPORTANT! -------. (139.) Make sure that your new Power Tech 340 washing machine is installed on a foundation that is strong ------- (140.) to support its weight when it is fully loaded. In order to prevent noise and vibration, the appliance should be leveled. This is done by ------- (141.) the height of the small feet at the bottom corners of the machine. Be sure to attach the water-supply hoses at the back of the machine ------- (142.) to the hot and cold water valves.

139 (A) I believe that technology will contribute to improving our customers' experience.
(B) We're famous for our speedy and efficient process.
(C) I don't know exactly how many people will turn up.
(D) Carefully read the following instructions before operating your new washing machine.

140 (A) enough
(B) very
(C) so
(D) hard

141 (A) adjusting
(B) examining
(C) recording
(D) describing

142 (A) are secured
(B) securely
(C) secures
(D) security

GO ON TO THE NEXT PAGE

Questions 143-146 refer to the following article.

As flu season ------- (143.) once again, people wonder what they can do to keep from contracting the miserable virus. Getting vaccinated is the best solution, but there are many other ------- (144.) that can be taken!

Remember to wash your hands well and often. ------- (145.). If you feel sick, don't be a hero — go home and rest! ------- (146.) you don't feel too bad yet, it's often in the earliest stages of illness that you can spread your flu.

143 (A) approach
(B) approaches
(C) approached
(D) approaching

144 (A) warnings
(B) symptoms
(C) precautions
(D) communities

145 (A) They give employees up to ten days of sick leave.
(B) The flu is spreading across borders through the area.
(C) Keep your immune system strong with plenty of vitamin C.
(D) Some people remain symptom-free for several years.

146 (A) Even if
(B) As if
(C) In case of
(D) Rather than

PART 7

Directions: In this part you will read a selection of texts, such as magazine and newspaper articles, e-mails, and instant messages. Each text or set of texts is followed by several questions. Select the best answer for each question and mark the letter (A), (B), (C), or (D) on your answer sheet.

Questions 147-148 refer to the following flyer.

Seattle Movie Club

The Seattle Movie Club is proud to present our first Bollywood Festival. From September 18 through November 6, a total of eight contemporary and classic movies by Bollywood filmmakers will be shown at Coleman Theater near Lloyd Mall. The free movies, shown with Spanish and English subtitles, will begin at 7:00 P.M. each Saturday. To view the complete program, please visit our Web site at seattlemovieclub.org.

147 What is being announced?

(A) The opening of a film festival
(B) An interview with a Bollywood actor
(C) A film production
(D) A movie series

148 According to the flyer, what can be found on the Seattle Movie Club Web site?

(A) Free tickets to a new film
(B) Directions to Coleman Theater
(C) A list of events
(D) Biographies of movie directors

Questions 149-150 refer to the following notice.

Air Gold

Air Gold offers special meals, free of charge on all flights lasting three hours or more. Whether you reserved your flight with Air Gold or through an authorized agency, please call our customer service hotline at 121-555-0987 at least 24 hours before your scheduled flight departure to request a special meal. Travelers with any dietary concerns or restrictions may wish to call the hotline. Our catering staff will do its utmost to accommodate your needs. For a list of special meals, sample dishes or common ingredients, visit our Web site, www.airgold.com.

149 For whom is the advertisement most likely intended?

(A) Tour guides
(B) Travel agents
(C) Airline passengers
(D) Flight attendants

150 What is the purpose of the notice?

(A) To advertise a benefit of a membership program
(B) To give information about dining options
(C) To announce the hiring of aircraft pilots
(D) To suggest some healthful eating guidelines

Questions 151-153 refer to the following advertisement.

Grand Opening Celebration!

Ashland Brothers Company

54 Thompson Plaza (Next to Kathryn's Bakery)
San Diego, CA 94789
512-555-0090

Grand Opening Specials:
30% off all desks and chairs
25% off sofa (leather only)
15% off any dining tables

Offers good from July 3 to August 3
(Free cleaning products with purchase of $30 or more: Thompson Plaza Store only)

Store hours 8:00 A.M. – 8:00 P.M.

Sign up for the Ashland Brothers Company membership — for just $25 per year, get an additional 10% off everything you buy at both our Thompson Plaza and Alina Mall store locations as well as online!

Visit our Web site at www.ashlandbrotherscompany.com.

This week only, order any bookcase online and get 40% off!

151 What type of merchandise does Ashland Brothers Company sell?
(A) Electronics
(B) Office supplies
(C) Clothing
(D) Furniture

152 What is indicated from Ashland Brothers Company?
(A) Its grand-opening specials are offered for only one week.
(B) It stays open until 10 P.M. on August 3.
(C) Its salespeople are highly trained.
(D) It has more than one location.

153 For which item will the customers get a discount only when they purchase it by online?
(A) Baked goods
(B) Cleaning products
(C) Bookcases
(D) Leather items

Test 04

GO ON TO THE NEXT PAGE

Questions 154-155 refer to the following text message chain.

Sally Kleinman **11:36 A.M.**
Ali, could you check to see whether order number A 321 been sent out yet? The customer has just asked us to add item ZDS12.

Ali Griffin **11:39 A.M.**
That's customized sneakers, right? The engravers usually require a minimum of 3 days to add the customer's personalized message.

Sally Kleinman **11:39 A.M.**
Can you do a rush job? The customer needs it as soon as possible.

Ali Griffin **11:41 A.M.**
How soon do you need it? Is tomorrow okay?

Sally Kleinman **11:44 A.M.**
Yes, that works. Thank you for your help!

Send

154 What does the customer want to do?

(A) Add an item to the order
(B) Exchange a product
(C) Receive a refund
(D) Use a discount code

155 At 11:44 A.M., what does Ms. Kleinman most likely mean when she writes "that works"?

(A) She plans to make a slide presentation at the meeting.
(B) She is informed that the equipment is repaired.
(C) The customer will be satisfied if the item is ready tomorrow.
(D) A shipping company will deliver the item by the end of the day.

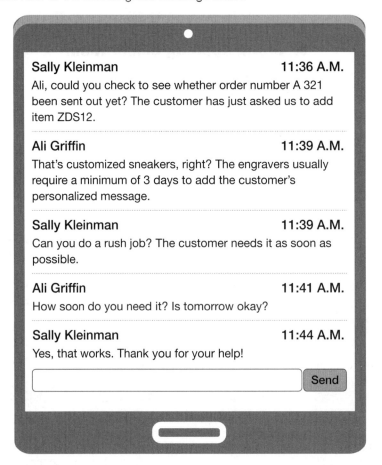

Questions 156-157 refer to the following information.

Brilliant ideas for cutting electricity expenses.

There are some helpful suggestions for high office utility costs.

Environment: Pull up the shades and blinds for more natural light, whenever possible. Use bright wall paper to reflect more natural light.

Lighting: Replace incandescent light bulbs with florescent light bulbs, which have the same brightness and use less energy, without replacing light fixtures. Use motion sensors to reduce the usage of electricity in non-working areas where light is not constantly used, such as storage rooms or closets.

Office Equipment: Turn off printers and copiers when they are not in use. Use a power strip. It will be very convenient to turn off all office equipment with the flip of the switch. A screen saver is not an energy saver. Please turn off your monitor when you leave the office. Use an auto timer to turn off electricity when the office is not occupied.

156 According to the information, how can light at the workplace be maximized?

(A) By relocating light fixtures
(B) By installing motion sensors in work areas
(C) By using brighter lightbulbs
(D) By letting more daylight enter the room

157 What is NOT mentioned as a way to limit energy consumption?

(A) Replacing office equipment with more efficient ones
(B) Turning off monitors instead of using screen savers
(C) Using power strips to turn off multiple devices
(D) Installing automatic timers

GO ON TO THE NEXT PAGE

Questions 158-160 refer to the following memo.

To	Julie Chan
From	Daniel Rhee
Date	March 14
Subject	Conference in Oakland

Your request to attend the landscaping conference in Oakland on March 28 has been approved by the vice president. In keeping with our travel policies, your plane ticket, rental car, and hotel room will be paid by the company in advance. –[1]–. Please plan to turn in receipts for meals, gasoline, and any other business-related expenses on your return. Please remember that company policy states that entertainment costs are not reimbursable. –[2]–.

A preliminary itinerary has you booked March 28 on Super Jet flight# 263, departing at 6:28 A.M. The return trip is for March 30 on flight 319, departing Oakland at 3:05 P.M. –[3]–. A compact vehicle has been reserved at Patel Autos at the airport; you can pick up the car there when you arrive. You will be staying at the Plaza Fisher Hotel on San Andreas Street. I hope all these arrangements meet with your approval. –[4]–. Please call me at extension 2326 between 9:15 A.M. and 4:30 P.M. tomorrow so that details can be finalized. I will email you a formal itinerary by the end of the week.

Thank you.

Daniel Rhee
Administrative Support Office

158 What is suggested about travel requests?
(A) They must have details about an itinerary.
(B) They must include a project proposal.
(C) They must estimate meal costs.
(D) They must be authorized by an executive.

159 What is NOT stated about Patel Autos?
(A) It accepts reservations.
(B) It is on San Andreas Street.
(C) It has a location in Oakland.
(D) It rents small cars.

160 In which of the positions marked [1], [2], [3], and [4] does the following sentence best belong?
"You will be reimbursed for any additional expenses you incur while in Oakland."
(A) [1]
(B) [2]
(C) [3]
(D) [4]

Questions 161-164 refer to the following e-mail.

From	Jane Kovar, President and CEO
To	All Bartel Financial Group Headquarters Staff
Date	February 3
Subject	Ellen Ortiz

After careful deliberation by the Bartel board of directors, I am pleased to announce that Ellen Ortiz, our current Director of Investor Relations, will take over as European Regional Manager when Andres Hildebrand retires next month. Ms. Ortiz's promotion comes at a time of increased emphasis on international markets. Working from our Rome office, she will oversee the continued growth of Bartel in Italy and its expansion into Germany and southwestern Europe.

Those of you who have worked with her know that Ms. Ortiz is an excellent choice for the job. After graduating from Kingston University in Dublin, she worked for Ostrava Finance in Italy for a number of years before joining Bartel over 20 years ago. She is a native Italian speaker and is fluent in several other languages. During her first years at Bartel, she worked in the Brussels office before being transferred to the Paris office, and finally to the headquarters here in London. Her outstanding leadership in investor relations has helped our client base grow by over 20 percent in the last 10 years.

Finally, to commemorate Mr. Hildebrand's many accomplishments during his years with Bartel, we have planned a farewell gathering for Friday, February 28, at the Prost Café near company headquarters from 6 P.M. to 8 P.M. For more information about the event, please contact my assistant Stan Milton at extension 1259. Any questions about these staffing changes should be directed to Bill Belmore, Director of Personnel, at extension 1286.

161 What position does Mr. Hildebrand currently have?

(A) Chief Executive Officer
(B) Manager of Investor Relations
(C) Director of Personnel
(D) European Regional Manager

162 What is indicated about Ms. Ortiz?

(A) She lived in Brussels for over twenty years.
(B) She speaks several languages.
(C) She has a degree in International Business.
(D) She is leaving Bartel to work for a company in Germany.

163 What is the purpose of the event on February 28?

(A) To discuss potential replacements for Mr. Hildebrand
(B) To share investment opinions with prospective clients
(C) To announce Bartel's plans for a merger with a competitor
(D) To recognize Mr. Hildebrand's contributions to Bartel

164 In which city will the event be held most likely?

(A) Brussels
(B) Paris
(C) London
(D) Rome

GO ON TO THE NEXT PAGE

Questions 165-167 refer to the following Web page.

http://easyservicestation.com

EASY SERVICE STATION

Easy Service Station owns and operates a large chain of truck stops and travel centers throughout Wisconsin. Our centers are conveniently located along most major highways and are open 24 hours a day, 365 days a year.

Easy Service Station center is equipped with fueling stations, a convenience store, a full-service restaurant and other amenities to make long-distance travel more comfortable.

- Automated teller machines are available 24 hours a day.
- Check cashing and money transfer services are available Monday to Friday, from 8 A.M. to 4 P.M.
- All locations have public laundries; some have public showers.
- Each location has an indoor lounge area with cable television and wireless Internet services.
- Hot food is available in our restaurants, and coffee and baked goods can be purchased in our convenience stores.

For a full list of Easy Service Station centers, click the link below.

www.easyservicestation.com/list

165 What does the Web page describe?
(A) Roadside facilities
(B) Car dealerships
(C) Relocation assistance
(D) Discounted hotels

166 What do only some locations offer?
(A) Shower rooms
(B) A lounge area
(C) Hot meals
(D) Laundry rooms

167 What information can most likely be found by clicking the link provided?
(A) Room rates
(B) Service charges
(C) Location information
(D) Reservation details

Questions 168-171 refer to the following article.

Munich (March 22) – Munich-based Steinmeier announced plans on Tuesday to build a second processing facility. Currently, the company's sole facility is located near Frankfurt, about 480 kilometers from its Munich corporate headquarters. The new facility, which is expected to cost upwards of €30 million, is part of a corporate strategy to boost profits by expanding into overseas markets.

Executives hope the ambitious expansion to Shanghai in China will help the company to become a major competitor in the China market. Once completed, the two processing plants together will have the capacity to meet the demands of both the Chinese and European markets. –[1]–. "An added benefit is that we would be able to maintain essential production for both markets in the event that one of the facilities is temporarily shut down for maintenance work or repairs," said company president Daniel Hoffman.

Mr. Hoffman's father, Jeremy Hoffman, founded Steinmeier in 1979 after graduating from business school in Beijing. –[2]–. In its first year of business, the company managed to turn a sizeable profit, which grew by 47% the following year. Today, Steinmeier is an internationally recognized beverage brand distributed in 30 countries across Europe. Despite its enormous success, however, sales have slowed recently as market share has dropped, and a new management team under Mr. Hoffman is aggressively trying to turn the company around. –[3]–.

The full range of Steinmeier's existing beverage products should be available in 20 cities in China by the end of the summer, according to regional sales manager Amy Garrett. –[4]–. Ms. Garrett envisions launching a line of fruit-based baked goods such as cookies and cakes to complement the company's current product line. "Our hope is that we continue to grow and develop new items that our customers will love." she said.

168 Where will the new facility be located?

(A) Munich
(B) Frankfurt
(C) Shanghai
(D) Beijing

169 What is mentioned about Steinmeier?

(A) Its competitors sell less products than Steinmeier.
(B) It sells products only in Munich.
(C) Product sales have declined recently.
(D) It is planning to recruit new board members.

170 What new type of product is Steinmeier planning to develop?

(A) Desserts
(B) Cosmetics
(C) Tableware
(D) Drinks

171 In which of the positions marked [1], [2], [3], and [4] does the following sentence best belong?

"Returning to northern German, he began selling fresh-squeezed fruit juice to restaurants and supermarkets across the region."

(A) [1]
(B) [2]
(C) [3]
(D) [4]

GO ON TO THE NEXT PAGE

Questions 172-175 refer to the following online chat discussion.

Almed Abedi

Almed Abedi [4:30 P.M.]	I'd like to re-examine the way we are currently advertising our line of vitamin supplements.
Saori Iwamoto [4:31 P.M.]	Marina, since you are new to our company, let me give you some background. In order to improve sales, we started making vitamin supplements specifically designed for women.
Almed Abedi [4:32 P.M.]	We began selling these supplements a year ago, and we allocated a substantial budget to advertising in order to promote them.
Marina Jordan [4:33 P.M.]	Thanks for the detailed explanation. I think I saw the commercials on TV. I've also driven by the billboards on the side of the road. That must have helped a lot with sales.
Almed Abedi [4:34 P.M.]	That's true. I've analyzed the sales data. The results are about 20% higher than we had projected.
Saori Iwamoto [4:35 P.M.]	Because the sales are so high, I think it's time to stop paying so much to advertise it. We don't need to continue running such a big campaign anymore.
Almed Abedi [4:36 P.M.]	I agree. We can do without it. Clearly the product has responded to a need in the market. I think customers will continue to buy these supplements even if we do less marketing.
Marina Jordan [4:37 P.M.]	You're right. And I think we have to start an advertising plan for our next product.
Saori Iwamoto [4:38 P.M.]	Do you mean our newest line of vitamin supplements intended for seniors?
Marina Jordan [4:39 P.M.]	Yes. We will start selling them in about three months.

Send

172 What is the purpose of the discussion?

(A) To assign specific duties
(B) To enhance employee productivity
(C) To write a budget proposal
(D) To modify a promotion strategy

173 What is indicated about Ms. Jordan?

(A) She is going to make a presentation.
(B) She is in charge of human resources.
(C) She has analyzed the sales data for the report.
(D) She has just started working at the company.

174 At 4:37 P.M., what does Ms. Jordan mean when she writes, "You're right"?

(A) She agrees it is time to develop a new product for women.
(B) She believes the product will sell well without less advertising.
(C) She thinks vitamins are essential for both women and children.
(D) She suggests that they start advertising on and off line.

175 What is true about the new products?

(A) They are specifically designed for women.
(B) They are easy to take.
(C) They are developed for older people.
(D) They must be consumed with food.

GO ON TO THE NEXT PAGE

Questions 176-180 refer to the following Web page information and e-mail.

http://www.citizensfirstbank.com

CITIZENS FIRST BANK

ANNOUNCEMENT | MY ACCOUNTS | FUNDS TRANSFER | EMPLOYMENT

Introducing Special Savings Starting!

Citizens First Bank now offers a new account, Special Savings Starting. This account offers several advantages over our Choice Savings account including favorable interest rates and increased options for transferring funds.

For a limited time, we are inviting our customers to convert their Choice Savings accounts into Special Savings Starting accounts without our usual account conversion fees. In addition, customers who make the change now will enjoy a special operation fee of only $5 per month for the first 12 months. After 12 months, the rate will increase to the regular Special Savings Starting rate of $8.25 per month.

For further details or to take advantage of this offer, please speak to one of our account representatives at 800-555-0111.

To	customerservice@citizensfirstbank.com
From	jtownsend@blakeleyryecable.com
Subject	New Savings Account
Date	April 2

I recently opened a Special Savings Starting account, and it was my understanding that the balance of my Choice Savings account would be transferred into the new account automatically. However, when I log in to my online banking profile, I see that available funds listed are $0 for the Special Savings Starting account. Could you please tell me when the funds will be transferred to the new account?

Thank you for your assistance.

Jessica Townsend

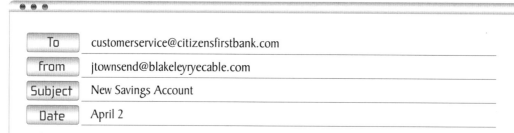

176 What is the purpose of the Web page information?

(A) To request customers for a payment
(B) To advertise a new type of bank service
(C) To review online banking procedures
(D) To report on the merger of two banks

177 What is stated about the operation fee?

(A) Customers can pay it in installments.
(B) It is offered at a discounted rate initially.
(C) It is lower than the fee at other banks.
(D) Customers can negotiate its due date.

178 Why is Ms. Townsend concerned?

(A) Because her money has not yet been moved to the new account
(B) Because she has been overcharged for an operation fee
(C) Because she was unable to update her bank transaction
(D) Because her account has been accessed without her permission

179 What is most likely true about Ms. Townsend?

(A) She will close her account because of this inconvenience.
(B) Her operation fee has been increased.
(C) She will not be charged a fee for the account change.
(D) She is a new customer to Citizens First Bank.

180 In the e-mail, the word "profile" in paragraph 1, line 3, is closest in meaning to?

(A) outline
(B) equality
(C) average
(D) stability

GO ON TO THE NEXT PAGE

Questions 181-185 refer to the following announcement and e-mail.

International Business Reconstruction Association (IBRA)

Opportunities for Information Storage

IBRA invites you to participate in a live, online seminar entitled "Strategies for Raising Corporate Funds." The seminar focuses on essential information to include in a grant proposal that will ensure your organization receives financial or other support from local and international companies.

This event will be presented by Michelle Conner, development director at the Rosario Foundation. The seminar, which will take place on July 22 from 1:30 P.M. to 3:00 P.M. GMT, will be moderated by Virginia Ross, a reporter for the television program World Business Reports. Registration is required by June 30; please visit www.ibra.org.uk/seminar0722 for information about fees and additional details.

At the time of your registration, you will be given the opportunity to submit a question for Ms. Conner. She will be able to respond to a limited number of these during the seminar. However, her answers to all relevant questions submitted by participants will be posted by August 1.

e-mail

From: mconner@rosariofoundation.org
To: keikomatusi@ibra.org.uk
Cc: swinkley@rosariofoundation.org
Subject: The Seminar
Sent: June 24

Dear Mr. Matusi:

I am very sorry to inform you that I am no longer able to fulfill my commitment to your organization. On the day I am scheduled to headline your event, I now, quite unexpectedly, need to travel to Barcelona on business. I have asked Smith Winkley, Associate Development Director, to present the seminar on my behalf as well as to participate in our video conference on July 31. He will be contacting you shortly by e-mail regarding these changes.

Mr. Winkley has planned and supervised fundraising campaigns for international firms for 25 years. Moreover, he is currently responsible for conducting our organization's online and in-person training sessions, so please rest assured that your seminar participants are in capable hands.

Again, my apologies for any inconvenience my cancellation causes.

Regards,

Michelle Conner

181 What is suggested about the event on July 22?

(A) It has been paid for with money from a charity organization.
(B) It is intended for international students.
(C) It will give advice about joining international corporations.
(D) It will be broadcast live by a television station.

182 What is indicated about seminar participants?

(A) They will receive professional development certificates.
(B) They should direct their questions to Ms. Ross.
(C) They must be members of the IBRA.
(D) They must sign up for the event in advance.

183 What date will Ms. Conner go on a business trip?

(A) June 24
(B) July 22
(C) July 31
(D) August 1

184 What has Ms. Conner arranged for the event?

(A) To have a financial donation sent to the IBRA
(B) To meet with Ms. Matusi in Barcelona
(C) To have her presentation video recorded
(D) To have a colleague substitute for her

185 What is suggested about the Rosario Foundation?

(A) It offers online training opportunities.
(B) It is seeking a new development director.
(C) It has been in business for 25 years.
(D) It is regularly featured on World Business Reports.

GO ON TO THE NEXT PAGE

Questions 186-190 refer to the following advertisement, e-mail and invoice.

GET YOUR DREAM CAR AT MADISON AUTOS.

If you want a nice car but don't want to spend a lot of money, then come to Madison Autos. We are in the business of buying and selling used vehicles. Our cars may not be brand-new, but we guarantee that they are in great condition. All vehicles are serviced when they arrive on our lot, and they are sold with a one-year warranty. We offer an extended two-year warranty with a purchase over $8,000. We also do repairs and order replacement parts right here on the lot.

Prices can be negotiated, so come visit Madison Autos and find your new car! Our address is 1807 Pine Street, Twin City, MN 00987.

To	Marco Colombo <marcocolombo@madisonautos.com>
From	Sydney Payton <sidneypayton@gmail.net>
Date	March 21
Subject	A Car Purchase

Dear Mr. Colombo:

I am contacting you because one of my colleagues recommended your services. Apparently you have a reputation as a kind and patient salesperson. I am looking to purchase a vehicle because mine keeps breaking down these days. I'd like to replace it with a newer model. I was hoping that you would be able to help me find something suitable.

However, I'm on a tight budget, so I don't want to pay any more than $10,000 for a used vehicle. According to an advertisement I saw recently, your company has a few that might be suitable. I'd like to schedule a time to meet with you. Then you can tell me more about it.

Sincerely,

Sydney Payton

MADISON AUTOS

1807 Pine Street, Twin City, MN 00987
555-7465

INVOICE #:	*123098*
DATE OF SALE:	*March 30*

Buyer INFO.

NAME:	*Sydney Payton*
ADDRESS:	*8912 South Hill Dr., Twin City, MN 00989*
PHONE:	*555-1423*
LICENSE NUMBER:	*K500-2507-0902-00*

Car INFO.

CAR:	*Prius Hybrid Z12*
REGISTRATION:	*J87F09876SS*
MILEAGE:	*82,000*
YEAR OF VEHICLE:	*2013*
SALES PRICE:	*$9,700*
WARRANTY:	*Extended*
METHOD OF PAYMENT:	___√___ *check* ______ *cash* ______ *credit*
Signature of Seller:	*Marco Colombo*
Signature of Buyer:	*Sydney Payton*

186 What is mentioned about cars in Madison Autos?

(A) They receive free servicing shortly after purchase.
(B) They can be paid for through financing plans.
(C) They were previously owned.
(D) They have the most popular features.

187 What is the purpose of the e-mail?

(A) To help design a car
(B) To distribute information
(C) To describe the process
(D) To ask for consultation

188 What is suggested about Ms. Payton's current vehicle?

(A) She bought it nearly 10 years ago.
(B) It is a four-door vehicle.
(C) She wishes to sell it to her colleague.
(D) It is not in perfect working order.

189 Why is Ms. Payton given an extended warranty?

(A) Because she spent over a certain amount of money
(B) Because she is a frequent customer
(C) Because she has joined a membership program
(D) Because Madison Autos is having a special event

190 What can be inferred about Ms. Payton?

(A) She paid for her vehicle with cash.
(B) Her colleague bought a car from Mr. Colombo.
(C) She chose a car that seats two people.
(D) She bought a Sport Utility Vehicle.

GO ON TO THE NEXT PAGE

Questions 191-195 refer to the following notice, e-mail, and article.

Fragment Master

If you have trouble getting rid of your old electronics, Fragment Master will come to you.

We are the region's largest recycler of electronic components. When you drop off your electronic devices, just put the materials in their proper place.

Box A: External hard devices, Miscellaneous
Box B: Monitors, Speakers, Laptop and Desktop computers
Box C: Keyboards, Accessories and Other devices

The current market for certain rare metals is strong. Therefore, for the time being, we will also be accepting small devices, including mobile phones, tablets, and hand-held video game systems through October 18.

We are here to help you. Please don't hesitate to ask for assistance at the service window.

To	dwerner@haverlyelectronics.com
From	Lgrove@fragmentmaster.org
Date	September 5
Subject	October Appointment

Dear Mr. Werner:

I'm reminding you that a Fragment Master representative, Matt Lovito, will visit Haverly Electronics on the morning of October 19. Please have your scrap electronics sorted to expedite the evaluation process. Be prepared to negotiate the price at that time.

As you are aware, prices offered are subject to daily market conditions. Let me fill you in a bit about what we are currently experiencing. Prices on reclaimed plastic have been trending downward. Similarly, because supplies of copper and silver are high now, there has been downward pressure on prices for recycled sources. You will be pleased to learn, however, that demand for titanium is unprecedented. The price has already doubled this year. A manufacturer called Baxon Ltd. in Singapore has been willing to buy all we can provide in the short term.

It continues to be a pleasure doing business with you.

Sincerely,

Lucia Grove
Fragment Master

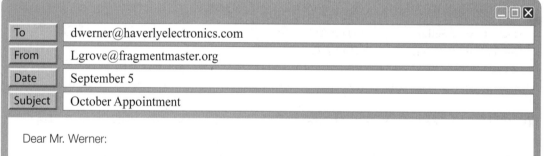

Singapore (Nov. 1) – Baxon Ltd. today announced the initial release of its newest model laptop computer, the Moonlight X10. The new product will be the fastest and lightest laptop in its class. These high-performance qualities are made possible by the use of newly designed rare-metal capacitors. The Moonlight X10 is also one of the first mass-produced laptops containing more than 50 percent recycled material, much of it salvaged from out-modeled consumer electronics. A limited number of model Moonlight X10s will be available tomorrow at the company's flagship store in Singapore. Although international customers must wait until November 30, Baxon plans to begin shipping the device to outlets throughout Singapore by November 10.

191 What does Ms. Grove most likely do for a living?

(A) Collect antiques for sale
(B) Sell computer accessories
(C) Develop software programs
(D) Run a recycling facility

192 In the notice, the word "strong" in paragraph 4, line 1, is closest in meaning to

(A) brilliant
(B) athletic
(C) bright
(D) active

193 What is probably true about Baxon Ltd.?

(A) It runs its own recycling center.
(B) It mainly manufactures external hard devices.
(C) It is Fragment Master's biggest customers.
(D) Some components of its latest laptops are from Fragment Master.

194 What is the main purpose of the article?

(A) To explain the cost of manufacturing a product
(B) To question a change in product development
(C) To introduce a new product in electronics
(D) To report on a product malfunction

195 What can be suggested about the Moonlight X10?

(A) It has more features compared to competitors' products.
(B) It will not be sold outside of Singapore for some time.
(C) It is the lightest product ever in the market.
(D) It is made out of recycled materials only.

GO ON TO THE NEXT PAGE

Questions 196-200 refer to following e-mails and schedule.

From	Scott Han <shan@dyscomventures.org>
To	All staff members of Dyscom Ventures
Date	January 9
Subject	Update
Attachment	deadline schedule.pdf

Dear colleagues:

Past editions of our company newsletter have focused only on developments in the IT industry and how they affect our company. This year I'd like to start including information about our employees in every issue. I have two features in mind.

The first will be announcements of professional achievements. If you have presented a paper in a conference, won an award, or completed a degree program, for example, please email me with your name and department and a description of your accomplishments in 40 words or less.

The goals of the second feature are to recognize employees who perform volunteer service in their communities and to bring attention to opportunities for community involvement. If you are a member of a local organization that needs help, please send me some information about the frequency and type of services and activities involved, whether they are one-time events like a charity golf tournament or more frequent events like volunteering in local schools. Attached is a complete list of the deadlines and publication schedules.

Sincerely,

Scott Han
Director, Internal Relations

DYSCOM VENTURES NEWSLETTER

Material	Deadline	For publication in
photo, illustrations articles, essays	February 8	March
photo, illustrations articles, essays	May 8	June
photo, illustrations articles, essays	August 8	September
photo, illustrations articles, essays	November 8	December

Any submissions that are received after the deadline will be published in the following issue. Please contact Scott Han at shan@dyscomventures.org if you have any questions.

e-mail

FROM: David Greenberg <dgreenberg@dyscomventures.org>
TO: Scott Han <shan@dyscomventures.org>
DATE: February 28
RE: Upcoming Event
ATTACHMENT: photo.jpg

Hi, Scott:

Sorry I did not get this to you earlier.

The Zuengler Library is currently accepting donations of gently used books for its annual book sale that will be held on July 8 from 10 A.M. to 4 P.M. I will be coordinating volunteer efforts to organize the books the day before. We tend to receive large boxes full of books, and they must be sorted into different categories so that customers can easily find whatever type of book they looking for during the sale. It is a lot of work, so we need your help.

I am sending you a photo of me at last year's event for the newsletter. I hope this will raise awareness of this great event. Let me know if you need any more information.

Thanks.

David Greenberg
Research and Development

196 What is the purpose of the first e-mail?

(A) To encourage Dyscom employees to submit papers for a conference
(B) To announce a job opening in the research department
(C) To explain procedures for the degree program
(D) To request information about Dyscom employees

197 What is NOT mentioned about the announcements?

(A) They are a new addition to the newsletter.
(B) They must be submitted by department supervisors.
(C) They honor award recipients.
(D) They can contain as many as 40 words.

198 What is suggested about the book sale?

(A) It is held in the library of the local community center.
(B) It carries both new and used books.
(C) People donate a large number of books.
(D) The proceeds will be donated to the children's charity.

199 When will a photo of Mr. Greenberg most likely appear in the newsletter?

(A) March
(B) June
(C) July
(D) September

200 What is Mr. Greenberg planning to do on July 7?

(A) To organize materials that the Zuengler Library received
(B) To participate in a sports competition
(C) To attend a lecture by an author at the Zuengler Library
(D) To write an article about the IT industry

Stop! This is the end of the test. If you finish before time is called, you may go back to Parts 5, 6, and 7 and check your work.

잠깐!! 시작 전 **꼭** 확인하세요!

- 실제 시험과 같이 책상을 정리하고 마음의 준비를 하세요.
- 핸드폰은 잠깐 끄고 대신 아날로그 시계를 활용해 보세요.
- 제한 시간은 120분입니다. 제한 시간을 꼭 지켜주세요.
- 어렵다고 넘어가지 마세요. 가능하면 차례대로 풀어 보세요.

Actual Test

05

시작 시간 :

종료 시간 :

▶정답 및 해설 P127

LISTENING TEST

In the Listening test, you will be asked to demonstrate how well you understand spoken English. The entire Listening test will last approximately 45 minutes. There are four parts, and directions are given for each part. You must mark your answers on the separate answer sheet. Do not write your answers in your test book.

PART 1

Directions: For each question in this part, you will hear four statements about a picture in your test book. When you hear the statements, you must select the one statement that best describes what you see in the picture. Then find the number of the question on your answer sheet and mark your answer. The statements will not be printed in your test book and will be spoken only one time.

Example

Sample Answer

Ⓐ ● Ⓒ Ⓓ

Statement (B), "The man is working at a desk," is the best description of the picture, so you should select answer (B) and mark it on your answer sheet.

1

2

GO ON TO THE NEXT PAGE

3

4

5

6

GO ON TO THE NEXT PAGE

▶정답 및 해설 P127

PART 2

Directions: You will hear a question or statement and three responses spoken in English. They will not be printed in your test book and will be spoken only one time. Select the best response to the question or statement and mark the letter (A), (B), or (C) on your answer sheet.

7 Mark your answer on your answer sheet.

8 Mark your answer on your answer sheet.

9 Mark your answer on your answer sheet.

10 Mark your answer on your answer sheet.

11 Mark your answer on your answer sheet.

12 Mark your answer on your answer sheet.

13 Mark your answer on your answer sheet.

14 Mark your answer on your answer sheet.

15 Mark your answer on your answer sheet.

16 Mark your answer on your answer sheet.

17 Mark your answer on your answer sheet.

18 Mark your answer on your answer sheet.

19 Mark your answer on your answer sheet.

20 Mark your answer on your answer sheet.

21 Mark your answer on your answer sheet.

22 Mark your answer on your answer sheet.

23 Mark your answer on your answer sheet.

24 Mark your answer on your answer sheet.

25 Mark your answer on your answer sheet.

26 Mark your answer on your answer sheet.

27 Mark your answer on your answer sheet.

28 Mark your answer on your answer sheet.

29 Mark your answer on your answer sheet.

30 Mark your answer on your answer sheet.

31 Mark your answer on your answer sheet.

▶정답 및 해설 P130

PART 3

Directions: You will hear some conversations between two or more people. You will be asked to answer three questions about what the speakers say in each conversation. Select the best response to each question and mark the letter (A), (B), (C), or (D) on your answer sheet. The conversations will not be printed in your test book and will be spoken only one time.

32 What does the woman want to discuss with the man?
(A) A remodeling project
(B) An advertising strategy
(C) An event plan
(D) A traffic problem

33 Where does the man say he is taking a client?
(A) To a manufacturing facility
(B) To a construction site
(C) To some properties
(D) To a client's office

34 What does the woman suggest?
(A) Calling a client
(B) Checking the schedule
(C) Taking public transportation
(D) Submitting a list

---

35 What are maintenance workers going to do by next Tuesday?
(A) Introduce the new system
(B) Install new equipment
(C) Clean the Conference room
(D) Submit the form

36 What is the woman concerned about?
(A) Testing a new device
(B) Meeting the deadline
(C) Using old equipment
(D) Rescheduling a presentation

37 What does the man suggest the woman do?
(A) Send an e-mail
(B) Try a bigger screen
(C) Go to the staff lounge
(D) Use another place

38 Why has the man come into the store?
(A) To bring back an item
(B) To get a gift
(C) To apply for a job
(D) To make a complaint

39 What does the woman ask the man to provide?
(A) Personal information
(B) Proof of purchase
(C) A gift voucher
(D) A store credit

40 What does the man let the woman know?
(A) He doesn't like the item.
(B) He is a regular customer.
(C) He came with his coworker.
(D) He lives near the store.

---

41 What are the speakers discussing?
(A) The completion of a project
(B) The commencement of the fiscal year
(C) The construction of a street
(D) The restoration of a bridge

42 What does the woman mean when she says, "Absolutely"?
(A) The tunnel should be renovated again.
(B) The transportation expenses will be increased.
(C) Kingston Avenue will be closed in September.
(D) There will be less traffic congestion.

43 According to the man, what will be offered in August?
(A) Discount fare
(B) New bus routes
(C) Free usage
(D) A travel card

GO ON TO THE NEXT PAGE

44 Where do the speakers most likely work?

(A) At a restaurant
(B) At a travel agency
(C) At a retail store
(D) At a hospital

45 What can be inferred about Daniel?

(A) He will handle the clothes.
(B) He is caught in traffic.
(C) He is out of town.
(D) He works as a cashier.

46 What will the man probably do next?

(A) Talk to Jasmine
(B) Restock some clothing
(C) Leave the office
(D) Put out some items

---

47 According to the woman, what will happen next month?

(A) A regional office will open.
(B) A Belgian firm will be acquired.
(C) An analysis will be conducted.
(D) A decision will be made.

48 What was the reason for the marketing director's decision?

(A) A lack of competition
(B) A certain industry regulation
(C) A shortage of hands
(D) An increase in efficiency

49 What does the man mean when he says, "I am not the right person to answer that"?

(A) He is unable to contact the CEO.
(B) He does not know the survey result.
(C) He is unable to answer the particular question.
(D) He is not in charge of the report.

50 What does Zoe ask of Isaac?

(A) If he can let her leave early
(B) If he can extend a deadline
(C) If he can give her a day off
(D) If he can buy her some new clothes

51 What does Sophia tell Zoe?

(A) She will take some time off.
(B) She can ask someone to help.
(C) She knows Rebecca.
(D) She knows Zoe's preferences.

52 By when must the work be finished?

(A) Monday
(B) Wednesday
(C) Friday
(D) Sunday

---

53 Who most likely is the woman?

(A) A charity organizer
(B) An office administrator
(C) A job candidate
(D) A research manager

54 Where does the conversation most likely take place?

(A) In a marketing office
(B) In an educational institution
(C) At a research institute
(D) At a fundraising event

55 According to the man, which group provides the most funding?

(A) Charitable organizations
(B) The government
(C) Corporations
(D) Private donors

56 What type of business do the speakers probably work for?

(A) An automobile company
(B) A financial firm
(C) An advertising agency
(D) An electronic manufacturer

57 Why does the woman say, "You're not going to believe this"?

(A) A project has made much progress.
(B) An unexpected decision has been made.
(C) An advertising campaign was very successful.
(D) The deadline will be moved forward.

58 What does the woman say about the clients?

(A) They are suffering from a lack of funds.
(B) They recently started their business.
(C) They are having difficulty exporting.
(D) They recently hired a new manager.

---

59 What is the topic of the conversation?

(A) A meeting plan
(B) A retirement event
(C) A sales presentation
(D) The latest car model

60 What has the woman recently done?

(A) Designed a car
(B) Updated the figures
(C) Created a chart
(D) Attended a meeting

61 What will the man do next?

(A) Contact a client
(B) Work on an estimate
(C) Revise data
(D) Attend a meeting

Department Manager Directory		
Dept.	Manager	Extension No.
Advertising	Nicole Martinez	210
Human Resources	Erica Lopez	324
Maintenance	Ethan Cabrera	420
Accounting	Lewis Moore	518

62 What is the main topic of the conversation?

(A) Plans for a seminar
(B) Adjustment of a document
(C) Ideas for a presentation
(D) Budgets for a project

63 Why does the man thank the woman?

(A) She gathered some information.
(B) She gave him a ride.
(C) She noticed some errors.
(D) She sent an e-mail.

64 Look at the graphic. In which department do the speakers most likely work?

(A) Advertising
(B) Human Resources
(C) Maintenance
(D) Accounting

GO ON TO THE NEXT PAGE

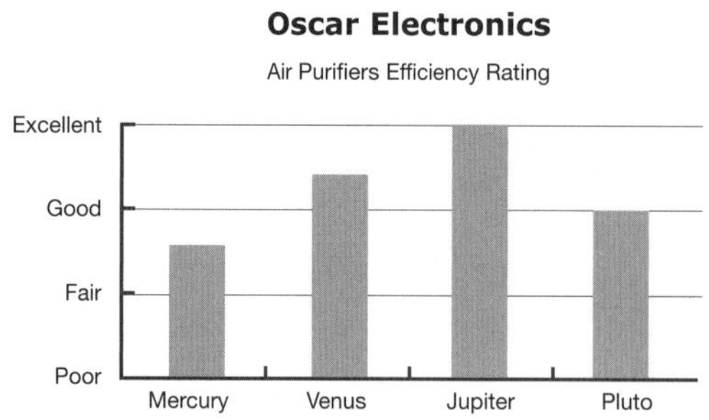

65 According to the woman, how was the sale advertised?

(A) On the Web site
(B) In the newspaper
(C) On the television
(D) On the radio

66 What does the man ask about?

(A) Where the item is displayed
(B) When a shipment will be made
(C) Whether a discount coupon is valid
(D) How a product will be used

67 Look at the graphic. Which model does the man say is the most expensive?

(A) The Mercury
(B) The Venus
(C) The Jupiter
(D) The Pluto

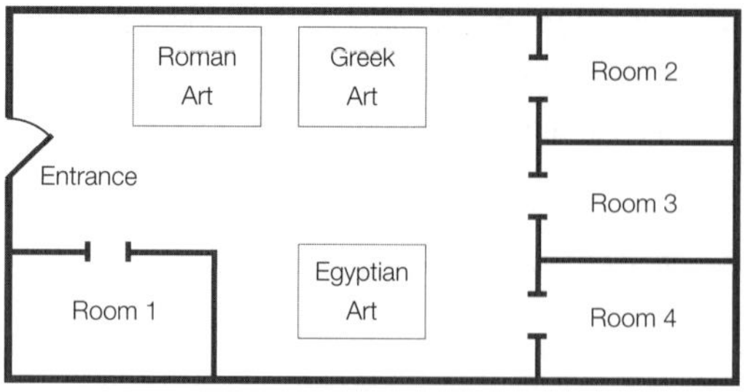

68 Who did the man meet yesterday?

(A) A museum director
(B) A town official
(C) A tour guide
(D) A department manager

69 How would the man like to promote the museum?

(A) In a newspaper
(B) On the television
(C) On the Web site
(D) On a street banner

70 Look at the graphic. Where will the collection of statues most likely be placed?

(A) In Room 1
(B) In Room 2
(C) In Room 3
(D) In Room 4

▶정답 및 해설 P139

PART 4

Directions: You will hear some talks given by a single speaker. You will be asked to answer three questions about what the speaker says in each talk. Select the best response to each question and mark the letter (A), (B), (C), or (D) on your answer sheet. The talks will not be printed in your test book and will be spoken only one time.

71 Who most likely are the tour participants?
(A) Natural Park tourists
(B) Restaurant owners
(C) New interns
(D) Local residents

72 Where will the tour begin?
(A) At the main entrance
(B) In the manufacturing facility
(C) In the warehouse
(D) In the marketing office

73 What will participants receive at the end of the tour?
(A) An item of clothing
(B) Food samples
(C) A carrier bag
(D) A booklet

---

74 What was announced yesterday?
(A) A proposal has been approved.
(B) A protest is going to be held.
(C) A new business has opened.
(D) A construction project has been completed.

75 What can be understood from the report?
(A) Construction has already started.
(B) The shopping mall will be torn down.
(C) Many residents are against the project.
(D) The tax will be increased next month.

76 What did the Mayor of Finsbury mean when he said, "This development will be a boon to our city"?
(A) The tax increase will be worth it.
(B) The project will generate more income.
(C) The land should remain as open space.
(D) The construction will cost a lot of money.

77 Who most likely is the speaker?
(A) A travel expert
(B) A personnel manager
(C) A recruitment officer
(D) A department head

78 What is the talk mainly about?
(A) Employee benefits
(B) Paid vacations
(C) Business travel expenses
(D) Travel schedules

79 What is on the first page of the booklet?
(A) A hiring contract
(B) An accounting report
(C) A set of rules
(D) A dress code

---

80 What does the speaker imply when he says, "Look for a host of yellow-marked items throughout the store"?
(A) Expiry dates are organized by color.
(B) Shoppers must go to the service desk.
(C) The store will be renovated soon.
(D) There are many bargain items.

81 Where can shoppers get lunch?
(A) In the deli department
(B) In the vegetables and fruit section
(C) In the food and beverage department
(D) In the meat and fish section

82 What item is fifty percent off?
(A) Beef
(B) Today's fish
(C) Lunch set
(D) Orange juice

GO ON TO THE NEXT PAGE

83 Why has the speaker made the call?

(A) To arrange an interview
(B) To find out when taxes are due
(C) To share work assignment
(D) To obtain more information

84 Who most likely is the speaker?

(A) An accountant
(B) A customer service representative
(C) A secretary
(D) A store clerk

85 What does the speaker let the listener know?

(A) His taxes are completed.
(B) He lives in Liverpool.
(C) He needs her signature.
(D) He owns a coffee shop.

---

86 What does the speaker mean when she says, "we need all hands on deck"?

(A) The listeners should applaud now.
(B) The event will be held on the ship.
(C) Everyone should work together.
(D) The listeners should submit the reports.

87 How many more chairs should the employees carry?

(A) 50
(B) 100
(C) 150
(D) 300

88 According to the speaker, what task will Nathan take on?

(A) Moving the chairs
(B) Printing the programs
(C) Preparing the tables
(D) Greeting the guests

89 What is Allegra's intended use?

(A) To treat back pain
(B) To stop coughing
(C) To ease allergy symptoms
(D) To help with sleeping problems

90 What is true of the medication?

(A) It is available in two flavors.
(B) It is not for children.
(C) It only comes in capsules.
(D) It has been discontinued.

91 What does the speaker say about Allegra?

(A) It will be available soon.
(B) It causes no side effects.
(C) It is good for long-term use.
(D) It should be taken three times a day.

---

92 Who most likely are the listeners?

(A) Security guards
(B) New employees
(C) Department heads
(D) Visitors

93 What aspect of the firm does the speaker emphasize?

(A) Its strong security
(B) Its generous pay
(C) Its friendly managers
(D) Its talented workers

94 What should listeners do if they temporarily misplace their badge?

(A) Call a guard
(B) Pay a fine
(C) Use a main entrance
(D) Request a receipt

Hotel Montana – Event Bookings	
Event Date(s)	Venue
September 1-4	The Euros Room
September 2-4	The Zepiros Room
September 5&6	The Notos Room
September 6	The Boreas Room

95 What did Chloe Adams do when she was a university student?

(A) She married an entrepreneur.
(B) She studied abroad.
(C) She created a software program.
(D) She founded a company.

96 What skill does Chloe Adams teach at her seminar?

(A) Software development
(B) Strategic thinking
(C) Decision making
(D) Risk analysis

97 Look at the graphic. In which venue will Chloe Adams' seminar probably be held?

(A) The Euros Room
(B) The Zepiros Room
(C) The Notos Room
(D) The Boreas Room

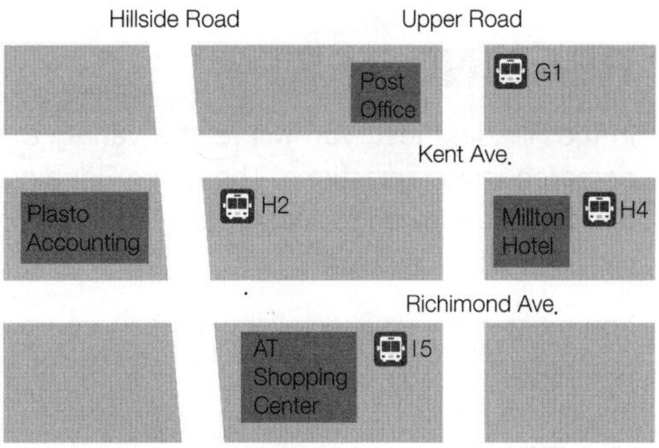

98 Look at the graphic. Which bus stop will no longer be available?

(A) G1
(B) H2
(C) H4
(D) I5

99 When is the change scheduled to occur?

(A) On Tuesday
(B) On Wednesday
(C) On Thursday
(D) On Friday

100 What are employees asked to do?

(A) Hand out some forms
(B) Renew their contracts
(C) Attend a conference
(D) Give their opinions

This is the end of the Listening test. Turn to Part 5 in your test book.

GO ON TO THE NEXT PAGE

READING TEST

In the Reading test, you will read a variety of texts and answer several different types of reading comprehension questions. The entire Reading test will last 75 minutes. There are three parts, and directions are given for each part. You are encouraged to answer as many questions as possible within the time allowed.

You must mark your answers on the separate answer sheet. Do not write your answers in your test book.

PART 5

Directions: A word or phrase is missing in each of the sentences below. Four answer choices are given below each sentence. Select the best answer to complete the sentence. Then mark the letter (A), (B), (C), or (D) on your answer sheet.

101 When attaching company contracts to an e-mail, keep these documents ------- by password-protecting them.

(A) secure
(B) security
(C) securely
(D) securing

102 Reasons for the increase in computer sales throughout the nation are not ------- clear.

(A) smoothly
(B) entirely
(C) justly
(D) tightly

103 Mr. Sherman is organizing the company banquet, so please let ------- know if you are able to attend.

(A) he
(B) his
(C) him
(D) himself

104 Before laying the new carpet, make sure the surface beneath it is completely -------.

(A) flat
(B) flatly
(C) flatter
(D) flatten

105 Customer service representatives are expected to respond within two hours to callers ------- leave a voice message.

(A) who
(B) they
(C) their
(D) when

106 Oldbrook Town's annual fashion fair helps residents learn about current trends while ------- having fun.

(A) formerly
(B) ever
(C) lastly
(D) also

107 At Copper Ltd., there are ------- opportunities for professional advancement.

(A) plenty
(B) each
(C) every
(D) many

108 Herman Printing Services uses higher quality paper ------- its competitors do.

(A) what
(B) that
(C) such
(D) than

109 Because of the unfavorable weather, the painters are not finished ------- the north side of the building.

(A) with
(B) out
(C) from
(D) of

110 Patients must sign an authorization form ------- medical records can be transferred to new insurance providers.

(A) except
(B) before
(C) instead
(D) rather

111 For security reasons, visitors to the Green Bay Science and Technology Research Institute must be ------- at all times.

(A) displayed
(B) estimated
(C) conferred
(D) escorted

112 The laboratory manual details our procedures for handling materials as ------- as possible.

(A) safety
(B) safely
(C) safer
(D) safest

113 In Ms. Bukowski's -------, the shift supervisor is in charge of the restaurant.

(A) duty
(B) absence
(C) instance
(D) event

114 Call Perrybridge Office Furniture representatives ------- immediate cost estimates over the phone.

(A) to receive
(B) receiving
(C) will receive
(D) receives

115 We are ------- to discuss your remodeling needs in detail via e-mail or telephone.

(A) delighting
(B) delighted
(C) delights
(D) delight

116 The Kerton Town Council ------- receives project proposals, so applicants should expect to wait several months for a decision.

(A) quickly
(B) recently
(C) regularly
(D) similarly

117 ------- Jung's Burger opened its newest franchise, the first 100 customers were given a free soda.

(A) Now
(B) When
(C) As if
(D) After all

118 Please include the serial number of your product in any ------- with the Customer Service Department.

(A) corresponds
(B) correspondence
(C) correspondingly
(D) correspondent

119 Fisher & Phillips Insurance Company offers coverage to ------- and commercial property owners in Barcelona.

(A) habitual
(B) residential
(C) necessary
(D) settled

120 Heike Construction Company is seeking a heavy equipment ------- with at least two years of related experience.

(A) operational
(B) operating
(C) operator
(D) operate

GO ON TO THE NEXT PAGE

121 A blue label indicates a package containing extra virgin olive oil, ------- a green label indicates it contains balsamic vinegar.

(A) whereas
(B) whether
(C) both
(D) about

122 If the Vogel Marathon is canceled, ------- who prepaid the registration fee will receive a full refund.

(A) those
(B) which
(C) them
(D) whichever

123 Orangedale Publishing's Chief of Staff meets regularly with the staff to ensure that procedures ------- correctly.

(A) to be performed
(B) would have performed
(C) had been performed
(D) are being performed

124 Technicians are trying to determine exactly ------- caused the building's power failure.

(A) what
(B) that
(C) whose
(D) those

125 ------- the popularity of our new wireless speaker, production will be increased fivefold next year.

(A) As a result of
(B) On behalf of
(C) Moreover
(D) Assuming that

126 ------- having the support of local officials, the Highbrook Library renovation project experienced numerous setbacks.

(A) Conversely
(B) Otherwise
(C) Whether
(D) Despite

127 Blakeley Architects noted that the community center ------- a one-story building for maximum accessibility.

(A) that remains
(B) should remain
(C) to remain
(D) remaining

128 Nelson Groth Institute offers an ------- of professional services to meet the needs of students.

(A) array
(B) entity
(C) article
(D) item

129 ------- events this year in the second and third quarters caused profits to differ significantly from the original projection.

(A) Total
(B) Marginal
(C) Representative
(D) Unforeseen

130 Mr. Hendley ------- authority to his most trusted employees in an emergency.

(A) aligned
(B) exercised
(C) delegated
(D) nominated

PART 6

Directions: Read the texts that follow. A word, phrase, or sentence is missing in parts of each text. Four answer choices for each question are given below the text. Select the best answer to complete the text. Then mark the letter (A), (B), (C), or (D) on your answer sheet.

Questions 131-134 refer to the following notice.

At Household Superstore, we sell major appliances from top brand names. We're the only store in the area that stocks replacement parts for all of our appliances. Parts ------- **131.** by phone at 032-555-2938 or online. Registration is not ------- **132.** for online orders. However, it will make the process faster the next time you shop with us. ------- **133.**. As a result, your order might arrive in several shipments. ------- **134.** will increase your shipping charges.

131 (A) should have ordered
(B) may be ordered
(C) were ordered
(D) to order

132 (A) advisable
(B) available
(C) required
(D) renewable

133 (A) To expedite delivery of your order, parts are sent directly from different suppliers.
(B) The company is currently interviewing candidates for the position.
(C) We offer all the supplies you need to prepare for any event.
(D) Please inquire at the service desk if it will be permitted on your flight.

134 (A) They
(B) Both
(C) Some
(D) This

GO ON TO THE NEXT PAGE

Questions 135-138 refer to the following e-mail.

To: Karen Karl
From: Liz Steinhauer
Subject: Special Project
Date: April 2

Good morning, Ms. Karl.

I have a list of special projects that must be completed, and I would like to assign you the job of ------- **135.** our collection of informational brochures. This will be one of your ongoing responsibilities because these pamphlets are revised periodically, and only the ------- **136.** versions are available to library patrons.

-------. **137.** Anything dated before February of this year should be replaced with the revised document, which can be printed from the library's internal Web page. Please complete this task -------, **138.** as a number of the brochures are quite outdated.

Thank you.

Liz Steinhauer
Head Librarian

135 (A) writing
(B) copying
(C) updating
(D) mailing

136 (A) initial
(B) current
(C) duplicate
(D) draft

137 (A) Thank you for becoming a member of our library organization.
(B) Check the information displays at the library entrance and the checkout desk.
(C) Our remodeled offices are due to open in April as scheduled.
(D) Your support has enabled us to improve our office products.

138 (A) promptly
(B) prompting
(C) prompted
(D) prompt

Questions 139-142 refer to the following article.

Windom Pharmacy Makes Prescription Orders Easier for Customers.

By Daniel Banaszek

Seattle (July 12) — Windom Pharmacy is about to make life easier for its tech-savvy customers. -------. (**139.**) Customers will be able to receive a text message ------- (**140.**) a prescription is ready for pickup. The previous notification system required pharmacy staff to make time-consuming phone calls.

"The old system was not very -------," (**141.**) CEO Jessica Windom said in a press release.

"People don't always listen to their voice mail in a timely manner. Text notifications will begin on July 15. -------, (**142.**) customers who prefer phone calls still have the option," Ms. Windom noted.

139 (A) Though we are now quite busy, my staff can handle the workload.
(B) I am writing to let you know that I have told all my friends about the service.
(C) One of these is creating a new line of women's vitamin supplements.
(D) The popular drugstore chain will soon offer mobile alerts for prescription orders.

140 (A) sooner
(B) despite
(C) when
(D) though

141 (A) fair
(B) efficient
(C) profitable
(D) clarifying

142 (A) As a result
(B) Therefore
(C) However
(D) Likewise

GO ON TO THE NEXT PAGE

Questions 143-146 refer to the following e-mail.

To: All members
From: Vanessa Kwan
Date: August 21
Subject: Good News

Balmer Theater at the Durian Art Center is pleased to share good news with season subscribers. The construction of an annex to the main building is almost finished and should be ready for the September 20 opening.

Last fall, the Durian Art Center ------- (143.) to add a studio to the theater auditorium so it can create sets for drama productions. The new ------- (144.) allows our theater to expand current events for all audiences. ------- (145.), it will be the home for classes and summer camps. ------- (146.).

Sincerely,

Vanessa Kwan
Art Director, Balmer Theater

143 (A) will decide
(B) decides
(C) decided
(D) has decided

144 (A) report
(B) space
(C) donor
(D) leadership

145 (A) In spite of this
(B) On the contrary
(C) Additionally
(D) Nevertheless

146 (A) I have attached a list of events that will take place at this year's trade fair.
(B) Located just an hour from busy downtown, we are an ideal destination for you.
(C) Please review the open positions at our Web site and contact me for further information.
(D) We thank you for your support and look forward to showing you our new facilities.

PART 7

Directions: In this part you will read a selection of texts, such as magazine and newspaper articles, e-mails, and instant messages. Each text or set of texts is followed by several questions. Select the best answer for each question and mark the letter (A), (B), (C), or (D) on your answer sheet.

Questions 147-148 refer to the following information.

This is to certify that

Jennifer Lloyd completed a series of three training sessions entitled "Issues of Online News Reporting: Neutrality in Economic and Political Stories" on May 25 at the Lamnan Professional Development Center.

Her series of sessions was rated very good by the course participants.

Mark Linksky, Training Director

Lamnan Professional Development Center

147 What did Ms. Lloyd do on May 25?

(A) She delivered a lecture.
(B) She underwent a training course.
(C) She appeared in a newspaper.
(D) She reported a technical problem.

148 Who most likely is Ms. Lloyd?

(A) A Web site designer
(B) A software developer
(C) A director of a development center
(D) A journalist

Questions 149-150 refer to the following warranty card.

Quentin Power Tools Inc.

WARRANTY CARD

Quentin Power Tools Inc., repairs, at no cost to our customers, any defective products, within a designated period of time. This warranty extends to the original purchaser of the product and lasts up to three weeks from the purchase date. If we are not able to repair the product, we may replace it with a comparable item.

The warranty does not cover any consumer negligence or accidental damage. It also does not cover part failure when someone other than a Quentin employee attempts to repair the product.

When sending an item for repair or replacement, you must include your name, street address and phone number for us to assist in returning shipment. It is recommended (although not required) to enclose a note explaining the problem you had using the item.

Once we receive your shipment, it normally takes 14 to 21 business days until we respond.

If you have further questions about product warranty or repair information, please call our Warranty Information Line at 1-800-555-4455.

Revised November 10

149 What information is stated on the warranty card?

(A) Names of dealers that provide replacement parts
(B) A list of tools that are covered
(C) Costs of specific types of repairs
(D) An estimation of the time needed to complete repairs

150 According to the warranty card, what must be included with a request for repair services?

(A) A copy of the warranty
(B) A photo of the product
(C) Shipping information
(D) A note explaining problems

Questions 151-153 refer to the following article.

Local Company Is Recognized

by Walter Vine

Milwaukee — In its December edition, *Adventure Wilderness Magazine* rated the Milwaukee-based Quest Out Tour Agency at number seven on its list of Top Ten Travel Companies for the upcoming year.

According to *Adventure Wilderness Magazine*, Quest Out made the list because it demonstrated a strong commitment to offering tour participants a rewarding and memorable experience. They range from canoeing, hiking, and cross-country skiing, to bird-watching, whale-watching, and dog sledding. Quest Out has developed fun-filled activities for every type of outdoor adventure.

The owner of Quest Out, Campbell Hargrove, was delighted to find out that his company had made the list. In a statement the company released yesterday, he said, "We are honored to be recognized as one of the preeminent travel companies in the country, alongside popular companies like Igloo Ice Explorer and Eco-World Travel Company, which have been in the eco-adventure business much longer than we have."

151 Why was the Quest Out Tour Agency selected by *Adventure Wilderness Magazine*?

(A) It is one of the most popular travel companies in the region.
(B) It is more committed to the environment than its competitors.
(C) It offers more outdoor activities than other travel companies.
(D) It organizes tours that are likely to be remembered for a long time.

152 What is NOT indicated about the Quest Out Tour Agency?

(A) Its trips cost a lot.
(B) It is based in Milwaukee.
(C) It takes travelers on ski trips.
(D) Its owner is Campbell Hargrove.

153 What is suggested about Eco-World Travel Company?

(A) It takes travelers to destinations outside the country.
(B) It has been in operation for quite a while.
(C) It does not offer outdoor activities.
(D) It is not as popular as the Quest Out Tour Agency.

GO ON TO THE NEXT PAGE

Questions 154-155 refer to the following online chat.

Sean Renault [2:30 P.M.]	I'm setting up the conference room for the board meeting but can't find the cable for the laptop.
Natalie Albright [2:32 P.M.]	I'm not sure which cable you mean.
Sean Renault [2:35 P.M.]	The one that hooks up a computer to the projector. I think it's missing.
Natalie Albright [2:37 P.M.]	That has happened before. I'll bring one down in a few minutes. Anything else?
Sean Renault [2:39 P.M.]	I think there's also a remote for the projector. I can't find that either.
Natalie Albright [2:43 P.M.]	I'll grab that as well.
Sean Renault [2:45 P.M.]	Thanks a lot.

Send

154 Why is Mr. Renault contacting Ms. Albright?

(A) To confirm the date of a board meeting
(B) To discuss a meeting agenda
(C) To ask for help with a piece of equipment
(D) To verify the event venue

155 At 2:37 P.M., what does Ms. Albright mean when she writes, "That has happened before"?

(A) She knows why the equipment is replaced.
(B) She knows which cable Mr. Renault needs.
(C) She thinks the computer is out of order.
(D) She acknowledges her mistakes.

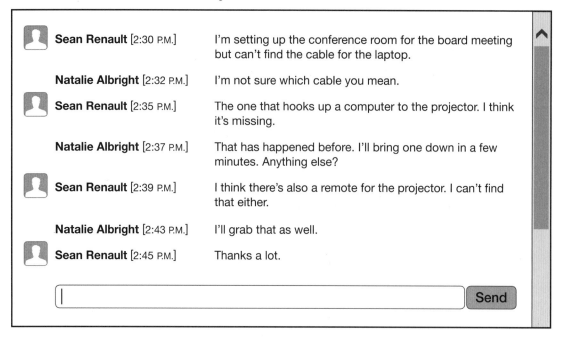

Questions 156-157 refer to the following text message.

Receiver: Sandy Baxter (001-555-0129)
Sender: Marco Connelly (002-555-9801)
Date: July 23, 10:01 A.M.

Hi, Sandy. I accidentally left my planner at the office. It has the address of Chester Systems. Could you send me the address? I am scheduled to meet the CEO there this afternoon. Also, I put the contract for Rogers and Master Express Ltd. on your desk. Please deliver the contract to Paul Rogers before noon. Thanks!

Marco

Send

156 What is the main purpose of the message?

(A) To cancel a meeting
(B) To ask for information
(C) To request a new planner
(D) To schedule an appointment

157 What should Ms. Baxter do?

(A) Send a message to a client
(B) Go to the office of Chester Systems
(C) Write a contract for Mr. Rogers
(D) Give someone a document

GO ON TO THE NEXT PAGE

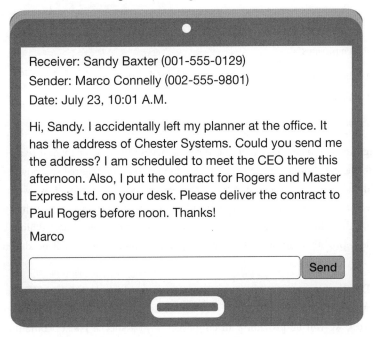

Questions 158-160 refer to the following memo.

To	All employees
From	Linda Meyerson, President, Meyerson Lighting Company
Subject	Office Relocation
Date	April 30

Meyerson Lighting Company has experienced phenomenal growth over the last two years, and while that is good for business, it also means that we have outgrown our original space here in the historic Creston Building. –[1]–. As discussed at the company meeting on March 29, we were in negotiation to purchase the recently renovated Barnet Building. I am happy to announce that we reached an agreement with the seller on April 14. The Barnet Building facility is almost double the size of our current location, providing additional offices, conference rooms, and much-needed manufacturing space. –[2]–.

The Barnet Building is just two kilometers away from our present location. We have contracted Kalamar & Murray Commercial Mover to assist us when we move on Thursday, May 16. –[3]–. Next week we will be providing all employees with a special packet containing information about the move, including a description of what each person will be responsible for packing and a comprehensive timeline for the week of the move. –[4]–. New office assignments and sketches of the Barnet Building that show the layout of offices, meeting rooms, and production space will also be provided. On May 13, all employees are welcome to visit the new building to become acquainted with the interior. Our goal is to resume work as soon as possible.

I look forward to seeing you all in our new facility.

158 What is suggested about the Creston Building?

(A) It was renovated to have more space.
(B) It was sold to another lighting company in April.
(C) It is where Meyerson Lighting Company first started doing business.
(D) It was originally intended to be a storage facility for Meyerson Lighting Company.

159 What is NOT mentioned as being included in the packet that employees will receive?

(A) Instruction for packing
(B) Detailed schedules
(C) A diagram of a building
(D) Directions to the new location

160 In which of the positions marked [1], [2], [3], and [4] does the following sentence best belong?

"We will now be able to increase production to meet the rapidly growing demand for our custom-designed lightings."

(A) [1]
(B) [2]
(C) [3]
(D) [4]

Questions 161-164 refer to the following e-mail.

To	altongilman@carroltonbusinesspost.com
From	agonzalez@endayafoundation.org
Subject	Today's Article
Date	June 12

Dear Mr. Gilman:

Thank you for your article in today's issue of the Carrolton Business Post. Our organization is pleased that you wrote about our upcoming fundraising event in so much detail, and we loved the picture of our building that your photographer took. We're looking forward to the publicity that your articles bring. I do, however, want to clarify one point. Our speaker's name is Milo Ferris, and not "Ferriz," as written in the article.

I realize that you face deadline pressure every day, but I'm hoping that it is not too late to print a small correction notice in tomorrow's issue. We would like to avoid a situation in which another reporter might reference your article, and inaccurately list the name of Mr. Ferris. In addition, I would appreciate if you could please update the original version and email it to us once the change has been made. We would like to make the article available as part of our online media kit, which will be accessible to other news organizations.

Thank you.

Alicia Gonzalez
Ben Knight

161 What is the purpose of the e-mail?
(A) To cancel a subscription
(B) To request a correction
(C) To promote an upcoming event
(D) To recommend a new organization member

162 What is probably true about the Carrolton Business Post?
(A) It has a reader's column.
(B) It recently funded a charity event.
(C) It is published daily.
(D) It releases information on business events.

163 The word "face" in paragraph 2, line 1, is closest in meaning to
(A) confront
(B) feature
(C) oppose
(D) overlook

164 What does Ms. Gonzalez request by e-mail?
(A) A revision of the publication guideline
(B) A list of media organizations
(C) A reference letter
(D) A copy of an article

GO ON TO THE NEXT PAGE

Questions 165-167 refer to the following information.

Drayton Music Festival

Interested in donating some of your time while enjoying all kinds of great music? Then volunteer at the fifteenth annual Drayton Music Festival! This year's festival runs from October 25 to 31 at the county fairgrounds in Drayton and features music from more than 50 talented groups, including local favorites Starroad Pop Band, Jazz Heroes, and Jackson's String Quartet.

Volunteers are needed to

- help with publicity — designing and posting a flyer and sending press release — starting in October.
- greet the musicians and help them locate their housing assignments from October 23 to 29. All out-of-town musicians will be hosted by area families.
- operate the ticket booth, direct guests to the parking areas during the festival, and provide general information.

In appreciation, each volunteer will receive a limited edition Drayton Music Festival T-shirt and four complimentary tickets.

If you are interested in volunteering, please contact Justin Brown at justinbrown@draytonmusicfest.org by September 17.

165 What is indicated about the event?

(A) It will take place on October 1.
(B) It features a variety of music types.
(C) It is run by a professional musician.
(D) It may be rescheduled because of rain.

166 What is suggested about some of the performers?

(A) They will be donating used instruments.
(B) They will be providing funds to the event.
(C) They will be staying at homes in Drayton.
(D) They will be receiving a major award at the event.

167 What task will NOT be done by volunteers?

(A) Selling tickets for festival performances
(B) Taking musicians to the fairground
(C) Giving audience directions to the parking area
(D) Distributing publicity materials

Questions 168-171 refer to the following text message chain.

Miranda Keo Hi, Lucy. Are you at headquarters? 10:30 A.M.

Lucy White Not yet. I'm heading there now, why? 10:31 A.M.

Miranda Keo We are running out of bricks for the walkway job here on Oakwood Street. Are there any left in the storehouse? If not, I can get some at the store on Hampton Plaza. 10:33 A.M.

Lucy White Patrick is in the office. I'm including him now. How many boxes do you need? 10:34 A.M.

Miranda Keo Twelve should cover it. 10:35 A.M.

Patrick Adams You got it! 10:36 A.M.

Miranda Keo Great. We'll need them by noon today. I'll come and get them. 10:40 A.M.

Lucy White Actually, I'm pulling in now and will be loading a truck for the house-siding jobs on Calvin Boulevard and Garner Road. The bricks should fit, too. When I'm done loading it, I'll come to you first. 10:41 A.M.

Miranda Keo Thanks, Lucy. And Patrick, could you add my name and the number of boxes to the log sheet? 10:42 A.M.

Patrick Adams Sure. 10:43 A.M.

168 Where does Ms. Keo probably work?

(A) At an architecture firm
(B) At a delivery service
(C) At a construction company
(D) At a home improvement store

169 At 10:36 A.M., what does Mr. Adams most likely mean when he writes, "You got it"?

(A) The traffic is running smoothly.
(B) He is free to help at noon.
(C) The truck Ms. White needs is available.
(D) There is enough material for the work.

170 Where does Ms. White say she will go?

(A) To Oakwood Street
(B) To Hampton Plaza
(C) To Calvin Boulevard
(D) To Garner Road

171 What does Ms. Keo ask Mr. Adams to do?

(A) Explain the directions to Ms. White
(B) Submit a request for time off
(C) Keep an accurate record of the items
(D) Calculate how much to bill a customer

GO ON TO THE NEXT PAGE

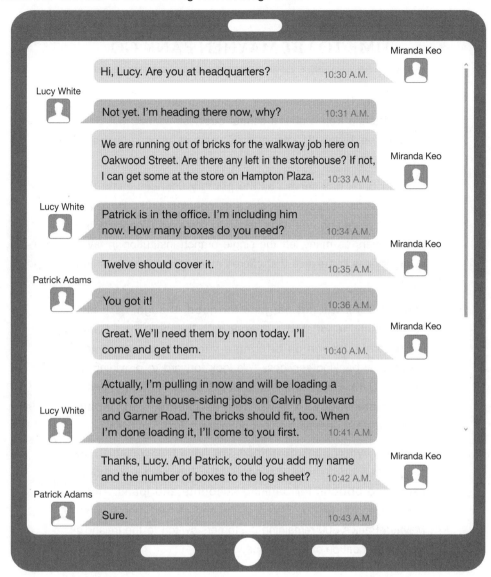

Questions 172-175 refer to the following article.

TIME TO LET MAYHEN BANK GO

Dublin (July 1) – Mayhen Bank, located in Broadstone, only a short distance from Dublin's central business district, will close its doors on August 31 after over 50 years of being in business. –[1]–.

Mayhen Bank has served as the primary financial institution for thousands of customers since its opening. –[2]–. However, about 10 years ago, the bank began to see a significant decline in customers as many left the single-branch institution in favor of larger ones in the area that offered more branch locations and services.

Mayhen Bank will not be gone for good, though, as it has successfully negotiated a merger with Ireland's First Bank, a multicity corporation offering a variety of personal and commercial banking services. "We look forward to providing all Mayhen Bank customers with a positive banking experience, and we are happy to have them as clients," said Adam Petrovich, chief operating officer of Ireland's First Bank. –[3]–.

Former Mayhen Bank customers will have the availability of several new products and services after the merger, including expanded options for banking accounts and loans. –[4]–. The merger will be completed at the end of next month when Mayhen Bank's 500 remaining customers switch to the Ireland's First Bank location of their choice.

172 What is the purpose of the article?

(A) To announce the opening of a bank
(B) To request consumer reviews of local businesses
(C) To report on new policies affecting customers
(D) To publicize the merger between two businesses

173 Why did Mayhen Bank lose a lot of customers?

(A) Because it charged too many fees
(B) Because it has too few locations
(C) Because its employees are not well trained
(D) Because it is closed too early on weekdays

174 What is stated about Mayhen Bank?

(A) It has about 500 customers.
(B) It opened 10 years ago.
(C) Its president will resign soon.
(D) It was formerly called Ireland's First Bank

175 In which of the positions marked [1], [2], [3], and [4] does the following sentence best belong?

"Additionally, all Mayhen customers will receive a complimentary $40 gift card from Ireland's First Bank as a welcome gift as soon as their accounts are transferred."

(A) [1]
(B) [2]
(C) [3]
(D) [4]

Test 05

GO ON TO THE NEXT PAGE

Questions 176-180 refer to following memo and form.

To	Parker Insurance staff
From	Aoto Kintoshita, Human Resource Department
Date	September 1
Subject	NWMS Partnership

As a part of its employee appreciation program, Parker Insurance Agency has partnered with New Way Mobile Service (NWMS) to offer employees discounted mobile phone service. Staff members who change to open either an individual or family service plan with NWMS will save 20% and 25%, respectively, off telephone charges for the first month of their subscription. Additionally, the account service charge will be waived. Subscription plans are for one year and will be automatically renewed for another year unless service is cancelled.

Employees wishing to take advantage of this offer should contact the NWMS Customer Service Department at 321-555-0123. Applications are also accepted electronically at www.nwms.com/corpsaving. To start the subscription process, employees must provide a work e-mail address and employee number. In addition, be ready to submit a valid credit card number as well as a government-issued document, such as a driver's license or passport, that carries a unique identification number.

NWMS CUSTOMER COMPLAINT FORM

Customer Details
Name: *Edward Boulanger*
Account Number: *BA834-1*
Date: *December 3*
E-mail address: *eboulanger@parkerinsurance.com*

Details of Complaint

Last October I opened a mobile phone plan account after learning about the special offer for Parker Insurance Agency employees. According to the promotional material distributed by my employer, I should not have been charged an account service charge to start the service. The NWMS representative I spoke with on the phone when I signed up also confirmed this. Nevertheless, the charge appeared on my first billing statement, dated November 30. Please remove the erroneous charge from the bill and send me an amended version. Of course, the new bill should continue to reflect a 25% discount on phone charges.

Thank you.

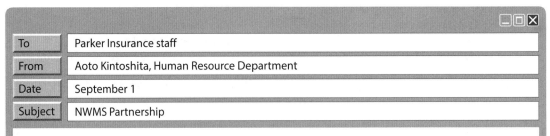

176 What is the memo mainly about?

(A) The addition of a benefit for employees
(B) Use of company phones for work purposes only
(C) The renewal of a mobile phone subscription
(D) Requirement for employees to register with NWMS

177 What is indicated about the account service charge?

(A) It can be paid in installments.
(B) It will be refunded if an account is cancelled.
(C) It usually costs $25.
(D) It will be complimentary.

178 What is NOT required for the NWMS application?

(A) An employee number
(B) A postal code
(C) A credit card number
(D) An e-mail address

179 What can be inferred about Mr. Boulanger?

(A) He works in Mr. Kintoshita's department.
(B) He has subscribed to the family service plan.
(C) He opened his account through the Parker Web site.
(D) He learned of NWMS' offer from one of his family members.

180 What does Mr. Boulanger request that NWMS do?

(A) Cancel his monthly plan
(B) Make changes to the revised company policy
(C) Send him a corrected billing statement
(D) Extend his discount to his friends

GO ON TO THE NEXT PAGE

Questions 181-185 refer to following schedule and e-mail.

Connelly Publishing House Presents Randy Carmichael's *The Art of Daydreaming*
National Book Tour
Southwestern Region - May Public Appearances

Thursday, May 10, 6 P.M.
Jessie's Book Haven – 500 Oak Terrace, Tucson, AZ 02116
A meet-and-greet with Mr. Carmichael will take place at 5 P.M.; by invitation only.
The reading session starts at 6 P.M. and is open to the public.

Saturday, May 12, 5 P.M.
Barnes and Nomads – 218 Maynard Street, Austin, TX 78704
Book reading begins at 5 P.M., followed by the book signing at 6 P.M. Due to a scheduling conflict, Mr. Carmichael will not be able to take questions at this presentation.

Wednesday, May 16, 6 P.M.
Café Reynolds – 685 Cherry Tree Avenue, Houston, TX 19103
Limited seating. Please visit www.cafereynolds.com to register for the event.
There is a $5 advance ticket fee. Tickets sold at the door will be $8.

Monday, May 21, 6 P.M.
Jefferson Public Library – 400 Jefferson Avenue, New Orleans, LA 21202
Attendees will have the opportunity to ask questions.
Afterward, a dinner reception for all attendees will be held in the library conference center.

Additional notes:
- All dates, times, and locations are subject to change.
- Unless otherwise indicated, Mr. Carmichael will read excerpts from *The Art of Daydreaming*, sign copies, and answer questions from the audience at each appearance.
- Copies of *The Art of Daydreaming* will be available for purchase at all venues.
- On June 1, future tour dates and cities will be announced on the publisher's Web site and in local newspapers.

To request an appearance by the author, please contact Cecilia Haywood at chaywood@connellypublishing.com.

To	Cecilia Haywood <chaywood@connellypublishing.com>
From	Jason King <jasonking@tucsonuniversity.com>
Date	May 25
Subject	Mr. Carmichael's Book Tour
Attachment	Inquiries.doc

Dear Ms. Haywood:

I want to thank Connelly Publishing for bringing Mr. Carmichael to Tucson and for inviting me to the private reception that preceded the public event. It was my honor to have an opportunity to meet one of my favorite authors in person and to exchange some words. I am planning to use *The Art of Daydreaming* in my introductory psychology class and had some questions for him. Since there was not enough time to discuss them all, he suggested I forward them to you. (See attached documents.) And I also want to speak with you about the possibility of having Mr. Carmichael visit my class to talk to my students. I try to bring in one guest lecturer each semester, and I think Mr. Carmichael is perfect. I hope to hear from you soon.

Sincerely,

Jason King

181 What is suggested about the book tour?

(A) All venues have a seating capacity of over 100.
(B) Invited guests will receive a copy of Mr. Carmichael's book.
(C) It will conclude on May 25.
(D) It is organized by Connelly Publishing.

182 What location requires an admission fee?

(A) Jessie's Book Haven
(B) Barnes and Nomads
(C) Café Reynolds
(D) Jefferson Public Library

183 What is the purpose of the e-mail?

(A) To give instructions about publishing a book
(B) To ask for assistance with making an arrangement
(C) To provide information on a psychology course
(D) To inquire about tours by other authors

184 What date did Mr. King meet Mr. Carmichael?

(A) May 10
(B) May 12
(C) May 16
(D) May 21

185 Who most likely is Mr. King?

(A) A textbook publisher
(B) A bookstore owner
(C) An university professor
(D) A newspaper correspondent

Questions 186-190 refer to the following memo, advertisement, and e-mail.

To	All Multiflex Gym Specialists
From	Donald Warren
Date	April 22
Subject	Promotion

As you know, many Dover College students stay in town during the summer, so we will be offering the yearly 30 percent summer discount for students who enroll during the first two weeks of June. However, Multiflex Gym is also considering offering two special discounts to new and continuing members during the upcoming summer season (June 1~August 1).

We would like to hear from our staff before making a final decision about the two possible offers. The first option would be to offer a family discount. This would mean that any current member could add a household member (age 16 or older) to his or her current membership for 20 percent less than the normal membership fee.

The second possible offer would be that Gold-level members could bring a friend for free from 6 A.M. until 4 P.M. on Tuesdays and Wednesdays. These friends would have access to the entire gym, including the yoga rooms. However, the driving range for golfers would be off limits to ensure that our members do not have to wait longer than they already do for their availability.

Please reply by May 3 with the promotion that you think would be most beneficial for our members.

Thank you for your help in making this decision.

Don't Miss Out on Our Special Offers Only for Dover College Students!

Sign up between June 1 and August 1 to receive a 30% discount on your summer membership at any level and get your own personalized water bottle for free.

Bring a friend on Tuesdays and Wednesdays:
Beginning June 1, all Gold- and Platinum-level members can bring a friend for free during their fitness visits on Tuesdays and Wednesdays. Friends must sign in and show a valid ID to the receptionist to use our facilities.

Multiflex Gym

To: Kevin Diego <ksukel@bvgfitness.com>
From: Bill Pullman <avelez@bvgfitness.com>
Date: August 2
Subject: Re: Numbers

Dear Kevin:

As always, thank you for sending the report. I was thrilled to see that the numbers of Gold- and Platinum-level members have each increased by 18 percent since the start of the summer promotion.

The large number of students from Dover College who have signed up for Gold-level memberships has led us to consider that we might want to offer the student discount again when classes begin in the fall. I have also heard that the fitness facility of the college is going to be remodeled over the next school year, which means students will be looking for alternative options. Even better, our main competitor is 10 kilometers farther from the school. So, we are looking into collaborating with the college to provide shuttle buses to help students get to and from the gym. This would hopefully encourage more students to choose Multiflex Gym.

I will keep you posted.

Bill Pullman, Sales Manager
Multiflex Gym Corporate Office

186 What is the purpose of the memo?

(A) To announce the hiring of new instructors
(B) To remind gym members of closing days
(C) To thank employees for their service
(D) To ask employees to give feedback

187 In the memo, the word "normal" in paragraph 2, line 4, is closest in meaning to

(A) standard
(B) average
(C) natural
(D) unusual

188 What is implied about the driving range?

(A) It will be converted into yoga rooms.
(B) It has popular features.
(C) It is located in a separate building.
(D) It will be temporarily unavailable during the summer.

189 What is indicated about Multiflex Gym?

(A) It offers free snacks on Tuesdays and Wednesdays.
(B) Every family member can get a discount.
(C) Platinum-level members can get T-shirts when they join.
(D) Many students were able to bring friends during the summer.

190 What will probably happen at Dover College?

(A) The sports competition will begin in the summer.
(B) Fitness specialists will be hired.
(C) The fitness facility will be renovated.
(D) Fitness classes will be provided to the community.

GO ON TO THE NEXT PAGE

Questions 191-195 refer to the following advertisement and e-mails.

Come and Visit Carolina Apartments Open House

Carolina Apartments are having an open house this Friday and Saturday, March 1 and 2. After two years of construction, Carolina Apartments are almost complete. So people will be able to move in at the beginning of May. There are still more than 100 units available for purchase or rent. These include apartments with two, three, and four bedrooms. There are both furnished and unfurnished apartments available. All furnished apartments are only available to rent, though. The facilities at Carolina Apartments are top notch, and the complex is located near outstanding schools and the main shopping district in London. Anyone is welcome to attend the open house. Tours of the available apartments will be given, and visitors will be shown around the entire building as well. Call 023-555-4321 for more information and to get directions to the open house.

To	inquiries@krausrealestate.com
From	teresawalters@gmail.net
Subject	Carolina Apartments
Date	March 6

To whom it may concern:

I attended the open house at the Carolina Apartments last Saturday. My sons and I were impressed with what we saw, and we have agreed that we would like to live there. We are going to move to London in June, and we intend to live in the city for the next three years. After that, I will be relocated to my company's headquarters in Manchester. That's why I am not interested in buying an apartment but would instead prefer to rent one. I would like to have a three-bedroom apartment so that each of my sons can have his own room.

I'm currently in Edinburgh, but I can arrange to fly to London whenever you need me to sign a contract. So please inform me of the availability of the apartments.

P.S. I have learned that the rent on a three-bedroom unit is £1,200 a month. Is it still in place?

Sincerely,

Teresa Walters

E-Mail Message

To: teresawalters@gmail.net
From: lindakraus@krausrealestate.com
Date: March 7
Subject: Re: Carolina Apartments

Dear Ms. Walters:

Thank you for inquiring about Carolina Apartments. Like you, many people are very pleased with how the apartments look, so it's one of the most popular properties in the region. Due to that fact, there are no longer any three-bedroom units available. The last three-bedroom apartment was just sold this morning. As a result, we have only a few four-bedroom apartments still available to rent. Of course, the rent for these apartments is a bit higher. It costs £600 more a month to rent a four-bedroom unit than it does to rent a three-bedroom unit. If you are still interested, please let me know immediately, and once I receive a nonrefundable payment of £100, I can reserve one for you until you are able to fly here to sign a contract. If you are no longer interested in Carolina Apartments, I can introduce you to several other properties in the same neighborhood that I'm sure you would approve of.

Regards,

Linda Kraus
Kraus Real Estate Agency

191 According to the advertisement, what will happen at the event?
(A) Visitors will be given tours.
(B) A film will be shown to the public.
(C) Contracts will be signed.
(D) Negotiations will be conducted.

192 In the first e-mail, the word "in place" in P.S., is closest in meaning to
(A) appropriate
(B) invalid
(C) efficient
(D) good

193 What is NOT mentioned about Carolina Apartments?
(A) It is conveniently located near a school.
(B) It is currently being constructed.
(C) It is a twenty-story building.
(D) Its rent for a four-bedroom apartment is £1,800.

194 What does Ms. Kraus suggest to Ms. Walters?
(A) Paying a fee to guarantee that she gets an apartment
(B) Flying to London this coming weekend
(C) Considering buying an apartment instead of renting one
(D) Getting a smaller apartment for a lower price

195 What is implied about Ms. Walters?
(A) She visited to the Open House on March 2nd.
(B) She has already sent her rental fee to Ms. Kraus.
(C) She is moving into a three-bedroom apartment next month.
(D) She is relocating to Manchester in two years.

GO ON TO THE NEXT PAGE

Questions 196-200 refer to the following flyer, Web page, and letter.

PLEASE SUPPORT THE STEWART DANCE COMPANY.

The Stewart Dance Company has been at the forefront of Australian Dance for 40 years. We offer great variety in repertoire and present more than 100 performances annually. To enable us to keep up the good work, your help is needed. Your financial support will allow us to maintain low ticket prices and keep dance performances accessible to everyone.

When you give to the Stewart Dance Company, we give back to you. The more you give, the more we return. For a complete list of our membership program, visit our Web site, www.stewartdancecompany.com. You can also view our performance schedule for this year.

www.stewartdancecompany.com

Our history | Schedule | **Membership Program** | Contact

Silver $49
Benefits: Receive tickets to our weekend matinee performances once a month, and a one-year subscription to the dance magazine *Movement* (published four times a year).

Gold $99
Benefits: Receive tickets to our weekend matinee performances once a month, a 20% discount on all weekday evening performances and a one-year subscription to the dance magazine *Movement*.

Platinum $199
Benefits: Receive Gold-level benefits, specially reserved seating, tickets to opening night performances, and the opportunity to dine with renowned choreographer Tom Roman, who directed the performance for our award-winning modern dance, *Dubliners*, at the annual Stewart Dance Company banquet.

You can send your donation to Elena Gibson, fund-raising manager, Stewart Dance Company, 199 Chestnut Street, Sydney.

199 Chestnut Street, Sydney

Dear Ms. Gibson:

As always, it is pleasure that I have the opportunity to support the Stewart Dance Company this year. I have enclosed a donation in the same amount of $199 as last year.

My colleagues, Karen Myers and Justin Copperfield, who are currently working in our travel agency, showed interest in supporting the Stewart Dance Company. They will contact you in the near future and you will be receiving donations of $99 from both of them.

I will definitely attend the Stewart Dance Company's banquet this year since I had a great time in joining last year's event. I look forward to another season of fine performances.

Yours sincerely,

Amy Hollister
Hollister Travel
187 Howell St. Birmingham, Sydney

196 What is the main purpose of the flyer?

(A) To encourage people to go to dance performances
(B) To ask the public for donations
(C) To announce a release of a new dance magazine
(D) To invite people to an awards ceremony

197 In the flyer, the word "variety" in paragraph 1, line 2, is closest in meaning to

(A) diversity
(B) difference
(C) entertainment
(D) change

198 What is implied about the Stewart Dance Company?

(A) It runs a dance performance twice every day.
(B) It recently hired a choreographer, Tom Roman.
(C) It hosts a banquet every year.
(D) It will hold a performance to raise funds.

199 What benefits will Ms. Hollister receive that Ms. Myers will not?

(A) Discounted admission prices
(B) Free tickets to opening-night performances
(C) A subscription to a magazine
(D) Tickets to weekend matinee performances

200 What is NOT true about Ms. Hollister?

(A) She is working with Ms. Myers.
(B) She has attended the Stewart Dance Company's banquet before.
(C) She donates more money than Mr. Copperfield.
(D) She will receive the magazine *Movement* every month.

Stop! This is the end of the test. If you finish before time is called, you may go back to Parts 5, 6, and 7 and check your work.

TOEIC® 점수 환산표

정답수	Listening Comprehension	정답수	Reading Comprehension
96-100	480-495	96-100	460-495
91-95	435-490	91-95	410-475
86-90	395-450	86-90	380-430
81-85	355-415	81-85	355-400
76-80	325-375	76-80	325-375
71-75	295-340	71-75	295-345
66-70	265-315	66-70	265-315
61-65	240-285	61-65	235-285
56-60	215-260	56-60	205-255
51-55	190-235	51-55	175-225
46-50	160-210	46-50	150-195
41-45	135-180	41-45	120-170
36-40	110-155	36-40	100-140
31-35	85-130	31-35	75-120
26-30	70-105	26-30	55-100
21-25	50-90	21-25	40-80
16-20	35-75	16-20	30-65
11-15	20-55	11-15	20-50
6-10	15-40	6-10	15-35
1-5	5-20	1-5	5-20
0	5	0	5

ANSWER SHEET

Actual **Test 1**

수험번호						

응시일자 : 년 월 일

성명	한글	
	한자	
	영자	

좌석번호
Ⓐ Ⓑ Ⓒ Ⓓ Ⓔ ① ② ③ ④ ⑤ ⑥ ⑦

LISTENING (Part I~IV)

NO.	ANSWER				NO.	ANSWER				NO.	ANSWER				NO.	ANSWER				NO.	ANSWER			
	A	B	C	D		A	B	C	D		A	B	C	D		A	B	C	D		A	B	C	D
1	Ⓐ	Ⓑ	Ⓒ	Ⓓ	21	Ⓐ	Ⓑ	Ⓒ		41	Ⓐ	Ⓑ	Ⓒ	Ⓓ	61	Ⓐ	Ⓑ	Ⓒ	Ⓓ	81	Ⓐ	Ⓑ	Ⓒ	Ⓓ
2	Ⓐ	Ⓑ	Ⓒ	Ⓓ	22	Ⓐ	Ⓑ	Ⓒ		42	Ⓐ	Ⓑ	Ⓒ	Ⓓ	62	Ⓐ	Ⓑ	Ⓒ	Ⓓ	82	Ⓐ	Ⓑ	Ⓒ	Ⓓ
3	Ⓐ	Ⓑ	Ⓒ	Ⓓ	23	Ⓐ	Ⓑ	Ⓒ		43	Ⓐ	Ⓑ	Ⓒ	Ⓓ	63	Ⓐ	Ⓑ	Ⓒ	Ⓓ	83	Ⓐ	Ⓑ	Ⓒ	Ⓓ
4	Ⓐ	Ⓑ	Ⓒ	Ⓓ	24	Ⓐ	Ⓑ	Ⓒ		44	Ⓐ	Ⓑ	Ⓒ	Ⓓ	64	Ⓐ	Ⓑ	Ⓒ	Ⓓ	84	Ⓐ	Ⓑ	Ⓒ	Ⓓ
5	Ⓐ	Ⓑ	Ⓒ	Ⓓ	25	Ⓐ	Ⓑ	Ⓒ		45	Ⓐ	Ⓑ	Ⓒ	Ⓓ	65	Ⓐ	Ⓑ	Ⓒ	Ⓓ	85	Ⓐ	Ⓑ	Ⓒ	Ⓓ
6	Ⓐ	Ⓑ	Ⓒ	Ⓓ	26	Ⓐ	Ⓑ	Ⓒ		46	Ⓐ	Ⓑ	Ⓒ	Ⓓ	66	Ⓐ	Ⓑ	Ⓒ	Ⓓ	86	Ⓐ	Ⓑ	Ⓒ	Ⓓ
7	Ⓐ	Ⓑ	Ⓒ		27	Ⓐ	Ⓑ	Ⓒ		47	Ⓐ	Ⓑ	Ⓒ	Ⓓ	67	Ⓐ	Ⓑ	Ⓒ	Ⓓ	87	Ⓐ	Ⓑ	Ⓒ	Ⓓ
8	Ⓐ	Ⓑ	Ⓒ		28	Ⓐ	Ⓑ	Ⓒ		48	Ⓐ	Ⓑ	Ⓒ	Ⓓ	68	Ⓐ	Ⓑ	Ⓒ	Ⓓ	88	Ⓐ	Ⓑ	Ⓒ	Ⓓ
9	Ⓐ	Ⓑ	Ⓒ		29	Ⓐ	Ⓑ	Ⓒ		49	Ⓐ	Ⓑ	Ⓒ	Ⓓ	69	Ⓐ	Ⓑ	Ⓒ	Ⓓ	89	Ⓐ	Ⓑ	Ⓒ	Ⓓ
10	Ⓐ	Ⓑ	Ⓒ		30	Ⓐ	Ⓑ	Ⓒ		50	Ⓐ	Ⓑ	Ⓒ	Ⓓ	70	Ⓐ	Ⓑ	Ⓒ	Ⓓ	90	Ⓐ	Ⓑ	Ⓒ	Ⓓ
11	Ⓐ	Ⓑ	Ⓒ		31	Ⓐ	Ⓑ	Ⓒ		51	Ⓐ	Ⓑ	Ⓒ	Ⓓ	71	Ⓐ	Ⓑ	Ⓒ	Ⓓ	91	Ⓐ	Ⓑ	Ⓒ	Ⓓ
12	Ⓐ	Ⓑ	Ⓒ		32	Ⓐ	Ⓑ	Ⓒ	Ⓓ	52	Ⓐ	Ⓑ	Ⓒ	Ⓓ	72	Ⓐ	Ⓑ	Ⓒ	Ⓓ	92	Ⓐ	Ⓑ	Ⓒ	Ⓓ
13	Ⓐ	Ⓑ	Ⓒ		33	Ⓐ	Ⓑ	Ⓒ	Ⓓ	53	Ⓐ	Ⓑ	Ⓒ	Ⓓ	73	Ⓐ	Ⓑ	Ⓒ	Ⓓ	93	Ⓐ	Ⓑ	Ⓒ	Ⓓ
14	Ⓐ	Ⓑ	Ⓒ		34	Ⓐ	Ⓑ	Ⓒ	Ⓓ	54	Ⓐ	Ⓑ	Ⓒ	Ⓓ	74	Ⓐ	Ⓑ	Ⓒ	Ⓓ	94	Ⓐ	Ⓑ	Ⓒ	Ⓓ
15	Ⓐ	Ⓑ	Ⓒ		35	Ⓐ	Ⓑ	Ⓒ	Ⓓ	55	Ⓐ	Ⓑ	Ⓒ	Ⓓ	75	Ⓐ	Ⓑ	Ⓒ	Ⓓ	95	Ⓐ	Ⓑ	Ⓒ	Ⓓ
16	Ⓐ	Ⓑ	Ⓒ		36	Ⓐ	Ⓑ	Ⓒ	Ⓓ	56	Ⓐ	Ⓑ	Ⓒ	Ⓓ	76	Ⓐ	Ⓑ	Ⓒ	Ⓓ	96	Ⓐ	Ⓑ	Ⓒ	Ⓓ
17	Ⓐ	Ⓑ	Ⓒ		37	Ⓐ	Ⓑ	Ⓒ	Ⓓ	57	Ⓐ	Ⓑ	Ⓒ	Ⓓ	77	Ⓐ	Ⓑ	Ⓒ	Ⓓ	97	Ⓐ	Ⓑ	Ⓒ	Ⓓ
18	Ⓐ	Ⓑ	Ⓒ		38	Ⓐ	Ⓑ	Ⓒ	Ⓓ	58	Ⓐ	Ⓑ	Ⓒ	Ⓓ	78	Ⓐ	Ⓑ	Ⓒ	Ⓓ	98	Ⓐ	Ⓑ	Ⓒ	Ⓓ
19	Ⓐ	Ⓑ	Ⓒ		39	Ⓐ	Ⓑ	Ⓒ	Ⓓ	59	Ⓐ	Ⓑ	Ⓒ	Ⓓ	79	Ⓐ	Ⓑ	Ⓒ	Ⓓ	99	Ⓐ	Ⓑ	Ⓒ	Ⓓ
20	Ⓐ	Ⓑ	Ⓒ		40	Ⓐ	Ⓑ	Ⓒ	Ⓓ	60	Ⓐ	Ⓑ	Ⓒ	Ⓓ	80	Ⓐ	Ⓑ	Ⓒ	Ⓓ	100	Ⓐ	Ⓑ	Ⓒ	Ⓓ

READING (Part V~VII)

NO.	ANSWER				NO.	ANSWER				NO.	ANSWER				NO.	ANSWER				NO.	ANSWER			
	A	B	C	D		A	B	C	D		A	B	C	D		A	B	C	D		A	B	C	D
101	Ⓐ	Ⓑ	Ⓒ	Ⓓ	121	Ⓐ	Ⓑ	Ⓒ	Ⓓ	141	Ⓐ	Ⓑ	Ⓒ	Ⓓ	161	Ⓐ	Ⓑ	Ⓒ	Ⓓ	181	Ⓐ	Ⓑ	Ⓒ	Ⓓ
102	Ⓐ	Ⓑ	Ⓒ	Ⓓ	122	Ⓐ	Ⓑ	Ⓒ	Ⓓ	142	Ⓐ	Ⓑ	Ⓒ	Ⓓ	162	Ⓐ	Ⓑ	Ⓒ	Ⓓ	182	Ⓐ	Ⓑ	Ⓒ	Ⓓ
103	Ⓐ	Ⓑ	Ⓒ	Ⓓ	123	Ⓐ	Ⓑ	Ⓒ	Ⓓ	143	Ⓐ	Ⓑ	Ⓒ	Ⓓ	163	Ⓐ	Ⓑ	Ⓒ	Ⓓ	183	Ⓐ	Ⓑ	Ⓒ	Ⓓ
104	Ⓐ	Ⓑ	Ⓒ	Ⓓ	124	Ⓐ	Ⓑ	Ⓒ	Ⓓ	144	Ⓐ	Ⓑ	Ⓒ	Ⓓ	164	Ⓐ	Ⓑ	Ⓒ	Ⓓ	184	Ⓐ	Ⓑ	Ⓒ	Ⓓ
105	Ⓐ	Ⓑ	Ⓒ	Ⓓ	125	Ⓐ	Ⓑ	Ⓒ	Ⓓ	145	Ⓐ	Ⓑ	Ⓒ	Ⓓ	165	Ⓐ	Ⓑ	Ⓒ	Ⓓ	185	Ⓐ	Ⓑ	Ⓒ	Ⓓ
106	Ⓐ	Ⓑ	Ⓒ	Ⓓ	126	Ⓐ	Ⓑ	Ⓒ	Ⓓ	146	Ⓐ	Ⓑ	Ⓒ	Ⓓ	166	Ⓐ	Ⓑ	Ⓒ	Ⓓ	186	Ⓐ	Ⓑ	Ⓒ	Ⓓ
107	Ⓐ	Ⓑ	Ⓒ	Ⓓ	127	Ⓐ	Ⓑ	Ⓒ	Ⓓ	147	Ⓐ	Ⓑ	Ⓒ	Ⓓ	167	Ⓐ	Ⓑ	Ⓒ	Ⓓ	187	Ⓐ	Ⓑ	Ⓒ	Ⓓ
108	Ⓐ	Ⓑ	Ⓒ	Ⓓ	128	Ⓐ	Ⓑ	Ⓒ	Ⓓ	148	Ⓐ	Ⓑ	Ⓒ	Ⓓ	168	Ⓐ	Ⓑ	Ⓒ	Ⓓ	188	Ⓐ	Ⓑ	Ⓒ	Ⓓ
109	Ⓐ	Ⓑ	Ⓒ	Ⓓ	129	Ⓐ	Ⓑ	Ⓒ	Ⓓ	149	Ⓐ	Ⓑ	Ⓒ	Ⓓ	169	Ⓐ	Ⓑ	Ⓒ	Ⓓ	189	Ⓐ	Ⓑ	Ⓒ	Ⓓ
110	Ⓐ	Ⓑ	Ⓒ	Ⓓ	130	Ⓐ	Ⓑ	Ⓒ	Ⓓ	150	Ⓐ	Ⓑ	Ⓒ	Ⓓ	170	Ⓐ	Ⓑ	Ⓒ	Ⓓ	190	Ⓐ	Ⓑ	Ⓒ	Ⓓ
111	Ⓐ	Ⓑ	Ⓒ	Ⓓ	131	Ⓐ	Ⓑ	Ⓒ	Ⓓ	151	Ⓐ	Ⓑ	Ⓒ	Ⓓ	171	Ⓐ	Ⓑ	Ⓒ	Ⓓ	191	Ⓐ	Ⓑ	Ⓒ	Ⓓ
112	Ⓐ	Ⓑ	Ⓒ	Ⓓ	132	Ⓐ	Ⓑ	Ⓒ	Ⓓ	152	Ⓐ	Ⓑ	Ⓒ	Ⓓ	172	Ⓐ	Ⓑ	Ⓒ	Ⓓ	192	Ⓐ	Ⓑ	Ⓒ	Ⓓ
113	Ⓐ	Ⓑ	Ⓒ	Ⓓ	133	Ⓐ	Ⓑ	Ⓒ	Ⓓ	153	Ⓐ	Ⓑ	Ⓒ	Ⓓ	173	Ⓐ	Ⓑ	Ⓒ	Ⓓ	193	Ⓐ	Ⓑ	Ⓒ	Ⓓ
114	Ⓐ	Ⓑ	Ⓒ	Ⓓ	134	Ⓐ	Ⓑ	Ⓒ	Ⓓ	154	Ⓐ	Ⓑ	Ⓒ	Ⓓ	174	Ⓐ	Ⓑ	Ⓒ	Ⓓ	194	Ⓐ	Ⓑ	Ⓒ	Ⓓ
115	Ⓐ	Ⓑ	Ⓒ	Ⓓ	135	Ⓐ	Ⓑ	Ⓒ	Ⓓ	155	Ⓐ	Ⓑ	Ⓒ	Ⓓ	175	Ⓐ	Ⓑ	Ⓒ	Ⓓ	195	Ⓐ	Ⓑ	Ⓒ	Ⓓ
116	Ⓐ	Ⓑ	Ⓒ	Ⓓ	136	Ⓐ	Ⓑ	Ⓒ	Ⓓ	156	Ⓐ	Ⓑ	Ⓒ	Ⓓ	176	Ⓐ	Ⓑ	Ⓒ	Ⓓ	196	Ⓐ	Ⓑ	Ⓒ	Ⓓ
117	Ⓐ	Ⓑ	Ⓒ	Ⓓ	137	Ⓐ	Ⓑ	Ⓒ	Ⓓ	157	Ⓐ	Ⓑ	Ⓒ	Ⓓ	177	Ⓐ	Ⓑ	Ⓒ	Ⓓ	197	Ⓐ	Ⓑ	Ⓒ	Ⓓ
118	Ⓐ	Ⓑ	Ⓒ	Ⓓ	138	Ⓐ	Ⓑ	Ⓒ	Ⓓ	158	Ⓐ	Ⓑ	Ⓒ	Ⓓ	178	Ⓐ	Ⓑ	Ⓒ	Ⓓ	198	Ⓐ	Ⓑ	Ⓒ	Ⓓ
119	Ⓐ	Ⓑ	Ⓒ	Ⓓ	139	Ⓐ	Ⓑ	Ⓒ	Ⓓ	159	Ⓐ	Ⓑ	Ⓒ	Ⓓ	179	Ⓐ	Ⓑ	Ⓒ	Ⓓ	199	Ⓐ	Ⓑ	Ⓒ	Ⓓ
120	Ⓐ	Ⓑ	Ⓒ	Ⓓ	140	Ⓐ	Ⓑ	Ⓒ	Ⓓ	160	Ⓐ	Ⓑ	Ⓒ	Ⓓ	180	Ⓐ	Ⓑ	Ⓒ	Ⓓ	200	Ⓐ	Ⓑ	Ⓒ	Ⓓ

1. 사용 필기구 : 컴퓨터용 연필(연필을 제외한 사인펜, 볼펜 등은 사용 절대 불가)
2. 잘못된 필기구 사용과 〈보기〉의 올바른 표기 이외의 잘못된 표기로 한 경우에는 당 위원회의 OMR기기가 판독한 결과에 따르며 그 결과는 본인 책임입니다. 1개의 정답만 골라 아래의 올바른 표기대로 정확히 표기하여야 합니다.
   〈보기〉 올바른 표기 : ● 잘못된 표기 : ✓ ✗ ◍
3. 답안지는 컴퓨터로 처리되므로 훼손하시면 안 되며, 상단의 타이밍마크(❚❚❚❚)부분을 찢거나, 낙서 등을 하면 본인에게 불이익이 발생할 수 있습니다.
4. 감독관의 확인이 없거나 시험 종료 후에 답안 작성을 계속할 경우 시험 무효 처리됩니다.

*서약 내용을 읽으시고 확인란에 반드시 서명하십시오.

서 약	확 인
본인은 TOEIC 시험 문제의 일부 또는 전부를 유출하거나 어떠한 형태로든 타인에게 누설 공개하지 않을 것이며 인터넷 또는 인쇄물 등을 이용해 유포하거나 참고 자료로 활용하지 않을 것입니다. 또한 TOEIC 시험 부정 행위 처리 규정을 준수할 것을 서약합니다.	

ANSWER SHEET

수험번호						

Actual **Test 2**

성명	한글	
	한자	
	영자	

좌석번호
Ⓐ Ⓑ Ⓒ Ⓓ Ⓔ ① ② ③ ④ ⑤ ⑥ ⑦

응시일자 : 년 월 일

LISTENING (Part I~IV)

NO.	ANSWER A B C D	NO.	ANSWER A B C D	NO.	ANSWER A B C D	NO.	ANSWER A B C D	NO.	ANSWER A B C D
1	Ⓐ Ⓑ Ⓒ Ⓓ	21	Ⓐ Ⓑ Ⓒ	41	Ⓐ Ⓑ Ⓒ Ⓓ	61	Ⓐ Ⓑ Ⓒ Ⓓ	81	Ⓐ Ⓑ Ⓒ Ⓓ
2	Ⓐ Ⓑ Ⓒ Ⓓ	22	Ⓐ Ⓑ Ⓒ	42	Ⓐ Ⓑ Ⓒ Ⓓ	62	Ⓐ Ⓑ Ⓒ Ⓓ	82	Ⓐ Ⓑ Ⓒ Ⓓ
3	Ⓐ Ⓑ Ⓒ Ⓓ	23	Ⓐ Ⓑ Ⓒ	43	Ⓐ Ⓑ Ⓒ Ⓓ	63	Ⓐ Ⓑ Ⓒ Ⓓ	83	Ⓐ Ⓑ Ⓒ Ⓓ
4	Ⓐ Ⓑ Ⓒ Ⓓ	24	Ⓐ Ⓑ Ⓒ	44	Ⓐ Ⓑ Ⓒ Ⓓ	64	Ⓐ Ⓑ Ⓒ Ⓓ	84	Ⓐ Ⓑ Ⓒ Ⓓ
5	Ⓐ Ⓑ Ⓒ Ⓓ	25	Ⓐ Ⓑ Ⓒ	45	Ⓐ Ⓑ Ⓒ Ⓓ	65	Ⓐ Ⓑ Ⓒ Ⓓ	85	Ⓐ Ⓑ Ⓒ Ⓓ
6	Ⓐ Ⓑ Ⓒ Ⓓ	26	Ⓐ Ⓑ Ⓒ	46	Ⓐ Ⓑ Ⓒ Ⓓ	66	Ⓐ Ⓑ Ⓒ Ⓓ	86	Ⓐ Ⓑ Ⓒ Ⓓ
7	Ⓐ Ⓑ Ⓒ	27	Ⓐ Ⓑ Ⓒ	47	Ⓐ Ⓑ Ⓒ Ⓓ	67	Ⓐ Ⓑ Ⓒ Ⓓ	87	Ⓐ Ⓑ Ⓒ Ⓓ
8	Ⓐ Ⓑ Ⓒ	28	Ⓐ Ⓑ Ⓒ	48	Ⓐ Ⓑ Ⓒ Ⓓ	68	Ⓐ Ⓑ Ⓒ Ⓓ	88	Ⓐ Ⓑ Ⓒ Ⓓ
9	Ⓐ Ⓑ Ⓒ	29	Ⓐ Ⓑ Ⓒ	49	Ⓐ Ⓑ Ⓒ Ⓓ	69	Ⓐ Ⓑ Ⓒ Ⓓ	89	Ⓐ Ⓑ Ⓒ Ⓓ
10	Ⓐ Ⓑ Ⓒ	30	Ⓐ Ⓑ Ⓒ	50	Ⓐ Ⓑ Ⓒ Ⓓ	70	Ⓐ Ⓑ Ⓒ Ⓓ	90	Ⓐ Ⓑ Ⓒ Ⓓ
11	Ⓐ Ⓑ Ⓒ	31	Ⓐ Ⓑ Ⓒ	51	Ⓐ Ⓑ Ⓒ Ⓓ	71	Ⓐ Ⓑ Ⓒ Ⓓ	91	Ⓐ Ⓑ Ⓒ Ⓓ
12	Ⓐ Ⓑ Ⓒ	32	Ⓐ Ⓑ Ⓒ Ⓓ	52	Ⓐ Ⓑ Ⓒ Ⓓ	72	Ⓐ Ⓑ Ⓒ Ⓓ	92	Ⓐ Ⓑ Ⓒ Ⓓ
13	Ⓐ Ⓑ Ⓒ	33	Ⓐ Ⓑ Ⓒ Ⓓ	53	Ⓐ Ⓑ Ⓒ Ⓓ	73	Ⓐ Ⓑ Ⓒ Ⓓ	93	Ⓐ Ⓑ Ⓒ Ⓓ
14	Ⓐ Ⓑ Ⓒ	34	Ⓐ Ⓑ Ⓒ Ⓓ	54	Ⓐ Ⓑ Ⓒ Ⓓ	74	Ⓐ Ⓑ Ⓒ Ⓓ	94	Ⓐ Ⓑ Ⓒ Ⓓ
15	Ⓐ Ⓑ Ⓒ	35	Ⓐ Ⓑ Ⓒ Ⓓ	55	Ⓐ Ⓑ Ⓒ Ⓓ	75	Ⓐ Ⓑ Ⓒ Ⓓ	95	Ⓐ Ⓑ Ⓒ Ⓓ
16	Ⓐ Ⓑ Ⓒ	36	Ⓐ Ⓑ Ⓒ Ⓓ	56	Ⓐ Ⓑ Ⓒ Ⓓ	76	Ⓐ Ⓑ Ⓒ Ⓓ	96	Ⓐ Ⓑ Ⓒ Ⓓ
17	Ⓐ Ⓑ Ⓒ	37	Ⓐ Ⓑ Ⓒ Ⓓ	57	Ⓐ Ⓑ Ⓒ Ⓓ	77	Ⓐ Ⓑ Ⓒ Ⓓ	97	Ⓐ Ⓑ Ⓒ Ⓓ
18	Ⓐ Ⓑ Ⓒ	38	Ⓐ Ⓑ Ⓒ Ⓓ	58	Ⓐ Ⓑ Ⓒ Ⓓ	78	Ⓐ Ⓑ Ⓒ Ⓓ	98	Ⓐ Ⓑ Ⓒ Ⓓ
19	Ⓐ Ⓑ Ⓒ	39	Ⓐ Ⓑ Ⓒ Ⓓ	59	Ⓐ Ⓑ Ⓒ Ⓓ	79	Ⓐ Ⓑ Ⓒ Ⓓ	99	Ⓐ Ⓑ Ⓒ Ⓓ
20	Ⓐ Ⓑ Ⓒ	40	Ⓐ Ⓑ Ⓒ Ⓓ	60	Ⓐ Ⓑ Ⓒ Ⓓ	80	Ⓐ Ⓑ Ⓒ Ⓓ	100	Ⓐ Ⓑ Ⓒ Ⓓ

READING (Part V~VII)

NO.	ANSWER A B C D	NO.	ANSWER A B C D	NO.	ANSWER A B C D	NO.	ANSWER A B C D	NO.	ANSWER A B C D
101	Ⓐ Ⓑ Ⓒ Ⓓ	121	Ⓐ Ⓑ Ⓒ Ⓓ	141	Ⓐ Ⓑ Ⓒ Ⓓ	161	Ⓐ Ⓑ Ⓒ Ⓓ	181	Ⓐ Ⓑ Ⓒ Ⓓ
102	Ⓐ Ⓑ Ⓒ Ⓓ	122	Ⓐ Ⓑ Ⓒ Ⓓ	142	Ⓐ Ⓑ Ⓒ Ⓓ	162	Ⓐ Ⓑ Ⓒ Ⓓ	182	Ⓐ Ⓑ Ⓒ Ⓓ
103	Ⓐ Ⓑ Ⓒ Ⓓ	123	Ⓐ Ⓑ Ⓒ Ⓓ	143	Ⓐ Ⓑ Ⓒ Ⓓ	163	Ⓐ Ⓑ Ⓒ Ⓓ	183	Ⓐ Ⓑ Ⓒ Ⓓ
104	Ⓐ Ⓑ Ⓒ Ⓓ	124	Ⓐ Ⓑ Ⓒ Ⓓ	144	Ⓐ Ⓑ Ⓒ Ⓓ	164	Ⓐ Ⓑ Ⓒ Ⓓ	184	Ⓐ Ⓑ Ⓒ Ⓓ
105	Ⓐ Ⓑ Ⓒ Ⓓ	125	Ⓐ Ⓑ Ⓒ Ⓓ	145	Ⓐ Ⓑ Ⓒ Ⓓ	165	Ⓐ Ⓑ Ⓒ Ⓓ	185	Ⓐ Ⓑ Ⓒ Ⓓ
106	Ⓐ Ⓑ Ⓒ Ⓓ	126	Ⓐ Ⓑ Ⓒ Ⓓ	146	Ⓐ Ⓑ Ⓒ Ⓓ	166	Ⓐ Ⓑ Ⓒ Ⓓ	186	Ⓐ Ⓑ Ⓒ Ⓓ
107	Ⓐ Ⓑ Ⓒ Ⓓ	127	Ⓐ Ⓑ Ⓒ Ⓓ	147	Ⓐ Ⓑ Ⓒ Ⓓ	167	Ⓐ Ⓑ Ⓒ Ⓓ	187	Ⓐ Ⓑ Ⓒ Ⓓ
108	Ⓐ Ⓑ Ⓒ Ⓓ	128	Ⓐ Ⓑ Ⓒ Ⓓ	148	Ⓐ Ⓑ Ⓒ Ⓓ	168	Ⓐ Ⓑ Ⓒ Ⓓ	188	Ⓐ Ⓑ Ⓒ Ⓓ
109	Ⓐ Ⓑ Ⓒ Ⓓ	129	Ⓐ Ⓑ Ⓒ Ⓓ	149	Ⓐ Ⓑ Ⓒ Ⓓ	169	Ⓐ Ⓑ Ⓒ Ⓓ	189	Ⓐ Ⓑ Ⓒ Ⓓ
110	Ⓐ Ⓑ Ⓒ Ⓓ	130	Ⓐ Ⓑ Ⓒ Ⓓ	150	Ⓐ Ⓑ Ⓒ Ⓓ	170	Ⓐ Ⓑ Ⓒ Ⓓ	190	Ⓐ Ⓑ Ⓒ Ⓓ
111	Ⓐ Ⓑ Ⓒ Ⓓ	131	Ⓐ Ⓑ Ⓒ Ⓓ	151	Ⓐ Ⓑ Ⓒ Ⓓ	171	Ⓐ Ⓑ Ⓒ Ⓓ	191	Ⓐ Ⓑ Ⓒ Ⓓ
112	Ⓐ Ⓑ Ⓒ Ⓓ	132	Ⓐ Ⓑ Ⓒ Ⓓ	152	Ⓐ Ⓑ Ⓒ Ⓓ	172	Ⓐ Ⓑ Ⓒ Ⓓ	192	Ⓐ Ⓑ Ⓒ Ⓓ
113	Ⓐ Ⓑ Ⓒ Ⓓ	133	Ⓐ Ⓑ Ⓒ Ⓓ	153	Ⓐ Ⓑ Ⓒ Ⓓ	173	Ⓐ Ⓑ Ⓒ Ⓓ	193	Ⓐ Ⓑ Ⓒ Ⓓ
114	Ⓐ Ⓑ Ⓒ Ⓓ	134	Ⓐ Ⓑ Ⓒ Ⓓ	154	Ⓐ Ⓑ Ⓒ Ⓓ	174	Ⓐ Ⓑ Ⓒ Ⓓ	194	Ⓐ Ⓑ Ⓒ Ⓓ
115	Ⓐ Ⓑ Ⓒ Ⓓ	135	Ⓐ Ⓑ Ⓒ Ⓓ	155	Ⓐ Ⓑ Ⓒ Ⓓ	175	Ⓐ Ⓑ Ⓒ Ⓓ	195	Ⓐ Ⓑ Ⓒ Ⓓ
116	Ⓐ Ⓑ Ⓒ Ⓓ	136	Ⓐ Ⓑ Ⓒ Ⓓ	156	Ⓐ Ⓑ Ⓒ Ⓓ	176	Ⓐ Ⓑ Ⓒ Ⓓ	196	Ⓐ Ⓑ Ⓒ Ⓓ
117	Ⓐ Ⓑ Ⓒ Ⓓ	137	Ⓐ Ⓑ Ⓒ Ⓓ	157	Ⓐ Ⓑ Ⓒ Ⓓ	177	Ⓐ Ⓑ Ⓒ Ⓓ	197	Ⓐ Ⓑ Ⓒ Ⓓ
118	Ⓐ Ⓑ Ⓒ Ⓓ	138	Ⓐ Ⓑ Ⓒ Ⓓ	158	Ⓐ Ⓑ Ⓒ Ⓓ	178	Ⓐ Ⓑ Ⓒ Ⓓ	198	Ⓐ Ⓑ Ⓒ Ⓓ
119	Ⓐ Ⓑ Ⓒ Ⓓ	139	Ⓐ Ⓑ Ⓒ Ⓓ	159	Ⓐ Ⓑ Ⓒ Ⓓ	179	Ⓐ Ⓑ Ⓒ Ⓓ	199	Ⓐ Ⓑ Ⓒ Ⓓ
120	Ⓐ Ⓑ Ⓒ Ⓓ	140	Ⓐ Ⓑ Ⓒ Ⓓ	160	Ⓐ Ⓑ Ⓒ Ⓓ	180	Ⓐ Ⓑ Ⓒ Ⓓ	200	Ⓐ Ⓑ Ⓒ Ⓓ

1. 사용 필기구 : 컴퓨터용 연필(연필을 제외한 사인펜, 볼펜 등은 사용 절대 불가)
2. 잘못된 필기구 사용과 〈보기〉의 올바른 표기 이외의 잘못된 표기로 한 경우에는 당 위원회의 OMR기기가 판독한 결과에 따르며 그 결과는 본인 책임입니다. 1개의 정답만 골라 아래의 올바른 표기대로 정확히 표기하여야 합니다.
   〈보기〉 올바른 표기 : ● 잘못된 표기 : ⊘ ✖ ◍
3. 답안지는 컴퓨터로 처리되므로 훼손하시면 안 되며, 상단의 타이밍마크(▮▮▮▮)부분을 찢거나, 낙서 등을 하면 본인에게 불이익이 발생할 수 있습니다.
4. 감독관의 확인이 없거나 시험 종료 후에 답안 작성을 계속할 경우 시험 무효 처리됩니다.

*서약 내용을 읽으시고 확인란에 반드시 서명하십시오.

서 약	확 인
본인은 TOEIC 시험 문제의 일부 또는 전부를 유출하거나 어떠한 형태로든 타인에게 누설 공개하지 않을 것이며 인터넷 또는 인쇄물 등을 이용해 유포하거나 참고 자료로 활용하지 않을 것입니다. 또한 TOEIC 시험 부정 행위 처리 규정을 준수할 것을 서약합니다.	

ANSWER SHEET

Actual **Test 3**

수험번호						

응시일자 :　　　년　　　월　　　일

성명	한글	
	한자	
	영자	

좌석번호
Ⓐ Ⓑ Ⓒ Ⓓ Ⓔ ① ② ③ ④ ⑤ ⑥ ⑦

LISTENING (Part I~IV)

NO.	ANSWER				NO.	ANSWER				NO.	ANSWER				NO.	ANSWER				NO.	ANSWER			
	A	B	C	D		A	B	C	D		A	B	C	D		A	B	C	D		A	B	C	D
1	Ⓐ	Ⓑ	Ⓒ	Ⓓ	21	Ⓐ	Ⓑ	Ⓒ		41	Ⓐ	Ⓑ	Ⓒ	Ⓓ	61	Ⓐ	Ⓑ	Ⓒ	Ⓓ	81	Ⓐ	Ⓑ	Ⓒ	Ⓓ
2	Ⓐ	Ⓑ	Ⓒ	Ⓓ	22	Ⓐ	Ⓑ	Ⓒ		42	Ⓐ	Ⓑ	Ⓒ	Ⓓ	62	Ⓐ	Ⓑ	Ⓒ	Ⓓ	82	Ⓐ	Ⓑ	Ⓒ	Ⓓ
3	Ⓐ	Ⓑ	Ⓒ	Ⓓ	23	Ⓐ	Ⓑ	Ⓒ		43	Ⓐ	Ⓑ	Ⓒ	Ⓓ	63	Ⓐ	Ⓑ	Ⓒ	Ⓓ	83	Ⓐ	Ⓑ	Ⓒ	Ⓓ
4	Ⓐ	Ⓑ	Ⓒ	Ⓓ	24	Ⓐ	Ⓑ	Ⓒ		44	Ⓐ	Ⓑ	Ⓒ	Ⓓ	64	Ⓐ	Ⓑ	Ⓒ	Ⓓ	84	Ⓐ	Ⓑ	Ⓒ	Ⓓ
5	Ⓐ	Ⓑ	Ⓒ	Ⓓ	25	Ⓐ	Ⓑ	Ⓒ		45	Ⓐ	Ⓑ	Ⓒ	Ⓓ	65	Ⓐ	Ⓑ	Ⓒ	Ⓓ	85	Ⓐ	Ⓑ	Ⓒ	Ⓓ
6	Ⓐ	Ⓑ	Ⓒ	Ⓓ	26	Ⓐ	Ⓑ	Ⓒ		46	Ⓐ	Ⓑ	Ⓒ	Ⓓ	66	Ⓐ	Ⓑ	Ⓒ	Ⓓ	86	Ⓐ	Ⓑ	Ⓒ	Ⓓ
7	Ⓐ	Ⓑ	Ⓒ		27	Ⓐ	Ⓑ	Ⓒ		47	Ⓐ	Ⓑ	Ⓒ	Ⓓ	67	Ⓐ	Ⓑ	Ⓒ	Ⓓ	87	Ⓐ	Ⓑ	Ⓒ	Ⓓ
8	Ⓐ	Ⓑ	Ⓒ		28	Ⓐ	Ⓑ	Ⓒ		48	Ⓐ	Ⓑ	Ⓒ	Ⓓ	68	Ⓐ	Ⓑ	Ⓒ	Ⓓ	88	Ⓐ	Ⓑ	Ⓒ	Ⓓ
9	Ⓐ	Ⓑ	Ⓒ		29	Ⓐ	Ⓑ	Ⓒ		49	Ⓐ	Ⓑ	Ⓒ	Ⓓ	69	Ⓐ	Ⓑ	Ⓒ	Ⓓ	89	Ⓐ	Ⓑ	Ⓒ	Ⓓ
10	Ⓐ	Ⓑ	Ⓒ		30	Ⓐ	Ⓑ	Ⓒ		50	Ⓐ	Ⓑ	Ⓒ	Ⓓ	70	Ⓐ	Ⓑ	Ⓒ	Ⓓ	90	Ⓐ	Ⓑ	Ⓒ	Ⓓ
11	Ⓐ	Ⓑ	Ⓒ		31	Ⓐ	Ⓑ	Ⓒ		51	Ⓐ	Ⓑ	Ⓒ	Ⓓ	71	Ⓐ	Ⓑ	Ⓒ	Ⓓ	91	Ⓐ	Ⓑ	Ⓒ	Ⓓ
12	Ⓐ	Ⓑ	Ⓒ		32	Ⓐ	Ⓑ	Ⓒ	Ⓓ	52	Ⓐ	Ⓑ	Ⓒ	Ⓓ	72	Ⓐ	Ⓑ	Ⓒ	Ⓓ	92	Ⓐ	Ⓑ	Ⓒ	Ⓓ
13	Ⓐ	Ⓑ	Ⓒ		33	Ⓐ	Ⓑ	Ⓒ	Ⓓ	53	Ⓐ	Ⓑ	Ⓒ	Ⓓ	73	Ⓐ	Ⓑ	Ⓒ	Ⓓ	93	Ⓐ	Ⓑ	Ⓒ	Ⓓ
14	Ⓐ	Ⓑ	Ⓒ		34	Ⓐ	Ⓑ	Ⓒ	Ⓓ	54	Ⓐ	Ⓑ	Ⓒ	Ⓓ	74	Ⓐ	Ⓑ	Ⓒ	Ⓓ	94	Ⓐ	Ⓑ	Ⓒ	Ⓓ
15	Ⓐ	Ⓑ	Ⓒ		35	Ⓐ	Ⓑ	Ⓒ	Ⓓ	55	Ⓐ	Ⓑ	Ⓒ	Ⓓ	75	Ⓐ	Ⓑ	Ⓒ	Ⓓ	95	Ⓐ	Ⓑ	Ⓒ	Ⓓ
16	Ⓐ	Ⓑ	Ⓒ		36	Ⓐ	Ⓑ	Ⓒ	Ⓓ	56	Ⓐ	Ⓑ	Ⓒ	Ⓓ	76	Ⓐ	Ⓑ	Ⓒ	Ⓓ	96	Ⓐ	Ⓑ	Ⓒ	Ⓓ
17	Ⓐ	Ⓑ	Ⓒ		37	Ⓐ	Ⓑ	Ⓒ	Ⓓ	57	Ⓐ	Ⓑ	Ⓒ	Ⓓ	77	Ⓐ	Ⓑ	Ⓒ	Ⓓ	97	Ⓐ	Ⓑ	Ⓒ	Ⓓ
18	Ⓐ	Ⓑ	Ⓒ		38	Ⓐ	Ⓑ	Ⓒ	Ⓓ	58	Ⓐ	Ⓑ	Ⓒ	Ⓓ	78	Ⓐ	Ⓑ	Ⓒ	Ⓓ	98	Ⓐ	Ⓑ	Ⓒ	Ⓓ
19	Ⓐ	Ⓑ	Ⓒ		39	Ⓐ	Ⓑ	Ⓒ	Ⓓ	59	Ⓐ	Ⓑ	Ⓒ	Ⓓ	79	Ⓐ	Ⓑ	Ⓒ	Ⓓ	99	Ⓐ	Ⓑ	Ⓒ	Ⓓ
20	Ⓐ	Ⓑ	Ⓒ		40	Ⓐ	Ⓑ	Ⓒ	Ⓓ	60	Ⓐ	Ⓑ	Ⓒ	Ⓓ	80	Ⓐ	Ⓑ	Ⓒ	Ⓓ	100	Ⓐ	Ⓑ	Ⓒ	Ⓓ

READING (Part V~VII)

NO.	ANSWER				NO.	ANSWER				NO.	ANSWER				NO.	ANSWER				NO.	ANSWER			
	A	B	C	D		A	B	C	D		A	B	C	D		A	B	C	D		A	B	C	D
101	Ⓐ	Ⓑ	Ⓒ	Ⓓ	121	Ⓐ	Ⓑ	Ⓒ	Ⓓ	141	Ⓐ	Ⓑ	Ⓒ	Ⓓ	161	Ⓐ	Ⓑ	Ⓒ	Ⓓ	181	Ⓐ	Ⓑ	Ⓒ	Ⓓ
102	Ⓐ	Ⓑ	Ⓒ	Ⓓ	122	Ⓐ	Ⓑ	Ⓒ	Ⓓ	142	Ⓐ	Ⓑ	Ⓒ	Ⓓ	162	Ⓐ	Ⓑ	Ⓒ	Ⓓ	182	Ⓐ	Ⓑ	Ⓒ	Ⓓ
103	Ⓐ	Ⓑ	Ⓒ	Ⓓ	123	Ⓐ	Ⓑ	Ⓒ	Ⓓ	143	Ⓐ	Ⓑ	Ⓒ	Ⓓ	163	Ⓐ	Ⓑ	Ⓒ	Ⓓ	183	Ⓐ	Ⓑ	Ⓒ	Ⓓ
104	Ⓐ	Ⓑ	Ⓒ	Ⓓ	124	Ⓐ	Ⓑ	Ⓒ	Ⓓ	144	Ⓐ	Ⓑ	Ⓒ	Ⓓ	164	Ⓐ	Ⓑ	Ⓒ	Ⓓ	184	Ⓐ	Ⓑ	Ⓒ	Ⓓ
105	Ⓐ	Ⓑ	Ⓒ	Ⓓ	125	Ⓐ	Ⓑ	Ⓒ	Ⓓ	145	Ⓐ	Ⓑ	Ⓒ	Ⓓ	165	Ⓐ	Ⓑ	Ⓒ	Ⓓ	185	Ⓐ	Ⓑ	Ⓒ	Ⓓ
106	Ⓐ	Ⓑ	Ⓒ	Ⓓ	126	Ⓐ	Ⓑ	Ⓒ	Ⓓ	146	Ⓐ	Ⓑ	Ⓒ	Ⓓ	166	Ⓐ	Ⓑ	Ⓒ	Ⓓ	186	Ⓐ	Ⓑ	Ⓒ	Ⓓ
107	Ⓐ	Ⓑ	Ⓒ	Ⓓ	127	Ⓐ	Ⓑ	Ⓒ	Ⓓ	147	Ⓐ	Ⓑ	Ⓒ	Ⓓ	167	Ⓐ	Ⓑ	Ⓒ	Ⓓ	187	Ⓐ	Ⓑ	Ⓒ	Ⓓ
108	Ⓐ	Ⓑ	Ⓒ	Ⓓ	128	Ⓐ	Ⓑ	Ⓒ	Ⓓ	148	Ⓐ	Ⓑ	Ⓒ	Ⓓ	168	Ⓐ	Ⓑ	Ⓒ	Ⓓ	188	Ⓐ	Ⓑ	Ⓒ	Ⓓ
109	Ⓐ	Ⓑ	Ⓒ	Ⓓ	129	Ⓐ	Ⓑ	Ⓒ	Ⓓ	149	Ⓐ	Ⓑ	Ⓒ	Ⓓ	169	Ⓐ	Ⓑ	Ⓒ	Ⓓ	189	Ⓐ	Ⓑ	Ⓒ	Ⓓ
110	Ⓐ	Ⓑ	Ⓒ	Ⓓ	130	Ⓐ	Ⓑ	Ⓒ	Ⓓ	150	Ⓐ	Ⓑ	Ⓒ	Ⓓ	170	Ⓐ	Ⓑ	Ⓒ	Ⓓ	190	Ⓐ	Ⓑ	Ⓒ	Ⓓ
111	Ⓐ	Ⓑ	Ⓒ	Ⓓ	131	Ⓐ	Ⓑ	Ⓒ	Ⓓ	151	Ⓐ	Ⓑ	Ⓒ	Ⓓ	171	Ⓐ	Ⓑ	Ⓒ	Ⓓ	191	Ⓐ	Ⓑ	Ⓒ	Ⓓ
112	Ⓐ	Ⓑ	Ⓒ	Ⓓ	132	Ⓐ	Ⓑ	Ⓒ	Ⓓ	152	Ⓐ	Ⓑ	Ⓒ	Ⓓ	172	Ⓐ	Ⓑ	Ⓒ	Ⓓ	192	Ⓐ	Ⓑ	Ⓒ	Ⓓ
113	Ⓐ	Ⓑ	Ⓒ	Ⓓ	133	Ⓐ	Ⓑ	Ⓒ	Ⓓ	153	Ⓐ	Ⓑ	Ⓒ	Ⓓ	173	Ⓐ	Ⓑ	Ⓒ	Ⓓ	193	Ⓐ	Ⓑ	Ⓒ	Ⓓ
114	Ⓐ	Ⓑ	Ⓒ	Ⓓ	134	Ⓐ	Ⓑ	Ⓒ	Ⓓ	154	Ⓐ	Ⓑ	Ⓒ	Ⓓ	174	Ⓐ	Ⓑ	Ⓒ	Ⓓ	194	Ⓐ	Ⓑ	Ⓒ	Ⓓ
115	Ⓐ	Ⓑ	Ⓒ	Ⓓ	135	Ⓐ	Ⓑ	Ⓒ	Ⓓ	155	Ⓐ	Ⓑ	Ⓒ	Ⓓ	175	Ⓐ	Ⓑ	Ⓒ	Ⓓ	195	Ⓐ	Ⓑ	Ⓒ	Ⓓ
116	Ⓐ	Ⓑ	Ⓒ	Ⓓ	136	Ⓐ	Ⓑ	Ⓒ	Ⓓ	156	Ⓐ	Ⓑ	Ⓒ	Ⓓ	176	Ⓐ	Ⓑ	Ⓒ	Ⓓ	196	Ⓐ	Ⓑ	Ⓒ	Ⓓ
117	Ⓐ	Ⓑ	Ⓒ	Ⓓ	137	Ⓐ	Ⓑ	Ⓒ	Ⓓ	157	Ⓐ	Ⓑ	Ⓒ	Ⓓ	177	Ⓐ	Ⓑ	Ⓒ	Ⓓ	197	Ⓐ	Ⓑ	Ⓒ	Ⓓ
118	Ⓐ	Ⓑ	Ⓒ	Ⓓ	138	Ⓐ	Ⓑ	Ⓒ	Ⓓ	158	Ⓐ	Ⓑ	Ⓒ	Ⓓ	178	Ⓐ	Ⓑ	Ⓒ	Ⓓ	198	Ⓐ	Ⓑ	Ⓒ	Ⓓ
119	Ⓐ	Ⓑ	Ⓒ	Ⓓ	139	Ⓐ	Ⓑ	Ⓒ	Ⓓ	159	Ⓐ	Ⓑ	Ⓒ	Ⓓ	179	Ⓐ	Ⓑ	Ⓒ	Ⓓ	199	Ⓐ	Ⓑ	Ⓒ	Ⓓ
120	Ⓐ	Ⓑ	Ⓒ	Ⓓ	140	Ⓐ	Ⓑ	Ⓒ	Ⓓ	160	Ⓐ	Ⓑ	Ⓒ	Ⓓ	180	Ⓐ	Ⓑ	Ⓒ	Ⓓ	200	Ⓐ	Ⓑ	Ⓒ	Ⓓ

1. 사용 필기구 : 컴퓨터용 연필(연필을 제외한 사인펜, 볼펜 등은 사용 절대 불가)
2. 잘못된 필기구 사용과 〈보기〉의 올바른 표기 이외의 잘못된 표기로 한 경우에는 당 위원회의 OMR기기가 판독한 결과에 따르며 그 결과는 본인 책임입니다. 1개의 정답만 골라 아래의 올바른 표기대로 정확히 표기하여야 합니다.
   〈보기〉 올바른 표기 : ●　　잘못된 표기 : ✓ ✗ ▨
3. 답안지는 컴퓨터로 처리되므로 훼손하시면 안 되며, 상단의 타이밍마크(❙❙❙❙)부분을 찢거나, 낙서 등을 하면 본인에게 불이익이 발생할 수 있습니다.
4. 감독관의 확인이 없거나 시험 종료 후에 답안 작성을 계속할 경우 시험 무효 처리됩니다.

＊서약 내용을 읽으시고 확인란에 반드시 서명하십시오.

서　약	확 인
본인은 TOEIC 시험 문제의 일부 또는 전부를 유출하거나 어떠한 형태로든 타인에게 누설 공개하지 않을 것이며 인터넷 또는 인쇄물 등을 이용해 유포하거나 참고 자료로 활용하지 않을 것입니다. 또한 TOEIC 시험 부정 행위 처리 규정을 준수할 것을 서약합니다.	

ANSWER SHEET

Actual **Test 4**

수험번호						

응시일자 :　　　년　　　월　　　일

성명	한글	
	한자	
	영자	

좌석번호
Ⓐ Ⓑ Ⓒ Ⓓ Ⓔ
① ② ③ ④ ⑤ ⑥ ⑦

LISTENING (Part Ⅰ~Ⅳ)

NO.	ANSWER				NO.	ANSWER				NO.	ANSWER				NO.	ANSWER				NO.	ANSWER			
	A	B	C	D		A	B	C	D		A	B	C	D		A	B	C	D		A	B	C	D
1	Ⓐ	Ⓑ	Ⓒ	Ⓓ	21	Ⓐ	Ⓑ	Ⓒ		41	Ⓐ	Ⓑ	Ⓒ	Ⓓ	61	Ⓐ	Ⓑ	Ⓒ	Ⓓ	81	Ⓐ	Ⓑ	Ⓒ	Ⓓ
2	Ⓐ	Ⓑ	Ⓒ	Ⓓ	22	Ⓐ	Ⓑ	Ⓒ		42	Ⓐ	Ⓑ	Ⓒ	Ⓓ	62	Ⓐ	Ⓑ	Ⓒ	Ⓓ	82	Ⓐ	Ⓑ	Ⓒ	Ⓓ
3	Ⓐ	Ⓑ	Ⓒ	Ⓓ	23	Ⓐ	Ⓑ	Ⓒ		43	Ⓐ	Ⓑ	Ⓒ	Ⓓ	63	Ⓐ	Ⓑ	Ⓒ	Ⓓ	83	Ⓐ	Ⓑ	Ⓒ	Ⓓ
4	Ⓐ	Ⓑ	Ⓒ	Ⓓ	24	Ⓐ	Ⓑ	Ⓒ		44	Ⓐ	Ⓑ	Ⓒ	Ⓓ	64	Ⓐ	Ⓑ	Ⓒ	Ⓓ	84	Ⓐ	Ⓑ	Ⓒ	Ⓓ
5	Ⓐ	Ⓑ	Ⓒ	Ⓓ	25	Ⓐ	Ⓑ	Ⓒ		45	Ⓐ	Ⓑ	Ⓒ	Ⓓ	65	Ⓐ	Ⓑ	Ⓒ	Ⓓ	85	Ⓐ	Ⓑ	Ⓒ	Ⓓ
6	Ⓐ	Ⓑ	Ⓒ	Ⓓ	26	Ⓐ	Ⓑ	Ⓒ		46	Ⓐ	Ⓑ	Ⓒ	Ⓓ	66	Ⓐ	Ⓑ	Ⓒ	Ⓓ	86	Ⓐ	Ⓑ	Ⓒ	Ⓓ
7	Ⓐ	Ⓑ	Ⓒ		27	Ⓐ	Ⓑ	Ⓒ		47	Ⓐ	Ⓑ	Ⓒ	Ⓓ	67	Ⓐ	Ⓑ	Ⓒ	Ⓓ	87	Ⓐ	Ⓑ	Ⓒ	Ⓓ
8	Ⓐ	Ⓑ	Ⓒ		28	Ⓐ	Ⓑ	Ⓒ		48	Ⓐ	Ⓑ	Ⓒ	Ⓓ	68	Ⓐ	Ⓑ	Ⓒ	Ⓓ	88	Ⓐ	Ⓑ	Ⓒ	Ⓓ
9	Ⓐ	Ⓑ	Ⓒ		29	Ⓐ	Ⓑ	Ⓒ		49	Ⓐ	Ⓑ	Ⓒ	Ⓓ	69	Ⓐ	Ⓑ	Ⓒ	Ⓓ	89	Ⓐ	Ⓑ	Ⓒ	Ⓓ
10	Ⓐ	Ⓑ	Ⓒ		30	Ⓐ	Ⓑ	Ⓒ		50	Ⓐ	Ⓑ	Ⓒ	Ⓓ	70	Ⓐ	Ⓑ	Ⓒ	Ⓓ	90	Ⓐ	Ⓑ	Ⓒ	Ⓓ
11	Ⓐ	Ⓑ	Ⓒ		31	Ⓐ	Ⓑ	Ⓒ		51	Ⓐ	Ⓑ	Ⓒ	Ⓓ	71	Ⓐ	Ⓑ	Ⓒ	Ⓓ	91	Ⓐ	Ⓑ	Ⓒ	Ⓓ
12	Ⓐ	Ⓑ	Ⓒ		32	Ⓐ	Ⓑ	Ⓒ	Ⓓ	52	Ⓐ	Ⓑ	Ⓒ	Ⓓ	72	Ⓐ	Ⓑ	Ⓒ	Ⓓ	92	Ⓐ	Ⓑ	Ⓒ	Ⓓ
13	Ⓐ	Ⓑ	Ⓒ		33	Ⓐ	Ⓑ	Ⓒ	Ⓓ	53	Ⓐ	Ⓑ	Ⓒ	Ⓓ	73	Ⓐ	Ⓑ	Ⓒ	Ⓓ	93	Ⓐ	Ⓑ	Ⓒ	Ⓓ
14	Ⓐ	Ⓑ	Ⓒ		34	Ⓐ	Ⓑ	Ⓒ	Ⓓ	54	Ⓐ	Ⓑ	Ⓒ	Ⓓ	74	Ⓐ	Ⓑ	Ⓒ	Ⓓ	94	Ⓐ	Ⓑ	Ⓒ	Ⓓ
15	Ⓐ	Ⓑ	Ⓒ		35	Ⓐ	Ⓑ	Ⓒ	Ⓓ	55	Ⓐ	Ⓑ	Ⓒ	Ⓓ	75	Ⓐ	Ⓑ	Ⓒ	Ⓓ	95	Ⓐ	Ⓑ	Ⓒ	Ⓓ
16	Ⓐ	Ⓑ	Ⓒ		36	Ⓐ	Ⓑ	Ⓒ	Ⓓ	56	Ⓐ	Ⓑ	Ⓒ	Ⓓ	76	Ⓐ	Ⓑ	Ⓒ	Ⓓ	96	Ⓐ	Ⓑ	Ⓒ	Ⓓ
17	Ⓐ	Ⓑ	Ⓒ		37	Ⓐ	Ⓑ	Ⓒ	Ⓓ	57	Ⓐ	Ⓑ	Ⓒ	Ⓓ	77	Ⓐ	Ⓑ	Ⓒ	Ⓓ	97	Ⓐ	Ⓑ	Ⓒ	Ⓓ
18	Ⓐ	Ⓑ	Ⓒ		38	Ⓐ	Ⓑ	Ⓒ	Ⓓ	58	Ⓐ	Ⓑ	Ⓒ	Ⓓ	78	Ⓐ	Ⓑ	Ⓒ	Ⓓ	98	Ⓐ	Ⓑ	Ⓒ	Ⓓ
19	Ⓐ	Ⓑ	Ⓒ		39	Ⓐ	Ⓑ	Ⓒ	Ⓓ	59	Ⓐ	Ⓑ	Ⓒ	Ⓓ	79	Ⓐ	Ⓑ	Ⓒ	Ⓓ	99	Ⓐ	Ⓑ	Ⓒ	Ⓓ
20	Ⓐ	Ⓑ	Ⓒ		40	Ⓐ	Ⓑ	Ⓒ	Ⓓ	60	Ⓐ	Ⓑ	Ⓒ	Ⓓ	80	Ⓐ	Ⓑ	Ⓒ	Ⓓ	100	Ⓐ	Ⓑ	Ⓒ	Ⓓ

READING (Part Ⅴ~Ⅶ)

NO.	ANSWER				NO.	ANSWER				NO.	ANSWER				NO.	ANSWER				NO.	ANSWER			
	A	B	C	D		A	B	C	D		A	B	C	D		A	B	C	D		A	B	C	D
101	Ⓐ	Ⓑ	Ⓒ	Ⓓ	121	Ⓐ	Ⓑ	Ⓒ	Ⓓ	141	Ⓐ	Ⓑ	Ⓒ	Ⓓ	161	Ⓐ	Ⓑ	Ⓒ	Ⓓ	181	Ⓐ	Ⓑ	Ⓒ	Ⓓ
102	Ⓐ	Ⓑ	Ⓒ	Ⓓ	122	Ⓐ	Ⓑ	Ⓒ	Ⓓ	142	Ⓐ	Ⓑ	Ⓒ	Ⓓ	162	Ⓐ	Ⓑ	Ⓒ	Ⓓ	182	Ⓐ	Ⓑ	Ⓒ	Ⓓ
103	Ⓐ	Ⓑ	Ⓒ	Ⓓ	123	Ⓐ	Ⓑ	Ⓒ	Ⓓ	143	Ⓐ	Ⓑ	Ⓒ	Ⓓ	163	Ⓐ	Ⓑ	Ⓒ	Ⓓ	183	Ⓐ	Ⓑ	Ⓒ	Ⓓ
104	Ⓐ	Ⓑ	Ⓒ	Ⓓ	124	Ⓐ	Ⓑ	Ⓒ	Ⓓ	144	Ⓐ	Ⓑ	Ⓒ	Ⓓ	164	Ⓐ	Ⓑ	Ⓒ	Ⓓ	184	Ⓐ	Ⓑ	Ⓒ	Ⓓ
105	Ⓐ	Ⓑ	Ⓒ	Ⓓ	125	Ⓐ	Ⓑ	Ⓒ	Ⓓ	145	Ⓐ	Ⓑ	Ⓒ	Ⓓ	165	Ⓐ	Ⓑ	Ⓒ	Ⓓ	185	Ⓐ	Ⓑ	Ⓒ	Ⓓ
106	Ⓐ	Ⓑ	Ⓒ	Ⓓ	126	Ⓐ	Ⓑ	Ⓒ	Ⓓ	146	Ⓐ	Ⓑ	Ⓒ	Ⓓ	166	Ⓐ	Ⓑ	Ⓒ	Ⓓ	186	Ⓐ	Ⓑ	Ⓒ	Ⓓ
107	Ⓐ	Ⓑ	Ⓒ	Ⓓ	127	Ⓐ	Ⓑ	Ⓒ	Ⓓ	147	Ⓐ	Ⓑ	Ⓒ	Ⓓ	167	Ⓐ	Ⓑ	Ⓒ	Ⓓ	187	Ⓐ	Ⓑ	Ⓒ	Ⓓ
108	Ⓐ	Ⓑ	Ⓒ	Ⓓ	128	Ⓐ	Ⓑ	Ⓒ	Ⓓ	148	Ⓐ	Ⓑ	Ⓒ	Ⓓ	168	Ⓐ	Ⓑ	Ⓒ	Ⓓ	188	Ⓐ	Ⓑ	Ⓒ	Ⓓ
109	Ⓐ	Ⓑ	Ⓒ	Ⓓ	129	Ⓐ	Ⓑ	Ⓒ	Ⓓ	149	Ⓐ	Ⓑ	Ⓒ	Ⓓ	169	Ⓐ	Ⓑ	Ⓒ	Ⓓ	189	Ⓐ	Ⓑ	Ⓒ	Ⓓ
110	Ⓐ	Ⓑ	Ⓒ	Ⓓ	130	Ⓐ	Ⓑ	Ⓒ	Ⓓ	150	Ⓐ	Ⓑ	Ⓒ	Ⓓ	170	Ⓐ	Ⓑ	Ⓒ	Ⓓ	190	Ⓐ	Ⓑ	Ⓒ	Ⓓ
111	Ⓐ	Ⓑ	Ⓒ	Ⓓ	131	Ⓐ	Ⓑ	Ⓒ	Ⓓ	151	Ⓐ	Ⓑ	Ⓒ	Ⓓ	171	Ⓐ	Ⓑ	Ⓒ	Ⓓ	191	Ⓐ	Ⓑ	Ⓒ	Ⓓ
112	Ⓐ	Ⓑ	Ⓒ	Ⓓ	132	Ⓐ	Ⓑ	Ⓒ	Ⓓ	152	Ⓐ	Ⓑ	Ⓒ	Ⓓ	172	Ⓐ	Ⓑ	Ⓒ	Ⓓ	192	Ⓐ	Ⓑ	Ⓒ	Ⓓ
113	Ⓐ	Ⓑ	Ⓒ	Ⓓ	133	Ⓐ	Ⓑ	Ⓒ	Ⓓ	153	Ⓐ	Ⓑ	Ⓒ	Ⓓ	173	Ⓐ	Ⓑ	Ⓒ	Ⓓ	193	Ⓐ	Ⓑ	Ⓒ	Ⓓ
114	Ⓐ	Ⓑ	Ⓒ	Ⓓ	134	Ⓐ	Ⓑ	Ⓒ	Ⓓ	154	Ⓐ	Ⓑ	Ⓒ	Ⓓ	174	Ⓐ	Ⓑ	Ⓒ	Ⓓ	194	Ⓐ	Ⓑ	Ⓒ	Ⓓ
115	Ⓐ	Ⓑ	Ⓒ	Ⓓ	135	Ⓐ	Ⓑ	Ⓒ	Ⓓ	155	Ⓐ	Ⓑ	Ⓒ	Ⓓ	175	Ⓐ	Ⓑ	Ⓒ	Ⓓ	195	Ⓐ	Ⓑ	Ⓒ	Ⓓ
116	Ⓐ	Ⓑ	Ⓒ	Ⓓ	136	Ⓐ	Ⓑ	Ⓒ	Ⓓ	156	Ⓐ	Ⓑ	Ⓒ	Ⓓ	176	Ⓐ	Ⓑ	Ⓒ	Ⓓ	196	Ⓐ	Ⓑ	Ⓒ	Ⓓ
117	Ⓐ	Ⓑ	Ⓒ	Ⓓ	137	Ⓐ	Ⓑ	Ⓒ	Ⓓ	157	Ⓐ	Ⓑ	Ⓒ	Ⓓ	177	Ⓐ	Ⓑ	Ⓒ	Ⓓ	197	Ⓐ	Ⓑ	Ⓒ	Ⓓ
118	Ⓐ	Ⓑ	Ⓒ	Ⓓ	138	Ⓐ	Ⓑ	Ⓒ	Ⓓ	158	Ⓐ	Ⓑ	Ⓒ	Ⓓ	178	Ⓐ	Ⓑ	Ⓒ	Ⓓ	198	Ⓐ	Ⓑ	Ⓒ	Ⓓ
119	Ⓐ	Ⓑ	Ⓒ	Ⓓ	139	Ⓐ	Ⓑ	Ⓒ	Ⓓ	159	Ⓐ	Ⓑ	Ⓒ	Ⓓ	179	Ⓐ	Ⓑ	Ⓒ	Ⓓ	199	Ⓐ	Ⓑ	Ⓒ	Ⓓ
120	Ⓐ	Ⓑ	Ⓒ	Ⓓ	140	Ⓐ	Ⓑ	Ⓒ	Ⓓ	160	Ⓐ	Ⓑ	Ⓒ	Ⓓ	180	Ⓐ	Ⓑ	Ⓒ	Ⓓ	200	Ⓐ	Ⓑ	Ⓒ	Ⓓ

1. 사용 필기구 : 컴퓨터용 연필(연필을 제외한 사인펜, 볼펜 등은 사용 절대 불가)
2. 잘못된 필기구 사용과 〈보기〉의 올바른 표기 이외의 잘못된 표기로 한 경우에는 당 위원회의 OMR기기가 판독한 결과에 따르며 그 결과는 본인 책임입니다. 1개의 정답만 골라 아래의 올바른 표기대로 정확히 표기하여야 합니다.
   〈보기〉 올바른 표기 : ●　　잘못된 표기 : ✓ ✗ ◍
3. 답안지는 컴퓨터로 처리되므로 훼손하시면 안 되며, 상단의 타이밍마크(▮▮▮▮)부분을 찢거나, 낙서 등을 하면 본인에게 불이익이 발생할 수 있습니다.
4. 감독관의 확인이 없거나 시험 종료 후에 답안 작성을 계속할 경우 시험 무효 처리됩니다.

*서약 내용을 읽으시고 확인란에 반드시 서명하십시오.

서　약	확 인
본인은 TOEIC 시험 문제의 일부 또는 전부를 유출하거나 어떠한 형태로든 타인에게 누설 공개하지 않을 것이며 인터넷 또는 인쇄물 등을 이용해 유포하거나 참고 자료로 활용하지 않을 것입니다. 또한 TOEIC 시험 부정 행위 처리 규정을 준수할 것을 서약합니다.	

ANSWER SHEET

수험번호						

Actual **Test 5**

성명	한글	
	한자	
	영자	

좌석번호
Ⓐ Ⓑ Ⓒ Ⓓ Ⓔ ① ② ③ ④ ⑤ ⑥ ⑦

응시일자 : 년 월 일

LISTENING (Part I~IV)

NO.	ANSWER				NO.	ANSWER				NO.	ANSWER				NO.	ANSWER				NO.	ANSWER			
	A	B	C	D		A	B	C	D		A	B	C	D		A	B	C	D		A	B	C	D
1	Ⓐ	Ⓑ	Ⓒ	Ⓓ	21	Ⓐ	Ⓑ	Ⓒ		41	Ⓐ	Ⓑ	Ⓒ	Ⓓ	61	Ⓐ	Ⓑ	Ⓒ	Ⓓ	81	Ⓐ	Ⓑ	Ⓒ	Ⓓ
2	Ⓐ	Ⓑ	Ⓒ	Ⓓ	22	Ⓐ	Ⓑ	Ⓒ		42	Ⓐ	Ⓑ	Ⓒ	Ⓓ	62	Ⓐ	Ⓑ	Ⓒ	Ⓓ	82	Ⓐ	Ⓑ	Ⓒ	Ⓓ
3	Ⓐ	Ⓑ	Ⓒ	Ⓓ	23	Ⓐ	Ⓑ	Ⓒ		43	Ⓐ	Ⓑ	Ⓒ	Ⓓ	63	Ⓐ	Ⓑ	Ⓒ	Ⓓ	83	Ⓐ	Ⓑ	Ⓒ	Ⓓ
4	Ⓐ	Ⓑ	Ⓒ	Ⓓ	24	Ⓐ	Ⓑ	Ⓒ		44	Ⓐ	Ⓑ	Ⓒ	Ⓓ	64	Ⓐ	Ⓑ	Ⓒ	Ⓓ	84	Ⓐ	Ⓑ	Ⓒ	Ⓓ
5	Ⓐ	Ⓑ	Ⓒ	Ⓓ	25	Ⓐ	Ⓑ	Ⓒ		45	Ⓐ	Ⓑ	Ⓒ	Ⓓ	65	Ⓐ	Ⓑ	Ⓒ	Ⓓ	85	Ⓐ	Ⓑ	Ⓒ	Ⓓ
6	Ⓐ	Ⓑ	Ⓒ	Ⓓ	26	Ⓐ	Ⓑ	Ⓒ		46	Ⓐ	Ⓑ	Ⓒ	Ⓓ	66	Ⓐ	Ⓑ	Ⓒ	Ⓓ	86	Ⓐ	Ⓑ	Ⓒ	Ⓓ
7	Ⓐ	Ⓑ	Ⓒ		27	Ⓐ	Ⓑ	Ⓒ		47	Ⓐ	Ⓑ	Ⓒ	Ⓓ	67	Ⓐ	Ⓑ	Ⓒ	Ⓓ	87	Ⓐ	Ⓑ	Ⓒ	Ⓓ
8	Ⓐ	Ⓑ	Ⓒ		28	Ⓐ	Ⓑ	Ⓒ		48	Ⓐ	Ⓑ	Ⓒ	Ⓓ	68	Ⓐ	Ⓑ	Ⓒ	Ⓓ	88	Ⓐ	Ⓑ	Ⓒ	Ⓓ
9	Ⓐ	Ⓑ	Ⓒ		29	Ⓐ	Ⓑ	Ⓒ		49	Ⓐ	Ⓑ	Ⓒ	Ⓓ	69	Ⓐ	Ⓑ	Ⓒ	Ⓓ	89	Ⓐ	Ⓑ	Ⓒ	Ⓓ
10	Ⓐ	Ⓑ	Ⓒ		30	Ⓐ	Ⓑ	Ⓒ		50	Ⓐ	Ⓑ	Ⓒ	Ⓓ	70	Ⓐ	Ⓑ	Ⓒ	Ⓓ	90	Ⓐ	Ⓑ	Ⓒ	Ⓓ
11	Ⓐ	Ⓑ	Ⓒ		31	Ⓐ	Ⓑ	Ⓒ		51	Ⓐ	Ⓑ	Ⓒ	Ⓓ	71	Ⓐ	Ⓑ	Ⓒ	Ⓓ	91	Ⓐ	Ⓑ	Ⓒ	Ⓓ
12	Ⓐ	Ⓑ	Ⓒ		32	Ⓐ	Ⓑ	Ⓒ	Ⓓ	52	Ⓐ	Ⓑ	Ⓒ	Ⓓ	72	Ⓐ	Ⓑ	Ⓒ	Ⓓ	92	Ⓐ	Ⓑ	Ⓒ	Ⓓ
13	Ⓐ	Ⓑ	Ⓒ		33	Ⓐ	Ⓑ	Ⓒ	Ⓓ	53	Ⓐ	Ⓑ	Ⓒ	Ⓓ	73	Ⓐ	Ⓑ	Ⓒ	Ⓓ	93	Ⓐ	Ⓑ	Ⓒ	Ⓓ
14	Ⓐ	Ⓑ	Ⓒ		34	Ⓐ	Ⓑ	Ⓒ	Ⓓ	54	Ⓐ	Ⓑ	Ⓒ	Ⓓ	74	Ⓐ	Ⓑ	Ⓒ	Ⓓ	94	Ⓐ	Ⓑ	Ⓒ	Ⓓ
15	Ⓐ	Ⓑ	Ⓒ		35	Ⓐ	Ⓑ	Ⓒ	Ⓓ	55	Ⓐ	Ⓑ	Ⓒ	Ⓓ	75	Ⓐ	Ⓑ	Ⓒ	Ⓓ	95	Ⓐ	Ⓑ	Ⓒ	Ⓓ
16	Ⓐ	Ⓑ	Ⓒ		36	Ⓐ	Ⓑ	Ⓒ	Ⓓ	56	Ⓐ	Ⓑ	Ⓒ	Ⓓ	76	Ⓐ	Ⓑ	Ⓒ	Ⓓ	96	Ⓐ	Ⓑ	Ⓒ	Ⓓ
17	Ⓐ	Ⓑ	Ⓒ		37	Ⓐ	Ⓑ	Ⓒ	Ⓓ	57	Ⓐ	Ⓑ	Ⓒ	Ⓓ	77	Ⓐ	Ⓑ	Ⓒ	Ⓓ	97	Ⓐ	Ⓑ	Ⓒ	Ⓓ
18	Ⓐ	Ⓑ	Ⓒ		38	Ⓐ	Ⓑ	Ⓒ	Ⓓ	58	Ⓐ	Ⓑ	Ⓒ	Ⓓ	78	Ⓐ	Ⓑ	Ⓒ	Ⓓ	98	Ⓐ	Ⓑ	Ⓒ	Ⓓ
19	Ⓐ	Ⓑ	Ⓒ		39	Ⓐ	Ⓑ	Ⓒ	Ⓓ	59	Ⓐ	Ⓑ	Ⓒ	Ⓓ	79	Ⓐ	Ⓑ	Ⓒ	Ⓓ	99	Ⓐ	Ⓑ	Ⓒ	Ⓓ
20	Ⓐ	Ⓑ	Ⓒ		40	Ⓐ	Ⓑ	Ⓒ	Ⓓ	60	Ⓐ	Ⓑ	Ⓒ	Ⓓ	80	Ⓐ	Ⓑ	Ⓒ	Ⓓ	100	Ⓐ	Ⓑ	Ⓒ	Ⓓ

READING (Part V~VII)

NO.	ANSWER				NO.	ANSWER				NO.	ANSWER				NO.	ANSWER				NO.	ANSWER			
	A	B	C	D		A	B	C	D		A	B	C	D		A	B	C	D		A	B	C	D
101	Ⓐ	Ⓑ	Ⓒ	Ⓓ	121	Ⓐ	Ⓑ	Ⓒ	Ⓓ	141	Ⓐ	Ⓑ	Ⓒ	Ⓓ	161	Ⓐ	Ⓑ	Ⓒ	Ⓓ	181	Ⓐ	Ⓑ	Ⓒ	Ⓓ
102	Ⓐ	Ⓑ	Ⓒ	Ⓓ	122	Ⓐ	Ⓑ	Ⓒ	Ⓓ	142	Ⓐ	Ⓑ	Ⓒ	Ⓓ	162	Ⓐ	Ⓑ	Ⓒ	Ⓓ	182	Ⓐ	Ⓑ	Ⓒ	Ⓓ
103	Ⓐ	Ⓑ	Ⓒ	Ⓓ	123	Ⓐ	Ⓑ	Ⓒ	Ⓓ	143	Ⓐ	Ⓑ	Ⓒ	Ⓓ	163	Ⓐ	Ⓑ	Ⓒ	Ⓓ	183	Ⓐ	Ⓑ	Ⓒ	Ⓓ
104	Ⓐ	Ⓑ	Ⓒ	Ⓓ	124	Ⓐ	Ⓑ	Ⓒ	Ⓓ	144	Ⓐ	Ⓑ	Ⓒ	Ⓓ	164	Ⓐ	Ⓑ	Ⓒ	Ⓓ	184	Ⓐ	Ⓑ	Ⓒ	Ⓓ
105	Ⓐ	Ⓑ	Ⓒ	Ⓓ	125	Ⓐ	Ⓑ	Ⓒ	Ⓓ	145	Ⓐ	Ⓑ	Ⓒ	Ⓓ	165	Ⓐ	Ⓑ	Ⓒ	Ⓓ	185	Ⓐ	Ⓑ	Ⓒ	Ⓓ
106	Ⓐ	Ⓑ	Ⓒ	Ⓓ	126	Ⓐ	Ⓑ	Ⓒ	Ⓓ	146	Ⓐ	Ⓑ	Ⓒ	Ⓓ	166	Ⓐ	Ⓑ	Ⓒ	Ⓓ	186	Ⓐ	Ⓑ	Ⓒ	Ⓓ
107	Ⓐ	Ⓑ	Ⓒ	Ⓓ	127	Ⓐ	Ⓑ	Ⓒ	Ⓓ	147	Ⓐ	Ⓑ	Ⓒ	Ⓓ	167	Ⓐ	Ⓑ	Ⓒ	Ⓓ	187	Ⓐ	Ⓑ	Ⓒ	Ⓓ
108	Ⓐ	Ⓑ	Ⓒ	Ⓓ	128	Ⓐ	Ⓑ	Ⓒ	Ⓓ	148	Ⓐ	Ⓑ	Ⓒ	Ⓓ	168	Ⓐ	Ⓑ	Ⓒ	Ⓓ	188	Ⓐ	Ⓑ	Ⓒ	Ⓓ
109	Ⓐ	Ⓑ	Ⓒ	Ⓓ	129	Ⓐ	Ⓑ	Ⓒ	Ⓓ	149	Ⓐ	Ⓑ	Ⓒ	Ⓓ	169	Ⓐ	Ⓑ	Ⓒ	Ⓓ	189	Ⓐ	Ⓑ	Ⓒ	Ⓓ
110	Ⓐ	Ⓑ	Ⓒ	Ⓓ	130	Ⓐ	Ⓑ	Ⓒ	Ⓓ	150	Ⓐ	Ⓑ	Ⓒ	Ⓓ	170	Ⓐ	Ⓑ	Ⓒ	Ⓓ	190	Ⓐ	Ⓑ	Ⓒ	Ⓓ
111	Ⓐ	Ⓑ	Ⓒ	Ⓓ	131	Ⓐ	Ⓑ	Ⓒ	Ⓓ	151	Ⓐ	Ⓑ	Ⓒ	Ⓓ	171	Ⓐ	Ⓑ	Ⓒ	Ⓓ	191	Ⓐ	Ⓑ	Ⓒ	Ⓓ
112	Ⓐ	Ⓑ	Ⓒ	Ⓓ	132	Ⓐ	Ⓑ	Ⓒ	Ⓓ	152	Ⓐ	Ⓑ	Ⓒ	Ⓓ	172	Ⓐ	Ⓑ	Ⓒ	Ⓓ	192	Ⓐ	Ⓑ	Ⓒ	Ⓓ
113	Ⓐ	Ⓑ	Ⓒ	Ⓓ	133	Ⓐ	Ⓑ	Ⓒ	Ⓓ	153	Ⓐ	Ⓑ	Ⓒ	Ⓓ	173	Ⓐ	Ⓑ	Ⓒ	Ⓓ	193	Ⓐ	Ⓑ	Ⓒ	Ⓓ
114	Ⓐ	Ⓑ	Ⓒ	Ⓓ	134	Ⓐ	Ⓑ	Ⓒ	Ⓓ	154	Ⓐ	Ⓑ	Ⓒ	Ⓓ	174	Ⓐ	Ⓑ	Ⓒ	Ⓓ	194	Ⓐ	Ⓑ	Ⓒ	Ⓓ
115	Ⓐ	Ⓑ	Ⓒ	Ⓓ	135	Ⓐ	Ⓑ	Ⓒ	Ⓓ	155	Ⓐ	Ⓑ	Ⓒ	Ⓓ	175	Ⓐ	Ⓑ	Ⓒ	Ⓓ	195	Ⓐ	Ⓑ	Ⓒ	Ⓓ
116	Ⓐ	Ⓑ	Ⓒ	Ⓓ	136	Ⓐ	Ⓑ	Ⓒ	Ⓓ	156	Ⓐ	Ⓑ	Ⓒ	Ⓓ	176	Ⓐ	Ⓑ	Ⓒ	Ⓓ	196	Ⓐ	Ⓑ	Ⓒ	Ⓓ
117	Ⓐ	Ⓑ	Ⓒ	Ⓓ	137	Ⓐ	Ⓑ	Ⓒ	Ⓓ	157	Ⓐ	Ⓑ	Ⓒ	Ⓓ	177	Ⓐ	Ⓑ	Ⓒ	Ⓓ	197	Ⓐ	Ⓑ	Ⓒ	Ⓓ
118	Ⓐ	Ⓑ	Ⓒ	Ⓓ	138	Ⓐ	Ⓑ	Ⓒ	Ⓓ	158	Ⓐ	Ⓑ	Ⓒ	Ⓓ	178	Ⓐ	Ⓑ	Ⓒ	Ⓓ	198	Ⓐ	Ⓑ	Ⓒ	Ⓓ
119	Ⓐ	Ⓑ	Ⓒ	Ⓓ	139	Ⓐ	Ⓑ	Ⓒ	Ⓓ	159	Ⓐ	Ⓑ	Ⓒ	Ⓓ	179	Ⓐ	Ⓑ	Ⓒ	Ⓓ	199	Ⓐ	Ⓑ	Ⓒ	Ⓓ
120	Ⓐ	Ⓑ	Ⓒ	Ⓓ	140	Ⓐ	Ⓑ	Ⓒ	Ⓓ	160	Ⓐ	Ⓑ	Ⓒ	Ⓓ	180	Ⓐ	Ⓑ	Ⓒ	Ⓓ	200	Ⓐ	Ⓑ	Ⓒ	Ⓓ

1. 사용 필기구 : 컴퓨터용 연필(연필을 제외한 사인펜, 볼펜 등은 사용 절대 불가)
2. 잘못된 필기구 사용과 〈보기〉의 올바른 표기 이외의 잘못된 표기로 한 경우에는 당 위원회의 OMR기기가 판독한 결과에 따르며 그 결과는 본인 책임입니다. 1개의 정답만 골라 아래의 올바른 표기대로 정확히 표기하여야 합니다.
   〈보기〉 올바른 표기 : ● 잘못된 표기 : ⊘ ⊗ ◍
3. 답안지는 컴퓨터로 처리되므로 훼손하시면 안 되며, 상단의 타이밍마크(❙❙❙❙)부분을 찢거나, 낙서 등을 하면 본인에게 불이익이 발생할 수 있습니다.
4. 감독관의 확인이 없거나 시험 종료 후에 답안 작성을 계속할 경우 시험 무효 처리됩니다.

*서약 내용을 읽으시고 확인란에 반드시 서명하십시오.

서 약	확 인
본인은 TOEIC 시험 문제의 일부 또는 전부를 유출하거나 어떠한 형태로든 타인에게 누설 공개하지 않을 것이며 인터넷 또는 인쇄물 등을 이용해 유포하거나 참고 자료로 활용하지 않을 것입니다. 또한 TOEIC 시험 부정 행위 처리 규정을 준수할 것을 서약합니다.	

나혼자 끝내는 新 토익

FINAL 실전 모의고사

LC+RC 5회

제이드 김 · 김선희 지음

MP3 바로 듣기
정답 자동 채점
모바일 단어장
받아쓰기 테스트

혼공족들을 위한 막강 부가자료
www.nexusbook.com

3가지 버전 MP3
영국·호주식 발음 MP3
모바일 단어장
온라인 받아쓰기
어휘 리스트 & 테스트

스크립트+정답 및 해설

Actual Test

01

Listening Comprehension

본책 P14

PART 1

1 (A)	2 (C)	3 (C)	4 (B)	5 (B)	6 (A)

PART 2

7 (B)	8 (C)	9 (C)	10 (C)	11 (C)	12 (C)	13 (B)	14 (A)	15 (B)	16 (B)
17 (B)	18 (C)	19 (B)	20 (C)	21 (A)	22 (B)	23 (C)	24 (A)	25 (A)	26 (B)
27 (C)	28 (B)	29 (B)	30 (C)	31 (B)					

PART 3

32 (C)	33 (B)	34 (B)	35 (A)	36 (D)	37 (B)	38 (D)	39 (C)	40 (B)	41 (C)
42 (C)	43 (B)	44 (D)	45 (C)	46 (D)	47 (B)	48 (C)	49 (D)	50 (D)	51 (B)
52 (D)	53 (A)	54 (B)	55 (D)	56 (D)	57 (D)	58 (C)	59 (A)	60 (D)	61 (C)
62 (C)	63 (D)	64 (B)	65 (B)	66 (D)	67 (C)	68 (D)	69 (A)	70 (C)	

PART 4

71 (B)	72 (A)	73 (B)	74 (A)	75 (C)	76 (B)	77 (B)	78 (B)	79 (C)	80 (C)
81 (B)	82 (D)	83 (C)	84 (A)	85 (A)	86 (B)	87 (D)	88 (C)	89 (B)	90 (D)
91 (C)	92 (B)	93 (C)	94 (A)	95 (C)	96 (B)	97 (B)	98 (C)	99 (A)	100 (D)

Reading Comprehension

본책 P26

PART 5

101 (C)	102 (A)	103 (A)	104 (B)	105 (A)	106 (B)	107 (D)	108 (D)	109 (D)	110 (C)
111 (D)	112 (B)	113 (B)	114 (B)	115 (C)	116 (A)	117 (C)	118 (C)	119 (B)	120 (D)
121 (A)	122 (A)	123 (A)	124 (B)	125 (D)	126 (C)	127 (A)	128 (C)	129 (C)	130 (A)

PART 6

131 (A)	132 (C)	133 (B)	134 (D)	135 (D)	136 (A)	137 (B)	138 (A)	139 (C)	140 (D)
141 (A)	142 (D)	143 (B)	144 (B)	145 (D)	146 (C)				

PART 7

147 (D)	148 (C)	149 (B)	150 (D)	151 (A)	152 (B)	153 (C)	154 (D)	155 (C)	156 (C)
157 (A)	158 (A)	159 (B)	160 (D)	161 (B)	162 (A)	163 (C)	164 (C)	165 (B)	166 (B)
167 (A)	168 (B)	169 (A)	170 (D)	171 (C)	172 (C)	173 (D)	174 (B)	175 (C)	176 (B)
177 (A)	178 (C)	179 (B)	180 (A)	181 (D)	182 (C)	183 (D)	184 (C)	185 (B)	186 (B)
187 (B)	188 (D)	189 (A)	190 (A)	191 (C)	192 (B)	193 (D)	194 (D)	195 (C)	196 (B)
197 (B)	198 (A)	199 (D)	200 (D)						

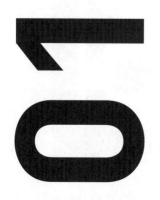

PART 1

P14

1 미W
(A) He is jotting something down.
(B) He is selecting a notebook.
(C) He is looking through some files.
(D) He is putting on eyeglasses.

(A) 남자가 무언가를 적고 있다.
(B) 남자가 공책을 고르고 있다.
(C) 남자가 파일들을 훑어보고 있다.
(D) 남자가 안경을 쓰고 있다.

해설 1인 사진은 인물의 동작과 복장에 집중한다. 남자가 무엇인가 적는 모습을 묘사한 (A)가 가장 적절한 답이다. 남자가 안경을 착용하고는 있으나, (D)의 putting on은 착용하는 동작의 묘사이므로 이미 착용하고 있는 상태의 사진에서는 정답이 될 수 없다. 사진에서 남자가 공책을 고르거나, 파일을 훑어보는 행위 역시 하고 있지 않으므로 (B)와 (C)는 모두 오답이다.

어휘 jot down 쓰다, 적다 select 고르다, 선택하다 look through 훑어보다, 살펴보다

2 미M
(A) The man is preparing some food.
(B) The woman is pointing to something.
(C) People are helping themselves to some food.
(D) People are placing their orders.

(A) 남자가 음식을 준비하고 있다.
(B) 여자가 무엇인가 가리키고 있다.
(C) 사람들이 음식을 접시에 담고 있다.
(D) 사람들이 주문을 하고 있다.

해설 뷔페에서 남자와 여자가 음식을 담고 있는 모습이므로 (C)가 정답이다. 손가락으로 무언가 가리키는 사람은 남자이므로 여자의 동작으로 잘못 묘사한 (B)는 오답이다. 앞의 주어를 놓치고 뒷부분의 행동만 듣고 오답을 고르지 않도록 주의한다. 또한 남자가 음식을 만들거나, 주문을 하는 것이 아니므로 (A)와 (D)도 모두 오답이다.

어휘 point to ~을 가리키다 help oneself to (음식물 등을) 자유로이 집어먹다, 자유로이 먹다 place an order 주문하다

3 영M
(A) The vendor is filling containers with produce.
(B) Customers are exiting a supermarket.
(C) Some jars have been arranged on a stand.
(D) Some women are holding flags.

(A) 상인이 용기에 농산물을 채우고 있다.
(B) 고객들이 슈퍼마켓에서 나오고 있다.
(C) 몇 개의 병들이 가판대 위에 정렬되어 있다.
(D) 몇 명의 여자들이 깃발을 들고 있다.

해설 다수의 인물 사진은 다양한 어휘가 주어로 사용되니 사진에 등장하지 않는 어휘가 들리면 빠르게 소거해야 한다. 가판대 위에 여러 물건들과 함께 병들이 진열된 모습을 묘사한 (C)가 가장 적절한 답이다. 사진에 상인과 손님은 등장하지만 상인이 용기에 무엇인가를 채우거나, 손님이 슈퍼마켓을 나가는 모습은 확인되지 않으므로 (A)와 (B)는 오답이며, 깃발이 보이지만 여자들이 들고 있는 모습은 보이지 않으므로 (D) 또한 오답이다.

어휘 vendor 행상인, 상인 container 그릇, 용기, (화물 수송용) 컨테이너 produce 생산물, 농산물 exit 나가다 jar (잼, 꿀을 담아 두는) 병, 단지 stand 가판대, 좌판

4 호M
(A) Some people are sunbathing at the beach.
(B) Some people are wading in the water.
(C) Large waves are hitting the beach.
(D) A parasol is being opened on the shore.

(A) 몇 명의 사람들이 해변에서 일광욕을 하고 있다.
(B) 몇 명의 사람들이 물속을 걷고 있다.
(C) 큰 파도가 해변에 치고 있다.
(D) 파라솔이 해안에 펼쳐지고 있다.

해설 다수의 사람과 사물이 혼재된 사진 유형으로, 사물과 배경의 묘사는 물론 사람 묘사도 출제되기 때문에 사진 관찰에 각별히 신경을 써야 한다. 몇 명의 사람들이 물속을 걷고 있는 동작을 묘사하는 (B)가 정답이다. 일광욕을 하는 사람과 큰 파도는 모두 사진 속에 나타나 있지 않으므로 (A)와 (C)는 오답이며, 파라솔은 이미 펴진 상태이므로 펴지고 있는 동작을 묘사한(is being opened) (D)도 오답이다.

어휘 sunbath 일광욕을 하다 wade 헤치며 걷다 hit 때리다, 치다 shore (바다, 호수 등의) 기슭, 해안

5 영M
(A) Sunlight is streaming through the clouds.
(B) Some tall buildings are located near the shoreline.
(C) The scenery is reflected on the surface of the water.
(D) A bridge is being built across the water.

(A) 햇빛이 구름 사이로 비치고 있다.
(B) 높은 건물들이 해안가에 있다.
(C) 경치가 물의 표면에 반사된다.
(D) 다리가 물을 가로질러 건설되고 있다.

해설 물가 근처에 건물과 배가 보이며 사람이 없는 전형적인 풍경 사진이다. 다양한 어휘가 주어로 등장할 것을 염두에 두고 사진에 보이지 않는 주어가 들리면 빠르게 소거해야 한다. 해안가 건물들의 위치를 가장 적절하게 묘사한 (B)가 정답이다. 구름 사이로 햇빛이 비치는 모습을 묘사한 (A)와 물에 비친 풍경 모습을 묘사한 (C)는 사진에서 확인되지 않으므로 오답이다. (D)는 사진에 다리(bridge)가 보이지 않으며, 사람이 없는 사진에서 사물을 주어로 하는 수동태 진행형(be being p.p.)을 사용해서 동작을 묘사하고 있으므로 오답이다. 풍경 사진은 사물이 주어로 된 수동태가 주로 정답이 된다.

어휘 stream 흐르다, 흘러나오다 shoreline 해안선 scenery 풍경, 경치 reflect 비추다 surface 표면, 수면

6 미W
(A) A path leads through a tunnel.
(B) A footbridge extends over a hill.
(C) A grassy area is surrounded by rocks.
(D) Rocks are being gathered into piles.

(A) 길이 터널로 이어진다.
(B) 육교가 언덕 너머로 뻗어 있다.
(C) 풀로 덮인 지역이 바위들로 둘러싸여 있다.
(D) 바위들이 더미로 쌓이고 있다.

해설 길이 터널 쪽으로 뚫려 있는 사진을 가장 적절히 묘사한 (A)가 정답이다. 육교는 전혀 보이지 않으므로 (B)는 오답이며, 바위는 보이지만 풀로 덮인 지역은 확인되지 않으므로 (C)도 오답이다. 또한 바위를 모아서 쌓고 있는 동작도 보이지 않으므로 (D) 역시 오답이다.

어휘 lead through ~로 이어지다 footbridge 보행자 전용다리, 육교 extend 늘이다, 늘리다, 펼치다 grassy area 잔디가 있는 공간

PART 2

P18

7 미M 미W
How can I reach City Hall from here?
(A) City Hall is crowded these days.
(B) A taxi will be the best option.
(C) Yes, he comes from a very rich family.

제가 여기서 시청까지 어떻게 가야 하나요?
(A) 시청은 요즘 붐빕니다.
(B) 택시가 가장 좋은 방법입니다.
(C) 네, 그는 아주 부유한 가정 출신이에요.

해설 특정 장소에 가는 방법을 묻는 How 의문문이므로 교통수단을 언급한 (B)가 가장 적절하다. (A)는 질문의 city hall을 반복 사용하여 혼동을 유도하는 오답이며, (C)는 의문사 의문문에 Yes/No로 대답할 수 없으므로 오답이다.

8 영M 미W
Will you attend the workshop, or do you have too much work?
(A) John will finish his work later.
(B) Sorry, but I didn't see it.
(C) I will definitely be there.

워크숍에 참석하실 건가요, 아니면 일이 너무 많으신가요?
(A) John은 일을 나중에 끝낼 거예요.
(B) 죄송하지만, 못 봤어요.
(C) 저는 꼭 갈 거예요.

해설 참석 여부를 묻는 선택의문문에 꼭 갈 것이라는 대답을 한 (C)가 정답이다. (A)는 질문의 work를 반복 사용하여 정답인 듯 혼동을 유도한 오답이며, (B)는 미래의 참석 여부를 묻는 질문과 상관없이 과거로 대답하고 있다.

어휘 attend 참석하다 definitely 확실히, 분명히

9 미W 미M
Where have you been?
(A) Not really.
(B) It's from New York.
(C) With my friend at the store.

지금까지 어디에 계셨어요?
(A) 별로예요.
(B) 이것은 뉴욕에서 왔어요.
(C) 친구와 함께 상점에요.

해설 어디에 있었는지를 묻는 Where 의문문에 장소로 대답한 (C)가 정답이다. (A) Not really는 의미상 No에 가까운 부정적 대답으로 의문사 의문문에 적절한 답이 될 수 없으며, (B)는 장소를 사용하여 혼동을 유도하고 있지만 질문과 상관없는 답변이므로 오답이다.

어휘 so far 지금까지, 여태

10 Which flight are you taking?
미W (A) Absolutely, I'll take it.
호M (B) No, are you?
(C) The one at seven.

어떤 비행기를 타실 건가요?
(A) 물론이죠, 제가 그것을 살게요.
(B) 아니요, 당신은요?
(C) 7시 비행기요.

해설 비행편을 묻는 Which 의문문에 특정 시간을 언급하며, 그때 떠나는 비행기라고 대답한 (C)가 정답이다. (A)는 질문의 taking을 활용한 take를 사용하여 발음 혼동을 유도하는 오답이며, (B)는 의문사 의문문에 Yes/No로 대답할 수 없으므로 오답이다.

어휘 absolutely (강한 동의, 허락) 물론, (사실임을 강조) 틀림없이

11 Don't you need this note for your presentation?
영M (A) No, I don't take notes during the lecture.
미M (B) I will turn in my paper.
(C) Thanks, I almost forgot it.

발표에 이 노트가 필요하지 않으신가요?
(A) 아니요, 저는 강의 시간에 메모를 하지 않아요.
(B) 제 서류를 제출할 거예요.
(C) 감사합니다, 잊을 뻔 했어요.

해설 이 노트가 필요하지 않은지 확인하는 부정의문문에 상기시켜 준 것에 감사하다고 인사한 (C)가 가장 적절한 답이다. (B)는 질문의 note를 반복 사용하고 있는 발음 오답이다. (C)는 질문의 note에서 연상되는 paper를 사용하고 있으며 질문의 내용과도 연관성이 없다.

어휘 take notes 메모하다 lecture 강의, 강연 turn in 제출하다

12 What about playing tennis together?
미M (A) I don't want to play darts.
미W (B) He is one of the best tennis players in this country.
(C) This week is full of deadlines.

함께 테니스 치는 것이 어떨까요?
(A) 저는 다트 놀이를 하고 싶지 않아요.
(B) 그는 이 나라 최고의 테니스 선수 중 하나예요.
(C) 이번 주는 마감일로 가득 찼어요.

해설 테니스를 치자는 제안의문문에 바쁘다며 거절하는 표현을 우회적으로 전달한 (C)가 가장 적절한 답이다. 질문의 tennis를 반복 사용한 (B)와 질문의 tennis와 무관한 다트 게임을 언급한 (A)는 오답이다.

어휘 full of ~로 가득 찬 deadline 마감일

13 Have you been to the art gallery yet?
영M (A) She's a scientist.
미W **(B) No, can we go?**
(C) Yes, it is.

미술관에 이미 가 보셨나요?
(A) 그녀는 과학자예요.
(B) 아니요, 가실래요?
(C) 네, 그거 맞아요.

해설 특정 장소에 가 보았는지 경험을 묻는 질문에 같이 가자는 의미로 되물으며 제안하는 (B)가 정답이다. (A)는 질문과 전혀 연관성이 없는 직업 설명일 뿐만 아니라, 2인칭(You) 질문에 3인칭(She)으로 답하는 주어 불일치 오답이며, (C) 또한 질문의 내용과 무관하다.

어휘 yet 이미, 벌써(의문문에서), 아직(부정문에서)

14 How long have you been staying in this condominium?
미W **(A) Since I got a new job in this city.**
호M (B) I sold my condominium a long time ago.
(C) My cousin will live in this apartment with me.

이 아파트에 머무신 지 얼마나 오래 되셨어요?
(A) 제가 이 도시에 새 직장을 가진 이후부터요.
(B) 저는 오래 전에 아파트를 팔았어요.
(C) 제 사촌이 이 아파트에서 저와 함께 살 거예요.

해설 기간을 묻는 How long 의문문에 Since(~부터)를 사용하여 특정 시점부터 머물고 있음을 설명하는 (A)가 정답이다. (B)는 과거의 특정 시점을 언급했으므로 기간을 묻는 How long 질문에 부적절한 대답일 뿐만 아니라, 질문의 condominium과 long을 반복 사용하고 있으며, (C)는 condominium에서 연상할 수 있는 apartment를 사용하여 혼동을 유도하는 오답이다.

어휘 condominium 아파트 cousin 사촌

15 Why doesn't this printer work?
미W (A) Ms. Brown asked me to print some documents.
영M **(B) See, you have not pressed the power button.**
(C) I don't think the printer is mine.

이 프린터가 왜 작동하지 않나요?
(A) Brown 씨가 저에게 문서 출력을 요청했어요.
(B) 보세요, 전원 버튼을 누르지 않으셨잖아요.
(C) 그 프린터는 제 것이 아닌 것 같은데요.

해설 이유를 묻는 Why 의문문에 버튼을 누르지 않았기 때문이라고 설명해 주는 (B)가 가장 적절한 답이다. (A)는 질문의 printer와 어근이 동일한 print를 사용하여 혼동을 유도하는 오답이며, (C) 또한 printer를 반복 사용한 오답이다.

16 Would you send our agreement letter with International Tech. to me?
미M (A) The agreement will be revised soon.
영M **(B) I'll fax it directly after this meeting.**
(C) They made a new contract with other company.

저에게 International Tech와 체결한 합의서를 보내 주시겠어요?
(A) 그 합의서는 곧 수정될 거예요.
(B) 제가 회의 후에 바로 팩스로 보내드릴게요.
(C) 그들이 다른 회사와 새로운 계약을 체결했어요.

해설 서류를 보내 달라고 요청하는 일반의문문에 팩스로 보내겠다고 긍정적인 답변을 한 (B)가 가장 적절한 답이다. (A)는 질문의 agreement를 반복 사용하고 있으며, (C)는 질문의 agreement에서 연상할 수 있는 contract를 사용하여 혼동을 유도하고 있다. 또한 (A)는 내용상 요청하는 합의서가 곧 수정될 것이므로 보내 줄 수 없다고 혼동을 유도하고 있으나, 질문은 합의서의 수정 여부와 상관없이 보내 달라는 요청이므로 정답이 될 수 없다.

어휘 agreement 협정, 합의 revise 수정(변경)하다 directly 곧, 곧장

17 When were the changes to the budget submitted?
미M (A) To the department mailing list.
미W **(B) They haven't been done yet.**
(C) That's what I'd submit.

언제 예산 변경안이 제출된 건가요?
(A) 부서의 우편 목록으로요.
(B) 아직 제출되지 않았어요.
(C) 그게 바로 제가 제출할 거예요.

해설 제출한 시점을 묻는 When 의문문에 아직 하지 않았다고 대답한 (B)가 정답이다. (A)는 Where 의문사에 적절한 답변이며, (C)는 질문의 submit과 동일한 단어 사용으로 혼동을 유도하는 오답이다.

18 Who is in the meeting room right now?
영M (A) The meeting room is being renovated right now.
미W (B) The shareholders will invite you.
(C) I think I've just seen Monica there.

누가 지금 회의실 있나요?
(A) 회의실은 지금 보수 중이에요.
(B) 주주들이 당신을 초대할 거예요.
(C) 방금 Monica 씨가 그곳에 있는 걸 본 것 같아요.

해설 누가 회의실에 있는지를 묻는 Who 의문문에 특정인을 언급하는 (C)가 가장 적절한 답이다. (A)는 질문의 meeting room과 동일한 단어 사용으로 혼동을 유도하고 있으며, (B)는 Who 의문문에 사람(shareholders)을 언급하며 오답을 고르도록 유도하고 있지만 질문과는 상관없는 대답이다.

어휘 renovate 개조(보수)하다 shareholder 주주

19 He is going to sign a new contract with us, isn't he?
미W (A) The contract documents are brought by our manager.
미M **(B) I think so. He's satisfied with our presentation.**
(C) Our last contract was cancelled.

그는 우리와 새로운 계약을 체결할 거예요, 그렇지 않아요?
(A) 그 계약서는 우리 매니저가 가져온 거예요.
(B) 저도 그렇게 생각해요. 그는 우리의 발표에 만족하고 있어요.
(C) 우리의 지난 계약은 취소되었어요.

해설 그가 계약을 맺을 것인지 확인하는 부가의문문에 관련된 발표에 만족스러워하므로 그럴 것이라는 긍정의 의미를 전달하는 (B)가 정답이다. (A)와 (C) 모두 질문과 의미상 상관없는 답변이며 또한 질문의 contract를 반복 사용한 발음 오답 유형이다.

어휘 sign a contract 계약을 맺다 be satisfied with ~에 만족하다

20 Can we postpone the deadline for the annual report?
미W (A) Sure, give me his phone number.
영M (B) There is a long line.
(C) Yes, for a day or two.

연례 보고서의 마감을 연기할 수 있을까요?
(A) 물론이죠, 저에게 그의 전화번호를 주세요.
(B) 줄이 기네요.
(C) 네, 하루나 이틀 정도요.

해설 마감일 연장을 요청하는 일반의문문에 하루, 이틀 정도 미루는 것은 가능하다고 대답하는 (C)가 가장 적절한 답이다. (A)는 제안의문문의 단골 정답 유형인 Sure를 언급하여 혼동을 유도하고 있으나, 뒤에 질문과 관련 없는 3인칭(his)을 사용한 내용이 이어지고 있으며, (B)는 질문과 무관한 답변이므로 오답이다.

어휘 for a day or two 하루나 이틀 동안

21 Have you already prepared the press release?
영M **(A) It will be done shortly.**
미M (B) One of our biggest clients from the UK.
(C) Many journalists will come.

보도자료 준비하셨나요?
(A) 곧 완성될 거예요.
(B) 영국에서 가장 큰 우리 고객 중에 하나예요.
(C) 많은 기자들이 올 거예요.

해설 자료 준비 여부를 묻는 일반의문문에 곧 완성될 것이라며 긍정적인 의미를 전달하는 (A)가 가장 적절한 답이다. (B)는 질문과 의미상 상관없는 오답이며 (C)는 질문의 press release에서 연상되는 journalists(기자들)를 사용하여 혼동을 유도하고 있다.

어휘 press release 보도자료, (기관의) 대언론 공식 발표 journalist 저널리스트, 기자

22 How was your previous trip to London?
미M (A) Have you gone to London before?
미W **(B) No words can describe it.**
(C) The trip will be cancelled, I think.

London으로의 이전 여행은 어땠어요?
(A) London에 가 본 적 있어요?
(B) 어떤 말로도 설명할 수 없어요.
(C) 제 생각에, 그 여행은 취소될 거예요.

해설 여행이 어땠냐는 상대방의 의견을 묻는 How 의문문에 어떤 묘사로도 부족할 정도로 좋았다고 답변한 (B)가 정답이다. No word로 시작하는 구문을 부정 대답의 No와 혼동하지 않도록 주의해야 한다. (A)와 (C) 모두 질문의 London과 trip을 각각 반복 사용한 오답이다.

어휘 previous 과거의, 이전의

23 I don't have any appointments tomorrow, do I?
영M (A) He did it last time.
미W (B) The results were promising.
(C) No, you're available all day.

제가 내일은 약속이 전혀 없어요, 그렇죠?
(A) 그는 지난번에 그것을 했어요.
(B) 결과가 조짐이 좋아요.
(C) 없습니다, 당신은 하루 종일 시간적 여유가 있어요.

해설 내일 일정이 있는지를 확인하는 부가의문문에 하루 종일 시간적 여유가 있다고 자연스럽게 대화가 이어지는 (C)가 정답이다. (A)의 주어는 질문의 주어와 불일치하며, (B)는 질문의 약속(appointment)에서 연상 가능한 promise(약속하다)를 사용하여 혼동을 유도하고 있다.

어휘 promising 유망한, 조짐이 좋은 available 시간(여유)이 있는, (사물을) 이용할 수 있는

24 When can I expect to hear from you about the interview?
미W **(A) Within the next few days.**
호M (B) At the end of the street.
(C) I found it right here.

언제 면접에 대한 연락을 받을 수 있을까요?
(A) 며칠 내에요.
(B) 그 길 끝이요.
(C) 바로 여기에서 그것을 찾았어요.

해설 연락 받을 시점을 묻는 When 의문문에 때를 언급하며 적절히 대답한 (A)가 정답이다. (B)와 (C)는 모두 Where 의문문의 정답 유형인 장소를 언급하고 있으므로 질문과는 연관이 없으나, 질문의 When 의문사를 Where로 착각하게끔 혼란을 유도하고 있으니 청취 시 주의해야 한다.

어휘 expect to do ~하기를 기대하다

25 It's the most unique tower design in this city, isn't it?
미W **(A) None can be compared to this tower, for sure.**
영M (B) This city has a beautiful view.
(C) Did your team design this wide room?

이것은 도시에서 가장 독특한 건물 디자인이에요, 그렇지 않나요?
(A) 이 건물에 견줄 만한 것은 없다고 확신합니다.
(B) 이 도시는 아름다운 경관을 가졌군요.
(C) 당신 팀이 이 넓은 방을 디자인했나요?

해설 건물 디자인이 독특한지 확인하는 부가의문문에 다른 것과 비교할 수 없을 정도로 특별하다고 우회적인 긍정의 답변을 하고 있는 (A)가 정답이다. (B)와 (C)는 질문의 의도와도 상관없으며 각각 city와 design을 반복 사용한 오답이다.

어휘 unique 독특한, 특별한 for sure 확실히, 틀림없이 compare to ~와 비교하다

26 Have you chosen the new photographer or are you still deciding?
미M (A) I'll be happy to take a picture of you.
영M **(B) We have two more candidates to interview.**
(C) The chief photographer's name is Arthur Gonzalez.

새로운 사진작가를 선택했나요, 아니면 아직도 생각 중이신가요?
(A) 제가 기꺼이 당신의 사진을 찍어드릴게요.
(B) 면접을 봐야 할 후보가 두 명 더 있어요.
(C) 수석 사진작가 이름은 Arthur Gonzalez예요.

해설 사진작가를 결정했는지 여부를 묻는 선택의문문에 면접을 봐야 할 사람이 더 있다고 언급함으로써 아직 결정하지 못했다는 것을 우회적으로 표현한 (B)가 가장 적절한 답이다. (A)는 photographer에서 연상되는 take a picture(사진 찍다)를 사용하여 혼동을 유발하고 있으며 (C)는 선택의문문의 적절한 정답 유형인 동일한 단어 photographer를 사용하고는 있으나 의미상 질문과 무관한 답변을 하고 있다.

어휘 candidate 후보자, 출마자 chief (계급, 직급상) 우두머리, 상관

27 Mr. Miller will be writing the training manual.
미M (A) They were just hired.
미W (B) Yes, a few employees did.
(C) I know he'll do a good job.

Miller 씨가 교육 매뉴얼을 작성할 겁니다.
(A) 그들은 방금 채용되었어요.
(B) 네, 소수의 직원들이 했어요.
(C) 저는 그가 잘 할 거라는 것을 알아요.

해설 특정인이 매뉴얼을 작성할 것이라는 사실을 전달하는 평서문에 그 사람이 잘할 거라고 맞장구의 형식으로 말하는 (C)가 가장 적절한 답이다. (A)와 (B) 모두 평서문의 주어와 불일치하며 의미상으로도 질문과 무관한 답변을 하고 있으므로 오답이다.

28 What was the name of the book you recommended?
영M (A) Thanks, I enjoyed it.
미W **(B) Do you mean the one on proposal writing?**
(C) Yes, in the library.

당신이 추천했던 책의 이름이 뭐였죠?
(A) 감사합니다, 재미있었어요.
(B) 제안서 작성에 관한 책 말인가요?
(C) 네, 도서관에서요.

해설 책 이름을 묻는 What 의문문에 특정 책을 언급하며 우회적으로 되묻는 (B)가 가장 적절한 답이다. (A)는 질문과 무관한 답변을 하고 있으며, (C)는 의문사 의문문에 Yes/No의 답변은 불가하므로 오답이다.

29 Why didn't Brian submit his budget proposal yesterday?
미W (A) Yes, it's more expensive than I thought.
미M **(B) It's possible that he forgot.**
(C) I'll submit the sales figures tomorrow.

왜 Brian은 어제 그의 예산 제안서를 제출하지 않았나요?
(A) 네, 제가 생각했던 것보다 더 비싸네요.
(B) 그가 잊어버렸을 가능성이 있어요.
(C) 제가 내일 매출액을 제출하겠습니다.

해설 제출하지 않은 이유를 묻는 Why 의문문에 Brian이 잊어버렸을 거라고 설명한 (B)가 정답이다. (B)는 의문사 의문문에 Yes/No로 대답할 수 없으므로 오답이며, (C)는 질문의 submit과 같은 단어를 반복 사용하여 혼동을 유도하고 있다.

어휘 sales figures 매출액

30 The facilities manager is out of town for family matters.
미W (A) That building is empty.
영M (B) It's fine with me.
(C) Who's covering for her?

시설 관리자는 가족 문제로 다른 곳에 있습니다.
(A) 그 건물은 비었어요.
(B) 저는 괜찮아요.
(C) 그녀의 일을 누가 대신하고 있나요?

해설 시설 관리자가 자리를 비웠다는 사실을 전달하는 평서문에 누가 그 일을 대신하고 있는지 되묻는 (C)가 정답이다. (A)는 질문의 〈out of + 명사(~이 다 떨어진)〉에서 연상할 수 있는 empty를 사용하여 혼동을 유도하고 있으며, (B)는 의미상 평서문과 상관없는 문장으로 모두 오답이다.

어휘 out of town (출장 등으로) 도시를 떠나서, 타지에 family matters 가정 사정

31 I think you should try a shorter hair cut this time.
영M (A) Why don't you try this?
미W **(B) Yes, I have been considering that.**
(C) One o'clock on Thursday.

이번에는 더 짧은 머리를 해 보는 것이 좋을 것 같습니다.
(A) 이것을 해 보는 건 어떨까요?
(B) 네, 그것도 생각 중이었어요.
(C) 목요일 한 시 정각이요.

해설 머리 스타일을 제안하는 의미의 평서문에 considering을 사용하여 우회적으로 긍정 대답을 하고 있는 (B)가 정답이다. (A)는 질문의 try를 반복 사용한 오답이며 (C)는 의미상 질문과 상관없는 답변이다.

PART 3

Questions 32-34 refer to the following conversation. 미W 영M

W Matt, ㉜ I noticed that you were reading this month's issue of Business Circle in the staff lounge earlier. Can I have it when you're finished? There's an article that I'd like to look at.
M ㉝ Is it the one about the global trade agreement that's currently under negotiation?
W That's right, if that deal goes through, it's likely to have a major impact on our industry.
M You're right. ㉞ We'll need to keep a close eye on the situation as it develops. We want to make plans to try to take advantage of potential opportunities, and we should also be prepared for any negative effects that could result from the deal.

여 Matt, 조금 전 당신이 직원 휴게실에서 〈비즈니스 서클〉의 이번 달 호를 읽고 계신 것을 보았어요. 다 보시면 제가 볼 수 있을까요? 보고 싶었던 기사가 있거든요.
남 현재 협상이 진행 중인 국제 무역 협정에 대한 거죠?
여 맞아요. 만약 그 거래가 성사된다면, 우리 산업에 큰 영향을 줄 것 같아요.
남 당신 말이 맞아요. 어떻게 진행되는지 상황을 잘 지켜봐야 할 필요가 있어요. 우리는 잠재적인 기회를 활용할 수 있는 계획을 세워야 해요. 그리고 협상으로 발생할 수 있는 부정적인 영향에도 대비해야 하고요.

어휘 this month's issue 이번 달 호 article 글, 기사 global 세계적인 trade agreement 무역 협정 under negotiation 교섭 중, 협상 중 impact 영향, 충격 keep a close eye on ~을 잘 지켜보다 take advantage of ~을 이용하다 negative effects 부정적 효과 suspend 유예하다, 연기하다

32 What most likely is Business Circle?
(A) A trade conference
(B) A Web site
(C) A magazine
(D) A radio program

Business Circle은 무엇인가?
(A) 무역 회의
(B) 웹 사이트
(C) 잡지
(D) 라디오 프로그램

해설 〈구체적 정보 파악 – 언급〉
문제에서 언급한 Business Circle에 주목해서 문제를 풀어야 한다. 여자가 첫 대사에서 'Business Circle'의 이번 달 호라고 언급한 부분에서 잡지라는 것을 알 수 있다. 따라서 정답은 (C)이다.

33 What is the current status of the trade agreement?
(A) It has gone through.
(B) It is being discussed.
(C) It has been suspended.
(D) It will soon expire.

무역 협정의 현재 상황은 어떠한가?
(A) 그것은 통과되었다.
(B) 그것은 논의 중이다.
(C) 그것은 보류되었다.
(D) 그것은 곧 기한이 만료될 것이다.

해설 〈구체적 정보 파악 – 특정 사항〉
trade agreement를 키워드로 잡고 이에 집중해야 한다. 남자가 첫 대사에서 현재 논의 중에 있는 국제 무역 협정을 언급하고 있으므로 (B)가 정답이다.

34 What does the man suggest doing?
(A) Preparing an alternative proposal
(B) Monitoring the situation closely
(C) Advertising job opportunities
(D) Analyzing the negative result

남자가 제안하는 것은 무엇인가?
(A) 대안을 준비하는 것
(B) 상황을 주의 깊게 지켜보는 것
(C) 취업 기회를 광고하는 것
(D) 부정적인 결과를 분석하는 것

해설 〈구체적 정보 파악 – 제안〉
남자의 제안 사항을 묻는 문제로 남자의 대사에 주목해야 한다. 남자가 마지막 대사에서 제안을 의미하는 We'll need to의 표현으로 문장을 시작하고 있으며, 이어서 상황을 잘 지켜봐야 한다고 말하므로 정답은 (B)이다.

패러프레이징 keep a close eye on ~을 잘 지켜보다
→ monitoring the situation closely 상황을 예의주시하다

Questions 35-37 refer to the following conversation. (미W) (미M)

W ㉟ Did you hear that Jamal is going to be elevated to sales manager soon, and then transferred to our headquarters in Prague next month?

M Yes, he deserves it. Since joining the company, ㊱ he's made some outstanding contributions which have helped us become one of the leading pharmaceutical firms in Eastern Europe.

W That's true. And he's a great team player, so I'm sure that he will be able to lead his own team and deal with them well.

M ㊲ Why don't we hold some kind of leaving party for him?

여 Jamal이 곧 영업 부장으로 승진해서 다음 달에 프라하에 있는 본사로 전근 간다는 얘기 들었어요?

남 네, 그는 그럴 만한 자격이 있어요. 그는 회사에 입사한 이후로 우리가 동유럽 선두의 제약 회사가 되는 일에 큰 기여를 했어요.

여 맞아요. 그리고 그는 훌륭한 팀 플레이어이기도 해요. 그래서 저는 그가 팀을 이끌고 팀원들과 잘 지낼 거라고 생각해요.

남 그를 위한 송별회 같은 걸 여는 것은 어떨까요?

어휘 be elevated to ~로 관등에 오르다, 승진하다 be transferred to ~로 전근되다 deserve ~을 받을 만하다 outstanding 뛰어난, 두드러진 contribution 기여, 이바지 pharmaceutical 약학의, 제약의 advancement 승진

35 What are the speakers mainly talking about?
(A) The advancement of a coworker
(B) The retirement of a manager
(C) A recent business agreement
(D) The relocation of a headquarters

화자들은 주로 무엇에 대해 이야기하고 있는가?
(A) 동료의 승진
(B) 관리자의 은퇴
(C) 최근의 업무 협약
(D) 본사의 이전

해설 〈기본 정보 파악 – 주제〉
대화의 주제를 묻는 문제로, 대화의 전반부에서 정답의 근거를 찾을 수 있다. 여자가 첫 대사에서 Jamal이 영업 부장으로 승진한다는 소식을 전하고 있으므로 (A)가 정답이다.

패러프레이징 be elevated to 승진하다, ~로 관등에 오르다
→ advancement 승진, 출세

36 What type of company do the speakers most likely work for?
(A) A legal office
(B) A marketing firm
(C) A travel agency
(D) A medical firm

화자들이 근무하는 회사는 어떤 종류의 회사이겠는가?
(A) 법률 회사
(B) 마케팅 회사
(D) 여행사
(D) 제약 회사

해설 〈기본 정보 파악 – 장소〉
남자가 첫 대사에서 그들의 회사가 동유럽 선두의 제약 회사가 되는 일에 동료가 큰 기여를 했다고 평가하고 있으므로 화자들이 근무하는 회사가 제약 회사임을 알 수 있다. 따라서 (D)이다.

패러프레이징 pharmaceutical firms 제약 회사
→ medical firm 제약 업체

37 What does the man suggest?
(A) Leading a workshop
(B) Holding a farewell event
(C) Checking a report
(D) Asking for more information

남자가 제안하는 것은 무엇인가?
(A) 워크숍을 인솔하는 것
(B) 송별회를 여는 것
(C) 보고서를 확인하는 것
(D) 더 많은 정보를 요청하는 것

해설 〈구체적 정보 파악 – 제안 관련〉
마지막 대사에서 남자가 송별회를 열자고 제안하고 있으므로 정답은 (B)이다.

패러프레이징 leaving party 작별 파티, 송별회
→ farewell event 고별회, 송별회

Questions 38-40 refer to the following conversation. (영M) (미W)

M Glenside Suites. How may I help you?

W Diego, it's Lisa from housekeeping. Sorry to call you at the front desk, but there's a problem. ㊳ The guest who just checked in to 709 told me that her room is too cold. It looks like the heater isn't working. ㊴ I tried calling maintenance but no one answered.

M Oh, ㊴ Chris had to go to the hardware store to pick up a few things. I'm afraid he won't be back for a while.

W Well, what should I tell the guest?

M ㊵ Please send her back to the front desk, and we'll put her in a different room.

남 Glenside Suites입니다. 어떻게 도와 드릴까요?

여 Diego, 객실 관리부 Lisa입니다. 프론트 데스크로 전화해서 미안하지만, 여기 문제가 있습니다. 709호에 방금 투숙한 손님이 방이 너무 춥다고 하십니다. 아마도 히터가 고장난 것 같아요. 관리부에 전화해 봤는데, 아무도 받질 않습니다.

남 아, Chris는 철물점에 몇 가지 물건을 사러 갔어요. 한동안은 돌아오지 않을 텐데요.

여 그럼, 손님에게는 뭐라고 얘기해야 할까요?

남 손님을 프론트 데스크로 보내 주세요. 우리가 그분께 다른 방을 드리겠습니다.

어휘 housekeeping 객실 관리부, 가사 노동 maintenance 유지, 관리 hardware store 철물점 for a while 얼마 동안은

38 Why is the woman calling?
(A) To announce a plan
(B) To offer an apology
(C) To request some supplies
(D) To pass along a complaint

여자가 전화한 이유는 무엇인가?
(A) 계획을 알려주기 위해서
(B) 사과하기 위해서
(C) 몇 가지 물품을 요청하기 위해서
(D) 불평을 전달하기 위해서

해설 〈기본 정보 파악 – 전화 목적〉
전화 목적을 묻는 문제로, 대화의 전반부에서 정답의 근거를 찾을 수 있다. 남자가 전화를 받은 후, 여자가 객실의 히터가 고장이라 방이 춥다는 투숙객의 말을 전달하고 있으므로 정답은 (D)이다.

39 In which department does Chris probably work?
(A) Housekeeping
(B) Reception
(C) Maintenance
(D) Security

Chris는 어느 부서에서 일하겠는가?

(A) 객실 관리 부서
(B) 접수처
(C) 관리 부서
(D) 보안 부서

해설 〈구체적 정보 파악 – 언급〉
여자가 첫 대사에서 문제 해결을 위해 시설 관리부에 연락했으나 아무도 전화를 받지 않는다고 말하자 남자가 Chris는 철물점에 갔다고 대답하고 있으므로 Chris가 시설 관리부와 관련이 있음을 알 수 있다. 따라서 정답은 (C)이다.

40 What will the woman probably do next?
(A) Make some repairs
(B) Speak to a guest
(C) Call a hardware store
(D) Clean a guest's suite

여자는 다음에 무엇을 할 것인가?
(A) 수리를 한다.
(B) 손님에게 말한다.
(C) 철물점에 전화한다.
(D) 객실을 청소한다.

해설 〈구체적 정보 파악 – 미래〉
앞으로의 일을 묻는 문제로 후반부에 정답의 단서가 제시된다. 남자가 마지막 대사에서 여자에게 손님을 프런트 데스크로 보내 달라고 부탁하고 있으며 여자는 손님에게 이 말을 전달할 것이므로 정답은 (B)이다.

Questions 41-43 refer to the following conversation with three speakers. 영W 미M 호M

W Hi, Peter, you look worried.
M1 ㊶ I have to get over to Tribien French Restaurant to pick up some food for our party this evening.
M2 You don't have much time. What do you think, Alice?
W You'll make it. ㊷ It's only about 5 minutes from here.
M1 Yeah, but that's 5 minutes by car. I rode my bicycle to work today, and I can't carry all that food on my bike. ㊸ The train doesn't run very often around here.
M2 ㊸ And it's too far from the station. A lot of their customers complain about it.
W Why don't you use my car? I was planning to walk home anyway.
M1 Really? Thanks, Alice.

여 안녕하세요, Peter, 걱정이 있어 보이네요.
남1 오늘 저녁 파티를 위해 음식을 가지러 Tribien 프랑스 식당에 가야 하거든요.
남2 시간이 별로 없네요. Alice, 어떻게 생각해요?
여 당신은 해낼 수 있어요. 여기서 5분밖에 안 걸리잖아요.
남1 맞아요, 하지만 차로 5분이에요. 저는 오늘 자전거를 타고 출근했고 제 자전거로는 음식을 모두 실을 수가 없을 거예요. 기차는 여기에 자주 운행되지도 않고요.
남2 그리고 여기는 역에서 너무 멀어요. 여러 고객들도 그 점에 대해서 불평하고 있어요.
여 제 차를 쓰는 건 어때요? 저는 집까지 걸어서 가려고 했거든요.
남1 정말요? 고마워요, Alice.

어휘 get over (장거리)를 가다, ~을 건너다 run (버스, 기차 등이 특정 노선으로) 운행하다, 다니다 evaluation 평가

41 Why does Peter want to go to a restaurant?
(A) To meet some clients
(B) To arrange an event
(C) To pick up an order
(D) To book a place

Peter는 왜 식당에 가길 원하는가?
(A) 고객을 만나기 위해
(B) 행사를 준비하기 위해
(C) 주문품을 가져오기 위해
(D) 장소를 예약하기 위해

해설 〈구체적 정보 파악 – 특정 사항〉
남자 두 명과 여자 한 명이 대화하는 3인 대화 유형이다. 여자가 Peter에게 인사를 하고 바로 남자1이 대답했으므로 그가 Peter라는 것을 알 수 있으며, 그는 식당에 가야 하는 이유로 음식을 가지러 가야 한다고 말하고 있으므로 정답은 (C)이다.

42 What does the woman mean when she says, "You'll make it"?
(A) She expects a coworker will attend a gathering.
(B) She knows who will prepare a meal.
(C) She thinks a colleague has enough time.
(D) She believes an evaluation will go well.

여자가 "갈 수 있어요"라고 말한 의미는 무엇인가?
(A) 여자는 동료가 모임에 참석할 것이라고 생각한다.
(B) 여자는 누가 음식을 준비할 것인지 알고 있다.
(C) 여자는 동료에게 충분한 시간이 있다고 생각한다.
(D) 여자는 평가가 잘 진행될 것이라고 믿고 있다.

해설 〈구체적 정보 파악 – 화자 의도〉
화자의 의도 파악을 묻는 문제 유형은 해당 표현과 주변의 문맥을 종합하여 답을 선택해야 한다. 남자2가 Peter에게 시간이 별로 없다고 하자, 여자는 문제에 언급된 표현을 말하며 여기에서 식당까지는 5분밖에 걸리지 않는다고 대답한다. 따라서 충분한 시간이 있다는 의미를 제시한 (C)가 정답이다.

43 What do the men imply about the neighborhood?
(A) It has some nice restaurants.
(B) It is inconvenient.
(C) It is growing rapidly.
(D) It was featured in a magazine.

남자들은 인근 지역에 대해 무엇이라고 암시하는가?
(A) 그곳엔 훌륭한 레스토랑이 있다.
(B) 그곳은 불편하다.
(C) 그곳은 급격히 성장했다.
(D) 그곳은 잡지에 특집으로 실렸다.

해설 〈구체적 정보 파악 – 언급〉
3인 대화에서 출제되는 화자의 공통 의견 문제로, 이 지역에 관한 두 남자의 공통적 의견을 묻고 있다. 남자1이 기차가 자주 운행되지 않는다고 언급하자 남자2가 역에서도 멀다고 말하며 동의한다. 두 남자 모두 이 지역은 통행이 불편하다고 지적하고 있으므로 정답은 (B)이다.

Questions 44-46 refer to the following conversation. 영M 미W

M I've been reading the reviews of the Finesound car stereo system. ㊹ Thanks to our campaign, their initial sales were good, ㊺ but the people who bought them seem really disappointed.

W So, you mean that our strategy was successful, but the main problem is the client's product quality?

M That's right. I think it's up to the manufacturer to address the issue.

W ㊻ Let's ask the clients to find some time to discuss our concerns. I really believe this product has a lot of potential if they can overcome this problem.

남 제가 Finesound 카 스테레오 시스템의 후기를 읽어 봤는데요. 우리 캠페인 덕분에 초기 매출은 좋았지만, 그것을 구입한 사람들의 실망은 컸던 것으로 보입니다.

여 그럼, 우리의 전략은 성공했지만, 고객 회사의 제품 품질이 문제라는 말씀이신가요?

남 맞아요. 이 문제를 해결하는 것은 제조업체에 달려 있다고 생각합니다.

여 고객 회사에 문제를 논의할 시간을 내 달라고 요청합시다. 이 문제를 극복할 수 있다면, 이 제품은 정말 많은 잠재력을 가지고 있다고 생각해요.

어휘 review 평가, 비평 initial 처음의, 초기의 strategy 전략, 계획 address the issue 문제를 해결하다 potential 가능성, 잠재력 overcome 극복하다

44 Who most likely are the speakers?
(A) Potential clients
(B) Car dealers
(C) Product designers
(D) Advertising executives

화자들은 누구인가?
(A) 잠재적 고객
(B) 자동차 판매업자
(C) 제품 디자이너
(D) 광고 회사 임원

해설 〈기본 정보 파악 – 직업〉
화자들의 직업을 묻는 문제는 초반에 단서가 제시되는 편이다. 첫 대사에서 남자가 화자들의 캠페인으로 인해 스테레오 시스템의 매출이 올랐다고 말하고 있으므로 광고 회사임을 유추할 수 있다. 따라서 정답은 (D)이다.

45 What problems are the speakers discussing?
(A) Sales figures are unimpressive.
(B) Advertising is becoming more expensive.
(C) Customer satisfaction is low.
(D) Production is behind schedule.

화자들이 논의하고 있는 문제는 무엇인가?
(A) 매출액이 특별하지 않다.
(B) 광고가 더 비싸지고 있다.
(C) 고객 만족도가 낮다.
(D) 생산이 늦어지고 있다.

해설 〈기본적 정보 파악 – 문제점〉
문제점을 묻는 문제 역시 초반에 단서가 제시되는 편이다. 남자가 첫 대사에서 고객들의 후기에 따르면 매출은 올랐으나 구매한 사람들이 실망했다고 밝히고 있으므로 (C)가 가장 적절한 답이다.

패러프레이징 disappointed 실망한 → satisfaction is low 만족도가 낮다

46 What does the woman suggest?
(A) Reading customer feedback
(B) Reviewing an instruction manual
(C) Reducing prices
(D) Calling a client meeting

여자가 제안하는 것은 무엇인가?
(A) 고객의 의견을 읽는 것
(B) 사용 설명서를 보는 것
(C) 가격을 낮추는 것
(D) 고객과의 회의를 소집하는 것

해설 〈구체적 정보 파악 – 제안 관련〉
여자의 제안 사항을 묻는 문제이다. 여자가 마지막 대사에서 고객들에게 논의할 시간을 요청하자고 의견을 제시하고 있으므로 정답은 (D)이다.

Questions 47-49 refer to the following conversation. 미M 미W

M Excuse me. ㊽ I'd like to get one of those prepaid lunch cards. ㊼ I've just joined the company, and a colleague told me to apply for one here at the personnel office.

W Do you have your employee identification card with you? We can't issue a prepaid card without it.

M Actually, I just had my photo taken for the ID, and apparently it won't be ready until the end of this week.

W Well, ㊾ I'll give you the application form so you can fill that out now. Please return to our office later with your identification card when you get it. The lunch card will be issued within five business days after we receive your application.

남 실례합니다. 선불 급식 카드를 받고 싶은데요. 제가 회사에 막 입사했는데, 동료가 이곳 인사부에 요청하라고 알려줬어요.

여 사원증 가지고 계신가요? 사원증 없이는 선불 카드를 발행해 드릴 수가 없습니다.

남 사실은 사원증에 사용할 사진을 방금 찍었는데, 듣기로는 이번 주말은 되어야 준비가 된다고 합니다.

여 그럼 우선 신청서를 드릴 테니 지금 작성해 주세요. 나중에 사원증을 받으면 사무실에 방문해 주세요. 급식 카드는 저희가 신청서를 받은 후로 5일 안에 발행될 겁니다.

어휘 prepaid 선불된 apparently 듣자 하니, 보아하니 not A until B B하고 나서야 비로소 A하다 fill out (서류, 신청서를) 작성하다 issue 발부하다, 발행하다

47 Who most likely is the man?
(A) A receptionist
(B) A new recruit
(C) A store clerk
(D) A security officer

남자는 누구인가?
(A) 접수원
(B) 신입 직원
(C) 상점 점원
(D) 경비원

해설 〈기본적 정보 파악 – 직업〉
남자의 신분을 묻는 문제로, 대화 초반에 주목해야 한다. 남자가 첫 대사에서 회사에 막 입사했다고 말하는 부분을 통해 남자가 신입 사원이라는 것을 유추할 수 있으므로 정답은 (B)이다.

48 Why does the man visit the woman?
(A) To get a refund
(B) To have an interview
(C) To apply for a card
(D) To pay for items

남자가 여자를 방문한 이유는 무엇인가?
(A) 환불을 받기 위해
(B) 면접을 보기 위해
(C) 카드를 신청하기 위해
(D) 제품을 결제하기 위해

해설 〈기본 정보 파악 – 목적〉
남자가 방문한 목적을 묻는 문제로 대화 초반에 정답의 단서가 등장한다. 남자가 첫 번째 대사에서 선불 카드를 신청하러 왔다고 언급하고 있으므로 정답은 (C)이다.

49 What will the man probably do next?
(A) Send an application form
(B) Have his photo taken
(C) Talk to a colleague
(D) Complete the document

남자가 다음에 할 일은 무엇인가?
(A) 신청서를 보낸다.
(B) 사진을 찍는다.
(C) 동료에게 이야기한다.
(D) 서류를 작성한다.

해설 〈구체적 정보 파악 – 미래〉
미래 정보 문제이므로 대화 후반부에서 정답의 단서를 찾을 수 있다. 여자가 마지막 대사에서 신청서를 줄 것이라 말하면서 신청서를 지금 작성할 수 있다고 했으므로 남자가 서류 작성을 할 것임을 알 수 있다. 따라서 정답은 (D)이다.

패러프레이징 fill the application form out 신청서를 작성하다
→ complete the form 서류를 작성하다

Questions 50-52 refer to the following conversation with three speakers. (영W) (영M) (호M)

W Chris and Greg! ㊿ I appreciate the both of you taking time out of your busy schedules today to discuss this consumer survey.
M1 It's no trouble at all.
M2 We know how important the research will be in developing a successful promotional strategy.
W What do you think of the initial draft of our questionnaire?
M1 Well, the questions are all very good, but some seem a bit repetitive. ㊿1 I'd recommend dropping a few.
M2 ㊿1 That makes two of us. Plus, you'll probably get a lot more responses if the form doesn't take long to complete.
W Those are convincing points. ㊿2 I'll be sure to pass them along to the project manager at our next meeting.

여 Chris and Greg! 이 소비자 설문 조사 논의를 위해 바쁜 일정에도 시간을 내주신 두 분께 감사드려요.
남1 전혀 어려운 일이 아닙니다.
남2 저희는 성공적인 프로모션 전략을 개발하는 데 있어서 이 조사가 얼마나 중요한지 알고 있어요.
여 우리 설문지의 초안에 대해 어떻게 생각하시나요?
남1 음, 질문들이 아주 좋긴 하지만 몇 가지가 약간 반복되는 부분이 있는 것 같아요. 조금 삭제할 것을 추천해 드립니다.
남2 저도 같은 생각입니다. 게다가, 아마도 이 양식을 작성하는 데 시간이 오래 걸리지 않는다면, 더 많은 응답을 받게 될 겁니다.
여 설득력 있는 지적이네요. 다음 회의에서 프로젝트 매니저에게 꼭 전달하겠습니다.

어휘 consumer survey 소비자 설문 조사 promotional strategy 광고 전략 initial 처음의, 초기의 draft 원고, 초안 questionnaire 설문지 repetitive 반복적인, 반복되는 drop ~을 빼다 That makes two of us 나도 마찬가지이다, 같은 생각이다 convincing 설득력 있는 pass along 전달하다, 알리다

50 What are the speakers mainly discussing?
(A) A research budget
(B) A consumer campaign
(C) A managerial promotion
(D) A marketing survey
화자들이 주로 논의하는 것은 무엇인가?
(A) 연구 예산
(B) 소비자 캠페인
(C) 경영 촉진
(D) 마케팅 설문 조사

해설 〈기본적 정보 파악 – 주제〉
대화의 주제를 묻는 문제로 초반부에서 정답의 근거를 찾아야 한다. 첫 대사에서 여자가 바쁜 일정 중에도 설문 조사 논의를 위해 시간을 내 준 것에 대해 감사 인사를 하고 있으므로 정답은 (D)이다.

51 What do the men suggest?
(A) Emphasizing particular points
(B) Shortening a form
(C) Conducting longer interviews
(D) Extending a deadline
남자들이 제안하는 것은 무엇인가?
(A) 특정 포인트 강조하는 것
(B) 양식을 단축시키는 것
(C) 더 긴 인터뷰를 실시하는 것
(D) 마감일을 연장하는 것

해설 〈구체적 정보 파악 – 제안 관련〉
3인 대화에서 출제되는 화자의 공통 의견을 묻는 문제이다. 대화 후반에 남자1이 설문 조사에 반복되는 부분이 있으니 조금 뺄 것을 추천하자 남자2가 남자1의 의견에 동의하며 부연 설명하고 있다. 따라서 (B) 정답이다.

패러프레이징 drop a few 몇 개를 빼다 → shorten 짧게 하다, 단축하다

52 What does the woman decide to do?
(A) Make a few revisions to a document
(B) Find a way to satisfy customers
(C) Alter the schedule for a meeting
(D) Relay some feedback
여자는 무엇을 하기로 결심하는가?
(A) 문서를 몇 군데 수정하는 것
(B) 고객들을 만족시킬 방법을 찾는 것
(C) 회의 일정을 변경하는 것
(D) 피드백을 전달하는 것

해설 〈구체적 정보 파악 – 특정 사항〉
여자의 결정 사항에 관한 구체적 정보를 묻는 질문이므로 여자의 말에서 단서가 제시될 것임을 예측할 수 있다. 여자가 마지막 대사에서 앞서 남자들이 지적한 사항들을 다음 회의에서 프로젝트 매니저에게 전달할 것이라고 말하고 있으므로 정답은 (D)이다.

Questions 53-55 refer to the following conversation. (미W) (미M)

W Hi, Joseph. ㊿3 Do you have time to go over this press release I just drafted?
M Certainly. What's it about?
W It describes some updates that we plan for our Web site.
M Oh, yeah? I read about that in the company newsletter. ㊿4 I bet a lot of our customers will be making use of the new financial services we'll be offering. So many people are doing their banking online these days.
W Well, who can blame them? ㊿5 It's so much more convenient than going into a branch.

여 안녕하세요, Joseph, 제가 방금 작성한 보도 자료 초안을 검토해 주실 시간이 있으신가요?
남 물론입니다. 무엇에 관한 거죠?
여 우리가 계획한 웹 사이트 업데이트에 관한 내용입니다.
남 아, 그런가요? 사보에서 그에 대해 읽었어요. 많은 고객들이 우리가 제공할 새로운 금융 서비스들을 사용할 거라고 저는 장담해요. 요즘 많은 사람들이 온라인 뱅킹을 하고 있잖아요.
여 맞아요, 누가 그들을 탓할 수 있겠어요? 그것이 지점에 가는 것보다 훨씬 더 편리하니까요.

어휘 press release 보도 자료 newsletter 소식지 blame ~을 탓하다, ~책임으로 보다

53 What does the woman ask the man to do?
(A) Review her work
(C) Draft a report
(D) Release some records
(D) Update a Web site
여자는 남자에게 무엇을 하라고 요청하는가?
(A) 여자의 작업을 검토하는 것
(B) 보고서 초안을 작성하는 것
(C) 음반을 발매하는 것
(D) 웹 사이트를 업데이트하는 것

해설 〈구체적 정보 파악 – 요청 관련〉
여자의 요청 사항을 묻는 문제이므로 여자의 대사에서 단서를 찾아야 한다. 여자가 첫 대사에서 보도 자료를 검토할 시간이 있는지 남자에게 묻고 있으므로 정답은 (A)이다.

54 What kind of organization do the speakers work for?
(A) A marketing company
(B) A banking firm
(C) A newspaper
(D) A software company
화자들이 근무하는 곳은 어떤 종류의 회사인가?

(A) 마케팅 회사
(B) 금융 회사
(C) 신문사
(D) 소프트웨어 회사

해설 〈기본 정보 파악 – 장소〉
화자들이 일하는 장소를 묻는 문제는 대화 초반에 단서가 나오는 경우가 많으나, 이 문제는 중반부에 근거가 제시되므로 주의해야 한다. 남자가 두 번째 대사에서 우리가 제공할 금융 서비스를 많은 고객들이 사용하게 될 것이라며 화자들의 업무를 설명하고 있다. 따라서 정답은 (B)이다.

패러프레이징 financial services 금융 서비스 → banking firm 금융 회사

55 What does the woman mean when she says, "who can blame them"?
(A) Customers did not cause the problem.
(B) Customers are likely to make some complaints.
(C) Customers' confusion was expected.
(D) Customers' behavior is understandable.

여자가 "누가 그들을 탓할 수 있겠어요?"라고 말하는 의미는 무엇인가?
(A) 고객들이 문제를 일으키지 않았다.
(B) 고객들이 불만을 제기할 가능성이 있다.
(C) 고객들의 혼란이 예상되었다.
(D) 고객들의 행동은 당연한 것이다.

해설 〈구체적 정보 파악 – 화자 의도〉
화자의 의도 파악 문제 유형은 해당 표현과 주변의 문맥을 종합하여 답을 선택해야 한다. 문제의 표현 앞뒤를 살펴보면, 먼저 남자가 요즘 많은 사람들이 인터넷 뱅킹을 사용한다고 말하자 여자도 그것이 훨씬 더 편리하다며 부연 설명을 하고 있으므로 정답은 (D)이다.

Questions 56-58 refer to the following conversation with three speakers. 미W 영W 영M

W1 Can I ask you guys a favor? ⑯ I'm scheduled to wait tables on Monday from 7 A.M. to 3 P.M., but I have a doctor's appointment at noon. ⑰ Could someone possibly cover my breakfast shift?
M Sorry, Heather, but I can't. I'm off both Monday and Tuesday this week.
W1 Oh, thanks anyway.
M I wish I could help.
W1 Olivia, do you think you could do it?
W2 Well, I start my shift at 11 A.M. that day. What time do you think you can be here?
W1 I don't expect the appointment to last more than an hour, so I'm sure I'll be in by about 1:30 P.M. Does that work for you?
W2 You bet. ⑱ Maybe you could cover one of my shifts next month when I go on my camping trip.

여1 여러분에게 부탁 좀 해도 될까요? 제가 월요일 오전 7시에서 오후 3시까지 서빙 근무를 하기로 되어 있는데, 12시에 병원 진료 예약이 있어요. 아침 근무를 대신해 주실 분 있으세요?
남 Heather, 미안하지만, 저는 안 돼요. 이번 주는 월요일과 화요일 모두 쉬는 날이거든요.
여1 아, 어쨌든 감사해요.
남 제가 도울 수 있으면 좋을 텐데요.
여1 Olivia, 해줄 수 있어요?
여2 음, 저는 그날 오전 11시에 근무를 시작해요. 몇 시에 오실 수 있어요?
여1 진료가 1시간 이상은 안 걸릴 테니, 대략 오후 1시 반까지는 올 수 있어요. 괜찮을까요?
여2 물론이죠. 다음 달에 제가 캠핑 여행 갈 때는 당신이 교대 근무를 대신 해 주면 되겠네요.

어휘 wait tables (웨이터, 웨이트리스가) 서빙하다 cover (자리 비운 사람의 일을) 대신하다 You bet 물론이죠

56 What best describes the speakers' jobs?
(A) They are medical staff.
(B) They are cashiers.
(C) They are office employees.
(D) They are restaurant servers.

화자의 직업에 대해 가장 잘 묘사한 것은 무엇인가?
(A) 그들은 의료진이다.
(B) 그들은 계산원들이다.
(C) 그들은 사무실 직원들이다.
(D) 그들은 레스토랑에서 서빙하는 사람들이다.

해설 〈기본 정보 파악 – 직업〉
화자들의 직업을 묻는 문제로 대화 초반에 집중해야 한다. 여자1이 첫 대사에서 월요일에 서빙 근무 일정이 잡혀 있다고 언급하고 있으므로 정답은 (D)이다.

57 What does Heather ask the other two people to do?
(A) Assign her different hours
(B) Have breakfast with her
(C) Go on a camping trip with her
(D) Fill in for her at work

Heather가 다른 두 사람에게 해 달라고 요청하는 것은 무엇인가?
(A) 여자에게 다른 시간들을 할당하는 것
(B) 여자와 아침 식사를 함께 하는 것
(C) 여자와 캠핑 여행을 같이 가는 것
(D) 여자 대신 근무를 해 주는 것

해설 〈구체적 정보 파악 – 요청〉
3인 대화에서 특정인이 나머지 두 사람에게 요청하는 사항을 묻는 질문이므로 우선 질문에 언급된 Heather가 누구인지 파악해야 한다. 여자1이 첫 대사에서 교대 근무를 대신해 줄 수 있는 사람을 구하고 있다고 언급하자 남자가 이름을 부르며 대답하고 있으므로 여자1이 Heather임을 알 수 있다. 따라서 여자1이 요청하는 내용을 적절히 묘사한 (D)가 정답이다.

패러프레이징 cover 대신하다 → fill in for ~을 대신(대리)하다

58 What does Olivia imply?
(A) She cannot accommodate the request.
(B) She'll be off that day.
(C) Heather should return the favor.
(D) Heather should change her appointment.

Olivia가 암시하는 것은 무엇인가?
(A) 그녀는 요청을 수용할 수 없다.
(B) 그녀는 그날 쉬는 날이다.
(C) Heather가 호의에 보답해 주어야 한다.
(D) Heather가 예약을 바꿔야 한다.

해설 〈구체적 정보 파악 – 언급〉
제3자의 이름을 언급하며 이 사람이 말하는 의미를 묻는 문제이다. 문제에서 언급된 이름의 사람이 대화의 화자가 될 가능성과 제3자일 가능성이 있는데, 3인 대화에서는 많은 경우 대화에 등장하는 화자일 가능성이 높다. 그러므로 이름이 언급된 후 대답하는 사람이 당사자이므로 그 대사에서 답을 찾아야 한다. 대화 중반부에서 여자1이 Olivia를 부른 후 여자2가 대답하므로 여자2가 Olivia임을 알 수 있으며, 여자2가 마지막 대사에서 요청을 들어주면 다음 달에 교대 근무를 대신해 달라고 말하고 있다. 따라서 정답은 (C)이다.

Questions 59-61 refer to the following conversation. 미W 영M

W Thomas, I was wondering if you could help me. (59) I'm thinking of changing my Internet service provider. Could you give me some advice?

M Which Internet company are you using now? There are several service providers with different packages, depending on both the length of contract and voice service bundles.

W Actually, (60) high-speed Internet is what I'm considering the most. That's the bottom line. Also I'm being transferred to overseas in about a year so I just want the short-term agreement.

M (61) Why don't you check a Internet provider comparison Web site? There are a few sites that show the different options and packages.

여 Thomas, 당신이 좀 도와줄 수 있는지 궁금해요. 제가 인터넷 서비스 제공 업체를 바꿀까 생각 중인데, 조언해 주실 수 있나요?

남 지금 어떤 인터넷 업체를 사용하고 있나요? 서로 다른 패키지들을 제공하는 여러 서비스 업체들이 있어서 당신이 선택하는 계약 기간과 전화 서비스 묶음에 따라 달라져요.

여 사실, 빠른 인터넷 속도가 제가 가장 중요하게 여기는 부분이에요. 그게 핵심이죠. 게다가 저는 1년 후에 외국으로 전근 갈 거예요. 그래서 단기 약정을 원해요.

남 인터넷 제공 업체 비교 사이트를 확인해 보는 것은 어때요? 다양한 옵션 및 패키지를 보여 주는 몇 군데가 있어요.

어휘 Internet service provider 인터넷 서비스 제공 업체 bundle 묶음 depending on ~에 따라 bottom line 핵심, 요점, 중요한 요소 seldom 거의 ~하지 않는

59 Why does the woman ask for advice?
(A) To replace a current service
(B) To purchase a computer
(C) To provide a new device
(D) To design a Web site

여자가 조언을 요청한 이유는 무엇인가?
(A) 현재 서비스를 바꾸기 위해서
(B) 컴퓨터를 구입하기 위해서
(C) 새로운 기기를 제공하기 위해서
(D) 웹 사이트를 디자인하기 위해서

해설 〈구체적 정보 파악 – 요청 관련〉
여자가 요청하는 내용은 여자의 대사에서 찾아야 한다. 여자가 첫 대사에서 인터넷 서비스 제공 업체를 바꾸려고 한다고 말하며 조언을 구하고 있으므로 정답은 (A)이다.

60 Why does the woman say, "That's the bottom line"?
(A) She wants the long-term plan.
(B) She wants a cheap price.
(C) She uses Internet frequently.
(D) She wants fast online access.

여자는 왜 "그것이 핵심이다"라고 말하는가?
(A) 여자는 긴 기간의 약정을 원한다.
(B) 여자는 저렴한 가격을 원한다.
(C) 여자는 자주 인터넷을 사용한다.
(D) 여자는 빠른 온라인 접속을 원한다.

해설 〈구체적 정보 파악 – 화자 의도〉
제시된 문장을 주변 문맥과 함께 종합하여 여자의 의도를 파악해야 한다. 여자가 문제 표현 바로 앞에 가장 중요하게 여기는 것은 빠른 인터넷 속도라고 언급하고 있으므로 정답은 (D)이다.

패러프레이징 high speed Internet 고속 인터넷 → fast online access 빠른 온라인 접속

61 What is the woman advised to do?
(A) Transfer to an overseas branch
(B) Get some feedback
(C) Compare options on the Internet
(D) Read some product instructions

여자는 어떻게 하라고 충고받고 있는가?
(A) 해외 지사로 전근 가기
(B) 피드백 받기
(C) 인터넷에서 옵션을 비교하기
(D) 제품 설명서를 읽기

해설 〈구체적 정보 파악 – 제안 관련〉
수동태형 질문으로 남자가 제안하는 내용을 묻는 문제이다. 대화 후반부의 남자의 말에서 근거를 찾아야 하는데 남자가 온라인에서 비교 사이트를 확인하라고 말하고 있으므로 정답은 (C)이다.

Questions 62-64 refer to the following conversation and table. 미M 미W

Model	Price ($)
Modern 765 (Black and White)	1,530
Solusi 300 (Color)	1,720
Primark 200 (Black and White)	1,940
Allthatprint 500 (Color)	2,250

M (62) I have received a request from the advertising department for a new printer. They need one that can handle banners and really large posters.

W Yeah, (63) I spoke with Mr. Warren, their department head, about that yesterday. He said he wants to be able to produce color documents.

M Hmm...They're not cheap.

W Well, (64) the most we can afford is $2,000 so get the best one you can within the budget. Do you have the brochure I sent you yesterday?

M OK. I'm looking at it right now. The next most expensive one only prints black and white.

W I'll leave it up to you.

모델	가격(달러)
Modern 765(흑백)	1,530
Solusi 300(컬러)	1,720
Primark 200(흑백)	1,940
Allthatprint 500(컬러)	2,250

남 광고부로부터 새 프린터에 대한 요청을 받았어요. 그들은 현수막과 아주 큰 포스터를 다룰 수 있는 프린터가 필요하답니다.

여 네, 제가 어제 부서의 책임자인 Warren 씨와 그것에 관련된 얘기를 했어요. 그는 컬러 문서들을 제작하고 싶다고 말하더군요.

남 음... 비용이 싸지 않은데요.

여 우리가 감당할 수 있는 금액은 최대 2천 달러이니 그 예산 안에서 살 수 있는 가장 좋은 것으로 구입해 주세요. 제가 어제 보내드린 책자를 가지고 있나요?

남 네, 지금 보고 있어요. 두 번째로 비싼 것은 흑백만 프린트하는 거네요.

여 당신에게 맡길게요.

어휘 handle 다루다, 처리하다 banner 플래카드, 현수막

62 According to the man, what has the advertising department requested?
(A) A client list

(B) A customer code
(C) An office device
(D) An e-mail address

남자에 따르면, 광고부가 요청한 것은 무엇인가?
(A) 고객 리스트
(B) 사용자 코드
(C) 사무기기
(D) 이메일 주소

해설 〈구체적 정보 파악 – 요청 관련〉
advertising department를 키워드로 잡고, 남자가 광고부를 언급하는 부분에서 단서를 찾아야 한다. 첫 대사에서 남자가 광고부로부터 새 프린터를 요청을 받았다고 언급하고 있으므로 정답은 (C)이다.
패러프레이징 printer 프린터 → office device 사무기기

63 Who most likely is Mr. Warren?
(A) A client
(B) A supplier
(C) A manufacturer
(D) A supervisor

Warren 씨는 누구인가?
(A) 고객
(B) 공급업자
(C) 제조업자
(D) 관리자

해설 〈구체적 정보 파악 – 언급〉
Mr. Warren을 키워드로 잡고, 앞뒤를 잘 들어야 한다. 여자가 첫 번째 대사에서 부서 책임자인 Mr. Warren과 얘기했다고 말하고 있으므로 정답은 (D)이다.

64 Look at the graphic. How much will the company most likely pay for the order?
(A) $1,530
(B) $1,720
(C) $1,940
(D) $2,250

시각 자료를 보시오. 회사는 그 주문에 얼마의 비용을 지불할 것인가?
(A) 1,530달러
(B) 1,720달러
(C) 1,940달러
(D) 2,250달러

해설 〈구체적 정보 파악 – 시각 자료 연계〉
가장 먼저 선택지와 시각 자료의 관계를 파악해야 한다. 상품의 가격이 선택지로 제시되어 있으므로 정답의 단서는 가격별로 달라지는 상품의 종류가 될 것으로 예측할 수 있다. 여자가 대화 중반에 최대 2,000달러 범위 내의 예산에서 가장 좋은 것을 구입하자고 제안했다. 따라서 컬러 프린터이면서 2,000달러 예산 안에서 구입할 수 있는 프린터는 Solusi 300이므로 해당 가격인 (B)가 정답이다.

Questions 65-67 refer to the following conversation and coupon.
영M 미W

Jade's Diner
Present this coupon for
30% off lunch
or
20% off dinner
Valid for parties of up to 3
Expires June 18

M How was everything today? Did you enjoy your lunch?
W Everything was great, and your service was excellent, as always.
M 65 We really appreciate your repeat business. Can I get you anything else? Dessert perhaps?
W No, thanks. I'm ready for my check. 66 My lunch break's almost over and I need to head back to the office.
M All right. I'll be right back.
W Oh, that reminds me. I have this coupon for a discount. Should I give it to you now?
M Sure. The coupon's still valid. 67 Let me go calculate your charges and I'll bring you your bill.

제이드 식당
이 쿠폰을 제시하면
점심 30% 할인
또는
저녁 20% 할인
일행 3명까지 유효
만료일 6월 18일

남 오늘 음식은 어떠셨나요? 점심 식사는 맛있게 하셨어요?
여 모두 다 좋았어요. 항상 그런 것처럼 서비스도 훌륭하고요.
남 다시 찾아 주셔서 정말 감사드립니다. 다른 것 좀 가져다 드릴까요? 디저트 같은 거 드릴까요?
여 아니요. 괜찮습니다. 계산서 주세요. 제 점심시간이 거의 끝나가고 있어서 사무실로 돌아가야 하거든요.
남 알겠습니다. 금방 오겠습니다.
여 아, 그러고 보니 생각나네요. 할인 쿠폰이 있는데 지금 드려도 될까요?
남 그럼요. 이 쿠폰은 아직 사용 가능하네요. 제가 가서 당신의 비용을 계산하고 청구서를 가지고 오겠습니다.

어휘 appreciate 고마워하다 repeat business 지속적인 거래 check 계산서 valid 유효한 bill 청구서, 계산서

65 What does the man indicate about the woman?
(A) She ordered a dessert.
(B) She is a regular customer.
(C) She owns a business.
(D) She works near the restaurant.

남자는 여자에 대해 무엇을 암시하는가?
(A) 여자는 디저트를 주문했다.
(B) 여자는 단골 고객이다.
(C) 여자는 사업체를 소유하고 있다.
(D) 여자는 레스토랑 근처에서 일하고 있다.

해설 〈구체적 정보 파악 – 언급〉
남자가 여자에 대해 언급한 사항에 대한 질문이므로 남자의 말에서 정답을 찾아야 한다. 식사를 마친 여자에게 남자는 다시 찾아주셔서 감사하다는 인사를 하고 있으므로 여자가 이 식당에 종종 방문한다는 것을 알 수 있다. 따라서 정답은 (B)이다.
패러프레이징 repeat business 지속적인 거래
→ regular customer 단골 고객

66 Look at the graphic. How much of a discount will the woman receive?
(A) 5%
(B) 10%
(C) 20%
(D) 30%

시각 자료를 보시오. 여자는 얼마의 할인을 받게 되는가?
(A) 5%
(B) 10%
(C) 20%
(D) 30%

해설 〈구체적 정보 파악 – 시각 자료 연계〉
대화를 듣기 전에 문제와 시각 자료를 보고 단서를 예측할 수 있어야 한다. 선택지가 할인율로 구성되어 있으며 시각 자료인 쿠폰에는 식사 종류에 따라 할인율이 다르게 표시되어 있으므로 점심식사인지 저녁식사인지를 통해 단서가 제시될 가능성이 높다. 첫 대사에서 점심식사에 대한 언급이 있었으며 중반부에 여자가 점심시간이 끝나간다고 말하는 부분에서 이 쿠폰이 점심식사에 사용될 것을 알 수 있다. 따라서 정답은 (D)다.

67 What does the man say he will do?
(A) Speak to a manager
(B) Accept a credit card
(C) Make a calculation
(D) Fax an invoice

남자는 무엇을 하겠다고 말하는가?
(A) 관리자에게 말한다.
(B) 신용 카드를 받는다.
(C) 계산을 한다.
(D) 영수증을 팩스로 보낸다.

해설 〈구체적 정보 파악 – 미래〉
앞으로 일어날 일을 묻는 문제는 후반부에 단서가 제시된다. 남자가 계산 후에 청구서를 가지고 오겠다고 언급하므로 (C)가 정답이다.

Questions 68-70 refer to the following conversation and chart. 미M 미W

Candidate Test Score

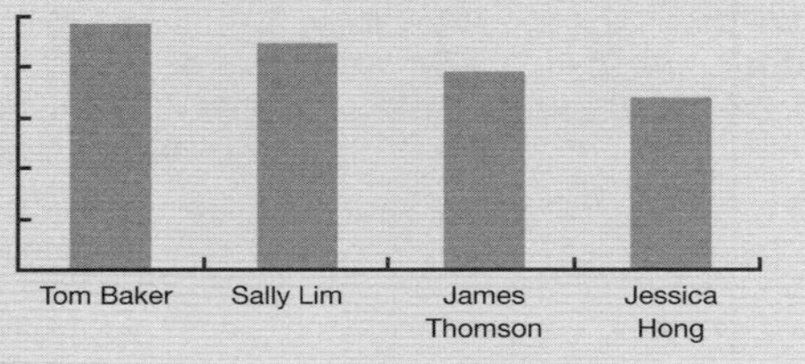

M ⑱ We just got an e-mail from Besthires.com reminding us that our job advertisement is due to be removed from their Web site tomorrow. They asked whether we want to keep it posted for another month.
W No, we have four strong candidates who all qualify for the position. One of them will certainly get the offer. I just haven't decided which one.
M Okay, ⑲ I'll write back to Besthires.com and let them know.
W Thanks, Dean. I'd appreciate that.
M No problem. So, is the man you interviewed today among the four you're considering?
W Yes, he is. ⑳ Two candidates scored higher on the test than he did, but his interview was the most impressive.

후보자 테스트 점수

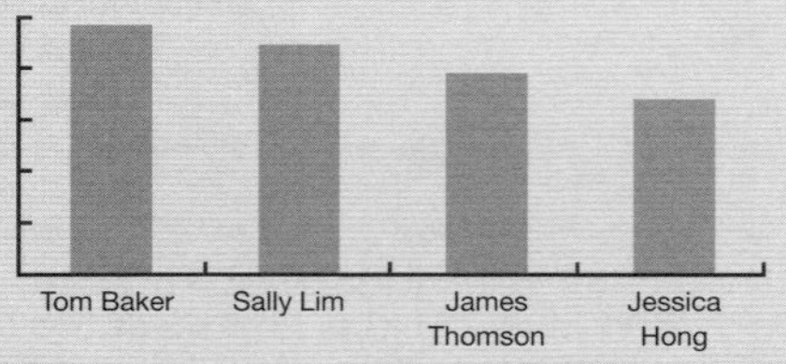

남 방금 Besthires.com으로부터 이메일을 받았는데, 내일 그들의 웹 사이트에서 우리의 채용 공고가 삭제될 예정이랍니다. 한 달 더 공지를 게시하기를 원하는지 물었습니다.
여 안 할 겁니다. 그 직책에 적합한 4명의 유력한 후보자가 있거든요. 그들 중 한 명은 분명히 제안을 받게 될 거예요. 제가 아직 누구를 선택할지 결정하지 않았어요.
남 알겠습니다. 그럼 Besthires.com에 답장을 써서 알려야겠네요.
여 고마워요. Dean. 그래 주면 고맙겠어요.
남 알겠습니다. 그래서 오늘 면접 본 남자가 당신이 고려 중인 네 명 중에 있나요?
여 네, 맞아요. 두 명의 후보자가 테스트에서 그보다 더 높은 점수를 받긴 했지만 그의 면접이 가장 인상적이었어요.

어휘 post 게시하다 candidate 후보자 score 점수, 득점 screen 확인하다, 가려내다 job description 직무 설명서

68 How was the job opening probably advertised?
(A) In a trade journal
(B) On some posters
(C) In a newspaper
(D) On a Web site

채용 공고는 어떻게 광고되었는가?
(A) 무역 저널에
(B) 포스터에
(C) 신문에
(D) 웹 사이트에

해설 〈구체적 정보 파악 – 특정 사항〉
구인 광고가 어디에 실렸는지 묻는 질문이다. Job opening, advertised를 키워드로 잡고 이 단어들이 언급되는 부분에서 정답을 찾아야 한다. 남자의 첫 대사에서 채용 공고가 웹 사이트에서 삭제될 것이라고 언급했으므로 정답은 (D)이다.

69 What does the man offer to do?
(A) Reply to an organization
(B) Screen résumés from applicants
(C) Write a job description
(D) Extend a deadline for a project

남자는 무엇을 하겠다고 제안하는가?
(A) 한 회사에 회신을 한다.
(B) 지원자들의 이력서를 가려낸다.
(C) 직무 설명서를 작성한다.
(D) 프로젝트의 마감 기한을 연장한다.

해설 〈구체적 정보 파악 – 제안 관련〉
남자가 제안하는 내용이므로 남자의 말에서 단서를 찾아야 한다. 남자가 두 번째 대사에서 해당 회사에 답장을 쓰겠다고 말하므로 정답은 (A)이다.

패러프레이징 write back 답장을 쓰다 → reply 답장을 보내다

70 Look at the graphic. Who does the woman say gave the most impressive interview?
(A) Tom Baker
(B) Sally Lim
(C) James Thomson
(D) Jessica Hong

시각 자료를 보시오. 여자는 누구의 면접이 가장 인상적이었다고 말하는가?
(A) Tom Baker
(B) Sally Lim
(C) James Thomson
(D) Jessica Hong

해설 〈구체적 정보 파악 – 시각 정보〉
문제의 선택지가 그래프의 가로축인 후보자의 이름이다. 따라서 정답의 단서는 그래프의 세로축이 되어야 하지만, 주어진 그래프의 세로축에는 숫자 정보가 없으므로 그래프의 높낮이가 정답의 단서가 될 것을 인지하고 대화를 들어야 한다. 그래프의 높낮이는 후보자들의 테스트 점수이므로 이 부분과 문제의 키워드인 most impressive가 언급되는 곳에 집중한다. 대화의 마지막에 여자가 높은 점수를 받은 두 사람이 있지만, 그의 인터뷰가 가장 인상적이었다고 언급하므로 세 번째로 높은 점수를 받은 (C)가 정답임을 알 수 있다.

PART 4

Questions 71-73 refer to the following advertisement. 호M

Whether you're on the road for work or traveling on vacation, there's a Travel Lodge just where you need it. ⑪ ⑫ With over 250 Travel Lodges across the country, we can provide you with a clean, comfortable room nearly anywhere you travel. All locations include free Wi-Fi Internet access, free satellite TV, and complimentary coffee and toast in the morning. ⑬ Throughout August, if you make a reservation through our Web site at www.travellodge.com, we'll take ten percent off our regular nightly rates. Next time you make travel plans, be sure to include a stay at Travel Lodge.

출장 중이거나, 휴가차 여행 중이거나 당신이 필요로 하는 곳 어디든지 Travel Lodge가 있습니다. 저희는 전국에 250개가 넘는 Travel Lodge로 당신이 가는 어느 곳에서나 깨끗하고 편안한 숙소를 제공합니다. 모든 지점에는 무료 와이파이 인터넷 사용, 무료 위성 텔레비전 그리고 무료 커피와 토스트 조식이 포함됩니다. 8월 한 달 동안, 저희 웹 사이트 www.travellodge.com으로 예약을 하시면, 기본 숙박 요금에서 10% 할인을 받으실 수 있습니다. 당신의 다음 여행 계획에는 Travel Lodge에 숙박하는 것을 반드시 포함시켜 주시기 바랍니다.

어휘 on the road 여행(이동) 중인 lodge 오두막, 산장 satellite 위성 complimentary 무료의 catering 음식 출장 courteous 친절한, 공손한

71 What is being advertised?
(A) A tour agency
(B) A hotel chain
(C) A catering service
(D) An airline company

무엇을 광고하고 있는가?
(A) 여행사
(B) 호텔 체인
(C) 음식 출장 서비스
(D) 항공사

해설 〈기본 정보 파악 – 주제〉
무엇에 대한 광고인지를 묻는 주제 문제이므로 담화의 전반부에서 답을 찾아야 한다. 담화의 전반부에 어디로 여행을 가든 깨끗하고 편안한 방을 제공한다고 설명하고 있으므로 숙소 광고라는 것을 알 수 있다. 따라서 정답은 (B)이다.

72 According to the advertisement, what advantage does the business offer?
(A) Easy access
(B) Courteous service
(C) Corporate rates
(D) Membership bonuses

광고에 의하면, 이 업체는 어떤 혜택을 제공하는가?
(A) 편리한 접근성
(B) 친절한 접객
(C) 법인 요금
(D) 회원 보너스

해설 〈구체적 정보 파악 – 특정 사항〉
광고하는 구체적 내용에 관한 문제이다. 담화의 초반에 숙박 시설이 전국에 250개가 넘는다고 설명하며 접근이 편리한 점을 언급을 하고 있다. 따라서 정답은 (A)이다.

73 What will happen in August?
(A) A facility will be expanded.
(B) A discount will be offered.
(C) A Web site will be upgraded.
(D) A selection will be widened.

8월에 무슨 일이 있을 것인가?
(A) 시설이 확장될 것이다.
(B) 할인이 제공될 것이다.
(C) 웹 사이트가 업그레이드될 것이다.
(D) 선택 옵션이 확대될 것이다.

해설 〈구체적 정보 파악 – 시점〉
in August를 키워드로 잡고 그 주위에 언급되는 내용을 단서로 정답을 찾아야 한다. 대화 후반부에 8월 동안 웹 사이트를 통해 예약을 하면 10%의 할인을 제공한다고 설명하고 있으므로 정답은 (B)이다.

패러프레이징 ten percent off 10% 할인 → discount 할인

Questions 74-76 refer to the following announcement. 영M

Attention, all passengers. On behalf of FlyBE Airlines, I'd like to offer my sincere apologies for the delay. ⑭ Due to the weather conditions, the runway is extremely crowded. ⑮ It looks like we won't be able to take off until 6 P.M., 30 minutes after our scheduled time of 5:30 P.M. This means our arrival will also be late. Those of you with connecting flights can speak to our flight crew. We will be serving a meal once we get in the air, but before takeoff, ⑯ I suggest you read our in-flight magazine that has been recently updated. Once again, I apologize for the inconvenience.

승객 여러분께 알려드립니다. FlyBE 항공을 대표하여 지연에 대해 진심으로 사과의 말씀을 전합니다. 기상 조건으로 인하여, 활주로가 극심하게 혼잡한 상태입니다. 이로 인해 예정된 5시 30분보다 30분 늦은 오후 6시는 되어서야 이륙이 가능할 것으로 보입니다. 이것은 우리의 도착도 늦어짐을 의미합니다. 비행기를 갈아타실 승객 여러분들께서는 저희 승무원에게 얘기해 주시기 바랍니다. 저희 비행기가 상공에 진입하게 되면 식사를 제공해 드릴 예정입니다. 그러나 이륙 전까지는 최신 업데이트된 기내 잡지를 읽어보실 것을 권해드립니다. 다시 한 번, 불편을 드린 점 대단히 죄송합니다.

어휘 sincere apologies 진심 어린 사과 runway 활주로 extremely 극도로 not A until B B가 되어서야 A하다 in the air 공중에 takeoff 출발, 이륙

74 Why has the fight been delayed?
(A) The runway is busy.
(B) The plane has a mechanical problem.
(C) The fog prevented the plane from departing.
(D) Boarding took a long time.

비행기가 지연된 이유는 무엇인가?
(A) 활주로가 복잡하다.
(B) 비행기에 기계적 결함이 있다.
(C) 안개로 인하여 비행기가 이륙하지 못했다.
(D) 탑승에 시간이 오래 걸렸다.

해설 〈구체적 정보 파악 – 이유〉
delayed를 키워드로 잡고 비행기 지연에 관한 이유를 들어야 한다. 담화 전반부에 지연에 대한 사과의 말을 한 후, 날씨로 인해 활주로가 혼잡하다고 알리고 있으므로 정답은 (A)이다. 활주로의 혼잡 이유는 날씨 때문이지만 선택지에 기상 조건을 의미하는 것은 없으므로 가장 적절한 (A)가 정답이다. 또한 기상 조건 중의 하나인 안개(fog)를 담화에서 언급하지는 않았으므로 (C)와 혼동하지 않도록 주의한다.

패러프레이징 crowded 혼잡한 → busy 복잡한

75 What time will the flight depart?
(A) 5:00 P.M.
(B) 5:30 P.M.
(C) 6:00 P.M.
(D) 6:30 P.M.

비행기는 몇 시에 이륙할 것인가?
(A) 오후 5시
(B) 오후 5시 30분
(C) 오후 6시
(D) 오후 6시 30분

해설 〈구체적 정보 파악 – 시간〉
비행 이륙 시간 관련 문제이므로 depart를 키워드로 잡고 담화에서는 같은 의미인 take off(이륙)를 언급할 때 답을 찾아야 한다. 6시는 되어서야 이륙할 것이라고 언급하고 있으므로 정답은 (C)이다. Not A until B(B가 되어서야 A한다)의 의미 파악과, 정답 언급 이후에 나오는 다른 시간 표현들에 혼동하지 않도록 주의한다.

76 What does the speaker suggest the listeners do?
(A) Relax in the lounge
(B) Take a look at some reading materials
(C) Fill out a form
(D) Revise their schedule

화자는 청자에게 무엇을 하라고 권하는가?
(A) 라운지에서 쉬는 것
(B) 읽을거리를 보는 것
(C) 양식을 채우는 것
(D) 일정을 수정하는 것

해설 〈구체적 정보 파악 – 요청 관련〉
요청 사항을 묻는 문제이므로 suggest를 키워드로 잡고 담화 후반부에서 답을 찾아야 한다. 담화 후반부에 화자가 기내 잡지를 읽으라고 권유하고 있으므로 정답은 (B)이다.

패러프레이징 magazine 잡지 → reading materials 읽을거리

Questions 77-79 refer to the following telephone message. 영W

Hello, Mr. Aston. My name is Lisa Rodriguez and I represent Dantos Incorporated. ⑰ We're organizing a five-day seminar on how to maximize employees' potential and we're looking for people with management experience to lead workshops during the event. ⑱ You were referred to us by Jennifer Ward. She told me that she used to work under you at General Consulting, and said you would be ideally suited to this position. We'd be very interested in having you join us. The seminar runs from Monday, June 18 to Friday 22. ⑲ If you're interested, please get back to me at your convenience. I can be reached on my cell phone at 303-555-9935. I'm looking forward to hearing from you.

안녕하세요. Aston 씨. 저는 Dantos 사의 Lisa Rodriguez입니다. 저희는 직원들의 잠재력을 극대화시키는 방법에 대한 5일 간의 세미나를 계획하고 있는데, 행사 중 워크숍 안내를 담당할 관리 경험이 있는 사람을 찾고 있습니다. Jennifer Ward가 당신을 언급했는데, General Consulting에서 일할 당시 당신 밑에서 일을 했었고, 당신이 이 자리에 적합할 것이라고 저에게 말해 주었습니다. 우리는 당신이 우리와 함께해 주기를 바랍니다. 세미나는 6월 18일 월요일부터 22일 금요일까지 진행됩니다. 관심이 있으시다면, 편하신 시간에 연락해 주시기 바랍니다. 제 전화번호는 303-555-9935입니다. 연락해 주시길 기대하고 있겠습니다.

어휘 incorporated 주식회사의 potential 가능성이 있는, 잠재적인 be referred to ~로 언급되다 ideally 이상적으로 be suited to ~에 적합하다, 맞다 get back to ~에게 나중에 다시 연락하다 solicit 간청하다, 요청하다 found 설립하다

77 Why has the speaker called Mr. Aston?
(A) To ask for some personal information
(B) To solicit his participation
(C) To arrange an interview
(D) To finalize a job offer

화자가 Aston 씨에게 전화한 이유는 무엇인가?
(A) 개인 정보를 요청하기 위해
(B) 그의 참가를 요청하기 위해
(C) 면접 일정을 잡기 위해
(D) 일자리 제의를 마무리 짓기 위해

해설 〈기본 정보 파악 – 목적〉
전화 메시지의 기본적인 목적 파악 문제이므로 담화 초반부에 집중해야 한다. 초반에 세미나를 준비 중이며 이와 같은 행사를 담당할 사람을 찾고 있다고 말하며 함께 해 주시면 좋을 것 같다고 중반부에 한 번 더 언급하고 있으므로 화자는 청자의 행사 참가 권유를 위해 전화하고 있다. 따라서 정답은 (B)이다. 특정 행사 일정에만 합류 요청을 하기 위한 메시지이다. 이 행사와 관련해서는 처음 연락하는 것이므로 일자리 제의를 마무리 짓는 것이나 면접 일정 잡는 것과는 연관이 없으므로 다

78 What did Jennifer Ward do?
(A) She was Mr. Aston's supervisor.
(B) She recommended Mr. Aston.
(C) She is organizing the seminar.
(D) She founded Dantos Incorporated.

Jennifer Ward는 무엇을 했는가?
(A) 그녀는 Aston 씨의 상사였다.
(B) 그녀는 Aston 씨를 추천했다.
(C) 그녀는 세미나를 기획하고 있다.
(D) 그녀는 Dantos 사를 설립했다.

해설 〈구체적 정보 파악 – 언급〉
키워드인 Jennifer Ward가 언급되는 부분에 집중해야 한다. 화자는 Jennifer Ward가 청자인 Mr. Aston을 언급하며 그 직책에 추천했다고 설명하고 있으므로 정답은 (B)이다.

79 According to the speaker, what should Mr. Aston do next?
(A) Contact General Consulting
(B) Register for the seminar
(C) Return Ms. Rodriguez's call
(D) Submit the document

화자에 따르면, Aston 씨는 다음에 무엇을 해야 하는가?
(A) General Consulting에 연락한다.
(B) 세미나에 등록한다.
(C) Rodriguez 씨의 전화에 회신한다.
(D) 서류를 제출한다.

해설 〈구체적 정보 파악 – 요청〉
담화문 요청 사항의 단서는 대부분 후반부에 제시된다. 후반부에서 화자가 관심이 있으면 연락 달라고 했으므로 정답은 (C)이다.

패러프레이징 get back to ~에게 나중에 다시 연락하다
→ return a call 회답 전화를 하다

Questions 80-82 refer to the following speech. 호M

I'm very pleased to accept this award for Charity of the Year. ⑳ After retiring as a chef, I started the Slow Cooker Foundation to promote healthy, economical home-cooked dishes. I asked some of my former colleagues in the restaurant industry to contribute tasty but affordable recipes for a cookbook. They responded with more ideas than one book could hold. ㉑ So, the Foundation produced a free weekly magazine, *The Slow Cooker Gazette*, which is available in supermarkets throughout the country. This magazine has been a huge hit regionally, ㉒ so next month we're going to distribute it nationwide. Thank you to everyone who has supported us, and we look forward to your continued support in the years ahead.

올해의 자선단체 상을 수상하게 되어 매우 기쁩니다. 요리사에서 은퇴한 이후에 저는 건강하고 경제적인 집밥 요리의 홍보를 위해 Slow Cooker 재단을 시작했습니다. 저는 요리책을 위해 외식업계에 있는 저의 예전 동료들에게 맛있고 적당한 가격의 조리법을 기고해 달라고 요청했습니다. 그들은 책 한 권을 내고도 남을 만큼의 많은 아이디어를 보내 주었습니다. 그로 인해 저희 재단에서는 국내 도처의 슈퍼마켓에서 이용할 수 있는 무료 주간 잡지인 〈The Slow Cooker Gazette〉을 만들게 되었습니다. 이 잡지는 지역적으로 크게 성공을 거두었으며 다음 달에 전국적으로 배포될 예정입니다. 저희를 지원해 주신 모든 분들께 감사드리며 앞으로도 여러분의 지속적인 성원을 기대하겠습니다.

어휘 accept 받아들이다, 수락하다 award 상 foundation 재단 promote 홍보하다 economical 경제적인 home-cooked 가정에서 요리한, 손으로 만든 contribute 기부하다, 기여하다 tasty 맛있는 recipe 요리법 throughout the country 국내 도처에서 regionally 국지적으로, 지역적으로 nationwide 전국적인 critic 비평가 complimentary 무료의 fundraising 자금 조달, 모금 nutrition 영양 expand 확장시키다, 확대시키다

80 Who most likely is the speaker?
(A) An author
(B) A food critic
(C) A charity founder
(D) A restaurant manager

화자는 누구이겠는가?
(A) 작가
(B) 음식 비평가
(C) 자선 단체 설립자
(D) 레스토랑 매니저

해설 〈기본 정보 파악 – 화자〉
화자의 신분을 묻는 문제는 지문 초반에 언급된다. 요리사를 그만둔 후 재단을 설립했다고 언급하고 있으므로 정답은 (C)이다.

81 What has the speaker's organization created?
(A) A documentary film
(B) A complimentary publication
(C) A fundraising competition
(D) A nutrition workshop

화자의 단체는 무엇을 만들었는가?
(A) 다큐멘터리 영화
(B) 무료 간행물
(C) 기금 모으기 대회
(D) 영양 학회

해설 〈구체적 정보 파악 – 특정 사항〉
화자의 조직, 단체가 무엇을 만들었는지를 묻는 문제이므로 speaker's organization을 키워드로 잡고 담화를 들어야 한다. 화자의 재단이 무료 주간 잡지를 만들었다고 언급했으므로 정답이 (B)임을 알 수 있다.

패러프레이징 free weekly magazine 무료 주간 잡지
→ complimentary publication 무료 출판물

82 According to the speaker, what will happen next month?
(A) A new product will be developed.
(B) An event venue will change.
(C) A new branch will open.
(D) A project will be expanded.

화자에 의하면, 다음 달에 무슨 일이 있을 것인가?
(A) 새로운 제품이 개발될 것이다.
(B) 행사 장소가 변경될 것이다.
(C) 새로운 지점을 열 것이다.
(D) 프로젝트가 확대될 것이다.

해설 〈구체적 정보 파악 – 특정 사항〉
Next month를 키워드로 잡고 담화를 들어야 한다. 담화 후반부에 다음 달에 무료 잡지가 전국적으로 배포될 것이라고 말하고 있으므로 이를 적절하게 묘사한 (D)가 정답이다.

Questions 83-85 refer to the following radio broadcast. (미W)

(83) And for today's weather news. Today marks not only the coldest day we've had so far this month, but the coldest December ever recorded in Ipswich County. We had a high today of two degrees below zero, and a low of minus 18. The second coldest December on record was exactly three decades ago when the high was three degrees above zero and the low hit minus 15. That date was also marked by huge blizzard, which virtually stopped the city for two entire days with 2.5 feet of snow that closed streets, businesses and schools. We don't have the same situation tonight, since there's no moisture in the forecast, but you never know what might happen in such bitter cold. (84) The electrical grid is definitely prone to outages when temperatures get this low. (85) So stay indoors and be sure to listen to our hourly reports.

오늘의 날씨입니다. 오늘은 이번 달 중 가장 추운 날일 뿐 아니라, Ipswich 지역에서 가장 추운 12월로 기록되기도 했습니다. 오늘의 최고 기온 영하 2도, 최저 기온은 영하 18도를 보였습니다. 두 번째로 추운 12월로 기록된 것은 정확히 30년 전이며 이때 최고 기온은 영상 3도, 최저 기온은 영하 15도를 보였습니다. 그날은 또한 2.5피트의 눈을 동반한 엄청난 눈보라로 인해 거리와 상점, 학교가 문을 닫아 이틀 동안 도시가 사실상 멈춰 있기도 했습니다. 오늘 밤 일기 예보에 습도는 없기 때문에 같은 상황이 벌어지지는 않겠지만, 이렇게 매섭게 추운 날씨에는 어떤 일이 일어날지 알 수 없습니다. 기온이 이렇게 낮을 때에는 배전망의 전력 공급이 정지되기 쉬우므로 실내에 머무시면서 저희의 매 시간 보도에 귀 기울여 주시기 바랍니다.

어휘 mark 표시하다 record 기록하다 degree (온도 단위) 도 blizzard 눈보라 virtually 사실상, 거의 feet 피트(약 12인치) bitter 혹독한, 매서운 electrical grid 배전관(망) be prone to ~하기 쉽다 outage 정전 shortage 부족

83 What is true of the weather today?
(A) It is expected to warm up later.
(B) Heavy snowfall is forecast.
(C) It hit a record low temperature.
(D) Heavy rain is expected.

오늘 날씨에 대해 사실인 것은 무엇인가?
(A) 곧 따뜻해질 것이 예상된다.
(B) 폭설이 예측된다.
(C) 최저 기온을 기록했다.
(D) 폭우가 예상된다.

해설 〈구체적 정보 파악 – 특정 사항〉
오늘 날씨에 대한 질문이므로 today를 키워드로 잡고 단서를 찾아야 한다. 첫 문장에서 오늘이 가장 추운 날임을 언급하며 날씨에 대한 부연 설명이 이어지고 있으므로 정답은 (C)이다.

84 What potential hazard does the speaker mention?
(A) Loss of power
(B) Lack of fuel
(C) Shortage of supplies
(D) Health issues

화자가 언급한 잠재적 위험은 무엇인가?
(A) 전원 상실
(B) 연료 부족
(C) 비품 부족
(D) 건강 문제

해설 〈구체적 정보 파악 – 특정 사항〉
일기예보 지문이므로 날씨로 인해 일어날 수 있는 위험 요소에 집중해야 한다. 담화의 후반부에 기온이 이렇게 낮을 때는 배전망의 전력 공급이 정지되기 쉽다고 언급하고 있으므로 이 말을 바꾸어 표현한 (A)가 정답이다.

패러프레이징 electrical grid is prone to outages 전력 공급이 정지되기 쉽다 → loss of power 전원 상실

85 What suggestion does the speaker make?
(A) Listeners should stay home.
(B) Listeners should exercise regularly.
(C) People should drive carefully.
(D) People should purchase supplies.

화자가 제안하는 것은 무엇인가?
(A) 청자들은 집에 머물러야 한다.
(B) 청자들은 정기적으로 운동을 해야 한다.
(C) 사람들이 운전을 조심해야 한다.
(D) 사람들이 비품들을 구매해야 한다.

해설 〈구체적 정보파악 – 제안 관련〉
일기 예보의 제안 관련 문제는 그 날의 날씨와 밀접한 연관이 있으며 담화의 후반부에 언급된다. 후반부에서 실내에 머물며 일기 예보를 들으라고 말하고 있으므로 정답은 (A)이다

Questions 86-88 refer to the following excerpt from a meeting. 영W

86 We're going to start today with an initial training session for all of you who've just joined our firm. First, you'll view a video detailing the history of the organization, from our founding over fifty years ago up until the present. Then, Mr. Ambrose, who directs our personnel department, will speak with you about some basic company policies and our general expectations from the staff. 87 He'll also issue you each a copy of the employee handbook, which you should take home and try to become familiar with as soon as possible. You will be separated into groups for the afternoon sessions. So, before we break for lunch, make sure to report back to me. 88 I'll need to tell you which group you'll be part of.

우리는 오늘 회사에 막 입사한 여러분들을 위한 첫 트레이닝 세션을 시작할 예정입니다. 우선, 50년 전의 창립부터 현재까지 회사의 역사를 담은 비디오를 볼 예정입니다. 그러고 나서, 저희 인사부 부장님이신 Ambrose 씨가 회사의 기본 정책과 직원들의 일반적인 기대 사항들에 대해 말씀해 주실 것입니다. 그는 또한, 여러분이 가능한 한 빨리 적응할 수 있도록 각자 집으로 가지고 갈 직원 안내책자를 모두에게 지급해 드릴 것입니다. 오후 세션을 위해 여러분을 그룹으로 나눌 예정입니다. 그러니, 점심 식사하러 가시기 전에 반드시 저에게 알려 주시기 바랍니다. 당신이 어떤 그룹에 속하게 될 것인지 말씀 드리겠습니다.

어휘 initial 처음의, 초기의 personnel department 인사부 policy 정책, 방침 general 보통의, 일반적인 expectation 예상, 기대 issue 지급하다 employee handbook 직원 안내서 be part of ~의 일부분이다 a series of 일련의 be eager to ~을 하고 싶어 하다

86 Who is the speaker addressing?
(A) University instructors
(B) Newly hired employees
(C) Potential clients
(D) Survey participants

화자는 누구에게 연설하고 있는가?
(A) 대학 강사들
(B) 새로 고용된 직원들
(C) 잠재적 고객들
(D) 설문 참가자들

해설 〈기본 정보 파악 – 청자〉
청자의 신분에 관한 문제의 단서는 지문 초반에 나온다. 오늘 일정을 소개하면서 회사에 막 입사한 여러분을 위한 세션을 시작한다고 말하고 있으므로 정답은 (B)이다.

87 According to the speaker, what will Mr. Ambrose do today?
(A) Conduct a series of interviews
(B) Show a video presentation
(C) Introduce the company founder
(D) Distribute guidebooks

화자에 의하면, Ambrose 씨는 오늘 무엇을 할 것인가?
(A) 연속 면접을 진행한다.
(B) 비디오 자료를 보여준다.
(C) 회사 설립자를 소개한다.
(D) 가이드북을 배포한다.

해설 〈구체적 정보 파악 – 특정 사항〉
키워드인 Mr. Ambrose가 언급되는 부분에서 정답을 찾아야 한다. 담화의 중반에 해당 이름을 언급하면서 그가 사원 안내 책자를 나누어 줄 것이라고 언급하고 있으므로 정답은 (D)이다.

패러프레이징 handbook 직원 안내서 → guidebook 안내서

88 What does the speaker mean when she says, "make sure to report back to me"?
(A) She is eager to see some results.
(B) She requires feedback from all attendees.
(C) She wants to give further information.
(D) She works as a department supervisor.

화자가 말한 "반드시 저에게 알려 주시기 바랍니다"가 의미하는 것은 무엇인가?
(A) 그녀는 결과를 보고 싶어 한다.
(B) 그녀는 모든 참석자들에게 피드백을 요청한다.
(C) 그녀는 추가 정보를 주려고 한다.
(D) 그녀는 부서 관리자로 근무하고 있다.

해설 〈구체적 정보 파악 – 화자 의도〉
문제에 언급된 문장을 주변 문맥과 함께 종합하여 화자의 의도를 파악해야 한다. 해당 표현 앞에서 그룹으로 나누어 오후 세션을 진행할 것임을 언급하며 화자에게 오면 그룹 배정에 대해 알려줄 것이라고 말하고 있다. 따라서 화자가 배정된 그룹 정보를 청자들에게 알려줄 것을 의미하는 (C)가 정답이다.

Questions 89-91 refer to the following announcement. 미M

89 Hamilton Enterprises today announced that it has decided to purchase the site of the former town center and establish a new manufacturing plant. The work is scheduled to begin as early as April and expected to be completed within two years. 90 The new facility will enable the company to manufacture its complete range of products at just one location, rather than its present three, which will help it distribute its products more promptly. 91 Company spokesperson Ian Douglas has said that the site is the perfect location for Hamilton and that the local community will also benefit from its use.

Hamilton Enterprises는 오늘 예전 시민 회관 부지를 매입하고 그곳에 새로운 제조 공장을 설립하기로 결정했다고 발표했습니다. 공사는 이르면 4월부터 시작될 예정이며, 2년 안에 완공될 것으로 기대하고 있습니다. 새로운 시설은 현재의 세 곳이 아닌 단 한 곳에서 전 기종의 완성품을 생산할 수 있게 해 줄 것이며, 그것은 제품을 좀 더 신속하게 유통시키는 데 도움이 될 것입니다. 회사 대변인인 Ian Douglas 씨는 그 부지가 Hamilton을 위한 최적의 장소이고, 그 지역 사회 역시 그것을 이용함으로써 이익이 될 것이라고 말했습니다.

어휘 enterprise 기업, 회사 site 부지 former 이전의, 과거의 town center 시민 회관 establish 설립하다 complete range 전 기종 distribute 나누어주다, 유통시키다 promptly 지체 없이 spokesperson 대변인 local community 지역 사회 benefit 혜택, 이득

89 What is the report mainly about?
(A) The renovation of a town center
(B) The construction of a new facility
(C) The introduction of a new product
(D) The relocation of a stadium

주로 무엇에 대한 보도인가?
(A) 시민 회관의 보수 공사
(B) 새로운 시설의 건설
(C) 새로운 제품의 소개
(D) 경기장 이전

해설 〈기본 정보 파악 – 주제〉
담화의 주제는 대부분 초반에 언급된다. 초반에 특정 회사가 새로운 제조 공장 설립을 발표했다고 언급하고 있으므로 정답은 (B)이다. Town center의 부지를 매입하여 공장을 세우는 것이므로 (A) 시민 회관의 보수 공사와 혼동하지 않도록 주의해야 한다.

90 What is an advantage of the plan?
(A) It will accommodate more people.
(B) It will reduce expenses.
(C) It will generate more income.
(D) It will improve delivery times.

이 계획의 장점은 무엇인가?
(A) 더 많은 사람을 수용할 것이다.
(B) 경비를 감소시킬 것이다.
(C) 더 많은 수입을 발생시킬 것이다.
(D) 배달 시간을 개선시킬 것이다.

해설 〈구체적 정보 파악 – 특정 사항〉
문제에서 언급한 계획은 제조 공장의 설립이고, 설립 후의 장점을 언급하는 부분에서 답을 찾아야 한다. 담화의 중반부에서 생산을 한 곳에서 할 수 있게 될 것이라고 언급하며, 이것은 신속한 유통에 도움이 될 것이라는 긍정적 평가를 하고 있으므로 정답은 (D)이다.

패러프레이징 distribute its products more promptly 물건을 신속하게 유통하다 → improve delivery times 배송 시간을 개선하다

91 Who is Ian Douglas?
(A) A factory manager
(B) A local land owner
(C) A company spokesperson
(D) A real estate agent

Ian Douglas는 누구인가?
(A) 공장 관리자
(B) 지역 지주
(C) 회사 대변인
(D) 부동산 중개업자

해설 〈구체적 정보 파악 – 특정 사항〉
Ian Douglas가 키워드이므로 해당 이름이 언급되는 부분에 집중해야 한다. 담화 후반에 해당 이름과 직책이 함께 언급되므로 정답은 (C)이다.

Questions 92-94 refer to the following telephone message. (호M)

Hello, Mr. Wallace. This is Mavis Stevens at Homeworld Cooling and Refrigeration. (92) I'm returning the message you left earlier regarding your air-conditioning system. (92) Based on your description, you may be able to solve the problem without a technician by resetting the unit manually. (93) Just press the power button for about three seconds. That will shut down the system, (93) and it should restart automatically after about fifteen seconds. The procedure is also explained in the product manual. If you no longer have that, (94) I'd be happy to email a copy of the relevant section. Your unit is still under warranty, so if resetting the system doesn't fix the problem, we'll send a technician to make any necessary repairs at no charge.

안녕하세요, Wallace 씨. 저는 Homeworld Cooling and Refrigeration의 Mavis Stevens입니다. 에어컨과 관련하여 이전에 남기신 메시지에 대해 답변해 드립니다. 귀하께서 설명하신 대로라면, 기술자 없이도 귀하께서 기계를 수동으로 재설정하여 문제를 해결하실 수 있습니다. 3초 정도 전원 버튼을 눌러 주세요. 그러면 시스템이 정지되고, 약 15초 후에 자동으로 재가동될 겁니다. 이 방법은 제품 설명서에도 설명되어 있습니다. 만약 제품 설명서를 가지고 있지 않으시면, 제가 이메일로 관련 항목을 보내 드리겠습니다. 귀하의 제품은 아직 보증 기간이 남아 있으므로 시스템 재설정으로 문제가 수정되지 않을 경우, 기술자를 보내 필요한 수리를 무료로 진행해 드리도록 하겠습니다.

어휘 cooling 냉각 refrigeration 냉동, 냉장 regarding ~에 관해서 based on ~에 근거하여 unit (상품의) 한 개 단위 manually 손으로, 수동으로 shut down 정지시키다 automatically 자동으로 manual 설명서 under warranty 보증 기간 중인 at no charge 무료로, 비용의 청구 없이

92 Why is the speaker calling?
(A) A change in schedule
(B) An equipment malfunction
(C) A policy proposal
(D) A revision to a manual

화자가 전화한 이유는 무엇인가?
(A) 일정 변경
(B) 기기 고장
(C) 정책 제안
(D) 매뉴얼 수정

해설 〈기본 정보 파악 – 주제〉
전화 메시지의 주제는 담화 초반, 화자 소개 이후에 언급된다. 전화를 회신하는 이유가 에어컨 때문이라고 말한 후 이에 대한 문제점 해결 방법이 설명되고 있으므로 정답은 (B)이다.

93 Why does the speaker say, "That will shut down the system"?
(A) To upgrade a system
(B) To change a suggestion
(C) To explain a process
(D) To make a complaint

화자가 "시스템이 정지될 것입니다"라고 말한 이유는 무엇인가?
(A) 시스템을 업그레이드하기 위해
(B) 제안을 변경하기 위해
(C) 과정을 설명하기 위해
(D) 항의를 하기 위해

해설 〈구체적 정보 파악 – 화자 의도〉
문제에 언급된 문장을 주변 문맥과 함께 종합하여 화자의 의도를 파악해야 한다. 해당 표현 앞에서 에어컨을 수동으로 재가동 시키라고 말한 후, 시스템을 정지하는 방법을 설명하고 있으므로 재가동 과정을 설명하는 것임을 알 수 있다. 따라서 (C)가 정답이다.

94 What does the speaker offer to do?
(A) Email a document
(B) Issue a refund
(C) Install a system
(D) Deliver a new unit

화자는 무엇을 하겠다고 제안하는가?
(A) 서류를 이메일로 보낸다.
(B) 환불을 해 준다.
(C) 시스템을 설치해 준다.
(D) 새 기기를 배송해 준다.

해설 〈구체적 정보 파악 – 제안 관련〉
제안과 요청 사항은 담화의 후반부에 주로 언급된다. 담화의 후반부에서 안내서에 방법이 설명되어 있다고 말한 후 가지고 있지 않다면 이메일로 보내 주겠다고 제안하고 있으므로 정답은 (A)이다.

Questions 95-97 refer to the following announcement and form. 영W

Reservation Slip
See Dinosaurs at Whiterose!

Name of child: *Alex Hunt*

Parent of child: *Susan Hunt*

Age of child: *Six*

Your visit will take place at *1:30 P.M.*
Thank you and enjoy your shopping!

Thank you for selecting Whiterose! We have everything you need from sturdy plates to wine glasses. Our in-house designers craft quality pieces, made for everyday living. Fill your home with people, laughter, memories and something from Whiterose. We'd like to remind customers with young children that there is a childcare center located on the third level. 95 Children 7 and under may stay in the childcare center for up to two hours. So get ready for a hassle-free shopping experience! 96 And today we have a special event for children — come see dinosaurs from 10 A.M. to 5 P.M. They're on the second level. Reservation forms are available at the information desk by the entrance. 97 Parents, please come 5 minutes before the time of your child's reservation for the smooth running of the event.

예약 용지
Whiterose에서 공룡을 만나 보세요!

아이 이름: *Alex Hunt*

아이의 부모: *Susan Hunt*

아이 연령: *Six*

귀하의 방문 시간은 *오후 1:30*입니다.
감사드리며, 즐거운 쇼핑되세요!

Whiterose를 선택해 주셔서 감사합니다. 저희는 견고한 접시에서 와인 잔에 이르기까지 당신이 필요한 모든 것을 갖추고 있습니다. 우리의 사내 디자이너들은 일상생활에 필요한 우수한 품질의 제품을 제작합니다. 사람들, 웃음, 기억들 그리고 Whiterose의 제품으로 당신의 집을 채우세요. 아이들과 함께 오신 고객들에게 3층에 어린이 돌봄 센터가 있음을 알려드립니다. 7세 이하 어린이들은 이 돌봄 센터에서 2시간까지 머물 수 있습니다. 그러니 편안한 쇼핑을 위한 준비를 하십시오! 그리고 오늘은 어린이를 위한 특별 이벤트가 있습니다. 오전 10시부터 오후 5시까지 공룡들을 보러 오세요. 공룡은 2층에 있습니다. 예약 용지는 입구 옆 안내 데스크에서 이용이 가능합니다. 이벤트의 원활한 진행을 위해 부모님들은 아이들의 예약 시간 5분 전에 와 주시기 바랍니다.

어휘 sturdy 튼튼한, 견고한 craft 공들여 만들다 hassle 귀찮은 일, 번거로운 상황 smooth running 순조로운 진행 exclusive ~ 전용의

95 What is mentioned about the childcare center?
(A) It is on the second floor.
(B) It is exclusive to members.
(C) Children over 7 are not allowed.
(D) Children may stay for a day.

어린이 돌봄 센터에 대해 언급된 내용은 무엇인가?
(A) 그것은 2층에 있다.
(B) 그것은 회원 전용이다.
(C) 7세가 넘는 아동은 입장할 수 없다.
(D) 아이들은 하루 동안 머무를 수 있다.

해설 〈구체적 정보 파악 – 특정 사항〉
childcare center가 키워드이므로 이 부분이 언급되는 문장에 집중해야 한다. 담화 중반에 돌봄 센터를 언급하면서 7세 이하 어린이들은 2시간까지 머물 수 있다고 안내하고 있으므로 정답은 (C)이다.

96 What can be found on the second floor?
(A) A reservation form
(B) A special event
(C) A childcare center
(D) An information desk

2층에서 무엇을 찾을 수 있는가?
(A) 예약 용지
(B) 특별 행사
(C) 어린이 돌봄 센터
(D) 안내 데스크

해설 〈구체적 정보 파악 – 특정 사항〉
second floor가 키워드이므로 이 부분에 집중해야 한다. 어린이를 위한 특별 이벤트가 2층에서 열린다고 했으므로 정답은 (B)이다.

97 Look at the graphic. By when should Susan arrive at the special event?
(A) 1:20
(B) 1:25
(C) 1:30
(D) 1:35

시각 자료를 보시오. Susan은 특별 행사에 언제까지 도착해야 하는가?
(A) 1시 20분
(B) 1시 25분
(C) 1시 30분
(D) 1시 35분

해설 〈구체적 정보 파악 – 시각 자료 연계〉
시각 자료와 선택지를 대조해야 한다. 문제의 키워드인 Susan이 예약 용지의 부모 이름이라는 것과 선택지가 시간으로 제시되어 있는 것을 확인하고 담화를 들어야 한다. 후반부에서 이벤트의 원활한 진행을 위해 부모님들은 예약 시간 5분 전에 오라고 안내하고 있으므로 예약 용지의 지정된 시간 1시 30분보다 5분 이른 (B)가 정답이다.

Questions 98-100 refer to the following talk and schedule. 영M

Christchurch Tour – Day One		
Time	Location	Activity
09:00-10:30	Waitomo Caves	Morning walk
11:00-12:00	Central Square	Shopping
12:00-14:00	Victoria Park	Afternoon picnic
14:00-17:00	Bay of Islands	Boat ride

Everyone, I want to point out that from here you can see the Goff Bridge to the south in the distance. 98 The bridge is named after Phil Goff, who was elected as Christchurch's first mayor shortly after the founding of the city. Due to its unique architecture, the bridge was considered a marvel of modern engineering at the time of its construction. 99 Before we cross it tomorrow on the way to Mission Bay for our cycling tour, we'll stop so you can see its beautiful features up close and take pictures. 100 Let's pack up our picnic baskets and head to our next activity. Make sure not to leave any beverage containers or food wrappers behind.

Christchurch 여행 – 첫째 날		
	장소	활동
09:00-10:30	Waitomo 동굴	아침 산책
11:00-12:00	중앙 광장	쇼핑
12:00-14:00	Victoria 공원	오후 소풍
14:00-17:00	Islands 만	보트 타기

여러분, 여기서 저 멀리 남쪽에 있는 Goff 다리를 볼 수 있다는 것을 강조해 드리고 싶습니다. 이 다리는 도시 건설 직후 Christchurch의 첫 번째 시장으로 선출되었던 Phil Goff의 이름을 따서 지어졌습니다. 독특한 건축 양식 때문에 건축 당시 이 다리는 현대 기술의 경이로운 업적으로 여겨졌습니다. 내일 우리는 자전거 여행을 위해 Mission Bay로 가는 도중 이 다리를 건너게 되는데, 잠시 멈추어 아름다운 특징들을 가까이에서 보고 사진 촬영을 하게 될 것입니다. 그러면 피크닉 가방을 챙겨서 다음 일정으로 넘어갑시다. 음료 용기나, 음식 포장지를 놓고 가지 마시기 바랍니다.

어휘 point out 지적하다, 주목하다 elect 선출하다, 선택하다 unique 유일무이한, 독특한 architecture 건축학, 건축양식 marvel 경이로운 업적 on the way ~하는 중에 feature 특색, 특징 head to ~로 향하다 leave behind 두고 가다, 둔 채 잊고 가다 food wrapper 식품 포장지 civil engineer 토목 기사

98 Who most likely is Phil Goff?
(A) A civil engineer
(B) A famous celebrity
(C) A local politician
(D) A renowned architect

Phil Goff는 누구이겠는가?
(A) 토목 기사
(B) 유명 인사
(C) 지역 정치가
(D) 유명한 건축가

해설 〈구체적 정보 파악 – 특정 사항〉
Phil Goff를 키워드로 잡고, 해당 이름이 언급되는 부분에서 정답의 단서를 찾아야 한다. 다리에 대한 설명을 하는 부분에서 이 다리의 이름은 Christchurch의 첫 번째 시장의 이름을 따서 지었다고 설명하고 있으므로 정답은 (C)이다.

패러프레이징 mayor 시장 → local politician 지역 정치가

99 According to the speaker, what is the purpose of the trip to Mission Bay?
(A) To ride bicycles
(B) To photograph wildlife
(C) To shop for souvenirs
(D) To visit a castle

화자에 의하면, Mission Bay로의 여행 목적은 무엇인가?
(A) 자전거를 타기 위해
(B) 야생동물 사진을 찍기 위해
(C) 기념품을 사기 위해
(D) 성에 방문하기 위해

해설 〈구체적 정보 파악 – 특정 사항〉
키워드인 Mission Bay가 언급되는 부분에서 정답의 단서를 찾아야 한다. 내일 일정을 설명하는 부분에서 자전거 여행을 위해 Mission Bay로 갈 것임을 언급하고 있으므로 정답은 (A)이다.

패러프레이징 cycling tour 자전거 여행 → ride bicycles 자전거 타기

100 Look at the graphic. Where will listeners probably go next?
(A) Waitomo Caves
(B) Central Square
(C) Victoria Park
(D) Bay of Islands

시각 자료를 보시오. 청자들이 다음에 갈 곳은 어디이겠는가?
(A) Waitomo 동굴
(B) 중앙 광장
(C) Victoria 공원
(D) Islands 만

해설 〈구체적 정보 파악 – 시각 자료 연계〉
먼저 주어진 선택지와 시각 자료의 연관성을 파악해야 한다. 여행의 장소들이 선택지로 제시되어 있으므로 장소에 따른 활동 사항이 정답에 대한 단서로 제시될 것임을 예측하고 듣는다. 후반부에 피크닉 바구니를 챙긴 후 다음 일정으로 이어 가자고 말하고 있으므로 현재 청자들은 피크닉 장소인 빅토리아 공원에 있다는 것을 알 수 있다. 따라서 피크닉 이후의 장소인 (D)가 정답이다.

PART 5

101 **해석** Brooks 서점은 주문을 집, 직장 혹은 지역 우체국으로 24시간 안에 배송 가능합니다.
해설 빈칸은 명사 business와 local post office 사이이므로 등위접속사가 와야 한다. '직장 혹은 지역 우체국'이 적절하므로 (C) or가 정답이다.
어휘 ship 배송하다 local 지역의

102 **해석** 고품질이지만 저렴한 원자재의 사용은 Walton 씨의 공장에서 비용 인하로 이어졌다.
해설 빈칸 앞의 yet은 등위접속사로 '그러나'의 의미로 사용되었으므로 high-quality와 대조되는 의미의 (A) inexpensive가 정답이다.
어휘 raw material 원자재 lead to ~로 이어지다 cost reduction 비용 인하 inexpensive 저렴한 incomplete 완성되지 않은 undecided 결정되지 않은

103 **해석** Jason Flowers는 귀하의 특별한 행사에 멋진 장식을 배달할 준비가 항상 되어 있습니다.
해설 빈칸 뒤 to부정사와 어울리는 형용사 단어는 (A) ready이다.
어휘 be ready to ~할 준비가 되어 있다 decoration 장식 skillful 숙련된

104 **해석** Kate Vausden은 Lindsey 전시장에 현재 진열 중인 그녀의 멋진 그림으로 최고의 새로운 예술가로 선정되었다.
해설 빈칸 뒤에 명사가 왔으므로 전치사가 와야 한다. 이유를 나타내는 뜻으로 (B) for가 정답이다.
어휘 be nominated as ~로 임명되다, 선정되다 elaborate 멋진, 훌륭한 on display 전시 중인

105 **해석** 이번 달 할인을 이용하고 싶으면 다음 주에 끝나므로 빨리 해야만 한다.
해설 빈칸은 as절 안의 주어 자리이고 if절의 sale을 가리키는 것이므로 대명사 (A) it이 정답이다.
어휘 take advantage of ~을 이용하다

106 **해석** 비디오 자료를 출판물에 추가하는 것은 회사가 홍보 상품을 만드는 것을 도울 수 있다.
해설 video가 publication에 추가된다는 내용이므로 (B)가 정답이다.
어휘 publication 출판물 promotional 홍보의 merchandise 상품 content 내용 addition 추가

107 **해석** 그 시장의 반대자들은 그녀가 지역 경제를 부흥시켰다는 주장을 부인했다.
해설 Opponents가 주어이므로 that 이하를 부정한다는 의미의 (D)가 정답이다.
어휘 opponent 반대자 claim 주장 revive 되살리다 regional 지역의 reject the claim 주장을 부인하다

108 **해석** 우리 Sisco 디자인은 여러분의 필요에 맞는 각각의 스타일을 표현하는 일련의 이미지를 만들어 낸다.

해설 뒤에 복수 명사(images)가 오고 빈칸 앞뒤로 a, of가 있으므로 이와 어울리는 (D) series가 정답이다.

어휘 individual 각각의, 개인의 suitable for ~에 적합한 needs 필요함 frequency 빈번함, 횟수 length 길이 shortage 부족 a series of 일련의

109 **해석** Isaac 신발 가게에서는 대부분의 고객 맞춤 신발들은 영업일 기준 2일 이내로 제작될 수 있다.

해설 2일 이내라는 기간의 제한을 나타내는 전치사가 적절하므로 (D)가 정답이다.

어휘 customized 고객 맞춤의 business day 영업일

110 **해석** Sanders 씨는 음성 메일을 자주 확인하지 않으므로 당신은 그의 응답이 늦을 것임을 예상할 수 있다.

해설 의미상 적절한 부사를 고르는 문제이다. '자주' 확인하지 않아서 응답이 늦다는 뜻이 적절하므로 (C)가 정답이다. (A) scarcely는 부정적 의미의 부사이므로 부정문에 사용하지 않고 (B)와 (D)는 문맥상 어울리지 않는다.

어휘 scarcely 거의 ~하지 않게 similarly 유사하게 partially 부분적으로

111 **해석** 교통 정체를 피하기 위해서 Pleasant Valley 도심 복구는 전체적인 계획이 필요하다.

해설 빈칸은 정관사 the와 전치사 of 사이이므로 명사형이 와야 한다. 따라서 (D)가 정답이다.

어휘 traffic congestion 교통 정체 extensive 전체적인, 광범위한 planning 계획 (세우기) restore 복구하다 restorative 복원하는 restoration 복구

112 **해석** 학교 봉사 활동 프로그램은 Twin City를 돕기 위해 자신의 시간을 자원한 학생들에 대해 경의를 표한다.

해설 명사 students와 동사 volunteer를 연결하는 자리로 주격 관계대명사 (B)가 정답이다.

어휘 outreach 봉사 (활동) honor 존중하다, 경의를 표하다 volunteer 자원하다

113 **해석** 평가 보고서는 기술자들이 실험 장비를 검사한 후에만 완료될 것이다.

해설 빈칸은 부사절인 after 이하를 강조하고 있으므로 (B) only가 정답이다.

어휘 evaluation 평가 complete 완성하다, 완료하다 inspect 점검하다 lab equipment 실험 장비 still 여전히

114 **해석** Grunburg 빌딩 건설 공사는 원래 도면의 수정 때문에 연기되었다.

해설 빈칸은 문장의 동사 자리로 뒤에 목적어가 없으므로 수동형인 (B)가 정답이다.

어휘 modification 수정 original 원본의 floor plan 도면, 청사진

115 **해석** 모든 승객들은 되찾은 짐이 실제로 자신의 것인지 확인하기 위해 수화물 보관표를 확인하도록 권고받는다.

해설 빈칸에는 '실제로 자신의 짐인지'라는 뜻이 되어야 하므로 소유대명사 (C) theirs(= their bags)가 정답이다.

어휘 be advised to ~를 권고받다 baggage claim tag 수화물 보관표 verify 확인하다 retrieve 찾다

116 **해석** Charleston 은행의 고객들은 자금을 하나의 계좌에서 다른 계좌로 쉽게 이체할 수 있다.

해설 account를 나타내는 대명사 자리로 정해지지 않은 또 다른 계좌를 의미하므로 (A)가 정답이다.

어휘 easily 쉽게 transfer from A to B A에서 B로 이체하다

117 **해석** Henry Bonaducci의 제안은 실행 가능성으로 인해 놀랍게도 짧은 시간에 승인되었다.

해설 빈칸은 형용사 short를 수식하고 있으므로 부사형인 (C)가 정답이다.

어휘 feasibility 실행 가능성 surprised 놀란 surprising 놀라운

118 **해석** 1885년에 지어진 St. Petersburg 대성당은 역사적 중요성 때문에 보존되어 왔다.

해설 전치사 for와 형용사 historical 뒤의 빈칸으로 명사형이 적절하므로 (C)가 정답이다.

어휘 cathedral 성당 preserve 보존하다 historical 역사적인 signify 의미하다, 뜻하다 significant 중요한, 의미를 가진 significance 중요함

119 **해석** 제안된 개선안이 실행된 후에 생산 과정이 더 효율적으로 운영되어야 한다.

해설 한정사 the와 명사 사이의 빈칸에는 형용사가 와야 하므로 (B)와 (C) 중에서 골라야 한다. improvement는 수동의 의미인 과거분사의 수식을 받아야 하므로 (B)가 정답이다.

어휘 improvement 개선 implement 실행하다 efficiently 효율적으로

120 **해석** 고객들은 대기 주문의 가장 최신 상태를 공지받기 위해서 이메일 주소와 전화번호를 모두 제공해야만 한다.

해설 orders를 수식하는 형용사 자리로 '대기 중인' 주문이라는 뜻이 문맥상 적절하므로 (D) pending이 정답이다.

어휘 notify 공지하다 current 현재의 status 상태 dependent 의존적인 representative 대표하는 practical 실질적인 pending 대기 중인, 보류인

121 **해석** RT Technology Services는 사전 등록 참가자의 수가 350명 이상이면 Austin에 있는 훈련 센터를 사용할 것이다.

해설 빈칸 이하의 number는 동사로 사용되어 부사절 접속사가 필요한 문장이므로 (A)가 정답이다.

어휘 training center 훈련 센터 preregistered 사전 등록된 attendee 참석자 number ~ 수에 이르다, 되다 despite (전치사) ~에도 불구하고

122 **해석** Ortega 철물점의 새로운 고객들은 첫 번째 주문에서 관례적으로 10퍼센트 할인을 받는다.

해설 동사 receive를 수식하는 부사 자리이며 문맥상 '할인을 받는다'는 내용을 수식할 수 있는 (A)가 정답이다.

어휘 customarily 관례적으로, 전통적으로, 보통 repeatedly 반복적으로 obediently 고분고분하게

123 **해석** McAfee 제조업체는 건설업계에서는 독보적으로 정확한 도구를 만들어내는 회사로 알려져 있다.

해설 빈칸은 부사 uniquely와 명사 tools 사이로 형용사 자리이므로 (A)가 정답이다.

어휘 be known as ~로서 알려져 있다 uniquely 유례없이, 특특하게 precise 정확한 precision 정확성, 신중함 preciseness 정밀함

124 **해석** 인사부장인 Hogan 씨가 내일 회의에서 인턴 고용에 대한 회사의 수정된 지침서를 얘기할 것이다.

해설 빈칸은 동사 자리로서 목적어가 있으므로 능동형 동사가 정답이며 내일 회의를 언급했으므로 (A)는 정답이 될 수 없다. 현재 진행형이 가까운 미래를 나타내는 데 사용될 수 있으므로 (B)가 정답이다.

어휘 personnel 인사부 revised 수정된 address 연설하다, 말하다, 다루다

125 **해석** 고속 프린터가 아무리 느리다 하더라도 여전히 우리 목적에 적합한 복사물을 만들어 내고 있다.

해설 빈칸 뒤의 형용사 slow 다음에 주어 high-speed printer와 동사 may be를 취하고 있으므로 절인 것을 알 수 있다. 접속사가 필요한 문장으로 however는 양보의 뜻(아무리 ~하더라도)을 갖는 복합관계부사절 접속사이므로 (D)가 정답이다. However는 '그러나'의 뜻으로 접속부사로도 사용된다.

어휘 make a copy 복사하다 adequate 적절한 rather 다소 seldom 거의 ~하지 않는 thoroughly 철저히

126 **해석** 〈Wisconsin Daily〉가 이제 디지털 방식으로 이용 가능하므로 구독자들은 일반 대중보다 하루 먼저 기사를 읽을 수 있다.

해설 one day와 함께 '하루 먼저'가 문맥상 적당하므로 (C)가 정답이다. between은 둘 사이이므로 복수 명사를, during은 시간을 나타내는 명사와 사용해야 한다.

어휘 since (접속사) ~이므로 subscriber 구독자 general public 일반 대중 ahead of ~보다 먼저 away from ~에서 멀리 떨어진

127 **해석** 조명이 배송되는 동안에 손상되었다면 회사가 Oakley 씨에게 교체품을 보냈을 것이다.

해설 가정법 과거완료 문장으로 if절의 시제가 had p.p.로 과거완료 시제이므로 주절에는 조동사와 have p.p.를 사용한 (A)가 정답이다.

어휘 damage 손상시키다 replacement 교체, 대체품

128 **해석** 지원금 제안서에 대한 모든 필수 서류들을 일단 제출하면 평가를 위한 결정 위원회가 소집될 것이다.

해설 두 문장을 연결하는 부사절 접속사 자리이며 선택지 중에는 (C) Once가 유일한 접속사이다.

어휘 grant 지원금 decision committee 결정 위원회 convene 소집하다

129 해석 가게 매니저들은 성수기 동안에는 보통 직원들에게 휴가를 승인해 주지 않을 것이다.

해설 〈조동사+부정어〉인 will not과 일반동사 approve 사이이므로 부사가 와야 한다. 따라서 (C)가 정답이다.

어휘 time off 휴가 peak season 성수기 generalization 일반화 generalize 일반화하다 generally 보통, 일반적으로

130 해석 회사 이전에 대한 결정은 다음 달에 예정되어 있는 특별 회의 때까지 미뤄질 것이다.

해설 빈칸은 수동태 문형의 과거분사 자리로서 주어인 decision과 문맥상 의미가 통하고 until과 연결되는 (A) deferred가 정답이다.

어휘 relocation 이전 defer 미루다, 연기하다 resolve 해결하다

[131-134]

속보

2월 2일 - P. H. Manning은 1월에 은퇴한 Sandy Connelly를 대신하여 최고 재무 책임자로 Sean Renault를 임명한다고 발표한다.

P. H. Manning에 131 입사하기 전에, Renault 씨는 KUB Systems에서 일했었다. 그곳에 있는 동안에 그는 최고 재무 책임자의 역할을 포함해서 다양한 회계부와 재무부 일을 해왔다. 그는 Adams Financial Group의 감사부서에서 그의 경력을 132 시작했다.

"Renault 씨의 경력과 리더십은 우리가 다음 성장 단계에 돌입하는 데 있어서 매우 유용할 것이다"라고 P. H. Manning의 대표 이사인 Marco Colombo가 말했다.

133 이전 최고 재무 책임자인 Connelly 씨는 17년 동안 P. H. Manning에서 일했다. 134 그녀는 이사회 고문으로 남아 있을 것이다.

어휘 appointment 임명 replace 대체하다 prior to ~ 이전에 treasury 재무부 audit 감사 invaluable 매우 유용한 phase 단계

131 해설 빈칸 앞에 'prior to(이전에)'가 있고 빈칸 이하로 P. H. Manning 회사 이름이 나오며 이어서 Renault 씨의 이전 이력이 나오므로 입사하기 전을 뜻하는 단어가 적절하다는 것을 알 수 있다. 따라서 (A)가 정답이다.

어휘 join 합류하다 found 설립하다 promote 홍보하다, 승진시키다 complete 완료하다

132 해설 동사의 시제 문제로서 Adams Financial Group은 Renault 씨가 이전에 일했던 회사이므로 과거 시제가 적절하다. 따라서 (C)가 정답이다.

133 해설 첫 번째 문장에서 Connelly가 은퇴했다고 언급했으므로 Chief Financial Officer라는 직책 앞의 빈칸은 '이전'이라는 어휘가 적절하다. 따라서 (B)가 정답이다.

어휘 former 이전의 alternate 대체의 potential 잠재적인

134 (A) 회계 부서는 아직 새로운 사람들을 고용하고 있다.
(B) 모든 직원들은 내일부터 일을 시작할 것이다.
(C) 그녀를 CEO로 승진시키기 위해 많은 노력을 했다.
(D) 그녀는 이사회 고문으로 남아 있을 것이다.

해설 앞 문장에서 Connelly 씨에 대한 이야기를 하고 있으므로 그녀가 계속해서 회사 고문으로 남아 있을 것이라는 내용이 연결되는 것이 적절하다.

[135-138]

수신: 출판부 직원들
발신: Hans Shuler
날짜: 2월 18일
주제: 새 복사기

동료 여러분,

어제 135 지속적으로 고장 나던 복사기를 대체하기 위해서 새로운 복사기가 자료실에 설치되었습니다. 136 우리는 새로운 복사기가 더 믿을 만할 것이라고 믿습니다. 이것은 산업용 모델이므로 앞으로 몇 년 동안 우리들을 위해 잘 작동할 것이라고 기대합니다.

이 복사기가 제대로 작동하는 것을 보장하기 하기 위해 종이클립이나 스테이플러 137 같은 작은 물건들은 (복사기의) 종이 넣는 곳에서 멀리 떨어뜨려 두세요.

새로운 복사기를 작동하는 방법에 대해 배우는 동안에 질문이 있으실 수 있습니다. 그렇다면 복사기 옆 캐비닛 안에 있는 설명서를 138 참고하세요.

Hans

어휘 resource room 자료실 broke down 고장 나다 industrial-grade 산업용의 ensure 보장하다 working order 정상적으로 작동하는 object 물건, 물체 paper feed (복사기의) 종이 놓는 곳

135 해설 빈칸은 조동사 had와 과거분사 broken 사이이므로 부사가 와야 한다. 따라서 (D)가 정답이다.

136 (A) 우리는 새로운 복사기가 더 믿을 만할 것이라고 믿습니다.
(B) 상점에는 다양한 종류의 복사기가 있습니다.
(C) 약속을 정하고 싶은 시간을 우리에게 알려 주세요.
(D) 나중에 정확한 견적서를 줄 수 있습니다.

해설 빈칸 앞 문장에서 새로운 복사기의 설치를 언급하고 다음 문장에서 산업용 수준의 모델임을 언급하고 있으므로 복사기의 신뢰성을 언급하는 것으로 문장을 연결하는 (A)가 적절하다.

어휘 set up an appointment 약속을 잡다 accurate 정확한 estimate 견적서

137 해설 빈칸은 small objects와 paper clips and staples를 연결하는 전치사가 필요하다. as well은 '또한'이라는 부사이고 (C)와 (D)는 명사구를 연결하기에는 적절하지 않은 형태이다. 종이클립과 스테이플러는 작은 물건의 예에 해당하는 것이므로 (B) such as가 정답이다.

138 해설 빈칸 뒤에 manual이 등장하므로 설명서를 참고해서 사용하라는 문맥이 적절하다. 따라서 (A)가 정답이다.

어휘 consult 참고하다 discard 버리다 revise 수정하다

[139-142]

2월 28일 — 2년간의 공사 후에 Milwaukee 역사상 가장 큰 호텔이 문을 열 준비가 되었다. Cherish River 강둑에 위치한 Mendota 호텔은 방문객을 위한 1,200개의 방이 있을 것이다. 최대 300명 단체를 위한 2개의 회의실도 있을 것이다. (139) 첫 번째 고객이 의료 기술 컨퍼런스의 일행으로 곧 도착할 것이다. 이 프로젝트는 현재 (140) 공사 중인 도심 지역 호텔 중의 하나이다. Milwaukee Hotel & Lodging Association의 회장인 Sanjay Singh에 따르면 이 새로운 발전은 (141) 필수인 것이다. "지난 몇 년 동안 우리는 대규모 방문객들의 유입을 겪었다"라고 Singh 씨가 말했다. "(142) 결과적으로, 도시의 거의 모든 호텔이 완전히 다 찼다. 확실히 추가적인 호텔 방이 필요하다."

어휘 massive 대규모 influx 유입

139 (A) 예약받는 것이 오픈될 것인지 확실하지 않다.
(B) 건물 보수는 원래 일정대로 내년에 시작될 것이다.
(C) 첫 번째 고객이 의료 기술 컨퍼런스의 일행으로 곧 도착할 것이다.
(D) 몇몇 회사들이 그 프로젝트에 입찰할 것이라는 추론이 있다.

해설 앞 문장에서 호텔의 시설이 완성된 것에 대해 설명하고 있으므로 곧 손님들이 올 것이라는 (C)가 정답이다.

어휘 speculation 추론 bid on ~에 입찰하다

140 해설 문장에 이미 is라는 동사가 있으므로 본동사 형태인 (B)과 (C)는 적절치 않으며 빈칸 앞 hotels를 수식할 준동사가 필요하다. (A)는 construct의 능동 형태이므로 목적어 없이 사용할 수 없다. 따라서 수동의 분사형인 (D)가 정답이다.

141 해설 빈칸 다음 문장은 Singh 씨의 말로서 앞의 문장에서 언급한 호텔 공사 프로젝트가 필요한 이유로 대규모 방문객(massive influx of visitors)을 언급하고 있으므로 필수라는 (A)가 적절하다.

어휘 necessity 필수 nuisance 골칫거리 risk 위험 bargain 거래

142 해설 빈칸 뒤는 Singh 씨의 말로 앞 문장과 인과 관계에 있으므로 (D)가 적절하다.

어휘 likewise 이처럼 otherwise 그렇지 않으면 additionally 추가로 consequently 결과적으로

[143-146]

예술가, 공예가 여러분 집중해 주세요!

(143) 이 지역에서 당신의 재능을 처음으로 보여줄 특별한 기회에 관심 있으신가요? 그렇다면, 5월 17일에 있는 Bloomberg County 예술 박람회에 당신의 작품을 전시할 기회에 지원해 보세요.

지원서는 www.bloombergfair.org에서 가능하며 지역 대학 예술 부문 교수들 몇몇 분이 검토할 것입니다. 작성한 지원서 서류와 함께 작품 (144) 사진을 올려 주세요. 이미지는 심사위원들의 검토 과정을 도울 것입니다.

지원 마감 날짜는 2월 15일이며 심사위원들의 결정은 3월 30일까지 완료될 것입니다. (145) 초대받은 지원자들은 5 x 5미터 크기의 전시 부스를 사용할 수 있으며 박람회 하루 종일 (146) 내내 참가할 것으로 예상됩니다.

어휘 craftspeople 공예가 apply for 지원하다 artwork 예술 작품 aid 돕다, 보조하다

143 (A) 가능하다면 행사 조사를 위해서 집으로 초대장을 보내고 싶습니다.
(B) 이 지역에서 당신의 재능을 처음으로 보여줄 독특한 기회에 관심 있으신가요?
(C) 단골 고객으로서 연장된 6년의 보상 기간에 자격이 되십니다.
(D) 우리 웹 사이트에서 다른 종류의 예술 작품들을 볼 수 있습니다.

해설 박람회 참가를 권유하는 첫 번째 문장이며 빈칸 뒤 문장에서 'if so(그렇다면)'라고 언급했으므로 관심을 유발하는 내용의 (B)가 정답이다.

어휘 unique 독특한 showcase 처음으로 보여주다 qualify for ~할 자격이 되다 extended 연장된 coverage (보험, 배상) 적용 범위

144 해설 빈칸 뒤의 문장에서 The image라고 언급했으므로 업로드해야 할 것은 사진임을 알 수 있다. 따라서 (B)가 정답이다.

어휘 description 설명 requirement 요구 사항

145 해설 지원자 applicants를 수식하는 분사로서 문맥상 과거분사 형태인 '초대받은'이 적절하다. 따라서 (D)가 정답이다.

146 해설 하루 종일이라는 기간을 나타내는 전치사이므로 (C)가 정답이다.

[147-148]

FANCY 스키 리조트

주말 행사

Fancy 스키 리조트는 여러분의 가족이나 단체가 다음 주말 휴가를 즐길 수 있는 완벽한 장소입니다.

침실 1개가 있는 콘도미니엄이나 1인당 240달러까지 내려가는 저렴한 가격의 스위트룸에서 3박을 보내세요. 우리 숙소는 경치가 좋은 Lyon 산에서 2마일 떨어진 편리한 장소에 위치해 있고, (148) 실내 수영장, 사우나, 아이스 스케이팅 링크가 구비되어 있습니다. (147) 셔틀 차량이 우리 숙소와 Lyon 산 사이에서 오전 5시부터 오후 8시까지 30분마다 운행됩니다.

주말 특별가에는 Lyon 산에서 이틀 동안 스키를 타는 것을 포함합니다. 이 서비스는 11월 11일부터 2월 20일까지, 주중과 공휴일을 제외하고 이용할 수 있습니다. 더 많은 정보를 원하시면 www.skifancy.com을 방문해 주세요.

어휘 suite 스위트룸 per person 1인당 lodging 숙박 시설 scenic 경치가 좋은 valid 유효한 excluding 제외하고

147 고객들은 숙소에서 Mount Lyon까지 어떻게 갈 수 있는가?
(A) 걸어서
(B) 운전해서
(C) 택시를 타고
(D) 셔틀버스를 타고

해설 지문에서 'A shuttle service operates between our lodgings and Mount Lyon'이라고 언급하였으므로 (D)가 정답이다.

148 숙박 시설에 포함되어 있지 않은 시설은 무엇인가?
(A) 사우나
(B) 수영장
(C) 스키 대여 서비스
(D) 아이스 스케이팅 링크

해설 지문에서 'include an indoor swimming pool, sauna, and ice skating rink'라고 언급되어 있으므로 (C)가 정답이다.

[149-150]

ALTON CITY 주차장

(149) 차량을 회수하여 돌아갈 때 지불금액과 함께 이 표를 담당자(직원)에게 제시하세요.

날짜: 3월 7일

시간: 오전 9시 15분

직원은 현금과 신용 카드 지불만 받습니다.

*월 요금이 가능합니다. 20퍼센트까지 절약하세요.

(150) 세부 사항을 알기 위해서는 028-555-3421로 전화하거나, 웹 사이트 altoncitygarage.co.uk를 방문하세요.

어휘 present 제시하다 payment 지불 monthly rates 한 달 요금

149 고객들은 주차 비용을 어떻게 지불하는가?
(A) 주차 미터기에 돈을 넣음으로써
(B) 비용을 직원에게 지불해서
(C) 사전에 지불된 주차 카드를 사용해서
(D) 온라인으로 지불함으로써

해설 초반에 'present this ticket with your payment to the attendant'에서 (B)가 정답임을 알 수 있다.

어휘 deposit 맡기다, 넣다, 지불하다 parking meter 주차 미터기 prepaid 사전에 지불된

150 고객들은 왜 표에 있는 전화번호로 전화할 것을 권장받는가?
(A) 다른 지불 방법을 요청하기 위해서
(B) 하루 동안의 주차 공간 확보를 위해서
(C) 직원에 대한 정보를 주기 위해서
(D) 주차 요금에 대한 정보를 더 얻기 위해서

해설 지문의 'To obtain details, call 028-555-3421'에서 (D)가 정답임을 알 수 있다.

어휘 alternative 차선의 reserve 예약하다 parking spot 주차 공간

[151-153]

주목해 주세요!

Capricorn 도서관 자원 봉사 연합은 11월 3일부터 6일까지 단 4일 동안 중고 도서 판매를 제공합니다. (153-B) 여러분들은 대부분 좋은 상태의 수천 권의 책을 살펴보실 수 있습니다. (153-A) 모든 연령대가 좋아할 만한 것들이 있습니다.

목요일: 사전 세일
오후 6시 ~ 오후 9시
(152) 입장료 5달러

금요일: 일반 세일
오후 6시 ~ 오후 9시

토요일: 일반 세일
오전 9시 ~ 오후 3시

일요일: 정리 세일
오전 11시 ~ 오후 2시
(153-D) 모든 책이 20% 할인됩니다.

수익금은 Capricorn 도서관의 별관 공사에 도움이 됩니다.

(151) 위치: 15 Harper Street, Capricorn 커뮤니티 센터의 중앙 이벤트 홀

질문이 있으시면 Capricorn 도서관 자원 연합 회장인 Leslie Ling에게 555-0173으로 연락주세요.

더 이상 판매용 책의 기부는 받지 않는다는 것을 알아 주세요.

어휘 present 제공하다 browse 훑어 보다, 찾다 of interest 재미있는 proceeds 수익금 benefit ~에 도움이 되다

151 행사 장소는 어디인가?
(A) 커뮤니티 센터
(B) 지역 서점
(C) Ling 씨의 거주지
(D) Capricorn 도서관

해설 지문의 'Location: Capricorn Community Center'에서 (A)가 정답임을 알 수 있다.

어휘 take place 일어나다, 발생하다 residence 주거지

152 목요일 판매에 대해 언급된 것은?
(A) 행사 수익금은 자선 단체로 갈 것이다.
(B) 입장료가 부과될 것이다
(C) 현금이 유일한 지불 수단이다.
(D) 하루 종일 운영될 것이다.

해설 가장 먼저 목요일 판매에 대해 나오는데 '$5 admission fee'에서 목요일에는 입장료를 지불해야 하므로 (B)가 정답이다.

어휘 charity 자선 단체 entrance fee 입장료

153 판매되는 책에 대해 알 수 없는 것은?
(A) 몇몇 책은 어린 아이들에게 적합하다.
(B) 많은 책들이 좋은 상태이다.
(C) 모든 책은 도서관 회원들이 기부했다.
(D) 일요일에는 할인된 가격으로 판매될 것이다.

해설 지문의 첫 번째 단락에서 'There is something of interest for readers of all ages'라고 언급했으므로 어린 아이들 도서도 있을 것으로 추정되고 'You can browse thousands of books, most in excellent condition!'에서 (B)도 언급되고 있고, 요일별 할인 안내에서 'Sunday: Clearance Sale – All books 20% off'라고 하였으므로 (D)도 해당되는 내용임을 알 수 있으나 (C)에 대한 내용은 찾을 수 없다.

어휘 be suitable for ~에 적합하다 reduced price 할인된 가격

[154-155]

Douglas Carter 오전 10시 05분
Carolina 아파트의 B호에서 전화를 받았어요. (154) 세입자가 7월 말에 이사 가고 싶어 해요. 그러나 그들 계약은 10월 31일에 만료됩니다.

Mia Sanders 오전 10시 06분
흠, 계약서에는 계약이 끝나기 전에 나가는 세입자는 벌금을 내야 한다고 명시되어 있어요. 그러나 때때로 (155) 부동산 소유주들은 새로운 세입자를 즉시 구할 수 있다면 비용을 면제해 줄 거예요. 예외로 해 줄 수 있는지 건물주에게 전화해 보는 게 어때요?

Douglas Carter 오전 10시 07분
한번 해 볼게요. 건물주에게 그곳을 임대하기 위해 대기 중인 사람이 많다는 것을 알려 줄 거예요.

Mia Sanders 오전 10시 08분
그래요, Carolina 아파트는 지역 주민들 사이에서 꽤 인기가 많아요. 세입자 구하는 것은 어렵지 않을 거예요.

Douglas Carter 오전 10시 10분
곧 다시 얘기할게요.

어휘 tenant 세입자 lease 임대 계약 expire 만료되다 waive the fee 수수료를 면제하다 property 부동산, 건물 right away 즉시 make an exception 예외를 만들다 quite 꽤

154 세입자가 원하는 것은 무엇인가?
(A) 주택 구입
(B) 가까운 다른 아파트 임대
(C) 식당 개조
(D) 계약 조기 종결

해설 Carter 씨의 10시 05분 메시지 'The tenants would like to move out at the end of July, but their lease doesn't expire until 31 October'에서 정답이 (D)인 것을 알 수 있다.

어휘 nearby 근처의

155 오전 10시 07분에 Carter 씨가, "한번 해 볼게요"라고 한 것은 어떤 뜻인가?
(A) 임대료가 너무 비싸다고 생각한다.
(B) 세입자들이 더 오래 머물기를 요청할 계획이다.
(C) 부동산 소유주에게 연락할 것이다.
(D) 기꺼이 벌금을 지불할 것이다.

해설 오전 10시 07분의 Carter 씨의 메시지는 10시 06분의 Sanders 씨의 'What about calling the owner and seeing if they'll make an exception?'에 대한 답변이므로 제안한 대로 소유주에게 전화해 보겠다는 뜻이므로 (C)가 정답이다.

어휘 rent 임대료 be willing to 기꺼이 ~하다

[156-157]

5번 플랫폼 근처의 Garland 대기실 티켓 기계가 수리를 위해 치워져 있습니다. 4월 14일 월요일까지 새 기계를 배치할 것을 바라고 있습니다. (156) 그때까지 철도 승객들은 7번 플랫폼 근처의 Midvale 대기실에 있는 기계를 사용하시거나 안내 부스 옆에 있는 메인 로비에 있는 카운터 직원들을 만나실 수 있습니다. 불편을 드려서 죄송합니다. (157) 승객 여러분들은 주간 패스나 월간 패스를 구매함으로써 10퍼센트나 20퍼센트 절약하실 수 있고 티켓 기계의 줄도 피할 수 있다는 것을 기억해 주세요. 패스는 www.fasttrackservice.com으로 온라인에서만 가능합니다.

어휘 replacement 교체 apologize 사과하다 inconvenience 불편함

156 공지는 어디에 게시되어 있는가?
(A) 극장
(B) 렌터카 업체
(C) 기차역
(D) 공항

해설 세 번째 문장에서 'railroad passengers'라고 언급하였으므로 기차역인 것을 알 수 있다. 따라서 (C)가 정답이다.

157 티켓 기계에 대해 알 수 있는 것은?
(A) 주간 패스나 월간 패스는 판매하지 않는다.
(B) 신용 카드 고객들만을 위한 것이다.
(C) 10에서 20퍼센트 할인된 표를 제공한다.
(D) 7번 플랫폼에서는 아직 설치되지 않았다.

해설 마지막 문장에서 'Passes are only available online'이라고 언급하였으므로 티켓 기계를 통해서는 주간 패스나 월간 패스 구매가 불가능함을 알 수 있다. 따라서 (A)가 정답이다.

[158-160]

발신: Carrie Fenway
수신: Harper Randolph
주제: 대화를 계속 이어서
날짜: 12월 22일

Harper 씨에게,

지난주 지역 매니저들 수련회에서 만나서 반가웠어요. 그쪽 사무실 이동과 관련해서 우리가 했던 대화를 계속 이어 가고 싶어요. 작년 Bristol 사무실 이동은 사무실 이전을 운영하는 데 있어서 제게 많은 것을 가르쳐 주었고 (158) 제가 배운 것을 당신에게 전해주고 싶어요. -[1]-.

첫 번째, 나는 당신이 사무실을 며칠간 문을 닫을지 아니면 점차적으로 이사를 하면서 이전과 같이 열어 둘지에 대해 아직 생각 중인 것을 알아요. 나는 가능하다면 열어두는 것을 추천하고 싶어요. -[2]-. Bristol 사무실은 열어두고 2주에 걸쳐서 점차적으로 이사를 했는데 그것이 이사를 꽤 쉽게 만들었어요. 물론, (159) 그 시기 동안에 몇몇 직원들은 그들의 팀 동료들이 옛 사무실에 남아 있는 동안 새 사무실로 이전해야 해서 정상적인 작업 스케줄을 유지하는 것이 어려웠어요. -[3]-. 이 방법을 선택한다면 혼란을 최소화하기 위해서 한 팀의 모든 멤버들을 동시에 이동시킬 것을 제안해요.

두 번째, 사무실 이전은 모든 사람들에게 시간 소비적인 일이라는 것을 기억하세요. (160) 직원들에게 이사하는 동안에 당신이 정상적인 작업량을 이행하는 것을 기대하지 않는다는 메시지를 분명하게 전달하세요. -[4]-. (160) Bristol 사무실이 했던 것처럼 미리 이 단계를 거친다면 작업의 흐름을 개선하고 스트레스를 누그러뜨리는 데 많은 도움이 될 거예요.

이 주제에 대해 더 이야기하기 위해 이번 주 후반에 전화할게요.

Carrie Fenway

사장, Situation Consulting

어휘 retreat 수련회 follow up 후속으로 따라가다 pass on 전달하다 as usual 늘 그렇듯이 gradually 점차적으로 minimize ~을 최소화하다 confusion 혼란 time-consuming 시간이 걸리는 deliver the message 소식을 전하다 take on (일을) 맡다 workload 작업량 take a step 조치, 단계를 취하다 ahead of time 사전에 workflow 일의 흐름 greatly 많이, 상당히 give a call 전화하다

158 Fenway 씨가 Randolph 씨에게 편지를 쓴 이유는 무엇인가?
(A) 조언하기 위해서
(B) 서류를 신청하기 위해서
(C) 새로운 프로젝트를 제안하기 위해서
(D) 결정에 대해 불만을 얘기하기 위해서

해설 첫 번째 문단, 세 번째 문장에서 'I wanted to pass on what I learned to you'에서 자신의 알고 있는 것을 조언해 주는 편지임을 알 수 있다.

어휘 appeal 반대하다, 불만을 얘기하다

159 Fenway 씨가 실수라고 생각했던 것은?
(A) 보수하는 동안 사무실을 일찍 닫지 않은 것
(B) 팀 직원들을 함께 유지하지 않은 것
(C) 이전하는 동안에 직원들에게 휴가를 주지 않은 것
(D) 직원들 개개인과 새 정책에 대해 이야기하지 않은 것

해설 두 번째 문단의 세 번째 문장에서 'maintaining the normal work schedule during that time was difficult because some employees had relocated to the new office while their team members remained at the old office'에서 자신이 힘들었던 이유에 대해 설명했으므로 (B)가 정답이다.

어휘 time off 휴가 individually 각각

160 [1], [2], [3], [4]로 표시된 위치들 중 다음 문장이 들어가기 적절한 곳은?
"대신 직원들과 이전하는 시기 동안 각자의 작업량을 줄이는 것에 대해서 자세하게 이야기하세요."
(A) [1]
(B) [2]
(C) [3]
(D) [4]

해설 'Instead'로 문장을 시작하므로 이전의 문장과 대조를 이루는 내용임을 알 수 있다. 앞 문장 'you will not be expecting to take on normal workloads during the move'에서 작업량을 정상 수준으로 유지하기 힘들다는 점이 언급되고 이어서 제시 문장을 this step이라고 언급하고 있으므로 (D)가 정답이다.

어휘 in detail 자세하게

[161-163]

http://www.lowell.edu

교수 프로파일
Edinburgh 캠퍼스

안내	홈	연락하기	**교수진**

Margaret Pullman 박사
경영 관리
Pullman@lowell.edu

Margaret Pullman 박사는 Manchester에 있는 Arlington 대학에서 경영과 역사 복수 전공으로 졸업했습니다. (162) 그녀는 Liverpool에 있는 Duncan 대학의 대학원 과정 학생으로서 경영 입문 과정에 있는 학생들을 개인 지도했을 때 교육자로서의 그녀의 경력을 시작했습니다. Duncan 대학에서 경영 관리로 박사학위를 받은 후에, Edinburgh 캠퍼스에 있는 Lowell 대학의 경영학부 교수로 합류하게 되었습니다. 그녀는 〈어떻게 사업이 성공하는가〉의 저자입니다(앞으로 Lowell 대학 출판부에서 나오게 됩니다). 그녀는 또한 Great Lake Business Council의 회원이기도 합니다. (163) 현재 Pullman 박사는 Lowell 대학에서 휴직 중이며 London에 위치한 Global Business Affairs Institute에서 국제 경영 사업 관련 세미나를 진행 중입니다.

어휘 dual 이중의 복수의 embark on ~을 착수하다, 시작하다 introductory course 입문 과정 doctorate 박사학위 forthcoming 임박한, 곧 다가올 on leave 휴가 중인

161 위의 정보의 목적은 무엇인가?
(A) 사업 세미나 날짜를 공지하기 위해서
(B) 어떤 직원에 대한 사실을 알리기 위해서
(C) 사업가들에게 책 구입을 권장하기 위해서
(D) 지원자에 대한 세부 사항을 제공하기 위해서

해설 지문은 Pullman 교수의 이력을 알리는 Lowell 대학의 웹 페이지이므로 (B)가 정답이다.

어휘 publicize 알리다

162 Pullman 교수는 강의 경력을 어디에서 시작했는가?
(A) Liverpool
(B) Edinburgh
(C) Manchester
(D) London

해설 'She embarked on her career as an educator when, as a graduate student in Duncan University in Liverpool'로부터 Liverpool에서 처음 강의 시작을 한 것을 알 수 있다. 따라서 (A)가 정답이다.

163 Pullman 교수에 대해 알 수 있는 것은?
(A) 현재 대학에서 역사를 강의하고 있다.
(B) Business Council 회원에 지원했다.
(C) 현재 London에서 잠시 일하고 있다.
(D) 전 세계에서 사업을 운영하고 있다.

해설 마지막 문장에서 'Dr. Pullman is conducting a series of international business seminars at the Global Business Affairs Institute in London'에서 현재 London에서 일하고 있음을 알 수 있으므로 (C)가 정답이다.

[164-167]

Meyers 단지

164 새롭게 개조된 Meyers 단지에서 Mendota 만의 아름다운 경치를 즐기세요. 이전에 봉제 공장이었던 건물은1900년대 초반을 대표하는 특징과 현대적 편리함과 기술을 결합하여 완전히 새롭게 되었습니다. 165 2년 전에 시카고에 기반을 둔 수상 경력이 있는 건축 회사인 Gerund Remodeling 주식회사가 Fargo의 봉제 공장을 상업과 주거 공간으로 전환하는 프로젝트를 맡았습니다. 166-A 다음 달 개회 행사는 이 개조의 완성을 기념할 것입니다.

Meyers 단지는 대부분이 Fargo 항구를 내려다보는 240개의 아파트와 4,500평방미터에 달하는 사무실과 상점들을 제공합니다. 전면적인 전망과 더불어 이 건물은 항구를 따라 아름답게 조성된 조경 정원을 제공합니다. 이렇게 멋진 다용도 건물은 167 중심지에 위치하고 있습니다. 166-C Meyers 단지는 부티크 상점, 미술관 그리고 레스토랑이 있는 Fargo Maple 거리에서 단지 한 블럭 떨어져 있습니다. 166-D 또한 23킬로미터의 Chanda 만의 자전거 도로의 끝에 위치하고 있는데, 이 도로는 오래된 철로에서 탄생했고 Fargo에서 Alton 시를 연결하고 있습니다. 이 지역에는 몇몇 잘 관리된 자전거 도로가 더 있습니다. 남쪽으로는 여러 관광명소가 있는 Jacksonville이 30분 운전으로 가능합니다.

상업 또는 주거 공간에 대해 문의하시려면 301-555-3241의 Meyers 단지 부동산 관리부로 연락해 주시거나 rentalinfo@meyerscomplex.com으로 이메일을 보내 주세요. 각 아파트의 평면도는 다양합니다. 상업 공간은 고객에 맞추어져 있습니다. 더 많은 세부 사항은 웹 사이트 www.meyerscomplex.com을 방문해 주세요.

어휘 scenic 경치가 좋은 formerly 과거에는, 이전에는 sewing factory 봉제 공장 combine ~을 연계하다 features 특징 representative of ~을 대표하는 award-wining 수상 경력이 있는 undertake 이행하다 convert 전환하다 mark ~을 기념하다 completion 완성 overlook ~을 내려다보다 sweeping 전체적인, 광범위한 appealing 매력적인 prime 중심부의 trail 길 attraction 관광지 inquire about ~에 대해 문의하다 floor plan 평면도 vary 다양하다 customize 주인이 원하는 대로 만들다

164 광고의 목적은 무엇인가?
(A) 최근에 승인된 프로젝트를 공지하기 위해서
(B) 건축 상 행사를 홍보하기 위해서
(C) 새로운 사무용과 주거용 공간을 홍보하기 위해서
(D) 개점 지연의 이유를 설명하기 위해서

해설 첫 번째 문장에서 'Enjoy the scenic beauty of Mendota Bay from the newly renovated Meyers Complex'라고 시작하며 건물을 홍보하고 있다.

어휘 approved 승인된 publicize 홍보하다, 알리다

165 Gerund Remodeling 주식회사에 대해서 언급된 것은?
(A) 가족 소유의 사업체이다.
(B) 작업으로 인정받은 적이 있다.
(C) 상업 건물을 전문으로 한다.
(D) 독특한 봉제 기술로 알려져 있다.

해설 첫 번째 문단의 세 번째 문장에서 'Gerund Remodeling Inc., the award-winning architecture firm'이라고 언급한 것으로 이 건축 회사가 상을 받은 것을 알 수 있으므로 (B)가 정답이다.

어휘 recognize 인정하다 specialize in ~을 전문으로 하다 be known for ~로 유명하다

166 Meyers 단지에 대해서 언급되지 않은 것은?
(A) 다음 달에 문을 연다.
(B) 지하철역 바로 옆이다.
(C) 쇼핑 지역에서 멀지 않다.
(D) 자전거 도로에서 가깝다.

해설 첫 번째 문단의 마지막 문장에서 'Next month's opening reception'이라고 언급하였으므로 (A)는 언급하였고 두 번째 문단에서 'Meyers Complex is just a block away from Fargo's Maple Street, lined with boutique shops'에서 (C)도 언급되었고 'It also sits at the end of the 23 kilometer Chanda Bay Bicycle Path'에서 (D)도 언급된 것을 알 수 있으므로 언급되지 않은 (B)가 정답이다.

167 두 번째 단락, 네 번째 줄의 prime과 뜻이 가장 가까운 것은?
(A) 중앙의
(B) 무거운
(C) 앞서가는
(D) 우수한

해설 'prime location'에서 prime은 중심이 되는 중요한 지역임을 나타내고 있으므로 (A)가 정답이다.

[168-171]

Rebecca Walton [오후 04시 17분]	168 오늘 이른 오후에 있었던 지역 매니저 회의에 참석해 줘서 고마워요. 추가 질문이 있나요?
Kelly Stevens [오후 04시 18분]	Juan과 저는 새로운 판매 구역이 현재 고객들에게 어떻게 영향을 끼치는지 확실하지 않아요. 새로운 구역이 새로운 고객들에게만 적용되나요?
Rebecca Walton [오후 04시 20분]	아니요. 새 구역은 새 고객과 현재 고객 모두에게 적용됩니다.
Kelly Stevens [오후 04시 21분]	그럼, 제가 더 이상 Perot Publishing 같은 현재 고객들로부터 인센티브를 못 받는다는 것인가요?
Rebecca Walton [오후 04시 22분]	맞아요. 5구역에 있는 현재 고객들은 모두 Juan에게 갑니다.
Juan Rubble [오후 04시 23분]	170 그러나 만약 제가 Kelly가 Perot Publishing을 관리하는 데 동의한다면요?
Rebecca Walton [오후 04시 25분]	Perot Publishing은 큰 고객이에요.
Juan Rubble [오후 04시 26분]	네. 그러나 169 생산적인 관계를 방해하고 싶지 않아요. 제게는 Perot Publishing이 큰 의미는 아니에요.
Rebecca Walton [오후 04시 27분]	저는 그게 꼭 방해하는 것이라고 생각하지는 않아요. 171 그러나 Juan이 그렇게 말한다면 구역 매니저가 동의하면 예외로 할 수 있을 것 같아요.
Kelly Stevens [오후 04시 28분]	제가 직접 고객에게 이야기하는 건 어떨까요?
Rebecca Walton [오후 04시 30분]	그건 적절한 것 같지 않아요.
Kelly Stevens [오후 04시 31분]	알겠어요.
Juan Rubble [오후 04시 32분]	좋아요. 우리 모두 소식 듣기를 기다릴게요.

어휘 regional 지역의 be unclear about 확실하지 않다 existing 현재의 district 구역, 지역 apply to ~에 적용되다 interrupt ~을 방해하다 productive 생산적인 make an exception 예외를 만들다 appropriate 적절한

168 Walton 씨는 누구인 것 같은가?
(A) 서점 주인
(B) 판매 매니저
(C) 여행사 직원
(D) 작가

해설 4시 17분에 Walton 씨가 지역 매니저 회의에 참석했다고 한 것으로부터 (B)가 정답임을 알 수 있다.

169 Stevens 씨에 대해 암시하는 것은?
(A) Perot Publishing과 좋은 관계를 갖고 있다.
(B) 5구역에 있는 사무실로 이전하고 싶어 한다.
(C) 새로운 구역 배정에 몹시 만족한다.
(D) 오전 회의에 참석하지 않았다.

해설 오후 4시 26분에 Rubble 씨가 'I'd rather not interrupt a productive relationship'이라고 하였으므로 Stevens 씨가 고객과 좋은 관계를 유지하고 있었음을 알 수 있다. 따라서 (A)가 정답이다.

어휘 transfer 전근 가다 assignment 배정

170 4시 25분에 Walton 씨가 "Perot Publishing은 큰 고객이에요"라고 한 것은 어떤 뜻인가?
(A) Rubble 씨가 Perot Publishing의 필요를 맞출 수 있을지 의심한다.
(B) Rubble 씨가 혼란을 겪고 있다고 생각한다.
(C) Rubble 씨가 5구역을 방문하기를 바란다.
(D) Rubble 씨의 생각이 의아하다고 생각한다.

해설 바로 앞 문장에서 Rubble 씨는 Kelly가 Perot Publishing을 관리하는 것에 동의하겠다는 의사를 표시했는데 이에 대해 큰 고객이라고 말한 것은 그렇게 큰 고객을 맡지 않겠다는 Rubble 씨의 생각에 대해 의아함을 나타내는 것이다. 따라서 (D)가 정답이다.

어휘 doubt 의심하다 meet needs 필요를 맞추다 confused 혼란스러운

171 다음에 일어날 일은?
(A) Stevens 씨가 새 판매 구역 지도를 검토할 것이다.
(B) Stevens 씨가 고객을 만날 것이다.
(C) Walton 씨가 동료에게 연락할 것이다.
(D) Rubble 씨가 Perot Publishing의 일자리 제안을 받아들일 것이다.

해설 Walton 씨가 4시 27분에 'I might be able to make an exception if our district manager approves it'이라고 말한 것으로부터 구역 매니저에게 연락할 것임을 알 수 있으므로 (C)가 정답이다.

[172-175]

172 McClellan 극장은 Dublin의 가장 소중한 역사적 명소 중의 하나이고 보존될 필요가 있다. 이 건물은 Dublin 중앙 광장에 거의 2세기 전에 지어졌고 많은 두드러지고 독특한 특징들을 갖고 있다. -[1]-. 앞면의 화려한 석고 장식은 건물이 건설된 시기의 장엄한 건축의 예이다. 로비의 벽면은 Wendy Ramsey와 Madeline Estes를 포함하여 수년 동안 그곳에서 공연해 온 많은 유명한 배우들이 등장하는 아름다운 벽화로 덮여 있다. 이 극장은 건축적인 보석일 뿐만 아니라 지역 주민들에게 매우 높은 가치를 지니고 있는 엔터테인먼트 장소이며 그 지역에 여행객들을 유입시킴으로서 지역 경제를 지원한다. -[2]-.

172 173 175 최근 건물의 노화 때문에 더 이상 대규모 극장 공연과 뮤지컬 작품들을 이끌지 못하고 있다. 극장을 계속해서 사용하는 것을 보장하려면 전면적인 보수가 필요하다. -[3]-. 175 앞으로 6개월 동안, 시의 주민, 지역 사업가들, 시민 지도자들로 구성된 이 위원회는 복구 계획을 최종적으로 마무리 짓고 이 프로젝트를 완성하기 위한 자금을 모금할 것이다. 위원회는 또한 Dublin 전체에서 기업과 지역 후원금을 찾기 위해 일할 것이다. -[4]-.

174 복구 계획을 따르는 데 관심이 있는 주민들을 위해 위원회는 매달 첫 번째 화요일에 Dublin 공공 도서관의 지역 회의실에서 공공 정보 세션을 열 것이다. 프로젝트의 자세한 계획과 이 노력에 대해 기부하는 것에 대한 정보는 www.restoretheMcClellantheater.com에서 이용할 수 있다.

어휘 treasured 소중한 landmark 명소, 이정표 preserve 보존하다 feature ~을 특징으로 갖다 striking 눈에 띄는, 두드러지는 unique 독특한 attribute 속성, 특징 ornate 화려하게 장식된 plasterwork 석고세공 facade 정면 장식 magnificent 장엄한 mural 벽화 gem 보석, 보배 venue (행사) 장소 deterioration 악화, 퇴화 no longer 더 이상 ~하지 않다 extensive 광범위한, 전체적인 restoration 복구 composed of ~로 구성된 civic 시민의 finalize ~을 최종 승인하다 raise the capital 자금을 모금하다 corporate 기업의 sponsorship (재정적) 후원, 협찬

172 이 기사는 주로 무엇에 대한 것인가?
(A) 건축물로 마을이 받은 상
(B) 위원회 투표 결과
(C) 곧 있을 시 프로젝트에 대한 정보
(D) 극장 공연 일정 날짜

해설 첫 번째 문단에서 McClellan 극장의 가치와 중요성에 대해 언급하고 두 번째 문단에서 복구의 필요성과 위원회 설립 등 진행 과정에 대해 설명하고 있으므로 (C)가 정답이다.

어휘 upcoming 다음의, 곧 있을

173 McClellan 극장에 대해서 암시하는 것은?
(A) Dublin에서 가장 큰 건물이다.
(B) Dublin 주민들에게 할인된 표를 제공한다.
(C) 더 이상 대중에게 공개되지 않는다.
(D) 한 때는 대규모 관객을 이끌었다.

해설 두 번째 문단 첫 번째 문장 'it no longer attracts large theater productions and musical acts'에서 이전에는 대규모 공연으로

관객들이 모였었다는 것을 알 수 있다. 따라서 (D)가 정답이다.

174 기사에 따르면 사람들은 McClellan 극장의 변화에 대한 정보를 어떻게 알 수 있는가?

(A) 시 정부에 요청서를 제출한다.
(B) 월별 회의에 참석한다.
(C) 직접 Ramsey 씨에게 이야기한다.
(D) 월간 사보를 신청한다.

해설 세 번째 문단의 첫 번째 문장에서 'For residents interested in following the restoration efforts, the committee will hold public information sessions on the first Tuesday of each month'에서 한 달에 한 번 회의에서 자세한 상황이 설명되어진다는 것을 알 수 있으므로 (B)가 정답이다.

어휘 sign up for ~을 신청하다, 등록하다 newsletter 사보

175 [1], [2], [3], [4]로 표시된 위치들 중 다음 문장이 들어가기 적절한 곳은?
"이러한 이유로 McClellan 극장 복구 위원회가 극장을 복구하겠다는 야심찬 계획을 갖고 지난달 구성되었다."

(A) [1]
(B) [2]
(C) [3]
(D) [4]

해설 [3]의 앞 문장에서 'Ensuring the theater's continued use would require extensive restoration'에서 처음으로 복구가 언급되고 [3]의 다음 문장에서 this committee라며 위원회가 처음 언급된다. 이전 문장에서는 위원회가 언급된 적이 없으므로 주어진 문장 위치는 [3]인 것을 알 수 있다. 따라서 (C)가 정답이다.

어휘 form 구성하다 ambitious 야심찬 restore 복구하다

[176-180]

4월 4일

180-A 국제 플라스틱 제조업자 연합(NAPW)은 6월 6일부터 8일까지 Sydney에서 연례 컨퍼런스를 개최할 것이다. 다시 한 번 Sydney의 상업 지역에 있는 Stone 컨퍼런스 센터에서 개최될 것이다. NAPW 회장인 Stan Keating은 편리한 위치와 그곳에서 제공하는 편의 시설들 때문에 그 행사 장소로 돌아갈 것이라고 말했다. Stan은 176 "이 컨퍼런스 센터는 최신식이며 직원들은 매우 지식이 많고 도움이 된다"라고 말했다.

올해의 주제는 "플라스틱 주조와 형성에 있어서 떠오르는 기술"이다. 177 6월에 있을 기조연설은 Plastigic Innovators 주식회사의 대표 이사인 Colleen Allen이 하게 될 것이다. Allen 씨의 연설에 더해서 3일 동안의 행사 기간 동안 20건의 발표가 있으며 Keating 씨가 폐회 연설을 하게 될 것이다.

컨퍼런스에 등록하기 위해서 NAPW 웹 사이트(www.napw.com/conference)를 방문하라. 180-D 컨퍼런스 비용은 회원에게는 85달러, 비회원에게는 120달러이다. 178 학생들은 할인 정보를 알기 위해 자신의 기관에 연락해 보라. NAPW는 많은 대학 및 기술 대학과 가격 협정을 유지하고 있다. 179 호텔 예약 또한 웹 사이트를 통해 할 수 있다. 참석자들은 다양한 가격 범위에서 6개의 지역 호텔 중에서 선택할 수 있다. NAPW는 참여하는 호텔과 컨퍼런스 현장을 오고 가는 무료 셔틀 서비스를 제공할 것이다.

Mastuki 제조업체
비용 환급 양식

직원 이름: Rodney Kruger
급여 지급 ID#: 129856
매니저/관리자 이름: Michelle Robertson
목적: National Association of Plastic Workers Conference

각 품목 비용:
180-D 컨퍼런스 비용: 85달러
180-C 버스 비용: (Melbourne/Sydney 왕복) 43.34달러
180-A 숙박: (6월 6일에 Jefferson Inn 숙박 1일) 126.78달러

총계: 255.12달러

모든 비용 영수증을 첨부하시오. 처리까지 2주에서 3주 소요됩니다.

직원 서명: R. Kruger
매니저/관리자 서명: M. Robertson
제출 날짜: 180-B 6월 12일

어휘 business district 상업 지구 venue 행사 장소 amenities 편의 시설, 물품 state-of-the-art 최첨단의 extremely 매우, 몹시 knowledgeable 박식한 keynote address 기조연설 closing address 폐회 연설 register for 신청하다 institution 기관, 학원 maintain 유지하다 pricing agreement 가격 협정 as well 또한 price range 가격 범위 site 장소, 현장 reimbursement 환급 payroll 급여 지급 itemize 품목화하다 round-trip 왕복 fare 요금 accommodation 숙박 process 처리하다

176 Stone 컨퍼런스 센터에 대해 언급된 것은?

(A) 공항에 가깝다.
(B) 직원들이 능숙하다.
(C) 회의실 할인을 제공한다.
(D) 최근에 개조가 되었다.

해설 기사에서 Stan Keating이 the staff members are extremely knowledgeable and helpful이라고 언급한 것으로부터 직원들이 능력 있음을 알 수 있으므로 (B)가 정답이다.

어휘 competent 능력 있는 undergo 겪다

177 Allen 씨는 누구인가?

(A) 초청 연사
(B) 컨퍼런스 기획자
(C) Kruger 씨의 매니저
(D) NAPW 회장

해설 기사의 두 번째 단락에서 'The keynote address on June will be given by Colleen Allen CEO of Plastigic Innovators, Inc.'라고 언급하였으므로 Collen Allen은 컨퍼런스의 초청 연설자임을 알 수 있다. 따라서 (A)가 정답이다.

178 기사에서 학생들에 대한 할인에 대해 언급한 것은?

(A) 대학원 학생들에게만 제공된다.
(B) 인턴으로 일하고 있는 학생들에게 제공된다.
(C) 특정 학교들에서 유용하다.
(D) 외국인 학생들에게 유용하다.

해설 기사의 세 번째 단락에서 할인을 언급한 'Students, please contact your institution for discount information; the NAPW maintains pricing agreements with a number of universities and technical colleges'에서 할인을 제공하는 대학이 있음을 알 수 있다. 따라서 (C)가 정답이다.

179 NAPW 웹 사이트에서 찾을 수 있는 것은?

(A) 셔틀 시간
(B) 호텔 목록
(C) 컨퍼런스 센터 지도
(D) 발표 내용

해설 기사의 세 번째 단락에서 'Hotel reservations can be made through the Web site as well'이라고 언급하였으므로 (B)가 정답이다.

180 Kruger 씨에 대해 알 수 있는 것은?

(A) 폐회 연설을 듣지 않았다.
(B) 6월 12일에 비용을 환급받았다.
(C) NAPW 컨퍼런스에 운전해서 갔다.
(D) NAPW의 회원이 아니다.

해설 연계 지문 문제이다. 환급 양식에 따르면 6월 12일은 지불 신청 날짜이고 비용 목록에 버스비가 있으므로 운전하지 않았다는 것을 알 수 있고, 컨퍼런스 비용이 85달러라는 것은 기사의 세 번째 단락에서 'The cost of the conference is $85 for NAPW members'에서 알

수 있듯이 Kruger가 NAPW 회원이라는 것을 알 수 있다. 환급 양식에서 첫 날 1박만 숙박했다는 것을 알 수 있고, 기사에서 폐회사는 세 번째 마지막 날 6월 8일 진행된다는 것을 알 수 있으므로 (A)가 정답이다.

[181-185]

발신: customerservice@lowndeselectronics.com
수신: meredithclose@mail.com
날짜: 10월 4일
주제: 주문 번호 98345

Close 씨에게,

총 899달러에 Power Shot X12 디지털 카메라를 구매해 주셔서 감사합니다. 와이드 광학 렌즈가 탑재된 신형 카메라는 추가 배터리, 충전기와 함께 갖춰져 있습니다. 182 700달러 이상 구매하신 특별 보너스로 특별한 목줄이 달린 무료 휴대 케이스 또한 받게 될 것입니다.

184 구매 물품은 10월 15일 배송 예정입니다만 특급 배송 제안 자격이 있다는 것을 알려드립니다. 단지 7달러 50센트의 추가 비용으로 5일 빠른 10월 10일에 구매품을 받아보실 수 있습니다. 181 이번 업그레이드 제안을 받기 위해서는 이 제안이 만료되는 10월 6일 이전에 답장해 주셔야 합니다.

Lowndes 전자에서 구매해 주셔서 다시 한 번 감사드립니다.

Jeremy Harris
소비자 센터

발신: meredithclose@mail.com
수신: customerservice@lowndeselectronics.com
날짜: 10월 6일
주제: 회신: 주문 번호 98345

Harris 씨에게,

184 제 주문을 특급 배송으로 업그레이드해 주시고 이에 따라 제 계좌에 청구해 주세요.

추가로 저는 2주 안에 이사를 가게 되어서 물품이 제 사무실로 배송되기를 원합니다. 183 정확한 주소는 제 주문 양식에 있는 '청구서는 이곳으로' 부분에 명시되어 있습니다. 팩스로 처음 주문한 양식에 기입한 '배송은 이곳으로' 정보는 무시해 주세요.

감사합니다.
Meredith Close

어휘 optical 시각적인 equipped with 갖춰진 charger 충전기 complimentary 무료의 be aware that ~을 인지하다, 알다 be eligible for ~할 자격이 있다 expire 만료되다 accordingly 이에 따라 specify 명시하다 disregard 무시하다 place an order 주문하다 initial 처음에

181 Harris 씨가 이메일을 쓴 이유는 무엇인가?
(A) 고객에게 실수를 공지하기 위해서
(B) 초대장을 발송하기 위해서
(C) 배송 지연에 대해 사과하기 위해서
(D) 단기 제안을 하기 위해서

해설 첫 번째 이메일 두 번째 단락 'In order to receive this upgrade offer, you must reply on or before October 6, after which the offer will expire'에서 10월 6일에 만료되는 제안을 하고 있으므로 (D)가 정답이다.

182 첫 번째 이메일에 따르면 Close 씨가 무료 제품을 받게 되는 이유는 무엇인가?
(A) 사업 계좌를 열어서
(B) 10월 6일 이전에 구매해서
(C) 명시된 금액 이상을 소비해서
(D) 오랜만에 돌아온 고객이므로

해설 첫 번째 이메일의 'a special bonus for spending over $700'에서 700달러 이상을 구매하면 무료 제품을 받는다고 했으므로 (C)가 정답이다.

183 Close 씨에 대해 알 수 있는 것은?
(A) 디지털 카메라를 업그레이드하고 싶어 한다.
(B) 해외로 이사 간다.
(C) 2개의 품목을 취소하고 싶어 한다.
(D) 배송이 다른 곳으로 되기를 원한다.

해설 두 번째 이메일 두 번째 단락에서 처음 팩스에 쓴 주소 대신, 주문 양식에 있는 주소로 배송해 달라고 했으므로 정답은 (D)이다.

184 Close 씨는 주문품을 언제 받을 것 같은가?
(A) 10월 5일
(B) 10월 6일
(C) 10월 10일
(D) 10월 15일

해설 연계 지문 문제이다. 첫 번째 이메일에서 원래 배송 날짜는 10월 15일이지만 10월 6일까지 신청하면 10월 10일에 배송된다고 공지했고 두 번째 이메일에서 Close 씨가 특급 배송을 신청했으므로 10월 10일에 배송된다는 것을 알 수 있다. 따라서 (C)가 정답이다.

185 두 번째 이메일의 두 번째 단락, 네 번째 줄의 entered와 뜻이 가장 가까운 것은?
(A) 들어가다
(B) 입력하다
(C) 시작하다
(D) 생각하다

해설 이 문장에서 entered는 양식에 기입한 것을 나타내므로 (B)가 정답이다.

[186-190]

발신: Thomas Reilly
수신: 모든 학생들
날짜: 2월 26일

Stein 대학 기숙사에 오신 걸 환영합니다.

우리 기숙사에 오신 신입생과 복학생 모두 환영합니다. 우리는 올해가 작년보다 더 좋지는 않더라도 그만큼은 좋기를 바랍니다. 4개의 당구대와 새로운 다트판이 있는 새로운 라운지를 포함해서 여러분들이 좋아할 만한 몇 가지 보수를 했습니다. 이 라운지는 오전 10시부터 오후 11시까지 열려 있으며 여러분들의 즐거움을 위해 다양한 종류의 음료와 간식을 제공하는 카페와 함께 할 것입니다.

186 190 우리 모두가 즐겁고 안전한 한 해를 보내기 위해 여러분들의 행동에 대한 몇 가지 기본적인 규칙을 정하는 것은 중요합니다. 세 가지 규칙을 어기게 되면 특혜의 중단, 기숙사 방출에서 학교 퇴학까지 가능하다는 점을 반드시 알아 두시기 바랍니다. 추가로, 여러분들이 기숙사로 데려 오는 손님들의 행동도 여러분의 책임입니다. 이것은 여러분들이 함께 지내고 싶은 모든 게스트가 기숙사를 입실과 퇴실할 때 반드시 기록해야 한다는 것을 의미합니다. 1인당 최대 게스트의 수는 2명입니다.

더 자세한 기숙사 세부 규칙과 규정은 로비에 있는 게시판의 공지를 참고해 주세요.

Stein 대학 기숙사 규정

1. 189-B 기숙사 방 이외의 공공장소에서의 음주는 금지합니다.
2. 어떤 종류이든 불법 약품은 금지합니다.
3. 어떤 종류의 폭력이든 금지합니다.
4. 건물에 대한 상해도 금지합니다.
5. 건물 안에서의 흡연은 허가되지 않습니다.
6. 189-B 10시 이후 복도의 소음은 금지합니다.

이 중요한 규칙들이 Stein 대학에서 모두가 안전하고 교육적인 한 해를 보내는 데 도움이 되기를 바랍니다.

질문이 있으시면 102호의 189-A 기숙사 사감인 Thomas Reilly에게 문의주세요.

5월 1일

Smith 씨에게,

188 이 편지는 공식적으로 당신이 이번 주 금요일 5월 6일의 기숙사 위원회 회의에 소환되었다는 것을 알리기 위한 것입니다. 4월 21일 밤에 벌어진 당신 게스트의 행동은 우리 규칙과 맞지 않으며 메모에서 명시된 것처럼 당신은 책임이 있습니다.

전해진 바에 의하면, 당신 게스트들은 189-B 새벽 1시에 벌어진 12층 복도의 음주와 싸움에 관련되었습니다. 189-A 기숙사 사감이 도착했을 때, 그들은 무례했고 그를 밀기까지 했습니다. 이것은 용납될 수 없는 일이며 조치를 취해야 하는 일입니다. 기숙사 이사회 위원회와 함께 Johnson Hall 11층에서 하게 될 회의에 참석해야 합니다. 190 이 회의가 당신의 최종 운명을 결정할 것입니다.

Vanessa Burkowits
기숙사 매니저

어휘 returning student 복학생 set up 정하다 ground rules 기본 규칙 suspension 중단 privilege 혜택 eviction 방출 expulsion 퇴학 by-law 규정 bulletin board 게시판 common space 공공장소 ban 금하다 prohibit 금지하다 illegal 불법의 violence 폭력 tolerate 인내하다, 참다 formally 공식적으로 summon 소환하다 in line with 일치하다 as stated 명시된 것처럼 allegedly 전해진 바에 의하면 be involved in ~에 관련하다 disrespectful 무례한 shove around 거칠게 밀다 unacceptable 받아들일 수 없는 take action 조치를 취하다 ultimate 궁극적인

186 메모를 보낸 이유는 무엇인가?
(A) 학생들에게 양식 작성을 요청하기 위해서
(B) 학생들에게 규정을 지킬 것을 상기시키기 위해서
(C) 학생들에게 위원회 참석을 상기시키기 위해서
(D) 학생들에게 기숙사 입실 방법을 알려주기 위해서

해설 메모의 두 번째 단락에서 'It is very important to note that breaking three rules can result in suspension of privileges, eviction from the residence, and possibly expulsion from school'이라고 언급하여 규정의 중요성을 강조하고 있으므로 정답은 (B)이다.

어휘 complete the form 양식을 작성하다 follow the rule 규정을 따르다

187 메모의 두 번째 단락, 두 번째 줄의 suspension과 뜻이 가장 가까운 것은?
(A) 연기
(B) 중단
(C) 재판
(D) 어려움

해설 이 문장에서 suspension은 기숙사 입주민으로서의 권리가 유보된다는 것을 의미하므로 '중단'을 뜻하는 (B)가 정답이다.

어휘 interruption 중단 trial 시도

188 편지의 목적은 무엇인가?
(A) 기숙사 폐쇄를 공지하기 위해서
(B) 기숙사에서 나갈 것을 제안하기 위해서
(C) Smith 씨를 커뮤니티 행사에 초대하기 위해서
(D) Smith 씨를 위원회 회의에 부르기 위해서

해설 편지의 첫 문장에서 'This letter is being sent to formally notify you that you are being summoned to the residence committee meeting'이라고 언급하였으므로 (D)가 정답이다.

189 Smith 씨의 손님에 대해 알 수 있는 것은?
(A) Thomas Reilly와 접촉하였다.
(B) 규칙 3번과 5번을 위반하였다.
(C) 4월 21일 이전에 기숙사를 방문한 적이 있다.
(D) 9시 이전에 기숙사를 떠나야만 한다.

해설 연계 지문 문제이다. 편지에서 'your guests were involved in drinking and fighting in the hallway of the 12th floor at 1 o'clock in the morning'이라고 언급했으므로 기숙사 규정 1번과 6번을 위반했음을 알 수 있다. 'Upon arrival of the resident tutor they were disrespectful and were shoving him around'에서 규정 3번을 위반하였고 resident tutor와 만났다는 것을 알 수 있다. 두 번째 지문에서 resident tutor가 Reilly 씨임을 알 수 있으므로 (A)가 정답이다. (C)와 (D)는 언급되지 않은 사항이다.

어휘 approach 접근하다 be supposed to ~하기로 되어 있다

190 금요일 회의에 대해 추정할 수 있는 것은?
(A) Smith 씨가 기숙사에 남아 있을지를 결정할 것이다.
(B) Stein 대학 모든 학생들에게 공개되어 있다.
(C) 매 금요일에 정기적으로 열린다.
(D) Smith 씨가 위원회 의원을 선택하기 위해서 참석한다.

해설 연계 지문 문제이다. 메모에서 언급한 'breaking three rules can result in suspension of privileges, eviction from the residence'와 편지에서 언급한 They will decide your ultimate fate를 종합하면 (A)가 정답임을 알 수 있다.

[191-195]

http://www.communityboard.com/housing

이름: Donovan Swayze
날짜: 1월 23일

191 Kensington의 새로운 일자리를 받아들여서 도심 지역으로 5월 15일 시작일 이전에 이사 가야만 합니다. 단순하고 깨끗한 방 1개 혹은 가격에 따라 더 큰 임대 장소를 찾고 있습니다. 친구들이나 가족들이 앉을 만한 편안한 야외 공간이 있다면 추가점이 될 것입니다. 차량은 있으나 대중교통에 접근하기 쉬우면 좋겠습니다. 192 공과금을 포함해서 모든 주거 비용이 월 1,200파운드 정도의 예산을 갖고 있습니다.

KENSINGTON에 있는 당신만의 집에서 쉬세요

전면적인 수리가 끝나면 2개의 침실이 있는 아파트를 처음으로 임대해 보세요. 195 이 건물은 5월 1일에 이사 올 수 있습니다. 이 건물은 깨끗하고 현대적인 외관, 전체적으로 깐 새 바닥, 그리고 모두 새로운 전자제품을 특징으로 하고 있습니다. 도심에 위치해 있으며 도시 교통 센터에서 Trinity 대학까지 버스로 10분도 걸리지 않으므로 학생들을 환영합니다. 193 고양이와 작은 강아지들은 조건부로 허가될 수 있으므로 문의해 주시기 바랍니다. 192 1,200파운드는 수도, 하수, 쓰레기 수거 그리고 일반적인 건물의 유지 비용입니다. 전기와 가스는 세입자의 책임이 될 것입니다. 임대 계약에 서명하면 1달치 임대료를 보증금으로 지불해야 합니다.

관심이 있다면 nancyphan@kensingtonpalace.com으로 연락주세요.

수신: Nancy Phan
발신: Donovan Swayze
날짜: 1월 24일
주제: 아파트

Phan 씨에게

우연히 아파트 임대 광고 전단지를 보았습니다. 설명에 따르면 꼭 제가 원하던 아파트처럼 보입니다. 194 195 아파트를 직접 보고 싶습니다. 이번 주 내내 일 때문에 Kensington에 있을 겁니다. 1월 30일 일요일이 제가 마지막으로 있는 날입니다. 장소가 제게 맞는다면 입주가 가능한 바로 그날에 이사 가고 싶습니다. 시기가 완벽할 것 같습니다. 소식 기다리겠습니다.

감사합니다.
Donovan Swayze

어휘 depend on ~에 달려 있다 relaxing 편안한 seating 좌석, 자리 have good access to ~에 접근하기 좋다 housing cost 주거 비용 utility 공과금 completion 완성 extensive 전면적인 property 부동산 feature ~을 갖고 있다 throughout 전체에 걸쳐서 appliance 가전제품 situated 위치한 potentially 잠재적으로 with conditions 조건부로 inquire 문의하다 sewer 하수 garbage pickup 쓰레기 수거 upkeep 유지 tenant 세입자 security deposit 보증금 rental agreement 임대 계약 happen to 우연히 ~하다 description 설명 be eager to 열심히 ~하고 싶어 하다 suit ~에 적합하다, 맞다

191 Swayze 씨가 이전하는 이유는 무엇인가?
(A) 자신의 사업을 시작하기 위해서
(B) 고향으로 돌아가기 위해서
(C) 새로운 직장에서 일하기 위해서
(D) 은퇴를 시작하기 위해서

해설 웹 페이지에서 첫 번째 문장 'I accepted a new position in Kensington and need to relocate'에서 이사 이유를 언급하고 있으므로 (C)가 정답이다. accept라는 표현을 사용하였으므로 (A)가 아님을 알 수 있다.

192 부동산의 어떤 면이 Swayze 씨의 선호에 맞지 않는가?
(A) 위치
(B) 공과금 비용
(C) 규모
(D) 가능한 날짜

해설 연계 지문 문제이다. 웹 페이지 마지막 문장에서 Swayze 씨는 '£1,200 monthly to cover all housing costs, including utilities'라고 언급하였는데 전단지에서는 'The electricity and natural gas will be the responsibility of the tenant'라고 명시되어 있으므로 (B)가 정답이다.

193 Phan 씨가 추가 정보가 필요하다고 언급한 이유는 무엇인가?
(A) 장식의 변화가 필요해서
(B) 보증금을 내지 않는 세입자를 위해서
(C) 아파트 리모델링을 위해서
(D) 애완동물을 키우는 사람들을 위해서

해설 광고에서 'Cats and small dogs are potentially permitted but with conditions, so please inquire'라고 언급하였으므로 (D)가 정답이다.

194 이메일의 목적은 무엇인가?
(A) 계약 조건에 동의하기 위해서
(B) 주거 광고의 세부 사항을 변경하기 위해서
(C) 아파트의 특징에 대해 문의하기 위해서
(D) 건물을 볼 날짜를 정하기 위해서

해설 이메일에서 'I'm eager to look over the apartment'라고 언급하며 'I hope to hear from you soon'이라며 연락을 바라고 있으므로 (D)가 정답임을 알 수 있다.

어휘 terms of the contract 계약 조건 view 보다

195 Swayze 씨가 주거지에서 살기 시작하는 날짜로 원하는 것은?
(A) 1월 24일
(B) 1월 30일
(C) 5월 1일
(D) 5월 15일

해설 연계 지문 문제이다. 전단지에서 5월 1일부터 입주할 수 있음을 명시하고 있고, Swayze 씨의 이메일에서 'I'd want to move in the same day that it's expected to be available'이라며 입주 가능한 날과 같은 날짜에 이주하기 원한다고 말하므로 정답은 (C)이다.

[196-200]

발신: Elise Manning <emanning@ml.com>
수신: Sandra McGowan, Easy Travel <easytravel@gm.com>
주제: 자전거 투어
날짜: 5월 23일
197 첨부: 사진 (scan #1)

안녕하세요, Sandra

저는 이제 다시 한 번 당신과 함께 Andalucía를 여행할 준비가 되었어요! 이번에는 상품이 있다면 자전거 투어 중의 하나를 시도하고 싶어요. 자전거에서 Almeria 폭포의 또 다른 모습을 보고 싶지만 199 저는 자전거 초보자라 힘든 투어에는 준비가 되어 있지 않아요. 199 또 올해는 Valencia로 돌아올 때 비행기보다는 기차를 타고 싶어요. 하지만 솔직히 말해서 Huelva에서부터의 긴 여행은 별로 내키지 않아요. 196 이번 여름 제가 합류할 만한 적당한 여행 상품이 있을까요?

소식을 기다립니다.

Elise

추신: 197 Andalucía 여행 비자용 업데이트된 사진을 첨부했어요. 여행 상품 신청할 때 파일에 갖고 있어 주세요.

From: Sandra McGowan, Easy Travel <easytravel@gm.com>
To: Elise Manning <emanning@ml.com>
주제: 회신: 자전거 투어
날짜: 5월 24일

안녕하세요, Elise

문의와 업데이트 고마워요. 마침 다행스럽게도 Andalucía에 있는 우리 비즈니스 파트너가 방금 우리에게 올 가을 더 많은 자전거 투어를 운영할 수 있는 허가를 주었어요. 200 여름 회사 사보를 이번에는 무료로 보내 드리니 영업일 기준 3일 안에 받으실 거예요. 한번 봐 주세요. 마음에 드는 여행 상품을 발견할 수 있을 거예요.

이번 여름에 다시 만나기를 바라요.

Sandra

EASY TRAVEL 회사 사보 Andalucía의 새로운 자전거 여행 기회!

지난주 국경일 투어 동안에 Amelia 호텔에서 198-B 우리의 20주년을 축하한 후에 EASY TRAVEL은 다시 한 번 멀리 떨어진 198-C Andalucía 지역에 자전거 여행 상품을 제공할 세계에서 유일한 여행사가 될 권리를 확보했습니다. 우리 여행 상품은 1,100유로의 좋은 가격이며 모든 식사, Valencia로 출발/도착하는 비행기/기차를 모두 포함하며 198-D 산악자전거도 포함하고 있습니다. 이제는 채식주의 식단 요청까지 수용 가능하다는 것도 주목해 주세요.

날짜와 일정표

TOUR A
7월 3일-8일
Cadiz – Darya – Lenza – Slakotov – Cadiz
난이도: 하(Cadiz에서 비행기로 Andalucía 떠남)

TOUR B
7월 3일-8일
Cadiz – Darya – Lenza – Almeria Falls – Cadiz
난이도: 상(Cadiz에서 비행기나 기차로 Andalucía 떠남)

TOUR C
7월 3일-8일
Cadiz – Darya – Almeria Falls – Huelva
난이도: 중(Huelva에서 기차로 Andalucía 떠남)

195 TOUR D
7월 3일-8일
Cadiz – Darya – Almeria Falls – Cadiz
199 난이도: 하(Cadiz에서 비행기나 기차로 Andalucía 떠남)

주목: '난이도 하'나 '난이도 중'이라고 평가된 모든 여행 상품은 가벼운 자전거와 차량 이동의 결합입니다. 만약 능숙한 자전거 선수라면 '난이도 상'이라고 평가된 여행 상품을 선택하세요.

어휘 be ready to ~할 준비가 되다 tough 힘든 rather than 차라리 ~보다는 be up to ~을 좋아하다, 열망하다 suitable 적합한 inquiry 질문 as chance would have it 마침 다행스럽게도 permission 허가 at no charge 무료로 business day 영업일 secure the right to ~할 권리를 확보하다 remote 멀리 떨어진 a good value at ~에 비해 좋은 가치, 가격 transport 이동, 운송 accommodate 수용하다 dietary request 식단 요청 itinerary 일정표 rate 평가하다, 등급을 정하다 moderate 온순한, 적당한 combination 조화, 조합 keen 능숙한 challenging 도전적인, 힘든

196 첫 번째 이메일의 목적은 무엇인가?
(A) 회의 일정을 잡기 위해서
(B) 정보를 요청하기 위해서
(C) 호텔 예약을 하기 위해서
(D) 계획의 변화를 공지하기 위해서

해설 첫 번째 이메일에서 'Would there be any suitable tours for me to join this summer?'라면서 여행 상품을 문의했으므로 (B)가

정답이다.

197 Manning 씨가 이메일에 첨부한 것은 무엇인가?
(A) 프로젝트 제안서
(B) 비자용 사진
(C) 여행 일정표
(D) 여행 신청서

해설 첫 번째 이메일의 추신에서 'I've enclosed an updated photo'라고 하였으므로 (B)가 정답이다.

198 EASY TRAVEL에 대해서 언급되지 않은 것은?
(A) 호텔 체인을 운영한다.
(B) 20년 동안 운영되어 왔다.
(C) 어떤 여행 상품은 독점적 권리를 갖고 있다.
(D) 어떤 투어에는 타는 장비를 제공한다.

해설 사보의 첫 번째 단락의 'our 20th anniversary'에서 (B)를 언급하였고, 'once again become the world's only tour company to offer cycling tours'에서 (C)도 언급되었으며, 'use of mountain bikes'에서 (D)가 언급되었다. 언급되지 않은 (A)가 정답이다.

199 Manning 씨가 선택할 것 같은 여행 상품은?
(A) Tour A
(B) Tour B
(C) Tour C
(D) Tour D

해설 연계 지문 문제이다. 첫 번째 이메일에서 기차를 이용하고, 별로 어렵지 않은 자전거 여행 상품을 원했으므로 Tour A와 Tour B는 해당되지 않고 Huelva에서 출발하는 것도 좋아하지 않는다고 했으므로 선호하는 상품은 (D) Tour D임을 알 수 있다.

200 Manning 씨에 대해 알 수 있는 것은?
(A) Huelva를 방문한 적이 있다.
(B) 겨울에 여행하는 것을 좋아한다.
(C) 부동산 중개업자로 일하고 있다.
(D) Easy Travel 회사 사보를 정기 구독하고 있지 않다.

해설 두 번째 이메일에서 Sandra가 이번에는 무료로 사보를 보내 주겠다고 하였으므로 Manning 씨는 정기 구독하고 있지 않음을 알 수 있으므로 (D)가 정답이다.

Actual Test 02

Listening Comprehension

본책 P56

PART 1

1 (C)	2 (A)	3 (D)	4 (D)	5 (B)	6 (A)

PART 2

7 (C)	8 (A)	9 (A)	10 (C)	11 (B)	12 (B)	13 (A)	14 (A)	15 (C)	16 (A)
17 (B)	18 (A)	19 (C)	20 (C)	21 (B)	22 (B)	23 (A)	24 (A)	25 (B)	26 (A)
27 (B)	28 (A)	29 (B)	30 (A)	31 (B)					

PART 3

32 (C)	33 (D)	34 (B)	35 (A)	36 (C)	37 (C)	38 (C)	39 (C)	40 (B)	41 (B)
42 (C)	43 (D)	44 (D)	45 (A)	46 (C)	47 (B)	48 (A)	49 (D)	50 (B)	51 (A)
52 (C)	53 (B)	54 (C)	55 (C)	56 (D)	57 (C)	58 (A)	59 (B)	60 (B)	61 (D)
62 (D)	63 (D)	64 (A)	65 (C)	66 (D)	67 (B)	68 (D)	69 (B)	70 (D)	

PART 4

71 (C)	72 (A)	73 (D)	74 (B)	75 (B)	76 (A)	77 (D)	78 (B)	79 (A)	80 (D)
81 (B)	82 (B)	83 (D)	84 (B)	85 (D)	86 (A)	87 (C)	88 (A)	89 (D)	90 (A)
91 (B)	92 (D)	93 (B)	94 (B)	95 (D)	96 (A)	97 (B)	98 (B)	99 (D)	100 (A)

Reading Comprehension

본책 P68

PART 5

101 (A)	102 (A)	103 (D)	104 (B)	105 (B)	106 (C)	107 (B)	108 (A)	109 (B)	110 (C)
111 (A)	112 (A)	113 (C)	114 (C)	115 (C)	116 (D)	117 (C)	118 (A)	119 (D)	120 (D)
121 (A)	122 (C)	123 (A)	124 (B)	125 (C)	126 (B)	127 (D)	128 (A)	129 (D)	130 (C)

PART 6

131 (A)	132 (D)	133 (B)	134 (C)	135 (D)	136 (A)	137 (B)	138 (B)	139 (A)	140 (B)
141 (B)	142 (A)	143 (A)	144 (C)	145 (C)	146 (D)				

PART 7

147 (D)	148 (A)	149 (C)	150 (A)	151 (A)	152 (D)	153 (C)	154 (A)	155 (B)	156 (D)
157 (C)	158 (C)	159 (A)	160 (D)	161 (A)	162 (D)	163 (B)	164 (B)	165 (A)	166 (B)
167 (C)	168 (D)	169 (C)	170 (B)	171 (B)	172 (A)	173 (C)	174 (B)	175 (B)	176 (C)
177 (B)	178 (A)	179 (C)	180 (B)	181 (B)	182 (A)	183 (D)	184 (B)	185 (C)	186 (C)
187 (D)	188 (C)	189 (C)	190 (A)	191 (B)	192 (B)	193 (D)	194 (A)	195 (B)	196 (A)
197 (D)	198 (C)	199 (B)	200 (A)						

1 미W
(A) She's putting on glasses.
(B) She's putting a sign on the wall.
(C) She's connecting a cable.
(D) She's plugging in a copier.

(A) 여자가 안경을 쓰고 있다.
(B) 여자가 표지판을 벽에 붙이고 있다.
(C) 여자가 전선을 연결하고 있다.
(D) 여자가 복사기에 전원을 연결하고 있다.

해설 1인 사진은 인물의 동작에 집중한다. 여자가 컴퓨터에 케이블을 연결하는 모습을 묘사하고 있는 (C)가 정답이다. 여자가 안경을 착용하고는 있으나, (A)의 putting on은 착용하는 동작의 묘사이므로 정답이 될 수 없고, 표지판과 복사기는 사진에서 전혀 볼 수 없으므로 (B)와 (D) 모두 오답이다.

어휘 put on ~을 입다, 쓰다, 걸치다, ~에 붙이다 connect 잇다, 연결하다 plug in ~의 전원을 연결하다

2 미M
(A) They're walking alongside one another.
(B) They're waiting to cross the street.
(C) They're facing in opposite directions.
(D) They're headed into the building.

(A) 그들은 서로 나란히 걷고 있다.
(B) 그들은 길을 건너려고 기다리고 있다.
(C) 그들은 반대 방향으로 향하고 있다.
(D) 그들은 건물을 향해 가고 있다.

해설 남자와 여자가 나란히 같은 방향으로 길을 건너고 있는 모습을 묘사한 (A)가 정답이다. 길을 건너가려고 기다리거나, 서로 다른 방향이 아닌 같은 방향으로 걷고 있으므로 (B)와 (C)는 오답이며, 또한 건물로부터 멀어지고 있으므로 (D)도 오답이다.

어휘 alongside ~옆에, 나란히 one another 서로 opposite 맞은편의, 반대의 head ~로 가다, 향하다

3 영M
(A) A plane is about to land on the runway.
(B) Passengers are checking their baggage.
(C) Mechanics are working on an engine.
(D) A vehicle is parked next to an aircraft.

(A) 비행기가 활주로에 착륙하려고 한다.
(B) 승객들이 짐을 확인하고 있다.
(C) 기술자들이 엔진을 수리 중이다.
(D) 자동차가 항공기 옆에 주차되어 있다.

해설 여러 사물이 보이는 야외 사진으로 각 선택지의 주어에 집중해야 한다. 활주로에 있는 비행기 옆에 차량 한 대가 있으므로 이를 적절히 묘사한 (D)가 정답이다. 비행기는 이미 착륙해 있으므로 (A)는 오답이며, 사진에 없는 승객과 기계공을 각각 주어로 묘사하고 있는 (B)와 (C)는 정답이 될 수 없다.

어휘 be about to 막 ~하려는 참이다 runway 활주로 baggage 수화물, 짐 aircraft 항공기

4 미W
(A) Baked goods have been put in the boxes.
(B) The woman is tying her apron.
(C) Some baskets are being cleared.
(D) The customer is being served at the counter.

(A) 제빵류들이 상자에 담겨 있다.
(B) 여자가 앞치마를 묶고 있다.
(C) 몇 개의 바구니들이 치워지고 있다.
(D) 손님이 카운터에서 서비스를 받고 있다.

해설 실내를 배경으로 한 다수의 인물 사진이다. 각 인물들의 동작이 서로 엇갈리게 출제되므로 주의해야 한다. 제과점에서 일하는 사람이 손님에게 구매를 하도록 돕는 행위를 serve로 표현한 (D)가 정답이다. 제빵류들이 상자가 아닌 바구니에 담겨 있고, 바구니가 치워지는 동작은 사진에서 보이지 않으므로 (A)와 (C)는 오답이다. 또한 앞치마를 착용한 것은 남자이므로 주어의 혼동을 유도한 (B)도 오답이다.

어휘 baked 오븐에 구운 apron 앞치마 serve (상점에서 손님의) 시중을 들다, 구매를 돕다

5 영M
(A) Some armchairs are being occupied.
(B) Books have been arranged on multiple shelves.
(C) There is a lamp beneath the door.
(D) A rug has been placed on the floor.

(A) 팔걸이의자 몇 개가 사용 중이다.
(B) 책들이 여러 선반 위에 배열되어 있다.
(C) 문 아래에 램프가 있다.
(D) 깔개가 바닥 위에 놓여 있다.

해설 전형적인 사물 사진 유형으로 사진 속 모든 사물의 위치나 상태에 주목해야 한다. 선반 위에 배열된 책을 묘사한 (B)가 정답이다. 사물 사진에는 인물이 없으므로 사람을 뜻하는 단어와 동작을 나타내는 수동현재 진행형(be being p.p.)은 소거해야 한다. 의자에 아무도 앉아 있지 않으며, 램프, 깔개 등이 사진에서 보이지 않으므로 나머지는 모두 오답이다.

어휘 occupied 사용되는, 사용 중인 multiple 많은, 다수의 beneath 아래에 rug 깔개, 작은 양탄자

6 호M
(A) The building is located behind an open-air market.
(B) A vendor is unfolding a large parasol.
(C) Some goods are being packed into a basket.
(D) A price tag is being attached to the box.

(A) 건물이 야외 시장 뒤에 위치하고 있다.
(B) 상인이 큰 파라솔을 펼치고 있다.
(C) 몇몇 상품들이 바구니에 포장되고 있다.
(D) 가격표가 상자에 붙여지고 있다.

해설 다수의 인물과 사물/배경이 혼재된 사진이다. 사람들의 동작뿐 아니라 사물과의 관계, 배경 등도 반드시 확인해야 한다. 야외 시장 뒤쪽에 건물이 위치한 것을 볼 수 있으므로 (A)가 정답이다. 상인으로 보이는 사람들은 있으나 파라솔을 펴고 있지 않으며, 물건들을 바구니에 넣지도 않으므로 (B)와 (C)는 오답이다. 또한 가격표도 사진에서는 확인되지 않으므로 (D)도 오답이다.

어휘 open air 옥외, 야외 vendor 행상인, 매도인 price tag 가격표

7 미M 미W
Where are the best available seats for tonight's play?
(A) Yes, they are the best.
(B) It's Mr. Monroe.
(C) There are some in the second row.

오늘 밤 연극 공연에 남아 있는 가장 좋은 자리는 어디인가요?
(A) 네, 그들이 최고예요.
(B) Monroe 씨입니다.
(C) 두 번째 줄에 있는 몇 자리입니다.

해설 좌석의 위치를 묻는 Where 의문문으로 두 번째 줄에 있다는 〈전치사 + 장소〉의 패턴을 제시한 (C)가 가장 적절한 답이다. (A)는 의문사 의문문에 Yes/No로 대답할 수 없으며, (B)도 질문과 상관없는 사람을 지칭하고 있다.

어휘 available 구할 수 있는, 이용할 수 있는 row (극장 등의 좌석) 줄

8 영M 미W
Isn't Mr. Chan on vacation?
(A) Actually his trip was cancelled.
(B) He's from Zurich.
(C) No, she still has some.

Chan 씨는 휴가를 가지 않았나요?
(A) 사실 그의 여행은 취소되었어요.
(B) 그는 Zurich에서 왔어요.
(C) 아니요, 그녀가 아직 가지고 있어요.

해설 특정인이 휴가를 가지 않았냐고 확인하는 부정의문문에 가지 않은 이유를 언급하며 확인시켜 주는 (A)가 정답이다. (B)는 특정 도시를 언급하며 휴가와 연관지어 혼동을 유도한 오답이며, (C)는 주어 불일치 오답이다.

어휘 actually 실제로, 정말로

9 미W 미M
When will dessert be served?
(A) Right away.
(B) The head chef.
(C) It was a week ago.

디저트는 언제 나오나요?
(A) 곧바로요.
(B) 주방장이요.
(C) 일주일 전이었어요.

해설 디저트가 언제 나오는지 묻는 When 의문문에 시점을 의미하는 표현으로 적절히 대답한 (A)가 정답이다. (B)는 시점을 묻는 질문 내용과 무관한 사람을 언급하고 있으므로 오답이며, (C)는 미래 시점 질문에 과거로 답변하고 있으므로 시제 불일치 오답이다. When 의문문에 대한 정답을 고를 때 시제 일치와 불일치는 정답의 중요한 단서가 되므로 주의해야 한다.

어휘 right away 즉시, 곧바로

10 Are you satisfied with your new car?
미W (A) Sorry, I can't.
영M (B) They're very sophisticated.
(C) Yes, it runs well.

새 차에 만족하세요?
(A) 죄송하지만, 전 할 수 없어요.
(B) 그것들은 아주 세련됐어요.
(C) 네, 아주 잘 나가요.

해설 새 차에 대한 만족도를 묻는 be동사 의문문에 긍정의 의미로 응답한 뒤, 잘 작동된다고 부연 설명하고 있는 (C)가 정답이다. (A)는 만족하냐는 질문에 조동사 can을 사용하여 질문과 무관한 답변을 하고 있으며 (B)는 질문의 satisfied와 발음이 유사한 sophisticated를 사용하여 혼동을 유도하는 오답이다.

어휘 be satisfied with ~에 만족하다 sophisticated 세련된, 교양 있는 run 작동하다

11 Why did he leave the office so early?
영M (A) By taxi.
미M **(B) Didn't he tell you?**
(C) In an hour or so.

그는 왜 일찍 퇴근했나요?
(A) 택시로요.
(B) 그가 말 안 했어요?
(C) 대략 한 시간 후요.

해설 일찍 퇴근한 이유를 묻는 Why 의문문에 퇴근한 사람이 이유를 말해 주지 않았느냐고 되묻는 (B)가 정답이다. (A)는 방법을 묻는 How 의문문에 적절한 답변이며, (C)는 〈전치사 + 시점〉을 사용하여 시점을 묻는 When 의문문에 적절한 답변이므로 모두 오답이다.

어휘 leave the office 퇴근하다 an hour or so 약 한 시간

12 Wasn't Bruce at the sales conference in Dallas last week?
미M (A) Yes, I'm in excellent health.
미W **(B) I didn't see him there.**
(C) Where is Conference Room C?

Bruce 씨가 지난주 Dallas 영업 회의에 없었죠?
(A) 네, 저는 아주 건강해요.
(B) 저는 거기서 그를 보지 못했는데요.
(C) 회의실 C가 어디인가요?

해설 제3자의 회의 참석 여부를 확인하는 부정의문문에 그 장소에서 그를 보지 못했다며 불참한 것을 우회적으로 말하고 있는 (B)가 가장 적절한 답이다. (A)는 Yes로 답하면 Bruce 씨가 회의에 참석했다는 의미는 되지만, 관련 없는 내용이 이어지고 있으므로 오답이며, (C)는 질문의 conference를 반복 사용하여 혼동을 유도하는 오답이다.

어휘 conference 회의, 학회 excellent 훌륭한, 탁월한

13 Who is helping Mr. Winslow schedule the night shifts?
영M **(A) He's doing it by himself.**
미W (B) From 9 A.M. to 6 P.M.
(C) Visitors are welcome.

Winslow 씨가 야간 교대 일정 짜는 것을 누가 도와주고 있나요?
(A) 그 분 스스로 하고 있습니다.
(B) 오전 9시부터 오후 6시까지요.
(C) 방문객들을 환영합니다.

해설 누가 Winslow 씨를 돕고 있는지 묻는 Who 의문문에 그 사람 스스로 하고 있다고 대답한 (A)가 정답이다. Who 의문문에 3인칭 대명사가 언급되는 선택지는 오답일 경우가 많으나 문제에 제3자가 있으면 3인칭 대명사가 정답이 될 수 있으므로 주의해서 들어야 한다. (B)는 시점을 제시하는 답변이므로 질문과 어울리지 않는 오답이며, (C)는 Who 의문문에 visitor를 언급함으로써 적절한 답변인 것처럼 혼동을 유도하고 있지만 전혀 무관한 내용을 말하고 있으므로 오답이다.

어휘 by oneself 혼자, 다른 사람 없이

14 Why isn't Helena working on the newspaper advertisement?
미W
미M **(A) I thought she was.**
(B) On the last page.
(C) Next Thursday, I think.

Helena는 왜 신문 광고 작업을 하지 않나요?
(A) 하고 있을 거라고 생각했는데요.
(B) 마지막 페이지에요.
(C) 제 생각에는 다음 주 목요일입니다.

해설 Helena가 하지 않는 이유를 묻는 Why 의문문에 그녀가 했다고 생각한다며 대답하는 (A)가 가장 적절한 답이다. (B)는 장소를 묻는 Where 의문문에 어울리는 대답이며 (C)는 때를 묻는 When에 적절한 답변이므로 오답이다.

어휘 work on 작업하다, 공들이다

15 The managers are taking a long time to come to a decision.
미W
영M (A) I'll ask for directions.
(B) Within a month.
(C) I wonder why.

매니저들이 결정을 내리는 데 시간이 오래 걸리고 있어요.
(A) 제가 길을 물어볼게요.
(B) 한 달 안에요.
(C) 왜 그런지 궁금하네요.

해설 매니저들의 결정이 오래 걸렸다고 말하는 평서문에 왜 그런지 모르겠다고 우회적으로 답변한 (C)가 정답이다. (A)는 회피성 답변으로 자주 쓰이는 〈ask + 사람〉 구문을 연상시키는 ask를 사용하여 혼동을 유도하고 있는 오답이며, (B)는 결정하는 데 걸리는 기간으로 혼동을 유도하고 있지만, 질문과 전혀 어울리지 않는 답변이다.

어휘 come to a decision 결정을 내리다 directions 길 안내 wonder 궁금하다

16 When will we release the updated software?
미M **(A) It's too early to tell.**
영M (B) At least six.
(C) At the auditorium.

언제 우리가 최신 소프트웨어를 출시하나요?
(A) 아직 말씀 드리기는 너무 이르네요.
(B) 적어도 여섯이요.
(C) 강당에서요.

해설 소프트웨어 출시 일정을 묻는 When 의문문에 언제인지 정확히 말할 수 없다는 것을 우회적으로 답변한 (A)가 정답이다. (B)는 개수를 언급하는 숫자를 사용하여 시간처럼 들리도록 혼동을 유도한 오답이며, (C)는 장소를 묻는 질문에 어울리는 응답이다.

어휘 release 공개하다, 발표하다 auditorium 객석, 강당

17 Should I send the contract now or after the workshop?
미M (A) I believe there is.
미W **(B) Wait until after.**
(C) Both of the pages.

계약서를 지금 보내야 하나요, 아니면 워크숍 후에 보내야 하나요?
(A) 있다고 생각해요.
(B) (워크숍 끝날 때까지) 기다리세요.
(C) 양쪽 페이지 모두요.

해설 계약서를 보내는 시점을 묻는 선택의문문에 워크숍이 끝나면 보내라는 의미로 언급한 (B)가 정답이다. (A)는 의미상 질문과 전혀 어울리지 않으며, (C)는 선택의문문의 전형적인 정답 유형인 both를 사용하여 혼동을 유도하고 있으나 질문과 무관한 답변이다.

어휘 contract 계약(서) both 둘 다

18 I'm just reviewing the quarterly sales report.
영M **(A) How do the figures look?**
미W (B) Sara will be leading it.
(C) After reviewing it.

저는 분기 매출 보고서를 검토하고 있어요.
(A) 수치가 어때 보이나요?
(B) Sara가 지휘할 거예요.
(C) 이것을 검토한 후에요.

해설 매출 보고서를 검토 중이라는 평서문에 보고서의 수치가 어떠냐고 되묻는 (A)가 정답이다. (B)는 제3자를 언급하며 질문과 무관한 내용을 말하고 있으며 (C)는 질문의 review를 반복 사용한 오답이다.

어휘 review 검토하다 quarterly 분기별의 figure 수치, 계산 lead 지휘하다, 이끌다

19 Would you be interested in designing our in-house newsletter?
미W
미M (A) Online research.
(B) Yes, I use several.
(C) When do you need it done?

... 회사 자료를 디자인하는 데 관심 있으세요?
(A) 온라인 연구요.
(B) 네, 저는 여러 개를 사용합니다.
(C) 언제 끝내기를 원하세요?

해설 특정 업무에 관심 여부를 묻는 조동사 의문문에 그 일을 언제까지 끝내야 하는지를 되물으면서 조건이 맞으면 관심이 있다는 의미로 응답하는 (C)가 정답이다. (A)는 질문과 전혀 연관성이 없는 답변을 하고 있으므로 오답이며, (C)는 관심이 있냐는 질문에 Yes로 답하면서 관심이 있다는 의미는 전달이 되지만, 뒤에 이와 관련 없는 내용이 이어지고 있으므로 오답이다.

어휘 in-house 내부의 research 연구, 조사 several 몇(몇)의

20 미W 영M
How much will it cost to reprint the brochures?
(A) There should be twelve.
(B) To make it easier to print.
(C) It depends on the design.
책자를 다시 인쇄하는 데 비용이 얼마나 드나요?
(A) 12개 정도 있을 거예요.
(B) 인쇄를 더 쉽게 하기 위해서요.
(C) 디자인에 따라 다르죠.

해설 비용을 묻는 How much 의문문에 디자인에 따라 결정된다는 전형적인 회피성 답변을 하는 (C)가 정답이다. (A)는 비용 대신 개수를 언급하면서 혼동을 유도하고 있는 오답이며, (B)는 이유를 묻는 Why 의문문에 대한 답변이므로 오답이다.

어휘 brochure (안내, 광고용) 책자 depend on ~에 달려 있다

21 영M 미M
Which train goes to the Natural History Museum?
(A) About a mile.
(B) The green line stops there.
(C) Yes, we saved them for large events.
어떤 기차가 자연사 박물관으로 가나요?
(A) 1마일 정도요.
(B) 녹색 노선이 거기에 섭니다.
(C) 네, 저희가 큰 행사를 위해서 모았어요.

해설 어떤 버스가 박물관에 가는지를 묻는 Which 의문문에 특정 노선을 언급하는 (B)가 정답이다. (A)는 얼마나 멀리 떨어져 있는지에 대한 답변으로 질문과 무관하며, (C)는 의문사 의문문에 Yes/No로 대답할 수 없으므로 오답이다.

어휘 line (기차) 선로, 노선 save (좋아하는 것, 특정 목적용으로) 모으다

22 미M 미W
This eatery has a wireless Internet connection, doesn't it?
(A) A reservation for three.
(B) Of course, and it's free for customers.
(C) In a connecting flight.
이 음식점은 무선 인터넷 연결이 됩니다, 그렇지 않아요?
(A) 세 명 예약이요.
(B) 물론이죠. 그리고 고객에게는 무료예요.
(C) 연결 비행 편에서요.

해설 식당에 무선 인터넷의 유무를 확인하는 부가의문문에 긍정의 Of course로 응답하고, 무료라는 추가 정보를 제공하고 있는 (B)가 가장 적절한 답이다. (A)는 질문의 식당(eatery)에서 연상이 가능한 reservation을 사용하여 혼동을 유도하고 있으나 예약 인원을 언급하는 답변으로 질문과 어울리지 않으며, (C)는 질문의 connection을 반복 사용하여 혼동을 유도하고 있으므로 오답이다.

어휘 eatery 음식점, 식당 connection 연결, 접속 connecting flight 연결 항공편

23 영M 미W
What are you bringing in to the celebration event?
(A) I won't be attending.
(B) I had some already.
(C) Yes, I went there last year.
기념행사에 무엇을 가지고 오실 건가요?
(A) 저는 참석하지 않을 거예요.
(B) 저는 이미 가지고 있어요.
(C) 네, 작년에 그곳에 갔었어요.

해설 행사에 무엇을 가져 오는지를 묻는 What 의문문에 행사 자체에 불참할 것이라고 우회적인 대답을 하는 (A)가 가장 적절한 답이다. (B)는 질문과 상관없는 답변을 하고 있으며, (C)는 의문사 의문문에 Yes/No로 대답할 수 없으므로 오답이다.

어휘 celebration 기념(축하) 행사 attend 참석하다, ~에 다니다

24 미W 미M
Who is the director of your firm?
(A) You'll be meeting her at noon.
(B) You're welcome to sit here.
(C) Herbert Foster will order it.
누가 당신 회사의 대표 이사인가요?
(A) 그녀를 정오에 만나게 되실 거예요.
(B) 여기에 앉으셔도 됩니다.
(C) Herbert Foster가 주문할 거예요.

해설 회사의 대표 이사가 누구인지를 묻는 Who 의문문에 그 사람을 곧 만나게 될 것이라는 우회적인 답을 하고 있으므로 (A)가 정답이다. (B)는 요청하는 질문에 적절한 답변으로 사용되는 허락의 표현이므로 오답이고, (C)는 Who 의문문에 전형적이 정답인 사람 이름을 언급하고 있지만 질문과 상관없는 답변이다. Who 의문문에 오답으로 출제되는 '이름, 직책' 등을 사용한 함정에 혼동되지 않도록 문제의 핵심 의미를 파악해야 한다.

어휘 director 대표 이사, 중역

25 미W 영M
Did you send them the notice about the project timeline?
(A) I'll go look for a projector.
(B) I thought Rio was going to do it.
(C) To save money.
프로젝트 일정에 대한 공지를 그들에게 보내셨나요?
(A) 제가 가서 프로젝터를 찾아볼게요.
(B) Rio가 할 거라고 생각했는데요.
(C) 돈을 절약하기 위해서요.

해설 공지를 보냈는지 묻는 조동사 의문문에 제3자를 언급하며 그가 할 것으로 알고 있었다고 회피성 언급을 하는 (B)가 가장 적절한 답이다. (A)는 질문의 project와 발음이 유사한 projector를 사용하여 혼동을 유도하고 있으나 질문과 무관한 답변을 하고 있으며, (C)는 이유를 묻는 Why 의문문의 전형적인 답변 유형이므로 해당 질문에는 어울리지 않는다.

어휘 notice 공고, 안내문 timeline 연대표, 시간별 상황표 save (돈을) 모으다, 저축하다

26 미M 영M
Would you like some help with the presentation or can you finish it by yourself?
(A) I'm almost done.
(B) She is a good speaker.
(C) Yes, I can see it.
발표에 도움이 필요하신가요, 아니면 혼자 끝내실 수 있으세요?
(A) 거의 다했어요.
(B) 그녀는 좋은 연설자예요.
(C) 네, 보여요.

해설 도움이 필요한지 아니면 혼자 할 수 있는지를 묻는 선택의문문에 거의 다했기 때문에 혼자 할 수 있다는 말을 우회적으로 표현한 (A)가 정답이다. (B)는 질문의 presentation에서 연상이 가능한 speaker를 이용하여 혼동을 유도하는 오답 유형이며, (C)는 질문의 내용과 무관한 답변이다.

어휘 by oneself 혼자, 다른 사람 없이

27 미M 미W
How can I change the password?
(A) I don't have any change, sorry.
(B) Chris will show you later.
(C) Whenever you like.
어떻게 비밀번호를 바꿀 수 있나요?
(A) 잔돈이 없어요. 죄송합니다.
(B) Chris가 나중에 알려줄 거예요.
(C) 언제든지 당신이 원하면요.

해설 방법을 묻는 How 의문문에 다른 사람이 알려 줄 거라고 답변하는 (B)가 가장 적절한 답이다. 제3자가 알려준다고 말하는 표현은 How 의문문에 자주 등장하는 우회적인 답변이다. (A)는 질문의 change(바꾸다)와 발음이 같은 change(잔돈)를 사용하여 혼동을 유도하는 오답으로 전혀 다른 의미로 사용되었음에 유의해야 한다. (C)는 당신이 원하면 언제든지 바꿀 수 있다는 의미로 방법을 묻는 질문에는 적절하지 않은 표현이다.

어휘 password 암호, 비밀번호

28 영M 미W
Let's try the new deli that opened near the office.
(A) I've already eaten lunch.
(B) The office is closed today.
(C) It's by the copier.
사무실 근처에 새로 개업한 델리에 가 봅시다.
(A) 저는 이미 점심을 먹었어요.

(B) 그 사무실은 오늘 닫았어요.
(C) 그것은 복사기 옆에 있어요.

해설 사무실 근처에 새로 생긴 샌드위치 가게에 가 보자는 제안 성격의 평서문에 이미 점심식사를 했으므로 가지 않겠다는 뜻을 우회적으로 답변하는 (A)가 가장 적절한 답이다. (B)는 질문의 office를 반복 사용할 뿐만 아니라, open-close의 연상어를 사용해 혼동을 유도하는 오답이며, (C)는 질문과 무관한 답변이다.

어휘 deli delicatessen의 줄임말, 육가공 식품 가게, 간단한 조리 샌드위치를 파는 상점

29 Where did you learn to make such delicious meatballs?
미W (A) I'd like the pasta, thanks.
미M **(B) My aunt showed me her recipe.**
(C) I saw you at the restaurant.

이렇게 맛있는 미트볼을 만드는 것을 어디서 배웠어요?
(A) 저는 파스타가 좋아요. 감사합니다.
(B) 제 이모가 요리법을 알려주셨어요.
(C) 당신을 레스토랑에서 봤어요.

해설 요리법을 배운 곳을 묻는 Where 의문문에 장소가 아닌 정보의 출처를 언급하는 (B)가 정답이다. Where 의문문 답변으로 장소뿐 아니라 정보의 출처를 뜻하는 사람이나 직책 등을 언급할 수 있으므로 이 점에 유의해야 한다. (A)는 질문의 meatballs에서 연상이 가능한 pasta로 답변한 오답이며, (C)는 Where 질문에 어울리는 장소로 대답하고 있지만 해당 질문과는 무관한 답변이다.

어휘 recipe 조리(요리)법

30 Do you know whether our Monday meeting is still on?
미W **(A) No, it's been called off.**
영M (B) Because she didn't have enough time.
(C) That doesn't work for me.

월요일 회의가 여전히 계획되어 있는지 알고 계시나요?
(A) 아니요. 취소되었어요.
(B) 그녀는 충분한 시간이 없었기 때문이죠.
(C) 저한테는 맞지 않네요.

해설 월요일 회의 여부를 묻는 간접의문문에 No로 부정적인 응답을 한 후, 취소되었다는 적절한 부연 설명을 하고 있으므로 (A)가 정답이다. (B)는 이유에 대한 대답이므로 질문과는 무관하며, (C)는 제안에 대한 거절의 의미이므로 질문과 상관없는 답변이다.

어휘 call off ~을 취소, 철회하다

31 Because of the rain, we've rescheduled the company picnic for next Friday instead.
미M (A) It sure was a lot of fun.
영M **(B) Okay, I'll change the date on my calendar.**
(C) I loved meeting everyone there.

비 때문에 다음 주 금요일로 회사 야유회 일정을 재조정했어요.
(A) 정말 재미있었어요.
(B) 알겠습니다. 제 달력에 날짜를 수정해 놓을게요.
(C) 저는 그곳에서 모두를 만나는 것이 좋았어요.

해설 날씨로 인해 야유회 일정을 조정했다는 정보를 알려주는 평서문에 달력에 표시하겠다며 다음 행동을 적절히 언급하고 있는 (B)가 정답이다. (A)는 질문의 picnic에서 연상이 가능한 fun으로 답변했으나 시제 불일치일 뿐만 아니라 내용상 연관성이 없으며, (C)는 만나서 좋았다며 과거로 언급하고 있으므로 질문의 시제와 맞지 않다.

PART 3

P61

Questions 32-34 refer to the following conversation. 미W 영M

W Excuse me. ㉜ I really like the pattern on this scarf. Are there any other color variations in the same style? I looked, but I didn't see any on display.
M Yes, actually, there are several color combinations that all have the same pattern. But I'm afraid we've already sold out of nearly everything from our original order. ㉝ We have more on the way, though. The complete selection will be back in stock by the end of this week.
W Great. Well, ㉞ I guess I'll go ahead and take this one today. I'll stop by again this weekend to look at the others once they've arrived.
M That sounds reasonable. I'll wrap it up for you.

여 실례합니다. 이 스카프의 패턴이 정말 맘에 드는데요. 같은 스타일로 다른 색상이 있나요? 제가 찾아봤지만, 진열된 것 중에 보지 못해서요.
남 네, 사실, 같은 패턴을 가진 다양한 색상 조합이 있는데요. 저희가 주문한 거의 모든 제품이 이미 다 팔렸습니다. 추가 상품이 들어오긴 할 텐데요. 이번 주말까지 모든 상품들이 들어올 겁니다.
여 훌륭하네요. 그럼, 오늘은 이것을 사야겠네요. 이번 주말에 다시 들러서 물건이 다 도착했을 때 다른 것들을 봐야겠어요.
남 일리 있는 말씀이시네요. 이건 제가 포장해 드릴게요.

어휘 variation 변화, 차이 combination 조합, 결합 sold out 다 팔린, 매진된 though ~이긴 하지만 selection 선정, 구색 go ahead 일어나다, 진행되다 reasonable 합리적인, 타당한 wrap 싸다, 포장하다 patron 고객 a range of 다양한 run out 다 떨어지다

32 Who is the woman talking to?
(A) A graphic designer
(B) A patron
(C) A sales clerk
(D) An interior decorator

여자는 누구와 대화하고 있는가?
(A) 그래픽 디자이너
(B) 고객
(C) 판매 사원
(D) 실내 장식가

해설 〈기본 정보파악 – 직업〉
화자의 직업을 묻는 문제는 초반에 단서가 제시되는 편이다. 첫 대사에서 여자가 스카프가 맘에 든다고 하면서 다른 색상이 있는지 묻고 있으므로 남자가 상점의 판매 사원임을 알 수 있다. 따라서 정답은 (C)이다.

33 What does the man expect to happen by the end of this week?
(A) An order will be placed.
(B) A range of new patterns will be designed.
(C) Some supplies will run out.
(D) Additional merchandise will be delivered.

남자는 이번 주말까지 무슨 일이 일어날 것으로 예상하는가?
(A) 주문이 이루어 질것이다.
(B) 다양한 새로운 패턴이 디자인될 것이다.
(C) 일부 상품이 다 떨어질 것이다.
(D) 추가 상품이 배송될 것이다.

해설 〈구체적 정보 파악 – 특정 사항〉
by the end of this week를 키워드로 잡고 남자가 이번 주말을 언급하는 부분에서 단서를 찾아야 한다. 대화 중반에 남자가 주문한 상품이 들어 오고 있으며 주말까지 모든 상품들이 갖추어질 것이라고 설명하고 있으므로 정답은 (D)이다.

34 What will the woman probably do next?
(A) Visit a different store
(B) Make a purchase
(C) Call a regular customer
(D) Look at color samples

여자가 다음으로 할 일은 무엇인가?
(A) 다른 상점에 방문한다.
(B) 결제를 한다.
(C) 단골 고객에게 전화한다.
(D) 색상 샘플을 확인한다.

해설 〈구체적 정보 파악 – 미래〉
앞으로 일어날 일을 묻는 문제는 후반에 단서가 제시된다. 여자가 대화 마지막에 다음 주에 와서 다시 살펴본다는 말을 하면서 오늘은 이것만 구입한다고 했으므로 정답은 (B)이다.

Questions 35-37 refer to the following conversation. (미M) (미W)

M Hi, Nancy. This is Alex Park from the sales department. ㉟ Has production started on the jerseys for the Brighton hockey team yet?

W No, it's not scheduled to start until tomorrow. We need to finish making the new uniforms for Elias Diner first. Why do you ask?

M ㊱ A team representative called me this morning and asked if it was too late to alter the design. He sent me the new specifications by e-mail, and the changes look pretty minor.

W Well, ㊲ go ahead and forward the new specifications to me right away. I'll take a look and see whether we can make the changes without affecting the production schedule.

남 안녕하세요, Nancy. 영업부의 Alex Park입니다. Brighton 하키팀을 위한 셔츠가 제작되기 시작했나요?

여 아니요, 내일은 되어서야 시작될 예정입니다. Elias Diner의 새 유니폼 제작을 먼저 끝내야 해서요. 왜 물어보시는 건가요?

남 오늘 아침에 팀 대표가 디자인을 변경하려면 너무 늦은 것인지 전화로 문의해 와서요. 새 시안을 이메일로 보내주었는데, 변경 사항이 많지는 않습니다.

여 음, 새로운 시안을 저에게 지금 바로 보내 주세요. 제가 확인해 보고 제작 일정에 영향을 주지 않는 선에서 변경할 수 있는지 한번 볼게요.

어휘 jersey (운동 경기용) 셔츠 not A until B B가 되어서야 A하다 alter 변하다, 바꾸다 specification 설명서, 사양 minor 작은, 별로 중요하지 않은 forward (물건, 정보를) 보내다, 전달하다 affect ~에 영향을 미치다 draft 초안을 작성하다

35 Where do the speakers probably work?

(A) At a manufacturing company
(B) At a hockey field
(C) At a department store
(D) At a storage facility

화자들이 일하는 곳은 어디인가?

(A) 제조 회사
(B) 하키 필드
(C) 백화점
(D) 저장 시설

해설 〈기본 정보 파악 – 장소〉
화자들이 일하는 장소를 묻는 문제로 대화 초반에 집중해야 한다. 남자가 첫 대사에서 셔츠 생산이 시작되었는지 확인하는 부분에서 옷을 만드는 공장이라는 것을 알 수 있다. 따라서 가장 적절한 정답은 (A)이다.

36 According to the man, what did a representative ask to do?

(A) Increase an order
(B) Delay a shipment
(C) Revise a design
(D) Reschedule a visit

남자에 의하면, 대표가 요청한 것은 무엇인가?

(A) 주문량 증가
(B) 배송 연기
(C) 디자인 수정
(D) 방문 일정 변경

해설 〈구체적 정보 파악 – 특정 사항〉
representative를 키워드로 잡고 남자가 이 단어를 언급하는 부분에서 정답의 단서를 찾아야 한다. 남자가 두 번째 대사에서 디자인을 수정하는 것에 대해서 팀 대표가 전화했다고 설명하고 있으므로 정답은 (C)이다.

패러프레이징 alter the design 디자인을 수정하다
→ revise a design 디자인을 변경(수정)하다

37 What does the woman want the man to do?

(A) Draft another design
(B) Arrange a meeting
(C) Send some information
(D) Change a plan

여자는 남자가 무엇을 하기를 원하는가?

(A) 다른 디자인의 초안을 만들기
(B) 회의 준비하기
(C) 정보 제공하기
(D) 계획 변경하기

해설 〈구체적 정보 파악 – 요청 관련〉
여자가 남자에게 무엇인가를 원하는 요청 관련 문제이므로 여자의 말에서 단서를 찾아야 한다. 여자가 마지막에 디자인 수정과 관련된 새로운 설명을 보내 달라고 요청하고 있으므로 정답은 (C)이다.

패러프레이징 forward the specifications 설명을 전달하다
→ send some information 정보를 보내다

Questions 38-40 refer to the following conversation. (영M) (미W)

M Hi, Ms. Kammerick. My name is Brad Simon and I'm from the Westside Theater in London. ㊳ I enjoyed your company's performance of *The Phantom of the Opera* last month.

W Thanks for coming. ㊳ I've produced several plays in London in the past. I'm sure we've met before.

M Well... ㊴ I'm not sure because I recently moved there from Manchester. By the way, I'd like to invite you to London with your cast and crew. The Westside Theater is very interested in hosting you for two or three months.

W ㊵ That sounds wonderful but we've just made an agreement with a theater in New York. Our schedule is full until the end of this year.

남 안녕하세요, Kammerick 씨, 저는 London에 있는 Westside 극장에서 온 Brad Simon입니다. 지난주 당신 회사의 '오페라의 유령' 공연을 잘 봤습니다.

여 와 주셔서 감사합니다. 저도 과거에 London에서 여러 연극을 제작 했었어요. 예전에 우리가 분명히 만난 적이 있을 겁니다.

남 글쎄요, 제가 최근에 Manchester에서 London으로 이사해서 잘 모르겠어요. 그건 그렇고, 제가 귀하의 배우들 및 제작진을 London으로 초청하려고 하는데요, 저희 Westside 극장은 2~3개월 동안 귀하를 초대하는 것에 매우 관심 있거든요.

여 아주 흥미로운 제안이지만, 저희가 New York에 있는 극장과 최근에 계약을 맺었어요. 저희 일정은 올해 말까지 가득 차 있습니다.

어휘 host ~를 초대하다, 열다 be interested in 관심이 있다, 의향이 있다 cast 배역

38 Who most likely is Ms. Kammerick?

(A) An actor
(B) A writer
(C) A producer
(D) A critic

Kammerick 씨는 누구인가?

(A) 배우
(B) 작가
(C) 제작자
(D) 비평가

해설 〈구체적 정보 파악 – 언급〉
문제에 제시된 제3자 이름을 언급할 때 정답의 단서를 찾아야 한다. 첫 대사에서 남자가 해당 이름을 부르며 인사하는 부분에서 Ms. Kammerick은 대화에 등장하는 여자임을 알 수 있으며, 남자가 이어서 여자 회사의 '오페라의 유령' 공연을 잘 보았다고 언급하는 부분과 여자가 과거에 런던에서 연극을 제작했다고 말하고 있으므로 정답은 (C)이다.

39 What does Mr. Simon say about London?
(A) He will meet a publisher there.
(B) He went to university there.
(C) He recently moved there.
(D) He used to work there.

Simon 씨는 London에 대해 무엇이라고 말하는가?
(A) 그는 출판업자를 그곳에서 만날 것이다.
(B) 그는 대학을 그곳에서 다녔다.
(C) 그는 최근에 그곳으로 옮겼다.
(D) 그는 그곳에서 일한 적이 있다.

해설 〈구체적 정보 파악 – 언급〉
Mr. Simon과 London을 동시에 키워드로 잡고 해당 키워드가 나오는 대사에 주목해야 한다. 첫 대사에서 남자가 자신을 런던에서 온 Mr. Simon이라고 소개한다. 또한 남자가 대화 중반에 Manchester에서 London으로 최근에 옮겼다고 말하고 있으므로 정답은 (C)이다.

40 What problem does Ms. Kammerick mention?
(A) The cost of living is too high.
(B) Her schedule is full.
(C) The theater is fully booked.
(D) She cannot meet a deadline.

Kammerick 씨가 언급한 문제는 무엇인가?
(A) 거주 비용이 너무 비싸다.
(B) 그녀의 일정이 가득 찼다.
(C) 극장 예약이 모두 끝났다.
(D) 그녀는 마감일을 맞출 수 없다.

해설 〈구체적 정보 파악 – 문제점〉
38번 문제를 통해 Ms. Kammerick이 대화에 등장하는 여자임을 인지하고 여자가 문제점을 언급하는 대사에 주목해야 한다. 남자의 제안에 여자는 마지막 대사에서 올해 말까지 일정이 많다고 거절하고 있기 때문에 정답은 (B)이다. 대화 중에 언급되는 반전의 표현은(but, however, actually, unfortunately) 정답을 언급하는 중요한 단서이므로 주목해야 한다.

Questions 41-43 refer to the following conversation. 미W 미M

W Frank, I got your e-mail with the materials you've created for our presentation to the board of directors next week. ㊶ You asked me to get back to you with my opinions. Do you have a moment now?
M Sure, Annabel. I've been looking forward to hearing from you.
W Well, for the most part, everything looks good. ㊷ But I would recommend including some graphs.
M Oh, that sounds good. What type of graphs?
W I'll leave that to you. ㊸ Whatever you think will make it easier to understand the figures we'll be reporting.

여 Frank, 다음 주에 있을 이사회 보고를 위해 만든 자료가 담긴 당신의 이메일을 받았어요. 제 의견을 달라고 요청하셨는데, 지금 시간 있으세요?
남 그럼요. Annabel. 회신을 기다리고 있었어요.
여 거의 모든 부분이 좋아 보이긴 하지만 그래프를 포함시키는 걸 추천하고 싶네요.
남 아, 그거 좋겠네요. 어떤 종류의 그래프요?
여 그건 당신에게 맡길게요. 보고해야 할 수치들을 더 이해하기 쉽게 만들 수 있다면 무엇이든 생각해 보세요.

어휘 material 자료, 소재 board of directors 이사회 look forward to ~을 기대하다 figures 수치 length 길이 visual 시각적인 accompany 동행하다

41 What did the man ask the woman to do in his e-mail?
(A) Confirm the length of a presentation
(B) Provide some feedback on his work
(C) Offer some presentation materials
(D) Contact the board of directors

남자는 이메일에 여자에게 무엇을 하라고 요청했는가?
(A) 프레젠테이션의 길이를 확정하는 것
(B) 그의 작업에 대한 피드백을 제공하는 것
(C) 발표 자료를 제공하는 것
(D) 이사회에 연락하는 것

해설 〈구체적 정보 파악 – 요청 관련〉
e-mail을 키워드로 잡고 앞뒤를 잘 들어야 한다. 남자가 요청하는 것에 관한 문제이므로 남자의 말에서 정답이 언급되는 경우가 많으나 이 문제는 키워드인 e-mail을 여자가 언급하고 있으므로 주의해야 한다. 여자는 남자가 보낸 이메일을 확인했다고 말하며 남자가 의견을 요청했다고 언급하고 있으므로 정답은 (B)이다.

패러프레이징 get back to you with my opinions 의견을 주다
→ provide some feedback 피드백을 제공하다

42 What does the woman suggest?
(A) Contacting a coworker
(B) Increasing a budget
(C) Adding a visual aid
(D) Shortening a document

여자가 제안하는 것은 무엇인가?
(A) 동료에게 연락하는 것
(B) 예산을 증가시키는 것
(C) 시각 자료를 추가하는 것
(D) 문서를 축약하는 것

해설 〈구체적 정보 파악 – 제안 관련〉
여자의 제안 사항을 묻는 문제로 여자의 대사에 주목해야 한다. 여자는 두 번째 대사에서 그래프를 추가하라고 추천하고 있으므로 정답은 (C)이다.

패러프레이징 including some graphs 그래프를 포함하다
→ adding visual aid 시각 자료를 추가하다

43 What does the woman mean when she says, "I'll leave that to you"?
(A) She plans to give an item to the man.
(B) She does not intend to stay for much longer.
(C) She will not accompany the man.
(D) She will allow the man to make a decision.

여자가 "그건 당신에게 맡길게요"라고 말한 의미는 무엇인가?
(A) 여자는 남자에게 제품을 줄 예정이다.
(B) 여자는 오래 머물 생각이 없다.
(C) 여자는 남자와 동행하지 않을 것이다.
(D) 여자는 남자가 결정을 내리도록 할 것이다.

해설 〈구체적 정보 파악 – 화자 의도〉
화자의 의도 파악을 묻는 문제 유형으로 여자가 해당 표현을 말하는 주변의 문맥을 종합하여 답을 선택해야 한다. 남자가 어떤 그래프를 포함해야 하는지 묻자 여자는 문제에 언급된 표현을 하며 보고할 수치들의 이해를 돕는 무엇이든 생각해 보라고 추가 설명한다. 남자에게 스스로 생각해서 결정을 하라는 의미이므로 (D)가 가장 적절한 답이다.

Questions 44-46 refer to the following conversation. (영M) (미W)

M Hi, Ashley. Did you order the additional boxes? We're almost out of stock.
W I was going to, 44 but I noticed that the price has gone up by about 20% from the last time we ordered.
M Oh, is that true?
W Yeah. And the discount rates for bulk orders have gone down as well.
M 44 We can't afford to spend more than what we're paying now. 45 We should definitely start looking for a different company.
W I think so. 46 I'll get some price estimates from several suppliers and make a list. Let's think about all the possibilities.

남 안녕하세요, Ashley. 추가 상자들을 주문했나요? 거의 다 떨어져 가거든요.
여 하려고 했는데, 가격이 지난번 우리가 주문했을 때보다 거의 20%가 올랐어요.
남 오, 정말이요?
여 네. 그리고 대량 구매 할인율도 떨어졌고요.
남 우리가 지금 지불하고 있는 것보다 더 많은 금액을 쓸 여유가 없어요. 다른 회사를 찾아봐야겠어요.
여 저도 그렇게 생각해요. 제가 여러 공급 업체로부터 비용 견적을 받아서 목록을 만들게요. 모든 가능성에 대해서 생각해 봅시다.

어휘 additional 추가의 out of stock 품절되어, 매진되어 bulk order 대량 발주, 일괄 주문 afford 여유(형편)가 되다 definitely 분명히, 틀림없이 estimate 추정, 견적서 defective 결함이 있는 price quote 견적서

44 What are the speakers concerned about?
(A) Defective items
(B) Wrong orders
(C) Lack of staff
(D) Rising expenses

화자들은 무엇에 대해 걱정하는가?
(A) 제품 불량
(B) 잘못된 주문
(C) 직원 부족
(D) 비용 상승

해설 〈구체적 정보 파악 – 걱정 관련〉
주문 상황을 묻는 남자의 질문에 여자가 하려고 했으나 가격이 올랐다고 말하며 주문하지 않은 이유를 설명하자, 남자가 돈을 더 지불할 수 없다고 말하고 있으므로 정답은 (D)이다.

45 What does the man suggest?
(A) Changing a supplier
(B) Checking the order form
(C) Reporting to a manager
(D) Discussing a problem

남자가 제안하는 것은 무엇인가?
(A) 공급 업체를 변경하는 것
(B) 주문 양식을 확인하는 것
(C) 관리자에게 보고하는 것
(D) 문제점을 논의하는 것

해설 〈구체적 정보 파악 – 제안 관련〉
남자의 제안 사항에 대한 문제이므로 남자의 말에서 정답을 찾아야 한다. 남자의 두 번째 대사에서 현재 거래하는 회사의 가격이 상승하여 다른 회사를 찾아봐야 한다고 말하고 있으므로 정답은 (A)이다.

패러프레이징 looking for a different company 다른 회사 찾기
→ changing a supplier 공급 업체 변경하기

46 What does the woman decide to do?
(A) Cancel orders
(B) Work overtime
(C) Get some price quotes
(D) Help her coworker

여자는 무엇을 하기로 결정하는가?
(A) 주문을 취소하기
(B) 추가 근무하기
(C) 견적서 받기
(D) 동료를 도와주기

해설 〈구체적 정보 파악 – 특정 사항〉
여자의 결정 사항에 대한 문제이므로 여자의 말에서 정답을 찾아야 한다. 여자의 마지막 대사에서 여러 공급 업체로부터 비용 견적을 받아서 목록을 만들 것이라고 하므로 정답은 (C)이다.

패러프레이징 get some price estimates 가격 견적 받기
→ get some price quote 견적서 받기

Questions 47-49 refer to the following conversation. (미W) (미M)

W Excuse me. I'm looking for journals on agriculture. Could you tell me where they are?
M Ah, sure. They're in aisle 2, next to the sale items display. 47 Unfortunately, our selection is quite small at the moment; the publisher has been having trouble with shipping.
W I see. 48 I suppose that could be a result of the terrible weather in the East Coast.
M That's probably the case. Anyway, we hope to be getting more journals next week. 49 If you'd like to leave your name and number, I can give you a call as soon as they come in.

여 실례합니다. 농업 관련 저널을 찾고 있는데요. 어디에 있는지 알려주시겠어요?
남 아, 그럼요. 할인 제품 진열대 옆 2번 통로에 있습니다. 안타깝게도, 현재 출판사가 운송에 어려움을 겪고 있어서 선택의 폭이 좀 좁으실 겁니다.
여 그렇군요. 동부 해안의 험한 날씨 때문에 그런 거군요.
남 아마 그럴 겁니다. 어쨌든, 다음 주에 더 많은 저널들을 받을 수 있을 거예요. 번호와 이름을 남기시면, 들어오는 대로 전화 드릴게요.

어휘 journals 저널, 학술지 agriculture 농업 aisle 통로 publisher 출판사 under construction 공사 중인

47 What is the problem?
(A) The store is under construction.
(B) Only a few items are available.
(C) Some equipment is not working.
(D) A sale has just ended.

무엇이 문제인가?
(A) 가게가 공사 중이다.
(B) 일부 제품만 이용 가능하다.
(C) 몇몇 기구가 작동하지 않는다.
(D) 할인이 막 끝났다.

해설 〈구체적 정보 파악 – 문제점〉
문제점을 묻는 구체적 정보 파악 유형이지만 문제점은 초반에 단서가 제시될 가능성이 높다. 저널을 찾고 있는 여자에게 해당 위치를 알려주며 운송에 문제가 있어 고객의 선택 폭이 좁다고 부연 설명하고 있으므로 정답은 (B)이다.

패러프레이징 selection is quiet small 선택의 폭이 좁다 → only a few items are available 일부 제품만 이용 가능하다

48 Why does the man say, "That's probably the case"?
(A) He agrees with the woman.
(B) He is searching in a display case.
(C) He hopes the weather will clear up.
(D) He is offering his idea.

남자가 "아마 그럴 겁니다"라고 말하는 이유는 무엇인가?
(A) 남자는 여자에게 동의한다.
(B) 남자는 진열장 안을 찾고 있다.
(C) 남자는 날씨가 좋아지길 바란다.
(D) 남자는 그의 아이디어를 제안한다.

해설 〈구체적 정보 파악 – 화자 의도〉
화자의 의도를 묻는 문제로, 주변 문맥과 함께 남자가 한 말의 의도를 파악해야 한다. 여자가 마지막 대사에서 출판사가 겪고 있는 운송 문제는 동부 해안의 악천후 때문이라고 언급하자 남자가 동의하고 있으므로 정답은 (A)이다.

49 Why does the man request the woman's personal information?
(A) To give her details of another location
(B) To tell her about upcoming sale
(C) To offer a membership discount
(D) To notify her when more stock arrives

남자가 여자의 개인 정보를 요청하는 이유는 무엇인가?
(A) 다른 위치의 세부 사항을 여자에게 알려주기 위해
(B) 다가오는 할인에 대해 여자에게 알려주기 위해
(C) 회원 할인을 제공하기 위해
(D) 재고품이 도착하면 알려주기 위해

해설 〈구체적 정보 파악 – 특정 사항〉
personal information을 키워드로 잡고 유사어가 나오는 부분에 집중해야 한다. 대화 마지막에 남자가 이름과 번호를 남기면 저널이 들어오는 대로 전화하겠다고 말한다. 따라서 정답은 (D)이다.

패러프레이징 name and number 이름과 전화번호
→ personal information 개인 정보

Questions 50-52 refer to the following conversation with three speakers. 미W 영W 영M

W1 Hey, Charles. I just heard about your art exhibition opening this weekend. You must be excited.
W2 What's this? Charles, I didn't know you were an artist.
M It's just a hobby, really. 50 In fact, this will be my first time to exhibit my art in public.
W1 Are you nervous?
M I hate to admit it, but I'm very nervous.
W2 What type of artwork do you do? Paintings or photographs?
M No, sculpture. 51 I make all my pieces out of recycled material.
W2 Sounds very interesting.
M 52 Why don't you guys come to the gallery and check it out? It'd be nice to have some coworkers show up to give me some emotional support.

여1 Charles, 이번 주말에 열리는 당신의 미술 전시회에 대해 방금 들었습니다. 좋으시겠어요.
여2 무슨 얘기예요? Charles, 저는 당신이 예술가인지 몰랐어요.
남 그냥 취미예요. 사실, 공개적으로 제 작품을 전시하는 것은 이번이 처음입니다.
여1 긴장되시나요?
남 인정하기는 싫지만, 사실, 정말 긴장돼요.
여2 어떤 종류의 작품을 만드시나요? 그림 아니면 사진인가요?
남 아니요, 조각입니다. 모든 작품들을 재활용품으로 만들죠.
여2 아주 흥미롭네요.
남 갤러리에 오셔서 보시는 것이 어떨까요? 동료들이 와서 저에게 정서적 지원을 해 준다면 기쁠 겁니다.

어휘 exhibition 전시회 excited 신이 난, 들뜬 hobby 취미 in public 공개적으로 nervous 불안해 하는 recycle 재활용하다 show up ~을 나타내다, 눈에 띄다 emotional 정서의, 감정적인 support 지원, 지지 auction 경매 collaborate 협력하다

50 What is the man nervous about?
(A) Making a public speech
(B) Showing his work
(C) Entering a competition
(D) Leading a discussion

남자는 무엇에 대해 긴장하는가?
(A) 공개 연설하는 것
(B) 그의 작품을 보여주는 것
(C) 경쟁에 참여하는 것
(D) 토론을 이끄는 것

해설 〈구체적 정보 파악 – 특정 사항〉
남자가 긴장하는 이유이므로 남자의 말에서 정답을 찾아야 한다. 남자가 처음 여는 전시회라고 언급하자 여자1이 긴장되는지 묻고 남자가 그렇다고 말하고 있으므로 정답은 (B)이다.

패러프레이징 exhibit one's art in public ~의 작품을 공개적으로 전시하다 → show one's work ~의 작품을 보여주다

51 What does the man say about his work?
(A) It is made from recycled material.
(B) It is being sold at an auction.
(C) It consists mainly of paintings.
(D) It has recently won an award.

남자는 그의 작품에 대해 무엇이라고 말하는가?
(A) 재활용품으로 만들었다.
(B) 경매에서 판매 중이다.
(C) 주로 그림으로 구성되어 있다.
(D) 최근에 상을 받았다.

해설 〈구체적 정보 파악 – 언급〉
작품에 대해 말하는 남자의 설명에 주목해야 한다. 남자가 조각 작품을 만든다고 말하면서 모든 작품은 재활용품을 이용해서 만든다고 했으므로 정답은 (A)이다.

52 What does the man suggest the women do?
(A) Collaborate on a design
(B) Support an artist
(C) Attend an exhibition
(D) Cast a vote online

남자는 여자들에게 무엇을 하라고 제안하는가?
(A) 디자인 협력하기
(B) 예술가 지원하기
(C) 전시회 참석하기
(D) 온라인 투표하기

해설 〈구체적 정보 파악 – 제안 관련〉
남자가 두 여자들에게 제안하는 사항이므로 남자의 말에서 단서를 찾아야 한다. 마지막 대사에서 남자가 직접 와서 작품을 볼 것을 제안하고 있으므로 정답은 (C)이다.

Questions 53-55 refer to the following conversation. 미W 미M

W Welcome back to the lunch hour show here on Radio Five. 53 Today we're talking with documentary filmmaker Ernest Schmidt, 54 who's just come back from an excursion to Congo. Tell us about that, Ernest.

M It was a thrilling experience. I went rafting on the River Ivindo. It's even more thrilling than any other places. Of course, my favorite thing was interacting with the locals, although it can be challenging when few people speak English.

W Sounds interesting! Can you tell us little more about what's in your upcoming film?

M Well, 55 it'll feature a lot of interviews, mostly with very low-income people. There's still a lot of poverty even as the government and economy improve.

여 Radio Five의 점심시간 방송에 다시 오신 것을 환영합니다. 오늘 우리는 콩고 여행에서 방금 돌아온 다큐멘터리 제작자 Ernest Schmidt 씨와 이야기를 나눌 것입니다. 말씀해 주시죠, Ernest 씨.

남 그것은 흥미진진한 경험이었습니다. Ivindo 강에 래프팅하러 갔었어요. 그 어떤 장소보다도 훨씬 더 스릴 있었지요. 물론, 제가 가장 좋아했던 것은 주민들과 소통하는 것이었습니다. 비록 영어를 말하는 사람들이 거의 없을 때는 어려운 일이 될 수 있지만 말이죠.

여 흥미롭네요! 새로 나올 영화에 대해 조금 더 말씀해 주실 수 있을까요?

남 음, 대부분 저소득 계층 사람들과의 인터뷰를 가장 크게 다루었어요. 정권과 경제가 향상되어도 여전히 빈곤한 사람들이 많이 있습니다.

어휘 filmmaker 영화 제작자, 영화 회사 excursion (단체로 짧게 하는) 여행 thrilling 흥분되는, 신 나는 interact 소통하다, 교류하다 challenging 도전적인, 어려운 although (비록) ~이긴 하지만 feature 프로그램의 특색으로 삼다, ~을 크게 다루다 low-income 저소득의 poverty 가난, 빈곤, 부족

53 What type of business does the man work for?
(A) A tour service
(B) A film production company
(C) A radio station
(D) An airline company

남자는 어떤 종류의 회사에 근무하는가?
(A) 여행 서비스
(B) 필름 제작 회사
(C) 라디오 방송국
(D) 항공사

해설 〈기본 정보 파악 – 장소〉
남자가 일하는 장소를 묻는 문제이므로 첫 대사의 단서에 주목해야 한다. 여자가 첫 대사에서 남자를 소개하며 오늘 다큐멘터리 제작자 Ernest Schmidt 씨와 이야기를 나눌 것이라고 예고하고 있으므로 정답은 (B)이다.

54 What has the man recently done?
(A) Written a book
(B) Attended an international seminar
(C) Returned for a trip abroad
(D) Started his own business

남자가 최근에 한 것은 무엇인가?
(A) 책을 썼다.
(B) 국제 세미나에 참석했다.
(C) 해외여행에서 돌아왔다.
(D) 자신의 회사를 시작했다.

해설 〈구체적 정보 파악 – 특정 사항〉
남자가 최근에 한 일이지만 여자가 남자를 소개하면서 언급하므로 주의해야 한다. 키워드를 recently로 잡고 비슷한 표현이 나오는 부분에서 답을 찾아야 하는데 여자가 just와 현재완료 시제로 얘기하는 부분에서 답이 언급된다. 여자는 남자가 방금 콩고 여행에서 돌아왔다고 했으므로 정답은 (C)이다.

패러프레이징 come back from an excursion to Congo 콩고 여행에서 돌아오다 → return for a trip abroad 해외여행에서 돌아오다

55 Who does the man say he talked with?
(A) Volunteer aid workers
(B) Government officials
(C) Many poor people
(D) Newspaper journalists

남자는 누구와 이야기를 나누었다고 말하는가?
(A) 자원봉사 구조원들
(B) 공무원들
(C) 많은 가난한 사람들
(D) 신문 기자들

해설 〈구체적 정보 파악 – 특정 사항〉
남자가 마지막 대사에서 다큐멘터리에 저소득 계층 사람들과의 인터뷰가 많이 실려 있다고 했으므로 정답은 (C)이다.

패러프레이징 low-income people 저소득층 사람들
→ poor people 가난한 사람들

Questions 56-58 refer to the following conversation with three speakers. 영M 미W 호M

M1 56 We need to get the rest of these packages sent out today. I'll check that each box's contents are correct, and Melissa, you tape them shut.

W Okay, I'll get the tape.

M1 Jack, will you check the address labels?

M2 You bet. I have the final list right here.

W What time does the post office close today?

M1 57 At 6. Don't worry, we've still got two hours until then, and we only have 6 more boxes to do. We've got lots of time.

M2 Brian, 58 we have to finish more than 6, there's a big stack of them over there too.

W Really? Let's get on with it, then.

남1 우리는 오늘 남은 소포들을 발송해야 해요. 제가 각 상자의 내용물이 맞는지 확인할 테니, Melissa는 테이프를 붙여 주세요.

여 좋아요. 테이프를 가져올게요.

남1 Jack, 주소 라벨을 확인해 줄래요?

남2 물론이죠. 최종 리스트가 바로 여기 있어요.

여 오늘 우체국이 몇 시에 닫나요?

남1 6시요. 걱정하지 마세요. 그때까지 아직 두 시간이 남아 있고, 여섯 상자만 더 하면 돼요. 시간은 많아요.

남2 Brian, 여섯 개 이상을 끝내야 해요. 저쪽에 무더기로 쌓여 있어요.

여 정말인가요? 그럼 어서 서두릅시다.

어휘 contents 내용물 stack 무더기, 더미 parcel 소포

56 What activity are the speakers participating in?
(A) Driving to the post office
(B) Operating some office equipment
(C) Placing an order of supplies
(D) Preparing parcels to mail

화자들은 어떤 활동을 하고 있는가?
(A) 우체국으로 운전해서 가기
(B) 사무기기를 작동시키기
(C) 상품 발주하기
(D) 소포 발송 준비하기

해설 〈구체적 정보 파악 – 특정 사항〉
화자들이 무슨 일에 참여하고 있는지를 묻는 구체적 문제이지만, 주제와 동일하게 첫 대사에 정답이 등장한다. 남자1이 첫 대사에서 소포를 보내야 한다고 말하고 있으므로 (D)가 정답이다.

패러프레이징 send out a package 소포를 부치다
→ mail a parcel 소포를 우편으로 부치다

57 At what time does the conversation most likely take place?
(A) 2:00
(B) 3:00
(C) 4:00
(D) 5:00

대화가 이루어지는 시간은 언제인가?
(A) 2시
(B) 3시
(C) 4시
(D) 5시

해설 〈구체적 정보 파악 - 특정 사항〉
구체적 시간을 언급하는 부분에 주목해야 한다. 여자가 남자에게 우체국의 닫는 시간을 묻자 남자1이 6시라고 답하며 아직 두 시간이 남아 있다고 말하는 부분에서 현재 대화를 나누고 있는 시간은 4시임을 알 수 있다. 그러므로 정답은 (C)이다.

58 What does the woman mean when she says, "Let's get on with it, then"?
(A) Everyone should work faster.
(B) The labels are all ready.
(C) There is plenty of time left.
(D) They need to leave right now.

여자가 "그럼 어서 서두릅시다"라고 말한 의미는 무엇인가?
(A) 모든 사람들이 더 빨리 일해야 한다.
(B) 라벨은 모두 준비되었다.
(C) 시간이 많이 남았다.
(D) 그들은 지금 바로 떠나야 한다.

해설 〈구체적 정보 파악 - 화자 의도〉
문제에 언급된 말 앞뒤의 내용을 살펴보면, 시간이 많다는 남자1에게 남자2가 작업해야 할 상자들이 쌓여 있다고 말한다. 이어서 여자가 문제에 언급된 표현을 하고 있으므로, 시간은 정해져 있고 일은 많이 남았으니 서두르자는 의도를 가장 적절히 설명한 (A)가 정답이다.

Questions 59-61 refer to the following conversation. 미M 미W

M Hi, Naomi. 59 Has there been any progress on the year-end function?
W Actually, yes. We've booked the Kingston Auditorium.
M That big place?
W That's right. To be honest, it's a little expensive to rent, but it has enough space to accommodate the large numbers we're expecting, as well as plenty of free parking.
M Great! 60 We had some problems with last year's venue, especially the fact that it wasn't easily accessible. A lot of people have told me Kingston is very easy to get to. Have the tickets gone on sale yet?
W They went on sale yesterday. 61 I heard around 35% have already been sold. We've managed to keep prices the same as last year, which is proving to be attractive.
M Wow, that's a very good idea.

남 안녕하세요, Naomi. 연말 행사에 진전이 있나요?
여 네, 있어요. Kingston 강당을 예약했거든요.
남 그 큰 장소를요?
여 맞아요. 솔직히 말하면 임대 비용이 좀 비싸기는 했지만, 우리가 예상하고 있는 많은 인원을 수용하기에 충분한 장소예요. 뿐만 아니라, 무료 주차 공간도 많고요.
남 훌륭하네요! 작년에는 장소에 문제가 좀 있었잖아요. 특히 접근이 용이하지 않았던 것도 사실이었고요. 많은 사람들이 Kingston은 아주 가기 쉽다고 했어요. 표는 이미 판매하고 있죠?
여 어제 판매를 시작했어요. 제가 듣기로는 이미 35% 가량 팔렸대요. 작년과 동일한 가격을 유지한 것이 매력적이었던 것 같아요.
남 와, 아주 좋은 생각이네요.

어휘 progress 진전, 진척, 진행 function 기능, 행사, 의식 accommodate 공간을 제공하다, 수용하다 venue 장소 accessible 접근, 입장이 가능한 attractive 멋진, 매력적인

59 What is the conversation mainly about?
(A) Preparation for an award ceremony
(B) Plans for an event
(C) The cost of supplies
(D) Directions to a venue

이 대화의 주제는 무엇인가?
(A) 시상식 준비
(B) 행사 계획
(C) 공급 제품의 비용
(D) 특정 장소로 가는 길 안내

해설 〈기본 정보 파악 - 주제〉
대화의 목적을 묻는 문제는 초반에 단서가 나온다. 남자가 첫 대사에서 연말 행사에 대해 언급하고 있으므로 정답은 (B)이다.

60 What does the man say about the previous year's event?
(A) It had enough space.
(B) It was hard to get to.
(C) It was expensive to rent.
(D) It had free parking.

남자는 작년 행사에 대해 무엇이라고 말하는가?
(A) 공간이 충분했다.
(B) 가기가 어려웠다.
(C) 임대 비용이 비쌌다
(D) 무료 주차가 가능했다.

해설 〈구체적 정보 파악 - 언급〉
previous year's event를 키워드로 잡고 비슷한 표현이 언급되는 부분에 주목해야 한다. 대화 중반부에 남자가 작년 행사의 장소에 문제가 있었다고 말하며, 접근이 쉽지 않았다고 부연 설명하고 있으므로 정답은 (B)이다.

패러프레이징 It wasn't easily accessible. 접근이 쉽지 않았다
→ It was hard to get to. 가기가 어려웠다

61 What is indicated about the tickets?
(A) They are quite expensive.
(B) They have already sold out.
(C) The prices are lower than before.
(D) They are selling well.

표에 대해 무엇이 언급되고 있는가?
(A) 꽤 비싸다.
(B) 이미 다 팔렸다.
(C) 가격이 이전보다 싸다.
(D) 잘 팔리고 있다.

해설 〈구체적 정보 파악 - 언급〉
대화 중에 표가 언급되는 부분에서 단서가 나온다. 대화 후반에 남자가 표를 판매하는 중인지 묻자, 여자가 어제부터 판매 중이며 이미 35% 가량이 판매되었다고 대답하고 있으므로 표가 아주 잘 팔린다는 의미의 (D)가 정답이다.

Questions 62-64 refer to the following conversation and floor plan.
미W 영M

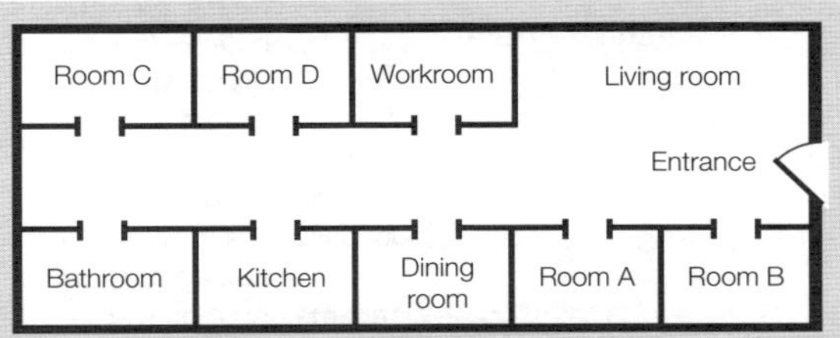

W Thanks for coming so quickly.
M Not at all. ⓺② Actually I was working on the renovation on an apartment a couple of blocks away.
W I see. Well, I'd like to get an estimate on some remodeling work. Do you think it would be possible to remove this wall between the workroom and the living room?
M That should be a simple job.
W Great. ⓺③ Also the bathroom is far from the workroom. I'd like to put it next to where the workroom is now.
M Good idea. ⓺④ I should tell you that this will take around five weeks to complete though. There is a lot of plumbing and electrical work to do. That kind of work is quite expensive, too.

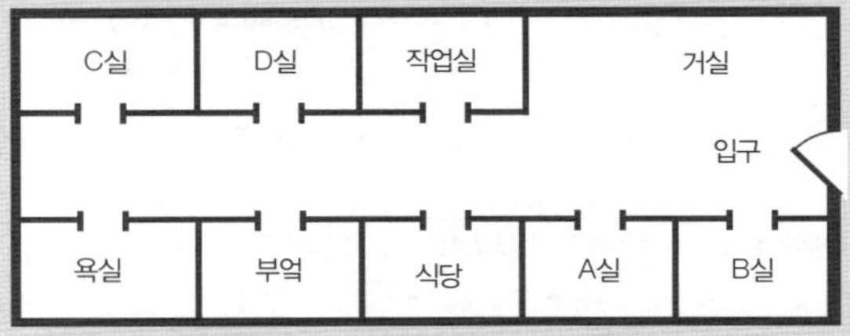

여 이렇게 빨리 와 주셔서 감사합니다.
남 아닙니다. 사실, 몇 블록 근처에서 아파트 수리 작업을 하고 있었어요.
여 그렇군요. 저는 리모델링 작업에 대한 견적을 받고 싶은데요. 작업실과 거실 사이에 있는 이 벽을 제거하는 것이 가능할까요?
남 간단한 작업입니다.
여 다행이네요. 또 욕실이 작업실과 너무 멀어요. 현재 작업실이 있는 곳 옆에 욕실을 두고 싶어요.
남 좋은 생각이네요. 이 작업을 완료하는 데 5주 정도 걸릴 거라는 것을 말씀 드려야겠네요. 배관과 전기 작업들이 많거든요. 이런 종류의 작업은 비용도 좀 많이 듭니다.

어휘 renovation 개조, 수리 get an estimate 견적 받기 plumbing 배관, 수도시설 electrical work 전기 작업

62 Who most likely is the man?
(A) A plumber
(B) An electrician
(C) A real estate agent
(D) A builder
남자는 누구인가?
(A) 배관공
(B) 전기 기사
(C) 부동산 중개인
(D) 건축업자

해설 〈기본 정보 파악 – 직업〉
화자의 직업을 묻는 문제는 대화의 전반부에서 답을 찾아야 한다. 여자가 남자의 방문에 고마움을 전하자 남자는 근처에서 수리 작업을 하고 있다고 말한다. 따라서 남자는 renovation과 관련된 일을 하는 사람이므로 (D)가 가장 적절한 답이다.

63 Look at the graphic. Where does the woman say she would like to put the bathroom?
(A) Room A
(B) Room B
(C) Room C
(D) Room D
시각 자료를 보시오. 여자는 욕실을 어디에 두고 싶다고 말하는가?
(A) A실
(B) B실
(C) C실
(D) D실

해설 〈구체적 정보 파악 – 시각 자료 연계〉
대화를 듣기 전에 문제와 시각 자료를 보고 단서를 예측할 수 있어야 하며, 배치 관련 문제이므로 위치 관계 묘사를 통해 단서가 제시될 가능성이 높다. 여자가 욕실과 작업실이 멀어서 욕실을 작업실 옆으로 옮기고 싶다고 설명하고 있으므로 작업실 바로 옆에 위치한 (D)가 정답이다.

64 What does the man say about the project?
(A) It will take a long time.
(B) It requires a lot of travel.
(C) It will be started next week.
(D) It will be cheap to complete.
남자는 계획에 대해 무엇이라고 말하는가?
(A) 시간이 오래 걸릴 것이다.
(B) 많은 출장이 필요할 것이다.
(C) 다음 주에 시작할 것이다.
(D) 완료하는 데 가격이 저렴할 것이다.

해설 〈구체적 정보 파악 – 언급〉
남자가 개조 공사에 대해 언급하는 부분에서 답을 찾아야 한다. 대화 마지막에 남자는 배관과 전기 공사 때문에 비싸다는 말과 함께 완료까지 5주가 걸릴 것임을 알리고 있다. 따라서 (A)가 정답이다.

Questions 65-67 refer to the following conversation and schedule.
미W 미M

SCHEDULE	
Tuesday, October 6	Financial Reports Due
Wednesday, October 7	Plant Inspection
Thursday, October 8	Plant Inspection
Friday, October 9	New Item Introduction

W Hi, Martin. ⓺⑤ I'm wondering when we should hold the welcoming reception for Ms. Sato.
M Her first day here will be on Tuesday, but I don't think we should hold it then because people will be too tired to work the next day.
W Besides, the financial reports are due then so we'll probably have to work until late.
M Yeah, and some of the staff members have to take a trip to inspect the factory in Portland on the seventh and eighth.
W And they won't want to go out on the evening they get back.
M Right, ⓺⑥ so the day of the product release is our only option. ⓺⑦ Would you mind making a reservation at a local restaurant — for twenty people, I guess.
W Sure, ⓺⑦ I'll see if Gino's can accommodate us.

일정	
10월 6일 화요일	재무 보고서 마감
10월 7일 수요일	공장 점검
10월 8일 목요일	공장 점검
10월 9일 금요일	새로운 제품 소개

여 안녕하세요, Martin. Sato 씨를 위한 환영회를 언제 해야 하는지 궁금해서요.
남 그녀의 첫 출근이 화요일이긴 하지만 그때 할 수는 없을 것 같아요. 왜냐하면 사람들이 다음 날 일하는데 많이 피곤해 할 거예요.
여 게다가, 재무 보고서 마감 때라서 우리는 아마도 늦게까지 일해야 할 거예요.
남 맞아요. 그리고 직원 몇 명은 7일과 8일에 점검을 위해 Portland에 있는 공장에 가야 해요.
여 그리고 그들은 돌아온 날 저녁에 외출하고 싶어 하지 않을 겁니다.
남 맞아요. 그래서 제품이 출시되는 날이 우리가 선택할 수 있는 유일한 날이에요. 근처 식당에 예약 좀 해 주시겠어요? 20명 정도로요.
여 물론이죠. Gino에 우리가 모두 갈 수 있는지 알아볼게요.

어휘 welcoming reception 환영회 inspect 조사하다 release 출시 accommodate 수용하다, 공간을 제공하다

65 What is the main topic of the conversation?
(A) A guest speaker
(B) A sporting competition
(C) A welcome event
(D) A local festival
이 대화의 주요 주제는 무엇인가?
(A) 객원 연설자
(B) 스포츠 경기
(C) 환영 행사
(D) 지역 축제

해설 〈기본 정보 파악 – 주제〉
대화의 주제는 초반을 잘 들어야 한다. 첫 대사에서 여자가 환영회 개최에 대해 묻고 있으므로 정답은 (C)이다.

66 Look at the graphic. When most likely will the event be held?
(A) On Tuesday
(B) On Wednesday
(C) On Thursday
(D) On Friday
시각 자료를 보시오. 행사는 언제 열리겠는가?
(A) 화요일
(B) 수요일
(C) 목요일
(D) 금요일

해설 〈구체적 정보 파악 – 시각 자료 연계〉
행사가 열리는 날짜와 요일이 선택지로 제시되고 있으므로 정답의 단서는 요일별로 달라지는 행사와 관련해서 언급된다는 것을 예측하고 들어야 한다. 대화 후반부에 남자가 제품이 출시되는 날이 선택할 수 있는 유일한 날이라고 했으므로 제품 출시일 즉, 새 제품 소개 행사가 예정된 금요일인 (D)가 정답이다.

패러프레이징 product release 제품 출시
→ New Item introduction 새 제품 소개

67 What does the woman say she will do?
(A) Attend a conference
(B) Book a venue
(C) Prepare an inspection
(D) Reserve a hotel room
여자는 무엇을 하겠다고 말하는가?
(A) 학회에 참석한다.
(B) 장소를 예약한다.
(C) 점검을 준비한다.
(D) 호텔을 예약한다.

해설 〈구체적 정보 파악 – 미래〉
대화 후에 일어날 일이므로 대화의 후반부에서 정답을 찾아야 한다. 남자가 예약을 해 달라고 부탁한 후, 여자가 마지막 대사에서 특정 장소를 언급하며 행사에 참석할 인원 수용이 가능한지 알아보겠다고 했으므로 장소 예약을 할 것임을 알 수 있다. 따라서 (B)가 가장 적절한 답이다.

패러프레이징 make a reservation at the restaurant 식당을 예약하다
→ book a venue 장소를 예약하다

Questions 68-70 refer to the following conversation and bill.
영M 미W

Name: Joyce Hahn Patient# 002875		
Wednesday 9/13	Examination	$40.00
	2x Gum Treatment	$200.00
	2x Dental Filling	$260.00
	Toothpaste	$10.00
	Balance Due	$510.00

M Thank you for calling the Union Town Dental Clinic. How may I help you?
W Hello. This is Joyce Hahn. I'm a patient of Dr. Betts. I just received the bill for my visit last Wednesday, and it looks like I've been charged twice for the same treatment. ⓺⓼ Dr. Betts just filled a cavity in one tooth during my visit, but my bill shows the cost for two fillings.
M Oh, I'm terribly sorry, Ms. Hahn. ⓺⓽ We recently installed new accounting and billing software. The error must have been made when I transferred your information into the new system. ⓻⓪ I'll make the correction to your records and issue a new bill right away.

이름: Joyce Hahn 환자 번호 002875		
수요일 9/13	진료비	40달러
	2x 잇몸 치료	200달러
	2x 치과용 충전	260달러
	치약	10달러
	지불액	510달러

남 Union Town 치과에 전화해 주셔서 감사합니다. 무엇을 도와 드릴까요?
여 안녕하세요. 저는 Betts 선생님의 환자 Joyce Hahn입니다. 제가 지난주 수요일 진료 청구서를 방금 받았는데, 동일한 치료에 비용이 두 번 청구된 것 같습니다. 제가 이번에 방문했을 때 Betts 선생님이 치아 하나에 있는 구멍을 메웠는데요, 제 청구서에는 두 번 메운 것으로 되어 있어요.
남 오, 정말 죄송합니다, Hahn 씨. 저희가 최근에 새로운 계산 및 청구용 소프트웨어를 설치했는데요, 그 실수는 제가 새 시스템에 귀하의 정보를 이전하면서 발생했을 겁니다. 기록을 수정하고, 지금 바로 새로운 계산서를 발행해 드리겠습니다.

어휘 charge 청구하다 treatment 치료, 처치 cavity 구멍, 빈 부분 bill 계산서, 청구서 transfer 이전하다 correction 정정, 수정 issue 발급하다 gum 잇몸 statement 내역서

68 Look at the graphic. Which charge on the bill is incorrect?
(A) $10
(B) $40
(C) $200
(D) $260
시각 자료를 보시오. 청구서의 어떤 비용이 잘못되었는가?
(A) 10달러
(B) 40달러
(C) 200달러
(D) 260달러

해설 〈구체적 정보 파악 – 시각 자료 연계〉
가장 먼저 선택지와 시각 자료의 관계를 파악해야 한다. 선택지에 가격이 제시되어 있으므로 대화 속의 진료 종류가 정답 단서로 언급될 것을 염두에 두고 들어야 한다. 여자의 말에 따르면 의사는 치아 충전을 하나만 했으나 청구서에는 두 개를 채운 것으로 되어 있다고 설명한다. 따라서 충전 비용의 청구가 잘못되어 있다는 것을 알 수 있으므로 정답은 (D)이다.

69 What does the man say about the clinic?
(A) It changed its phone number.
(B) It installed a new program.
(C) It hired new staff members.
(D) It purchased new equipment.
남자는 병원에 대해 무엇이라고 말하는가?
(A) 전화번호가 변경되었다.
(B) 새로운 프로그램을 설치했다.
(C) 새로운 직원을 고용했다.
(D) 새로운 기구를 구매했다.

해설 남자가 병원에 대해 말하는 대사에서 정답을 찾아야 한다. 남자가 최근에 새 프로그램을 설치했다고 설명하고 있으므로 정답은 (B)이다.

70 What does the man say he will do?
(A) Upgrade a system
(B) Issue a refund
(C) Update software
(D) Send another statement
남자는 무엇을 하겠다고 말하는가?
(A) 시스템을 업그레이드한다.
(B) 환불을 해준다.
(C) 소프트웨어를 업데이트한다.
(D) 다른 내역서를 보낸다.

해설 〈구체적 정보 파악 – 미래〉
대화 후반의 남자 대사를 듣고 근거를 찾는 미래 문제이다. 남자가 마지막 대사에서 기록을 수정하고, 바로 새로운 계산서를 발행하겠다고 말하고 있으므로 정답은 (D)이다.

패러프레이징 issue a new bill 새 청구서를 발행하다
→ send another statement 다른 내역서를 보내다

PART 4

P65

Questions 71-73 refer to the following announcement. 영M

71 This is the Metropolitan Express bound for Watford and Amersham stations. 72 The next stop is Pinner station. There will be a five-minute stop while the train is separated into two sections. Cars one through five will then proceed to Watford, and cars six through twelve will continue on to Amersham. 73 Please check your car number to ensure that you are in the right section. Once again, the front sections, cars one through five, are bound for Watford. The rear sections, cars six through twelve, are bound for Amersham.

이 열차는 Watford와 Amersham로 가는 Metropolitan 급행열차입니다. 다음 역은 Pinner 역입니다. 거기서 기차가 두 구간으로 나뉘므로 5분간 정차할 예정입니다. 1번에서 5번 차량은 Watford를 향해 가고, 6번에서 12번 차량은 Amersham으로 계속 이동합니다. 승객 여러분의 차량 번호를 체크하여 알맞는 구간에 계신지 반드시 확인해 주시기 바랍니다. 다시 한 번 말씀드립니다. 앞쪽 구간, 1번부터 5번 차량은 Watford 행입니다. 뒤쪽 구간, 6번부터 12번 차량은 Amersham 행입니다.

어휘 bound for ~ 행의 car (기차의) 차량, 칸 proceed to ~로 향하다 ensure 반드시 ~하게 하다 rear 뒤쪽의

71 Where does the announcement take place?
(A) In a train station
(B) At an airport
(C) On an express train
(D) At an express bus terminal

방송이 나오는 곳은 어디인가?
(A) 기차역
(B) 공항
(C) 급행열차 안
(D) 급행 버스 터미널

해설 〈기본 정보 파악 – 장소〉
장소를 묻는 문제의 단서는 담화 초반에 등장한다. 담화의 첫 문장에서 특정 지역으로 가는 급행열차임을 알리고 있으므로 정답은 (C)이다.

72 Why is the announcement being made?
(A) To provide information on destinations
(B) To explain a schedule change
(C) To ask passengers to start boarding
(D) To apologize for a delay

안내는 왜 이루어지고 있는가?
(A) 목적지에 관한 정보를 제공하기 위해
(B) 일정 변경을 설명하기 위해
(C) 승객들에게 탑승을 요청하기 위해
(D) 지연에 대해 사과하기 위해

해설 〈기본 정보 파악 – 목적〉
기차에서 다음 정차할 역을 알리며, 그곳에서 기차가 나뉘어 운행될 것이라고 안내하고 있다. 따라서 안내의 목적은 차량별로 서로 다른 목적지를 알리는 것이므로 정답은 (A)이다.

73 What are listeners asked to do?
(A) Proceed to a different platform
(B) Present their documents
(C) Wait for more instructions
(D) Confirm they are in the correct place

청자들이 요청받는 것은 무엇인가?
(A) 다른 플랫폼으로 갈 것
(B) 서류를 제시하는 것
(C) 다음 지시를 기다리는 것
(D) 알맞은 장소에 있는지 확인하는 것

해설 〈구체적 정보 파악 – 요청 관련〉
요청 관련 문제의 답은 담화의 후반부에 please, make sure 등의 표현과 함께 등장하는 경우가 많다. 차량 번호를 체크하고 알맞은 구간에 위치하고 있는지 확인할 것을 요청하고 있으므로 정답은 (D)이다.

패러프레이징 in the right section 알맞은 구간
→ in the correct place 올바른 위치

Questions 74-76 refer to the following announcement. 영W

Fifteen years ago this week, the Ormer Mayfair restaurant opened its doors to the public and has been a proud member of the Kensington community ever since. To mark the occasion, 74 we're inviting our patrons to join us for a special anniversary celebration. 75 This coming Friday we'll present live band performances from open to close in our courtyard dining area. In addition, we'll be preparing a special menu selection just for the event. As always, 76 we'll be using only the finest quality, locally grown vegetables in all of the dishes we serve. Join us this Friday at Ormer Mayfair. Located at 8 Patriot Square, Kensington.

15년 전 이번 주, Ormer Mayfair 식당이 대중에게 문을 열었고 그 이후로 Kensington 지역의 자랑스러운 구성원이 되었습니다. 그날을 기념하기 위해 특별 기념행사에 저희와 함께 할 고객들을 초대합니다. 다가오는 금요일에 개장부터 폐장 때까지 우리의 야외 식사 공간에서 라이브 밴드 공연을 선보일 예정입니다. 게다가, 이번 행사를 위해 특별한 메뉴들을 준비합니다. 언제나 그랬듯이, 우리가 제공하는 모든 요리에는 현지에서 재배한 최고급 채소만을 사용할 것입니다. 이번 주 금요일 Ormer Mayfair에서 우리와 함께 해 주세요. Kensington 8 Patriot Square에 위치하고 있습니다.

어휘 be opened to the public 대중에게 공개되다 proud 자랑스러운 community 지역사회, 공동체 mark 기념하다 occasion 때, 행사 patron 고객, 손님 anniversary 기념일 celebration 기념행사, 축하 행사 courtyard 뜰, 마당 dish 요리 complimentary 무료의 renowned 유명한 ownership 소유

74 What is being celebrated?
(A) An opening of a new branch
(B) A business anniversary
(C) A retirement ceremony
(D) A special award

무엇을 기념하고 있는가?
(A) 새로운 지점의 오픈
(B) 사업체 기념일
(C) 퇴임식
(D) 특별 시상

해설 〈구체적 정보 파악 – 특정 사항〉
celebrated를 키워드로 잡고 해당 단어가 언급되는 부분을 주목해야 한다. 담화 초반에 특별한 기념행사에 함께 할 고객들을 초대한다고 말하고 있으므로 정답은 (B)이다.

75 What is the restaurant planning to do on Friday?
(A) Extend its hours of operation
(B) Offer musical entertainment
(C) Provide complimentary meals
(D) Discount certain items

레스토랑은 금요일에 무엇을 할 계획인가?
(A) 운영 시간의 연장
(B) 음악 연주 제공
(C) 무료 음식 제공
(D) 특정 상품의 할인

해설 〈구체적 정보 파악 – 특정 사항〉
Friday를 키워드로 잡고 문제를 풀어야 한다. 금요일에 라이브 밴드 공연이 있을 것이라고 말하고 있으므로 정답은 (B)이다.

패러프레이징 live band performances 라이브 밴드 공연
→ musical entertainment 음악 연주, 음악회

76 What does the speaker say about the restaurant?
(A) It uses local produce.
(B) It hired a renowned chef.
(C) It has multiple locations.
(D) It is under new ownership.

화자는 레스토랑에 대해 무엇이라고 말하는가?
(A) 지역 농작물을 이용한다.
(B) 유명한 주방장을 고용했다.
(C) 많은 지점이 있다.
(D) 주인이 바뀌었다.

해설 〈구체적 정보 파악 – 언급〉
식당 소개를 하는 부분에서 정답의 근거를 찾아야 한다. 담화 후반부에 이 식당에서 제공하는 모든 요리는 이 지역에서 재배하는 최고급 채소만을 사용할 것이라고 언급하고 있으므로 정답은 (A)이다.

패러프레이징 locally grown vegetables 현재에서 자란 채소
→ local produce 현지 농작물

Questions 77-79 refer to the following talk. (미M)

Good afternoon, and welcome to the future site of Walton electronics' newest production facility. ⑦⑦ As you can see, construction work is ongoing but nearing its completion. In fact, installation of our assembly equipment is scheduled to begin in just one month, and we expect production to begin by early next month. ⑦⑧ As investors, you'll be happy to know that everything about this facility has been designed to maximize efficiency and reduce costs. The lighting system, for example, will consume about twenty percent less energy than those at our other plants. For your own safety, ⑦⑨ I'd like to remind everyone to keep your hardhats on at all times as we tour the site. Now, let's get started.

안녕하십니까, 미래 Walton electronics의 새로운 생산 시설 현장에 오신 것을 환영합니다. 보시다시피, 공사 작업은 진행 중에 있지만 마무리가 되어가고 있습니다. 실제로 조립 장비의 설치는 한 달 있으면 시작될 예정이며, 생산 시작은 다음 달 초로 기대하고 있습니다. 투자자로서, 이 공장의 모든 것은 효율을 극대화시키고 비용을 줄이기 위해 디자인되었다는 것을 아시면 기쁘실 겁니다. 여기의 조명 시스템을 예로 들면, 우리의 다른 공장들보다 20% 적은 에너지를 소비하게 될 것입니다. 스스로의 안전을 위해 공장을 견학하는 동안에는 항상 안전모를 착용해 주시기 바랍니다. 이제, 시작합시다.

어휘 site 현장, 부지 production facility 생산 공장 ongoing 계속 진행 중인 investor 투자자 maximize 극대화하다, 최대한 활용하다 efficiency 효율, 능률 reduce costs 비용을 줄이다 hardhat 안전모 fill out 작성하다

77 Where is the talk probably taking place?
(A) At an electronics store
(B) In a research center
(C) In a conference room
(D) At a construction site

이 담화가 진행되는 곳은 어디인가?
(A) 전자제품 매장
(B) 연구 센터
(C) 회의실
(D) 건설 현장

해설 〈기본 정보 파악 – 장소〉
장소에 관한 단서는 담화의 초반에 등장한다. 앞부분에서 미래의 공장 부지에 온 것을 환영한다는 인사말과 함께 공사가 진행 중임을 언급하고 있으므로 정답은 (D)이다.

78 Who most likely are the listeners?
(A) New employees
(B) Company investors
(C) Store patrons
(D) Factory workers

청자들은 누구인가?
(A) 새로운 직원들
(B) 회사 투자자들
(C) 상점 고객들
(D) 공장 근로자들

해설 〈기본 정보 파악 – 청자〉
청자에 대한 정답의 단서는 담화의 초반에 언급하는 것이 대부분이나, 해당 지문에서는 초반에 특별한 언급이 없다가 투자자로서 알게 되면 기쁠 것이라고 말하는 부분이 중반에 등장하고 있으므로 주의해야 한다. 투자자를 언급한 부분에서 정답이 (B)임을 알 수 있다.

79 What does the speaker mean when he says, "let's get started"?
(A) A tour is about to begin.
(B) Some delivery is ready to be shipped.
(C) Listeners should go back to work immediately.
(D) Listeners should fill out some forms.

남자가 "시작합시다"라고 말한 의미는 무엇인가?
(A) 견학을 막 시작하려고 한다.
(B) 몇 개의 배송품이 발송될 예정이다.
(C) 청자들은 즉시 다시 일하러 가야 한다.
(D) 청자들은 양식을 작성해야 한다.

해설 〈구체적 정보 파악 – 화자 의도〉
주변 문맥과 문제에 언급된 문장을 종합하여 의도를 파악해야 한다. 담화 후반에 공장을 견학하는 동안 계속해서 안전모를 착용하길 바란다고 말한 후, 문제의 표현을 언급하고 있으므로 견학을 시작할 것임을 유추할 수 있다. 따라서 정답은 (A)이다.

Questions 80-82 refer to the following recorded message. (미W)

80 You have reached Domus Design Institute's administration office. 81 Due to the approaching blizzard, all morning classes today have been canceled. The National Weather Service has issued a severe weather alert for the Florence metropolitan area. Our school's policy is to cancel morning classes when a severe weather alert is in effect for the region as of 6 A.M. If this alert is still in effect at 10:30 A.M., afternoon classes will be canceled as well. 82 Look for updates on our Web site at www.domusdesign.com, or call this number again for the latest news.

Domus 디자인 학교 행정실입니다. 눈보라의 접근으로 인하여 오늘 모든 오전 수업은 취소되었습니다. 국립 기상청은 Florence 수도권 지역에 심각한 기상 특보를 발령했습니다. 저희 학교의 정책은 오전 6시를 기준으로 심각한 기상 경보가 지역에 영향을 미칠 경우, 오전 수업을 취소하는 것입니다. 만약 이 경보가 오전 10시 30분까지 지속될 경우, 오후 수업도 취소될 예정입니다. 저희 웹 사이트 www.domusdesign.com의 업데이트를 확인하시거나, 새로운 소식을 들으시려면 이 번호로 다시 전화주시기 바랍니다.

어휘 institute 교육기관, 학교 administration 관리, 행정 업무 blizzard 눈보라 severe 심각한, 극심한 alert 경계 경보 metropolitan area 수도권, 대도시권 in effect 시행(발효) 중인 repave 재포장하다

80 What type of organization recorded this message?
(A) A radio station
(B) A transportation service
(C) The National Weather Service
(D) A local school

어떤 종류의 기관이 이 메시지를 녹음한 것인가?
(A) 라디오 방송국
(B) 운송 서비스
(C) 국립 기상청
(D) 지역 학교

해설 〈기본 정보 파악 – 화자〉
메시지 녹음을 남겨 둔 기관을 묻고 있으므로 초반의 인사말과 더불어 회사 또는 기관의 상호에서 정답을 유추할 수 있다. 담화의 처음에 디자인 학교임을 알리는 인사말이 언급되고 있으므로 정답은 (D)이다.

81 What does the speaker say about Florence?
(A) Its roads have been repaved.
(B) It will experience a snowstorm.
(C) Its schools will all be closed.
(D) It is the largest city in the region.

화자는 Florence에 대해 무엇이라고 말하는가?
(A) 도로들이 재포장되었다.
(B) 눈보라를 경험할 것이다.
(C) 지역의 학교가 모두 닫을 것이다.
(D) 지역 내에서 가장 큰 도시이다.

해설 〈구체적 정보 파악 – 언급〉
키워드인 지명 이름 Florence를 담화의 중반에서 확인할 수 있는데, 이 담화의 전체 주제가 날씨로 인한 수업 취소이기 때문에 Florence가 언급되기 전 이미 정답은 날씨와 관련이 있다는 것을 유추할 수 있다. 또한 기상청은 Florence 수도권 지역에 심각한 기상 특보를 발령했다고 전하고 있으므로 정답은 (B)이다.

패러프레이징 blizzard 눈보라 → snowstorm 눈보라

82 What are listeners asked to do?
(A) Attend the afternoon classes
(B) Check for updated information
(C) Design a new Web site
(D) Listen to an upcoming broadcast

청자들이 요청받은 것은 무엇인가?
(A) 오후 수업에 참여하는 것
(B) 새로운 소식을 확인하는 것
(C) 새 웹 사이트를 디자인하는 것
(D) 다음 방송을 듣는 것

해설 〈구체적 정보 파악 – 요청 관련〉
담화의 요청 관련 정답은 후반에 언급될 확률이 높다. 담화의 끝부분에 업데이트된 소식을 웹 사이트에서 확인하라고 설명하고 있으므로 정답은 (B)이다.

Questions 83-85 refer to the following talk. (호M)

Good afternoon, everyone. 83 First, I regret to inform you that Jacob Lansing is retiring at the end of the month, ending his 25 years of service at Dover Sport Equipment. Jacob originally joined us as a sales assistant, and over the years he's demonstrated outstanding ability. In the past five years as a project director, he has led many projects to success. 84 Especially successful was his recent advertisement which gained widespread media attention. 85 I'll send you an e-mail shortly with details of a farewell ceremony we're planning. Please attend if you can.

여러분, 안녕하세요. 우선 Jacob Lansing이 Dover 스포츠 장비에서의 25년의 근무 경력을 끝으로, 이번 달 말에 은퇴하는 것을 알려 드리게 되어 유감스럽습니다. Jacob은 원래 판매 사원으로 입사하여, 수년간 뛰어난 능력을 보여주었습니다. 지난 5년 동안은 프로젝트 관리자로서 많은 기획들을 성공적으로 이끌었습니다. 특히 성공한 것은 언론의 집중 보도를 받았던 그의 최근 광고였습니다. 제가 곧 계획 중인 송별회의 자세한 사항을 이메일로 보내 드리겠습니다. 가능하다면 참석해 주시기 바랍니다.

어휘 service (특히 오래 계속되는) 근무, 봉사 demonstrate 발휘하다, 보여주다 outstanding 뛰어난, 두드러진 ability 능력, 재능 gain (이익, 혜택을) 얻다 widespread 광범위한, 널리 퍼진 media attention 언론의 집중 보도 farewell 작별(인사) resignation 사직

83 What is the purpose of the talk?
(A) To introduce a new employee
(B) To reschedule a farewell party
(C) To explain about new policy
(D) To announce the resignation of an employee

이 연설의 목적은 무엇인가?
(A) 새로운 직원을 소개하기 위해
(B) 송별회의 일정을 조정하기 위해
(C) 새로운 정책을 설명하기 위해
(D) 직원의 사직을 알리기 위해

해설 〈기본 정보 파악 – 목적〉
목적 문제 정답의 단서는 담화의 초반에 나온다. 특정인의 은퇴를 알리고 있으므로 정답은 (D)이다.

패러프레이징 retire 은퇴하다, 퇴직하다 → resignation 사직, 사임

84 What has Mr. Lansing recently done?
(A) Accepted a promotion
(B) Created an advertisement
(C) Submitted a report
(D) Attended a seminar

Lansing 씨는 최근에 무엇을 했는가?
(A) 승진을 받아들였다.
(B) 광고를 만들었다.
(C) 보고서를 제출했다.
(D) 세미나에 참석했다.

해설 〈구체적 정보 파악 – 특정 사항〉
담화에서 소개하고 있는 인물 Mr. Lansing의 업적을 묻는 문제이며 키워드로 recently가 주어져 있다. 담화 후반에 언론의 집중 보도를 받았던 그의 최근 광고가 성공적이었음을 소개하고 있으므로 이와 동일한 표현의 (B)가 정답이다.

85 What will the speaker probably do next?
(A) Join a conference
(B) Talk to a supervisor
(C) Receive an electronic mail
(D) Send detailed information

화자는 다음에 무엇을 할 것인가?
(A) 학회에 참여한다.
(B) 관리자에게 말한다.
(C) 전자 메일을 받는다.
(D) 자세한 정보를 보낸다.

해설 〈구체적 정보 파악 – 미래〉
미래 시제로 언급된 문장에 주목해야 하는데 담화의 마지막에 화자가 송별회의 상세한 사항을 이메일로 보내겠다고 했으므로 정답은 (D)이다.

Questions 86-88 refer to the following telephone message. 영W

Mr. Gupta, this is Tammy Hughes from Meyer Estate about a location for your office in Lancaster. We've just listed a commercial space on the second floor of Acton Building, on Abbey Road. ⑧⑥ This business center has recently been refurbished. It offers fully furnished, immediately operational space for between 5 and 18 work stations. ⑧⑦ Also, it is equipped with a cutting-edge office technology system and high-speed Internet, which is something you said you'd wanted. This luxury serviced office is set in a spacious modern building and offers a comfortable business environment. ⑧⑧ This property is quite popular on the market, so if you're interested in seeing it, please let me know as soon as possible. Thank you.

Gupta 씨, 저는 Meyer 부동산의 Tammy Hughes입니다. Lancaster에 있는 사무실 때문에 전화드립니다. Abbey 가의 Acton 건물 2층 상업 용지가 저희 목록에 올라와 있습니다. 이 비즈니스 센터는 최근에 새 단장 되었습니다. 그곳은 가구가 완비되어 있으며 5개에서 18개까지의 즉시 사용 가능한 작업 공간이 제공됩니다. 또한 이곳은 최첨단 사무 시스템과 고속 인터넷을 갖추고 있으며, 이것은 당신이 원한다고 말씀하신 것입니다. 이 호화로운 서비스를 제공하는 사무실은 넓은 현대식 건물에 있으며, 편안한 근무 환경을 제공합니다. 이 부동산은 시장에서 꽤 인기가 있습니다. 그러니 만약 보시려면, 가능한 한 빨리 저에게 알려주시기 바랍니다. 감사합니다.

어휘 commercial space 상업 공간 refurbish 새로 꾸미다, 재단장하다 furnish 가구를 배치하다 cutting-edge 최첨단의 spacious 넓은 property 부동산, 재산 adequate 적절한

86 What is mentioned about the property?
(A) It's newly renovated.
(B) It is for up to 15 persons.
(C) It offers on-site parking.
(D) It is close to the station.

이 부동산에 대해 언급된 것은 무엇인가?
(A) 최근에 개조되었다.
(B) 최대 15명까지 사용할 수 있다.
(C) 주차 공간을 제공한다.
(D) 역에서 가깝다.

해설 〈구체적 정보 파악 – 언급〉
건물에 관해 설명하는 부동산 관계자의 전화 메시지이다. 화자는 이 비즈니스 센터가 최근에 새 단장되었다고 말하고 있으므로 정답은 (A)이다.

패러프레이징 recently refurbished 최근에 재단장한
→ newly renovated 새로 단장한

87 According to the message, what feature is Mr. Gupta looking for?
(A) A fully furnished office
(B) A convenient location
(C) Modern equipment
(D) Adequate parking

메시지에 의하면, Gupta 씨가 찾는 특징은 무엇인가?
(A) 가구가 완비된 사무실
(B) 편리한 위치
(C) 현대식 장비
(D) 충분한 주차장

해설 〈구체적 정보 파악 – 특정 사항〉
전화 메시지에서 문제에 언급된 이름은 화자 또는 청자인 경우가 많다. 담화의 첫 대사에서 문제에 언급된 Mr. Gupta가 청자임을 알 수 있으므로, 그 후로는 이름이 언급되지 않고 You라고 지칭되고 있음을 알아야 한다. 대화 중반에 이 사무실은 최첨단 사무 시스템과 고속 인터넷을 갖추고 있으며 이것은 청자가 원하는 조건이었다고 말하고 있으므로 정답은 (C)이다.

88 Why does the speaker recommend viewing the building as soon as possible?
(A) It will rent out quickly.
(B) Its price will go up soon.
(C) It will be renovated shortly.
(D) It will be advertised on TV.

화자가 가능한 한 빨리 건물을 보라고 추천하는 이유는 무엇인가?
(A) 임대가 빨리 될 것이다.
(B) 곧 가격이 오를 것이다
(C) 곧 개조될 것이다
(D) TV에 광고될 것이다.

해설 〈구체적 정보 파악 – 특정 사항〉
건물을 둘러보라는 것을 이미 요청했으므로 recommend가 아닌 viewing을 키워드로 잡고 풀어야 하지만, 제안/요청과 연관이 있는 문제이므로 담화의 후반부에서 단서를 찾아야 한다. 후반부에 해당 건물은 꽤 인기가 있으므로 관심이 있다면 전화하라는 요청을 하고 있으므로 정답은 (A)이다.

Questions 89-91 refer to the following talk. 호M

Welcome to the organizing committee for the 2018 Memorial Golf Tournament. ⑨⓪ Male golfers from all over the country will be competing in this tournament, and you are all here to help things run smoothly over the next five days. ⑧⑨ You and your fellow student volunteers from Cleveland High School will make certain the golfers and caddies have everything they need, so they can focus on the competition. Remain on the sidelines and be alert at all times, but ⑨① unless specifically asked, please stay off the fairways. You must remain silent while play is in progress, and don't talk to the golfers or caddies unless they speak to you first. Keep up with your assigned athlete as he progresses through the course. And, last but not least, let's hope for sunny skies over these next five days.

2018 Memorial Golf Tournament 조직 위원회에 오신 것을 환영합니다. 전국의 모든 남자 골퍼들이 이 시합에 참가하여 겨루게 될 것이며, 여러분은 앞으로 5일간의 순조로운 진행을 돕기 위해 이곳에 오셨습니다. 여러분과 Cleveland 고등학교에서 온 동료 학생 자원봉사자들은 골퍼들과 캐디들이 필요한 모든 것들을 확실하게 챙겨서, 그들이 경기에만 집중할 수 있도록 해야 합니다. 경기장 밖에 머물러 있을 때도 항상 긴장하셔야 하며, 별도의 요청이 없는 한, 페어웨이에서 떨어져 있어 주시기 바랍니다. 경기가 진행되는 동안은 조용히 하셔야 하며, 골퍼나 캐디들이 먼저 당신에게 말하지 않는 한 말씀을 삼가 주시기 바랍니다. 코스를 진행하는 동안 지정된 선수와 보조를 맞춰 주세요. 마지막으로 말씀 드리지만 역시 중요한 것은 앞으로 5일 동안은 화창한 날씨가 되기를 희망합시다.

어휘 tournament 토너먼트, 시합 run smoothly 순조롭게 되어가다 be alert 경계하다, 긴장하다 sidelines 경기장 밖 stay off 삼가다, 멀리하다 fairways 골프에서의 페어웨이 (티와 그린 사이의 커다란 잔디밭) keep up with 처지지 않고 따라가다 athlete 운동선수

89 Who is the intended audience for this talk?
(A) Golfers
(B) Caddies
(C) Teachers
(D) Volunteers

이 담화의 의도된 청중은 누구인가?
(A) 골퍼
(B) 캐디
(C) 선생님
(D) 자원봉사자

해설 〈기본 정보 파악 – 청자〉
청자에 대한 정보는 담화의 앞부분에서 출제된다. 담화 초반에 여러분과 동료 학생 자원봉사자들은 골퍼들과 캐디들이 필요한 것들을 확실히 챙겨야 한다고 설명하고 있으므로 정답은 (D)이다.

90 What is mentioned about the tournament?

(A) It is a national competition.

(B) It will last three days.

(C) It is an annual event.

(D) It will be rescheduled.

경기에 대해 무엇이라고 언급되어있는가?

(A) 전국 경기이다.

(B) 3일 동안 지속될 것이다.

(C) 연례 행사이다.

(D) 일정이 재조정될 것이다.

해설 〈구체적 정보 파악 – 언급〉
tournament를 키워드로 담화를 잘 들어야 한다. tournament 가 첫 부분에 언급되므로 89번 문제에만 집중하느라 놓치지 않도록 주의해야 한다. 첫 문장에서 전국의 모든 남자 골퍼들이 이 시합에 참가하여 겨루게 될 것이라고 설명하고 있으므로 이를 바꾸어 표현한 (A)가 정답이다.

패러프레이징 all over the country 전국에 → national 전국적인

91 What is one instruction given to the listeners?

(A) Speak loudly during play

(B) Stay off the greens

(C) Ask questions to the athletes

(D) Check out the schedule

화자들에게 지시된 것은 무엇인가?

(A) 경기 동안 크게 이야기할 것

(B) 잔디에서 떨어져 있을 것

(C) 선수에게 질문을 할 것

(D) 일정을 확인할 것

해설 〈구체적 정보 파악 – 요청 관련〉
요청이나 제안 유형 문제의 단서는 후반부에 주로 please, be sure to 등의 표현과 함께 정답의 단서가 나온다. 별도의 요청이 없는 한, 페어웨이에서 떨어져 있어 달라고 요구하고 있으므로 이를 적절하게 표현한 (B)가 정답이다.

Questions 92-94 refer to the following news report. 영M

Hello. I'm Kevin Taylor with your seven o'clock business news update. 92 United Textiles announced today that it intends to open a new factory in New Delhi. 93 Jack Wentworth, the company CEO, said that United Textiles will transfer its central operation to the new factory. He also said that the new factory will help United Textiles to continue growing on sales, which have more than tripled over the last three years. 94 Industry insiders say the local government has encouraged the project. That would make perfect sense. The factory will help ease local unemployment while bringing in much-needed hard currency.

안녕하세요. 저는 7시 정각 비즈니스 뉴스 소식의 Kevin Taylor입니다. United Textiles은 오늘 New Delhi에 새로운 공장을 개설할 예정이라고 발표했습니다. 회사의 대표 이사인 Jack Wentworth 씨는 United Textiles의 중앙 운영부를 새 공장으로 이전할 것이라고 말했습니다. 그는 또한, 새로운 공장이 지난 3년에 걸쳐 3배 증가한 United Textiles의 지속적인 매출 성장에 도움을 줄 것이라고 말했습니다. 업계 관계자는 지방 정부가 이 프로젝트를 장려했다고 합니다. 확실히 타당성이 있는데요. 이 공장은 많은 필요한 통화 자금을 들여오는 동시에, 지역 실업 문제를 해결하는 데 도움이 될 것입니다.

어휘 triple 3배의 insiders 내부자 ease 덜어주다 unemployment 실업, 실업률 hard currency 경화, 통화 acquisition 인수 spokesperson 대변인 executive 임원 favor 찬성하다 textile 직물

92 What is the report mainly about?

(A) A planned closure of a facility

(B) An acquisition of two companies

(C) A new line of product

(D) A company's expanded operation

이 보도는 주로 무엇에 관한 것인가?

(A) 시설의 폐쇄 계획

(B) 두 회사의 인수

(C) 새로운 제품 라인

(D) 회사의 사업 확장

해설 〈기본 정보 파악 – 주제〉
주제를 묻는 질문은 초반에 정답의 단서를 찾을 수 있다. 첫 대사에서 특정 회사가 New Delhi에 새 공장을 열 것이라고 보도하고 있으므로 이를 바꾸어 표현한 (D)가 정답이다.

패러프레이징 open a new factory 새 공장을 열다
→ expand one's operation 사업을 확장하다

93 Who is Jack Wentworth?

(A) A company spokesperson

(B) A corporate executive

(C) A broadcast reporter

(D) A news reader

Jack Wentworth는 누구인가?

(A) 회사 대변인

(B) 회사 임원

(C) 방송 리포터

(D) 뉴스 앵커

해설 〈구체적 정보 파악 – 언급〉
이름이 언급되는 부분에서 정답을 찾아야 한다. 해당 이름을 말하며 CEO라고 소개하고 있으므로 정답은 (B)이다.

94 What does the speaker mean when he says, "That would make perfect sense"?

(A) United Textiles is an international company.

(B) Any local government would favor such a plan.

(C) Textile sales are strong in the local area.

(D) United Textiles is famous in the region.

화자가 "확실히 타당성이 있다"라고 말한 의미는 무엇인가?

(A) United Textiles는 국제적인 회사이다.

(B) 어떤 지방 정부라도 그런 계획을 지지할 것이다.

(C) 직물의 판매량이 지역 내에서 강세다.

(D) United Textiles는 이 지역에서 유명하다.

해설 〈구체적 정보 파악 – 화자 의도〉
담화 후반에 업계 관계자는 지방 정부가 이 프로젝트를 장려했다고 전한 후 해당 표현을 언급했으므로 가장 적절하게 표현한 (B)가 정답이다.

Questions 95-97 refer to the following talk and graph. 영W

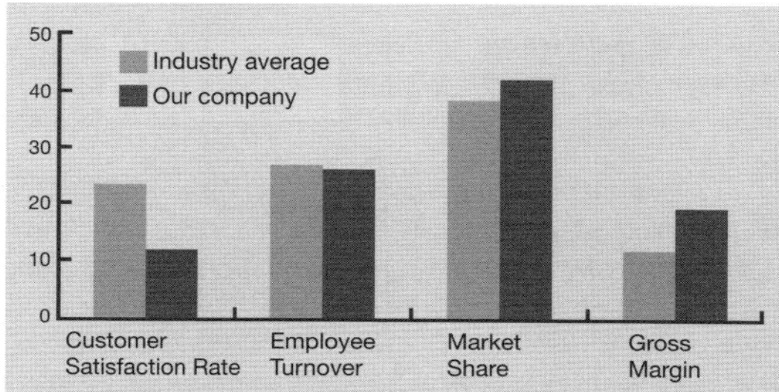

Everyone, I would like to thank all of you for coming here today. 95 I know that I asked you here on short notice. The board of directors went over last year's management report and unfortunately I can't say they were altogether happy with it. 96 Specifically, they weren't pleased with the area where we performed the worst. They want us to develop a strategy as to how we're going to do better in this area and they want it by Thursday morning. That means that we're probably going to spend the next three days here in the office. We'll spend a lot of time brainstorming this issue and draw up some proposals. 97 After that Ashley Gallagher will write up a final submission.

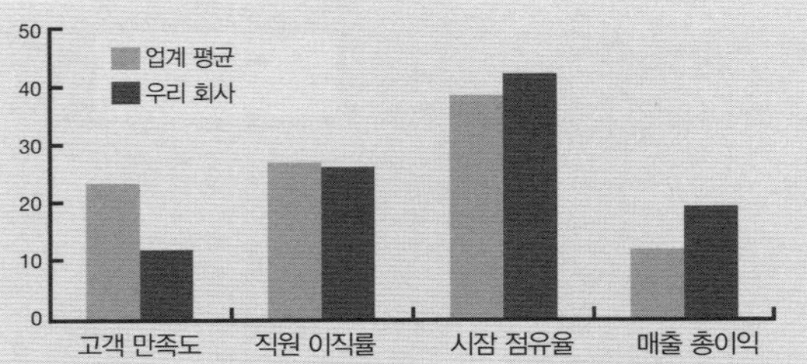

여러분, 오늘 여기에 오신 모든 분들께 감사드리고 싶습니다. 제가 여러분들께 갑작스러운 요청을 드렸다는 것을 알고 있습니다. 이사회에서 작년 경영 보고서를 검토했고, 안타깝게도 그들이 전적으로 만족했다고 말할 수는 없습니다. 구체적으로 그들은 우리가 최악의 성과를 낸 분야에 대해 마음에 들어 하지 않았습니다. 그들은 우리가 그 분야에서 어떻게 더 잘 할 수 있는지에 관한 전략을 목요일 오전까지 수립하기를 원하고 있습니다. 이것은 아마도 우리가 앞으로 3일 동안 여기 이 사무실에서 보내야 할지도 모른다는 것을 의미합니다. 우리는 오랜 시간 동안 이 문제에 대해 브레인스토밍을 하고 계획서를 작성할 것입니다. 그 후에 Ashley Gallagher가 최종 제안서를 쓰게 될 것입니다.

어휘 short notice 촉박한 통보 go over 검토하다 specifically 구체적으로 말하면 strategy 계획, 전략 as to ~에 관한 brainstorming 브레인스토밍, 아이디어 창출 단계 draw up 만들다, 작성하다 submission 제안서

95 Why does the speaker thank the listeners?
(A) They formed a committee.
(B) They finished a quarterly report.
(C) They distributed a notice.
(D) They gathered quickly.

화자는 청자들에게 왜 감사하는가?
(A) 위원회를 조직했다.
(B) 분기별 보고서를 끝냈다.
(C) 안내문을 배포했다.
(D) 빠르게 모였다.

해설 〈구체적 정보 파악 – 특정 사항〉
담화의 첫 인사말로 와 주셔서 감사하다고 말하며 갑작스러운 통보였음을 인정하고 있으므로 이를 바꿔 말한 (D)가 정답이다.

96 Look at the graphic. What area does the board of directors most want to improve?
(A) Customer satisfaction rate
(B) Employee turnover
(C) Market share
(D) Gross margin

시각 자료를 보시오. 이사회에서는 어떤 분야를 가장 향상시키고 싶어 하는가?
(A) 고객 만족도
(B) 직원 이직률
(C) 시장 점유율

해설 〈구체적 정보 파악 – 시각 자료 연계〉
선택지와 시각 자료의 관계를 파악하는 것이 중요하다. 가로축에 해당되는 항목들이 선택지로 제시되어 있으므로 담화에서는 세로축인 숫자에 대한 단서가 제시되거나, 업계 평균치와 해당 회사의 가장 높거나 가장 낮은 그래프를 언급하는 부분에서 정답의 단서가 제공된다. 이사회가 최악의 성과를 낸 분야에 대해 마음에 들어 하지 않는다고 말하며, 그 분야에서 어떻게 더 잘할 수 있는지에 관한 전략을 모색하기를 원한다고 했다. 따라서 평균 대비 가장 성과가 나지 않은 고객 만족도인 (A)가 정답이다.

97 What will Ms. Gallagher have to do?
(A) Use a different facility
(B) Create a document
(C) Report a current issue
(D) Contact a manager

Gallagher 씨는 무엇을 해야 하는가?
(A) 다른 시설을 이용하기
(B) 문서 만들기
(C) 현재 이슈 보고하기
(D) 관리자에게 연락하기

해설 〈구체적 정보 파악 – 특정 사항〉
문제의 Ms. Gallagher가 언급되는 부분을 주목한다. 후반에 Gallagher 씨가 최종 제안서를 작성할 것임을 언급하고 있으므로 (B)가 정답이다.

패러프레이징 write up a final submission 최종 제안서 작성
→ create a document 문서 만들기

Questions 98-100 refer to the following talk and table. (호M)

Alice Spring Regional Weather Report		
Day	**Skies**	**Temperature**
Tuesday	Sunny	Hot
Wednesday	Sunny	Warm
Thursday	Sunny	Warm
Friday	Cloudy	Cool

Welcome to Alice Spring Desert Park. We'll be covering over eight kilometers today, so I hope you all remembered to bring plenty of water and wear practical shoes. (98) Today we'll see wild native animals and plants that have made the park famous. It also offers us the opportunity to experience the variety of the deserts of central Australia, exploring the inter-relationships between the plants, animals and people. By the way, (99) a cloudy day like today is rare for this area and provides a great opportunity for us. The highly reflective surfaces of some areas in the park make photographing the plants from certain angles difficult when it's sunny. (100) Make sure to take advantage of the cloud cover by getting plenty of pictures during today's hike.

Alice Spring 지역 일기 예보		
요일	**기상**	**기온**
화요일	화창함	더움
수요일	화창함	따뜻함
목요일	화창함	따뜻함
금요일	흐림	시원함

Alice Spring Desert 공원에 오신 것을 환영합니다. 우리는 오늘 8킬로미터가 넘는 여정을 가게 됩니다. 그러니 충분한 물과 알맞은 신발을 가지고 오셨기를 바랍니다. 오늘 우리는 이 공원을 유명하게 만든 야생 동물들과 식물을 보게 될 것입니다. 이것은 또한 우리에게 중앙 오스트레일리아 사막의 다양성을 경험하고 식물과 동물, 그리고 사람 간의 상호 관계를 탐험하는 기회를 제공해 줄 것입니다. 오늘과 같이 흐린 날이 이 지역에서는 드물지만 우리에겐 좋은 기회를 제공해 줄 것입니다. 공원 내 일부 지역의 고도로 반사되는 지면들은 화창한 날씨에서는 특정 각도에서 식물들의 사진을 찍는 일을 어렵게 합니다. 흐린 날의 장점을 이용하셔서 오늘 하이킹에서 많은 사진을 찍으시기 바랍니다.

어휘 cover 가다, 이동하다 practical 현실적인, 실용적인 native 원주민의, 토박이의 inter-relationships 상호 관계 rare 드문, 희귀한 reflective 반사하는 surface 표면, 지면 angle 각도 take advantage of ~을 이용하다 exotic 이국적인

98 According to the speaker, what is the park known for?
(A) Impressive rock formations
(B) Native species
(C) Exotic flowers
(D) High numbers of visitors

화자에 의하면, 공원은 무엇으로 알려져 있는가?
(A) 인상 깊은 암석 형성
(B) 야생종
(C) 이국적인 꽃
(D) 많은 방문자들

해설 〈구체적 정보 파악 – 특정 사항〉
키워드인 be known for를 바꾸어 말하는 부분을 주목하자. 담화 초반에 이 공원을 유명하게 만든 야생 동물들과 식물을 보게 될 것이라고 말하므로 정답은 (B)이다.

패러프레이징 wild native animals and plants 야생 동식물
→ native species 야생종

99 Look at the graphic. When does the talk probably take place?
(A) On Tuesday
(B) On Wednesday
(C) On Thursday
(D) On Friday

시각 자료를 보시오. 이 담화는 언제 일어났겠는가?

(A) 화요일
(B) 수요일
(C) 목요일
(D) 금요일

해설 〈구체적 정보 파악 – 시각 자료 연계〉
담화를 듣기 전에 문제의 선택지와 일기 예보를 살펴보아야 한다. 문제의 선택지에는 요일이 나오고 있으므로 기상 상황이나 기온이 정답의 단서로 언급될 것을 예상하고 들어야 한다. 대화 후반에 날씨는 흐리지만 사진을 찍기에 좋은 기회를 제공해 줄 것이라고 말하고 있다. 그러므로 날씨가 흐린 요일에 해당하는 날은 금요일이므로 정답은 (D)이다.

100 What does the speaker advise listeners to do?
(A) Take a lot of photographs
(B) Draw some pictures
(C) Wear sunglasses
(D) Stay on the hiking trail

화자는 청자들에게 무엇을 하라고 조언하는가?
(A) 사진을 많이 찍을 것
(B) 그림을 그릴 것
(C) 선글라스를 착용할 것
(D) 하이킹 코스에 남아 있을 것

해설 〈구체적 정보 파악 – 요청 관련〉
요청, 제안 관련 문제의 정답은 후반부에 please, make sure 등의 표현과 함께 언급되는 경우가 많다. 흐린 날의 장점을 이용해서 많은 사진을 찍길 바란다고 조언하고 있으므로 정답은 (A)이다.

패러프레이징 get plenty of pictures 많은 사진을 찍다
→ take a lot of photographs 사진을 많이 찍다

PART 5

P68

101 해석 Bergeson's는 작은 소매점으로 시작했으나 큰 도매상으로 빠르게 변화했다.
해설 동사 transitioned를 수식하는 부사 자리이므로 (A)가 정답이다. quite, well, highly는 동사를 수식하지 않는다.
어휘 retail store 소매점 transition 변하다 wholesaler 도매상

102 해석 공동 자료는 Jefferson Electronics의 일자리 기회를 찾기 위해 사용된다.
해설 search 뒤에는 for를 사용하여 '~을 수색하다'라는 뜻으로 사용된다. 따라서 (A)가 정답이다.
어휘 open access 공동으로 오픈된 job opportunity 일자리 기회

103 해석 공급 부족이 생길 때 매니저들이 인지하고 있어야 하는 것은 중요하다.
해설 that절 안에 동사원형 be가 사용되고 있으므로 조동사 should가 생략된 것으로 추측할 수 있고 그렇다면 that절 앞에 주장, 제안, 필수 등의 의미를 나타낼 수 있는 형용사를 사용하여야 하므로 (D) critical이 정답이다. 〈It is important/imperative/essential that ~〉에서 that절에는 should가 생략된 동사원형이 쓰일 수 있다.
어휘 aware of ~을 인지하는 a shortage of ~의 부족 supply 공급 occur 발생하다 sudden 갑작스러운 eventful 다사다난한, 특별한 critical 중요한

104 해석 대부분의 회사 직원들은 업무 경험이 있지만, 우리들 중 단지 일부만이 현재 흐름의 미래적 중요함을 볼 수 있다.
해설 전치사 of 뒤에는 목적격 us를 사용한다. 따라서 (B)가 정답이다.
어휘 a handful of 소수의 current 현재의

105 해석 마지막 페이지에 서명하기 전에 모든 계약서의 각 페이지를 꼼꼼히 읽으세요.
해설 빈칸 뒤의 page가 단수이므로 수량 형용사 (B) each가 정답이다. whole/complete는 일반 형용사이므로 앞에 관사가 필요하고, all은 가산명사라면 복수형과 사용해야 하므로 오답이다.
어휘 read through 정독하다 whole 전체의 complete 완전한

106 해석 튼튼한 쇼핑 가방은 식료품점의 일반적인 비닐봉지를 좋아하지 않는 사람들에게는 필수 아이템이다.
해설 bag을 수식하는 적절한 형용사는 (C) durable이다.
어휘 ordinary 일상적인 plastic bag 비닐봉지 grocery store 식료품점 rigorous 엄격한 comparable 비교할 만한, 필적할 만한 durable 튼튼한 vigorous 활기 찬

107 해석 올해 토론 대회 심사위원들은 방송국 대표들도 포함한다.
해설 include가 타동사이므로 명사가 필요하고 representative는 형용사와 명사 두 가지로 사용되는 단어이므로 (B)가 정답이다.
어휘 judge 심사위원 debate 토론 competition 대회 include 포함하다 broadcasting station 대회 representative 대표자

108 해석 Total Water Purifier의 필터는 제품을 제대로 작동시키기 위해서 적어도 한 달에 한 번은 청소해야만 한다.
해설 조동사 must 뒤에 사용하고 빈칸 뒤에 목적어가 없으므로 원형의 수동태 형태인 (A) be cleaned가 정답이다.
어휘 water purifier 정수기 at least 적어도 appliance (가전) 제품 function 작동하다 properly 적절히

109 해석 O'Neil 씨는 원고를 프린트하지 않은 것을 깨닫자, 즉석 연설을 했다.
해설 원고를 프린트하지 않았다는 것은 연설을 원고 없이 해야 함을 뜻한다. 따라서 즉석 연설을 했다는 (B)가 정답이다.
어휘 achieve 성취하다 improvise a speech 즉석 연설을 하다 command 명령하다 officiate 공무, 임무를 수행하다 realize 깨닫다 draft 원고

110 해석 Varner Bank는 장기간의 파트너 관계를 형성하기 위해 고객들과 긴밀히 협력한다.
해설 문맥상 고객들과의 관계가 가까운 것을 나타내는 (C) closely가 정답이다.
어휘 establish 만들다, 설립하다 long-term 장기간의 nearly 거의 closely 가깝게, 긴밀히

111 해석 업데이트된 안전 분석 보고서는 Russell Software System 내의 현장 감독자들에게 제한되어 있다.
해설 빈칸 뒤의 Russell Software System은 회사명을 나타내는 고유명사이므로 '회사 내부의'라는 뜻을 만들 수 있는 (A) within이 정답이다. until/since는 전치사로 사용될 때 시간 표현과 사용해야 하므로 오답이다.
어휘 analysis report 분석 보고서 be limited to ~에 제한되다 site supervisor 현장 감독자

112 해석 강조되어야 하는 것은 농업과 천연 자원 분야이다.
해설 빈칸 뒤에 두 개의 동사 needs와 is가 나오므로 빈칸은 주어 역할과 접속사 역할을 함께 할 수 있는 (A) What이 정답이다. which는 '어느 것'을 의미하고 whichever는 '어느 것이든지'의 양보의 의미를 가지므로 오답이다.
어휘 highlight 강조하다 agriculture 농업 natural resources 천연자원

113 해석 San Remo 레모네이드는 여름철 음료로 홍보되었지만, 일 년 내내 꾸준한 판매량을 유지했다.
해설 all year around로부터 꾸준히 판매되었다는 것이 적절하므로 (C) steady가 정답이다.
어휘 maintain 유지하다 all year around 일 년 내내 promote 홍보하다 summertime 여름철 steady 꾸준한 seasoned 양념을 한, 경험 많은

114 해석 Morrison Electronics는 Yearwood Tech를 주식과 현금으로 약 3백 5십만 달러에 인수한다.
해설 숫자 $35 million을 수식하는 부사 자리이므로 (C)가 정답이다.
어휘 acquire 인수, 획득하다 in stocks 주식으로 approximate ~에 비슷하다, 가깝다 approximation 근사치 approximately 거의

115 해석 그 건물은 지원 교육에 참가했던 인원들만이 들어갈 수 있을 것이다.
해설 명사 personnel과 have attached를 연결할 수 있는 관계대명사 주격 (C) who가 정답이다.
어휘 access 이용하다 personnel 인력 employee orientation 직원 교육

116 해석 새로운 기술은 Poland Cell Tech가 네트워크를 확장하고 판매 기회를 찾는 것을 가능하게 했다.
해설 목적어 Poland Cell Tech 뒤에 to부정사 보어가 있으므로 5형식이 가능한 (D) enabled가 정답이다.
어휘 expand 확장하다 explore 찾다, 탐험하다 sales opportunities 판매 기회 emerge 모습을 드러내다 enable ~을 가능하게 하다

117 **해석** Long 씨는 지난 금요일, 관리 부서 직원이 부족해서 직접 팩스기를 수리했다.

해설 문장에 필요한 구성이 다 있으므로 강조 역할을 할 수 있는 재귀대명사 (C) himself가 정답이다.

어휘 repair 수리하다 maintenance 관리, 정비 be short on ~이 부족하다

118 **해석** 계절과 상관없이 실내 워터 파크에서 일 년 내내 즐길 수 있다.

해설 빈칸부터 of the season까지가 부사구이므로 전치사구를 만들 수 있는 (A) regardless가 정답이다.

어휘 indoor 실내의 regardless of ~와 상관없이

119 **해석** 심사위원단은 디자인 제출 마감이 지났기 때문에 출품작 검토를 시작할 것이다.

해설 문장 전체에 동사가 may begin, has passed로 2개가 있고, 빈칸부터는 부사절을 구성하고 있으므로 부사절 접속사 (D) now that이 정답이다.

어휘 panel 심사위원단 entry 출품작 now that (접속사) ~ 때문에

120 **해석** 결과가 설득력이 있기 위해서는 실험실 내부 온도와 습도는 실험 내내 정확하게 똑같이 유지되어야만 한다.

해설 문장 구성에 필요한 구성이 다 있으므로 부사 (D) exactly가 정답이다.

어휘 convincing 설득력 있는 humidity 습도 laboratory 실험실 remain the same 똑같이 유지하다 throughout 내내 exact 정확한 exactness 정확성 exactly 정확하게

121 **해석** Motohashi 씨는 기차를 놓쳤지만 다행히도 시상식에 제시간에 갈 수 있었다.

해설 기차를 놓쳤다는 내용과 시상식에 제시간에 도착했다는 내용이 반대이므로 양보를 나타내는 접속사 (A) Though가 정답이다.

어휘 miss ~을 놓치다 fortunately 다행히 on time 제시간에 awards ceremony 시상식 despite (전치사) ~에도 불구하고

122 **해석** 영국 회사인 Gordon Architecture의 Karl Byquist가 올해의 Master Architects Award의 수상자이다.

해설 빈칸 앞에 정관사 the가 있으므로 명사형이 정답이고 문맥상 사람 주어인 Karl Byquist의 보어로 사용될 수 있는 (C) recipient가 정답이다.

어휘 architecture 건축 architect 건축가 receive ~을 받다 recipient 수령자, 수혜자 receipt 수령, 영수증

123 **해석** 2개의 감사 지적 보고서의 결과는 이사의 기대를 넘었다.

해설 문장에 적절한 동사가 없으므로 과거 동사인 (A) surpassed가 정답이다.

어휘 audit findings report 감사 지적 보고서 surpass expectations 기대를 넘다

124 **해석** 최근에 Valley Restaurant을 방문하지 않았다면 인테리어가 바뀐 것을 보고 기뻐할 수도 있다.

해설 빈칸 앞에 be동사가 있고 뒤에 to부정사가 있으므로 '~해서 기쁘다'는 뜻의 'be pleased to'가 적절하다. 따라서 (B)가 정답이다.

어휘 be pleased to ~해서 기뻐하다

125 **해석** Norview Road와 Harriot Avenue 사이의 9마일의 Fosberg Road 구간은 9월에 다시 재포장될 것이다.

해설 9마일의 수식어와 함께 쓸 수 있고 동사 resurface의 대상이 될 수 있는 (C) stretch가 정답이다.

어휘 resurface 재포장하다 duration (시간의) 지속, 구간 stretch (길게 늘어져 있는) 구간 instance 사례, 경우

126 **해석** Explore Nature 저널에 기사를 제출할 때 참고 목록을 제외하고 2,000자를 넘어서는 안 된다.

해설 빈칸 앞은 완전한 문장 구성을 이루므로 references를 목적어로 취할 수 있는 준동사(분사) (B) excluding이 정답이다.

어휘 exceed 초과하다 exclude 제외하다 exclusive 독점적인, 전용의 exclusion 제외

127 **해석** 지역 사회 프로그램 등록이 주민들에게 시작될 것인데 그들 중 대부분은 학생이다.

해설 빈칸 뒤의 구성이 동사 are로 시작되므로 주어와 접속사를 모두 포함한 (D) most of whom이 정답이다. (B) the reason being과 (C) because of them은 동사와 함께 쓸 수 없는 구문이다.

어휘 registration 등록 resident 주민 inasmuch as (접속사) ~인 점을 고려하면

128 **해석** 이사회 회의가 너무 갑자기 끝나서 회원들이 도로 건설 프로젝트에 대해서 언급할 기회를 거의 갖지 못했다.

해설 동사 ended를 수식하는 부사로 that절 이하의 내용과 이어져야 하므로 (A) abruptly가 문맥상 적절하다.

어휘 have an opportunity to ~할 기회를 갖다 comment on ~에 대해 언급하다 proposed 제안된 abruptly 갑자기 broadly 대략, 대체로 practically 현실적으로 obviously 명백히

129 **해석** Abraham 씨는 그녀의 경험 부족 때문에 우주 비행사 훈련에 자원하는 것을 꺼려했다.

해설 be동사 뒤의 보어 자리이므로 형용사 (D) reluctant가 정답이다.

어휘 lack of ~이 부족한 volunteer for ~에 자원하다 astronaut 우주 비행사 reluctance 꺼려함 be reluctant to ~하기를 꺼려하다

130 **해석** 공식적인 구매 협정을 하기 위해서 매니저는 적어도 세 명 이상의 자격을 갖춘 전문가의 견적서를 제출하여야 한다.

해설 동사가 submit이므로 목적어가 제출할 수 있는 것이므로 서류(견적서)를 나타내는 (C) estimates가 정답이다.

어휘 make an agreement 협약/계약하다 official 공식적인 qualified

PART 6

[131-134]

수신: 모든 직원

Light Cloud 항공 이사회는 Roberto Rinaldi가 떠난 **131** 후에 이사회 의장인 Mathew Mavens를 재단의 새로운 임시 회장으로 임명하는 것을 기쁘게 공지합니다. **132** 이사회와 직원들은 지난 7년 동안 Rinaldi 씨가 우리 일에 헌신한 것에 매우 감사합니다. 우리는 또한 그에게 미래의 노력에 최고만을 바랍니다. 그동안 새로운 정식 회장을 위한 임명회가 구성되었습니다. Mavens 씨는 조직의 새로운 회장이 **133** 결정되면 자신의 원래 임무인 이사회 의장을 재개할 것입니다.

질문이나 염려가 있으시다면 우리가 리더십에 과도기를 **134** 겪는 동안에 제게 자유롭게 연락 주시기 바랍니다.

감사합니다.

Rajiv Shrestha

홍보국장

어휘 be pleased to 기쁘게 ~하다 board chair 이사회 의장 appoint 임명하다 interim 중간의, 잠정의 foundation 조직, 업체 endeavor 노력 in the meantime 그러는 동안 form 구성하다 resume 재개하다 transition 이동, 변환

131 **해설** 빈칸은 'the departure of Roberto Rinaldi'를 앞의 문장에 연결해야 하는 전치사 자리이므로 (A)가 정답이다. 동사 follow는 동사이나 following은 전치사로도 사용하며 '~ 이후에'로 해석된다.

132 (A) 그가 찾던 상품을 찾았고 주문했다는 것을 알려드리게 되어서 기쁩니다.

(B) 제가 몇몇 이사회 회원을 만나야 해서 회의에 갈 수 없다는 이야기를 한다는 것을 잊어버렸습니다.

(C) 고용 과정을 부드럽게 운영하기 위해 제가 할 수 있는 게 있다면 알려 주세요.

(D) 이사회와 직원들은 지난 7년 동안 Rinaldi 씨가 우리 일에 헌신한 것에 대해 매우 감사합니다.

해설 빈칸 앞에 Rinaldi 씨가 처음 언급되었고 이 빈칸 뒤에 'We also wish him the best in his future endeavors'라며 계속해서 Rinalid 씨를 계속 언급하므로 정답은 (D)이다.

133 **해설** 빈칸은 'Mr. Mavens will resume his duty as board chair'와 'the new president of the organization is chosen'을 연결하는 부사절 접속사 자리이며 두 동사의 시제가 will과 is로 나타내고 있으므로 시제 일치의 예외에 해당하는 시간(때)을 의미하는 부사절 접속사 (B)가 정답이다.

134 **해설** 목적어 transition과 연결되어 '과정을 겪다'라는 문맥이 자연스러우므로 (C)가 정답이다.

어휘 reconsider 재고하다 undergo 겪다 avoid 피하다

[135-138]

이제 자격을 갖춘 지원자들을 Gibson 주식회사의 수석 웹 디자이너 직책에 고려하고 있습니다.

잘 알려진 광고 회사인 Gibson 주식회사는 사업체들에게 인터넷에서 회사의 존재를 극적으로 증가시킬 (135) 수 있는 혁신적인 기술 지원을 제공합니다. 이러한 특별한 서비스에 대한 수요가 늘어남에 따라 Gibson 주식회사 (136) 지점의 수도 늘어나고 있습니다. 사실, Berlin, Tokyo, Abu Dhabi처럼 아주 먼 곳에도 최근 새 사무실을 열었습니다.

Gibson 주식회사의 생산 부서의 일원으로서 새 수석 웹 디자이너는 고객들의 웹 사이트를 개발하고 유지하는 책임을 맡은 팀을 (137) 감독하게 될 것입니다. (138) 지원자들에게 필요한 업무에 대한 설명과 다른 정보들은 모두 www.gibson.com/jobs에서 찾아볼 수 있습니다.

어휘 qualified 자격을 갖춘 be considered 고려되다 innovative 혁신적인 dramatically 극적으로 presence 존재 unique 독특한 maintain 유지하다

135 해설 be동사 뒤의 보어 자리인데, be capable of는 '~할 능력이 있다'라는 뜻으로 쓰이므로 (D)가 정답이다.

어휘 capable 가능한, 능력 있는 capability 능력 capably 유능하게

136 해설 다음 문장에서 'new offices have recently opened'라고 언급하고 있으므로 '지점, 사무실'을 뜻하는 (A)가 정답이다.

어휘 instruction 지도, 안내

137 해설 새 웹 디자이너는 아직 결정되지 않았으므로 일하게 되면 미래에 일을 하게 될 것이라는 (B)가 정답이다.

어휘 oversee 감독하다

138 (A) 이메일을 보내 주시고 고객으로부터의 긍정적인 의견을 나누어 주셔서 감사합니다.
(B) 지원자들에게 필요한 업무에 대한 설명과 다른 정보들은 모두 www.gibson.com/jobs에서 찾아볼 수 있습니다.
(C) 당신과 Gibson의 전 직원과 함께 일하게 되어서 큰 기쁨이었습니다.
(D) 우리의 작업이 당신 기준에 맞지 않는다면 우리가 보장해 드린다는 것을 지킬 것입니다.

해설 앞의 내용에서 새 웹 디자이너의 채용을 공지했으므로 세부 사항을 안내하는 (B)가 정답이다.

어휘 share 나누다, 함께 하다 positive feedback 긍정적인 반응 description 설명 meet the standard 기준에 맞다 honor 존중하다, 지키다

[139-142]

11월 29일 — Sheboygan 거리에 있는 Jake 레스토랑이 최근에 오락 허가증 신청서를 제출했습니다. 만약 (139) 승인된다면, 그 허가증으로 레스토랑은 야간에 라이브 음악 공연을 열 수 있게 될 것입니다.

이 레스토랑은 주로 주거 지역인 곳에 위치해 있으므로 몇몇 이웃들은 정기적 (140) 으로 시끄러운 음악에 노출될 것을 염려하고 있습니다. 다른 사람들은 큰 (141) 문제가 될 거라고 생각하지는 않습니다. "문제없을 거예요"라고 주민 Beth Martinez가 말했습니다.

(142) 주민들은 그들의 염려를 나타내기 위해 시의회에 연락할 수도 있습니다. 그러나 결정은 결국에는 시 면허 사무실 직원들에게 놓여 있습니다.

어휘 entertainment 오락, 여흥 permit 허가증 enable ~을 가능하게 하다 performance 공연 nightly 밤에 primarily 주로 residential 주거지의 be concerned that ~을 염려하다 be exposed to ~에 노출되다 resident 주민 voice 목소리를 내다 ultimately 결국에는 lie with ~에 놓여 있다 licensing office 면허 사무실

139 해설 if절 안의 빈칸으로 주어가 없는 형태이므로 본동사는 사용할 수 없는 분사구문이다. approve는 타동사인데 빈칸 뒤에 목적어가 없으므로 과거분사를 이용한 분사구문임을 알 수 있으므로 정답은 (A)이다.

140 해설 빈칸은 뒤의 명사 basis와 어울리는 전치사 자리이다. 'on a regular basis'는 '정기적으로'라는 의미로 사용되므로 (B)가 정답이다.

141 해설 앞 문장에서 어떤 주민들이 걱정하고 있지만 다른 이들은 큰 문제가 아니라고 생각한다는 문맥을 이루므로 (B)가 정답이다.

어휘 investment 투자 act 행동

142 **(A) 주민들은 그들의 염려를 나타내기 위해 시의회에 연락할 수도 있습니다.**
(B) 레스토랑에서 일하는 것을 도울 자원봉사자를 찾고 있습니다.
(C) 전환이 더 빨리 이루어지게 하기 위해 개인 용품들은 치워 주세요.
(D) 경영진이 실행하려고 하는 변화 중의 하나입니다.

해설 뒤 문장의 'the decision ultimately lies with the staff in the city licensing office'를 However를 이용하여 연결하고 있으므로 대조되는 내용의 (A)가 정답이다.

어휘 transition 전환 personal 개인용의 implement 실행하다

[143-146]

수신: Fred Jaspers 〈fjaspers@westfordmarketing.com〉
발신: Winnie Price 〈WPrice@lapimaelectronics.com〉
날짜: 4월 8일
주제: 새로운 마케팅 캠페인
첨부: 전자 제품

안녕, Fred.

Lapima 전자 상가는 곧 여름 상품 목록을 받습니다. (143) 이에 따라, 새 제품을 홍보하기 위해 지면과 온라인 광고를 새로 시작하고 싶어요.

100퍼센트 재활용 제품으로 제조된 Mason의 새로운 가정용 가전제품 라인을 특징으로 잡고 싶어요. Lapima 전자 상가는 이 제품 라인을 제공하는 단 둘뿐인 소매업체 중 (144) 하나이니 광고에서 이점을 (145) 강조하고 싶어요. (146) 전자 제품 사진을 첨부했어요. 이 이미지는 마음대로 사용하실 수 있습니다.

감사합니다.

Winnie Price
영업 부사장, Lapima 전자 상가

어휘 inventory 상품 목록 shortly 곧 promote 홍보하다 print 서면, 지면 feature 특징으로 하다 recycled materials 재활용 물품 retailer 소매업자 at will 마음대로

143 해설 앞뒤 문장을 연결하는 접속부사 자리로서 앞 문장 'Lapima Electronic Store will receive its summer inventory shortly'와 이어져야 하므로 (A)가 정답이다

어휘 accordingly 이에 따라 likewise 이처럼 moreover 더욱이 nevertheless 그럼에도 불구하고

144 해설 두 소매업체 중 하나를 가리키므로 (C)가 정답이다.

145 해설 want 동사의 목적어인 it(앞 문장)을 설명하는 목적격 보어 자리이며 '강조되어지는'의 수동의 의미로 사용되어야 하므로 과거분사형 (C)가 정답이다.

어휘 emphasis 강조 emphasize 강조하다

146 (A) 주문이 어떻게 되어가고 있는지 알고 싶습니다.
(B) 행사 전에 우리가 만날 것이라는 것을 알려드리고 싶습니다.
(C) 지난 금요일에 온라인 가게에서 난방기를 주문했어요.
(D) 전자제품 사진을 첨부했어요.

해설 다음 문장에서 'these images'를 언급했으므로 images와 연결될 수 있는 photos를 언급한 (D)가 정답이다.

[147-148]

안녕하세요, Finkel 씨.

Pleasantville 부동산의 Jeff입니다. 그 사무실을 좋아해서 다행이에요.

147 이사 날짜를 잘못 알았어요.

7월 1일이 아니라 6월 1일입니다. 148 계약서는 아직 당신 서명이 필요해요. 되도록 빨리 사무실에 들러 주세요.

어휘 realty 부동산 lease 임대 계약 come by 잠깐 방문하다

147 메시지의 목적은 무엇인가?
(A) 아파트를 구매하기 위해서
(B) 이사 업체를 소개하기 위해서
(C) 사무실로 가는 길안내를 하기 위해서
(D) 정보를 정정하기 위해서

해설 'I was wrong about the move-in date. It's not July 1 but June 1'에서 이사 날짜를 정정하므로 정답은 (D)이다.

148 Finkel 씨에게 요청한 것은?
(A) 서류에 서명하기
(B) 소포 발송하기
(C) 기부하기
(D) 수수료를 지불하기

해설 지문의 'The lease still needs your signature'에서 서명을 요청하는 것이므로 정답은 (A)이다.

[149-150]

http://www.sanremowellbeingfoundation.com

149 San Remo 복지 재단은 올해 지원금에 대한 신청자를 받고 있다는 것을 기쁘게 알립니다. 매년 우리는 전 세계에서 지역의 건강과 복지를 개선하는 데 전념하고 있는 프로젝트에 대해 4개의 지원금을 증정합니다.

상금 총액은 아래에 자세하게 기술되어 있습니다.
- 1등 2,000파운드
- 2등 1,500파운드
- 3등 1,000파운드
- 4등 500파운드

비영리 재단만이 우리 지원금에 자격이 있습니다. 영리 추구 업체는 자격이 주어지지 않습니다. 이전 우승자들은 성인 수영 프로그램, 학생들을 위한 점심 프로그램, 150 일련의 애완동물 관리 워크숍 프로그램이 해당되었습니다.

링크를 클릭해서 지원금 신청서를 다운로드받아 주세요.

어휘 well-being 복지 be pleased to 기쁘게 ~하다 annual 연간 grant 지원금 throughout the world 전 세계에서 be committed to ~에 전념하다 amount 총액 entity 단체, 조직 be eligible for ~할 자격이 되다 ineligible 자격이 되지 않는 pet care 애완동물 관리

149 웹 페이지의 목적은?
(A) 정부 지원금을 유치하기 위해서
(B) 스포츠 행사의 우승자를 발표하기 위해서
(C) 행사 참여를 권장하기 위해서
(D) 새로운 학교의 개교를 상기시키기 위해서

해설 첫 번째 문장 'we are now accepting applicants for our annual grants'에서 지원금 신청자를 유치하기 위한 목적을 나타내고 있으므로 (C)가 정답이다.

어휘 solicit 간청하다

150 과거에 San Remo 복지 재단 지원금이 쓰인 용도는?
(A) 사람들에게 애완동물 관리 방법 교육하기
(B) 아이들을 위한 노래 대회 기획하기
(C) 지역 병원을 위해 의료 기기 구매하기
(D) 건강에 대한 국제 회의 개최하기

해설 'Previous years' winners include an adult swim program, a lunch program for schoolchildren, and a series of pet care workshops'에서 우승자가 상금을 쓴 분야를 알 수 있으므로 이중 하나에 해당되는 (A)가 정답이다.

[151-152]

Carol Lewis 오후 2시 29분
안녕, Anthony. 시간 있나요? 151 재고 목록 문제로 당신과 이야기를 하고 싶어요.

Anthony Ribisi 오후 2시 30분
좋아요. 계속 하세요.

Carol Lewis 오후 2시 31분
자료에 따르면, 프린터 용지가 한 상자 남았네요. 더 주문해야 할까요?

Anthony Ribisi 오후 2시 32분
그럴 필요없어요. 새로운 공급업체로 바꿨어요. 가격이 덜 비싼 브랜드로 갈 거예요. 152 지난주 당신이 없는 동안 새로운 제품 25상자를 주문했어요. 제품들이 아직 안 왔지만요.

Carol Lewis 오후 2시 33분
처리해 줘서 고마워요!

어휘 inventory 재고 목록 switch 바꾸다

151 오후 2시 30분에 Ribisi 씨가 "Go ahead"라고 쓴 의미는 무엇인가?
(A) Lewis 씨의 질문에 답할 시간이 있다.
(B) Lewis 씨가 요청했던 것을 했다.
(C) Lewis 씨와 만나는 것에 동의한다.
(D) Lewis 씨에게 프로젝트 진행을 허가해 주었다.

해설 오후 2시 29분 'I want to talk with you about the inventory issue'에 대한 응답이므로 계속해서 이야기하자는 의미로 (A)가 정답이다.

152 Lewis 씨에 대해 언급된 것은?
(A) 새로운 데이터를 만들었다.
(B) 오늘 배송을 받았다.
(C) 지난주에 주문을 했다.
(D) 최근에 휴가를 다녀왔다.

해설 오후 2시 32분에 Ribisi 씨가 'While you were out last week'라고 한 것으로 보아 (D)가 정답임을 알 수 있다.

[153-155]

153 최신 Cosmos 7 휴대폰을 구매해 주셔서 감사합니다. 구매하신 물품에 추가 배터리도 포함되어 있습니다. 모든 종류의 휴대폰 용품은 Cosmos 온라인 매장인 www.cosmoscellphone.com에서 직접 구매하실 수 있습니다. 154 영업일 7일 이내에 주문 상품을 수령하실 것이며, 그렇지 않으면 주문 상품은 무료입니다.

155 우수 고객으로서 휴대폰 용품을 처음 구매하실 때 20% 할인받으실 수 있습니다. 주문하실 때 홍보 코드 BHURRY를 입력해 주세요. 소매점을 통해서 용품을 구매하고 싶으시다면 저희 휴대폰 용품들은 모든 주요 전자제품 가게에서 이용 가능합니다. 대부분의 소매업체들은 저희 기업 할인을 받지 않는다는 것을 알아 두십시오.

새로운 휴대폰에 대해 의견이나 질문이 있으신가요? 기술 지원을 위해서는 24시간 800-555-9876로 전화해 주시고 판매나 계정 상담은 월요일부터 금요일까지 오전 7시부터 오후 8시까지 800-555-9878로 전화해 주세요.

어휘 brand-new 최신의 additional 추가의 directly from ~에서 직접 free of charge 무료로, 공짜로 preferred customer 우수 고객 retail 소매점 leading 주도적인, 선두의 honor 존중하다, 지키다 corporate 기업의 technical support 기술 지원

153 이 정보의 대상자는 누구인가?
(A) 기술 지원 전문가
(B) 제품 디자이너
(C) 새로운 휴대폰 구매자
(D) 연구원

해설 첫 번째 단락에서 'Thank you for purchasing a brand-new Cosmos 7'이라고 하였으므로 (C)가 정답이다.

154 정보로부터 무엇을 알 수 있는가?
(A) 배송이 늦으면 주문 상품은 무료이다.
(B) 판매원들은 항상 이용 가능하다.
(C) 제품은 1년 동안 보증된다.
(D) 기술자들이 가능한 한 빨리 답신 전화를 할 것이다.

해설 첫 번째 단락에서 'We guarantee that you will receive your order within seven working days or the order is free of charge라고 하였으므로 (A)가 정답이다.

어휘 at all times 항상 under warranty 보증 하에

155 할인받는 방법으로 추천되는 것은?
(A) 고객 서비스부에 전화하기
(B) 웹 사이트에 단어 입력하기
(C) 전자 상가 방문하기
(D) 쿠폰 발송하기

해설 두 번째 단락에서 'you will receive a 20 percent discount off your first purchase of cellphone accessories. Simply type in promo code BHURRY when placing your order'라고 하였으므로 (B)가 정답이다.

[156-157]

Easton 서점은 8월 12일 수요일 오후 3시에서 5시까지 156 작가 Annette Lyons의 낭독회를 개최합니다. 최고의 공상 과학 소설로 권위 있는 Reily 상을 2회 수상한 Lyons 씨가 〈문 뒤에서〉의 발췌본을 읽을 것입니다. 이 소설은 그녀의 157 〈알려지지 않은 자들의 왕국〉 시리즈의 5회이자 마지막 권이며 베스트셀러 목록에서 1위가 되었고 비평가들로부터 열정적인 칭찬을 받았습니다. 지난 10년 동안 가장 있기 있는 공상 과학 소설 작가 중의 한 명의 최신작 낭독을 놓치지 마세요.

입장권은 5달러이고 주소가 27 Grey Lane, Memphis인 Easton 서점에서 구매 가능합니다. 아니면 소비자 서비스 전화번호인 080-555-4834로 전화해 주세요.

어휘 host 개최하다 public reading 낭독회 prestigious 권위 있는, 명망 있는 excerpt 요약, 추출본 installment 연재물 top 최고를 차지하다 enthusiastic 열정적인 praise 칭찬 decade 10년

156 Lyons 씨는 누구인가?
(A) 유명 대학의 도서관 사서
(B) Easton 서점의 소유주
(C) 출판사의 문학 평론가
(D) 인기 있는 책의 작가

해설 첫 번째 문장의 'a public reading by writer Annette Lyons'에서 작가임을 알 수 있다. 따라서 (D)가 정답이다.

어휘 librarian 도서관 사서 critic 평론가

157 〈문 뒤에서〉에 대해 언급된 것은?
(A) 10년 동안 쓰여졌다.
(B) 중요한 상을 받았다.
(C) 연작의 마지막 권이다.
(D) 50만 부가 판매되었다.

해설 첫 번째 단락에서 'the fifth and final installment in her *Kingdoms of the Unknown* series'라고 하였으므로 (C)가 정답이다. 작가인 Lyons 씨가 상을 받았지만 〈문 뒤에서〉로 상을 받은 것인지는 알 수 없으므로 (B)는 오답이다.

[158-160]

Edgerton의 새로운 출발

Vernon 시, 9월 2일 – 158 Edgerton 국제공항에 대한 수정된 계획이 8월 30일 프로젝트 수석 엔지니어인 Nina Grant에 의해서 Vernon City 교통 이사회에서 발표되었습니다. –[1]–.

Vernon City의 서쪽에 위치하게 될 새로운 공항에 대한 계획은 3년 전에 처음 승인되었습니다. 그러나 교통 이사회가 작년에 의뢰한 연구에 따르면 이 지역에 항공으로 여행 오는 승객들의 수가 앞으로 몇 년 안에 상당히 증가할 것으로 예상된다고 결론이 지어졌습니다. –[2]–. 이것은 상당 부분 Vernon City 북쪽으로 20 킬로미터 근방에 Marcus 호텔이 대형 비치 리조트를 열겠다는 결정의 결과입니다. –[3]–.

159 160 제안된 변화는 대형 비행기를 수용할 활주로의 연장, 승객들의 대기 구역 확장, 그리고 승객 터미널에 쇼핑 지역을 추가하는 것들을 포함합니다. –[4]–.

이사회 의장인 Jenny Mason은 이사회가 이달 안에 수정된 계획을 승인할 것 같고, 이것은 원래 예정 대로 1월에 공항에 대한 공사의 4단계의 첫 번째 단계가 시작될 것임을 언급했습니다.

어휘 revised plan 수정안 commission 의뢰하다 substantially 상당히 largely 주로 lengthen 길이를 연장하다 runway 활주로 expand 확장하다 chairperson 의장 be likely to ~할 것 같다 phase 단계 originally 원래

158 Grant 씨와 이사회의 만남의 이유는 무엇인가?
(A) 연구가 수행되어야 함을 요청하기 위해서
(B) 회사의 새로운 사장 임명을 공지하기 위해서
(C) 디자인 계획에 대해 새로운 소식을 알려주기 위해서
(D) 공사가 예정보다 늦은 이유를 설명하기 위해서

해설 첫 번째 단락에서 'Revised plans for the Edgerton International Airport were presented to the Vernon City Transportation Board by Nina Grant, the project's chief engineer, on August 30'을 보면 8월에 이사회에서 Grant 씨가 수정 계획을 발표한 것을 알 수 있으므로 (C)가 정답이다.

159 Edgerton 국제공항에 대해서 알 수 있는 것은?
(A) 대형 비행기도 수용할 수 있을 것이다.
(B) Vernon City의 북쪽에 위치할 것이다.
(C) 승객 터미널이 3개가 있을 것이다.
(D) 그 지역에서 가장 큰 배송 지역이 있을 것이다.

해설 세 번째 단락에서 'Proposed changes include lengthening the runways to accommodate the large-capacity planes'라고 언급하였으므로 (A)가 정답이다.

어휘 large-capacity 대용량, 대형

160 [1], [2], [3], [4]로 표시된 위치 중 다음 문장이 들어가기 적절한 곳은?
"공항 화물 터미널 디자인 계획은 이 지역에서는 가장 대규모가 될 것으로 예정되어 있고 변하지 않고 남아 있습니다."
(A) [1]
(B) [2]
(C) [3]
(D) [4]

해설 공항의 시설에 대한 계획을 언급하고 있으므로 세 번째 단락의 'Proposed changes include lengthening the runways to accommodate the large-capacity planes, expanding the passenger waiting areas, and adding shopping areas to the passenger terminal'과 이어지는 내용이므로 (D)가 정답이다.

어휘 on tract 진행 중인

[161-164]

Whitfield 식료품

7월 1일

고객님께

Whitfield 식료품에서 멋진 변화가 일어나고 있습니다! 161 이달 말에 저희 매장을 방문하셔서 여러분의 쇼핑 경험을 좀 더 향상시키기 위해 저희가 만든 개선 사항들을 봐주시기를 바랍니다.

162-B 아시다시피 저희는 매장에 8,000 평방미터를 더하는 커다란 개조를 진행해 왔습니다. 7월 10일부터 우리의 농산물 코너는 거의 2배가 더 커져서 162-A 다양한 종류의 과일과 야채를 제공해 드릴 수 있으며 고객 여러분들이 좀 더 편안하게 매장에서 이동할 수 있게 될 것입니다. 여러분께 좀 더 신선하게 구워진 빵을 제공하기 위해서 제과제빵 코너도 또한 확장 중에 있습니다.

7월 20일 토요일에 이 개조를 축하하게 될 것입니다. 요리 시연과 무료 시식도 있습니다. 또한 162-C 토요일에 오전 7시가 아니라 6시에 문을 열기 시작할 것입니다.

여러분들에게 새로운 Whitfield 식료품 방문을 권장하기 위해 할인 쿠폰을 동봉합니다. 이 쿠폰은 7월 31일까지 164 유효합니다. 163 또한 특별 할인 행사가 표시되어 있는 달력도 발견하실 수 있습니다.

Ann O'Connor
가게 매니저

어휘 improvement 개선, 발전 undergo 겪다 significant 상당한 nearly 거의 with ease 쉽게 expand 확장하다 bakery section 제과제빵 코너 free food tasting 무료 시식 enclose 포함시키다 indicate 나타내다

161 편지의 목적은?
(A) 매장 보수의 완공을 공표하기 위해서
(B) 주문 제작 제과제빵류를 홍보하기 위해서
(C) 가게 소유주의 변화를 알리기 위해서
(D) 새로운 가게 위치를 홍보하기 위해서

해설 지문의 첫 번째 단락에서 'We hope you will visit us later this month and see the improvements we are making in order to enhance your shopping experience'로부터 매장 보수 공사

가 완료됨을 알리는 편지임을 알 수 있으므로 (A)가 정답이다.

어휘 completion 완성 ownership 주인, 소유주

162 편지에 언급되지 않은 것은?
(A) 제품의 폭 넓은 선택
(B) 늘어난 매장 면적
(C) 영업 시간 연장
(D) 추가 출납원

해설 두 번째 단락의 'adding about 8,000 square meter to our store'에서 (B)가 언급이 되었고 'offer a variety of fruits and vegetables'에서 상품이 다양화된 것으로 (A)가 언급되었으며 'we will start opening on Saturdays at 6 A.M. instead of 7 A.M.'에서 (C)도 언급되었음을 알 수 있으므로 정답은 (D)이다.

163 편지에 동봉된 것은?
(A) 설문지
(B) 이벤트 일정
(C) 제품 리스트
(D) 제품 샘플

해설 지문의 네 번째 단락에서 'You will also find a calendar indicating special sale days'에서 할인 행사 일정을 알 수 있는 달력이 동봉되어 있다고 했으므로 (B)가 정답임을 알 수 있다.

164 편지의 네 번째 단락, 두 번째 줄의 good과 뜻이 가장 가까운 것은?
(A) 충분한
(B) 유효한
(C) 친절한
(D) 능률적인

해설 'The coupons are good until July 31'에서 good의 의미는 7월 31일까지 사용할 수 있다는 뜻이므로 (B)가 정답이다.

[165-167]

메모

수신: Clarion Market 프로젝트 팀 멤버
발신: Marijus Fitzgerald
날짜: 9월 4일
주제: 프로젝트 결과

먼저, 지난 주말 Jefferson 공원에서 열린 Clarion Outdoor Market에 대해 열심히 일해 주신 여러분 모두에게 감사하고 싶습니다. 행사는 우리가 바랐던 대로 의료 센터를 위해 큰 액수를 모금하며 전반적으로 성공적이었으며 확실히 계속될 것입니다. 그럼에도 불구하고, 165 우리는 2개월 후에 두 번째 행사를 진행하기 전에 몇 가지 분야에서 개선할 필요가 있을 것 같습니다.

주된 걱정거리는 좋지 못한 날씨입니다. 여러분 중 많은 분들이 보셨듯이 일요일에 비가 왔음에도 불구하고 멋지게도 많은 분의 손님들이 있었습니다. 안타깝게도 우리는 이것에 대해 준비를 하지 못했고 상인들과 고객들 모두에게서 부스에 166 보호 천막을 설치하지 않은 것에 대해 많은 불만을 받았습니다. 공원에서 이것을 직원들과 이야기했고 그들은 기꺼이 나중에 열릴 시장을 위한 몇몇 대형 텐트를 제공해 주기로 했습니다.

다른 이야기이긴 한데, 우리는 또한 몇몇 상인들이 부진한 판매에 대해 불만을 제기했기에 등록 수수료를 없애는 것을 고려하고 싶습니다. 대신에, 거래에서 생긴 수익의 일정 퍼센트를 걷는 것을 생각하고 있어요. 167 이 문제를 완화하기 위한 다른 제안이나 이 절차를 불필요하게 어렵게 하지 않고 이 생각을 실행할 수 있는 방법을 제시해 주었으면 좋겠어요. 아이디어가 있으면 야외 마켓 기획자인 Adam Mosley에게 보내 주세요.

Marijus Fitzgerald
이사, Clarion Market 프로젝트

어휘 overall 전반적으로 a large amount of 많은 양의 raise 모금하다 proceeds 수익금 definitely 반드시 installment 회차 the month after next 2개월 후 inclement 좋지 못한 turnout 참가자의 수 merchant 상인 covering 천막, 덮개 be willing to 기꺼이 ~하다 on another note 다른 이야기지만 consider 고려하다 eliminate 제거하다, 없애다 registration fee 등록비 lack 부족, 결여 transaction 거래 alleviate 누그러뜨리다, 완화하다 implement 실행하다 unnecessarily 불필요하게, 필요 이상으로

165 Market 프로젝트에 대해서 추론할 수 있는 것은?
(A) 단지 한 번만 개최되었다.
(B) 한 달에 한 번 열린다.
(C) 날씨 때문에 취소되었다.
(D) 장소를 바꿀 것이다.

해설 첫 번째 단락 'we will need to improve a few areas before conducting the second installment of the event the month after next'에서 다음 두 번째 행사라고 언급한 것으로 이번이 첫 번째 임을 알 수 있으므로 (A)가 정답이다. 2개월 후에 다음 행사가 열린다고 했으므로 행사는 두 달에 한 번 열린다는 것을 추론할 수 있다.

166 고객들이 불평한 것은?
(A) 비싼 등록 비용
(B) 비를 피할 장비 부족
(C) 적은 수의 상인
(D) 적은 양의 제품 다양성

해설 두 번째 단락의 'not having protective coverings on the booths'에서 (B)가 정답임을 알 수 있다.

167 Fitzgerald 씨가 프로젝트 회원들에게 요청하는 것은?
(A) 새로운 행사를 기획하기
(B) 공원 직원들에게 연락하기
(C) 의견을 제출하기
(D) 상인들과 이야기하기

해설 세 번째 단락 'I would like for everyone to propose another suggestion to alleviate this problem, or perhaps methods that could be used to implement this idea'에서 의견을 제안하기를 바라고 있음을 나타내므로 (C)가 정답이다.

[168-171]

이 달의 하이라이트

5월에 수석 회계사의 자리에서 내려오기로 결정한 Susie Murray는 지난 32년간 Harrison Accounting Firm의 많은 자리에서 일해 왔다. -[1]-. 회사의 사장인 Mario Vinchenso는 Harrison에서 Susie처럼 폭 넓은 경험을 가진 사람을 찾는 것은 드문 일이다"라고 말했다.

171 Murray 씨는 Milwaukee에 위치한 Miller Creek Accounting에서 임시 접수 담당자로 회계 경력을 시작했다. -[2]-. 171 그 후에 Harrison의 Norfolk 지점의 정규직 직원이 되었다. 2년 동안 전화 응답과 고객들의 전화를 안내하는 업무 후에 Murray 씨는 Harrison Accounting의 Richmond 지점의 매니저로 채용되었으며 1년도 되지 않아 수석 매니저로 승진했다.

-[3]-. 그러나 Murray 씨의 승진은 거기서 멈추지 않았다. 그녀는 "저는 숫자와 일하는 것을 즐겼고 회계부서로 옮기고 싶었어요. Richmond 지점 매니저인 Galen Broadbent가 어떻게 내 목표를 이룰 수 있는지 조언해 주었어요. Galen의 추천으로 Norfolk에 있는 Whitney 대학에서 169 Galen이 몇 년 전에 그랬던 것처럼 회계 학위를 추구하기로 결심했어요. -[4]-. 학생 대출을 신청하고 계속해서 파트타임으로 일하는 것으로 5년 만에 회계 프로그램을 끝마칠 수 있었어요."라고 말했다.

그녀는 Whitney 대학에서 학위를 받자마자 Harrison Accounting 본사 회계부에 합류했다. 3년 후에 그녀는 수석 회계사 Jean Archer의 보조로 임명되었다. 170 그리고 Archer 씨가 상업 회계 부서로 이동했을 때 Murray 씨는 그 자리를 채우도록 선택되어졌다. "생각해 보세요"라고 Murray 씨는 말했다. "저는 전화받는 업무에서 시작했는데 마침내 회사 본사의 수석 회계사가 되었네요."

어휘 step down 물러나다 capacity 능력 direct calls 전화를 안내하다 recount 말하다, 언급하다 achieve a goal 목표를 이루다 headquarters 본사 fill the position 자리를 채우다, 맡다 end up 결국 ~가 되다

168 기사는 무엇에 대한 것인가?
(A) 여론 조사 결과의 발표
(B) 은행의 다양한 빈자리
(C) 특별 훈련 프로그램 개최의 이유
(D) 회계 회사의 한 직원의 경력 안내

해설 글의 전체 내용이 모두 Susie Murray의 경력에 대한 것이므로 정답은 (D)이다

169 Broadbent 씨에 대해 알 수 있는 것은?
(A) Harrison에서 시간제로 일하고 있다.
(B) 기사를 위해서 인터뷰를 했다.
(C) 회계를 공부했다.
(D) 교수로서 경력이 있다.

해설 세 번째 단락에서 'I decided to pursue an accounting degree at Whitney College in Norfolk, just as Galen had done some years before'라고 언급한 것으로 Broadbent도 회계를 전공한 것을 알 수 있다. 따라서 (C)가 정답이다.

170 Harrison Accounting에 대해서 알 수 있는 것은?
(A) Richmond에 본사가 있다.
(B) 상업 회계 부서가 있다.
(C) 직원들은 대학 등록금 할인을 받는다.
(D) 최근에 Miller Creek Accounting과 합병했다.

해설 네 번째 단락에서 언급한 'Ms. Archer transferred to the commercial accounting division'에서 (B)가 정답임을 알 수 있다.

171 [1], [2], [3], [4]로 표시된 위치 중 다음 문장이 들어가기 적절한 곳은?
"그녀는 그 일이 매우 보람 있다고 생각하여 그녀의 계약 기간이 만료되었을 때 그 업계에서 정규직을 구하기 시작했다."
(A) [1]
(B) [2]
(C) [3]
(D) [4]

해설 제시된 문장은 일자리를 찾는다는 내용이므로 이전에 시간제로 일했다는 문장인 'Ms. Murray began her career in accounting as a temporary receptionist'와 정규직원이 되었다는 문장 'She was then hired as a full-time receptionist' 중간인 [2]에 들어가야 자연스러우므로 (B)가 정답이다.

어휘 rewarding 보람 있는

[172-175]

Sheila Paxton	오전 10시 13분
173 금요일 우리 워크숍에 Rob Housewell을 초청 연사 중 한 명으로 초대했어요.	
Emily Miller	오전 10시 14분
잘 됐네요! 그 분은 〈매력과 소비자〉라는 책으로 권위 있는 Paddington 상도 받았어요! 우리 분야에서 그의 통찰력의 깊이를 존경해요.	
Martin Richards	오전 10시 15분
그래요, 맞아요. 그분이 훌륭한 연설가라는 얘기도 들었어요.	
Sheila Paxton	오전 10시 25분
172 우리 직원들이 좀 더 독창적이고 매력적인 광고를 만들 수 있도록 영감을 줄 수 있다고 믿어요. 그런데 우리 모두가 그분이 이곳에 계시는 동안에 괜찮은 곳으로 모시고 가도 좋을 것 같아요.	
Emily Miller	오전 10시 26분
날씨가 좋다면 야외에서 무언가 해도 좋을 듯 해요.	
Martin Richards	오전 10시 28분
몇 시쯤으로 생각하고 있나요?	
Sheila Paxton	오전 10시 29분
173 Housewell 교수가 금요일 오후에는 계획이 있다고 했어요. 그분은 작업 중인 책에 대해서 출판업자를 만날 거예요.	
Emily Miller	오전 10시 30분
그럼 저녁에 할 수 있는 일을 계획해야겠네요.	
Martin Richards	오전 10시 32분
174 Mendota 호수 바로 옆에 있는 태국 레스토랑에서 저녁을 먹는 게 어때요?	
Emily Miller	오전 10시 33분
좋아요! 그곳에 주말에는 멋진 라이브 음악도 있어요.	
Martin Richards	오전 10시 34분
음식의 질도 또한 훌륭하고 도시 전망도 멋진 곳이에요. Housewell 씨는 분명히 이 태국 레스토랑을 좋아할 거예요.	
Sheila Paxton	오전 10시 35분
확실히 그럴 거예요! 고마워요 여러분. 구체적인 일정이 나오면 알려 줄게요.	

어휘 prestigious 권위 있는 insight 통찰력 inspire 영감을 주다 creative 독창적인 appealing 매력적인, 멋진 have in mind 생각해 두다 publisher 출판업자 definitely 분명히 specific 구체적인

172 대화자들은 어떤 회사에서 일하고 있는가?
(A) 광고 회사
(B) 회계 사무실
(C) 출판 회사
(D) 출장 연회 서비스

해설 오전 10시 25분 Paxton 씨가 'I believe he can inspire our employees to make more creative and appealing advertisements'라고 언급한 것으로 광고 회사 직원들임을 알 수 있다.

173 Housewell 씨에 대해서 추측할 수 있는 것은?
(A) 지역 대학에서 경영을 가르친다.
(B) 상을 받은 책을 몇 권 썼다.
(C) 같은 날에 연설과 만남을 가진다.
(D) 대화자들과 만난 적이 있다.

해설 오전 10시 13분 메시지에서 Housewell 씨는 금요일에 연설 일정이 잡혀 있는데, 오전 10시 29분 메시지에서 Housewell 씨가 금요일 오후에 출판업자와 만날 것이라고 했으므로 정답은 (C)이다. 상을 받은 책이 한 권 언급되긴 했지만 여러 권이 상을 받았는지는 알 수 없으므로 (B)는 오답이다.

174 태국 레스토랑에 대해서 알 수 있는 것은?
(A) 건물의 꼭대기 층에 위치해 있다.
(B) 물가에 있는 식당이다.
(C) 매일 밤 음악 공연이 있다.
(D) 예약 시에만 저녁에 연다.

해설 오전 10시 32분에 Richards 씨가 'Thai Restaurant right next to Mendota Lake?'라고 하였으므로 (B)가 정답이다.

175 오전 10시 35분에 Paxton 씨가 "I bet"이라고 한 것은 무엇을 의미하는가?
(A) 금요일 레스토랑 예약이 꽉 찼다고 생각한다.
(B) Housewell 씨가 그 장소를 좋아할 것을 확신한다.
(C) Housewell 씨에게 직접 연락할 것이다.
(D) 워크숍 기획을 서둘러서 해야만 한다.

해설 오전 10시 35분에 'Mr. Housewell definitely will love that restaurant'에 대한 동의를 나타내기 위해 'I bet(확실히 그럴 거야)'이라고 쓴 것이므로 (B)가 정답이다.

어휘 be confident that ~에 확신하다 in a hurry 서둘러서

[176-180]

수신: 전 직원
발신: Cathy Pinkerton, 운영 담당 부사장
날짜: 10월 2일
제목: 장비 재정비

176 사무 장비 주문 시기가 다시 왔습니다. 회사 정책은 컴퓨터, 전화기, 팩스 같은 일반 장비는 5년 사용 후 교체할 수 있다고 명시하고 있습니다. 178 5년이 안 된 장비를 교체하기 위해서는 수리 비용이 교체 비용을 초과하는 것으로 결론이 나야 합니다. 구매 부서 직원이 가격을 알아보는 것을 기꺼이 도와줄 것입니다.

장비 요청을 적으시려면 첨부된 양식을 이용해 주세요. 필요한 대로 이 양식의 복사본을 만들어 두어도 됩니다. 177 179 모든 요청서는 반드시 승인을 나타내는 부서 담당자의 서명이 필요합니다. 180 구매 부서는 정보가 누락되어 있으면 청구자에게 요청서를 반송할 것이라는 것을 알아 두세요. 목록에 적힌 물품의 일련번호나 ID 번호가 있어야 합니다. 작성된 양식은 C 건물 구매부 Frank Wong에게 10월 14일까지 보내 주세요. 이 날짜 이후에 접수된 요청서는 다음 분기로 넘어갑니다.

읽어 주셔서 감사합니다.

CONNOR CHEMICALS

사무 장비 주문 양식

직원 이름: Martin Jacobs
직책과 담당 부서: 179 생산부서 품질 검사자

장비 사양	일련번호	연차
사진용 프린터	8 HDQ5	5
180 컴퓨터 모니터		7
178 전력 선	PH-3 AL	4

승인자: 179 Daniel Donaldson
날짜: 10월 15일

어휘 state 명시하다 be eligible for ~할 자격이 주어지다 determine 결정하다 exceed 초과하다 attached form 첨부 양식 photocopy 복사본 indicate 나타내다 omit 누락하다 forward A to B A를 B로 보내다 consider 고려하다 inspector 검사자 description 설명, 사양

176 메모가 보내진 이유는?
(A) 직원들에게 사무 장비 예산 삭감을 공지하기 위해서
(B) 사무 장비 비용 계산하는 방법을 설명하기 위해서
(C) 사무 장비 신청 절차를 설명하기 위해서
(D) 사무 장비 설치 설명서를 수정하기 위해서

해설 메모의 첫 번째 문장 'Please be reminded that it is again time to place orders for office equipment'에서 (C)가 정답임을 알 수 있다.

어휘 notify 공지하다 budget reduction 예산 삭감 calculate 계산하다 setup 설치

177 양식에 대해 언급된 것은 무엇인가?
(A) 운영부가 5년에 한 번씩 검토한다.
(B) 제출하려면 부서 매니저의 서명이 필요하다.
(C) 10월 15일까지 구매 사무실로 제출되어야 한다.
(D) 다양한 양식으로 발행된다.

해설 메모의 두 번째 단락에서 'All requests must have the signature of your department manager indicating his or her approval'이라고 언급하였으므로 (B)가 정답임을 알 수 있다. 제출 날짜는 10월 14일로 명시하고 있으므로 (C)는 오답이다.

178 전력 선에 대해서 알 수 있는 것은?
(A) 구매 비용이 수리 비용보다 적다.
(B) 작년에 단종되었다.
(C) 연장된 보증서와 함께 나온다.
(D) 회사 컴퓨터와 호환 가능하지 않다.

해설 연계 지문 문제이다. 메모의 첫 번째 단락에서 5년이 안 된 장비를 교체하려면 수리 비용이 구입 비용보다 높아야 한다고 했는데, 주문 양식에서 전력 선이 4년된 물품임에도 교체 신청을 하고 있으므로 구매 비용이 수리 비용보다 더 적다는 것을 알 수 있다. 따라서 정답은 (A)이다.

어휘 discontinue 단종하다 extended 연장된 be compatible with ~와 호환 가능하다

179 Donaldson 씨는 어떤 직책을 갖고 있는 것 같은가?
(A) 구매부 책임자
(B) 수리 기술자
(C) 생산부 매니저
(D) 행정 보조

해설 연계 지문 문제이다. 메모의 두 번째 단락에서 양식을 제출하려면 부서 매니저의 서명이 필요하다고 하였다. 신청서를 작성한 사람인 Jacobs 씨가 생산부 직원이고, 서명한 사람은 Donaldson 씨이므로 (C)가 정답이다.

180 왜 Jacobs 씨가 이 양식이 되돌려 받을 것 같은가?
(A) 양식 복사본을 제출했기 때문에
(B) 필요한 정보를 누락했기 때문에
(C) 개인 사용 장비를 적었기 때문에
(D) Pinkerton 씨의 서명을 받아야 하기 때문에

해설 연계 지문 문제이다. 메모의 두 번째 단락에서 'Make sure that a serial number or ID number appears for the items listed'라고 언급하였는데 양식에는 컴퓨터 모니터의 일련번호가 없다. 두 번째 단락에서 누락된 내용이 있는 경우 보낸 사람에게 다시 반송된다고 했으므로 (B)가 정답이다.

어휘 leave out 누락시키다 personal use 개인 사용 obtain 획득하다

[181-185]

www.tartanairlines.com

Tartan 항공사	새로운 서비스와 특별 행사	**예약**	Tartan 항공 Plus 프로그램

Tartan 항공은 Nashik 공항에서 다음 목적지로 새로운 운행의 시작을 자랑스럽게 생각합니다.

181-A 184 Kolkata – 9월 5일
Agra – 9월 20일
Chennai – 9월 15일
Mumbai – 9월 25일

지금 바로 예약하고 돈을 절약하세요! 위에 언급한 처음 시작하는 비행기를 예약하시는 Tartan 항공 단골 비행 프로그램, Tartan 항공 Plus 회원들은 25%를 할인받으실 수 있습니다.

예약을 클릭해서 지금 당장 예약하세요.

제한 및 상기 사항

** 이 혜택은 Nashik 공항에서 위에 언급한 특정 날짜에 출발하는 편도나 왕복 항공에 해당됩니다.

** 182 단골 비행 고객들은 Tartan 항공 Plus 회원 번호를 예약 시 사용하시면 25% 할인받을 수 있습니다.

** 181-C Tartan 항공은 더 이상 종이 티켓은 발행하지 않습니다. 표를 구매하시면 승객들은 예약 확인 이메일을 받게 됩니다. 여기에는 8자리 단위의 예약 번호가 있습니다. 탑승 수속을 신속하게 하기 위해 반드시 이 번호를 소지해 주세요. 셀프 탑승 수속 시에도 입력하도록 요청받습니다.

** 가장 저렴한 항공 요금을 제공하기 위해서 Tartan 항공은 더 이상 무료 신문, 잡지, 헤드폰, 식사나 간식 등을 비행하는 동안에 제공하지 않습니다. 181-D 각 승객들은 한 잔의 무료 음료를 마실 수 있습니다. 음료 선택은 과일 주스, 커피, 차나 물이 있습니다.

발신: amcgosh200@dfmailer.com
수신: customersieveice@tartanairlines.ca
날짜: 7월 29일
주제: 최초 비행 할인

담당자께:

184 7월 8일에, Nashik 공항에서 처음으로 Chennai로 운행하는 Tartan 항공 좌석을 예약했습니다. 웹 사이트에 따르면, Tartan 항공 Plus 회원들은 이 비행에 대해 25% 할인받을 자격이 있습니다. 183 좌석을 예약할 때 단골 비행 고객 번호를 입력하였는데 신용 카드 명세서는 전체 금액이 청구된 것으로 나옵니다. 가능한 한 빨리 이 문제를 185 해결해 주시면 감사하겠습니다.

Alice McGosh

어휘 be proud to 자랑스럽게 ~하다 destination 목적지 inaugural 처음의, 개회의 restrictions 제약 reminder 상기 사항 round-way 왕복의 originate 시작하다, 유래하다 specified 명시된 issue 발급하다 digit 숫자 단위의 keep in handy ~를 소지하다 speed process 과정을 신속히 하다 airfare 항공 요금 be entitled to ~할 자격이 있다 complimentary 무료의 beverage 음료 statement 명세서 charge 청구하다 full fare 전체 금액

181 Tartan Airlines에 대해서 언급되지 않은 것은?
(A) 4개의 새로운 목적지를 운행한다.
(B) 일정을 바꾸려면 25달러의 벌금을 내야 한다.
(C) 고객들에게 종이 티켓을 제공하지 않는다.
(D) 비행 동안에 현재 음료수 한 잔을 제공한다.

해설 웹 사이트 상단에 Kolkata, Agra, Chennai, Mumbai의 4곳의 새로운 목적지를 명시하고 있으므로 (A)는 언급되었고, 후반부에 'Tartan Airlines is no longer issuing paper tickets'라고 언급하였으므로 (C)도 언급되었다. 마지막 단락에서 'Each passenger is entitled to one complimentary beverage'에서 (D)도 언급한 사항임을 알 수 있다. 그러므로 언급되지 않은 것은 (B)이다.

어휘 destination 목적지 penalty 벌금 itinerary 일정 at no charge 무료로

182 정보에 따르면 고객들은 광고된 할인을 받기 위해서 무엇을 해야만 하는가?
(A) 단골 비행 고객 프로그램 회원 번호를 제공한다.
(B) 적어도 2주 전에 예약한다.
(C) 단골 비행 고객 프로그램 멤버십을 신청한다.
(D) 기술된 여행지 중 두 곳에 대한 표를 구매한다.

해설 웹 사이트의 'Frequent Flyers can receive a 25% discount by using the Tartan Airlines Plus Membership number'에서 회원 번호를 사용하면 할인받을 수 있다고 했으므로 (A)가 정답이다.

어휘 at least 적어도 in advance 먼저, 사전에 apply for 신청하다

183 McGosh 씨가 이메일을 보낸 이유는?
(A) 최근 여행에서 겪은 지연에 대해 불평하기 위해서
(B) 출발 날짜를 바꾸기 위해서
(C) 대체 예약 확인 번호를 요청하기 위해서
(D) 예약의 금액 청구 실수를 알리기 위해서

해설 이메일에서 'my credit card statement shows that I was charged the full fare'라고 했으므로 (D)가 정답이다.

어휘 complain about ~에 대해 불평하다 billing mistake 청구 실수

184 McGosh 씨가 Nashik 공항에서 출발하기로 예정된 날짜는?
(A) 9월 5일
(B) 9월 15일
(C) 9월 20일
(D) 9월 25일

해설 연계 지문 문제이다. 이메일에서 'I booked a seat on Tartan Airlines' first flight to Chennai from Nashik Airport'라고 하였으므로 웹 사이트의 새로운 목적지 운항 날짜를 참고하면 9월 15일에 출발한다는 것을 알 수 있다. 따라서 정답은 (B)이다.

185 이메일의 첫 번째 단락, 네 번째 줄의 address와 뜻이 가장 가까운 것은?
(A) 말하다
(B) 발언하다
(C) 다루다
(D) 쓰다

해설 이메일의 address this issue는 '문제를 해결하다'의 뜻이므로 (C)가 정답이다.

어휘 remark 언급하다 deal with 다루다

[186-190]

Vancouver (3월 10일)

점점 커지고 있는 Regina Regency 리조트

186 Seattle에 기반을 둔 Regina 호텔 그룹이 작지만 지역 소유의 고급 호텔 체인인 Orchid 주식회사를 인수했습니다. Orchid 건물의 추가로 Regina는 이제 Vancouver 지역에서 800개 이상의 객실을 갖고 있는 11개의 호텔을 운영하게 되었습니다.

인수 이전에 Regina는 사업차 출장 온 여행객들을 염두에 두고 설계된 좀 더 작은 호텔인 Regina Travel Suites로 잘 알려져 왔습니다. Orchid의 4개의 건물은 1924년에 지어진 Grand Hall 호텔과 작년에 오픈한 고급 호텔인 Hotel Olivia도 포함하고 있습니다.

Regina 대변인인 Douglas Wong은 Orchid 호텔은 Regina 브랜드에는 환영할 만한 추가라고 말했습니다. 187 Orchid는 Vancouver에서는 확고한 명성을 갖고 있고 특히 여행객들에 매력적인 숙박 시설로 현재 Regina 호텔의 완벽한 보완점이 됩니다.

이제 Regina 로열 클럽 회원들은 이전 Orchid 호텔에 숙박할 때 포인트를 받을 수 있습니다.

Vancouver 도심에 있는 당신의 집

Vancouver를 방문하십니까? 188 도심에 머무르고 싶으신가요? Regina 호텔을 선택하세요. 우리 호텔은 이제 인기 있는 Orchid 호텔까지 포함하고 있습니다. 아래에 도심 지역에서 가장 인기 있는 몇몇 호텔이 나와 있습니다.

Moon Hotel
무료 무선 인터넷에서 고급 침대, 대형 스크린 TV 그리고 실내 수영장까지! 이 호텔은 여러분 모두를 위한 것입니다. 가족들에게 좋습니다!

Hotel Fantastic Plaza
'Fantastic'이라는 말은 이 호텔을 표현하기에 부족합니다. 새롭게 재단장된 호화스러운 객실, 최근에 보수된 식당에서의 멋진 식사 그리고 190 극장, 쇼핑, 관광지로의 편리한 접근을 즐겨 보세요.

Hotel South
공항까지의 무료 교통수단과 잘 갖춰진 비즈니스 센터로 이곳은 비즈니스 여행자들에게는 완벽한 호텔입니다. 컨퍼런스 회의실과 무료 무선 인터넷도 갖추고 있습니다. 이 호텔은 여행하는 동안에 일하는 것을 쉽게 만들어 줍니다.

Cozy Inn
모든 방에 전자레인지와 헤어드라이어 같은 현대적인 편리함을 갖추고 있는 옛날 스타일의 숙박 시설입니다. 매력적인 실내 장식, 무료로 제공되는 맛있는 아침식사와 대중교통에 189 가까운 위치로 이곳은 당신이 Vancouver에서 휴가를 즐기는 데 멋진 장소입니다.

이외에도 Vancouver 지역에 있는 우리의 다른 호텔 중 하나를 선택하세요. Regina를 선택하신다면 최고를 선택하신 겁니다!

http://vancouverdays.com/review

레스토랑	**호텔**	관광지	교통

190 Hotel Fantastic Plaza에서 최근의 숙박은 몹시 즐거웠습니다. 방은 편안했고 가구가 잘 갖추어져 있었고 호텔의 모든 식사는 훌륭하게 준비되어 있었습니다. 호텔 직원은 또한 멋진 서비스를 제공했습니다. 단지 셔틀 서비스가 있었다면 하고 바랄 뿐입니다. 공항까지 가는 택시를 잡는 데 어려움을 겪었고 매우 비쌌습니다. 이런 작은 불편함을 빼고는 숙박은 몹시 즐거웠습니다.

Shirley Rogers
London

어휘 acquire 인수하다 exclusive 고급의 addition 추가, 증가 property 부동산 operate 운영하다 prior to ~전에 acquisition 인수 luxurious 화려한 high-end 고급의 spokesperson 대변인 solid 견고한, 단단한 appeal to ~을 끌다, 매력이 되다 complement 보충 earn points 포인트를 얻다 former 이전의 complementary 무료의 refurbished 새로 갖춰진 fine dining 고급 식사 시설 feature ~이 있다, ~을 갖추다 charming 매력적인 decor 장식 tasty 맛있는 proximity 근교, 가까움 well furnished 가구가 갖춰진 expertly 훌륭하게, 전문적으로 outstanding 뛰어난 as well 또한 have a difficult time -ing ~하는 데 어려움을 겪다 aside from ~은 제외하고

186 기사는 무엇에 대한 것인가?
(A) 호텔 업계의 새로운 경향
(B) 위원회 선거의 결과
(C) 두 업체의 합병
(D) 새 공사 현장의 발표

해설 기사의 첫 번째 문장 'The Seattle-based Regina Hotel Group has acquired Orchid Inc.'에서 두 업체의 합병을 언급하고 있으므로 (C)가 정답이다.

어휘 merger 합병 construction site 공사 현장

187 Regina Regency 리조트에 대해서 알 수 있는 것은?
(A) 본사를 이전할 것이다.
(B) 회원제 프로그램을 중단했다.
(C) 고급 호텔 전문이다.
(D) 더 다양한 고객을 유치하려 한다.

해설 기사의 세 번째 단락에서 'accommodations that appeal especially to tourists, they are a perfect complement to Regina's existing hotels'에서 Regina 호텔이 더 다양한 고객 유치를 위해 노력하고 있다는 것을 알 수 있으므로 (D)가 정답이다.

어휘 specialize in ~을 전문으로 하다 attempt to ~을 시도하다

188 광고에서 호텔에 대해 알 수 있는 것은?
(A) 모두 수영장이 있다.
(B) 1920년에 지어졌다.
(C) 도심에 위치해 있다.
(D) 출장객들에게 할인을 제공한다.

해설 광고의 초반부에 'Want to be in the heart of the city? Choose Regina Hotel'에서 광고에 등장한 4개의 호텔은 모두 Vancouver 중심에 위치하고 있다는 것을 유추할 수 있다. 따라서 (C)가 정답이다.

189 광고의 다섯 번째 단락, 두 번째 줄의 proximity와 뜻이 가장 가까운 것은?
(A) 연속
(B) 근사치
(C) 가까움
(D) 가능성

해설 proximity to는 '~에 가까움'을 뜻하므로 (C)가 정답이다.

어휘 subsequence 연속, 지속 approximation 근사치, 추정

190 Rogers 씨가 묵었던 호텔에 대해 알 수 있는 것은?
(A) 쇼핑 장소에서 멀지 않다.
(B) 레스토랑에서 최근에 새로운 요리사를 채용했다.
(C) 휠체어로 접근 가능하다.
(D) 호텔 시설물에 무료로 입장할 수 있다.

해설 연계 지문 문제이다. 웹 페이지에서 Rogers 씨는 Hotel Fantastic Plaza에 투숙하였던 것을 알 수 있고, 광고에서 'convenient access to theaters, shopping and sightseeing'이라고 언급되어 있으므로 쇼핑 장소에서 멀지 않다고 한 (A)가 정답임을 알 수 있다.

어휘 not far from ~에서 멀지 않다

[191-195]

국제 자동차 박람회

191 올해 국제 자동차 박람회는 8월 6일부터 13일까지 Detroit에 있는 MXFM 컨벤션 센터에서 개최됩니다. 우리는 여러분이 보았던 것 중에 가장 멋진 자동차와 트럭을 하나의 지붕 아래 전시할 것입니다. 지금까지보다 더 많은 사전 보기, 더 많은 새로운 양산 모델, 더 많은 콘셉트 자동차들이 있습니다. 올해에 한해, Cervi 자동차사가 영화감독 Meredith Grazinski의 블록버스터 영화 〈태양이 지기 전에〉에 나왔던 모든 자동차들을 전시할 것입니다. 195 이 영화의 주인공 Peter Wiseman과 Alicia Michel은 8월 11일과 12일에 자동차의 멋진 효과들을 보여주기 위해 현장에 참석할 것입니다.

La Siesta

제9회 Detroit 국제 자동차 박람회

• 대중 관람일
8월 6일 금요일부터 8월 13일 금요일까지
오전 11시 - 오후 10시 30분 (일요일: 오전 10시 – 오후 7시 30분)

• 192 특별 대중 프리뷰
8월 6일 금요일 오전 11시 – 오후 10시 30분

• 공식 개점 행사
8월 7일 토요일
행사는 오전 9시에 시작됩니다.
전시장은 오전 11시에 열립니다.

• 언론 프리뷰
8월 11일 수요일, 8월 12일 목요일
언론인 자격증 필요

• 193 판매업자 프리뷰
8월 12일 목요일 오후 4시 – 오후 10시 (초대에 의해서만 가능)
자격증 필요

발신: Lenox Stewart
수신: Themba Iherjirka
날짜: 8월 1일
주제: 자동차 박람회 업데이트

Themba에게,

어제 못 만나서 미안해요. 올해 행사에 참여하는 여러 자동차 업체 대표들을 만나느라 바빴습니다. 오늘 Zen Motors의 홍보업자를 지역 판매업소 중 한 곳에서 만날 거예요.

몇 가지 이야기할 것이 있습니다. 195 첫 번째는 Michel 씨가 그녀가 찍고 있는 다른 영화와 일정이 겹쳐서 참석할 수 없다는 것입니다. 그녀의 매니저 Charles Levingston이 어제 전화로 내게 알려왔어요.

잠정적으로 더 좋지 않은 효과를 가진 다른 문제는 입장부에 있는 Woodward 씨가 나에게 알려준 일이에요. 분명히 사전 표 주문 분은 지역 호텔에서 할인받을 수 있는 상품권이 같이 나가기로 되어 있었어요. 안타깝게도 사전 티켓 구매자의 3분의 1만 제때 이 상품권을 받았어요. 194 Woodward 씨는 공연에 도착한 사람들에게 상품권을 주고 나중에 호텔 청구서에 적용될 수 있게 하는 방법을 사용할 수 있는지 알고 싶어 합니다. 나는 이 생각이 마음에 들지만 당신의 생각도 알려 주세요.

Lenox Stewart
홍보부 매니저

어휘 sneak peek 사전 관람, 보기 showcase 처음으로 보여주다, 전시하다 on hand 편리한, 도움을 주는, 옆에 있는 demonstrate 시연하다 credential 자격증 publicist 홍보업자 dealership 판매업소 schedule conflict 일정이 겹침 potentially 잠정적으로, 잠재적으로 damaging 해가 되는 to one's attention 관심을 끄는 apparently 명백히, 분명히 advance ticket 사전 표 be supposed to ~하기로 되어 있다 accompany 동반하다, 수반하다 certificate 상품권 be good for ~에 유효하다 in time 시간에 맞게 work out 방법을 내다 retroactively 소급적으로(나중에 적용될 수 있는)

191 공지의 목적은 무엇인가?
(A) 새로운 정책의 세부 사항을 설명하기 위해서
(B) 다가올 행사를 홍보하기 위해서
(C) 신제품을 홍보하기 위해서
(D) 단체를 위한 자금을 모금하기 위해서

해설 공지의 첫 번째 문장 'This year's International Auto Show will be held at the MXFM Convention Center in Detroit from March 6th through 15th'에서 (B)가 정답임을 알 수 있다.

어휘 upcoming 다가오는, 곧 있을 organization 단체 raise money 돈을 모금하다

192 행사에 대해 언급된 것은?
(A) 참석하려면 등록해야 한다.
(B) 공식 행사 전에 참석 가능하다.
(C) 초대장은 언론에게만 보내졌다.
(D) 지역 업체가 사회를 볼 것이다.

해설 일정표에 따르면 8월 7일 공식 행사 전에 8월 6일에 사전 행사(Special Public Sneak Preview)가 있으므로 (B)가 정답이다.

193 판매업자 프리뷰에는 누가 참석할 수 있는가?
(A) 모든 공인된 판매업자
(B) 모든 언론 담당자
(C) 사전 표를 구매한 사람들
(D) 초대받은 사람들

해설 일정표에서 8월 12일의 판매업자 프리뷰는 'by invitation only'라고 명시되어 있으므로 (D)가 정답이다.

어휘 certified 공인된, 자격을 갖춘 press official 언론 담당자 advance ticket 사전 표

194 Woodward 씨는 무엇을 제안하는가?
(A) 컨벤션 센터에서 상품권 발급하기
(B) 사과의 편지를 발송하기
(C) 가능한 한 빨리 고객들에게 연락하기
(D) 불만 사항이 있는지 기다려서 확인하기

해설 이 메일의 세 번째 단락에서 'Ms. Woodward wants to know if we can work out a system where we give the certificates to the people when they arrive for the show'라고 하였으므로 (A)가 정답이다.

어휘 issue 발급하다

195 8월 12일 행사에 누가 참석할 것 같은가?
(A) Granzinski 씨
(B) Wiseman 씨
(C) Michel 씨
(D) Levingston 씨

해설 연계 지문 문제이다. 공지의 마지막 문장에서 'Peter Wiseman and Alicia Michel, will be on hand on August 11th and 12th'라고 하였으나 이메일의 두 번째 단락에서 'Ms. Michel will not be able to attend the show'라고 언급하였으므로 Wiseman 씨만이 참석할 것이라는 것을 알 수 있으므로 (B)가 정답이다.

[196-200]

기자 구함

앞서 가는 출판 회사인 Daily Indiana가 Bloomington 시내 지점에서 근무할 기자를 찾고 있습니다. 성공적인 지원자는 이전에 기자로 일한 경험이 있으며, 가급적 주목할 만한 출판 회사였기를 바랍니다. 해야 할 일은 196 구독자들의 의견 검토하기, 기고가에게 연락하기, 메일 처리하는 것 등과 다른 일반 사무직 업무를 포함합니다. 197 이 시간제 일자리는 추가 근무 수당이 지불되는 저녁 시간과 토요일 근무를 포함하여 일주일에 20시간 업무입니다. 관심 있는 분들은 hr@dailyindiana.ca로 이력서를 보내 주시기 바랍니다.

수신: hr@dailyindiana.ca
발신: lstein@gmail.com
날짜: 8월 8일
주제: 기자 자리
첨부: Stein_이력서; Stein_샘플 작업

인사부 담당자님께,

기자 직책에 관심을 표현하기 위해 이메일을 쓰고 있습니다. 저는 전문 사진작가이기는 하지만 사무실 환경에서 4년 동안 일한 경험이 있습니다. 예술 학교에 있을 때 학교 신문사에서 편집자로 3년 동안 일했습니다. 또한 큰 기업의 우편실에서 일한 적도 있습니다. 추가로 기사 편집에 사용되는 몇몇 소프트웨어 프로그램에 능숙합니다.

현재 잡지사에서 기자이자 사진작가로서 일하고 있습니다. 197 일주일에 아침에 세 번 일하기 때문에 제 일정을 채울 다른 일을 원하고 있습니다. 198 이것이 처음으로 신문사에서 일하게 될 기회지만 기꺼이 새로운 기술을 배울 것이고 제가 가진 기술은 당신 회사에 자산이 될 수 있을 것입니다. 200 이력서와 대학 신문사에서 편집자로서 일한 샘플 작업을 보내 드립니다. 제 글쓰기와 인터뷰 기술을 보여 주고 있습니다. 소식 기다리고 있겠으며, 고려해 주셔서 감사드립니다.

Lucy Stein

수신: 면접관에게
발신: Fred Jaspers
날짜: 8월 13일
주제: 기자직 채용

여러분들께,

최종 면접이 내일 오전 9시 30분에 실시됩니다. Stein 씨를 인터뷰할 것입니다. 199 그녀가 보낸 자료들을 읽어 보시고 인터뷰 동안에 정보가 잘 생각나도록 해 주세요. 여러분 중 몇몇은 그녀의 자격 요건에 대해서 염려하고 있다는 것을 알고 있습니다만, 그녀는 일상적인 사무실 업무는 쉽게 훈련받을 수 있을 겁니다. 제 생각에는 그녀는 훨씬 더 많은 것을 줄 수 있습니다. 200 사실 그녀가 제출한 자료는 우리의 홍보 자료를 돋구어 줄 수 있는 창조력을 보여주고 있습니다. 인터뷰 전에 이야기하고 싶은 것이 있으면 제게 연락주세요.

Fred

어휘 reporter 기자 leading 앞서 가는 preferably 더 선호하는, 가급적 high-profile 주목을 끄는, 유명한 subscriber 구독자 correspondent 기고가, 통신원 clerical work 사무직 일 overtime rate 추가 근무 수당 setting 환경 mailroom 우편실 corporation 회사, 기업 be proficient at ~에 능숙하다, 잘하다 edit 편집하다 be willing to 기꺼이 ~하다 asset 자산 demonstrate 보여주다, 시연하다 consideration 고려 take place 일어나다, 발생하다 materials 자료 be concerned about 걱정하다, 염려하다 qualification 자격 요건 routine 일상적인 creativity 창조성 spice up 돋구다

196 광고에 따르면 기자직의 업무 내용은 무엇인가?
(A) 의견 검토하기
(B) 이사회 일정 잡기
(C) 사설 쓰기
(D) 구독자에게 전화하기

해설 광고에서 언급한 업무 내용인 'reading opinions from subscribers, contacting correspondents, processing mail, and other clerical work' 중에서 선택지에서 해당되는 것은 (A)이다. 따라서 (A)가 정답이다.

197 일자리의 어떤 면이 Stein 씨에게 가장 매력적으로 보였겠는가?
(A) 신문의 명성
(B) 시내 위치
(C) 업무
(D) 근무 시간

해설 연계 지문 문제이다. 광고에서 'This part-time position is 20 hours a week'라고 언급하였고 Stein 씨의 이메일에서 'Since I only work three mornings a week, I want additional work to fill out my schedule'이라고 언급하였으므로 근무 시간이 맞기에 지원했음을 알 수 있다. 따라서 (D)가 정답이다.

198 Stein 씨에 대해서 나타나 있는 것은?
(A) 현재 신문사에서 일하고 있다.
(B) 예술학부 학생으로 등록할 것이다.
(C) 신문사에서 일해 본 적이 없다.
(D) Bloomington으로 이사 올 것이다.

해설 첫 번째 이메일에서 'this would be my first job in a newspaper company'라고 언급했으므로 (C)가 정답임을 알 수 있다.

199 두 번째 이메일의 목적은 무엇인가?
(A) 더 많은 면접관들이 이사회에 참석할 것을 권장하기 위해
(B) 면접관들에게 자료 검토를 요청하기 위해
(C) 직원들에게 인터뷰가 취소된 것을 상기시키기 위해
(D) 새로운 직원들에게 연수를 공지하기 위해

해설 이메일의 두 번째 문장에서 'Please read the materials that she submitted'라고 요청하고 있으므로 (B)가 정답이다.

200 Jaspers 씨가 Stein 씨가 직책에 좋은 후보자라고 생각하는 이유는 무엇인가?
(A) 편집자로서의 그녀의 경력
(B) 연장 근무 시간에 대한 가능성
(C) 고객들을 다루는 그녀의 전문성
(D) 컴퓨터 프로그래머로서의 기술

해설 연계 지문 문제이다. Jaspers 씨는 'the materials she submitted demonstrate a creativity'라고 언급하며 Stein 씨가 보낸 자료에 만족한다는 것을 나타내고 있고, 첫 번째 Stein 씨가 보낸 이메일의 두 번째 단락에서 'I'm sending my résumé and my sample work when I worked as an editor in a university newspaper'라고 언급했으므로 자료가 바로 신문사에서 편집자로 일했던 경력을 나타내고 있으므로 (A)가 정답이다.

Actual Test 03

Listening Comprehension

본책 P98

PART 1

1 (B)	2 (C)	3 (D)	4 (A)	5 (B)	6 (A)				

PART 2

7 (A)	8 (B)	9 (A)	10 (C)	11 (C)	12 (A)	13 (B)	14 (C)	15 (A)	16 (C)
17 (A)	18 (A)	19 (A)	20 (C)	21 (C)	22 (C)	23 (C)	24 (A)	25 (C)	26 (A)
27 (B)	28 (C)	29 (A)	30 (A)	31 (B)					

PART 3

32 (B)	33 (D)	34 (A)	35 (C)	36 (C)	37 (D)	38 (B)	39 (A)	40 (C)	41 (B)
42 (B)	43 (B)	44 (B)	45 (C)	46 (A)	47 (A)	48 (C)	49 (D)	50 (B)	51 (D)
52 (A)	53 (C)	54 (A)	55 (B)	56 (B)	57 (A)	58 (A)	59 (B)	60 (A)	61 (D)
62 (B)	63 (B)	64 (C)	65 (C)	66 (B)	67 (A)	68 (A)	69 (C)	70 (B)	

PART 4

71 (A)	72 (A)	73 (A)	74 (D)	75 (C)	76 (A)	77 (B)	78 (B)	79 (C)	80 (B)
81 (D)	82 (A)	83 (A)	84 (C)	85 (D)	86 (D)	87 (B)	88 (A)	89 (B)	90 (B)
91 (A)	92 (C)	93 (B)	94 (C)	95 (D)	96 (A)	97 (A)	98 (D)	99 (B)	100 (A)

Reading Comprehension

본책 P110

PART 5

101 (B)	102 (A)	103 (B)	104 (C)	105 (D)	106 (A)	107 (D)	108 (C)	109 (A)	110 (C)
111 (D)	112 (D)	113 (B)	114 (D)	115 (D)	116 (C)	117 (A)	118 (A)	119 (C)	120 (C)
121 (B)	122 (D)	123 (A)	124 (D)	125 (B)	126 (B)	127 (C)	128 (B)	129 (D)	130 (A)

PART 6

131 (C)	132 (A)	133 (A)	134 (D)	135 (B)	136 (B)	137 (C)	138 (D)	139 (B)	140 (A)
141 (C)	142 (D)	143 (D)	144 (D)	145 (C)	146 (A)				

PART 7

147 (A)	148 (C)	149 (A)	150 (D)	151 (C)	152 (A)	153 (C)	154 (D)	155 (B)	156 (B)
157 (B)	158 (D)	159 (A)	160 (C)	161 (A)	162 (B)	163 (D)	164 (A)	165 (A)	166 (C)
167 (D)	168 (D)	169 (D)	170 (A)	171 (C)	172 (D)	173 (B)	174 (D)	175 (D)	176 (D)
177 (A)	178 (B)	179 (C)	180 (D)	181 (D)	182 (A)	183 (B)	184 (D)	185 (B)	186 (C)
187 (A)	188 (C)	189 (C)	190 (D)	191 (D)	192 (B)	193 (C)	194 (B)	195 (D)	196 (A)
197 (B)	198 (D)	199 (A)	200 (C)						

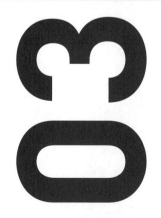

PART 1

1 미W
(A) She is holding a book in her hands.
(B) She is reclining in a field.
(C) She is reading to his companion.
(D) She is writing a book outdoors.

(A) 여자가 손에 책을 들고 있다.
(B) 여자가 들판에서 비스듬히 기대어 있다.
(C) 여자가 동료에게 책을 읽어주고 있다.
(D) 여자가 야외에서 책을 쓰고 있다.

해설 1인 사진은 인물의 동작에 주목한다. 여자가 나무에 기대어 노트북을 보고 있으므로 이를 가장 적절히 묘사한 (B)가 정답이다. (A)와 (D)는 사진에서 보이지 않은 책을 언급하고 있으며, 1인 사진에서 다른 사람을 언급한 (C)도 오답이다.

어휘 recline 비스듬히 기대다, 눕다 companion 동행, 친구

2 미M
(A) The man is browsing in a camera shop.
(B) The man is posing for a photograph.
(C) The man is kneeling down to take a picture.
(D) The man is placing his camera on the sidewalk.

(A) 남자가 카메라 상점 안을 둘러보고 있다.
(B) 남자가 사진 찍히기 위해 포즈를 취하고 있다.
(C) 남자가 사진을 찍으려고 무릎을 꿇고 있다.
(D) 남자가 카메라를 인도에 놓고 있다.

해설 남자가 무릎을 꿇고 사진 찍는 동작을 가장 알맞게 묘사한 (C)가 정답이다. (A)는 배경이 상점 안이 아닌 야외이므로 오답이며, (B)는 남자가 포즈를 취하는 것이 아니라 직접 사진을 찍고 있으므로 적절하지 않은 답이다. (D)는 남자가 카메라를 손에 쥐고 있기 때문에 오답이다.

어휘 browse 둘러보다, 훑어보다 kneel down 꿇어앉다 sidewalk (포장한) 보도, 인도

3 호M
(A) The meeting has gotten underway.
(B) The participants are sitting near the windows.
(C) Some of the seats are occupied.
(D) Identical chairs surround the table.

(A) 회의가 진행 중에 있다.
(B) 참석자들이 창문 근처에 앉아 있다.
(C) 몇몇 의자가 사용 중이다.
(D) 동일한 모양의 의자들이 테이블을 둘러싸고 있다.

해설 사람이 등장하지 않는 사진으로 각 사물들의 명칭을 집중해서 들어야 한다. 빈 회의실에 같은 모양의 의자가 놓여 있는 모습을 묘사한 (D)가 가장 알맞은 답이다. 인물이 없는 사물 사진에서 (A)는 회의가 진행 중이라고 묘사하며, (B)는 참가자를 언급하고 있다. 또한 (C)는 의자가 사용 중이라고 표현하고 있으므로 모두 오답이다.

어휘 underway 진행 중인, 이미 시작된 participant 참가자 occupy 차지하다, 사용하다 identical 동일한, 똑같은

4 영M
(A) Rows of shelves hold various products.
(B) The top rows are empty of merchandise.
(C) Shoppers are selecting different types of tea.
(D) All of the products are the same size.

(A) 여러 줄의 선반 위에 다양한 제품들이 진열되어 있다.
(B) 가장 윗줄에는 상품이 없다.
(C) 쇼핑객들이 다른 종류의 차를 고르고 있다.
(D) 모든 제품들의 크기가 동일하다.

해설 사람이 없는 상점 내부의 사진이다. 여러 칸의 선반에 서로 다른 물건들이 놓인 모습을 가장 적절히 묘사한 (A)가 정답이다. (B)는 모든 선반 위에 물건이 있으므로 답이 될 수 없고, (C)는 쇼핑객의 동작을 묘사하고 있으므로 오답이다. (D)는 물건들이 진열되어 있는 것은 맞으나 모두 같은 크기는 아니므로 오답이다.

어휘 row 열, 줄 various 여러 가지의 empty of ~이 없는 merchandise 물품, 상품

5 미W
(A) Passengers are unpacking some suitcases.
(B) People are facing a baggage carousel.
(C) Travelers are pushing carts along the floor.
(D) People are checking in their luggage.

(A) 승객들이 가방을 풀고 있다.
(B) 사람들이 수화물 컨베이어를 보고 있다.
(C) 여행객들이 통로를 따라 손수레를 밀고 있다.
(D) 사람들이 가방을 부치고 있다.

해설 여러 사람이 등장하는 실내 배경 사진으로 각 인물의 행동 묘사에 주목해야 한다. 사람들이 수화물 찾는 곳에서 컨베이어 벨트를 바라보며 짐을 기다리는 모습이므로 이를 묘사한 (B)가 정답이다. (A)는 사람들이 짐을 풀고 있는 모습은 보이지 않으므로 답이 아니며, (C)는 카트는 보이지만 사람들이 밀고 있지 않으므로 오답이다. (D)는 짐을 부치는 것을 묘사하고 있으므로 사진과 어울리지 않는다.

어휘 passenger 승객 unpack 꺼내다, 풀다 baggage carousel 수화물 컨베이어 check in (비행기 등을 탈 때) 짐을 부치다

6 영M
(A) The bedcover has been straightened.
(B) There are two pictures hung above the bed.
(C) Reading material has been placed on a couch.
(D) There are lamps on both sides of the desk.

(A) 침대 커버가 평평하게 펴져 있다.
(B) 침대 위에 그림이 두 개 걸려 있다.
(C) 읽을거리가 소파에 놓여 있다.
(D) 책상 양쪽에 전등이 있다.

해설 인물이 없는 사물 사진 유형으로, 사진 속 사물의 위치나 상태에 주목해야 한다. 침대 커버가 펴져 있다는 (A)가 정답이다. (B)는 침대 위의 그림 개수를 잘못 묘사하고 있고, (C)는 사진에 없는 소파를 언급했으므로 답이 될 수 없다. 또한 (D)는 전등은 보이지만 위치를 잘못 묘사하고 있다.

어휘 straighten 똑바르게 되다(하다), 바로 하다, 펴다 reading material (잡지, 책 등) 읽을거리 couch 긴 의자, 소파

PART 2

7 영M 미M
When do you move to the new building?
(A) Jade has the schedule.
(B) The regional office is in Delhi.
(C) Into the financial district.

새 건물로 언제 이사하나요?
(A) Jade가 그 일정을 가지고 있어요.
(B) 지사는 Delhi에 있어요.
(C) 금융가로요.

해설 이사를 가는 시점을 묻는 When 의문문에 일정을 알고 있는 특정인을 제시한 (A)가 가장 적절한 답이다. (B)와 (C)는 모두 Where 의문사 질문에 적합한 장소를 언급하고 있으므로 질문을 Where로 혼동하지 않도록 주의해야 한다.

어휘 regional 지방의 financial 금융의 district (특정한 특징이 있는) 지역, 지구

8 미M 미W
Does your manager use the company's intranet system?
(A) No, on the Internet.
(B) Yes, every day.
(C) Check the access code.

당신의 매니저가 회사 내부 전산 시스템을 사용하고 있나요?
(A) 아니요, 인터넷 상에서요.
(B) 네, 매일이요.
(C) 접속 코드를 확인해 보세요.

해설 매니저의 내부 전산망 시스템 사용 여부를 묻는 질문에 매일 사용한다는 긍정 대답을 하는 (B)가 정답이다. (A)는 No로 대답하면 사용하지 않는 것으로 이해할 수 있으나 이어지는 내용이 질문과 어울리지 않으며, (C)는 내용상 질문과 무관한 답변이다.

어휘 intranet 인트라넷, 내부 전산망 access 접속, 접근

9 영M 미M
Kyle Hanagami is the choreographer of this performance, isn't he?
(A) Yes and it's perfectly done.
(B) No, it's their performance reviews.
(C) He is a world-famous writer.

Kyle Hanagami가 이 공연의 안무가죠?
(A) 네, 아주 잘 되었어요.
(B) 아니요, 그들의 인사고과예요.
(C) 그는 세계적으로 유명한 작가입니다.

해설 질문에 언급한 사람이 공연의 안무 편성가가 맞는지 확인하는 부가의문문에 동의하며, 칭찬으로 이어지는 (A)가 가장 적절한 답이다. (B)는 질문의 performance에서 연상되는 reviews를 사용하여 혼동을 유도하고 있으나 질문과 무관한 대답이며, (C) 특정인의 직업을 말하고 있으므로 질문과 어울리지 않는다.

어휘 choreographer 안무가, 발레 편성가 review 비평, 평론

10 미M 미W Would you like me to bring copies of the customers' feedback for the meeting or email it to everyone?
(A) Listen to the customers.
(B) About two thousand Euros next year.
(C) We'll have to hand them out to everyone.

제가 고객들의 피드백 사본을 회의에 가지고 갈까요, 아니면 모두에게 이메일로 보낼까요?
(A) 고객들의 의견을 들으세요.
(B) 내년에 약 2천 유로입니다.
(C) 우리가 모두에게 나눠줘야 할 거예요.

해설 회의에 자료를 직접 가지고 갈지, 이메일로 보낼지 묻는 선택의문문에 모두에게 나누어 주어야 한다며 가지고 오라는 의미를 우회적으로 표현한 (C)가 가장 적절한 답이다. (A)는 질문에 사용한 customer를 반복 사용하여 혼동을 유도하고 있으며, (B)는 질문과 전혀 무관한 대답이다.

어휘 feedback 피드백 hand out 나누어 주다

11 영M 미M How many times have you relocated for work?
(A) Yes, I live in Berlin now.
(B) You should make twenty-five signs.
(C) This is my third move.

이직을 몇 번 하셨어요?
(A) 네, 저는 지금 Berlin에 살고 있어요.
(B) 25개의 표지판을 만들어야 해요.
(C) 이번이 세 번째예요.

해설 횟수를 묻는 How many 의문문에 이번이 세 번째라고 서수로 답하는 (C)가 정답이다. (A)는 의문사 의문문에 Yes/No로 대답할 수 없으며, (B)는 숫자를 언급하여 혼동을 유도하고 있지만 질문과 무관한 답변이므로 오답이다.

어휘 relocate 이전하다, 이동하다(시키다)

12 미M 미W Didn't you say you were a vegetarian?
(A) Yes, all my family is.
(B) Not too salty.
(C) Fresh fruits and vegetables.

채식주의자라고 하지 않으셨나요?
(A) 네, 저희 가족 모두요.
(B) 너무 짜지 않게요.
(C) 신선한 과일과 채소예요.

해설 채식주의자인지 확인하는 부정의문문에 동의하면서 부연 설명하고 있는 (A)가 가장 적절한 답이다. (B)는 맛에 대한 평가 또는 음식 주문 시 요청할 때 알맞은 표현이며, (C)는 질문의 vegetarian에서 연상되는 vegetables을 이용한 발음 오답이다.

어휘 vegetarian 채식주의자 salty 소금이 든, 짠

13 영M Why has the construction been delayed?
(A) A two-story building.
(B) We still need Mr. Marble's approval.
(C) I've read the introduction.

공사가 왜 연기되었나요?
(A) 2층짜리 건물이에요.
(B) Marble 씨의 승인이 아직 필요해요.
(C) 저는 설명서를 읽었어요.

해설 지연의 이유를 묻는 Why 의문문에 승인이 아직 필요하다며 지연의 이유를 말하는 (B)가 정답이다. (A)는 질문과 연관성 없는 단답형의 표현이고 (C)는 질문의 construction과 발음이 유사한 introduction을 사용하여 혼동을 유도하고 있다.

어휘 construction 건설, 공사 delay 미루다, 연기하다 approval 인정, 찬성, 승인 introduction 소개, 도입, 입문서

14 미W 미M Which attendees are missing from the guest list?
(A) Yes, I'm ready to leave.
(B) They're staying for a while.
(C) The new hires still haven't been added.

어떤 참석자들이 손님 명단에서 빠졌나요?
(A) 네, 저는 떠날 준비가 되었어요.
(B) 그들이 한동안 머무를 겁니다.
(C) 신입 사원들이 아직 추가되지 않았습니다.

해설 어떤 참석자들이 목록에서 누락되었는지 묻는 Which 의문사에 신입 직원들이 빠졌다고 설명한 (C)가 가장 적절한 답이다. (A)는 의문사 의문문에 Yes/No로 대답할 수 없으며, (B)는 질문과 전혀 무관한 답변이다.

어휘 attendee 참석자 for a while 한동안

15 미W 영M Will you continue to work here or move to the head office?
(A) I'm planning on staying.
(B) The boxes are in storage.
(C) I can work until 6.

여기서 계속 일을 하시겠어요, 아니면 본사로 옮기실 건가요?
(A) 여기에 있을 예정입니다.
(B) 상자들은 창고에 있어요.
(C) 6시까지 일할 수 있습니다.

해설 일할 장소를 묻는 선택의문문에 있던 곳에서 계속 일한다고 대답을 한 (A)가 정답이다. (B)는 질문과 전혀 무관한 내용으로 대답하고 있으며, (C)는 장소의 선택을 묻는 질문에 시간을 언급하고 있으므로 오답이다.

어휘 head office 본사 storage 저장고, 보관소, 저장

16 미M 영M I've completed all my assignments.
(A) Friday at noon.
(B) I missed Dane's signature.
(C) Could you help Aaron then?

제 모든 업무를 완료했습니다.
(A) 금요일 정오에요.
(B) Dane의 서명을 빠뜨렸네요.
(C) 그럼 Aaron을 도와주실래요?

해설 일을 끝냈다는 사실을 전달하는 평서문에 대해 그럼 다른 사람을 도와주라고 제안하는 (C)가 가장 적절한 답이다. (A)는 질문과 상관없는 시점으로 답하고 있으며, (B)는 질문의 assignments에서 확장 연상이 가능한 signature로 답변한 오답이다.

어휘 assignment 과제, 임무, 배정 signature 서명, 서명하다

17 미M 미W Who is the magazine targeted at?
(A) It's aimed at journalism experts.
(B) I write for magazines.
(C) I didn't attend, but Mary did.

잡지의 대상이 누구인가요?
(A) 언론 전문가들을 겨냥한 것입니다.
(B) 잡지에 글을 씁니다.
(C) 저는 참석하지 않았지만 Mary는 했어요.

해설 잡지의 대상을 묻는 Who 의문문에 특정 직업 군을 언급하며 대답한 (A)가 가장 적절한 답이다. (B)는 질문의 magazine을 반복 사용한 오답이며, (C)는 의문사 Who의 정답 유형인 제3자의 이름을 언급하면서 혼동을 유도하고 있지만 대상을 묻는 질문과는 어울리지 않는다.

어휘 target 목표로 삼다, 겨냥하다 journalism 저널리즘 expert 전문가

18 영M 미W Can anyone take these cylinders to the laboratory?
(A) I can do it in a minute.
(B) Look in those cabinets.
(C) No, I didn't take them.

이 실린더들을 실험실에 가져다 줄 사람이 있을까요?
(A) 제가 곧 할 수 있어요.
(B) 저 보관함을 보세요.
(C) 아니요, 제가 가져가지 않았어요.

해설 특정 물건을 가져다 줄 것을 요청하는 의문문에 곧 할 수 있다고 대답하는 (A)가 가장 알맞은 답이다. (B)는 laboratory에서 연상이 가능한 cabinet로 답변한 오답이며, (C)는 질문의 take를 반복 사용한 오답이다.

어휘 cylinder 실린더 laboratory 실험실

19 미W 미M Are you looking for a full-time or part-time position?
(A) I can work two days a week.
(B) We've been looking forward to it.
(C) I found it on my desk.

정규직을 찾고 있나요, 시간제 직업을 찾고 있나요?
(A) 저는 일주일에 이틀 일할 수 있어요.
(B) 저희는 그것을 기대하고 있어요.
(C) 제 책상에서 찾았어요.

해설 찾고 있는 직업의 종류를 묻는 선택의문문에 시간제 직책을 원한다는 말을 바꾸어 표현한 (A)가 정답이다. (B)는 looking을 반복 사용한 오답이며, (C)는 질문의 looking for에서 연상이 가능한 found를 사용해 혼동을 주고 있다.

어휘 look forward to ~을 기대하다, 고대하다

20 Weren't you expecting more people to come to the product demonstration?
미W
영M
(A) I received it yesterday.
(B) In the auditorium.
(C) No, this is everybody.

제품 시연회에 더 많은 사람들이 올 거라 기대했지 않으세요?
(A) 저는 어제 받았어요.
(B) 강당에서요.
(C) 아니요. 이것이 (올 수 있는 사람) 모두입니다.

해설 더 많은 사람들의 참석을 기대했는지 확인하는 부정의문문에 지금까지 모인 사람이 참석자의 전부라는 의미로 대답한 (C)가 가장 적절한 답이다. 확인 차 질문하는 부정의문문에 〈Yes/No + 부연 설명〉이 정답 패턴으로 자주 사용되니 기억하자. (A)는 질문의 expecting에서 연상이 가능한 received로 답변한 오답이며, (B)는 행사가 열리는 장소를 언급하고 있으므로 질문과 무관한 답변이다.

어휘 demonstration 설명, 입증 auditorium 객석, 강당

21 This year's award ceremony is being held in Singapore.
영M
미M
(A) We plan to board on time.
(B) Yes, a rewarding occupation.
(C) I didn't know they decided to move it.

올해 시상식은 Singapore에서 개최될 겁니다.
(A) 우리는 제시간에 탑승할 계획입니다.
(B) 네, 수입이 좋은 직업입니다.
(C) 저는 그들이 옮기기로 결정했다는 것을 몰랐어요.

해설 시상식 장소의 정보를 전달하는 평서문에 그곳에서 열리는지 몰랐다며 우회적인 표현을 사용한 (C)가 가장 알맞은 답이다. (A)는 Singapore에서 확장 연상이 가능한 board를 사용하여 혼동을 유도하고 있으며, (B)는 질문의 award와 rewarding의 유사 발음 오답이다.

어휘 award ceremony 시상식 on time 제시간에, 정각에 rewarding 수익이 많이 나는 occupation 직업

22 Could you tell me whether the marketing director can see me this morning?
미M
미W
(A) The interview went well.
(B) Take a left at the intersection.
(C) Certainly, she can meet with you at 10.

오늘 아침에 마케팅 이사님을 만날 수 있는지 알려주실 수 있어요?
(A) 면접은 잘 진행되었어요.
(B) 교차로에서 좌회전하세요.
(C) 물론이죠. 10시에 만날 수 있습니다.

해설 만남의 가능성을 묻는 간접의문문에 가능한 시간을 언급하며 긍정적으로 대답한 (C)가 가장 알맞은 답이다. (A)는 면접의 진행 여부를 묻는 질문에 알맞은 답이므로 주어진 질문과는 거리가 있으며, (B)는 질문과 무관한 답변이다.

어휘 go (on) well 잘 되다 intersection 교차로, 교차 지점 certainly 틀림없이, 분명히

23 How did you hear about the job?
영M
미W
(A) The volume is too high.
(B) Yes, I believe he started last week.
(C) It was advertised on the Web site.

그 직업에 대해 어떻게 아셨어요?
(A) 소리가 너무 크네요.
(B) 네, 그가 지난주에 시작했다고 알고 있어요.
(C) 웹 사이트에 광고가 났었어요.

해설 직업을 알게 된 경로를 묻는 How 의문문에 웹 사이트에서 광고를 보았다는 (C)가 정답이다. (A)는 질문의 hear에서 연상되는 volume으로 혼동을 유도하고 있으며 (B)는 질문과 전혀 무관한 답변이다.

어휘 advertise 광고하다

24 Have you seen the agenda?
미W
미M
(A) No, does it look interesting?
(B) To meet with an agent.
(C) Yes, generally it does.

안건을 보셨어요?
(A) 아니요, 흥미로워 보이나요?
(B) 대리인을 만나기 위해서요.
(C) 네, 일반적으로 그렇죠.

해설 회의 안건을 보았는지 묻는 조동사 의문문에 흥미로워 보이냐고 되묻는 (A)가 정답이다. (B)는 의문사 Why의 정답으로 적합하며, (C)는 Yes로 대답하면 본 적이 있는 것으로 이해할 수 있지만, 이어지는 문장이 질문과 무관하다.

어휘 agenda 안건, 의제 agent 대리인, 중개상 generally 일반적으로, 대개, 보통

25 Should we start the meeting now or wait for Ms. Lee?
미W
영M
(A) I don't know until tomorrow.
(B) I'm waiting for the 210 train.
(C) We have a lot to get through, so let's begin.

지금 회의를 시작해야 하나요, Lee 씨를 기다릴까요?
(A) 내일까지는 모르겠어요.
(B) 저는 210 열차를 기다리고 있어요.
(C) 해야 할 일이 많아요, 그러니 시작합시다.

해설 회의를 언제 시작하는 것이 좋은지 묻는 선택의문문에 해야 할 일이 많으니 지금 하자고 제안하는 (C)가 가장 적절한 답이다. (A)는 우회적인 표현으로 대답하고 있으나 뒤에 이어지는 부분이 질문과 무관하며, (B)는 질문의 wait을 반복 사용하여 선택의문문의 전형적 정답처럼 혼동을 유도하고 있으나 질문과 상관없는 내용이다.

어휘 get through ~을 하다, 끝내다

26 How often do you work overtime?
영M
미M
(A) Hardly ever.
(B) We're extremely busy.
(C) For a week or so.

얼마나 자주 야근을 하세요?
(A) 거의 안 해요.
(B) 우리는 아주 바빠요.
(C) 일주일 정도요.

해설 야근의 빈도를 묻는 How often 의문문에 거의 하지 않는다고 대답한 (A)가 정답이다. (B)는 질문과 무관한 내용이며, (C)는 How long 의문문에 어울리는 답변이다.

어휘 overtime 초과 근무, 야근 hardly ever 거의 ~하지 않는 extremely 극도로, 극히 or so ~쯤, ~ 정도

27 When was Ernest transferred to the Jakarta office?
미M
미W
(A) I opened before he started working.
(B) At least six years ago.
(C) Even I've never been there.

Ernest가 언제 Jakarta 사무실로 옮겨 갔나요?
(A) 저는 그가 일을 시작하기 전에 열었어요.
(B) 적어도 6년 전에요.
(C) 심지어 저는 거기 가 본 적도 없어요.

해설 옮겨간 시점을 묻는 When 의문사에 과거의 시점을 정확히 언급한 (B)가 정답이다. (A)는 before를 사용하여 When 의문문의 답인 것처럼 혼동을 유도하고 있으나 질문과 상관없으며, (C)도 질문과 무관한 답변이다.

어휘 transfer 옮기다, 이동하다

28 The price of stamps is going up next month, isn't it?
영M
미W
(A) No, she'll be back next week.
(B) A thousand-dollar prize.
(C) Not until next year, I think.

우표 가격이 다음 달에 올라가죠, 그렇지 않나요?
(A) 아니요, 그녀는 다음 주에 돌아올 거예요.
(B) 천 달러 상금이요.
(C) 내년은 되어야 할 겁니다.

해설 우표의 가격이 오를 것인지 확인하는 부가의문문에 가격 상승의 시점을 언급한 (C)가 정답이다. (A)는 질문의 next를 반복 사용한 오답이며 (B)는 질문의 price에서 연상이 가능한 A thousand dollar를 언급한 오답이다.

어휘 stamp 우표

29 What percentage of sales comes from advertising on the Internet?
미W
미M
(A) Around a third.
(B) They sell a lot of groceries.
(C) I sent several e-mails.

인터넷 광고로 들어오는 수입이 몇 퍼센트인가요?
(A) 대략 3분의 1 정도입니다.
(B) 그들은 많은 식료품을 판매합니다.
(C) 제가 여러 개의 이메일을 보냈어요.

해설 온라인 광고 수입의 비율을 묻는 What 의문문에 1/3이라고 대답을

한 (A)가 정답이다. (B)는 질문의 sales에서 연상이 가능한 sell로 답변한 오답이며, (C)도 질문의 Internet과 관련이 있는 e-mails로 혼동을 유도하고 있다.

어휘 advertise 광고하다, 알리다 grocery 식료품 및 잡화 several 몇몇의, 각각의

30 Where should I put all this paper?
미W 영M
(A) Just by the copier is fine.
(B) By Friday at the latest.
(C) I think it was Troy.

이 종이들을 모두 어디에 놓을까요?
(A) 복사기 옆에 두시면 돼요.
(B) 늦어도 금요일까지요.
(C) 제 생각에는 Troy 같아요.

해설 위치를 묻는 Where 의문문에 특정 장소를 언급한 (A)가 정답이다. (B)는 특정 시점을, (C)는 특정인을 언급하고 있으므로 질문과는 어울리지 않는 오답이다.

어휘 at the latest 늦어도

31 The keynote speaker hasn't arrived yet, has he?
미M 영M
(A) It shouldn't last more than two hours.
(B) No, apparently his plane was delayed.
(C) I'll check the microphone.

기조연설자가 아직 도착하지 않았어요, 그렇죠?
(A) 2시간 이상 지속되면 안 됩니다.
(B) 아니요, 듣기로는 그의 비행기가 연착됐대요.
(C) 제가 마이크를 확인해 보겠습니다.

해설 제3자의 도착 여부를 확인하는 부가의문문에 도착하지 않았다고 대답한 후 부연 설명이 이어지는 (B)가 가장 적절한 답이다. (A)는 기간에 대한 답변으로 질문과 무관하며 (C)는 keynote speaker에서 연상이 가능한 microphone으로 답변한 오답이다.

어휘 keynote speaker 기조연설자 apparently 듣자 하니, 보아 하니

PART 3

Questions 32-34 refer to the following conversation. 영M 미W

M Hello. ㉜ I'm calling about the high-speed color copier listed in your online ad. The advertisement said the device is only a year old. Is that right?
W Yes, and it's in perfect working condition. It's a great piece of equipment: it's fast and the image quality is exceptional. We're only selling it because ㉝ our company is relocating overseas next month.
M I see. Well, how soon could I drop by your office to take a look?
W If you could come sometime after 6 o'clock today, ㉞ I'd be happy to stay past the end of my shift to meet you. By the way, we also have some nice desks and drawers for sale if you're interested.

남 안녕하세요. 귀하의 온라인 광고에 올라온 고속 컬러복사기에 대해 문의하려고 전화했어요. 광고에는 겨우 1년 됐다고 하는데 맞나요?
여 네, 그리고 상태도 흠 잡을 데 없이 완벽합니다. 좋은 기기예요. 빠르고 화질도 우수합니다. 저희 회사가 다음 달에 해외로 이전하기 때문에 어쩔 수 없이 판매하는 것입니다.
남 알겠습니다. 그럼 언제쯤 제가 귀하의 사무실에 방문해서 볼 수 있을까요?
여 오늘 6시 이후로 오시면, 제가 근무가 끝난 후라도 기다리겠습니다. 그건 그렇고, 혹시 관심이 있으시다면 좋은 책상과 서랍장들도 가지고 있답니다.

어휘 advertisement 광고 equipment 장비, 용품, 설비 exceptional 우수한, 특출한 relocate 이전하다, 이동시키다 overseas 해외의(로), 국외의(로) drop by 잠깐 들르다, 불시에 찾아가다 resign 회사를 그만두다

32 What item does the man ask about?
(A) A color printer
(B) A copy machine
(C) A laptop
(D) A scanner

남자는 어떤 제품에 대해 묻고 있는가?
(A) 컬러 프린터
(B) 복사기
(C) 노트북
(D) 스캐너

해설 〈구체적 정보 파악 – 특정 사항〉
남자가 언급하는 물건이므로 남자의 대사에서 답을 찾아야 한다. 남자가 첫 대사에서 고속 컬러복사기 때문에 전화한다고 말하고 있으므로 정답은 (B)이다.

패러프레이징 copier 복사기 → copy machine 복사기

33 What does the woman say will happen next month?
(A) New equipment will be purchased.
(B) She will resign from her company.
(C) A new model will be released.
(D) Her work location will change.

여자는 다음 달에 무슨 일이 있을 것이라고 말하는가?
(A) 새로운 장비를 구매할 것이다.
(B) 그녀는 회사를 그만둘 것이다.
(C) 새로운 제품이 출시될 것이다.
(D) 직장 위치가 변경될 것이다.

해설 〈구체적 정보 파악 – 언급〉
문제의 키워드가 next month이고 여자가 말한다고 했으므로 여자가 next month를 언급할 때 정답을 찾아야 한다. 여자가 복사기를 파는 이유가 다음 달 회사의 이전 때문이라고 설명하고 있으므로 정답은 (D)이다.

패러프레이징 The company is relocating. 회사가 이전한다 → Her work location will change. 직장 위치가 변경될 것이다

34 What does the woman offer to do for the man?
(A) Remain after work
(B) Discount a price
(C) Speak with a seller
(D) Arrange a delivery

여자는 남자를 위해 무엇을 하겠다고 제안하는가?
(A) 업무가 끝난 후에 남아 있기
(B) 가격 할인하기
(C) 판매자와 이야기하기
(D) 배송 준비하기

해설 〈구체적 정보 파악 – 특정 사항〉
여자가 남자에게 제공하는 것이므로 후반부의 여자 대사에서 답의 근거를 찾아야 한다. 남자가 여자의 사무실에 방문하고 싶다고 하자, 여자가 근무를 마친 후라도 남자를 기다리겠다고 말하고 있다. 따라서 정답은 (A)이다.

Questions 35-37 refer to the following conversation. 미W 미M

W Hi, 36 Real Power Company. How can I help you?
M Hello. 35 36 I'd like to discuss my electricity account with someone.
W Would you mind giving me your account information?
M My name's Charles Tran, and my account number is, hold on a second… got it, it's CA56398, I think I've been overcharged.
W Okay, let me have a look. I'm looking at your account now. I see what's happened. You've been charged at the commercial rate rather than the residential rate. It must've been caused by the system upgrade last month.
M That's understandable.
W I'm sorry about the mistake. 37 Would you like a refund, or shall I give you a credit on your next month's bill?
M Actually, I'd prefer a refund, please.

여 안녕하세요. Real Power입니다. 어떻게 도와 드릴까요?
남 안녕하세요. 저의 전기세 청구서에 관해서 이야기하고 싶은데요.
여 고객님의 계정 정보를 알려주시겠어요?
남 이름은 Charles Tran이고요, 제 계정 번호는, 잠시만요... 여기 있네요, CA56398입니다. 비용이 과다 청구된 것 같아요.
여 알겠습니다. 제가 볼게요. 지금 고객님의 계정을 확인해 보고 있어요. 무슨 일이 있었는지 이제 알겠네요. 고객님에게 주거 요금이 아닌 상업 요금이 부과되었습니다. 지난달의 시스템 업그레이드가 원인임이 틀림없습니다.
남 그럴 수 있겠네요.
여 저희 실수에 사과 드리겠습니다. 환불을 원하시나요, 아니면 다음 달 청구서에 반영해 드릴까요?
남 사실 환불이 더 좋을 것 같습니다.

어휘 electricity 전기, 전력 account 계좌, 계정, 청구서 overcharge 많이 청구하다, 바가지를 씌우다 commercial 상업의, 상업적인 residential 주거의, 주거에 알맞은 understandable 정상적인, 당연한 credit 예금

35 What is the purpose of the man's call?
(A) To request a discount
(B) To make a payment
(C) To inquire about a bill
(D) To open an account

남자가 전화한 목적은 무엇인가?
(A) 할인을 요청하기 위해
(B) 금액을 지불하기 위해
(C) 청구서에 대해 문의하기 위해
(D) 계정을 개설하기 위해

해설 〈기본 정보 파악 – 목적〉
대화의 목적은 처음에 근거가 제시되는 것이 대부분이다. 전화를 받으며 응대하는 여자에게 남자가 전기세 청구서에 대해 얘기하고 싶다고 말하고 있으므로 이를 적절히 바꾸어 표현한 (C)가 정답이다.

36 What type of business is the man calling?
(A) A bank
(B) An Internet service provider
(C) An electric company
(D) An insurance company

남자가 전화한 곳은 어떤 종류의 회사인가?
(A) 은행
(B) 인터넷 서비스 제공업체
(C) 전기 회사
(D) 보험 회사

해설 〈기본 정보 파악 – 장소〉
장소는 전반부에 정답의 근거가 제시된다. 따라서 35번과 36번의 정답이 모두 앞부분에 언급될 것을 미리 예측하고 들어야 한다. 첫 대사에서 여자가 전화를 받으며 전력 회사라고 말했고 바로 다음에 남자가 전기세 청구서에 대해 이야기하고 싶다고 했으므로 정답은 (C)이다.

37 What does the woman offer to do?
(A) Give a discount
(B) Fix some device
(C) Provide new service
(D) Return a payment

여자가 제공하는 것은 무엇인가?
(A) 할인을 해 준다.
(B) 기기를 수리해 준다.
(C) 신규 서비스를 제공한다.
(D) 지불 금액을 돌려준다.

해설 〈구체적 정보 파악 – 특정 사항〉
여자의 대사에서 답을 찾아야 한다. 비용을 과다하게 청구받은 남자에게 여자는 환불 옵션을 선택하도록 제안하고 있다. 따라서 (D)가 정답이다.

Questions 38-40 refer to the following conversation with three speakers. 영W 영M 미M

W 38 That representative from Mitchell Cleaning was quite persuasive about the benefits of his cleaning service.
M1 I know the price they charge is attractive, too.
M2 That's right. It's considerably lower than what we're paying for the service we're using now.
W 39 Do you think we should switch, Oscar?
M1 Hmm... But we haven't had any problems with our current service. 39 They're very reliable and do a good job.
W What about you, Frank?
M2 I think we should go with Mitchell Cleaning. They have a good reputation, and we'd save our expenses.
W 40 In that case, let's think it over for a while.

여 Mitchell Cleaning 담당자가 말한 청소 서비스 혜택은 꽤 설득력 있었어요.
남1 맞아요. 그들이 청구하는 비용도 매력적이고요.
남2 저도 동의해요. 우리가 현재 이용하는 서비스에 지불하는 비용보다 훨씬 낮아요.
여 바꾸는 것이 좋을까요, Oscar?
남1 흠... 하지만 현재 이용 중인 서비스에 아무런 문제도 없잖아요. 그들은 아주 믿을 만하고, 일도 잘해 주고 있어요.
여 당신은 어때요, Frank?
남2 제 생각에는 Mitchell Cleaning으로 정해야 할 것 같아요. 평판도 좋고, 비용도 아낄 수 있잖아요.
여 그렇다면, 조금 더 생각해 봅시다.

어휘 representative 대표, 대리인 persuasive 설득력 있는 benefit 혜택, 이득 attractive 매력적인, 멋진 considerably 많이, 상당히 switch 바꾸다, 전환하다 reliable 믿을 수 있는, 신뢰할 만한 reputation 평판, 명성 expense 비용, 돈 negotiate 협상하다 postpone 연기하다

38 What does the woman say about the employee from Mitchell Cleaning?
(A) He was late for the meeting.
(B) He offered a persuasive deal.
(C) He left a product pamphlet.
(D) He will stop by the next day.

Mitchell Cleaning에서 온 직원에 대해 여자는 무엇이라고 말하는가?
(A) 그는 회의에 늦었다.
(B) 그는 설득력 있는 거래를 제안했다.
(C) 그는 제품 팸플릿을 두고 갔다.
(D) 그는 다음 날 들를 것이다.

해설 〈구체적 정보 파악 – 언급〉

여자의 말에서 해당 회사가 언급될 때 정답을 찾아야 한다. 첫 대사에서 여자가 Mitchell Cleaning의 서비스 혜택이 설득력 있다고 말하고 있으므로 정답은 (B)이다.

39 What does Oscar say about the company's current cleaning service?

(A) It is highly dependable.
(B) It charges less money.
(C) It has an international reputation.
(D) It offers a discount.

Oscar 씨는 회사의 현재 청소 서비스에 대해 무엇이라고 말하는가?
(A) 대단히 신뢰할 만하다.
(B) 비용이 덜 든다.
(C) 국제적인 명성이 있다.
(D) 할인을 제공한다.

해설 〈구체적 정보 파악 – 언급〉
전형적인 3인 대화의 문제 유형으로 문제에서 언급한 Oscar가 대화를 하는 인물 중 한 사람인지, 제3자인지 먼저 파악해야 한다. 여자가 두 번째 대사에서 Oscar를 부르며 의견을 묻자 남자1이 바로 대답하고 있으므로 남자1이 Oscar임을 알 수 있다. 남자1이 현재 이용 중인 서비스는 문제가 없으며 신뢰할 만하다는 의견을 제시하고 있으므로 정답은 (A)이다.

40 What does the woman suggest?

(A) Keeping the current service
(B) Negotiating better service
(C) Postponing a decision
(D) Searching for a different service

여자가 제안하는 것은 무엇인가?
(A) 현재 서비스를 유지하는 것
(B) 더 좋은 서비스를 협상하는 것
(C) 결정을 미루는 것
(D) 다른 서비스를 찾아보는 것

해설 〈구체적 정보 파악 – 제안 관련〉
여자의 제안 사항에 대한 문제이므로 여자의 말에서 정답을 찾아야 한다. 여자가 마지막 대사에서 조금 더 생각해 보자고 제안하고 있으므로 정답은 (C)이다.

패러프레이징 think it over for a while 생각할 시간을 갖다
→ postponing a decision 결정을 미루다

Questions 41-43 refer to the following conversation. 미M 미W

M Jasmine, just to remind you that ㊷ I'm off to London tomorrow to attend a COMDEX convention next Monday. I won't be back until Friday.
W Yes, ㊶ that'll be no problem at all. I arranged a taxi service from Heathrow airport but I haven't made a hotel reservation yet.
M Don't worry. ㊸ I'm planning to stay with a friend of mine for the whole week. He's lived there for more than five years now and he's going to show me around for a day or two once the convention is over.
W Sounds nice. I'm sure there's so much to see.

남 Jasmine, 제가 다음 주 월요일에 있을 COMDEX 컨벤션 참석을 위해 내일 런던으로 떠나는 것 잊지 말아요. 금요일은 되어야 돌아올 겁니다.
여 알고 있습니다. 전혀 문제없으실 거예요. 제가 Heathrow 공항에 택시 서비스는 준비했는데, 호텔은 아직 예약 못 했어요.
남 걱정 말아요. 그 주 내내 친구와 함께 머물 예정이에요. 그 친구가 지금 5년 넘게 그곳에 살고 있는데, 컨벤션이 끝나면 하루나 이틀 정도 저를 안내해 줄 예정이거든요.
여 잘됐네요. 그곳엔 볼 게 많을 거예요.

어휘 remind 상기시키다, 다시 한 번 알려주다 arrange 마련하다, 처리하다, 정리하다

41 Who most likely is the man talking to?

(A) A tour conductor
(B) A secretary
(C) A manager
(D) A taxi driver

남자는 누구에게 말하고 있는가?
(A) 여행 안내원
(B) 비서
(C) 관리자
(D) 택시 기사

해설 〈기본 정보 파악 – 직업〉
여자의 직업과 관련된 문제이므로 대화의 초반에 근거를 찾아야 한다. 남자가 첫 대사에서 자신의 출장에 대해 언급하자 여자가 택시와 호텔 예약에 대해 보고하고 있다. 그러므로 여자는 남자의 출장 일정 관련 업무를 담당하는 비서임을 알 수 있으므로 (B)가 정답이다. 직업을 파악하는 문제는 남자와 여자 중 누구의 직업을 묻는 것인지 주의해야 한다.

42 What will the man do next Monday?

(A) Tour the city
(B) Attend a convention
(C) Meet his friend
(D) See a client

다음 주 월요일에 남자는 무엇을 할 것인가?
(A) 도시 관광
(B) 컨벤션 참석
(C) 친구 만나기
(D) 고객 만나기

해설 〈구체적 정보 파악 – 특정 사항〉
남자가 Monday를 언급하는 대사에서 정답을 찾아야 한다. 남자는 첫 대사에서 컨벤션 참석을 위해 내일 런던으로 떠난다고 말하고 있으므로 정답은 (B)이다. 문제의 키워드가 요일, 시간 등 단답형일 경우 바로 앞 문제의 답과 함께 언급되는 경우가 많으므로 놓치지 않도록 주의해야 한다.

43 How long will the man be away?

(A) About three days
(B) About a week
(C) More than two weeks
(D) More than a month

남자는 얼마나 떠나 있을 것인가?
(A) 약 3일
(B) 약 일주일
(C) 2주 이상
(D) 한 달 이상

해설 〈구체적 정보 파악 – 특정 사항〉
남자가 일주일 동안 친구와 함께 머무를 것이라고 설명하므로 남자의 출장 기간이 일주일임을 알 수 있다. 따라서 정답은 (B)이다.

Questions 44-46 refer to the following conversation. (영M) (미W)

M Good afternoon, Ms. Bridges. This is Hugh Blair from Jade Architectural Design. ㊹ I'm calling to see if you'd seen the layout of your new store. I sent it to your office by express mail last week.

W Yes, I received it yesterday, and I really liked what you did. However, there is just one thing that worries me. ㊺ Do you think there are enough fitting rooms available? We expect a deluge of customers every weekend, so we need to avoid the clutter. Can you increase the number of changing rooms?

M Certainly, no problem. ㊻ I'll send you the revised version as soon as I make the change.

W That sounds perfect. I'll give you my feedback once I get it.

남 안녕하세요, Bridges 씨. Jade Architectural Design의 Hugh Blair입니다. 당신의 새 상점 배치도를 보셨는지 알아보려고 전화 드렸습니다. 제가 지난주에 빠른우편으로 사무실로 보냈거든요.

여 네, 어제 받았는데 당신이 해 준 작업이 정말 마음에 들었습니다. 그러나 한 가지 걱정되는 것이 있습니다. 탈의실이 충분하다고 생각 하시나요? 우리는 주말마다 고객들이 많이 올 것으로 예상하고 있어서 그로 인한 혼잡은 피해야 할 필요가 있어요. 탈의실 수를 늘려주실 수 있나요?

남 그럼요, 문제없습니다. 제가 변경한 후 가능한 한 빨리 수정본을 보내 드리겠습니다.

여 완벽하네요. 받자마자 피드백을 드리도록 할게요.

어휘 architectural 건축학의 layout 배치도 a deluge of 엄청난 양, 수 avoid 방지하다, 막다, 피하다 clutter 난잡, 혼란 revise 수정, 변경하다

44 What most likely did the man do last week?
(A) He emailed a document.
(B) He sent a floor plan.
(C) He changed the schedule.
(D) He analyzed the sales data.

남자는 여자에게 목요일에 무엇을 보냈는가?
(A) 그를 서류를 이메일로 보냈다.
(B) 그는 평면도를 보냈다.
(C) 그는 일정을 변경했다.
(D) 그를 판매자료를 분석했다.

해설 〈구체적 정보 파악 - 특정 사항〉
남자가 last week를 언급하는 대사에서 정답을 찾아야 한다. 첫 대사에서 남자가 지난주에 우편으로 보낸 상점의 평면도에 대한 언급을 하고 있으므로 정답은 (B)이다.

패러프레이징 layout (건물, 정원 등의) 배치도
→ floor plan (건물의) 평면도

45 What does the woman mean when she says, "there is just one thing that worries me"?
(A) The budget may not be sufficient.
(B) Information could have been missing.
(C) The layout might need adjusting.
(D) There may be a shortage of staff.

여자가 말한 "한 가지 걱정되는 것이 있다" 가 의미하는 것은 무엇인가?
(A) 예산이 충분하지 않을 수 있다.
(B) 정보가 누락되었을 수 있다.
(C) 배치도의 조정이 필요할 것 같다
(D) 직원이 부족할 수 있다.

해설 〈구체적 정보 파악 - 화자 의도〉
화자 의도 문제는 주어진 표현의 앞뒤 상황을 파악해야 한다. 여자가 해당 표현을 언급한 후 탈의실이 충분하다고 생각하는지 질문하고 있으므로 여자의 걱정은 탈의실의 수와 관련이 있음을 알 수 있다. 따라서 정답은 (C)이다.

46 What does the man say he will do?
(A) Send the woman the modified document
(B) Call the woman later in the day
(C) Give the woman his feedback
(D) Visit the woman's office

남자는 무엇을 하겠다고 말하는가?
(A) 여자에게 수정된 문서를 보낸다.
(B) 여자에게 오늘 늦게 전화를 건다.
(C) 여자에게 피드백을 준다.
(D) 여자의 사무실을 방문한다.

해설 〈구체적 정보파악 -미래〉
대화 후반에 남자가 말하는 부분에서 답을 찾아야 한다. 남자가 마지막 대사에서 변경한 후 수정본을 여자에게 보내겠다고 말하고 있으므로 정답은 (A)이다.

패러프레이징 revised version 수정(사항)본
→ modified document 수정된 서류

Questions 47-49 refer to the following conversation. (미M) (미W)

M Joyce, can I ask you something? I've heard that there are two management workshops. ㊽ One is for beginners and the other is at an advanced level. Someone told me that ㊼ you've attended both since you became a manager. ㊽ Which one would you suggest for me?

W ㊼ With your management experience, the beginner's course would be too basic for you. I'm sure you'll get more out of the advanced one.

M Thanks for your advice. I'll attend the advanced one then.

W ㊾ You should also speak to Ian Kline. He's the organizer of both workshops, so he should be able to tell you more information.

남 Joyce, 질문해도 될까요? 경영 관리 워크숍이 두 개가 있다고 들었거든요. 하나는 초보자를 위한 것이고, 다른 하나는 상급 단계래요. 당신이 매니저가 된 이후로 양쪽 모두 참석했다고 누군가가 얘기해 줬어요. 저에게 어떤 것을 제안하시나요?

여 당신의 경영 경험에 초보자 코스는 너무 기본적일 수 있어요. 상급 단계에서 더 많은 것을 얻을 수 있을 거라고 생각해요.

남 조언 고마워요. 그럼 상급 단계에 참석해야겠어요.

여 Ian Kline 씨에게도 얘기해 보세요. 그 분이 양쪽 워크숍의 조직위원이거든요. 당신에게 더 많은 정보를 줄 수 있을 거예요.

어휘 beginner 초보자 advanced 고급의, 상급의 suggest 추천하다, 제안하다 organizer 조직자, 주최자 executive 임원, 경영진

47 Who most likely are the speakers?
(A) Company executives
(B) Business consultants
(C) New interns
(D) Seminar organizers

화자는 누구이겠는가?
(A) 회사 운영진
(B) 회사 고문
(C) 신입 인턴
(D) 세미나 주최자

해설 〈기본 정보 파악 - 직업〉
화자들의 직업을 묻는 문제로 대화 초반에 집중해야 한다. 남자가 첫 대사에서 경영 관리 워크숍에 대해 언급한 후 워크숍 참석에 대한 대화가 이어지고 있으므로 화자는 경영 관리와 연관된 직책의 사람들이라는 것을 알 수 있다. 따라서 정답은 (A)이다.

패러프레이징 manager 매니저, 관리자 → executives 경영진

48 What does the man want to know about the workshops?
(A) The dates
(B) The registration fees
(C) The levels
(D) The attendees

남자는 워크숍에 대해 무엇을 알고 싶어 하는가?
(A) 날짜
(B) 등록비
(C) 수준
(D) 참석자

해설 〈구체적 정보 파악 – 특정 사항〉
키워드인 workshop을 언급하는 남자의 대사에 집중해야 한다. 남자가 첫 대사에서 두 단계의 워크숍이 있다고 언급하며 여자에게 추천해 달라고 말하고 있으므로 (C)가 정답이다.

49 What does the woman tell the man to do?
(A) Apply for the position
(B) Organize the event
(C) Speak to a manager
(D) Contact the person in charge

여자는 남자에게 무엇을 하라고 말하는가?
(A) 직책에 지원할 것
(B) 행사를 준비할 것
(C) 관리자에게 말할 것
(D) 책임자에게 연락할 것

해설 〈구체적 정보 파악 – 특정 사항〉
여자가 마지막 대사에서 워크숍의 조직위원인 Ian Kline과 이야기할 것을 제안하고 있으므로 가장 적절하게 바꾸어 표현한 (D)가 정답이다.

Questions 50-52 refer to the following conversation. 미W 영M

W Trevor, I just learned about your transfer to our Berlin branch. What will the company have you doing there?
M Mostly the same type of work I do here. ⑩ We'll be introducing our new menswear line throughout Europe starting this fall. ⑪ My project team has had a lot of success promoting the line here, so the company assigned me to oversee our European marketing efforts as well.
W That's great. Congratulations. That sounds very interesting. Have you arranged for a place to live yet?
M Actually, ⑫ someone I used to work with teaches at a university in Berlin. He invited me to stay with him and offered to help me find an apartment once I get there.

여 Trevor, 당신이 Berlin 지점으로 전근 간다는 것을 조금 전에 알게 되었어요. 그곳에서 무슨 일을 하게 되시나요?
남 대부분 여기서 하던 일과 똑같아요. 이번 가을을 시작으로 유럽에 새로운 남성 의류 제품을 선보이게 될 겁니다. 저희 프로젝트 팀이 여기서 그 제품을 홍보하는 데 큰 성공을 거두어서, 회사가 저에게 유럽 마케팅 담당을 맡겼어요.
여 대단하네요. 축하해요. 아주 흥미롭겠네요. 거주할 곳은 정하셨어요?
남 사실, 저랑 같이 일했던 분이 Berlin에 있는 대학에서 학생들을 가르치고 있어요. 그가 저에게 같이 지내자고 했고 제가 도착하면 아파트 찾는 것도 도와주실 겁니다.

어휘 transfer 옮기다, 이동하다 promote 홍보하다, 촉진하다 assign 맡기다, 배정하다 oversee 감독하다 effort 수고, 노력, 작업 enroll in ~에 등록하다

50 What will the speakers' company do in Europe during the fall?
(A) Conclude a research study
(B) Launch a product line
(C) Construct a new facility
(D) Open a new branch

화자들의 회사는 가을에 유럽에서 무엇을 할 것인가?
(A) 조사 연구를 완료한다.
(B) 제품 라인을 선보인다.
(C) 새로운 시설을 건설한다.
(D) 새로운 지점을 오픈한다.

해설 〈구체적 정보 파악 – 특정 사항〉
in Europe during the fall을 키워드로 잡고 앞뒤를 집중해야 한다. 남자가 가을에 유럽에서 남성복 제품을 선보일 것이라고 언급하고 있으므로 정답은 (B)이다.

51 Why does the woman say, "That's great. Congratulations"?
(A) The man was promoted to an executive position.
(B) The man finished a project ahead of schedule.
(C) The man enrolled in a well-known university.
(D) The man was given an important assignment.

여자가 "대단하네요. 축하해요"라고 말한 이유는 무엇인가?
(A) 남자가 임원으로 승진했다.
(B) 남자가 예정보다 일찍 프로젝트를 끝냈다.
(C) 남자가 잘 알려진 대학에 입학했다.
(D) 남자가 중요한 임무를 맡게 되었다.

해설 〈구체적 정보 파악 – 화자 의도〉
주어진 문장의 주변 문맥과 종합하여 여자의 의도를 파악해야 한다. 남자가 국내 홍보에 성공을 거두어서 회사가 유럽 마케팅 담당을 맡겼다고 말하자 여자가 해당 문장을 언급한다. 따라서 정답은 (D)이다.

52 According to the man, what will a former coworker help him do?
(A) Locate a residence
(B) Arrange transportation
(C) Prepare for a course
(D) Make professional contacts

남자에 의하면, 예전 동료가 무엇을 도와줄 것인가?
(A) 거주지를 찾는 것
(B) 교통편을 구하는 것
(C) 코스를 준비하는 것
(D) 직업상의 연줄을 만드는 것

해설 〈구체적 정보 파악 – 특정 사항〉
남자가 키워드인 former coworker를 언급할 때 집중한다. 남자가 마지막 대사에서 과거에 같이 일했던 동료가 아파트 찾는 것을 도와주기로 했다고 말하고 있으므로 정답은 (A)이다.

패러프레이징 find an apartment 아파트 찾기
→ locate a residence 거주지 찾기

Questions 53-55 refer to the following conversation. (미W) (미M)

W Hi. ⓹③ Could you tell me how far it is from here to the city center? This is my first time in Hanoi on business.
M Well, it's not too far. If you take a taxi, you'll probably get there in about half an hour. ⑤③ The airport shuttle bus takes almost twice as long, but it's considerably cheaper.
W If you say so, ⑤④ I'll take the shuttle bus. Do you know how often it goes?
M ⑤⑤ It departs every half hour from outside door B, which is at the end of the terminal by the foreign exchange counter.

여 안녕하세요. 여기에서 시내까지 얼마나 걸리는지 알려주실 수 있나요? 사업차 Hanoi를 방문한 것은 처음이라서요.
남 음, 그리 멀진 않아요. 택시를 타시면, 아마 거기까지 가는 데 30분 정도 걸릴 겁니다. 공항 셔틀 버스는 시간이 거의 두 배 정도 걸리지만 많이 싸죠.
여 그렇다면 셔틀 버스를 타야겠네요. 얼마나 자주 다니는지 아세요?
남 터미널 끝에 있는 환전소 옆 B 게이트 밖에서 30분마다 출발해요.

어휘 considerably 많이, 상당히 depart 떠나다, 출발하다, cheaper 값이 더 싼 foreign exchange 외화

53 Where does the conversation most likely take place?
(A) At a bus stop
(B) On a plane
(C) At an airport
(D) At a city center

이 대화가 일어나는 장소는 어디인가?
(A) 버스 정류장
(B) 비행기 안
(C) 공항
(D) 시내

해설 〈기본 정보 파악 – 장소〉
대화가 일어나는 장소를 묻는 문제는 초반에 단서가 제시되는 경우가 대부분이다. 여자가 첫 대사에서 길을 물으며 Hanoi에 처음 왔다고 말하고 있으므로 정답은 (C)이다.

54 What will the woman probably do next?
(A) Take a shuttle bus
(B) Purchase a ticket
(C) Exchange money
(D) Take a taxi

여자는 다음에 무엇을 하겠는가?
(A) 셔틀 버스를 탄다.
(B) 표를 구매한다.
(C) 돈을 환전한다.
(D) 택시를 탄다.

해설 〈구체적 정보 파악 – 미래〉
미래에 할 일과 연관된 문제는 마지막 대사에서 단서가 제시된다. 여자가 마지막 대사에서 셔틀 버스를 탈 것이라고 말하고 있으므로 정답은 (A)이다.

55 How many shuttle buses run per hour?
(A) One
(B) Two
(C) Three
(D) Four

셔틀 버스는 한 시간에 몇 번 운행하는가?
(A) 한 번
(B) 두 번
(C) 세 번
(D) 네 번

해설 〈구체적 정보 파악 – 특정 사항〉
Shuttle bus를 키워드로 잡고 주변 문장을 잘 들어야 한다. 여자가 셔틀 버스의 운행 빈도를 묻자 남자가 30분마다 한 대씩 다닌다고 대답하고 있으므로 정답은 (B)이다.

Questions 56-58 refer to the following conversation with three speakers. (영M) (미W) (미M)

M1 Angela, there are left-over materials after we've remodeled our office. It's a shame to get rid of them. Can we use them somehow?
W Well, ⑤⑥ we could use this paint to redo the sign on the entrance. It's just about the right color.
M2 You did a good job thinking it out, and we could put the extra cabinets in the staff lounge.
M1 Yeah! Smart thinking, Nathan! That would finally give us a place to store our clean cups and plates. Dealing with that tiny, cluttered area — it drives me up the wall.
W ⑤⑦ The sign on the entrance won't take long. I could do it tomorrow.
M2 ⑤⑧ Then I'll go and ask Ms. Morris to put the cabinets in the lounge.
M1 It's great that we can make good use of these things.

남1 Angela, 사무실을 개조하고 남은 재료들이 있어요. 그것을 버리자니 아깝네요. 어떻게든 사용할 수 있을까요?
여 이 페인트로 입구에 있는 간판을 다시 칠할 수 있겠네요. 색깔도 알맞아요.
남2 잘 생각해 냈어요. 그리고 휴게실에 여분의 캐비닛을 놓을 수도 있을 것 같아요.
남1 맞아요, 현명한 생각이에요. Nathan! 그러면 드디어 우리가 깨끗한 컵과 접시를 보관할 수 있는 장소가 생기겠네요. 작고 어수선한 곳을 처리하자니, 정말 미칠 지경이었어요.
여 그 입구 간판은 오래 안 걸릴 겁니다. 내일 할 수 있어요.
남2 그러면 제가 Morris 씨에게 가서 캐비닛을 놓는 것에 대해 물어볼게요.
남1 우리가 이런 것들이 잘 활용될 수 있다니 정말 좋아요.

어휘 left over 쓰고 남은 shame 애석한 일 redo 다시 하다 tiny 아주 작은 cluttered 어수선한 It drives me up the wall. 나를 미치게 하다, 나를 궁지로 몰아넣다

56 What does Angela suggest doing?
(A) Remodeling the office
(B) Repainting a sign
(C) Selecting colors
(D) Buying more paint

화자들이 근무하는 곳은 어떤 종류의 회사인가?
(A) 사무실 개조하기
(B) 간판 다시 칠하기
(C) 색상 선택하기
(D) 더 많은 페인트 구입하기

해설 〈기본 정보 파악 – 장소〉
첫 대사에서 남자가 문제의 키워드인 Angela를 부르며 남은 재료 사용에 대해 묻자 바로 이어서 여자가 대답하고 있으므로 대화에 등장하

는 여자가 Angela임을 알 수 있으며, 그녀가 남은 페인트로 입구 간판을 다시 칠하자고 제안하므로 정답은 (B)이다.

57 What will most likely happen tomorrow?
(A) Angela will use the paint.
(B) Nathan will throw away the materials.
(C) Ms. Morris will install the shelves.
(D) They will go to the head office.

내일 무슨 일이 일어 날 것인가?
(A) Angela가 페인트를 사용할 것이다.
(B) Nathan이 재료들을 버릴 것이다.
(C) Morris 씨가 선반을 설치할 것이다.
(D) 그들은 본사에 갈 것이다.

해설 〈구체적 정보파악 – 특정 사항〉
tomorrow를 키워드로 잡고 앞뒤를 집중해야 한다. 대화 중반에 여자가 간판은 두어 시간 밖에 안 걸리고 내일 할 수 있다고 말하므로 (A)가 가장 적절한 답이다.

58 What does the man say he will do?
(A) Consult with his colleague
(B) Hire a professional
(C) Attend a workshop
(D) Renovate a staff lounge

Nathan은 무엇을 할 것인가?
(A) 동료에게 이야기하기
(B) 전문가를 고용하기
(C) 워크숍에 참석하기
(D) 직원 휴게실 개조하기

해설 〈구체적 정보파악 – 미래〉
대화 중반에 남자1이 Nathan의 이름을 부르며 좋은 생각을 해냈다고 칭찬하고 있으므로 남자2가 Nathan임을 알 수 있다. 남자2가 대화 후반에 Ms. Morris에게 가서 선반을 놓는 것에 대해 물어본다고 말하고 있으므로 내용을 바꾸어 표현한 (A)가 가장 적절한 답이다. 3인 대화에서는 여러 명의 이름이 언급되는 경우가 많다. 그러므로 문제의 키워드가 이름일 경우, 해당 이름이 대화를 나누는 등장인물 중 한 명인지 아니면 제3의 인물인지 반드시 확인해야 한다.

Questions 59-61 refer to the following conversation. (미M) (미W)

M Excuse me. We've just arrived on a flight from Scotland but ⓹⓽ my son's suitcase is missing. We had four checked bags, but only three of them are here.
W Oh, have you checked the area thoroughly? Sometimes the attendants take bags off the carousels and place them over by that wall.
M Yes, we've looked everywhere but it's just not here. I wonder if another passenger took it by mistake. So many suitcases look alike these days.
W That's possible, ⓺⓪ but more likely it got misdirected somehow. I'll start looking into it. ⓺⓪ Here's a form for you to fill out. ⓺⓵ And can I have your baggage claim checks, please?
M Sure, here they are.

남 실례합니다. Scotland에서 비행기로 방금 도착했는데, 제 아들의 여행 가방이 없어졌습니다. 4개의 가방을 부쳤는데, 3개만 있어요.
여 오, 그 구역을 전부 확인해 보셨나요? 가끔 안내원들이 가방들을 컨베이어 벨트에서 내린 후에 벽 근처에 두거든요.
남 네, 전부 찾아봤지만 여기 없어요. 다른 승객이 실수로 가져간 건 아닌가 싶어요. 요즘 많은 여행 가방들이 비슷하게 생겼거든요.
여 그럴 수도 있지만, 어쩌다가 다른 곳으로 보내졌을 가능성이 더 큽니다. 제가 조사해 보겠습니다. 작성하실 서류를 드릴게요. 그리고 수화물표를 저에게 주시겠어요?
남 물론이죠. 여기 있습니다.

어휘 suitcase 여행 가방 thoroughly 대단히, 완전히, 철저히 attendant 종업원, 안내원 carousel 수하물 컨베이어 벨트 by mistake 실수로 alike 비슷한, 비슷하게 misdirect 다른 방향(곳)으로 보내다 somehow 어떻게든, 왜 그런지 baggage claim checks 수화물표 boarding pass 탑승권

59 What are the speakers mainly talking about?
(A) A missing flight
(B) A lost item
(C) A delayed flight
(D) A rude passenger

화자들은 주로 무엇에 대해 이야기하는가?
(A) 놓친 항공편
(B) 분실물
(C) 연착된 비행기
(D) 무례한 승객

해설 〈기본 정보 파악 – 주제〉
대화의 주제는 초반에 제시된다. 첫 대사에서 남자가 아들의 여행 가방이 분실되었음을 알리고 있으므로 정답은 (B)이다.

60 What does the woman mean when she says, "I'll start looking into it"?
(A) She will start an investigation.
(B) She will check out some information.
(C) She will book a flight.
(D) She will contact a colleague.

여자가 "제가 조사해 보겠습니다"라고 말한 의미는 무엇인가?
(A) 조사를 시작할 것이다.
(B) 몇몇 정보를 확인할 것이다.
(C) 항공편을 예약할 것이다.
(D) 동료에게 연락할 것이다.

해설 〈구체적 정보 파악 – 화자 의도〉
화자 의도 문제는 주어진 표현의 앞뒤 상황을 파악해야 한다. 여자가 해당 표현을 언급하기 전 여행 가방이 다른 곳으로 보내졌을 가능성을 제기하며 조사에 필요한 서류 작성을 요청하고 있다. 따라서 정답은 (A)이다.

61 What does the woman ask the man to give her?
(A) Some traveler's checks
(B) His boarding pass
(C) His passport
(D) Some documents

여자는 남자에게 무엇을 달라고 요청하는가?
(A) 여행자 수표
(B) 남자의 탑승권
(C) 남자의 여권
(D) 몇 가지 문서

해설 〈구체적 정보 파악 – 특정 사항〉
여자가 마지막 대사에서 수화물표를 달라고 요청하고 있으므로 이를 가장 적절히 바꾸어 표현한 (D)가 정답이다.

패러프레이징 your baggage claim checks 수화물표
→ some documents 몇 가지 문서

Questions 62-64 refer to the following conversation and building directory. 미W 영M

The Triumph Building Directory
5th Floor – Mark & Spencer Advisers 4th Floor – L&D Service 3rd Floor – Green Fingers Magazine 2nd Floor – Twingle Advertising 1st Floor – Lobby

W Hi, Jeff. 62 63 It's a shame that Mark & Spencer has moved out of the building. It was really convenient having a law firm on the floor right above us.

M Yeah, and I was a good friend with Charles, the lawyer. I'll miss having lunch with him. 63 He said that they didn't like having their offices on the top floor so they'd been searching for a right office for a while.

W They're right across 5th Street now. I hear they've settled in nicely.

M 64 Why don't we take a walk over there at lunchtime and say hello? I want to talk with Charles about a few things while we're there.

Triumph 건물 안내
5층 – Mark & Spencer 자문단 4층 – L&D 서비스 3층 – Green Fingers 잡지 2층 – Twingle 광고 1층 – 로비

여 안녕하세요, Jeff. Mark & Spence가 이 건물에서 이사 나갔다니 아쉽네요. 우리 바로 위층에 법률 회사가 있어서 무척 편리했거든요.

남 맞아요. 그리고 저는 변호사 Charles랑 친했거든요. 함께 점심 먹던 것이 그리울 겁니다. 그들은 사무실이 맨 위층에 있는 것을 좋아하지 않았다고 그가 말했거든요. 그래서 그들은 한동안 알맞은 사무실을 찾고 있었어요.

여 이제 그들은 바로 건너편 5번 가에 있어요. 좋은 곳을 정했다고 들었어요.

남 우리가 점심시간에 그쪽으로 가서 인사하는 것은 어떨까요? 거기서 Charles와 몇 가지 이야기를 하고 싶어요.

어휘 move out 이사를 나가다 convenient 편리한, 간편한 law firm 법률 사무소 settle 놓다, 앉히다, 자리를 잡다

62 What kind of company has moved out of the building?
(A) An accounting company
(B) A legal office
(C) An advertising agency
(D) A publishing company

어떤 종류의 회사가 건물에서 이사했는가?
(A) 회계 회사
(B) 법률 사무소
(C) 광고 대행사
(D) 출판 회사

해설 〈구체적 정보 파악 – 특정 사항〉
moved out을 키워드로 잡고 앞뒤를 잘 들어야 한다. 여자가 처음에 바로 위에 법률 회사가 있어 편리했었는데 이사 나갔다니 아쉽다고 말하고 있다. 따라서 정답은 (B)이다.

63 Look at the graphic. At what company do the speakers most likely work?
(A) Mark & Spencer Advisers
(B) L&D Service
(C) Green Fingers Magazine
(D) Tingle Advertising

시각 자료를 보시오. 화자들은 어떤 회사에서 일하는가?
(A) Mark & Spencer 자문단
(B) L&D 서비스
(C) Green Fingers 잡지
(D) Twingle 광고

해설 〈구체적 정보 파악 – 시각 자료 연계〉
대화 속에 언급된 내용과 제시된 시각 자료를 교차 확인하여 정답을 찾아야 하는데, 선택지에 회사명이 제시되어 있으므로 대화에서는 층이 언급되는 부분에 주목해야 한다. 법률 회사가 이사 나가는 이유가 가장 위층에 있는 것을 좋아하지 않기 때문이라고 했으므로 Mark and Spencer 자문단이 5층에 위치하고 있음을 알 수 있고 여자의 첫 번째 대사를 통해 그들이 화자들의 바로 위층에서 근무했음을 알 수 있다. 따라서 정답은 (B)이다.

64 What does the man suggest?
(A) Reviewing a document
(B) Planning an event
(C) Visiting a friend
(D) Hiring a lawyer

남자는 무엇을 제안하는가?
(A) 서류를 검토하는 것
(B) 행사를 계획하는 것
(C) 친구를 방문하는 것
(D) 변호사를 고용하는 것

해설 〈구체적 정보 파악 – 제안 관련〉
남자가 제안하는 것이므로 남자의 마지막 말에 주목해야 한다. 남자가 마지막 대사에서 점심시간에 이사 간 곳을 방문하자고 제안하고 있으므로 정답은 (C)이다.

Questions 65-67 refer to the following conversation and program. 미M 미W

Management & Marketing Conference Presentations in July
Dr. Edward Williamson, Risk Management
Dr. Raymond Gomez, Time Management
Dr. Hillary Palin, Decision Making
Dr. Jina Hong, Group Working

M Hello, I'm calling about the management and marketing conference being held at the Town Events Center in July. 65 I'm very interested in Dr. Hillary Palin's presentation. Is there any way for me to attend without registering for the entire conference?

W I'm sorry sir, but you cannot. In fact, due to limited seating, even conference attendees aren't guaranteed admission to every presentation. 66 If you really want to see Dr. Palin, you should probably register and reserve a seat as soon as possible.

M Okay, can you let me know how to do that?

W We can do it right now if you have a credit card handy, or 67 you can register online through our Web site.

7월 경영 & 마케팅 컨퍼런스 발표
Edward Williamson 박사, 위기 관리
Raymond Gomez 박사, 시간 관리
Hillary Palin 박사, 의사 결정
Jina Hong 박사, 공동 작업

남 안녕하세요. 7월에 Town Events Center에서 열리는 경영 및 마케팅 컨퍼런스 때문에 전화 드립니다. 저는 Hillary Palin 박사님의 발표에 아주 관심이 많은데요. 전체 컨퍼런스에 등록하지 않고 참석할 수 있는 방법이 있나요?

여 죄송하지만, 그건 어렵습니다. 사실 좌석이 제한적이기 때문에 컨퍼런스 참석자들조차도 모든 발표에 입장하는 것을 보장해드릴 수가 없거든요. Palin 박사님을 정말 보고 싶으시다면 가능한 한 빨리 등록하고 좌석 예약을 하셔야 합니다.

남 알겠습니다. 어떻게 하는지 알려주시겠어요?

여 신용 카드를 가지고 계시면 지금 바로 할 수 있습니다. 아니면 저희 웹 사이트를 통해서 온라인으로 등록하실 수도 있습니다.

어휘 register 등록하다, 기록하다 entire 전체의, 온 limited 제한된 guarantee 보장하다, 약속하다 admission 가입, 입장 reserve 예약하다 handy 유용한, 편리한, 가까운 곳에 있는 venue 장소

65 Look at the graphic. Which presentation is the man most interested in seeing?
(A) Risk Management
(B) Time Management
(C) Decision Making
(D) Group Working
시각 자료를 보시오. 남자가 가장 보고 싶어 하는 발표는 어떤 것인가?
(A) 위기 관리
(B) 시간 관리
(C) 의사 결정
(D) 공동 작업

해설 〈구체적 정보 파악 – 시각 자료 연계〉
선택지에 발표 주제가 제시되어 있으므로 대화에서는 발표자 이름이 언급되는 부분에 주목해야 한다. 남자가 첫 대사에서 Dr. Hillary Palin의 발표에 관심 있다고 언급하고 있으므로 해당 발표자 이름이 명시된 발표 주제가 답이다. 따라서 정답은 (C)이다.

66 What does the woman advise the man to do?
(A) Arrive at the venue early
(B) Make a reservation
(C) Contact a presenter
(D) Create a credit card
여자는 남자에게 무엇을 하라고 권고하는가?
(A) 장소에 일찍 도착하기
(B) 예약하기
(C) 발표자에게 연락하기
(D) 신용 카드를 만들기

해설 〈구체적 정보 파악 – 특정 사항〉
여자가 남자에게 조언하고 있는 부분에서 정답을 찾아야 한다. 대화 중반에 여자가 발표에 참석하고 싶다면 가능한 한 빨리 예약해야 한다고 권하고 있으므로 정답은 (B)이다.

패러프레이징 reserve a seat 자리를 예약하다
→ make a reservation 예약하다

67 According to the woman, what can the man do at the Web site?
(A) Sign up for the conference
(B) Access research data
(C) Check out the schedule
(D) Confirm the credit card number
여자에 의하면, 남자는 웹 사이트에서 무엇을 할 수 있는가?
(A) 컨퍼런스 등록
(B) 조사 자료 입수
(C) 일정 확인
(D) 신용카드 번호 확인

해설 〈구체적 정보 파악 – 특정 사항〉
여자가 문제의 키워드인 Web site를 언급할 때 집중해야 한다. 여자가 마지막 대사에서 웹 사이트를 통해 등록하라고 제안하고 있으므로 정답은 (A)이다.

패러프레이징 register 등록하다 → sign up 등록하다

Questions 68-70 refer to the following conversation and map. 미W 영M

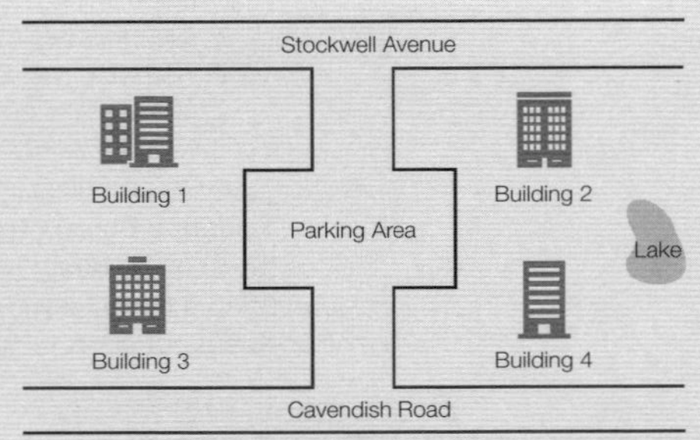

W This is the layout of the factory we're supposed to install the solar panels in, right?
M That's right. ⑥⑧ The company that owns the factory is trying to reduce energy costs. That's a near-term target for them.
W I see. Well, just looking at things, ⑥⑨ the locations seem ideal. It looks like we could do the installation almost anywhere. I mean, the roof is so flat and everything.
M Yes, ⑦⓪ but they only want us to cover the closest building to Stockwell Avenue, and it's right next to the lake. That catches the highest amount of average sunlight during the day year-round.

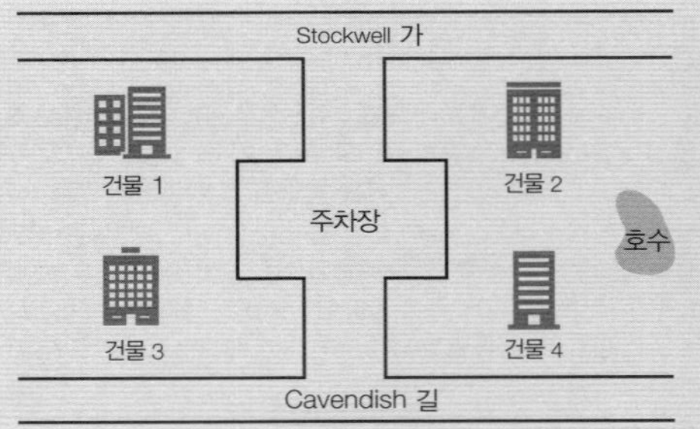

여 이것이 우리가 태양광 패널을 설치하기로 한 공장의 배치도네요, 그렇죠?
남 맞아요. 이 공장을 소유한 회사가 에너지 비용을 줄이려고 노력하는 중입니다. 그것이 그들의 단기 목표예요.
여 그렇군요. 음, 보기엔 위치가 이상적인 것 같아요. 거의 어디든지 설치할 수 있어 보입니다. 제 말은 지붕도 평평하고 이런 저런 것들 말이에요.
남 네, 그렇지만 그들은 Stockwell 가에서 제일 가까운 건물에 설치하기를 원하고 있어요. 바로 호수 옆이요. 연중 평균적으로 햇빛의 양을 가장 많이 받을 수 있어요.

어휘 layout 배치도 install 설치하다, 설비하다 solar 태양의, 태양열을 이용한 reduce 축소하다, 줄이다 near-term 근일의, 가까운 날의 ideal 이상적인 installation 설치, 설비 flat 평평한, 편평한 average 평균의

68 What does the man say is a near-term goal of the company?
(A) Reducing expenses
(B) Producing more energy
(C) Opening a new branch
(D) Completing a project
남자는 회사의 단기 목표가 무엇이라고 말하는가?
(A) 비용을 절감하는 것
(B) 더 많은 에너지를 생산하는 것
(C) 새로운 지점을 여는 것
(D) 프로젝트를 완성하는 것

해설 〈구체적 정보 파악 – 특정 사항〉
남자가 키워드인 near-term goal을 언급하는 부분에서 정답을 찾아야 한다. 남자가 첫 대사에서 회사의 단기 목표는 에너지 비용을 줄이는 것이라고 말하고 있으므로 정답은 (A)이다.

패러프레이징 reduce costs 비용을 줄이다
→ reducing expenses 비용 절감

69 What does the woman say is ideal?
(A) The amount of sunlight
(B) Weather condition
(C) The worksite
(D) The work hours
여자는 무엇이 이상적이라고 말하는가?

(A) 햇빛의 양
(B) 기상 상태
(C) 작업 장소
(D) 작업 시간

해설 〈구체적 정보 파악 – 특정 사항〉
여자가 키워드인 ideal을 언급하며 위치가 이상적이라고 말하고 있으므로 정답은 (C)이다.

70 Look at the graphic. Where will the installation be done?
(A) On building 1
(B) On building 2
(C) On building 3
(D) On building 4

시각 자료를 보시오. 설치는 어느 곳에 되겠는가?
(A) 1번 건물
(B) 2번 건물
(C) 3번 건물
(D) 4번 건물

해설 〈구체적 정보 파악 – 시각 자료 연계〉
지도의 건물이 선택지로 제시되어 있으므로 대화에서는 지도의 나머지 정보 즉 도로명, 주차장, 호수가 단서로 언급될 것을 예측하고 들어야 한다. 남자가 마지막 대사에서 Stockwell 가에서 제일 가까우며 호수 옆에 위치한 건물에 설치하기를 원하고 있다고 설명하므로 정답은 (B)이다.

PART 4

P107

Questions 71-73 refer to the following excerpt from a meeting.
미M

As you all know, (71) it is very crucial that we make a good impression at the presentation tomorrow. If the clients accept our proposal, it'll have a positive impact on our financial situation for years to come. Their building is at 247 Brompton Road, just down the street from Hyde Park. Our appointment is at 1:00 P.M., but (72) let's all try to get there early. (73) We'll meet up at the coffee shop next door and then go in together as a group. For those of you who will drive there, there's a pay garage on the corner across from Hyde Park.

여러분 모두 아시는 바와 같이, 내일 발표에서 우리가 좋은 인상을 남기는 것은 매우 중요합니다. 만약 고객들이 우리의 제안을 받아들인다면, 앞으로 몇 년간 우리 재정 상태에 긍정적인 영향을 끼칠 수 있을 것입니다. 건물은 Hyde 공원에서 바로 길을 따라 Brompton 길 247에 있습니다. 약속 시간은 오후 1시지만, 모두 일찍 도착하도록 합시다. 옆 건물의 커피숍에서 만나서 모두 함께 들어갈 것입니다. 운전해서 가실 분은 Hyde 공원 바로 맞은편 코너에 유료 주차장이 있습니다.

어휘 crucial 중대한, 결정적인 impression 인상, 느낌, 감동 accept 수락하다, 받아들이다 positive 긍정적인 impact 영향, 충격 financial situation 재정 상태 meet up (~와) 만나다 appoint 지정하다 postpone 연기하다

71 What is the purpose of the talk?
(A) To prepare for a meeting
(B) To vote on a proposal
(C) To change a presenter
(D) To appoint a project manager

담화의 목적은 무엇인가?
(A) 회의를 준비하기 위해서
(B) 제안서에 투표하기 위해서
(C) 발표자를 변경하기 위해서
(D) 프로젝트 관리자를 지정하기 위해

해설 〈기본 정보 파악 – 목적〉
담화의 목적은 앞부분에 언급된다. 담화 초반에 내일 발표에서 좋은 인상을 남기는 것을 강조하며 그 발표가 끼칠 긍정적 영향에 대해 언급하고 있으므로 고객과의 회의를 준비하고 있음을 알 수 있다. 따라서 (A)가 가장 적절한 답이다.

72 What does the speaker suggest?
(A) Arriving ahead of time
(B) Postponing a meeting date
(C) Making a presentation
(D) Cutting a budget

화자가 제안하는 것은 무엇인가?
(A) 일찍 도착하는 것
(B) 회의 날짜를 연기하는 것
(C) 발표를 하는 것
(D) 예산을 삭감하는 것

해설 〈구체적 정보 파악 – 제안 관련〉
담화 중반에 화자가 모두 일찍 도착하자고 제안하고 있으므로 정답은 (A)이다.

패러프레이징 get there early 일찍 도착하다
→ arriving ahead of time 예정보다 일찍 도착하는 것

73 Where are listeners asked to meet tomorrow morning?
(A) At a café
(B) In a parking lot
(C) At the park
(D) In a seminar room

청자들은 내일 아침에 어디에서 만나자고 요청받는가?
(A) 카페
(B) 주차장
(C) 공원
(D) 회의실

해설 〈구체적 정보 파악 – 특정 사항〉
화자가 마지막에 옆 건물의 커피숍에서 만나자고 언급하므로 정답은 (A)이다.

Questions 74-76 refer to the following excerpt from a meeting. 영W

There is something all of you need to do before returning to your workstations. 74 The new packaging machine arrived here at our factory yesterday and was installed by our technicians last night. 75 The new machine is capable of packaging our products at about twice the speed of our former equipment, but it's operated differently and uses a different system of mechanical processes. It won't take long, but everyone needs to learn how to use it. 76 My assistant, Ms Miller, is now going to hand out copies of the machine's instruction manual to everyone, and then we'll proceed to the packaging department and I'll demonstrate how to use it.

여러분들 모두 각자 자리로 돌아가시기 전에 해야 할 일이 더 있습니다. 어제 우리 공장에 새로운 포장 기기가 도착했고 기술자들이 지난밤에 설치를 모두 마쳤습니다. 새로운 기기는 기존 장비보다 약 두 배의 속도로 제품을 포장할 수 있습니다. 하지만 이 기기는 다르게 작동되고 기계적 처리도 다른 시스템을 사용합니다. 오래 걸리지 않을 테지만, 모든 분들이 어떻게 사용하는지 배워야 합니다. 저의 보조인 Miller 씨가 이제 여러분에게 기기의 사용 설명서를 배포할 것입니다. 그러고 나서 포장 부서로 옮겨 어떻게 사용하는지 시연해 드리겠습니다.

어휘 workstation 작업 장소 packaging machine 포장 기기 capable ~을 할 수 있는, 유능한 former 예전의, 이전의 operate 작동하다, 조작하다 hand out 나누어 주다, 배포하다 instruction manual 사용 설명서 demonstrate (행동으로) 보여주다, 입증하다 distribute 분배하다

74 Who most likely are the listeners?
(A) Office workers
(B) Computer technicians
(C) Packaging designers
(D) Factory workers

청자들은 누구이겠는가?
(A) 사무실 직원들
(B) 컴퓨터 기술자
(C) 포장 디자이너
(D) 공장 근로자들

해설 〈기본 정보 파악 – 청자〉
청자에 관한 정답 근거는 담화의 초반에 제시되는데, 초반에 어제 공장에 새로운 포장 기기가 도착해서 설치되었다고 알리고 있으므로 정답은 (D)이다.

75 What is an advantage of the new machine?
(A) It uses less power.
(B) It requires fewer operators.
(C) It performs more quickly.
(D) It is easier to maintain.

새로운 기계의 장점은 무엇인가?
(A) 전력을 적게 사용한다.
(B) 더 적은 수의 작업자가 필요하다.
(C) 더 빠르게 수행한다.
(D) 유지가 더 쉽다.

해설 〈구체적 정보 파악 – 특정 사항〉
새로운 기기를 설명하는 부분에서 기존보다 약 두 배의 속도로 제품을 포장할 수 있다고 말하고 있으므로 정답은 (C)이다.

76 According to the speaker, what will Ms. Miller do next?
(A) Distribute some documents
(B) Contact another department
(C) Give a demonstration
(D) Install some equipment

화자에 따르면, Miller 씨는 다음에 무엇을 할 것인가?
(A) 문서를 분배한다.
(B) 다른 부서에 연락한다.
(C) 시연을 한다.
(D) 기기들을 설치한다.

해설 〈구체적 정보 파악 – 특정 사항〉
Ms. Miller를 키워드로 잡고 앞뒤를 집중해야 한다. 해당 이름을 언급하며 그 사람이 사용 설명서를 나눠줄 것이라고 말하고 있으므로 정답은 (A)이다.

패러프레이징 hand out the instruction manual 설명서를 나누어 주다
→ distribute some documents 문서를 분배하다

Questions 77-79 refer to the following telephone message. 미W

Hello. This is Juliet Holton from Astoria Event Agency. I'm calling to let you know that 77 I've finished the outline for the *Discovering the Collection* event to be held at the Piccadilly Art Gallery. I've signed the contracts you faxed me, and we mailed them this afternoon. So that'll be all. 78 I think everything is ready for us to start. 79 I'd like to test the equipment and the designs at your gallery one day next week. I'm quite flexible with the time and date. So if you would contact me with a time that is suitable for you, I'll go there with my team and make sure everything works.

안녕하세요, Astoria 이벤트 대행사의 Juliet Holton입니다. Piccadilly 미술관에서 열리는 〈Discovering the Collection〉을 위한 기초 작업이 끝났다는 것을 알려 드리려고 전화합니다. 저에게 팩스로 보내주신 계약서에 서명했고 오늘 오후에 우편으로 발송했습니다. 비로소 다 되었네요. 제 생각에는 시작을 위한 모든 준비는 다 끝난 것 같습니다. 당신의 미술관에서 다음 주 중에 장비와 디자인을 시험해 보고 싶습니다. 저의 날짜와 시간은 변경이 가능하니 편하신 시간에 연락해 주시면 제 팀원들과 함께 가서 모든 것이 잘 작동되는지 확인하겠습니다.

어휘 outline 윤곽을 보여주다, 나타내다 contract 계약서 flexible 유연한, 융통성 있는 suitable 적합한, 적절한, 알맞은

77 What kind of business is Ms. Holton calling?
(A) An architectural firm
(B) An art gallery
(C) An event agency
(D) A real estate agency

Holton 씨는 어떤 종류의 회사에 전화하는가?
(A) 건축 회사
(B) 미술관
(C) 이벤트 대행사
(D) 부동산 중개 사무소

해설 〈기본 정보 파악 – 청자〉
화자가 전화하고 있는 회사를 묻고 있으므로 청자의 근무지를 찾아야 한다. 담화 초반에 Piccadilly 미술관에서 열리는 〈Discovering the Collection〉을 위한 기초 작업을 마쳤다고 연락하고 있으므로 (B)가 가장 적절한 답이다. 화자(Ms. Holton)의 근무지인 (C) An event agency와 혼동하지 말아야 한다.

78 What does the speaker mean when she says, "that'll be all"?
(A) She thinks the event will finish soon.
(B) She has completed preparations.
(C) She bought new equipment.
(D) She has found what she was looking for.

화자가 "다 되었네요"라고 말한 의미는 무엇인가?
(A) 여자는 행사가 곧 끝날 것이라고 생각한다.
(B) 여자는 준비를 완료했다.
(C) 여자가 새로운 장비를 샀다.
(D) 여자는 구하고 있던 것을 찾았다.

해설 〈구체적 정보 파악 – 화자 의도〉
문제에 언급된 문장의 앞뒤 문맥을 종합하여 화자의 의도를 파악해야 한다. 문제에 주어진 해당 표현 이후에 시작을 위한 모든 준비가 완료되었다고 언급하고 있으므로 정답은 (B)이다.

79 What does Ms. Holton say she will do next week?
(A) Sign a contract
(B) Contact a manager
(C) Visit a client
(D) Revise an estimate

Holton 씨는 다음 주에 무엇을 하겠다고 말하는가?
(A) 계약서에 서명하기
(B) 관리자에게 연락하기
(C) 고객 방문하기
(D) 견적서 수정하기

해설 〈구체적 정보 파악 – 특정 사항〉
화자가 문제의 키워드인 next week를 언급하는 부분에서 답을 찾아

험하고 싶다고 했으므로 정답은 (C)이다.

Questions 80-82 refer to the following news report. 영W

These are WTSZ evening updates. We have some good news for Wimbledon commuters. 80 The construction work on the Tower Bridge is nearly complete and all four lanes will be open starting tomorrow morning. Workers began resurfacing the bridge in June, and the project was expected to take seven weeks. 81 However, the heavy rainfalls the city experienced this summer slowed the pace of the work dramatically. Having only two lanes on the bridge open in each direction caused traffic congestion for miles during rush hour. The city has been under pressure to finish the work in time for the 82 Wimbledon Tennis Tournament, which begins in two weeks and is expected to bring thousands of sports fans to the city.

WTSZ 저녁 소식입니다. Wimbledon 통근자들에게 좋은 소식이 있습니다. Tower Bridge의 건설 공사가 거의 완료되어 내일 아침부터 4차선 모두 개통하게 됩니다. 작업자들은 6월에 다리 재포장 작업을 시작하였고 작업은 7주가 걸릴 것으로 예상했었습니다. 그러나 이번 여름에 겪었던 엄청난 폭우가 작업 속도를 급격히 지연시켰습니다. 다리의 양 방향으로 단 두 개의 차선만 이용하게 되면서, 출퇴근 시간 동안 수 마일에 걸쳐 교통 체증을 유발해 왔습니다. 시 당국은 수천 명의 스포츠 팬들이 방문할 것으로 예상되는 2주 후의 Wimbledon 테니스 경기를 위해 시간에 맞춰 공사를 완료해야 하는 압박감 속에 있었습니다.

어휘 commuter 통근자 construction 건설, 공사 lane 길, 도로 resurface (도로 등을) 재포장하다 heavy rainfall 폭우 dramatically 극적으로 traffic congestion 교통 혼잡, 교통 정체 under pressure ~하도록 강요당하는 insufficient 부족한 dispute 논쟁 inclement 궂은 on a regular basis 정기적으로

80 What is main topic of this report?
(A) The results of a sports match
(B) The completion of roadwork
(C) The expansion of a stadium
(D) The construction of a tennis court

보도의 주제는 무엇인가?
(A) 스포츠 경기의 결과
(B) 도로 공사의 완료
(C) 경기장의 확장
(D) 테니스 코트의 건설

해설 〈기본 정보 파악 – 주제〉
보도의 주제는 초반에 언급된다. 담화의 첫 부분에서 화자가 다리 건설 공사가 완료되었음을 알리고 있으므로 정답은 (B)이다.

81 According to the report, what caused the delay?
(A) Insufficient funding
(B) A legal dispute
(C) A supply shortage
(D) Inclement weather

보도에 따르면, 지연된 이유는 무엇인가?
(A) 자금 부족
(B) 법적 분쟁
(C) 공급 부족
(D) 궂은 날씨

해설 〈구체적 정보 파악 – 특정 사항〉
담화의 중반에 여름에 있었던 폭우 때문에 작업 속도가 급격히 느려져 공사가 지연되었음을 설명하고 있으므로 정답은 (D)이다.

패러프레이징 heavy rainfalls 폭우 → inclement weather 악천후

82 What does the speaker say about the Wimbledon Tennis Tournament?
(A) It will attract many people to the area.
(B) It will not start on schedule.
(C) It is causing some traffic detours.
(D) It is held on a regular basis.

화자는 Wimbledon 테니스 경기에 대해 무엇이라고 말하는가?
(A) 많은 사람들을 그 지역으로 유치할 것이다.
(B) 예정된 시간에 시작하지 못할 것이다.
(C) 교통 우회의 원인이 될 것이다.
(D) 정기적으로 열릴 것이다.

해설 〈구체적 정보 파악 – 언급〉
화자가 키워드인 Wimbledon Tennis Tournament를 언급할 때 집중해야 한다. 2주 후의 Wimbledon 테니스 경기에 수천 명의 스포츠 팬들이 방문할 것으로 예상된다고 보도하고 있으므로 정답은 (A)이다.

패러프레이징 bring thousands of sports fans 수천 명의 스포츠 팬을 데려 오다 → attract many people 많은 사람들을 유치하다

Questions 83-85 refer to the following telephone message. 호M

Hi, Emma. It's Jason. 84 I just wanted to make sure you haven't forgotten about your appointment with Oliver Smith on Friday morning. He just called me to say that he expects to be here sometime between ten and eleven, depending on when he finishes another sales call he's making. 83 He wanted me to mention that he has some samples from a new line that he's excited about showing you on Friday. By the way, I've really got to hand it to you. 85 The new store display you put together yesterday looks wonderful. I'm sure it's been attracting a lot of people into the shop.

안녕하세요, Emma, Jason입니다. Oliver Smith 씨와의 금요일 오전 약속을 잊지 않았는지 확인하고 싶어서요. 그가 방금 저에게 전화해서 다른 영업 상담이 언제 끝나는지에 따라 다르겠지만 금요일 10시에서 11시 사이에 도착할 것 같다고 알려주었습니다. 그가 당신에게 기대에 부풀어 금요일에 보여줄 새로운 라인의 샘플을 가지고 있다고 전해 달라고 했습니다. 그건 그렇고, 당신을 다시 보게 되었어요. 어제 당신이 만든 새로운 점포 디스플레이는 정말 훌륭해요. 디스플레이가 많은 사람들을 상점 안으로 들어오게 했다고 확신해요.

어휘 make sure 반드시 ~ 하다, 확실하게 하다 expect 예상하다, 기대하다 depend on ~에 달려 있다 have got to hand it to ~ ~를 칭찬할 만하다 put together 조립하다, 만들다

83 What will the listener most likely do on Friday morning?
(A) View product samples
(B) Reserve a place
(C) Make a phone call
(D) Create a window display

청자는 금요일 아침에 무엇을 할 것인가?
(A) 제품 샘플을 본다.
(B) 장소를 예약한다.
(C) 전화를 한다.
(D) 쇼윈도 디스플레이를 만든다.

해설 〈구체적 정보 파악 – 특정 사항〉
Friday morning을 키워드로 잡고 앞뒤에 집중한다. 화자는 초반에 Oliver Smith 씨와의 금요일 오전 약속을 상기시켜 주며 중반에 그가 보여줄 샘플에 대해 언급하고 있으므로 정답은 (A)이다.

84 Why is the speaker calling?
(A) To report an error
(B) To reschedule an appointment
(C) To give a reminder
(D) To make a sale

화자가 전화한 이유는 무엇인가?
(A) 오류를 알리기 위해
(B) 약속 일정을 재조정하기 위해

(C) 상기시켜 주기 위해
(D) 판매하기 위해

해설 〈기본 정보 파악 – 주제〉
주제에 대한 단서는 초반에 언급된다. 화자가 첫 부분에서 Oliver Smith 씨와의 금요일 오전 약속을 상기시켜 주고 있으므로 정답은 (C)이다. 주제 문제가 두 번째 문제로 출제되었으나 담화의 초반에 언급된다는 것을 미리 예측하고 들어야 한다.

85 What does the speaker mean when he says, "I've really got to hand it to you"?
(A) He wants to give an item to the listener.
(B) He needs to rearrange the window display.
(C) He wants to offer the listener help.
(D) He thinks the listener deserves praise.

남자가 "당신을 다시 보게 되었어요."라고 말한 의미는 무엇인가?
(A) 남자는 청자에게 물건을 주려고 한다.
(B) 남자는 쇼윈도 디스플레이를 재배치하고자 한다.
(C) 남자는 청자의 도움을 주길 원한다.
(D) 남자는 청자가 칭찬받을 만하다고 생각한다.

해설 〈구체적 정보 파악 – 화자 의도〉
언급된 문장의 주변 문맥을 통해 정답을 유추해야 한다. 언급된 문장 직후에 청자가 한 상점 디스플레이를 칭찬하고 있으므로 정답은 (D)이다.

Questions 86-88 refer to the following radio broadcast. (영M)

Welcome back to Developing Yourself. I'm Jack Dawson. (86) You are listening to the program for people who are eager to get ahead in the corporate world. (87) Today's guest is Sarah Parker, the former president of Metropolitan University's School of Business. Ms. Parker will tell us how furthering your education can improve your career. She'll look through some of the options that are available, such as attending short-term classes, taking online courses at a local community college, or even taking a break from work for a year or two to get an advanced degree. (88) At the end of the show, we'll open the phone lines so you can ask Ms. Parker questions about education and training.

Developing Yourself에 다시 오신 것을 환영합니다. 저는 Jack Dawson입니다. 지금 여러분께서는 기업 사회에서 앞서 나가고 싶은 열정을 가진 사람들을 위한 프로그램을 듣고 계십니다. 오늘의 초대 손님은 Metropolitan 대학의 경영대 전임 총장이신 Sarah Parker 씨입니다. Parker 씨는 당신의 배움이 당신의 경력을 어떻게 더 발전시킬 수 있는지 이야기해 주실 것입니다. 단기 수업에서부터 지역 전문대학의 온라인 강좌를 듣는 것, 또는 더 높은 수준의 학위를 받기 위해 1년이나 2년 정도 휴직하는 것까지 가능한 옵션들을 모두 살펴드릴 예정입니다. 방송의 마지막에는, Parker 씨에게 교육과 훈련에 대해 질문을 하실 수 있도록 전화 연결을 하도록 하겠습니다.

어휘 eager 열렬한, 간절히 바라는 former 예전의, 과거의 further 발전시키다 improve 개선되다, 향상시키다 available 구할 수 있는, 시간이 있는, 여유가 있는 short-term 단기의, 단기적인 college 대학, 전문대학 advanced degree (석사/박사) 고급 학위 questionnaire 설문지

86 What type of information does Developing Yourself probably focus on?
(A) Developing new products
(B) Fashion trends
(C) Technological innovations
(D) Career advice

Developing Yourself는 어떤 종류의 정보에 초점을 맞추고 있는가?
(A) 새로운 제품 개발
(B) 패션 트렌드
(C) 기술 혁신
(D) 경력 조언

해설 〈구체적 정보 파악 – 특정 사항〉
담화 첫 부분에 문제의 키워드인 Developing Yourself가 언급되는데 이 부분에서 해당 문구가 프로그램명임을 알 수 있다. 이 라디오 방송은 기업 사회에서 앞서 나가고 싶은 열정을 가진 사람들을 위한 프로그램이라고 말하며 경력 향상에 대해 언급하고 있으므로 (D)가 가장 적절한 답이다.

87 According to the broadcast, what has Sarah Parker done?
(A) She published a book.
(B) She ran a school.
(C) She took an online course.
(D) She owned a company.

방송에 따르면, Sarah Parker는 무엇을 했는가?
(A) 책을 출판했다.
(B) 학교를 운영했다.
(C) 온라인 강좌를 들었다.
(D) 회사를 소유했다.

해설 〈구체적 정보 파악 – 특정 사항〉
Sarah Parker를 키워드로 잡고 앞뒤를 잘 들어야 한다. 화자는 Sarah Parker가 오늘의 초대 손님이라고 말하며 Metropolitan 대학의 경영대 전임 총장이라고 소개하고 있으므로 정답은 (B)이다.

88 What will Ms. Parker do at the end of the show?
(A) Take calls from listeners
(B) Introduce another guest
(C) Attend the educational training
(D) Make a questionnaire

Parker 씨는 방송의 마지막에 무엇을 할 것인가?
(A) 청자들로부터 전화를 받는다.
(B) 다른 게스트를 소개한다.
(C) 교육 훈련에 참가한다.
(D) 설문지를 만든다.

해설 〈구체적 정보 파악 – 특정 사항〉
문제의 키워드인 end of the show를 언급한 후 Parker 씨에게 질문할 수 있도록 전화 연결을 할 것이라고 말하므로 정답은 (A)이다.

패러프레이징 open the phone lines (청자들과) 전화를 연결한다 → take calls from listeners 청자들의 전화를 받는다

Questions 89-91 refer to the following talk. (영W)

(89) Let me take this opportunity to introduce you all to Brian Price. He's replacing Glen Keys as a director of research and development department. Mr. Price comes to us from Warwick University, where he's been teaching business management for last fifteen years. He has worked in the industry far longer than any of us here in our company and won countless awards. As you can imagine, (90) many companies want to work with him. So, we're lucky! Before I ask him to talk about himself and his vision for us, (91) I'd like you to stand up one by one and tell Mr. Price your name and the position in the company.

이 자리를 빌려 여러분 모두를 Brian Price에게 소개합니다. 그는 연구 개발 부서의 이사인 Glen Key를 대신하게 될 것입니다. Price 씨는 지난 15년 동안 Warwick 대학에서 기업 경영 관리를 가르친 후 여기에 왔습니다. 그는 우리 회사의 어느 누구보다도 더 오래 이 분야에서 일했고, 수많은 상을 받았습니다. 여러분이 상상할 수 있는 것처럼, 많은 회사가 그와 함께 일하기를 원했습니다. 우리가 운이 좋았지요! 본인 소개와 그의 미래상에 대한 설명을 요청드리기 전에, 여러분이 차례로 일어서서 Price 씨에게 여러분의 이름과 회사에서 맡고 있는 직책을 말씀 드렸으면 좋겠습니다.

어휘 opportunity 기회 research and development 연구 개발 industry 산업, 공업 countless 무수한, 셀 수 없이 많은 personnel 직원

89 What is the purpose of the talk?
(A) To announce a new policy
(B) To introduce a new employee
(C) To plan a company event
(D) To inform about a business hour

이 담화의 목적은 무엇인가?
(A) 새로운 정책을 알리기 위해
(B) 새로운 직원을 소개하기 위해
(C) 회사 행사를 계획하기 위해
(D) 근무 시간을 알리기 위해

해설 〈기본 정보 파악 – 주제〉
담화의 첫 문장에서 특정인을 소개하고 있으므로 (B)가 가장 적절한 답이다.

90 What does the speaker mean when she says, "So, we're lucky"?
(A) The company has received the media attention.

(B) Brian Price has accepted the job offer.
(C) Glen Keys will join the company.
(D) The company has been highly ranked in the industry.

화자가 "우리는 운이 좋다"라고 말한 의미는 무엇인가?
(A) 회사가 미디어의 관심을 받았다.
(B) Brian Price 씨가 입사 제의를 받아들였다.
(C) Glen Keys 씨가 회사에 들어올 것이다.
(D) 회사가 업계 최고로 선정되었다.

해설 〈구체적 정보 파악 – 화자 의도〉
문제에 언급된 문장의 앞뒤 문맥을 종합하여 화자의 의도를 파악해야 한다. 화자가 해당 표현 바로 앞에서 많은 회사에서 탐내는 인재가 이 회사에 오게 된 것을 행운이라고 설명하고 있으므로 정답은 (B)이다.

91 What will most likely happen next?
(A) The employees will introduce themselves.
(B) There will be a discussion session.
(C) The staff will submit the forms.
(D) Mr. Price will speak about the company's future.

다음에 무슨 일이 일어날 것인가?
(A) 직원들이 자신들을 소개할 것이다.
(B) 토론회가 열릴 것이다.
(C) 직원들이 양식을 제출할 것이다.
(D) Price 씨가 회사의 미래에 대해 이야기할 것이다.

해설 〈구체적 정보 파악 – 특정 사항〉
다음에 일어날 일은 담화의 마지막에 언급된다. 담화의 끝에서 화자가 청자들에게 차례로 일어서서 소개하라고 말하고 있으므로 정답은 (A)이다.

Questions 92-94 refer to the following telephone message. 미M

Hi, Ivan. It's Jonathan. I got your message. 92 Thanks for inviting me to dinner, but I don't think I can make it. My laptop froze just as I was finishing my report this morning. 93 Since only half of the data was recovered, a lot has to be done over and over again. That's not the end because 94 the department manager called today asking for some last-minute changes to the sales figure. It is a terrible day. All this is gonna keep me up at night, so going out for dinner is out of the question. Let's try to get together soon, though. Bye!

안녕하세요, Ivan. Jonathan입니다. 당신의 메시지를 받았습니다. 저를 저녁식사에 초대해 주셔서 감사하지만, 못 갈 것 같습니다. 오늘 아침에 막 보고서를 끝내려던 참에 제 노트북이 멈춰버렸어요. 겨우 절반의 데이터만 복구했기 때문에, 많은 일을 반복해서 다시 해야만 합니다. 그게 다가 아니랍니다. 부서장이 오늘 전화를 해서 판매 수치에 대한 막바지 변경을 요청했어요. 끔찍한 날이네요. 이 모든 것이 저를 밤새도록 깨어 있게 할 거예요. 그래서 저녁 먹으러 나가는 건 불가능합니다. 그래도 조만간 다시 만나요. 안녕히 계세요.

어휘 freeze (시스템 고장으로 화면이) 동결되다, 멈추다 last-minute 막바지의, 마지막 순간의 terrible 심한, 끔찍한 keep somebody up ~를 잠자리에 들지 못하게 하다 out of the question 불가능한 (의논해 봐야 소용없는)

92 Why is the speaker calling?
(A) To congratulate on the success
(B) To complete the sales report
(C) To decline an invitation
(D) To confirm a meeting agenda

화자는 왜 전화하는가?
(A) 성공을 축하하기 위해
(B) 영업 보고서를 완성하기 위해
(C) 초대를 거절하기 위해서
(D) 회의 안건을 확인하기 위해서

해설 〈기본 정보 파악 – 주제〉
전화 메시지의 주제를 묻는 질문이므로 담화 첫 문장에 집중한다. 화자가 첫 문장에서 초대에 감사하지만 갈 수 없다고 말하고 있으므로 정답은 (C)이다.

93 What does the speaker mean when he says, "A lot has to be done over and over again"?
(A) He bought several computers.
(B) He lost some of his work.
(C) He attended a variety of workshops.
(D) He needed to call a manager repeatedly.

화자가 "많은 일을 다시 반복해서 해야만 합니다"라고 말하는 것은 무슨 의미인가?
(A) 그는 여러 대의 컴퓨터 샀다.
(B) 그는 그의 작업의 일부를 잃었다.
(C) 그는 다양한 워크숍에 참가했었다.
(D) 그는 매니저에게 여러 번 전화해야만 했다.

해설 〈구체적 정보 파악 – 화자 의도〉
언급된 문장의 주변 문맥을 통해 정답을 유추해야 한다. 언급된 문장 바로 전에 남자의 노트북이 멈추었고, 잃어버린 데이터의 절반만 복구했다고 말하고 있으므로 정답은 (B)이다.

94 According to the speaker, what did a department manager ask for?
(A) A deadline extension
(B) A personal visit
(C) Modification of information
(D) Completion of a questionnaire

화자에 따르면, 부서장은 무엇을 요청했는가?
(A) 마감일 연장
(B) 직접 방문
(C) 작업의 수정
(D) 설문지 완성

해설 〈구체적 정보 파악 –특정 사항〉
department manager를 키워드로 잡고 앞뒤를 들어야 한다. 담화의 마지막에 부서장이 전화를 해서 판매 수치에 대한 막바지 변경을 요청했다고 말하므로 이를 바꾸어 표현한 (C)가 가장 적절한 답이다.

패러프레이징 changes to the sales figure 판매 수치 변경
→ Modification of information 작업 수정

Questions 95-97 refer to the following talk and floor plan. 호M

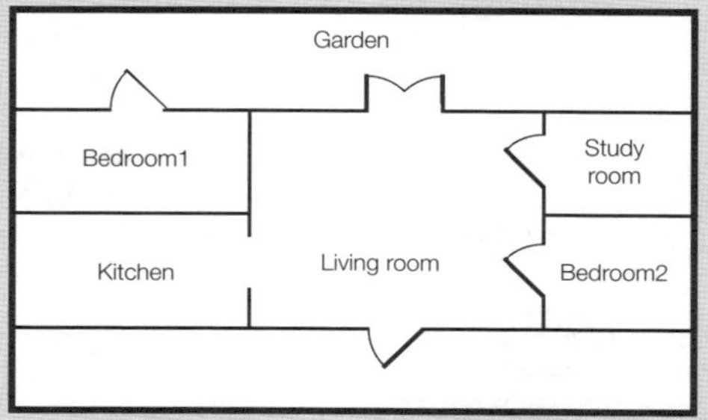

Before we start, I want to pass on to you a message from our customer Maggie Clarkson. Actually, 95 she left some instructions for where to put some of the things we're moving to her new home. 96 She said the green boxes should be placed in the bedroom in the back of the house, the one with access to the garden. And the rear door to the home connects directly with the living room. Plus, it's a lot wider than the front entrance, so it'll be easier if we bring the living room furniture in through the back. 97 Ms. Clarkson said she'd leave the gate to the fence unlocked for us.

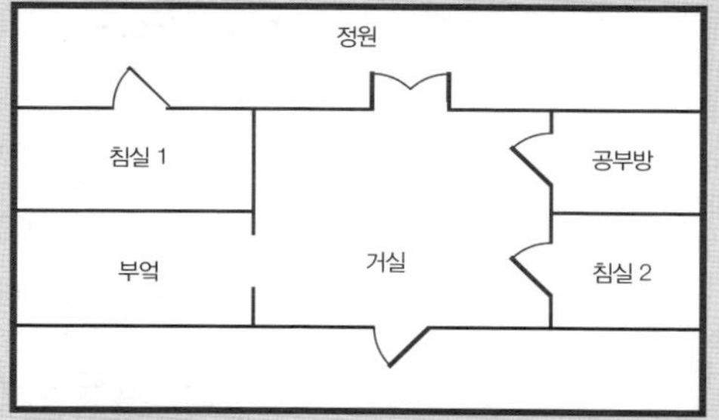

시작하기 전에, Maggie Clarkson 고객이 보낸 메시지를 전해 드리겠습니다. 사실 새 집으로 이사하면서 물건들을 어디에 놓을지에 대해 그녀는 몇 가지 지침을 남겼습니다. 녹색 상자들은 정원으로 들어갈 수 있는 집 뒤쪽 침실에 넣어 달라고 했어요. 그리고 집의 뒷문이 거실과 바로 연결됩니다. 게다가 앞쪽 정문보다 더 넓어서 뒤로 거실 가구를 들여오는 것이 더 쉬울 것입니다. Clarkson 씨가 우리를 위해 울타리 문을 열어 놓겠다고 했습니다.

어휘 instruction 설명, 지시 access 입장, 접근, 접속하다 rear 뒤쪽의, 뒤쪽 directly 곧장, 똑바로

95 What type of business do the listeners probably work for?
(A) A furniture dealer
(B) An interior design agency
(C) A cleaning service
(D) A moving company
청자들이 근무하는 회사는 어떤 종류인가?
(A) 가구 회사
(B) 인테리어 디자인 회사
(C) 청소 서비스
(D) 이삿짐 회사

해설 〈기본 정보 파악 – 장소〉
청자들의 근무지에 대한 단서는 담화의 앞부분에 언급되는 경우가 많다. 화자가 담화 초반에 고객이 이사하면서 물건들을 어디에 놓을지에 대한 지침을 남겼다고 설명하고 있으므로 정답은 (D)이다.

96 Look at the graphic. Where should the green boxes be placed?
(A) Bedroom 1
(B) Bedroom 2
(C) The study room
(D) The living room
시각 자료를 보시오. 녹색 박스는 어디에 놓아야 하는가?
(A) 침실1
(B) 침실2
(C) 서재
(D) 거실

해설 〈구체적 정보 파악 – 시각 자료 연계〉
대화를 듣기 전에 문제와 시각 자료를 보고 단서를 예측할 수 있어야 하는데, 배치 관련 문제이므로 위치 묘사를 통해 단서가 제시될 가능성이 높다. green boxes를 키워드로 잡고 평면도에 제시된 위치를 설명하는 부분에 집중해야 한다. 녹색 상자들은 정원에서 들어갈 수 있는 집 뒤쪽 침실에 넣어달라는 지시가 있었으므로 정원에서 가까운 침실인 (A)가 정답이다.

97 What does the speaker say Ms. Clarkson will do?
(A) Leave the entrance open
(B) Unpack some boxes
(C) Clean up the new home
(D) Lock up some valuable items
화자는 Clarkson 씨가 무엇을 할 것이라고 말하는가?
(A) 입구를 열어 둔다.
(B) 상자들을 푼다.
(B) 새 집을 청소한다.
(D) 귀중품들을 안전한 곳에 넣어 둔다.

해설 〈구체적 정보 파악 – 미래〉
Ms. Clarkson을 키워드로 잡고 마지막 부분에 집중한다. 화자가 마지막 문장에서 Clarkson 씨가 청자들을 위해 울타리 문을 열어 놓겠다고 말한 것을 전하고 있으므로 정답은 (A)이다.

Questions 98-100 refer to the following excerpt from a meeting and map. 영M

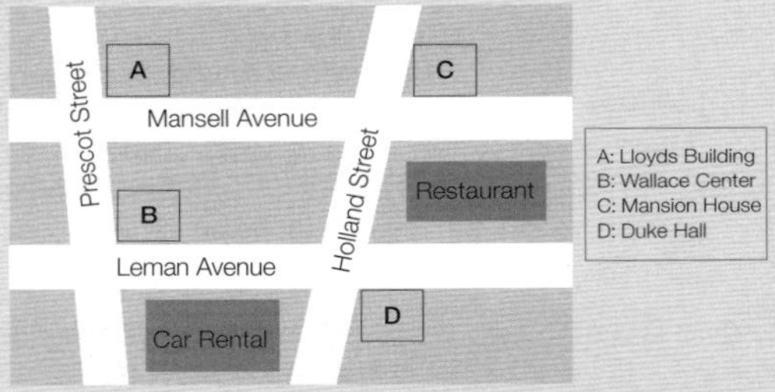

Unlike in previous years, 98 we're encouraging all of you to bring along a family member to this year's company banquet. This means we'll need a larger venue to accommodate more than 200 guests. Have a look at this map, which shows four potential locations. I'd like to get your input before making a final decision. Personally, 99 I think this one on the corner of Leman Avenue and Prescott Street is the best option. It's close to our office so we won't need to pay for parking and it's the cheapest one of the four, too. We don't have any time to discuss this now, so if you have any thoughts, 100 send me a text later this afternoon.

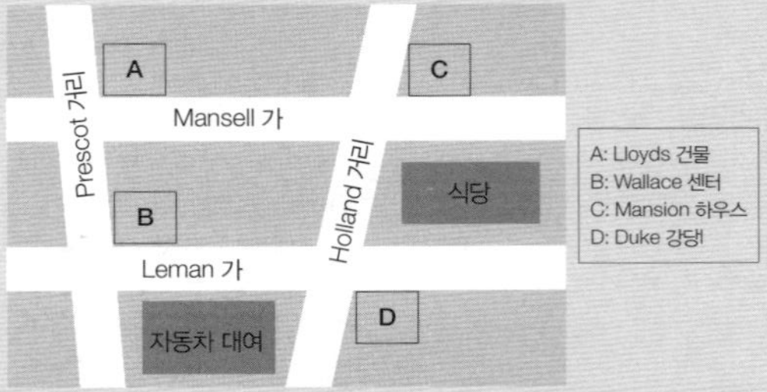

예년과 다르게, 올해 회사 연회에는 가족을 모두 데려오길 장려하고 있습니다. 이것은 우리가 200명 이상의 손님을 수용할 수 있는 큰 장소가 필요하다는 의미이기도 합니다. 이 지도를 보시면, 네 곳의 가능한 장소가 있습니다. 최종 결정을 하기 전에 여러분의 의견을 받고 싶습니다. 개인적으로는 Leman 가와 Prescott 거리 코너에 있는 곳이 가장 좋은 것 같습니다. 우리 사무실에서 가깝기 때문에 주차 비용도 필요없고 네 곳 중에 가장 저렴하기도 합니다. 지금은 토론할 시간이 없으니 만약 의견이 있으시면 오늘 오후에 저에게 문자를 보내 주세요.

어휘 previous 이전의 encourage 격려하다, 권장하다, 장려하다 banquet 연회, 만찬 venue 장소 accommodate 공간을 제공하다, 수용하다 potential 가능성 있는, 잠재적인 input 조언 gathering 모임 extension phone 내선 전화

98 What kind of event is going to be held?
(A) A product launch
(B) A business gathering
(C) A sales workshop
(D) A special dinner
어떤 종류의 행사가 열릴 것인가?
(A) 제품 출시
(B) 사업 모임
(C) 영업 워크숍
(D) 특별 정찬

해설 〈구체적 정보 파악 – 특정 사항〉
화자가 담화 초반에 회사 연회에 가족들을 데려 오라고 장려하고 있으므로 (D)가 가장 알맞은 답이다.

99 Look at the graphic. Which venue does the speaker recommend?
(A) Lloyds Building
(B) Wallace Center
(C) Mansion House
(D) Duke Hall
시각 자료를 보시오. 화자는 어떤 장소를 추천하는가?
(A) Lloyds 건물
(B) Wallace 센터
(C) Mansion 하우스
(D) Duke 강당

해설 〈구체적 정보 파악 – 시각 자료 연계〉
지도의 건물 이름들이 제시되어 있으므로 담화에서는 도로명이 단서로 언급될 것을 예측하고 들어야 한다. 화자는 Leman 가와 Prescott 거리 코너에 있는 곳을 추천하고 있는데 그 건물은 Wallace Center이므로 정답은 (B)이다.

100 How can the listeners contact the speaker?
(A) By text message
(B) By electronic mail
(C) By fax
(D) By extension phone
청자들은 화자에게 어떻게 연락해야 하는가?
(A) 문자 메시지로
(B) 전자 우편으로
(C) 팩스로
(D) 내선 전화로

해설 〈구체적 정보 파악 – 특정 사항〉
담화의 마지막 부분에서 의견이 있으면 화자에게 문자를 보내라고 제안하고 있으므로 정답은 (A)이다.

101 해석 우리 새 치과 사무실은 Mason 거리 새 빌딩의 3층에 입주할 예정이다.

해설 빈칸 뒤의 명사 office에 적절한 한정사가 없으므로 소유격 (B) Our가 정답이다.

어휘 occupy 차지하다

102 해석 자전거를 갖고 있는 버스 승객들은 자전거를 적절하게 보관하는 데 책임이 있다.

해설 passenger가 자전거를 소유하고 있는 것이므로 전치사 (A) with가 정답이다.

어휘 be responsible for ~에 대해 책임지다 secure 보관하다 appropriately 적절히

103 해석 사전 보증금은 임대 차량이 손상 없이 반납된다면 모두 다 환불 가능하다.

해설 be동사와 형용사 사이이므로 빈칸은 부사 자리이다. 따라서 (B) fully가 정답이다.

어휘 advance deposit 사전 보증금 refundable 환불 가능한 as long as (접속사) ~하는 한 without damage 손상 없이 fully 모두, 완전히

104 해석 아무도 Lisa Stanley보다 New Skin의 새로운 모발 관리 제품들을 홍보하기 위해 더 열심히 일한 사람은 없다.

해설 빈칸은 주어 자리이고 문맥상 동사 has worked와 어울려야 하므로 (C) Nobody가 정답이다.

어휘 hair treatment 모발 관리

105 해석 공사 프로젝트 비용이 몇몇 지역 기업가들의 후한 지원으로 충당되었다.

해설 cover the cost는 '비용을 충당하다'라는 뜻으로 사용되므로 수동형 동사 was covered의 주어로 cost가 적절하다. 따라서 (D)가 정답이다.

어휘 generous 넉넉한, 후한 entrepreneur 기업가 currency 통화

106 해석 서류를 수정할 때 Prichard 씨의 이름 철자를 다시 확인하는 것을 잊지 마세요.

해설 부사절 접속사 when 이하에는 〈주어+동사〉 구문 또는 분사구문이 가능한데, 빈칸 뒤에는 주어가 없으므로 목적어 the document를 취할 수 있는 능동의 현재분사인 (A) revising이 정답이다.

어휘 double-check 다시 확인하다 revise 수정하다

107 해석 인턴을 모집하는 것은 Cypher 은행의 시작(말단) 직원 자리를 나중에 채울 수 있는 합리적인 해결책이다.

해설 명사 solution을 수식하는 형용사 자리이므로 문맥상 '합리적인'을 의미하는 (D) sensible이 정답이다.

어휘 recruit 모집하다 eventually 마지막에 talented 재능 있는 various 다양한 willing 꺼리지 않는 sensible 합리적인

108 해석 개발업자들이 고대 장인들의 작품을 보존할 것인지에 대해 문의하기 위해 대표들이 시장을 방문했다.

해설 ask의 목적절이므로 명사절 접속사 (D) whether가 정답이다. although, since는 부사절 접속사이다

어휘 delegate 대표 preserve 보존하다 ancient 고대의 artisan 장인

109 해석 직원들은 여행 신청서를 이제 종이 서류 형태로 제출하는 대신 전자상으로 제출한다.

해설 빈칸 이하가 동명사구이므로 전치사가 필요하고 paper form과 electronically를 대조하고 있으므로 (A) instead of가 정답이다.

어휘 electronically 컴퓨터로 submit 제출하다 instead of ~대신에 through ~을 통해서

110 해석 임대 계약을 갱신하는 데 관심이 있는 세입자들은 Lakeview 아파트 웹 사이트에 정리되어 있는 절차를 따라야만 한다.

해설 빈칸은 be동사의 보어 자리로서 과거분사 (C) interested가 정답이다.

어휘 tenant 세입자 renew 갱신하다 lease 임대 계약 follow the process 절차를 따르다 outline 개요를 정리하다 be interested in ~에 관심이 있다 interesting 흥미진진한

111 해석 Manheim Film Production의 가장 새로운 직원인 Juan Reyes는 이전에 런던에서 8년 동안 일했다.

해설 과거 시제 동사 worked를 수식하는 부사로 문맥상 (D) previously가 정답이다.

어휘 consequently 결과적으로 previously 이전에

112 해석 Jenkins 씨가 주택 시장에 대한 논문을 썼기 때문에 그녀는 이윤을 낼 수 있는 부동산 투자 방법을 알고 있었다.

해설 빈칸은 부사절 접속사 자리로 선택지 중에 문맥상 이유를 나타내는 (D) Because가 정답이다.

어휘 thesis 논문 housing 주택 profitable 이익을 내는 property 부동산, 재산 investment 투자 rather (부사) 다소

113 해석 이사회 회의에서 Carmichael 아트센터가 폐쇄될 수 있는 약간의 가능성이 있다는 것이 언급되었다.

해설 빈칸은 관사 a 뒤의 자리로 형용사 slight의 수식을 받는 단수 명사 자리이다. 따라서 (B)가 정답이다.

어휘 slight 약간의

114 해석 명망 있는 Evangeline 상을 받자마자 Mehta 씨는 그녀의 오랜 동료들에게 감사를 나타냈다.

해설 upon -ing는 '~하자마자'의 뜻으로 사용될 수 있으므로 (D)가 정답이다.

어휘 prestigious 명망 있는 make a point of 반드시 ~하다 colleague 동료 unlike ~와 달리

115 해석 Wellington 호텔 요금이 매우 높았으므로 Logisoft 주식회사는 올해 워크숍을 다른 곳에서 개최할 것이다.

해설 seldom은 빈도부사로 동사 앞에 사용하여야 하고, recently는 과거 시제와 사용하여야 하며 somewhat은 형용사 수식 부사이므로 (D) elsewhere가 정답이다.

어휘 rates 요금 seldom (부정빈도부사) 거의 ~하지 않다 somewhat (부사) 다소 elsewhere 다른 곳에서

116 해석 Di Scala 박사는 자료 분석을 사용하면 중요한 쇼핑 경향이 예상 가능하다고 지적했다.

해설 become은 2형식 동사이므로 주어 trends를 설명하는 주격 보어로서 형용사형 (C) predictable이 정답이다.

어휘 indicate ~을 나타내다. data analysis 자료 분석 predict 예상하다 prediction 예상 predictable 예상할 수 있는 predictably 예상대로

117 해석 도로 작업이 다음 주에 시작되면 Braxton Drive로 가는 길은 거리의 한 쪽으로 제한된다.

해설 빈칸은 문장의 주어 자리이므로 명사형 (A)가 정답이다. access는 불가산명사이므로 (B) Accesses는 사용할 수 없다.

어휘 be limited to ~에 한정되다 road work 도로 작업 access 접속 accessible 접근 가능한

118 해석 Malkin 대학에서 가르치는 Hillsman 교수의 열정은 65세의 나이에도 여전히 강하다.

해설 빈칸 자리는 for teaching과 동사구인 remain strong과 어울리는 주어 자리이므로 (A) enthusiasm이 정답이다.

어휘 enthusiasm 열정 assortment 모음, 종합 likeness 유사성 inclusion 포함

119 해석 Jessie 전자에서 할인을 받기 위해서는 메일에 보내졌던 쿠폰을 제출해야만 한다.

해설 (A) has sent와 (B) have to send는 본동사이므로 접속사 없이 사용할 수 없고 (D) for sending은 빈칸 뒤에 목적어가 없으므로 사용할 수 없다. 관계대명사 that을 포함하고 수동태 동사형인 (C)가 정답이다.

어휘 be eligible for ~할 자격이 있다 submit 제출하다

120 해석 우기로 인해 Faye 자전거 대여점은 이번 달 고객이 거의 없을 것 같다.

해설 선택지에 있는 형용사 중에 customers 복수형 앞에 사용 가능한 수량형용사 (C) fewer가 정답이다. every는 단수 명사와 함께 사용한다.

어휘 rainy season 우기 most likely ~인 것 같은

121 해석 모든 인터뷰 과정이 끝나자마자 광고 담당자 자리에 적합한 세 명의 최종 후보에게 연락이 갈 것이다.

해설 빈칸은 부사절 접속사 자리이고 선택지 접속사 중 인터뷰 과정이 끝나자마자 연락이 갈 것이라는 (B) As soon as가 문맥상 가장 적합하다.

어휘 process 절차 complete 완료하다 contact 연락하다 compared to ~와 비교하여 as soon as ~하자마자 so that ~하기 위하여

122 해석 만약 할당된 발언 시간이 맞지 않으면 Everett 씨에게 알려 주세요. 그러면 그녀가 발표 일정을 재조정할 수 있습니다.

해설 빈칸부터 for you까지가 부사절이며, 부사절 안에 부정어 not이 조동사 없이 사용되었으므로 조동사와 접속사가 필요하다. 가정법에서 접속사 if가 생략되는 경우 조동사 should가 문두로 도치될 수 있으므로 (D)가 정답이다.

어휘 assigned 할당된 rearrange 다시 조정하다 as well as ~뿐만 아니라

123 해석 고용 위원회가 다음 월요일에 Dwan Willis에게 고용 제안을 할 것이다.

해설 동사구 자리로서 extend an offer(제안하다)가 가장 적절하다. 따라서 (A)가 정답이다.

어휘 hiring committee 고용 위원회 assign 할당하다 displace 대신하다, 대체하다

124 해석 만약 당신이 신분증을 분실하면 보안 담당 매니저가 무효화시킨 후 다른 것을 발급할 것입니다.

해설 동사 issue의 목적어 자리로 또 다른 신분증을 의미하는 것이므로 부정대명사 (D) another가 정답이다. other는 형용사이다.

어휘 identification card 신분증 security 보안 deactivate 무효화하다 issue 발급하다 one another 서로

125 해석 에너지 사용을 가장 잘 줄이는 방법을 결정하기 위해서 도시 검사관들이 다음 주에 5층에 있는 모든 사무실을 평가할 것이다.

해설 동사 determine 앞에 빈칸이 있으므로 선택지 중에 동사 앞에 사용할 수 있는 (B) in order to가 정답이다.

어휘 inspector 검사관 evaluate 평가하다 determine 결정하다 reduce 줄이다 energy usage 에너지 사용 in order to ~하기 위해서 after all 결국에는 given that ~를 고려하면

126 해석 감사 위원회 회원을 뽑기 위해서 Blake Techline 주식회사는 도전할 준비가 되어 있는 직원들을 찾고 있다.

해설 동사 자리가 비어 있고 목적어 employees가 있으므로 동사 능동형인 is seeking이 정답이다.

어휘 select 뽑다 audit committee 감사 위원회 be ready for 준비하다 challenge 도전 seek 구하다

127 해석 Perone 씨는 자금 배분 과정을 가능한 한 투명하게 유지하기 위하여 최근 변화에 대한 설명을 제공하였다.

해설 동사 keep의 목적어인 funding arrangement process를 설명하는 목적격 보어로서의 형용사가 필요하므로 절차를 수식할 수 있는 (C) transparent가 정답이다.

어휘 explanation 설명 funding arrangement 자금 배치, 분배 process 과정, 절차 forceful 단호한, 강력한 transparent 투명한 remarkable 놀랄 만한, 주목할 만한

128 해석 Glaxton-Jenner 회사의 작업장 안전은 절대 타협될 수 없는 것이다.

해설 명사 something과 동사 will을 연결할 수 있는 주격 관계대명사 (B) that이 정답이다. where, when은 관계부사, then은 일반 부사이다.

어휘 safety 안정성 compromise 절충하다, 협상하다

129 해석 일반적으로 관련 서류는 우리 법무 부서의 비서에 의해 변호사 사무실로 배달된다.

해설 동사 delivered를 수식하는 적절한 부사형을 찾는 문제로 (D) typically가 문맥에 가장 적절하다.

어휘 relevant 관련된 lawyer 변호사 legal 법률의 timely 시기적절한 identifiably 알아 볼 수 있게 highly 매우 typically 보통, 일반적으로

130 해석 역사적인 Karen Marx 건물이 여전히 건축물로서 튼튼한지 확인하기 위해 기술자들이 다음 주에 검사할 것이다.

해설 빈칸 뒤는 완전한 절인 것을 알 수 있으므로 빈칸 뒤에 명사절 접속사 that이 생략된 것을 알 수 있다. 선택지 동사 중 접속사 that을 생략할 수 있는 동사는 (A) ensure가 해당된다.

어휘 inspect 검사하다 historic 역사적인 architecturally 건축물로서 sound 튼튼한 ensure ~을 분명히 하다 measure 측정하다 modify 수정하다

PART 6

P113

[131-134]

발신: Jin Li Zhang
수신: 모든 직원
날짜: 4월 10일
주제: Natalie Albright

몇몇 여러분이 아시다시피 수석 조경가인 Natalie Albright가 곧 우리 회사를 떠납니다.

그녀는 주거 건설 업계의 일자리를 (131) 받아들였습니다. Natalie는 오랫동안 그 분야에 관심을 가져 왔습니다. (132) 그녀의 새로운 일은 건설 엔지니어가 되려는 그녀의 최종 목적과 조금 더 맞습니다. 그렇지만, 우리는 그녀를 보내는 것이 (133) 몹시 아쉽습니다.

Natalie가 우리와 함께 하는 마지막 날은 4월 25일 금요일입니다. 그날 오후 2시 30분에 회사 카페테리아에서 우리와 함께한 10년 동안을 (134) 감사하는 송별회를 갖습니다. 여러분 모두를 만날 것을 기대합니다.

Marry Rogers
시설 관리 책임자

어휘 landscaper 조경가 leave the company 회사를 그만두다 residential 주거지의 be in line of ~와 어울리다, 맞다 ultimate 궁극의, 최종의 farewell gathering 송별회

131 해설 동사 어휘 문제로서 목적어에 a position이 있고 문맥상 Natalie가 일자리를 받아들였다는 내용이므로 (C)가 정답이다.

어휘 advertise 홍보하다 support 지지하다 accept 받아들이다 indicate 나타내다

132 **(A) 그녀의 새로운 일은 건설 엔지니어가 되려는 그녀의 최종 목적과 조금 더 맞습니다.**
(B) 다음 월요일부터 매니저 회의가 오전 10시에서 오후 2시로 옮겨졌습니다.
(C) 인사부 이사가 회사가 제공하는 건강 보험을 설명할 것입니다.
(D) 직원들은 매일 최소한 오전 9시 5분 전에 출근하는 것이 필요합니다.

해설 앞 문장에서 Natalie가 새로운 직장으로 간다는 내용이 나오므로 새로운 일에 대해 부연 설명하는 (A)가 정답이다.

어휘 at least 적어도

133 해설 sorry를 수식하는 부사 자리이므로 (A)가 정답이다. too는 부정적인 내용에 적합하고 such는 형용사이므로 부적절하다.

134 해설 문장에 접속사가 없으므로 빈칸 앞 동사 have 다음에 (A), (B), (C)의 동사 형태는 부적절하며 준동사인 (D)가 정답이다.

[135-138]

(135) 정기적으로 일정이 잡혀 있는 4개의 도보 투어 중의 하나를 통해서 Bronxville 마을을 돌아보세요. Bronxville 관광국이 후원하는 각각의 투어는 박학다식한 가이드에 (136) 의해 이끌어지고 독특한 마을 지역을 둘러보는 것을 포함하고 있습니다.

가장 인기 있는 것은 도시의 극장 (137) 구역인 Cyrus 광장입니다.

3개의 극장과 2개의 음악 공연관뿐만 아니라 Cyrus 광장은 오페라 공연장과 상당한 건축 스타일을 대표하는 몇몇 역사적인 호텔도 포함하고 있습니다. 투어는 대략 2시간 정도 지속되며 Bronxville에서는 가장 유명한 식당 건물인 Waterfront 카페에서 맛있는 식사를 하는 것으로 (138) 마무리됩니다.

Cyrus 광장 투어를 신청하시거나 다른 투어에 대해서 알고 싶으시다면 555-0114로 Bronxville 관광국으로 문의해 주세요.

어휘 knowledgeable 지식이 풍부한 unique 독특한 focus on ~에 집중하다 playhouse 극장 approximately 대략 Visitors Bureau 관광국

135 (A) 소비자들은 새로운 가이드 책과 도시 지도를 구매하기 위해서 6시간 동안 기다렸습니다.
(B) 정기적으로 일정이 잡혀있는 4번의 도보 투어 중의 하나를 통해서 Bronxville 마을을 돌아보세요.
(C) 시립 갤러리는 봄 전시에서 당 왕조에 대한 유물을 특징으로 보여줍니다.
(D) 우리는 그것이 음식과 음료 판매로 수익을 만들어 내는 좋은 생각이라고 생각합니다.

해설 빈칸 뒤에 'Sponsored by the Bronxville Visitors Bureau, each tour'라고 언급하고 있으므로 tour를 언급하는 (B)가 정답이다.

어휘 relics 유물 exhibit 전시 generate 생성하다, 만들어 내다 revenue 수익

136 해설 수동태(is led)가 나오므로 주체자 앞에 쓰이는 전치사 (B)가 정답이다.

137 해설 Cyrus Square 뒤의 콤마로 'the town's theater ------'의 두 구가 동격을 이루고 있으므로 장소를 나타내는 (C)가 정답이다.

138 해설 주어가 tour인 동사 자리이므로 식사와 함께 끝난다는 의미가 될 수 있는 (D)가 정답이다.

어휘 exit 탈출하다 conclude 끝나다, 종결하다

[139-142]

발신: Gabrielle Rothschild, 건물 관리인
수신: 모든 직원들
날짜: 8월 9일 목요일
제목: 공사 작업

여러분 모두가 (139) 알고 있듯이, 우리 건물 보수가 8월 13일 월요일에 시작하며 8월 17일 금요일까지 지속될 것입니다. 따라서 여러분들은 (140) 불편을 겪으실 수 있습니다.

(141) 북쪽 승강기는 일주일 내내 작동하지 않을 것입니다. 이 승강기를 보통 사용하셨던 직원들은 계단을 이용하거나 남쪽 승강기를 사용하셔야 합니다.

(142) 또한 Ali Avenue 방면의 북동쪽 출입구는 화요일부터 목요일까지 폐쇄됩니다. 다른 모든 건물 출입구는 이 기간 동안 보통 때처럼 개방되어 있을 것입니다.

어휘 as a result 결과적으로 regularly 정기적으로, 항상 take the stairs 계단을 이용하다 entrance 입구 facing 바라보는, 직면하는 as usual 늘, 항상

139 해설 '뒤의 내용을 알고 있듯이'라는 의미로 (B)가 정답이다.

어휘 aware 인지하는 informing 정보를 주는

140 해설 공사로 인한 불편을 겪는다는 문맥으로 (A)가 정답이다.

어휘 inconvenience 불편 assignment 배정 addition 추가 interference 개입

141 (A) 소음 수준은 항상 최소로 유지되어야만 합니다.
(B) 적절한 용기에 쓰레기를 버리시기 바랍니다.
(C) 북쪽 승강기는 일주일 내내 작동하지 않을 것입니다.
(D) 직원들은 대표 이사에게 지정된 개인 공간에 입장하는 것이 금지되어 있습니다.

해설 뒤 문장에서 'this elevator'를 언급하므로 승강기 사용을 설명하는 (C)가 정답이다.

어휘 at a minimum 최소로 at all times 항상 dispose of 버리다 proper 적절한 receptacle 용기 out of service 작동하지 않는 forbid 금지하다 designated 지정된

142 해설 앞뒤 문장을 연결하는 접속부사 자리로서 앞 문장에서 언급한 내용에 추가가 되는 것이므로 (D)가 정답이다.

어휘 instead 대신 previously 이전에

[143-146]

7월 1일 – 9월부터 남부 중앙 학교 구역은 건강 관련 교육과 강의 자료에 있어서 Chester 교육 출판부(143)에만 의존하게 될 것이다. (144) 역사적으로 Chester는 이러한 내용물을 제공하는 선호하는 업체 세 군데 중 한 곳이었다.

7월 30일부터, 학교 이사회는 다른 2곳의 공급 업체와 계약을 (145) 종료하게 된다. 이 결정은 Chester 제품의 우수성을 입증한 교사와 학교 유모들의 의견 조사서에 기초를 둔 것이다. Chester 교재 비용은 (146) 높지만 학습서, 모형, 교사 가이드 등은 경쟁 업체보다 낮아서 예산 내에서 전체적인 비용을 유지하게 한다.

어휘 as of ~부로 be based on ~에 근거하다 attest to ~을 증명하다, 입증하다 competitor 경쟁 업체 overall 전반적인 expenditure 지출, 비용

143 해설 rely on에 사용되는 부사 자리로 뒤의 문맥을 살펴보면 Chester에서만 내용을 공급받기로 한 것이므로 (D)가 정답이다.

어휘 formally 공식적으로 periodically 정기적으로 initially 처음으로 solely 유일하게

144 (A) 모든 강의 규칙을 준수하며 협조해 주셔서 감사합니다.
(B) 웹 사이트 사용자는 강의 파일을 다운로드받을 수 있을 것이다.
(C) 필요하다면 Chester는 이중 언어 도움을 제공하기 위해 교사들과 또한 긴밀히 일하고 있다.
(D) 역사적으로 Chester는 이러한 내용물을 제공하는 선호하는 업체 세 군데 중 한 곳이었다.

해설 앞 문장에 언급한 'health-related learning and teaching materials'가 content에 해당하는 것으로 (D)가 정답이다.

어휘 abide by 준수하다, 지키다 bilingual 이중 언어의 historically 역사적으로, 이제껏 preferred 선호하는 vendor 공급업자

145 해설 기사가 쓰인 날짜가 7월 1일인데 7월 30일부터 계약이 종료된다고 했으므로 미래 시제인 (C)가 정답이다. (D)는 가정법 시제이다.

어휘 discontinue 중단하다

146 해설 빈칸 뒤에 두 절이 연결되는데, 내용상 서로 대조를 이루고 있으므로 정답은 (A)이다.

[147-148]

JUNG & JO 의류 회사
중간 사이즈
100% 울
손으로 세탁하거나 비슷한 색상과 함께 약세탁으로 기계 세탁해 주세요.
(147) 찬물에서만 세탁해 주세요.
온도가 낮은 설정으로 건조시켜 주세요.
색상 변화는 이 섬유의 원래 특징임을 알아 주세요.
(148) 반복 세탁으로 질감도 추후 변화될 수 있습니다.
Italy 생산품

어휘 apparel 의류 회사 gentle 부드러운 setting 설정 variation 변화 intended feature 원래 특징 fabric 섬유 repeated 반복된 alter 변화하다 further 추후, 나중에

147 상표에 따르면 이 물품은 어떻게 관리되어야 하는가?
(A) 낮은 온도에서 세탁해서
(B) 정해진 시간 동안 건조시켜서
(C) 따뜻한 물에 담가 두어서
(D) 축축한 천으로 닦아서

해설 지문에 'Wash in cold water only'라고 언급하였으므로 (A)가 정답이다.

어휘 specific 구체적인 soak 물에 담그다 wipe 닦다 damp 축축한 cloth 천

148 물품에 대해서 언급된 것은?
(A) 손으로 만들어졌다.
(B) 세탁 후에 줄어들 것이다.
(C) 질감이 바뀔 수도 있다.
(D) 프랑스에서 생산되었다

해설 'With repeated washing, texture also may alter further'라고 언급되어 있으므로 (C)가 정답이다.

어휘 shrink 줄어들다, 수축하다

[149-150]

Major Technical Institute

학교로 돌아가는 것을 고려 중이신가요? 교육은 경력에 있어서 중요한 부분이며 Major Tech는 기꺼이 바쁜 직장인들에게 다양한 지속적인 교육 과정을 제공해 드리고 있습니다. 정규 낮 수업 이외에도 149 이제 누구의 일정에도 편리하게 적합할 수 있는 온라인 수업을 제공합니다.

컴퓨터 네트워크, 음식 준비, 의료 기술 등을 포함한 많은 연수 수업 중에서 선택해 보세요. 150 이용할 수 있는 전체 수업 일정은 www.majortech.edu에서 참고하실 수 있습니다.

150 자격증 프로그램에 관한 더 자세한 정보를 원하시면 090-555-7890으로 연락 주시거나 info@majortech.edu로 이메일을 보내 주세요.

어휘 consider 고려하다 path 경로, 길 in addition to ~에 더해서 daytime 낮 동안 fit into ~에 딱 맞다 regarding ~에 관하여 certification 자격증, 자격 인증

149 광고에 따르면 Major Tech에서 최근 발전된 것은?
(A) 인터넷 수업
(B) 졸업생을 위한 무료 상담
(C) 입학 정책 개정
(D) 최신 컴퓨터와 모니터

해설 첫 번째 단락에서 'we now offer classes online that conveniently fit into anyone's schedules'라고 한 것으로 (A)가 정답임을 알 수 있다.

어휘 consultation 상담 graduate 대학 졸업생 brand-new 최신의

150 Major Tech에 대해서 더 알 수 있는 방법으로 언급되지 않은 것은?
(A) 전화하기
(B) 이메일 보내기
(C) 웹 사이트 방문
(D) 캠퍼스 방문

해설 두 번째 문단에서 'Consult our Web site www.majortech.edu for a complete list of courses available'라고 언급하고 세 번째 문단에서 'please contact admission at 090-555-7890 or send an e-mail to info@majortech.edu'라고 하였으므로 언급되지 않은 (D)가 정답이다.

[151-152]

http://fantasticspain.com

Fantastic Spain Travels

HOME	목적지	후기	연락처

최근에, 동료와 저는 Madrid로 출장을 갔고 하루 동안 관광할 시간이 있었습니다. 151 호텔 프론트 직원의 조언으로 Fantastic Spain Travels (FST)를 통해 왕궁 투어를 예약했습니다. 153 이 관광지를 보는 것은 제 동료에게는 첫 번째 경험이었고 제게는 두 번째였습니다. 처음 방문했을 때는 단체 관광객과 함께였습니다. 서둘러야 했고 왕궁을 제대로 감상하거나 원하는 만큼 많은 사진도 찍지 못했어요. 이번에는 가이드 Juan Dominguez가 이끄는 조금 더 가격이 비싼 개별 여행을 예약하게 되어서 너무 기뻤습니다.

152-C 교통편이 포함되지 않았던 지난 여행과는 달리, Dominguez 씨는 우리를 자동차로 왕궁까지 데리고 갔습니다. Dominguez 씨의 역사 지식이 방대하다는 것을 우리는 알 수 있었어요. 제 동료와 제가 유일한 고객이었기 때문에 우리는 많은 질문을 하고 여유 있는 시간을 가질 수 있었어요.

152-D 입장료가 투어 비용에 포함되어 있고 FST가 우리 표를 미리 구매해서 도착했을 때 줄을 설 필요가 없어서 너무 좋았습니다. 152-B 맛있는 지역 식당에서 점심식사가 제공되었기에 우리는 식사 장소를 찾기 위해 돌아다닐 필요도 없었어요.

이 투어는 정말 소중하고 가격 이상의 가치를 가지고 있답니다.

Jane Weatherly (Calcutta, Australia)

어휘 recently 최근에 colleague 동료 sightseeing 관광 clerk 직원 book a tour 투어를 예약하다 royal palace 왕궁 attraction 관광지 appreciate 감사하다, 감상하다 pricy 가격이 비싼 excursion 여행, 수련 in contrast to ~와 대조적으로 historical 역사적인 extensive 넓은, 방대한 entrance fee 입장료 cover 포함하다

151 FST를 Weatherly 씨에게 소개한 것은 누구인가?
(A) 여행사 직원
(B) 회사 동료
(C) 호텔 직원
(D) 현지 친구

해설 첫 번째 단락에서 'On advice from the clerk at the front desk of our hotel, we booked a tour of the royal palace through Fantastic Spain Travels (FST)'라고 언급하였으므로 (C)가 정답이다.

152 투어 비용에 포함되어 있지 않은 것은?
(A) 기념 사진
(B) 식사
(C) 교통
(D) 입장료

해설 지문의 세 번째 단락에서 'Lunch at a delicious local restaurant was provided'라고 언급되고 두 번째 단락에서 'Mr. Dominguez took us to the palace by car', 그리고 세 번째 단락에서 'the entrance fees were covered by the excursion price'라고 언급하였으므로 (A)가 정답임을 알 수 있다.

153 Weatherly 씨에 대해서 알 수 있는 것은?
(A) 출장을 자주 간다.
(B) Dominguez 씨의 동료이다.
(C) Madrid를 이전에 방문한 적이 있다.
(D) 스페인 역사에 관심이 있다.

해설 첫 번째 단락의 'It was my colleague's first chance to see this attraction and my second'에서 이전에 Madrid를 방문한 것을 알 수 있으므로 (C)가 정답이다.

[154-155]

Martina Androva [오후 7시 55분]	154 퇴근 후에 귀찮게 해서 미안해요. 그런데 출장 가기 전에 물어봐야 할 것을 깜박했어요.
Antonio Fuentez [오후 7시 57분]	괜찮아요. 무엇을 도와 드릴까요?
Martina Androva [오후 7시 59분]	지금 방금 Auto World Rentals에 도착했는데 보험에 대해 물어보네요. 155 제가 처음이라 회사 정책을 잘 모르겠어요. 보험이 필요한가요?
Antonio Fuentez [오후 8시 01분]	차를 운전하기 전에 반드시 보험을 구매해야 해요.
Martina Androva [오후 8시 03분]	회사 신용 카드와 개인 카드 중에 무엇을 쓰나요?
Antonio Fuentez [오후 8시 05분]	회사 카드가 편할 거예요. 하지만 반드시 영수증을 챙겨 두세요.
Martina Androva [오후 8시 07분]	전자 영수증을 주네요. 그래서 영수증 추적은 쉬울 것 같아요.

어휘 bother 귀찮게 하다 insurance 보험 absolutely 당연히, 확실히 off the lot 도로로, 주차장을 벗어나는 be sure to 반드시 ~하다 keep track of 흔적을 찾다, 추적하다

154 오후 7시 57분에 Fuentez 씨가 "괜찮아요"라고 한 것은 무슨 뜻인가?
(A) Androva 씨가 구매 증거를 전자상으로 제출할 수 있다.
(B) 출장 정보를 Androva 씨는 쉽게 얻을 수 있다.
(C) Androva 씨가 보험 구매를 하지 않기를 제안한다.
(D) Androva 씨의 질문에 기꺼이 답변을 할 것이다.

해설 오후 7시 55분에 Androva의 'I'm sorry to bother you after work, but I've got some questions I forgot to ask before going on my trip'에 대한 응답이므로 (D)가 정답이다.

어휘 proof of purchase 구매 증거 obtain 획득하다 be willing to 기꺼이 ~하다

155 Androva 씨에 대해 알 수 있는 것은?
(A) 신용 카드를 신청했다.
(B) 회사에 최근에 고용되었다.
(C) 여행 비용을 환불받기를 원한다.
(D) 공항까지 교통편을 원한다.

해설 오후 7시 59분에 'Since I am new to the company'라고 한 것으로 (B)가 정답임을 알 수 있다.

어휘 refund 환불 travel expense 여행 비용

[155-157]

Ranger 카펫
2389 Market 거리
Laramie, WY 39877
902-555-0145 www.rangercarpet.ca

10월 2일 특별 행사를 놓치지 마세요!

최고 고객 중 한 분으로 당신은 156 혁신적인 새로운 카펫 섬유를 특징으로 하는 새로운 라인의 Comfortzone 카펫을 소개하는 특별 홍보 행사에 초대되었습니다. 공장 테스트는 Comfortzone 카펫이 비슷한 가격대의 카펫보다 25%나 더 적은 양의 먼지를 흡수하고 내구성이 더 강하다는 것을 보여주었습니다. 157 10월 2일 우리 가게에서 Comfortzone 카펫을 구입하신다면 정가에서 40%를 절약하실 수 있으십니다. 10월 2일에 우리 가게로 이 공지를 가지고 오셔서 가게 직원에게 보여주시면 Comfortzone 전시장으로 가는 입장을 허가해 드립니다. 당신을 만나기를 기대합니다!

어휘 miss out 놓치다 be invited to ~을 권장받다 feature ~을 특징으로 하다 revolutionary 혁신적인 trap up 잡다, 가두다 comparably priced 비슷한 가격대의 regular price 정가 admission 입장

156 Comfortzone 카펫에 대해서 알 수 있는 것은?
(A) 다양한 색상의 제품이 있다.
(B) 특별한 새로운 재료로 생산된다.
(C) 가격이 더 비싼 카펫보다 40% 더 오래 간다.
(D) 무료 배달이 가능하다.

해설 지문에서 'Comfortzone, a new line of carpets featuring a revolutionary new carpet fiber.'라고 언급한 것으로 (B)가 정답이다.

어휘 a variety of 다양한 material 재료 complimentarily 무료로

157 고객들은 어떻게 Comfortzone 카펫 할인을 받을 수 있는 자격이 되는가?
(A) 카펫을 온라인으로 구매해서
(B) 가게 행사에 참여해서
(C) 허가증을 제시해서
(D) 소비자 의견 조사를 작성해서

해설 지문의 'if you purchase a Comfortzone carpet at our store on October 2, you can save up to 40 percent off the regular price'에서 10월 2일 행사에 와서 구매하게 되면 할인을 받을 수 있으므로 (B)가 정답이다.

어휘 qualify for ~에 자격이 되다 participate in ~에 참여하다 present 제시하다 customer survey 소비자 의견 조사

[158-160]

5월 10일

〈다른 사람을 보세요〉라는 유명한 전광판 광고로 작품에 기여했던 Media Tree가 158 지난 40년 동안 출판 예술 작품과 그림 분야의 획기성에 상을 수여해 왔던 권위 있는 Malta Awards에 후보로 올랐습니다. 거의 2,000점의 출품작에서 선택된 Media Tree는 예술 작품 후보로 오른 것 중에서는 첫 번째 Taipei의 삽화 스튜디오입니다. -[1]-. 올해 Malta Awards 수상자들은 모두 6월 15일 London에서 시상식에서 발표될 것입니다.

"우리는 이번 후보 지명에 대해서 매우 흥분하고 있습니다. 이것이 우리 직원들의 기술, 전문성, 독창성의 높은 수준의 증거이기 때문입니다."라고 회사의 설립자이며 CEO인 Melinda Bonner가 말했습니다.

-[2]-. 전 세계의 박물관과 미술관의 12명의 앞서가는 예술 분야 중역들로 구성되어 있는 Malta Award 심사위원들은 Media Tree가 작품의 다양성, 질, 세련됨에 기준을 두고 후보 임명되었다고 언급했습니다. "우리는 잡지, 아동 문학에서부터 화장품, 식품 포장까지 모든 것의 그림을 그립니다"라고 Bonner 씨가 언급했습니다. "그리고 우리는 완제품이 고객의 기대를 확실히 뛰어넘도록 확실히 하기 위해 그들과 가깝게 일하고 있습니다."

-[3]-. 160 후보자들의 이름이 발표된 이후로 스튜디오는 서비스 신청의 수가 많이 늘었습니다. 159 "더 많은 삽화가와 프로젝트 매니저를 고용하지 않는다면 늘어난 수요를 맞출 방법이 없습니다. 물론 그것이 바로 우리가 지금 하려고 하는 것입니다"라고 Bonner 씨가 말했습니다.

Media Tree에 대한 더 많은 정보는 www.mediatree.co.in에서 보실 수 있습니다. Malta Award에 대한 세부 사항은 www.maltaaward.org에 있습니다.
-[4]-.

어휘 artwork 예술 작품 contribute to ~에 기여하다 nominate 후보로 지명하다 billboard 전광판 campaign 광고 prestigious 명망 있는, 권위 있는 recognize 인정하다, 상을 주다 illustration 삽화, 그림 entrant 응시자, 출품자 testament 증거 expertise 전문성 creativity 독창성 founder 설립자 leading 앞서 가는, 주도하는 across the globe 전 세계에서 sophistication 세련됨 literature 문학 cosmetics 화장품 packaging 포장 end product 완제품 exceed one's expectations 기대를 뛰어 넘다 nominee 후보자 release 발표하다 growing 늘고 있는 illustrator 삽화자

158 Malta Award에 대해서 알 수 있는 것은?
(A) 개인에 의해 설립되었다.
(B) 이전에 광고 회사에 수여된 적이 있다.
(C) 수상자에게 현금으로 상을 준다.
(D) 40년 전에 처음으로 상이 주어졌다.

해설 첫 번째 단락에서 'Malta Award, which has been recognizing innovation in published artwork and illustration for over 40 years.'라고 언급하였으므로 (D)가 정답이다.

어휘 establish 설립하다 individual 개인 recipient 수령자, 수혜자, 수상자

159 기사에 따르면 Bonner 씨가 계획하고 있는 것은?
(A) 새로운 직원 모집
(B) 2번째 지점 개장
(C) 홍보 비용 축소
(D) Taipei 시상식 참여

해설 네 번째 단락에서 Bonner가 'There is no way we can meet the growing demand unless we hire more illustrators and project managers.'라고 말하였으므로 (A)가 정답임을 알 수 있다.

어휘 publicity 홍보

160 [1], [2], [3], [4]로 표시된 위치들 중 다음 문장이 들어가기 적절한 곳은?
"상을 받은 것과는 별개로, 후보 임명은 Media Tree에 언론의 관심이 쏟아지고 일감도 늘어나게 만들었습니다."
(A) [1]
(B) [2]
(C) [3]
(D) [4]

해설 업무가 증가했다는 언급이 나오는 것은 네 번째 단락으로 이후에 'Since the names of the nominees were released, the studio has seen a large increase in the number of requests for its services'라는 문장과도 연결되므로 (C)가 정답이다.

어휘 apart from ~와 상관없이, 따로 honor 명예, 상 publicity 홍보, 언론의 관심

[161-163]

Perfect Health and Fitness Center
이사회 회의 기록

* 재정

작년에는 3,100 파운드 흑자로 마감했습니다. 161 올해 예산은 6,291파운드 흑자가 예상됩니다.

* 회원권/보유

올해 회원 수에 있어서 강하게 시작했습니다. 1월 신년 행사가 176명의 새로운 회원을 유입시켰습니다.

1월 신년 행사를 포함하지 않고서도, 피트니스 센터 회원은 1월에 8% 상승했습니다. 회원 증가의 지속을 위해 162 무료 1주일 사용권을 실시하기 시작할 것입니다.

갱신하는 회원이 증가할 뿐 만 아니라 새로운 회원들도 반영해서 전체 회원권은 작년 1월부터 늘었습니다. 회원권 사용이 증가함으로 사무실 공원 근처에 위치한 시설물에 대해서는 몇 가지 주의해야 할 것이 있습니다. 163 가까운 미래에 주차와 락커룸 시설 유용성 문제를 다루어야 할 것입니다.

어휘 surplus 흑자 estimate 추정하다 retention 보유 in terms of ~에 있어서 bash 큰 파티 bring in 유입하다 in an effort to ~하려는 노력으로 implement 시행하다 trial period 시험기간 reflect 반영하다 as well as …뿐만 아니라 renew 갱신하다 usage 사용 address 다루다 availability 이용성 in the near future 가까운 미래에

161 올해 예산에 대해 알 수 있는 것은?
(A) 흑자가 날 것으로 예상된다.
(B) 몇몇 프로그램은 삭제될 필요가 있다.
(C) 회원권 판매가 예산의 60%를 차지하고 있다.
(D) 5년 만에 처음으로 수지를 맞추었다.

해설 첫 번째 단락에서 'This year's budget is estimated to have a surplus of £6291.'에서 (A)가 정답임을 알 수 있다.

어휘 balance 수입과 지출의 균형이 맞다.

162 Perfect Health and Fitness Center가 제공하는 것은?
(A) 무료 피트니스 테스트
(B) 1주일 무료 사용 기간
(C) 무료 3회 연수 수업
(D) 개인 수업 1회 지불

해설 세 번째 단락에서 'we are implementing a free one-week trial period'라고 언급하였으므로 (B)가 정답임을 알 수 있다.

어휘 individual class 개인 수업

163 Perfect Health and Fitness Center가 나중에 다루어야 할 필요가 있는 것은?
(A) 센터의 운영 시간 연장하기
(B) 피트니스 수업과 장비 추가하기
(C) 도심 가까이에 새로운 센터 열기
(D) 센터에 더 많은 저장 공간 만들기

해설 마지막 문장에서 'We will need to address parking and locker availability in the near future.'라고 언급한 것으로 (D)가 정답임을 알 수 있다.

어휘 operating hours 운영 시간

164 네 번째 단락, 첫 번째 줄의 reflecting과 뜻이 가장 가까운 것은?
(A) 보여주다
(B) 관여하다
(C) 돌려주다
(D) 궁금하다

해설 신규 회원 및 기존 회원의 갱신 건수를 보여준다는 내용이므로 (A)가 정답이다.

[165-167]

편집자 메모

이번 〈Cuisine in New Orleans〉 11월호는 잡지의 1년을 기념합니다. 정확히 1년 전에, 우리는 1호를 배포했고 그 이후로 이 지역에서 지역 요리에 있어서 가장 널리 읽히는 잡지 중의 한 권이 되었습니다. 166 최근 판매 부수는 5만 권에 이르고 숫자는 계속해서 오르고 있습니다. 지역 음식 애호가들은 우리 출판물을 칭찬했고 지난달 167 New Orleans 음식 축제에서 최고의 새로운 음식 잡지 상의 자랑스러운 수상자가 되었습니다. 165 편집장으로서, 열심히 일했던 직원, 기고가, 광고주, 지역 커뮤니티 독자 여러분 모두가 우리 성공에서 중요한 역할을 한 것에 대해 감사의 뜻을 나누고 싶습니다.

Colin Green

어휘 issue (잡지, 책) 호, 판 mark 기념하다 distribute 나눠주다, 분포하다 widely 널리 regional 지역의 circulation (신문, 잡지) 판매 부수 reach 다다르다 enthusiast 애호가 praise 칭찬하다 publication 출판 recipient 수령자, 수혜자 culinary 요리의 editor-in-chief 편집장 appreciation 감사 hardworking 열심히 일하는 contributor 기고가 advertiser 광고주 expanding 늘어나고 있는 play an important part in ~에 있어서 중요한 역할을 하다

165 메모의 목적은?
(A) 감사를 표현하기 위해서
(B) 제안을 하기 위해서
(C) 기고가를 소개하기 위해서
(D) 초대장을 보내기 위해서

해설 지문의 'I would like to share my appreciation'에서 (A)가 정답임을 알 수 있다.

166 〈Cuisine in New Orleans〉에 대해 알 수 있는 것은?
(A) 추가로 작가를 구하고 있다.
(B) 곧 국제적으로 배포될 예정이다.
(C) 인기가 늘어나고 있다.
(D) 광고 비용이 늘어났다.

어휘 distribute 분배하다, 나눠 주다 advertising rates 광고 비용

해설 지문의 'Our circulation recently reached 50,000, and the number continues to climb'에서 정답이 (C)임을 알 수 있다.

167 Green 씨가 New Orleans 음식 축제를 언급한 이유는?
(A) 그곳에서 요리 시연을 하기 위해서
(B) 그곳에서 자원 봉사할 직원들을 모집하기 위해서
(C) 잡지가 그 행사를 지원한다는 것을 나타내기 위해서
(D) 잡지가 그 행사에서 상을 받았다는 것을 나타내기 위해

해설 지문에서 'at last month's New Orleans Food Fest, we became the proud recipient of an award for best new culinary magazine'이라고 한 것으로, 정답은 (D)이다.

어휘 cooking demonstration 요리 시연 honor 상을 주다

[168-171]

Lydia Johnson 오전 11시 30분
168 Marie와 저는 12시 30분쯤 점심 먹으러 나갈 거예요. 같이 할 사람 있어요?

Joanie Lockhart 오전 11시 31분
아마도요. 아직 중간 보고서 작업할 게 있어요. 어디로 갈 거예요?

Lydia Johnson 오전 11시 32분
170 Lexington 가에 있는 새로운 태국 식당을 한 번 가 볼 생각이에요. Erawan Hit예요.

John Randolph 오전 11시 33분
운이 없네요. 169 거기 며칠 전에 문 닫았어요.

Lydia Johnson 오전 11시 34분
그 얘기를 들으니 안타깝네요. 170 사람들이 그 식당에 대해 좋은 얘기를 많이 하던데요.

John Randolph 오전 11시 36분
가까이에 있는 Kaosan 가는 어때요? 그곳에는 금요일에는 항상 특별 메뉴가 있어요.

Lydia Johnson 오전 11시 37분
좋은데요. 모두 Kaosan 가에 가고 싶나요?

Joanie Lockhart 오전 11시 38분
좋아요. 171 그런데 저는 1시는 되어야 도착할 거 같아요.

Marie Cantanzaro 오전 11시 39분
저도 좋아요. Joanie, 방금 보고서 업데이트 수치 보냈어요.

어휘 grab a bite 간단히 먹다 out of luck 운이 없는 around the corner 가까운 곳에 있는 figures 수치

168 사람들이 이야기하고 있는 것은?
(A) 시상식을 여는 장소
(B) 지역의 가장 좋은 식당
(C) Erawan Hit의 오늘의 요리
(D) 점심 먹으러 갈 장소

해설 오전 11시 30분 Johnson 씨의 'Marie and I are grabbing a bite to eat for lunch around 12:30. Anyone wants to join us?'에서 주제는 점심임을 알 수 있다

169 Randolph 씨가 Erawan Hit에 대해 제공하는 정보는?
(A) 해산물 음식에 대해 평판이 좋다.
(B) 일요일에는 열지 않는다.
(C) 음식 가격을 저렴하게 제공한다.
(D) 더 이상 영업하지 않는다.

해설 오전 11시 33분에 'That place closed a few days ago'라고 한

것으로 정답은 (D)이다.

170 오전 11시 34분에 Johnson 씨가 "그 얘기 들으니 안타깝네요"라고 한 것은 무엇 때문인 것 같은가?
(A) **그녀는 새로운 식당에 가보고 싶어 했다.**
(B) Randolph 씨는 프로젝트를 끝낼 수가 없다.
(C) 모두가 가기에는 식당이 너무 작다.
(D) 다른 일정이 있다.

해설 오전 11시 32분에 Johnson 씨가 'We're thinking of trying the new Thai Restaurant on Rexington Road'라고 하였으므로 새로운 식당에 가보고 싶어 했다는 것을 알 수 있으므로 정답은 (A)이다.

171 Lockhart 씨는 무엇을 하기로 결정하였는가?
(A) 근처 식당 둘러보기
(B) 내일 근무 시간 바꾸기
(C) **동료들과 함께 식사하기**
(D) Johnson 씨에게 샌드위치 부탁하기

해설 오전 11시 38분에 'OK. But I won't be able to get there until about one'이라고 하였으므로 늦게라도 간다는 것을 알 수 있다. 따라서 (C)가 정답이다.

어휘 browse 둘러보다

[172-175]

IOFF
국제 사무용 가구 재단
40 Block Road
Bloomington, IN 01398

5월 4일
Risa Daniels
Taylor 사무용 가구
14 Pine 거리
Belleville, IL 80214

Daniels 씨에게,

IOFF 이사회를 대표하여, 이번 여름 Bloomington에서 열리는 IOFF 무역 박람회에 일찍 등록해 주셔서 감사드립니다. 올해는 지금까지 열렸던 행사 중에 최고가 될 것을 확신합니다. (172) 더 넓은 행사 장소로 옮기는 것뿐만 아니라 행사 기조연설가가 저명한 가구 디자이너인 Lisa DeNoble이 될 것입니다.

항상 그렇듯이, IOFF는 최고의 가구 디자이너들이 그들의 작품을 전시하고 Bloomington 전역에서 최고급 소매업자들과 전문적인 관계를 발전시켜나갈 즐거운 분위기를 제공하고 싶습니다. -[1]-. 점점 늘어나고 있는 전시자들을 수용하기 위해서 (173) 올해의 행사는 Lafayette 컨벤션 센터에서 열릴 것입니다. 이 센터는 7만 평방미터의 전시장과 회의장을 갖추고 있으며 레스토랑, 상점, 극장에서 편리한 위치에 있는 (173) Bloomington 중심부의 상업 지역에서 단지 몇 분 거리에 위치하고 있습니다. -[2]-. 여러분의 대회 참가 준비를 돕기 위해 동봉된 책자를 자세히 읽어 보시기 바랍니다.

우리 목표 중 하나는 귀하께서 전시장에 설치하는 일을 원활히 하는 것입니다. -[3]-. 무역 전시회의 전시자 등록, 설치, 철거 시간과 날짜를 명심해 주시기 바랍니다. (174-A) (174-B) IOFF 자원 봉사자들은 8월 24일 일요일 정오부터 A홀 바깥에 있는 등록 데스크에서 현장 등록을 처리하고 신청한 전시자들의 등록, 이름표를 배포할 것입니다. A홀과 B홀은 같은 날 정오부터 7시까지 개장될 것입니다. 철거는 8월 28일 목요일 오후 1시부터 6시까지입니다. (174-C) (152-D) IOFF 자원 봉사자들이 여러분을 도와 같은 날 설치와 철거를 도울 것입니다.

행사 안내 책자에는 전체 행사 일정표가 있습니다: 지정 하역장 구역을 포함해서 컨벤션 센터 지도가 있습니다. -[4]-. (175) 이 편지와 안내 책자 이외에 질문이 있으시면 특별 지원팀이 어떤 문제든지 여러분을 돕기 위해 현장에 있습니다. 033-555-0011로 전화해 주세요.

여러분을 우리 대회에 모시게 되어 매우 명예롭게 생각하며, 행사가 가장 성공적인 행사가 되기를 바랍니다.

진심으로,

John Ellsworth
수석 행사 매니저

어휘 on behalf of ~을 대표해서 board 이사회 confident 자신감 있는 spacious 넓은, 여유로운 venue 행사 장소 keynote speaker 기조연설 renowned 저명한 as always 항상 그렇듯이 atmosphere 분위기 exhibit 전시하다, 전시, 전시장 high-end 최고급의 throughout ~에 걸쳐서 accommodate 수용하다 growing 늘어나는 exhibitor 전시자 enclosed 동봉된 facilitate 원활히 하다 teardown 철거 process 처리하다 on-site 현장의 set up 설치 complete 전체의 designated 지정된 unloading area 하역장, 짐 내리는 곳 beyond the scope of ~의 범위 외에 be honored to ~하게 되어 영광이다

172 편지에 따르면, IOFF 대회의 새로운 특징은 무엇인가?
(A) 오락 공연이 포함되어 있다.
(B) 더 이른 시간에 시작할 것이다.
(C) 더 넓은 범위의 행사를 제공할 것이다.
(D) **더 넓은 장소에서 열릴 것이다.**

해설 첫 번째 단락에서 'we moving to a more spacious venue'라고 했으므로 (D)가 정답이다.

173 대회 장소에 대해 알 수 있는 것은?
(A) 건물은 최근에 개조되었다.
(B) **Bloomington의 사업 지구 근처에 있다.**
(C) 가장 최신의 기술 장비를 갖고 있다.
(D) 건물에 레스토랑과 가게가 포함되어 있다.

해설 두 번째 단락에서 'this year's event will be held at the Lafayette Convention Centre'에서 행사 장소를 알 수 있고 다음 문장에서 'is located only minutes from Bloomington's central commercial area with easy access to restaurants, shops, and theatres'라고 언급하였으므로 (B)가 정답임을 알 수 있다.

어휘 district 구역

174 IOFF 자원 봉사자들이 대회에 도움을 주는 방법으로 언급되지 않은 것은?
(A) 참가자들을 등록하는 것
(B) 배지를 나눠주는 것
(C) 전시물에 도움을 주는 것
(D) **전화에 응답하는 것**

해설 지문의 세 번째 단락에서 'IOFF volunteers will process on-site registration, check in registered exhibitors'에서 (A)가 언급되었고 그 다음 'hand out name badges at the registration desk'에서 (B)도 언급하였으며 단락 마지막 문장에서 'IOFF volunteers will be available to assist you on both days for set up and teardown.'라고 하였으므로 (C)도 언급되었다. 언급되지 않은 (D)가 정답이다.

175 [1], [2], [3], [4]로 표시된 위치들 중 다음 문장이 들어가기 적절한 곳은?
"자주 언급하는 질문에 대한 응답 리스트 또한 포함되어 있습니다."
(A) [1]
(B) [2]
(C) [3]
(D) **[4]**

해설 [4] 뒤의 문장에서 편지와 안내 책자 내용에 없는 다른 문의 사항들은 특별 지원팀의 도움을 받으라는 내용이 나오므로 제시문은 이 내용 앞에 들어가야 한다.

[176-180]

5월 1일

(176) Aberman 출판사의 새로운 젊은 작가들의 책 소개

(180) Gabr Alfarsi의 〈Don't Look Back in Anger〉
바다에서 불어오는 태풍과 마을에 새로 등장한 인물로 등대를 배경으로 한, 눈을 뗄 수 없는 미스터리는 놀라운 반전이 가득합니다. 이것은 또한 멋진 시리즈물의 1편입니다.

(180) Kenneth Ling의 〈The Visigoths the Western Goths〉
이 에세이 전집에서 여행가 Kenneth Ling은 리베리아 반도의 탐험을 즐거운 소설처럼 읽히도록 (177) 설명했습니다. 교실 토론 가이드도 포함되어 있습니다.

(180) Ricardo Gomez의 〈All the Way Up〉
Geizan의 여왕이 사라지고 그녀의 어린 딸이 왕관을 이어받았을 때 어떤 일이 생길지 아무도 예상하지 못했습니다. 왕족 생활의 유머스러운 면이 최대한 쓰이고 있는 코미디물입니다.

(180) Joseph Gustaferro의 〈Sit Next to Me〉
조용한 바닷가 마을을 여행하던 한 무리의 지인들이 서로의 과거에 대해 알게 됩니다. Lennox Fiction Prize의 수상자가 쓴 이 이야기는 우정의 힘을 정교하게 분석합니다.

즉각적인 출판물 문의:
(212) 555-0130으로 Grover Misra에게.

Woodward 서점의 다음 행사

7월 12일 토요일

Woodward(455 Mason 가) 서점은 Writing & Publishing 잡지의 부편집장인 (179) Sanjay Dellegrio가 진행하는 공개 토론회를 진행할 것입니다. 올해 초에 Aberman Books에서 작품이 출판된 작가들인 (178) (180) Gabr Alfarsi, Kenneth Ling, Ricardo Gomez가 어떻게 그들이 책을 출판하는 작가가 되었는지에 대해 이야기할 것입니다. 같은 일을 바라고 있는 사람들을 위해 질문에 답을 하고 조언을 해 줄 것입니다. (180) 책 사인회는 이 행사 후에 진행됩니다. 더 많은 정보를 원하시면 (212) 555-0187로 전화 바랍니다.

어휘 brew 형성하다, 생겨나다 off the coast 해안가에서 떨어진 바다에서 gripping 시선을 사로잡는 lighthouse 등대 twist 반전 enchanting 황홀한, 멋진 anthology 전집 recount 말하다, 설명하다 expedition 탐험 delightful 기쁜 inherit 이어받다 throne 왕관 royal 왕족의, 왕가의 acquaintance 아는 사람, 지인 seaside 해안가의 deftly 솜씨 좋게 analyze 분석하다 panel 심사위원, 평가단 moderate 중재하다, 사회를 보다 associate editor 부편집장 book signing 책 사인회 take place 일어나다

176 공지에 있는 모든 책들의 공통점은?
(A) 추리 소설이다.
(B) 동시에 출판될 것이다.
(C) 젊은 층을 대상으로 만들어졌다.
(D) 젊은 작가들에 의해 쓰여졌다.

해설 공지의 첫 번째 문장에서 'Aberman Books Announces New Young Authors Titles'라고 언급하였으므로 (D)가 정답이다.

177 공지에서 세 번째 단락, 첫 번째 줄에서 recounts와 뜻이 가장 가까운 것은?
(A) 묘사하다
(B) 계산하다
(C) 추정하다
(D) 돌아가다

해설 recounts his expeditions는 '여행담을 이야기했다'라는 뜻이므로 (A)가 정답이다

178 7월 12일 행사의 주제는 무엇인가?
(A) 서점이 고객을 유치하는 방법
(B) 작가를 꿈꾸는 사람들이 출판하는 방법
(C) 잡지 편집자가 되는 방법
(D) 수업 계획서 작성 방법

해설 공지에서 'will speak about how they became published authors'라고 언급하였으므로 (B)가 정답이다

어휘 aspiring ~를 희망하는, 미래의

179 Dellegrio 씨는 행사에서 무엇을 할 것인가?
(A) 팬들을 위한 책 서명하기
(B) 강의 조언하기
(C) 단체 토론 이끌기
(D) 간식 제공하기

해설 공지에서 'a panel discussion moderated by Sanjay Dellegrio'라고 하였으므로 사회를 볼 것이라는 것을 알 수 있다. 따라서 (C)가 정답이다.

어휘 refreshments 간식

180 행사에서 작가가 서명하지 않는 책은 무엇인가?
(A) 〈Don't Look Back in the Anger〉
(B) 〈The Visigoths the Western Goths〉
(C) 〈All the Way Up〉
(D) 〈Sit Next to Me〉

해설 연계 지문 문제이다. 공지에서 Authors Gabr Alfarsi, Kenneth Ling, Ricardo Gomez를 언급하며 'They'll answer questions and give advice to those hoping to do the same. Book signing will take place after the event'라고 하였으므로 행사에 오지 않는 작가는 Joseph Gustaferro이므로 그의 작품인 (D)가 정답이다.

[181-185]

수신: Keith Blanchett
발신: Sam Brewer
주제: 감사 일정
날짜: 6월 10일

Blanchett 씨에게,

Environment Safe와 계약해 주셔서 감사합니다. 당신 회사의 기업 환경 기준 인증에 선택해 주셔서 자랑스럽게 생각하며 당신과 함께 일할 것을 기대하고 있습니다.

(181) 우리가 논의했던 것처럼, 감사는 당신의 회사가 깨끗한 공기, 깨끗한 물, 그리고 쓰레기 처리를 규제하는 정부 법규를 잘 준수하고 있는지 결정할 것입니다. 감사는 4개의 범위를 포함합니다: 일반 법규, 유출 공기 품질, 유출 수질, 쓰레기 처리와 재활용입니다. 각 범위에 대한 평가는 당신 업체의 전반적인 평가와 함께 보고서에 포함될 것입니다. (181) 우리는 제조 시설, 물품 보관소, 배송 센터 각각에 개별 감사와 평가를 실시할 것입니다.

아시다시피, 감사 기간은 2주가 걸리고 감사 기간 동안 반드시 모든 운영은 정상적으로 시행되고 있어야 합니다. (185) 등록 신청서에 감사가 8월 마지막 2주 동안 시행되는 것을 요청하셨습니다. 이 시간대는 우리에게도 아주 좋습니다. 다른 의견이 없다면, 이때 당신 회사의 환경 평가 일정을 잡는 것이 제일 좋다고 추정할 것입니다. 감사 준비의 세부 사항을 검토하기 위해서 편하실 때 연락해 주시기 바랍니다.

감사합니다.

Sam Brewer
홍보 담당 매니저
Environment Safe

수신: Keith Blanchett
발신: Tom McKnight
주제: 3분기 일정
(182) 날짜: 6월 12일
첨부: schedule.pdf

Keith 씨에게,

(182) 7월, 8월, 9월 회사 일정표의 현재 초안을 첨부했어요. 물류 창고 직원들은 Roberts Plumbing 주문 건에 따라서 이 기간 동안에 추가 근무할 필요가 있을 것 같다는 것을 알아 주세요. 우리는 이번 주말 안으로 주문이 다 들어오기를 바라고 어느 점에서든 일정을 마무리 지어야만 합니다. 다른 모든 주문들은 확정되어서 일정에 포함되었어요.

(185) 지난 회의에서 당신은 우리가 일정을 추가할 수도 있다고 말했어요. 이미 7월 안전 교육은 입력했지만 제가 또 따로 추가할 게 있는지 알려 주시겠어요?
(183) 다음 주 초에는 지역 매니저들에게 일정표를 보내고 싶어요.

Tom

어휘 audit 감사 corporate 기업의 standard 기준 certification 인증

determine 결정하다 in compliance with ~을 준수하는 regulation 규제 govern 지도하다, 관리하다 waste 쓰레기 disposal 처리 cover 포함하다 discharge 유출하다 waste removal 쓰레기 제거 rating 평가, 평점 separate 개별의, 각각의 along with ~와 함께 overall 전반적인 occur 일어나다, 발생하다 operation 운영 normally 정상적으로 enrollment 등록 time frame 시간대 otherwise 달리, 다르게 assume that ~ 이하를 추정하다, 예상하다 assessment 평가 at one's convenience 편리할 때 go over 훑어보다, 검토하다 prepare for 준비하다 current 현재의 draft 초안 warehouse 물류 창고 additional 추가의 depend on ~에 따라 finalize 마무리 짓다, 최종화하다 existing 존재하는, 현재의 enter into 입력하다 add to ~에 추가하다 regional 지역의

181 첫 번째 이메일에 따르면, Environment Safe는 어떤 서비스를 제공하는가?
(A) 제조업과 창고업 직원 고용
(B) 회사의 재정 보고서 준비
(C) 종이와 그 외 재료 재활용
(D) 회사 정부 규제 준수 평가

해설 첫 번째 이메일 두 번째 단락 마지막에서 'We will perform separate audits and ratings for your manufacturing facility, warehouse and shipping center'라고 하였는데, 이는 두 번째 단락 첫 문장처럼 정부의 규제를 잘 준수하는지 확인하기 위한 것이므로 (D)가 정답이다.

어휘 warehousing 창고업

182 두 번째 이메일에 따르면 창고에서 다음 달에 어떤 일이 생길 것 같은가?
(A) 몇몇 직원들이 추가 근무를 할 것이다.
(B) 몇몇 고급 사양 장비들이 작동될 것이다.
(C) 폐기물이 재가공을 위해 수집될 것이다.
(D) 개정된 회사 절차가 게시될 것이다.

해설 두 번째 이메일에서 'I have attached the current draft of the company schedule for July, August and September. Please note that the warehouse staff will most likely need to work additional hours during these months'라고 하였고 이메일은 6월에 쓰여졌으므로 7월에 추가 근무가 있을 것으로 예상되므로 (A)가 정답이다.

어휘 work extra hours 추가 근무하다 advanced 고급의 waste material 폐기물 reprocess 재가공하다 revised 개정된 post 게시하다

183 McKnight 씨는 이번 주말까지 무엇을 하기 바라는가?
(A) Environment Safe의 제안을 평가하기
(B) 회사 일정을 완료하기
(C) 환경 기준 평가를 시작하기
(D) Roberts Plumbing에서 물품을 주문하기

해설 McKnight 씨가 작성한 두 번째 이메일에서 'I'd like to send the schedule to the regional managers by the beginning of the next week'라고 언급하였으므로 (B)가 정답이다

어휘 evaluate 평가하다 complete 마무리하다

184 두 번째 이메일의 첫 번째 단락, 두 번째 줄의 note와 뜻이 가장 가까운 것은?
(A) 쓰다
(B) 줍다
(C) 가지고 나가다
(D) 명심하다

해설 'Please note that'에서 that 이하를 잘 명심하라는 의미이므로 (D) bear in mind (명심하다)가 정답이다.

185 Blanchett 씨가 두 번째 이메일에 대한 응답에서 무엇을 이야기할 것 같은가?
(A) 제조 시설이 늘어난 업무에 대비해야만 한다.
(B) 회사 감사가 일정에 추가되어야 한다.
(C) 안전 교육이 9월에 시행되어야 한다.
(D) 일정 업데이트 방법이 수정되어야 한다.

해설 연계 지문 문제이다. 두 번째 이메일 마지막 단락에서 McKnight 씨는 Blanchett 씨에게 7, 8, 9월 일정에 추가해야 하는 것이 있으면 알려달라고 했는데, 첫 번째 이메일에서 감사 기간을 8월 마지막 2주로 잡는 것에 동의하는 내용이 나오므로 (B)가 정답이다.

[186-190]

Crestport 댄스 아카데미

Crestport 댄스 아카데미는 다음 시즌 공연을 공지하게 되어 기쁩니다. 186 현대 무용, 힙합부터 고전 발레까지, 오셔서 우리가 드리는 모든 것을 봐 주세요! 전체 시즌이나 1회 공연 표 모두 구매하실 수 있습니다. 190 시즌 티켓 정기권 소유자는 같은 날 티켓 구매의 50%를 할인받으실 수 있습니다.

1월 18일-22일
- Shelburne 그룹이 힙합 음악을 제공합니다.

2월 7일
- Catelynn Martin이 상을 받은 적이 있는 댄스 공연을 합니다.

188 2월 15일-21일
- 188 Strauss 트리오가 놀라운 발레 공연을 선사합니다.

2월 22일-27일
- Zachary Keaton이 피아노 연주에 맞춰 춤을 춥니다.

수신: Tara Craft
발신: Jeanne Harris
참조: Ben Springer
주제: Belle Systems 방문
날짜: 12월 29일

Craft 씨에게

187 Belle Systems을 대표해서, 당신이 2월 21일과 22일 강의할 기록물 유지 프로젝트 채택을 저희가 얼마나 기대하고 있는지 알려 드리고 싶습니다. 요청하신 대로 강의실, 노트북, 프로젝터, 마이크를 준비했고, 발표하시는 데 있어서 더 도움이 필요하시면 알려 주시기 바랍니다.

우리 부서 팀장인 Ben Springer가 우리의 감사함을 표현하고 당신의 방문을 좀 더 즐겁게 하기 위해서 특별한 계획을 세웠습니다. 187 188 방문하신 첫째 날에 우리 지역에서 찬사를 받는 레스토랑에서 저녁식사를 한 뒤 Crestport 댄스 아카데미의 댄스 공연 관람을 계획했습니다.

Jeanne Harris
마케팅 매니저
Belle Systems

수신: Jeanne Harris
발신: Ben Springer
수신 시간: 오전 8시 33분

Craft 씨로부터 방금 들었어요. 연결편 비행기가 연착되었답니다. 그녀가 새로운 도착 시간을 확인해 주었고, 오늘 저희는 회의를 열 수 있을 거예요. 190 Craft 씨가 오늘 공연을 내일로 미뤄서 우리가 급해지지 않기를 요청했어요. 오늘 대신에 내일 표를 사면 상당히 할인받을 수 있어요. 189 공항 도착/출발 택시 서비스를 다시 조정해 주시겠어요? 저녁 예약은 제가 연기할게요.

어휘 be pleased to 기꺼이 ~하다 performance 공연 classical 고전의 entire 전체의 subscriber 정기구독자 award-winning 상을 받은 적이 있는 put on 상연하다 accompany 수반하다, 동반하다 on behalf of ~을 대표하여 look forward to ~을 기대하다, 고대하다 adopt 채택하다 maintain 유지하다 further assistance 추가 도움 gratitude 고마움 enjoyable 즐거운 acclaimed 찬사를 받는 outing 외출 connecting flight 연결편 rather than ~보다는 다소 rush 서두르다 substantial 상당한

186 Crestport 댄스 아카데미에 관해 암시된 것은?
(A) 지난 20년 동안 운영되어 왔다.
(B) 댄스 강사를 현재 모집 중이다.
(C) 다양한 스타일의 댄스를 선보인다.
(D) 대중에게 댄스 수업을 제공한다.

해설 광고의 첫 번째 단락에서 'From modern dance and hip-hop to classical ballet'로부터 (C)가 정답임을 알 수 있다.

어휘 operate 운영하다 instructor 강사 showcase 소개하다

187 이메일의 목적은 무엇인가?

(A) 일정에 대한 세부 사항을 알리기 위해서
(B) 장비 개선 상황을 설명하기 위해서
(C) 잠재 고객에게 정보를 주기 위해서
(D) 회의 날짜를 새롭게 제안하기 위해서

해설 이메일 첫 번째 단락에서 'you will teach us about on February 21 and 22'로 일정을 언급하고 두 번째 단락에서 'He has planned dinner with you at an acclaimed local restaurant on the first evening of your visit, followed by an outing to a musical performance' 등을 언급했으므로 정답이 (A)임을 알 수 있다.

어휘 potential 잠재의, 미래의

188 Craft 씨가 원래 참석하기로 되어 있었던 공연은 어떤 공연인가?

(A) Shelburne 그룹
(B) Catelynn Martin
(C) Strauss 트리오
(D) Zachary Keaton

해설 연계 지문 문제이다. 이메일에서 Craft 씨가 방문하는 날은 2월 21일, 22일인데 첫째 날에 댄스 공연을 관람한다고 했다. 광고에서 이 날짜에 해당하는 21일 공연은 Strauss 트리오의 공연이므로 정답은 (C)이다.

189 문자 메시지에 따르면 Springer 씨가 Harris 씨에게 요청한 것은?

(A) 회의실 예약
(B) 저녁 식사 준비
(C) 교통편 조정
(D) 공연 취소

해설 문자에서 마지막에 'Would you reschedule the taxi service to and from the airport?'라고 하였으므로 정답은 (C)이다.

190 Springer 씨에 대해 알 수 있는 것은?

(A) Craft 씨의 일정을 아직 확정하지 않았다.
(B) Craft 씨가 공연을 좋아할지 확신하지 못한다.
(C) 곧 지난 공연표의 크레딧(포인트)을 받을 것이다.
(D) Crestport 댄스 아카데미의 정기권을 갖고 있다.

해설 연계 지문 문제이다. 문자 메시지에서 'If I order the tickets myself tomorrow rather than today we can receive a substantial discount'라고 한 것에서 Springer 씨는 내일 표를 사면 할인을 받을 수 있다는 것을 알 수 있다. 광고에서 'Season ticket subscribers also receive 50 percent off same-day ticket purchases'라고 하였으므로 할인을 받을 수 있는 Springer 씨는 정기 구독자임을 알 수 있다. 따라서 (D)가 정답이다.

어휘 get a credit for ~의 신용(점수)를 얻다 subscription 정기권

[191-195]

Zentron 시스템

Zentron 시스템에서 우리 제품 시험자 의견은 시장 연구 조사의 중요한 부분입니다. 우리는 도시에 있는 가장 유명한 연구 센터 중의 하나이고 더 많은 수요에 맞추기 위해 직원과 제품 시험자들을 충원하고 있습니다. 우리는 음식, 장난감부터 전자제품까지 여러 회사들이 새롭고 혁신적인 제품을 개발하는 것을 돕습니다. 우리는 또한 엄격한 품질 기준을 따릅니다. Zentron 시스템에서 제품 시험자가 되시면 현금과 심지어 상품도 받을 수 있습니다. www.zentronsystems.org/tester를 클릭하시고 '보상 프로그램'을 참고하세요.

http://www.zentronsystems.org/tester/register

제품 시험자가 되는 방법

1단계
"새로운 시험자" 등록 양식을 작성하세요 (여기를 클릭하세요). 그리고 웹 사이트에 접속할 때마다 사용할 암호를 만드세요. 이 등록은 당신을 제품 시험자 목록에 올려놓습니다.

2단계
제품 테스트가 생기면 여러분들은 전화나 이메일로 공지를 받습니다. 어떤 사람들은 다른 사람들보다 많이 전화를 받을 수 있습니다; 경우에 따라 다릅니다. 그러나 194 우리는 등록된 시험자에게 한 달에 1회 이상 전화하지는 않습니다.

3단계
제품 테스트에 관심을 보이면 우리의 모집 전문가가 여러분이 연구에 적합한 상대인지 알아보기 위해 여러분께 몇 가지 질문을 할 것입니다.

4단계
제품 시험에 선택되면 모집 전문가가 여러분께 얼마나 지불되는지 알려드릴 것입니다. 대부분의 테스트는 1시간 정도 소요되고 195-C 30달러에서 40달러가 지급됩니다.

보상 프로그램
191 처음으로 등록하신 모든 제품 시험자들은 자동으로 100달러나 혹은 최신 디지털 카메라를 받을 수 있는 무작위 경품에 응모됩니다. 참가 신청서는 필요 없습니다. 친구를 Zentron 시스템으로 192 안내하는 현재 제품 시험자들은 그 친구가 첫 번째 연구를 마치면 25달러를 받게 됩니다. 더 많은 정보를 원하시면, 여기를 클릭해 주세요.

날짜: 10월 29일
Sandra Stable
Zentron 시스템의 시험자가 되는 것

193 저는 Zentron 시스템의 제품 시험자로 작년에 합류했고 그 이후로 음료, 소다 그외 여러 가지를 시도해 보는 것으로 급여를 받았습니다. 등록은 쉬워요 – 그냥 온라인 신청서를 작성하고 암호를 만들면 됩니다 – 그리고 테스트는 재미있고 흥미롭습니다. 저는 방문할 때마다 1시간 시험하고 40달러를 받았지만 194 그들은 전화를 자주 합니다! 제가 해외에 나가 있었던 한 달 동안 5통에서 6통의 전화가 왔었고 음성메시지는 가득 차 있었어요. 돈을 벌기에 좋은 방법이지만 당신이 좋아하는 제품에 대해서 많은 질문을 한답니다. 그것이 시험에 대한 자격 과정의 일부인 것 같아요.

제품 시험자로 참여하시려면, 여기서 등록하세요: www.zentronsystems.org.

합류하는 것을 추천해요! 195-A 195-B 실험 시설은 Napa Valley의 도시 버스 정류장 근처에 있고 건물 앞에는 무료 주차장도 많습니다.

어휘 key 중요한 meet a demand 수요를 맞추다 innovative 혁신적인 electronics 전자제품 rigorous 엄격한 standards 기준 work ethics 직업 윤리 registration form 등록 양식 place on a list 목록에 올리다 arise 일어나다 via ~을 통해서 depend 상황에 달려 있다 specialist 전문가 preference 선호 match for ~에 어울리는 짝 random 무작위의 drawing 뽑기, 추첨 entry form 참가 신청서 refer A to B A를 B로 보내다 qualifying 자격이 되는 sign up 등록하다

191 새로운 등록자가 Zentron 시스템에서 100달러를 받을 수 있는 방법으로 가능한 것은?

(A) 소비자 조사를 실시하여
(B) 제품 실험을 2가지 완료하여
(C) 참가 신청서를 작성하여
(D) 무작위로 뽑혀서

해설 웹 페이지 마지막 단락 REWARDS PROGRAM에서 'All product testers who register with us for the first time will automatically be entered into a random drawing to win $100 or an MP3 player'라고 언급되어 있으므로 정답은 (D)이다.

어휘 randomly 무작위로, 불특정하게

192 웹 페이지의 다섯 번째 단락, 세 번째 줄의 refer와 뜻이 가장 가까운 것은?

(A) 연설하다, 다루다
(B) 안내하다
(C) 약속하다
(D) 이동시키다

해설 웹 페이지에서 'refer a friend to Zentron Laboratory'는 친구를 Zentron 연구소로 소개한다는 뜻이므로 (B)가 정답이다.

193 Stable 씨에 대해 알 수 있는 것은?

(A) Zentron의 직원 모집자였다.
(B) 친구로부터 Zentron에 대해 들었다.
(C) 다양한 종류의 음료를 시음해 보았다.
(D) 제품 시험자로서 자격이 되지 않는다.

해설 후기의 첫 번째 문장 'I joined Zentron Laboratory as a product tester last year, and since then I've gotten paid to try beverages, soda, and much more'에서 1년 동안 여러 번 참여하였다는 것을 알 수 있다. 따라서 (C)가 정답이다.

어휘 used to ~였었다 various 다양한 qualify for ~할 자격이 되다

194 후기에 따르면 웹 페이지의 어떤 부분이 정확하지 않은가?
(A) 1단계
(B) 2단계
(C) 3단계
(D) 4단계

해설 웹 페이지에서 'we do not call any of our registered testers more than once a month'라고 하였으나 Stable 씨의 후기에서 'I received 5 to 6 calls a week during a month when I was out of the country'라고 하였으므로 (B)가 정답이다.

195 Zentron에 대해서 언급되지 않은 것은?
(A) 도시 안에 편리한 위치에 있다.
(B) 무료 주차 공간이 있다.
(C) 제품 검사자에게 현금 지급을 한다.
(D) 제품을 가지고 직접 방문한다.

해설 후기의 'The testing facility, in Napa Valley, is near a city bus stop'에서 (A)는 언급되었고, 후기의 'there is also plenty of free parking in the lot in front of the building'에서 (B)도 언급하였고 후기의 'I usually get paid $40 cash for just one hour of testing'에서 (C)도 언급되었다. 언급되지 않은 (D)가 정답이다.

어휘 conveniently 편리하게 available 이용 가능한 in person 직접

[196-200]

수신: Terzo Ventimiglia
발신: Augustine Liu
날짜: 6월 25일
주제: 인턴 대상 여름 행사
첨부: 행사 일정

안녕하세요, Terzo.

우리 인턴 대상 여름 행사 계획을 요청합니다. 제품 개발 부서보다 연구 개발 부서에 인턴수가 더 적으니 197 당신 부서 인턴들을 우리가 하는 주말과 저녁 활동들에 합류하도록 초청하고 싶어요. 재미있는 경험이 될 것이며 인턴들은 행사에 참여함으로써 직접적인 경험이 주어진다고 생각하게 할 거예요.

198 Brandington 일간지의 온라인 호에서 읽은 새로운 기회를 소개하고 싶어요. 다음은 올해 행사의 새로운 장소에 대한 정보가 있는 기사 링크에요: www.brandingtondailynews.com/mtduncan.

행사에 대해 너무 기대하고 있지만 걱정되는 점도 있으니 196 당신이 제안하는 어떤 의견도 중요하게 생각해요. 행사에 대해 생각하고 있는 점들을 알려 주세요. 미리 제안하는 어떤 충고에도 감사합니다. 올해 일정표는 첨부했어요.

Augustine Liu
제품 개발 부서

여름 캠프 일정

7월 6일: East Pleasantville의 Corners 농장에서 농업 박람회

7월 28일: Topenski 놀이공원에서 하루

8월 14일: Great Skies 관람하는 영화의 밤

198 9월 10일: 야외 하이킹 1일 여행

올해의 활동 일정표가 전년도와 약간 다르다는 것에 주목해 주세요.

Brandington 일간지

198 다음 주에 Duncan 산의 개선된 산책로가 개장됩니다.

6월 23일 – 금요일 공원 관리인은 3개의 새로운 하이킹 산책로가 7월 1일 개장된다고 발표했습니다. 지난 가을에 산책로에 공사가 시작되었습니다. 12월부터 3월까지 199 겨울 날씨 때문에 중단되었던 산책로 작업은 4월과 5월에 다시 진행되었습니다. 200 새로운 산책로는 초보자용으로 설계되었고 참가자들에게 경험과 전문성을 요구하지 않습니다.

공원과 여가 생활 담당자 Nancy Phan은 이 지역 여가 생활을 위해 산책로가 주는 새로운 기회로 "전율이 와요"라고 말했습니다. "Duncan 산은 항상 사랑받는 이 지역의 명소가 되어 왔습니다."라고 Phan 씨는 "이전에는 경력 있는 하이커들만 이용할 수 있었지만 이제는 커뮤니티에 있는 모든 사람들이 즐길 수 있을 거예요."라고 Phan 씨는 말하며, 이 산책로가 여행을 활성화시키고 휴가를 가는 가족들과 기업 수련회에 바람직한 장소도 제공할 수 있는 미래의 사업 기회를 만들어 낼 것을 바란다고 덧붙였습니다.

어휘 meaningful 의미 있는 first-hand 직접적인 recreational 여가의 edition 호, 판 value 소중히 여기다 input 의견 have in mind 생각하다 in advance 먼저, 사전에 attached 첨부된 agricultural 농업의 featuring 등장하는, 나오는 slightly 살짝, 약간 be different from ~과 다르다 previous 사전의 trail 산책로 suspend 중단시키다 ongoing 진행하고 있는 throughout ~에 걸쳐서 expertise 전문성 thrilled 전율이 오는 beloved 사랑 받는 landmark 명소, 주요 건물 previously 사전에 accessible 접근하기 쉬운 desirable 바람직한 corporate 기업의 excursion 여행

196 이메일의 주요 목적은?
(A) 동료들의 의견 요청하기
(B) 워크숍 기획 문의하기
(C) 행사 일정 정정하기
(D) 제품 시연 취소하기

해설 이메일의 두 번째 단락에서 'Please let me know what you have in your mind for the events. Thank you in advance for any advice you can offer'라고 하였으므로 (A)가 정답이다.

어휘 inquire about ~에 대해서 문의하다 organize 기획하다

197 Liu 씨가 이메일에서 제안한 것은?
(A) 연구부서 고용 인턴의 수를 늘이기
(B) 두 부서간의 여름 연합 캠프 계획하기
(C) 돈을 절약하기 위해 친목회의 수를 줄이기
(D) 인턴 중 한 명이 행사 기획을 이끌도록 임명하기

해설 이메일 첫 번째 단락 'I want to invite your interns to join ours'에서 제안하고 있는 것이 (B)임을 알 수 있다.

어휘 joint 연합 social gathering 친목(사교) 모임 appoint 임명하다 organization 기획

198 Liu 씨가 올해의 새로운 행사로 제안한 날짜는?
(A) 7월 6일
(B) 7월 28일
(C) 8월 14일
(D) 9월 10일

해설 연계 지문 문제이다. 이메일에서 'I'd like to introduce a new recreational opportunity I read about in the online edition of the Brandington Daily News'라고 언급되었는데, 기사에서 'Improved Trails on Mount Duncan'이라고 하였으므로 일정표에서 야외 활동을 진행하는 날짜인 (D)가 정답이다.

199 공사 중단의 원인은 무엇이었는가?
(A) 날씨
(B) 예산 고려
(C) 도시 허가증 획득 지연
(D) 능력 있는 직원의 결여

해설 기사의 첫 번째 단락에서 'Work on the trails, which had been suspended ... due to winter weather'라고 언급했으므로 정답은 (A)이다.

어휘 budgetary 예산의 obtain 획득하다 permit 허가(증)

200 Duncan 산에 대해서 알 수 있는 것은?
(A) 몇몇 스포츠 대회가 열리기로 예정되어 있다.
(B) 능숙한 하이커들이 산을 오르는 도전을 즐긴다.
(C) 일반 대중들이 쉽게 이용할 수 있게 되었다.
(D) 공사가 일정보다 앞서 완성되었다.

해설 기사의 두 번째 단락에서 그녀가 인터뷰한 내용을 보면 'it was previously accessible only to experienced hikers. Now, everyone in our community will be able to enjoy it'라고 언급하였으므로 (C)가 정답이다.

어휘 competition 대회 accessible 이용 가능한 ahead of schedule 일정보다 먼저

Actual Test 04

Listening Comprehension

본책 P140

PART 1

1 (C)	2 (D)	3 (A)	4 (C)	5 (A)	6 (A)				

PART 2

7 (C)	8 (C)	9 (A)	10 (C)	11 (C)	12 (B)	13 (C)	14 (B)	15 (B)	16 (B)
17 (B)	18 (A)	19 (C)	20 (A)	21 (C)	22 (C)	23 (A)	24 (B)	25 (B)	26 (A)
27 (A)	28 (C)	29 (A)	30 (B)	31 (C)					

PART 3

32 (C)	33 (B)	34 (A)	35 (A)	36 (D)	37 (C)	38 (A)	39 (D)	40 (B)	41 (C)
42 (B)	43 (B)	44 (A)	45 (C)	46 (B)	47 (A)	48 (A)	49 (C)	50 (C)	51 (D)
52 (B)	53 (C)	54 (D)	55 (C)	56 (B)	57 (D)	58 (C)	59 (A)	60 (B)	61 (C)
62 (D)	63 (C)	64 (A)	65 (C)	66 (C)	67 (C)	68 (D)	69 (B)	70 (D)	

PART 4

71 (C)	72 (A)	73 (B)	74 (C)	75 (A)	76 (B)	77 (A)	78 (D)	79 (B)	80 (D)
81 (C)	82 (A)	83 (D)	84 (A)	85 (A)	86 (B)	87 (C)	88 (A)	89 (C)	90 (A)
91 (B)	92 (C)	93 (A)	94 (A)	95 (D)	96 (A)	97 (B)	98 (D)	99 (A)	100 (C)

Reading Comprehension

본책 P152

PART 5

101 (B)	102 (C)	103 (A)	104 (D)	105 (A)	106 (C)	107 (B)	108 (D)	109 (A)	110 (C)
111 (A)	112 (D)	113 (A)	114 (D)	115 (D)	116 (B)	117 (D)	118 (C)	119 (D)	120 (A)
121 (D)	122 (C)	123 (C)	124 (D)	125 (B)	126 (C)	127 (D)	128 (A)	129 (B)	130 (B)

PART 6

131 (B)	132 (A)	133 (D)	134 (C)	135 (B)	136 (B)	137 (C)	138 (D)	139 (D)	140 (A)
141 (A)	142 (B)	143 (B)	144 (C)	145 (C)	146 (A)				

PART 7

147 (A)	148 (C)	149 (C)	150 (B)	151 (D)	152 (D)	153 (C)	154 (A)	155 (C)	156 (D)
157 (A)	158 (D)	159 (B)	160 (A)	161 (D)	162 (B)	163 (D)	164 (C)	165 (A)	166 (A)
167 (C)	168 (C)	169 (C)	170 (A)	171 (B)	172 (D)	173 (D)	174 (B)	175 (C)	176 (B)
177 (B)	178 (A)	179 (C)	180 (A)	181 (D)	182 (D)	183 (B)	184 (D)	185 (A)	186 (C)
187 (D)	188 (D)	189 (A)	190 (B)	191 (D)	192 (D)	193 (D)	194 (C)	195 (B)	196 (D)
197 (B)	198 (C)	199 (B)	200 (A)						

PART 1

1 미W
(A) She is making a photocopy.
(B) She is posting a notice on the board.
(C) She is operating a machine.
(D) She is holding some wires.

(A) 여자가 복사를 하고 있다.
(B) 여자가 게시판에 공지를 붙이고 있다.
(C) 여자가 기계를 작동시키고 있다.
(D) 여자가 전선들을 잡고 있다.

해설 1인 사진으로 인물의 동작이나 상태에 주목한다. 여자가 장비를 조작하고 있으므로 정답은 (C)이다. (A)는 여자가 작동시키는 기계는 복사기가 아니며, 게시판이나 전선 등도 사진에서 보이지 않으므로 (B)와 (D) 모두 오답이다.

어휘 make a photocopy 복사하다 post a notice 게시물을 붙이다 operate (기계를) 가동하다 wire 전선, 철사

2 영M
(A) A cyclist has pulled ahead of the bus.
(B) A cyclist and a bus have collided.
(C) A group of cyclists is traveling along the street.
(D) A cyclist is riding alongside a vehicle.

(A) 자전거를 타는 사람이 버스 앞으로 나가고 있다.
(B) 자전거를 타는 사람과 버스가 충돌했다.
(C) 자전거를 타는 무리들이 길을 따라 가고 있다.
(D) 자전거를 타는 사람이 차량 옆으로 나란히 달리고 있다.

해설 차량 옆으로 나란히 자전거 타는 모습을 묘사한 (D)가 가장 알맞은 답이다. 자전거와 버스가 충돌한 모습이나, 무리 지어서 자전거를 타는 모습은 보이지 않으므로 (B)와 (C) 모두 오답이다.

어휘 pull ahead of ~을 앞서다 collide 충돌하다, 부딪치다 travel along ~을 따라 가다 alongside ~ 옆에, 나란히

3 미W
(A) Merchandise is being displayed outside a shop.
(B) Postcards are being selected from a pair of racks.
(C) A cabinet has been stocked with supplies.
(D) Some items are being put onto hangers.

(A) 상품이 상점 외부에 진열되어 있다.
(B) 엽서들이 한 쌍의 걸이에서 선택되고 있다.
(C) 캐비닛이 물건들로 채워져 있다.
(D) 몇 개의 물건들이 옷걸이에 걸리고 있다.

해설 상점 외부에 상품들이 진열되어 있는 상태를 적절히 묘사한 (A)가 가장 알맞은 답이다. 사람이 등장하지 않는 사진에서도 정답이 될 수 있는 수동태 진행형 구문으로는 '전시, 진열' 등의 상태를 나타내는 be being displayed/shown/exhibited가 있음을 숙지하자. (B)와 (D)는 사람이 없는 사진에서 사물을 주어로 하는 수동태 진행형을 사용한 오답이며, (C)는 사진에서 보관장(cabinet)을 찾아볼 수 없으므로 오답이다.

어휘 merchandise 물품, 상품 postcard 우편엽서 rack (물건을 걸기 위한) 걸이 stock 채우다 hanger 옷걸이

4 미M
(A) Workers are emptying a trash can.
(B) Visitors are enjoying an outing.
(C) A path winds through a park.
(D) Plants are being planted along the path.

(A) 인부들이 쓰레기통을 비우고 있다.
(B) 방문자들이 야유회를 즐기고 있다.
(C) 공원 사이에 길이 굽어져 있다.
(D) 식물들이 길을 따라 심겨지고 있다.

해설 사진 속에 걸어가는 사람이 한 명이므로 여러 사람을 묘사한 (A)와 (B)는 주어 불일치 오류이며, (D)와 같이 사물을 주어로 하는 수동태 진행형(be being planted)은 그 사물이 사람이 행하는 동작의 대상이 되어야 정답이 될 수 있는데 사진에 식물을 심는 사람이 없으므로 오답이다.

어휘 trash can 쓰레기통, 휴지통 outing 야유회, 소풍 wind (도로, 강 등이) 굽이지다, 구불구불하다

5 미W
(A) A clerk is stationed behind a sales counter.
(B) A woman is handing a card to a cashier.
(C) An employee is stocking a store shelf.
(D) A woman is trying on necklaces.

(A) 점원이 카운터 뒤에 있다.
(B) 여자가 계산원에게 카드를 건네주고 있다.
(C) 직원이 선반에 물건을 채우고 있다.
(D) 여자가 목걸이를 걸어보고 있다.

해설 다수의 인물이 혼재된 실내 배경 사진으로 각 인물의 행동 묘사에 주목해야 한다. 상점 점원이 카운터에 서 있는 위치를 적절하게 묘사한 (A)가 정답이다. 여자의 행동 묘사가 어울리지 않는 (B)와 (D)는 오답이며 선반을 채우는 행동 또한 점원의 동작과 무관하므로 (C)도 오답이다.

어휘 station 배치하다, 위치하다 necklace 목걸이

6 영M
(A) A shelter has been erected by the water.
(B) Cargo ships are lined up at the docks.
(C) A container is suspended from a crane.
(D) Sailors are about to board a vessel.

(A) 물가에 쉼터가 세워져 있다.
(B) 화물선들이 부두에 줄 지어 있다.
(C) 컨테이너가 크레인에 매달려 있다.
(D) 선원들이 배에 승선하려고 한다.

해설 사람이 등장하지 않는 사물, 풍경 사진으로 각 사물들의 명칭을 집중해서 들어야 한다. 햇빛을 피할 수 있도록 만든 은신처가 해변에 세워져 있는 모습을 적절히 묘사한 (A)가 가장 알맞은 답이다. 멀리 화물선이 있으나 줄 지어 있다고 묘사한 (B)는 오답이며, 사진에 없는 사물(container)과 사람(sailors)을 언급한 (C)와 (D)도 오답이다.

어휘 shelter 은신처, 대피소 erect 세우다, 건립하다 cargo ship 화물선 dock 선착장, 부두 suspend 매달다, 걸다 vessel (대형) 선박, 배

PART 2

7 미M 미W
Which of these pictures would look better in the brochure?
(A) Thanks, I feel better.
(B) I got it in the mail.
(C) I don't like either one.

이 사진들 중에 어떤 것이 안내 책자에 더 나을까요?
(A) 감사합니다. 기분이 나아졌어요.
(B) 우편으로 받았어요.
(C) 둘 다 마음에 들지 않아요.

해설 어떤 사진이 좋아 보이는지를 묻는 Which 의문문에 좋은 사진이 없다고 답변한 (C)가 가장 적절한 답이다. (A)는 질문의 better를 반복 사용한 오답이며, (B)에서 의문사 질문에 감사하다는 인사는 전혀 무관한 답변이다.

어휘 brochure 안내 책자 mail 우편, 우편물

8 영M 미W
Is Mr. Kline back from his appointment yet?
(A) Are you all ready?
(B) Yes, he gave it back.
(C) I'm not certain.

Kline 씨가 약속에서 돌아왔나요?
(A) 모두들 준비되었나요?
(B) 네, 그가 돌려주었어요.
(C) 확실하지 않습니다.

해설 Mr. Kline이 돌아왔는지 여부를 묻는 be동사 의문문에 잘 모르겠다는 전형적인 회피성 답변을 하는 (C)가 정답이다. (A)는 질문의 의미와 연관 없을 뿐 아니라, 주어가 일치되지 않으며, (B)는 Mr. Kline이 돌아왔는지 묻는 질문에 Yes로 답변하면 돌아왔다는 의미는 전달이 되지만 뒤에 관련 없는 내용이 이어지고 있으므로 오답이다.

어휘 yet (의문문에서) 이미, 벌써 certain 확실한, 틀림없는

9 미W 미M
What type of firm are you working for?
(A) We provide a variety of financial services.
(B) Mostly during our regular office hours.
(C) Actually, I'm still working on it.

어떤 종류의 회사에서 근무하시나요?
(A) 저희는 다양한 금융 서비스를 제공하고 있어요.
(B) 대부분 우리 정규 근무 시간 동안이에요.
(C) 사실, 저는 아직 작업 중이에요.

해설 어떤 종류의 회사에서 일하는지 묻는 What 의문문에 단답형이 아닌 구체적으로 하는 일을 설명하는 (A)가 가장 적절하다. (B)는 기간을 묻는 How long 의문사에 어울리는 답변이며, (C)는 working을 반복 사용하여 혼동을 유도하고 있다.

어휘 firm 회사 a variety of 다양한 financial service 금융 서비스 office hours 영업 시간, 근무 시간

10 미W 영M

Do you think the guests would prefer Italian or Thai food?
(A) I'll just have a dessert.
(B) It's probably more popular.
(C) Why don't you ask them?

손님이 이탈리아 음식을 좋아할까요, 태국 음식을 좋아할까요?
(A) 저는 디저트만 먹을게요.
(B) 이것이 아마 더 유명할 거예요.
(C) 그들에게 물어보는 게 어떨까요?

해설 손님들이 어떤 음식을 좋아할지 묻는 선택의문문에 그들에게 물어볼 것을 제안하며 되묻고 있는 (C)가 가장 적절하다. 회피성 답변으로 자주 쓰이는 〈ask + 사람〉 구문을 사용한 전형적인 표현으로 답하고 있다. (A)는 선택의문문의 음식(Italian or Thai food)에서 연상 가능한 dessert를 사용하여 혼동을 유도하고 있으며 (B)는 질문의 내용과 전혀 무관하다.

어휘 guest 손님, 내빈 popular 인기 있는

11 영M 미M

Can you call to see if the accounts office received the report we sent?
(A) In the phone directory.
(B) Here's Tran's office.
(C) I'll do it right away.

우리가 보낸 보고서를 회계 사무소가 받았는지 전화로 알아봐줄 수 있나요?
(A) 전화번호부에서요.
(B) 여기가 Tran의 사무실입니다.
(C) 지금 바로 하겠습니다.

해설 확인을 요청하는 의문문에 바로 하겠다고 긍정적 대답을 하는 (C)가 가장 적절한 답이다. (A)는 장소를 묻는 질문에 어울리는 답변이며 (B)는 질문의 office를 반복 사용한 오답이다.

어휘 accounts office 회계 사무실 phone directory 전화번호부 right away 당장, 즉시

12 미M 미W

How late will you be working at the office today?
(A) Tomorrow morning instead.
(B) I plan to leave within a couple of hours.
(C) As long as I finish on time.

오늘 사무실에 얼마나 늦게까지 있을 거예요?
(A) 대신에 내일 아침이요.
(B) 두 시간 안에 갈 계획이에요.
(C) 제시간에 끝내기만 한다면요.

해설 얼마나 늦게까지 남아서 일을 할 것인지를 묻는 How late 의문문에 기간으로 적절히 답변한 (B)가 정답이다. (A)는 얼마나 늦은 시간까지 일할 것인지를 묻고 있는 질문에 상관없는 답변이다. 내일 아침까지 계속 일할 것이다(until tomorrow morning)로 혼동하지 않도록 주의해야 한다. (C)는 조건을 제시하며 질문에 어울리지 않는 표현을 하고 있으므로 오답이다.

어휘 instead 대신에 as long as ~하는 한, ~하는 동안은

13 영M 미W

Whose turn is it to clean the staff lounge?
(A) Rachael already placed that order.
(B) The company's new internship program.
(C) I'll have to check the schedule.

직원 휴게실 청소가 누구 차례인가요?
(A) Rachael이 이미 그 주문을 했어요.
(B) 회사의 새로운 인턴십 프로그램입니다.
(C) 제가 일정을 확인해 볼게요.

해설 누구의 차례인지를 묻는 Whose 의문문에 일정을 확인해 보겠다고 회피성 대답을 하는 (C)가 가장 적절한 답변이다. (A)는 Whose 의문사에 정답인 것처럼 제3자의 이름을 제시하며 혼동을 유도하고 있으나 질문과 연관성이 없는 답변이 이어지고 있으며, (B)는 질문의 staff에서 확대 연상 가능한 internship을 사용하여 혼동을 유도하고 있는 오답이다.

어휘 turn (무슨 일을 할) 차례, 순번 staff lounge 직원 휴게실

14 미W 미M

You discussed the marketing campaign with the supervisor, didn't you?
(A) Some of the new employees.
(B) I'm meeting with him later this afternoon.
(C) Certainly, whenever you'd like.

관리자와 마케팅 캠페인을 논의했지요, 그렇지 않아요?
(A) 몇 명의 새로운 직원들이요.
(B) 오늘 오후에 그를 만날 거예요.
(C) 물론이죠, 좋으실 때 언제든지요.

해설 관리자와 논의를 했는지 확인하는 부가의문문에 오후에 만나서 논의할 거라고 설명하는 (B)가 정답이다. (A)는 질문의 supervisor에서 연상 가능한 employees를 사용하여 혼동을 유도하고 있으며, (C)는 확인하는 질문에 Certainly로 답변하면 논의했다는 의미는 전달이 되지만 뒤에 관련 없는 내용이 이어지고 있으므로 오답이다.

어휘 supervisor 관리자, 감독관

15 미W 영M

Who'll be representing our firm at the seminar?
(A) With a marketing manager.
(B) Ms. Brenner will.
(C) That's a good idea.

누가 세미나에서 우리 회사를 대표할 건가요?
(A) 마케팅 관리자와 함께요.
(B) Brenner 씨가 할 겁니다.
(C) 좋은 생각이에요.

해설 대표자가 누구인지를 묻는 Who 의문문에 전형적인 제3자의 이름을 언급하며 그 사람이 할 것이라고 말하는 (B)가 가장 적절하다. (A)는 직책을 언급하며 Who 의문문에 알맞은 답인 것처럼 혼동을 유도하고 있으나 매니저와 함께 할 주체가 없으므로 오답이고, (C)은 제안의문문에 어울리는 답변으로 의문사의 답으로는 적절하지 않은 표현이다.

어휘 represent 대표하다, 대변하다

16 미M 영M

Will anyone accompany you to the convention, or are you going on your own?
(A) Yes, until I start my own company.
(B) A colleague is coming along with me.
(C) It's an amazing invention.

컨벤션에 누군가와 함께 가시나요 아니면 혼자 가실 예정인가요?
(A) 네, 제가 제 회사를 시작할 때까지요.
(B) 회사 동료가 저와 함께 갈 거예요.
(C) 훌륭한 발명품이에요.

해설 컨벤션 참석을 묻는 상황으로 혼자 갈지, 누군가와 함께 갈지를 묻는 선택의문문에 동료와 함께 갈 것이라고 답변하는 (B)가 가장 적절하다. (A)는 질문과 연관성 없는 시점을 언급하고 있으며, (C)는 질문의 convention과 발음이 유사한 invention을 사용하여 혼동을 유도하고 있으나 질문과 무관한 답변을 하고 있다.

어휘 accompany 동반하다, 동행하다 on one's own 혼자서, 단독으로

17 미M 미W

Why didn't you visit our plant in Cyprus?
(A) To visit with my nephew.
(B) We ran out of time.
(C) It went very well.

Cyprus에 있는 우리 공장에 왜 방문하지 않았나요?
(A) 제 조카와 함께 방문하기 위해서요.
(B) 우리는 시간이 부족했어요.
(C) 그것은 아주 잘 됐어요.

해설 공장에 방문하지 않은 이유를 묻는 Why 의문문에 시간이 없었다고 설명하는 (B)가 가장 적절한 답이다. (A)는 이유를 설명하기에 적합한 to 부정사를 사용하여 혼동을 유도하고 있지만 일에 관한 질문의 답으로는 의미상 어울리지 않으며 질문의 visit을 반복 사용한 발음 오답이다. (C)는 진행 상황을 묻는 How 의문문에 어울리는 답변이다.

어휘 nephew 남자 조카 run out of ~을 다 써버리다 go well 잘 되어 가다

18 영M 미W

We aren't allowed to park here, are we?
(A) Not at this time of day.
(B) It seems extremely long.
(C) The park used to be there.

우리는 이곳에 주차를 할 수 없어요, 그렇죠?
(A) 이 시간에는 안 됩니다.
(B) 매우 긴 것 같아요.
(C) 공원이 거기 있었어요.

해설 주차가 가능한지 확인하는 부가의문문에 지금은 불가능하다고 답변하는 (A)가 가장 적절하다. (B)는 질문과 전혀 어울리지 않는 답변이며, (C)는 질문의 park(주차하다)와 발음이 같은 park(공원)를 사용하여 혼동을 유도하는 오답으로 전혀 다른 의미로 사용되는 점에 유의해야 한다.

어휘 extremely 극도로, 극히

19 When will the new safety guidelines take effect?
미W (A) Very safe, in my opinion.
미M (B) Not according to the new tour guide.
(C) The date hasn't been announced yet.

새로운 안전 지침은 언제 실시되나요?
(A) 제 생각으론 아주 안전해요.
(B) 새로운 여행 가이드에 따르면 그렇지 않습니다.
(C) 날짜는 아직 공지되지 않았어요.

해설 적용이 되는 시점을 묻는 When 의문문에 날짜가 정해지지 않았다며 회피성으로 답변하고 있는 (C)가 가장 적절한 답이다. (A)는 질문의 safety와 어근이 동일한 safe를 사용하며, (B)는 문제의 guidelines와 유사한 guide를 사용하여 혼동을 유도한 오답이다.

어휘 safety 안전, 안전성 guideline 지침, 지도 규범 take effect 효과가 나타나다, (법률이) 실시되다

20 I hope the board meeting doesn't run late.
미W **(A) It usually doesn't.**
영M (B) He runs in the evening on most days.
(C) I was there until the end.

이사회가 늦게까지 진행되지 않길 바랍니다.
(A) 대체로 안 그러잖아요.
(B) 그는 보통 저녁에 뛰어요.
(C) 저는 끝까지 거기에 있었어요.

해설 이사회가 늦게까지 지속되지 않길 바란다는 평서문에 보통 그런 일은 없다고 긍정적인 답을 하는 (A)가 가장 적절하다. (B)는 질문의 run(진행하다)와 동음이의어인 run(뛰다)을 사용하여 혼동을 유도한 오답이며, (C)는 질문의 late에서 연상이 가능한 the end를 사용하여 답변한 오답이다.

어휘 board meeting 이사회 run 뛰다, 운영하다, 진행되다 usually 보통, 대체로 on most days 평상시, 보통

21 Didn't Mr. Palo make a copy of the sales report for the staff?
영M (A) Sales were higher than expected.
미M (B) He's buying a lot of stuff.
(C) No, I'm afraid we have to share.

Palo 씨가 직원들을 위한 영업 보고서를 복사하지 않았나요?
(A) 판매량이 기대한 것보다 높았어요.
(B) 그는 물건을 많이 사고 있어요.
(C) 아니요, 죄송하지만 공유해야 합니다.

해설 제3자가 직원들을 위해 복사를 했는지 확인하는 부정의문문에 모든 직원들에게 줄 만큼 충분히 복사가 되지 않았다는 의미로 공유해야 한다고 설명한 (C)가 가장 적절한 답변이다. (A)는 질문의 sales를 반복 사용한 오답이며, (B)는 질문의 staff와 발음이 유사한 stuff를 사용하면서 주어까지 일치시켜 혼동을 유도하고 있으나 질문과 무관한 답변을 하고 있으므로 오답이다.

어휘 make a copy 복사하다 stuff 것(것들), 물건 share 함께 쓰다, 공유하다

22 Has the board of directors reviewed the contract yet?
미M (A) Yes, I saw it last night.
미W (B) I'll have them contact you right away.
(C) They'll discuss it tomorrow.

이사회가 계약서를 이미 검토했나요?
(A) 네, 제가 지난밤에 그것을 봤어요.
(B) 제가 바로 그들이 당신에게 연락하도록 할게요.
(C) 그들은 내일 논의할 거예요.

해설 이사회가 계약서를 검토했는지 여부를 묻는 의문문에 아직 하지 않았으나 내일 할 계획이라고 대답한 (C)가 가장 적절한 답이다. (A)는 Yes로 대답하면 논의했다는 의미로는 연결이 되나 주어가 맞지 않으며, (B)는 질문의 contract와 발음이 유사한 contact를 사용하여 혼동을 유도한 오답이다.

어휘 board of directors 이사회, 임원회

23 I heard that Steve is being promoted next month.
영M **(A) Yes, his secretary said so.**
미W (B) He should be proud of you.
(C) No, he didn't do it.

Steve가 다음 달에 승진한다고 들었어요.
(A) 네, 그의 비서가 그렇게 얘기했어요.
(B) 그는 분명 당신을 자랑스러워할 거예요.
(C) 아니요, 그가 하지 않았어요.

해설 제3자의 승진에 관한 정보를 알려주는 평서문에 그의 비서가 얘기했다며 동의하는 답변을 하는 (A)가 가장 적절한 답이다. (B)는 질문의 promoted에서 연상이 가능한 be proud of로 답변한 오답이며, (C)는 No로 답하면 승진하지 않았다는 의미로는 이해할 수 있으나 부연 설명이 질문과 무관하므로 오답이다.

어휘 promote 승진, 진급시키다 be proud of ~을 자랑으로 여기다

24 When do you think we should start preparing presentation slides?
미W (A) I'll be in the office then.
미M **(B) By next Thursday, at the latest.**
(C) We already have enough materials.

프레젠테이션 슬라이드 준비를 언제 시작해야 한다고 생각하세요?
(A) 저는 그때 사무실에 있을 거예요.
(B) 늦어도 다음 주 목요일까지요.
(C) 우리는 이미 충분한 자료가 있어요.

해설 준비해야 할 시점을 묻는 When 의문문에 정확한 시점으로 대답한 (B)가 정답이다. (A)는 장소 답변으로 Where 의문문에 어울리며, (C)는 질문의 presentation에서 연상이 가능한 materials를 사용하여 혼동을 유도한 오답이다.

어휘 at the latest 늦어도 material 자료, 재료

25 We've run out of envelopes.
미W (A) I'll get some more letters.
영M **(B) Have you look in the stationery cabinet?**
(C) You should do some exercise.

우리는 봉투가 다 떨어졌어요.
(A) 제가 편지들을 더 가지고 올게요.
(B) 사무용품 캐비닛을 확인해 보셨나요?
(C) 당신은 운동을 좀 해야겠어요.

해설 봉투가 없다는 사실을 알리는 평서문에 있을 만한 장소를 확인해 보았는지 되묻고 있는 (B)가 가장 적절한 답이다. (A)는 질문의 envelopes와 연관성이 있는 letters를 사용하여 혼동을 유도하고 있으며 (C)도 질문의 run에서 연상이 가능한 exercise을 이용하여 혼동을 유도하고 있는 오답이다.

어휘 run out of ~을 다 써버리다 envelope 봉투 stationery 문구류

26 How's the discussion coming along?
영M **(A) It'll be finished shortly.**
미M (B) We'll talk about it later.
(C) They've been waiting a long time.

논의는 어떻게 되어가고 있나요?
(A) 잠시 후에 끝날 거예요.
(B) 우리는 그것을 나중에 얘기할 거예요.
(C) 그들이 오래 기다리고 있어요.

해설 토론 진행 상황을 묻는 How 의문문에 곧 끝날 것이라고 대답한 (A)가 가장 적절한 답이다. (B)는 문제의 discussion과 연관성이 있는 talk를 사용하여 혼동을 유도하고 있으며, (C)는 문제의 along과 비슷한 long을 사용한 전형적인 유사 발음 오답 유형이다.

어휘 come along (원하는 대로) 되어 가다, 함께 가다

27 Shouldn't you be attending the management workshop this afternoon?
미M **(A) I was told to work on this analysis instead.**
미W (B) Yes, I've been there last night.
(C) It's in Meeting Room 102.

당신은 오늘 오후에 경영 관리 워크숍에 참석해야 하지 않나요?
(A) 대신에 이 분석 작업을 하라는 당부를 받았어요.
(B) 네, 저는 지난밤에 거기에 갔었어요.
(C) 102회의실이에요.

해설 워크숍에 참석 여부를 확인하는 부정의문문에 다른 일을 하라는 당부를 받아서 참석하지 못할 거라는 불참의 이유를 적절히 설명한 (A)가 정답이다. (B)는 Yes로 대답하여 참석할 거라는 의미로 이해되지만 이미 다녀왔다는 부연 설명이 질문과 어울리지 않으며, (C)는 문제의 workshop과 연관성 있는 Meeting Room을 이용하여 혼동을 유도하고 있다.

어휘 management 경영 be told to ~하라고 당부를 받다 analysis 분석

28 What was your hotel like in Milan?
영M (A) Sure, I made a reservation.
미W (B) Sounds like a good plan.

(C) The rooms were tidy and spacious.

Milan에 있는 호텔은 어땠나요?
(A) 물론이죠, 예약했어요.
(B) 좋은 계획 같네요.
(C) 방들이 깨끗하고 넓었어요.

해설 숙소가 어땠는지를 묻는 What 의문문에 호텔 방에 대해 적절히 묘사하고 있는 (C)가 정답이다. (A)는 의문사 의문문에 Yes/No로 대답할 수 없으므로 긍정의 의미인 sure는 오답이며, (B)는 제안의문문에 어울리는 답변이므로 의문사 의문문의 답변으로 적절하지 않다. 제안의문문인 What about ~?(~하는 것이 어떨까?) 구문과 혼동하지 않도록 주의해야 한다.

어휘 tidy 깔끔한, 잘 정돈된 spacious 넓은

29 Did the camera you bought include batteries?
미W 미M
(A) No, they were extra.
(B) I'll take them, thank you.
(C) Yes, because it was full.

당신이 구입한 카메라에 배터리가 포함되어 있었나요?
(A) 아니요, 그건 별도였어요.
(B) 제가 살게요. 감사합니다.
(C) 네, 왜냐하면 가득 있었거든요.

해설 카메라에 배터리가 들어 있었는지 묻는 질문에 별도로 구입했다고 언급한 (A)가 적절한 답변이다. (B)는 물건을 구입할 때 사용하는 표현으로 이미 구입 물건에 대해 묻는 질문과는 연관이 없으며, (C)는 Yes로 답하면 배터리가 포함되어 있었다는 의미로 이해할 수 있지만 부연 설명으로 이유를 언급하고 있으므로 오답이다.

어휘 extra 여분의, 별도 계산의

30 Were you on vacation last week?
미W 영M
(A) I'll be back on Monday.
(B) I went up to Castalian Spring.
(C) I'll make sure to be on time.

지난주에 휴가 갔었어요?
(A) 저는 월요일에 돌아올 거예요.
(B) 저는 Castalian 샘에 올라갔어요.
(C) 꼭 제시간에 오도록 할게요.

해설 휴가를 갔었는지 묻는 질문에 특정 장소의 지명을 언급하며 그곳에 갔었다고 말하는 (B)가 가장 알맞은 정답이다. (A)는 시제 불일치로 정답이 될 수 없으며 (C)는 질문과 연관성 없이 답하고 있다.

어휘 Castalian Spring 그리스에 위치한 카스탈리아의 샘 on time 제시간에

31 Where did Mr. Williams say the training would be held?
영M 미M
(A) There are enough seats for everyone.
(B) Anytime would be great with me.
(C) Hasn't it been postponed until tomorrow?

William 씨가 교육이 어디에서 열린다고 말했나요?
(A) 모든 사람을 위한 충분한 자리가 있어요.
(B) 저는 언제든 좋습니다.
(C) 내일로 연기되지 않았나요?

해설 교육이 열리는 장소를 묻는 Where 의문문에 연기되지 않았냐고 되물으며 자연스럽게 대화가 이어지는 (C)가 정답이다. tomorrow와 같은 시점을 언급했다는 이유만으로 When의 정답으로만 여겨 혼동을 유도하는 문제에 주의해야 한다. (A)의 좌석에 대한 정보와 (B)의 시간에 대한 설명은 질문과 연관성이 없으므로 오답이다.

어휘 be held 열리다, 개최하다 postpone 연기하다, 미루다

PART 3

P145

Questions 32-34 refer to the following conversation. 영M 미W

M Hello. Can I speak to Ernest Ferrel?
W ㉜ I'm afraid he is not in at the moment. He should be here later on this afternoon. Can I take a message and ask who is calling, please?
M Yes, this is Andy Hunt from City Weekly Deliveries. I sent Mr. Ferrel an e-mail last night regarding changes that need to be made to the clients' delivery list. ㉝ I've just received the updated version from him in the mail, but three new clients still haven't been added to it.
W Oh, I'm sorry to hear that, Mr. Hunt. ㉞ I'll let Ernest know as soon as possible and ask him to call you back.

남 안녕하세요. Ernest Ferrel 씨와 얘기할 수 있을까요?
여 죄송하지만, 지금 안 계십니다. 오늘 오후 늦게나 오실 거예요. 메시지를 남겨 드릴까요? 전화 거신 분은 누구신지 여쭤봐도 될까요?
남 네, 저는 City Weekly Deliveries의 Andy Hunt라고 합니다. 제가 어젯밤 Ferrel 씨께 고객 배송 리스트에 필요한 변경 사항들을 이메일로 보내 드렸습니다. 그리고 방금 그에게 최신 버전을 메일로 받았는데, 3명의 신규 고객들이 아직도 추가되지 않았습니다.
여 아, 죄송합니다, Hunt 씨. 제가 가능한 한 빨리 Ernest 씨에게 알리고, 전화 드리라고 하겠습니다.

어휘 I'm afraid (유감이지만) ~이다 regarding ~에 관하여 updated version 최신 버전 misplace (제자리에 두지 않아서) 찾지 못하다 relevant 관련 있는

32 Who most likely is the woman?
(A) An instructor
(B) A customer
(C) A personal assistant
(D) A delivery person

여자는 누구이겠는가?
(A) 강사
(B) 고객
(C) 개인 비서
(D) 배송 기사

해설 〈기본 정보 파악 – 직업〉
화자의 직업을 묻는 문제는 대화 첫 부분에서 단서를 찾아야 한다. 특정인과 통화를 원하는 남자에게 그 사람의 부재를 알리며 언제 통화가 가능한지 정보를 주고 있으므로 여자는 특정인의 비서임을 유추할 수 있다. 따라서 정답은 (C)이다.

33 According to the man, what is the problem?
(A) A manager is not available.
(B) A list of customers is incomplete.
(C) A document has been misplaced.
(D) A meeting was postponed.

남자에 의하면, 무엇이 문제인가?
(A) 매니저가 자리에 없다.
(B) 고객 리스트가 미완성이다.
(C) 문서가 분실되었다.
(D) 회의가 연기되었다.

해설 〈구체적 정보 파악 – 문제점〉
남자가 말하는 문제점이므로 남자의 대사에서 단서를 찾아야 한다. 대화 중반부에 남자가 이메일을 받았으나 정보가 누락되었다고 언급하고 있으므로 그 표현을 가장 적절하게 바꾸어 표현한 (B)가 정답이다. Ernest Ferrel의 부재를 언급하는 것은 여자이므로 (A)와 혼동하지 말아야 한다.

34 What will the woman do next?
(A) Contact the relevant person
(B) Check the customer list
(C) Search the Internet
(D) Provide an e-mail address

여자는 다음에 무엇을 할 것인가?
(A) 담당자에게 연락한다.
(B) 고객 리스트를 확인한다.
(C) 인터넷을 검색한다.
(D) 이메일 주소를 제공한다.

해설 〈구체적 정보 파악 – 미래〉
미래 정보 문제는 대화의 후반부에서 정답의 근거를 찾을 수 있다. 여자가 마지막 대사에서 Ernest 씨에게 알려서 연락하게 하겠다고 말하고 있으므로 정답은 (A)이다.

패러프레이징 let someone know ~에게 알리다
→ contact a relevant person 담당자에게 연락하다

Questions 35-37 refer to the following conversation. 미W 미M

W Hello. 36 I'm a guest in the room 802 who checked in this morning. 35 I'm calling because I found a leak in the bathroom. When I ran the shower, the floor got all wet. I turned it off right away but the whole area is totally soaked.
M I apologize, ma'am. Unfortunately, our repair person has left for the day. Why don't I change your room to another? 36 We have some vacant rooms on the second floor.
W That would be nice. 36 But that's six stories below where I'm staying now, and 37 I have some heavy suitcases. Is there anyone who can help me?
M Sure, we'll be glad to do that. I'll call someone at once.

여 안녕하세요. 저는 오늘 아침에 802호실에 체크인한 손님입니다. 화장실에 물이 새서 전화드렸습니다. 샤워기를 틀었더니 바닥이 온통 젖어 버렸네요. 바로 껐지만 흠뻑 젖었습니다.
남 정말 죄송합니다, 손님. 죄송하지만 저희 수리 직원이 퇴근을 했습니다. 제가 손님 방을 다른 방으로 바꾸어 드리는 것은 어떨까요? 2층에 비어 있는 방이 몇 개 있습니다.
여 그게 좋겠습니다. 하지만 거기는 지금 제가 머물고 있는 곳보다 6층 아래이고, 저에게는 무거운 여행 가방이 있어서요. 저를 도와주실 분이 있나요?
남 물론입니다. 기꺼이 그렇게 해 드리죠. 제가 바로 보내 드리겠습니다.

어휘 leak 새는 곳 leave for the day 퇴근하다

35 What does the woman complain about?
(A) A water leakage
(B) A broken electrical wire
(C) A cracked bathtub
(D) A locked door

여자는 무엇에 대해 불만을 제기하는가?
(A) 누수
(B) 끊어진 전선
(C) 깨진 욕조
(D) 잠긴 문

해설 〈구체적 정보 파악 – 문제점〉
여자가 언급하는 불만 사항이므로 처음에 여자가 말하는 부분에서 답을 유추할 수 있다. 첫 대사에서 여자가 화장실에서 물이 새는 것을 발견했다고 말하고 있으므로 이를 바꾸어 표현한 (A)가 정답이다.

패러프레이징 a leak in a bathroom 화장실에 물이 샌다
→ a water leakage 누수

36 What floor is the woman staying on?
(A) The second floor
(B) The fourth floor
(C) The sixth floor
(D) The eighth floor

여자는 몇 층에 머물고 있는가?
(A) 2층
(B) 4층
(C) 6층
(D) 8층

해설 〈구체적 정보 파악 – 특정 사항〉
여자가 대화 초반에 방의 호수를 말하는 부분에서 머물고 있는 층을 알 수 있으며, 또한 대화 중반부에서 남자가 2층에 빈방이 있으니 옮겨 준다고 하자, 여자가 6층 아래로 내려가야 한다는 말에서도 정답을 유추할 수 있다. 따라서 정답은 (D)이다

37 What does the woman ask the man to do?
(A) Give her a wake-up call
(B) Bring her some refreshments
(C) Assist her with the luggage
(D) Pick up her laundry

여자가 요청하는 것은 무엇인가?
(A) 모닝콜해 주기
(B) 다과를 가져다주기
(C) 짐 들어주기
(D) 세탁물을 찾아 주기

해설 〈구체적 정보 파악 – 요청 관련〉
여자가 남자에게 요청하는 사항이므로 여자의 말에서 정답을 찾아야 한다. 여자가 마지막에 가방을 옮겨줄 사람을 보내 달라고 요청하고 있으므로 정답은 (C)이다.

Questions 38-40 refer to the following conversation. 미W 영M

W Mr. Cole, this is Naomi Grant from Walton Commercial. I noticed your résumé on a professional marketing communication, and 38 I'm calling about an opening at our firm. We're looking for someone to help manage our design team, and your experience as both a public relations manager and instructor makes you ideal.
M I'm certainly interested in hearing more, 39 but unfortunately I'm in a rush. I'm conducting a workshop at the community center in just under an hour, and I'm a bit behind schedule. Can I call you back afterwards?
W I'll be out of town on business this afternoon, so how about tomorrow instead? In the meantime, 40 I'll email some details about the position for you to look through. It's a great opportunity for someone with your background.

여 Cole 씨, Walton Commercial의 Naomi Grant입니다. 전문 마케팅 커뮤니케이션에 관한 당신의 이력서를 보았고요, 저희 회사의 공석에 대해 말씀 드리려고 전화했습니다. 저희는 디자인 팀의 관리를 도와줄 사람을 찾고 있는데, 당신의 홍보 매니저 경력과 강사 경험이 이 직책에 알맞을 것 같습니다.
남 정말 더 듣고 싶지만, 불행히도 제가 바빠서요. 한 시간 이내에 주민 센터에서 워크숍을 진행하는데, 좀 늦었거든요. 제가 나중에 다시 전화드려도 될까요?
여 제가 오후에 출장을 갈 예정인데 내일은 어떠세요? 그 사이에 검토하실 수 있도록 직책에 대한 세부 사항을 이메일로 보내 드리겠습니다. 당신과 같은 이력을 가진 분께는 아주 훌륭한 기회입니다.

어휘 commercial 광고 résumé 이력서 professional 전문적인 opening 공석 public relation 홍보 instructor 강사, 교사 ideal 알맞은, 완벽한 in a rush 바쁘게 conduct (특정 활동을) 하다, 지휘하다 behind schedule 예정보다 늦게 afterwards 나중에, 그 뒤에 in the meantime 그동안, 그 사이에 look through ~을 검토하다 background 배경, 배후 사정 flexible 유동적인 job description 직무 내용 설명서

38 What is the woman calling to discuss?
(A) An open position
(B) A university program
(C) A marketing proposal
(D) A fashion magazine

여자는 무엇을 논의하려고 전화했는가?
(A) 공석
(B) 대학 프로그램
(C) 마케팅 제안
(D) 패션 잡지

해설 〈기본 정보 파악 – 목적〉
전화의 목적은 대화의 전반부에서 정답의 근거를 찾을 수 있다. 여자가 첫 대사에서 회사 공석 때문에 전화한다고 이유를 말하고 있으므로 정답은 (A)이다.

39 What does the man tell the woman?
(A) He is out of town.
(B) He is on another line.
(C) He has a flexible plan.
(D) He is in a hurry.

남자는 여자에게 뭐라고 말하는가?
(A) 그는 타지에 있다.
(B) 그는 통화 중이다.
(C) 그는 유동적인 계획을 가지고 있다.
(D) 그는 서두르고 있다.

해설 〈구체적 정보 파악 – 언급〉
남자가 언급하는 것을 묻는 문제이므로 남자의 대사에서 답을 유추해야 한다. 남자가 전화 통화를 계속하고 싶지만 일정에 늦어서 서두르고 있다고 했으므로 이를 바꾸어 표현한 (D)가 정답이다. 대화 중 반전을 의미하는 표현들(But, However, Unfortunately, I'm sorry ~, I'm afraid ~) 뒤에 정답이 언급되는 경우가 많으므로 이 부분을 주목해야 한다.

패러프레이징 in a rush 바쁜 → in a hurry 서둘러, 급히, 바쁜

40 What does the woman want the man to review?
(A) A detailed résumé
(B) A job description
(C) A business report
(D) A magazine article

여자는 남자가 무엇을 검토하길 원하는가?
(A) 세부 이력서
(B) 직무 상세 정보
(C) 사업 정보
(D) 잡지 기사

해설 〈구체적 정보 파악 – 특정 사항〉
문제의 키워드가 review이고, 여자가 남자에게 바라는 것이므로 여자의 대사에서 검토하라는 부분을 들어야 한다. 여자가 마지막 대사에서 남자가 검토할 수 있도록 직책에 대한 세부 사항을 이메일로 보내겠다고 언급하고 있으므로 정답은 (C)이다.

패러프레이징 details about the position 직책에 대한 세부 사항
→ job description 직무 상세 정보

Questions 41-43 refer to the following conversation. 미M 미W

M ㊶ You have a much larger number of finance books and journals than I'd thought. In fact, I was thinking I'd actually join the library membership since I plan on moving around this area.
W We do have a pretty extensive collection. I could sign you up right away, if you'd like. All you need to do is fill out this form and then pay a five dollar registration fee.
M Just five dollars? Is that all? I saw an ad in a brochure indicating there is a $15 fee. I think it was something about the library membership program.
W Oh, that's right. That's kind of like a special program. ㊷ It allows you to borrow double the number of books, up to 20 at a time instead of the usual 10 under the standard card. ㊸ One thing that's great about either card, though, is that it never expires.

남 제가 생각했던 것보다 훨씬 더 많은 양의 금융 서적과 저널이 있군요. 사실, 제가 이 근처로 이사 올 예정이라서 도서관 회원에 가입하려고 생각하고 있었습니다.
여 저희는 대규모의 보유 서적을 구비하고 있답니다. 원하시면, 지금 바로 가입시켜 드리겠습니다. 이 양식을 작성하시고, 5달러 등록비만 지불하시면 됩니다.
남 5달러요? 그게 전부인가요? 팸플릿 광고에서 비용이 15달러라고 봤거든요. 그건 도서관 멤버십 프로그램에 관한 것이었나봐요.
여 오, 맞아요. 그건 특별 프로그램이에요. 이 프로그램은 한 번에 20권까지 두 배로 빌릴 수 있습니다. 기본 카드로는 보통 한 번에 10권의 책만 가능하거든요. 두 카드 모두 좋은 점은 유효 기간이 없다는 것입니다.

어휘 extensive 아주 넓은(많은), 대규모의 sign up 등록하다 fill out 기입하다 작성하다 registration fee 등록비 brochure 팸플릿, 책자 expire 만료되다, 만기가 되다 indefinitely 무기한으로

41 Why is the man impressed with the library?
(A) The membership fee is free.
(B) The library is open all year round.
(C) The library's selection is broad.
(D) The library is open until late.

남자가 도서관에 감탄한 이유는 무엇인가?
(A) 회원 가입비가 무료이다.
(B) 도서관은 1년 내내 문을 연다.
(C) 도서관 보유 서적의 폭이 넓다.
(D) 도서관이 늦게까지 연다.

해설 〈구체적 정보 파악 – 특정 사항〉
남자가 감탄한 이유이므로 남자의 대사에 주목해야 한다. 남자는 첫 대사에서 도서관의 구비 서적이 많은 것에 놀라고 있으므로 이를 적절히 묘사한 (C)가 정답이다.

42 How many books can the man borrow if he has a regular card?
(A) 5 books
(B) 10 books
(C) 15 books
(D) 20 books

남자가 보통 카드를 가지고 있다면 몇 권의 책을 빌릴 수 있는가?
(A) 5권
(B) 10권
(C) 15권
(D) 20권

해설 〈구체적 정보 파악 – 특정 사항〉
regular card를 키워드로 잡고 여기에 초점을 맞춰 들어야 한다. 대화 후반에 여자의 도서관 멤버십에 대한 설명 중 특별 프로그램과 기본 카드를 비교하는 부분에서 기본 카드로는 10권을 빌릴 수 있다고 설명한다. 따라서 정답은 (B)이다. 선택지가 숫자로 구성되어 있을 경우 대화 중 여러 숫자들이 언급될 것이므로 항상 주의해야 한다.

패러프레이징 standard 표준, 보통 → regular 보통

43 What does the woman say is special about the library card?
(A) It requires no payment.
(B) It can be used indefinitely.
(C) It expires every 10 months.
(D) It can be replaced with an ID card.

여자는 도서관 카드의 특별한 점이 무엇이라고 말하는가?
(A) 비용이 요구되지 않는다.
(B) 무기한으로 사용할 수 있다.
(C) 10개월마다 만료된다.
(D) 신분증으로 대체할 수 있다.

해설 〈구체적 정보 파악 – 언급〉
library card를 키워드로 잡고 여자의 대사에 주목해야 한다. 여자가 마지막 대사에서 도서관에서 발급하는 두 종류의 카드 모두 만기가 없다고 설명하고 있으므로 정답은 (B)이다.

패러프레이징 never expire 절대 만료되지 않는다
→ indefinitely 무기한으로

Questions 44-46 refer to the following conversation. 미W 영M

W Jason, ㊹ can you check the number of attendees we'll have tomorrow? And find out if the local brasserie prepared the appropriate number of croissants and beverages.
M Julie told me that she's already taken care of it.
W That's wonderful. Do you know how many croissants she's ordered exactly?
M Thirty, I heard, because we are expecting 25 guests.
W ㊺ I'm concerned that won't be enough. I've heard that about 12 more guests have registered because the managing director has been invited as one of the presenters.
M Really? I'll check the list of attendees, and alter the order accordingly. ㊻ Do you want me to arrange the delivery? I'm sure the brasserie will provide us the delivery service.

여 Jason, 내일 올 참석자들의 수를 확인해 주시겠어요? 또한 시내 식당에서 크루아상과 음료를 인원수에 맞게 준비했는지도 알아봐 주세요.
남 Julie가 이미 처리했다고 말해줬어요.
여 잘 했네요. 크루아상을 정확히 몇 개 주문했는지 알고 계세요?
남 30개라고 들었어요. 예상되는 저희 손님이 25명이거든요.
여 충분하지 않을 것 같아서 걱정이네요. 약 12명 정도 손님이 더 등록했다고 들었어요. 왜냐하면 상무 이사가 발표자 중 한 명으로 초대되었거든요.
남 정말이요? 제가 참석자 리스트를 확인해 보고 그것에 맞춰 주문을 변경하겠습니다. 배달해 달라고 할까요? 그 식당은 배달 서비스를 제공할 거예요.

어휘 attendee 참석자 brasserie 식당 prepare 준비하다, 준비시키다 appropriate 적절한 register 등록하다, 기록하다 alter 바꾸다 accordingly 부응해서, 그에 맞춰 arrange 마련하다, 처리하다 enrollment 등록

44 What are the speakers discussing?
(A) The number of participants
(B) A registration fee
(C) Enrollment in a course
(D) The process of a survey

화자들이 논의하는 것은 무엇인가?
(A) 참가자의 수
(B) 등록비
(C) 강좌 등록
(D) 설문 조사 과정

해설 〈기본 정보 파악 – 주제〉
대화의 주제는 첫 대사를 주목해야 한다. 여자가 첫 대사에서 남자에게 참석자 수를 확인해 달라는 요청을 하고 있으므로 정답은 (A)이다.
패러프레이징 attendee 참석자 → participant 참가자

45 What information does the woman give the man?
(A) A location of a brasserie
(B) Details of the delivery
(C) An updated number of guests
(D) The name of managing director

여자는 남자에게 어떤 정보를 주는가?
(A) 식당 위치
(B) 배송의 상세 정보
(C) 변경된 손님의 수
(D) 상무 이사의 이름

해설 〈구체적 정보 파악 – 특정 사항〉
여자가 남자에게 알려주는 정보이므로 여자의 대사에서 정답을 유추해야 한다. 여자가 대화 중반에 손님들이 더 등록했기 때문에 음식이 부족할 것 같아 걱정된다고 언급하고 있으므로 정답은 (C)이다.

46 What does the man ask the woman about?
(A) If the woman has spoken with the managing director
(B) Whether food will be delivered
(C) Whether the woman has gotten any messages
(D) If the woman contacted a guest

남자는 여자에게 무엇에 대해 묻고 있는가?
(A) 여자가 상무 이사와 대화를 나누었는지
(B) 음식을 배달시킬 것인지
(C) 여자가 메시지를 받은 것인지
(D) 여자가 손님에게 연락했는지

해설 〈구체적 정보 파악 – 질문〉
남자가 여자에게 질문하는 형식의 대사를 주목해야 한다. 남자가 대화 마지막에 음식을 배달시킬 것을 원하는지 묻고 있으므로 정답은 (B)이다.

Questions 47-49 refer to the following conversation with three speakers. 미W 미M 영M

W I'm so pleased that our sales have doubled since our store was featured in the local newspaper.
M1 That's right, Jessica. ㊼ But on the other hand, our workload has increased too because we're shorthanded.
M2 I agree. I wonder if we can afford to hire a few more employees.
M1 I believe that we can, Frank. How about putting it on our next meeting's agenda?
W Well, ㊽ before that, let me talk directly to the regional manager for permission.
M2 As soon as we get permission, ㊾ I'll contact Steve to arrange job advertisements to be sent out.

여 지역 신문에 우리 상점이 실린 이후로 판매가 두 배나 늘어서 정말 기뻐요.
남1 맞아요 Jessica. 하지만 다른 한편으로는, 직원 부족으로 인해 우리의 업무량이 너무 많이 늘었어요.
남2 동감입니다. 우리가 직원을 더 고용할 수 있는 여유가 되는지 궁금하네요.
남1 할 수 있을 거예요, Frank. 다음 회의 안건으로 올려 보는 것이 어때요?
여 음, 그 전에 제가 지점장에게 승인을 받을 수 있는지 직접 물어볼게요.
남2 승인을 받는 즉시, 제가 구인 광고가 나갈 수 있도록 Steve에게 연락해서 준비해 놓을게요.

어휘 be featured in ~에 특집으로 실리다 on the other hand 다른 한편으로는 workload 업무량, 작업량 be shorthanded 일손이 모자라다 can afford to ~할 수 있다 agenda 안건, 주제 permission 허가, 허락, 승인 workforce 인력

47 What are the speakers concerned about?
(A) The size of the workforce
(B) New regulations
(C) The newspaper subscription
(D) The store location

화자들은 무엇을 걱정하는가?
(A) 인력 규모
(B) 새로운 규정
(C) 신문 구독료
(D) 가게 위치

해설 〈구체적 정보 파악 – 특정 사항〉
화자들의 걱정거리는 대화의 전반적인 주제와 연결되는 경우가 많으므로 대화의 앞부분에 주목해야 한다. 대화 초반에 여자가 판매가 늘었다며 기뻐하자 남자가 판매가 증가한 것은 맞지만 직원의 부족으로 인해 해야 할 일이 많다고 언급하고 있으므로 정답은 (A)이다.

48 What does the woman offer to do?
(A) Contact an executive
(B) Place an order
(C) Speak with a customer
(D) Give a raise

여자는 무엇을 해 주겠다고 하는가?
(A) 경영진에게 연락하는 것
(B) 주문하는 것
(D) 고객에게 이야기하는 것
(D) 월급을 올리는 것

해설 〈구체적 정보 파악 – 제공 관련〉
여자가 제공하는 것이므로 여자의 대사에서 단서를 찾아야 한다. 마지막 대사에서 여자가 매니저에게 승인을 받기 위해 직접 이야기하겠다는 의견을 제시하고 있으므로 (A)가 가장 적절한 답이다.

패러프레이징 regional manager 지점장 → executive 경영 간부

49 Why will Frank contact Steve?
(A) To correct an error
(B) To set up a meeting
(C) To create an advertisement
(D) To conduct an interview

Frank가 Steve에게 왜 연락할 것인가?
(A) 오류를 수정하기 위해
(B) 회의를 잡기 위해
(C) 광고를 만들기 위해
(D) 면접을 진행하기 위해

해설 〈구체적 정보 파악 – 특정 사항〉
대화 중반에서 M2 의견에 M1이 Frank라고 부르며 대답하고 있으므로 M2가 Frank임을 알 수 있다. 그 이후로 M2가 마지막 대사에서 Steve에게 연락해서 광고 만들 준비를 할 것이라고 언급하고 있으므로 정답은 (C)이다. 3인 대화에서는 여러 명의 이름이 언급되는 경우가 많다. 그러므로 문제의 키워드가 이름일 경우, 해당 이름이 대화를 나누는 등장인물 중 한 명인지 아니면 제3의 인물인지 반드시 확인해야 한다.

Questions 50-52 refer to the following conversation. 미W 영M

W Hey, Oliver, I'm glad you're finally here. (50) I can't access the Internet, and I have an e-mail I need to send by 2 o'clock. Could you please help me out?
M Certainly. Ashley, let me have a look. Ah, (51) you're connected to the wrong network. You have to use the one named "real-time-connection."
W (52) So that's all! It kept asking for a password, and I couldn't figure out why, since the office computers all connect automatically. How can I fix it?
M Do you see this icon? Click on that, and then click on "real-time-connection." That's all you should do. You're now online.

여 Oliver, 드디어 당신을 찾았군요. 2시까지 보내야 할 이메일이 있는데 인터넷에 연결이 안 됩니다. 좀 도와주시겠어요?
남 그럼요. Ashley, 한번 볼게요. 아, 잘못된 네트워크에 연결했네요. "실시간 접속"이라는 이름을 사용해야 해요.
여 바로 그거군요! 계속 비밀번호를 묻는데 도저히 왜 그런 것인지 알 수가 없었어요. 사무실 컴퓨터는 모두 자동으로 연결되잖아요. 어떻게 고쳐야 하나요?
남 이 아이콘 보이죠? 그걸 누른 다음에 "실시간 접속"을 눌러 보세요. 그렇게만 하면 되요. 이제 연결되었어요.

어휘 access 접속하다 figure out 생각해내다, 알아내다 automatically 자동적으로

50 What is the man asked to do?
(A) Provide a new password
(B) Help writing an e-mail
(C) Assist with getting online
(D) Analyze some data

남자는 무엇을 요청받고 있는가?
(A) 새로운 비밀번호를 제공하는 것
(B) 이메일 작성을 돕는 것
(C) 인터넷 접속을 도와주는 것
(D) 몇몇 자료를 분석하는 것

해설 〈구체적 정보 파악 – 요청 관련〉
남자가 요청을 받는 것에 대한 문제이므로 여자의 말에서 정답의 단서를 찾아야 한다. 첫 대사에서 여자가 인터넷 접속에 문제가 있어서 도와달라고 요청하고 있으므로 (C)가 정답이다. 수동태 문제는 문장에 언급되는 주어가 아닌 상대방의 말에서 답을 찾아야 하므로 수동태 의문문에 주의해야 한다.

51 What was the issue?
(A) The computer was broken.
(B) The password had been changed.
(C) The e-mail address was wrong.
(D) The connection was wrong.

무엇이 문제였는가?
(A) 컴퓨터가 고장 났다.
(B) 비밀번호가 바뀌었다.
(C) 이메일 주소가 잘못되었다.
(D) 연결이 잘못되었다.

해설 〈구체적 정보 파악 – 특정 사항〉
도움을 요청하는 여자에게 남자는 잘못된 네트워크에 연결했기 때문에 인터넷에 접속이 되지 않았던 것이라고 설명하고 있으므로 정답은 (D)이다.

52 Why does the woman say, "So that's all!"?
(A) She found an e-mail address.
(B) She understood the problem.
(C) She fixed the laptop.
(D) She had to restart the computer.

여자가 "바로 그거군요!"라고 말한 이유는 무엇인가?
(A) 이메일 주소를 찾았다.
(B) 문제점을 이해했다.
(C) 노트북을 수리했다.
(D) 컴퓨터를 다시 시작해야 한다.

해설 〈구체적 정보 파악 – 화자 의도〉
화자 의도 문제는 주어진 표현의 앞뒤 상황을 파악해야 한다. 남자가 문제점의 원인을 알려주자 여자는 해당 표현을 언급하며 사무실의 모든 컴퓨터는 자동으로 온라인에 연결되기 때문에 스스로 문제점을 찾지 못했다고 설명하고 있다. 따라서 남자의 말을 듣고 문제의 원인을 파악했음을 알 수 있으므로 (B)가 정답이다.

Questions 53-55 refer to the following conversation. (미M) (미W)

M How is the new Brewer Street property coming along?
W Well, everything is going okay. ⑬ The electricians should finish updating the wiring in three of the condominiums by Wednesday. After that, they'll need painting. ⑭ You called the painters, right?
M ⑭ Yeah, they're coming next week on Tuesday. I have the carpet layers scheduled to come in on the following Thursday. That should be enough time for the paint to dry. Have all of the units been rented?
W Renters have signed contracts for five of them. The other three are still listed on our Web site, ⑮ but I'm also going to place an ad all next week in the *Sun Daily*.

남 새로운 Brewer 가의 건물은 어떻게 되어 가고 있나요?
여 네, 모든 것이 잘 되어 가고 있어요. 전기 기술자가 수요일까지 3군데의 아파트 배선 공사를 마무리할 거예요. 그 후에는 페인트를 칠해야 하고요. 페인트 작업하는 사람에게 연락하셨죠, 그렇죠?
남 네, 다음 주 화요일에 올 거예요. 카펫 작업자들은 그 주 목요일에 오는 것으로 되어 있어요. 그 사이 페인트가 충분히 마를 거예요. 모든 호 수가 임대되었나요?
여 5개는 세입자들이 계약서에 사인했어요. 나머지 3개는 우리 웹 사이트에 여전히 올라가 있고요. 하지만 제가 다음 주 내내 〈Sun Daily〉에 광고를 낼 거예요.

어휘 property 재산, 부동산 come along 되어 가다, 나아지다 electrician 전기 기사 condominium 콘도미니엄, 아파트 renter 세입자, 임차인 floor plan 평면도 reasonable 합리적인 commence 시작하다 pass out 배포하다 leaflet 전단지 tenant 세입자

53 What work will be finished by Wednesday?
(A) Wall painting
(B) A floor plan
(C) Electrical construction
(D) A promotional campaign

수요일까지 완료될 작업은 무엇인가?
(A) 벽 페인팅 작업
(B) 평면도
(C) 전기 공사
(D) 홍보 캠페인

해설 〈구체적 정보 파악 – 특정 사항〉
키워드인 Wednesday가 나오는 문장에 집중해야 한다. 여자의 첫 번째 대사에서 전기 기술자가 수요일까지 아파트의 배선 공사를 마무리할 것이라고 언급하므로 정답은 (C)이다.

패러프레이징 updating the wiring 배선 작업하기
→ electrical construction 전기 공사

54 What does the man say about the painting?
(A) The cost is reasonable.
(B) The work takes a long time.
(C) The painters delayed the schedule.
(D) The work will commence next Tuesday.

남자는 페인팅에 대해 무엇이라고 말하는가?
(A) 가격이 합리적이다.
(B) 작업이 오래 걸린다.
(C) 페인트 작업자가 일정을 미뤘다.
(D) 작업은 다음 주 화요일에 시작될 것이다.

해설 〈구체적 정보 파악 – 언급〉
키워드인 painting이 남자의 대사에서 언급될 때 답을 찾아야 한다. 여자가 남자에게 페인트 칠하는 사람들에게 연락했는지 묻자 남자는 다음 주 화요일에 올 것이라고 대답한다. 따라서 정답은 (D)이다. 남자는 두 번째 대사에서 페인트가 건조되는 데 충분한 시간이 필요하므로 카펫 설치업자들을 목요일에 불렀다는 설명을 한다. 즉, 페인트칠 후 마르는 데 걸리는 시간을 설명한 것이므로 페인트 칠하는 데 시간이 오래 걸린다고 표현한 (B)에 혼동하지 않도록 주의한다.

55 How does the woman say she will find more tenants?
(A) By passing out leaflets
(B) By designing a new Web site
(C) By advertising in a newspaper
(D) By talking to other tenants

여자는 더 많은 세입자를 찾기 위해 어떻게 할 것인가?
(A) 전단지를 배포해서
(B) 새로운 웹 사이트를 디자인해서
(C) 신문에 광고를 내서
(D) 다른 세입자에게 이야기해서

해설 〈구체적 정보 파악 – 언급〉
여자가 키워드 tenants를 언급하는 부분에서 정답을 찾아야 한다. 여자는 마지막 대사에서 세입자들이 계약서에 서명한 것에 대해 설명하며 〈Sun Daily〉 신문에 다음 주 내내 광고를 낼 것이라는 계획을 언급하고 있으므로 (C)가 정답이다.

Questions 56-58 refer to the following conversation. (미W) (영M)

W Kevin, I tried to get you a Monday flight to Bangkok, ⑯ but there are no seats on any flights from Boston, even in first class. You'll either have to leave on Thursday if you want to fly direct, or you can depart on Tuesday afternoon with a five-hour layover in San Diego.
M ⑰ I can't leave on Thursday. I need to lead a workshop on Friday morning Bangkok time, and that wouldn't get me there by then.
W You are right. You'll lose 11 hours just with the time change, plus you'll be exhausted when you finally get there.
M Well, I hate stopovers but I don't see any other alternative. ⑱ I guess I'll have to take the Tuesday flight.

여 Kevin, 월요일 방콕행 비행기를 예약하려고 했지만 보스턴에서 출발하는 어떤 비행기도 좌석이 없습니다. 심지어 1등석도요. 직항을 원하시면 목요일에 출발하셔야 하고, 아니면 샌디에이고에서 5시간 경유하는 비행기로 화요일 오후에 출발할 수 있습니다.
남 목요일에 떠날 순 없어요. 제가 방콕 시간으로 금요일 아침에 워크숍을 진행해야 해서 그때까지 그곳에 도착할 수 없을 겁니다.
여 맞아요. 당신은 시차로만 11시간을 잃게 되고, 게다가 그곳에 도착했을 때는 정말 피곤하실 거예요.
남 음. 제가 경유하는 것을 싫어하긴 하지만, 다른 방법이 없어 보이네요. 화요일 비행기를 타야 할 것 같아요.

어휘 depart 떠나다, 출발하다 layover (잠깐 동안) 머무르다, 들르다 exhausted 기진맥진한, 진이 다 빠진 stopover 단기 체류 alternative 대안

56 Which city does the man probably work in?
(A) Bangkok
(B) Boston
(C) San Diego
(D) Los Angeles

어느 도시에서 남자는 근무하는가?
(A) 방콕
(B) 보스턴
(C) 샌디에이고
(D) 로스앤젤레스

해설 〈구체적 정보 파악 – 특정 사항〉
여자가 처음에 남자의 비행기 예약에 대해 말하는 부분에서 보스턴을 떠나는 어떤 비행기에도 좌석이 없다고 한다. 따라서 (B)가 정답이다. 특정 장소나 시점 등 단답형으로 구성된 선택지는 혼동을 유도하는 문제가 대부분이므로 선택지의 단어가 언급될 때마다 집중한다. Bangkok은 목적지이며, San Diego는 경유지로 언급되고 있으므로 주의해야 한다.

57 Why can't the man leave on Thursday?
(A) He has other plans.
(B) He can't afford the price.
(C) He doesn't like a layover.
(D) He would arrive too late.
남자는 왜 목요일에 떠날 수 없는가?
(A) 그는 다른 계획이 있다.
(B) 그는 경제적 여유가 없다.
(C) 그는 경유하는 것을 싫어한다.
(D) 그는 너무 늦게 도착하게 된다.

해설 〈구체적 정보 파악 – 특정 사항〉
남자의 대사에서 Thursday가 언급되는 부분에 주목해야 한다. 남자가 대화 중반에 방콕에서 열리는 금요일 워크숍에 맞추어 도착하려면 목요일에 떠나면 안 된다고 설명한다. 따라서 이를 적절히 바꿔 표현한 (D)가 정답이다.

58 What decision does the man make?
(A) To postpone his workshop
(B) To pay for first class
(C) To depart on Tuesday
(D) To arrive on Friday
남자가 결정한 것은 무엇인가?
(A) 워크숍을 연기하는 것
(B) 1등석을 구매하는 것
(C) 화요일에 출발하는 것
(D) 금요일에 도착하는 것

해설 〈구체적 정보 파악 – 특정 사항〉
남자의 결정이므로 남자의 대사에서 답을 유추해야 한다. 마지막 대사에서 남자가 다른 방법이 없으니 화요일 비행기를 타겠다고 말했으므로 정답은 (C)이다.

Questions 59-61 refer to the following conversation. 미W 미M

W Hello, Dr. Leon's office. How can I help you?
M Hi. My name is Timothy Johnson, and 59 I have an appointment with Dr. Leon tomorrow at 3 P.M., but unfortunately something has come up and I won't be able to make it by then. Does Dr. Leon have anything else open — say later tomorrow or the next day?
W Well, let me check his schedule. 60 61 It looks like he's fully booked tomorrow, and the next day is Saturday, so he doesn't work. Oh, wait! 61 It looks like he has an opening at five-twenty tomorrow. Does it work for you?
M Certainly, yes. That works for me. I could make it by then. Thanks for your help.
W See you tomorrow, Mr. Johnson.

여 안녕하세요, Leon 의원입니다. 어떻게 도와 드릴까요?
남 안녕하세요, 저는 Timothy Johnson입니다. 제가 내일 오후 3시에 Leon 박사님과 진료 예약이 있는데, 안타깝게도 일이 생겨서 그때까지 갈 수 없을 것 같습니다. Leon 박사님이 시간이 비는 때가 있을까요, 그러니까 내일 오후나 그 다음 날은 어떨까요?
여 음, 제가 그의 일정을 확인해 볼게요. 내일은 예약이 꽉 차 있네요. 그리고 그 다음 날은 토요일이라서 근무하지 않아요. 아, 잠시만요! 내일 5시 20분에 시간이 비는 것 같습니다. 괜찮으신가요?
남 물론이죠. 괜찮아요. 그때까지 가겠습니다. 도와주셔서 감사합니다.
여 내일 뵙겠습니다, Johnson 씨.

어휘 unfortunately 불행하게도, 유감스럽게도　come up 생기다, 발생하다　say 가령, 예를 들어　physician 의사

59 What is the purpose of the man's call?
(A) To reschedule a visit
(B) To change his physician
(C) To get a prescription
(D) To make an appointment
남자가 전화한 목적은 무엇인가?
(A) 방문 일정을 다시 잡기 위해
(B) 담당 의사를 바꾸기 위해
(C) 처방전을 받기 위해
(D) 예약을 하기 위해

해설 〈기본 정보 파악 – 목적〉
전화의 목적은 대화 초반에 단서가 제시되는 경우가 대부분이다. 여자가 인사말을 하며 전화를 받자, 남자가 예약한 시간에 갈 수 없다는 설명을 하고 있으므로 (A)가 정답이다.

60 What does the woman mean when she says, "the next day is Saturday"?
(A) Dr. Leon usually works on weekends.
(B) The office is closed on weekends.
(C) Saturday is available for a reservation.
(D) Mr. Johnson is fully booked on Saturday.
여자가 "그다음 날은 토요일이다"라고 말한 의미는 무엇인가?
(A) Leon 박사는 보통 주말에 근무한다.
(B) 병원은 주말에 닫는다.
(C) 토요일은 예약이 가능하다.
(D) Johnson 씨는 토요일에 예약이 가득 찼다.

해설 〈구체적 정보 파악 – 화자 의도〉
주변 문맥과 종합하여 여자의 의도를 파악해야 한다. 대화의 중반에 남자가 내일 또는 그 다음 날로 예약 변경이 가능한지 묻자 여자는 내일은 예약이 찼고, 그 다음 날은 토요일인데 의사는 토요일에 근무하지 않는다고 설명하고 있다. 따라서 정답은 (B)이다.

61 On what day will the man visit the office?
(A) Tuesday
(B) Thursday
(C) Friday
(D) Saturday
남자는 무슨 요일에 병원에 방문할 것인가?
(A) 화요일
(B) 목요일
(C) 금요일
(D) 토요일

해설 〈구체적 정보 파악 – 특정 사항〉
60번 문제에서 남자가 예약 변경을 원하자 여자가 내일은 예약이 찼으며 그 다음 날은 토요일이라 진료를 하지 않는다고 말하는 부분에서 내일이 금요일이라는 것을 알려주는 단서가 이미 제시되었다. 그 후 여자가 내일 5시 20분에 진료가 가능하다고 하자 남자가 그 시간에 가겠다고 말하고 있다. 따라서 (C)가 정답이다.

Questions 62-64 refer to the following conversation and coupon. 미W 영M

Harvey Nichols Department Store

Clothing Department

€10.00 OFF

Any piece of clothing priced over €50

Expires Oct 19

W ⑫ Can you tell me where I can find the clothing department here? I'm looking for it because I saw an ad about a sale on skirts in a magazine.

M It's behind the escalators, and yes, we're currently offering great savings on some items. ⑬ If you'd like to stop by our customer help desk, they'll give you all sorts of coupons you can use.

W Oh, sounds great. Thanks. I wonder if there are any coupons for skirts. ⑭ There's a certain one I'd like to buy. I remember it sells for €60.

M Of course, I know we've definitely got discounts on skirts, but I suggest you hurry. They're going pretty fast. We're down to about half of the inventory we started with before the sale.

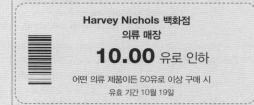

Harvey Nichols 백화점

의류 매장

10.00 유로 인하

어떤 의류 제품이든 50유로 이상 구매 시

유효 기간 10월 19일

여 의류 매장이 어디에 있는지 알려 주시겠어요? 제가 잡지에서 스커트 세일에 대한 광고를 봤기 때문에 찾고 있는 중이거든요.

남 에스컬레이터 뒤에 있습니다. 그리고 맞습니다. 저희는 현재 일부 제품을 큰 폭으로 할인하고 있는 중입니다. 고객 서비스 창구에 들르시면, 사용하실 수 있는 모든 종류의 쿠폰을 드릴 겁니다.

여 좋네요. 감사합니다. 스커트 쿠폰도 있는지 궁금하네요. 제가 꼭 사고 싶은 게 있거든요. 60유로에 판매한다고 기억하거든요.

남 물론이죠, 스커트도 할인하고 있는 것으로 알고 있습니다. 하지만 서두르시는 것이 좋겠어요. 굉장히 빠르게 팔리고 있거든요. 세일 시작하기 전에 가지고 있던 재고가 거의 반으로 줄었습니다.

어휘 currently 현재, 지금 certain 확실한, 틀림없는 definitely 분명히, 확실히 suggest 제안하다, 권하다 inventory 물품 목록 fitting room 탈의실

62 What does the woman ask the man about?
(A) The hours of operation
(B) The price of a certain item
(C) The duration of a sale
(D) The location of a section

여자가 남자에게 묻고 있는 것은 무엇인가?
(A) 영업 시간
(B) 특정 제품 가격
(C) 세일 기간
(D) 매장의 위치

해설 〈구체적 정보 파악 – 특정 사항〉
첫 대사에서 여자가 의류 매장의 위치를 묻고 있으므로 정답은 (D)이다.

63 Where does the man suggest the woman go?
(A) To a staff lounge
(B) To a fitting room
(C) To a service desk
(D) To the main entrance

남자는 여자에게 어디로 가라고 제안하는가?
(A) 직원 휴게실
(B) 탈의실
(C) 서비스 창구
(D) 정문

해설 〈구체적 정보 파악 – 특정 사항〉
대화의 중반에 남자가 할인 쿠폰을 받으려면 고객 서비스 창구에 가라고 제안하고 있다. 따라서 정답은 (C)이다.

패러프레이징 stop by (잠깐) 들르다 → go 가다

64 Look at the graphic. How much would the woman have to pay for the skirt?
(A) €50
(B) €60
(C) €70
(D) €80

시각 자료를 보시오. 여자는 스커트를 얼마에 구매하겠는가?
(A) 50유로
(B) 60유로
(C) 70유로
(D) 80유로

해설 〈구체적 정보 파악 – 시각 자료 연계〉
대화에 언급된 내용과 제시된 시각 자료를 교차 확인하여 정답을 찾아야 하는데, 선택지에 가격이 제시되어 있으므로 대화에서는 가격이 언급되는 부분에 주목해야 한다. 가격은 여자의 대사에서 언급되며 여자는 60유로짜리 스커트를 사고 싶다고 말한다. 이 가격은 쿠폰에 제시된 조건인 [50유로 이상 구매 시 10유로 할인 받기]에 충족되므로 여자는 60유로의 스커트를 50유로에 구매할 수 있다. 따라서 정답은 (A)이다.

Questions 65-67 refer to the following conversation and map. 미M 미W

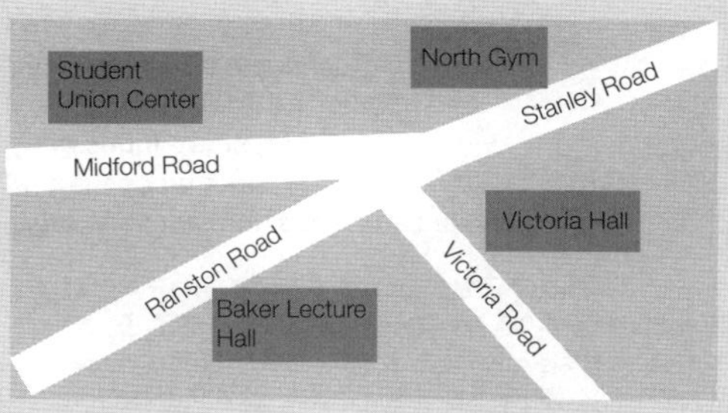

M Hi. I've been offered a position here at Karachi Education Center next month, ⑮ but I'd like to take a look around the facilities before I start the job. Is it possible?

W ⑯ I'm sorry but no one is available to show you around right now. I recommend you make an appointment and come back another day.

M Hmm, but I don't live in this town and I'm not sure when I'll be able to come back this month.

W In that case, why don't I give you this map? You should be able to find your way easily. Remember to take this guest pass with you. ⑰ Also, there's no point going down Ranston Road. The only building there is closed for renovation.

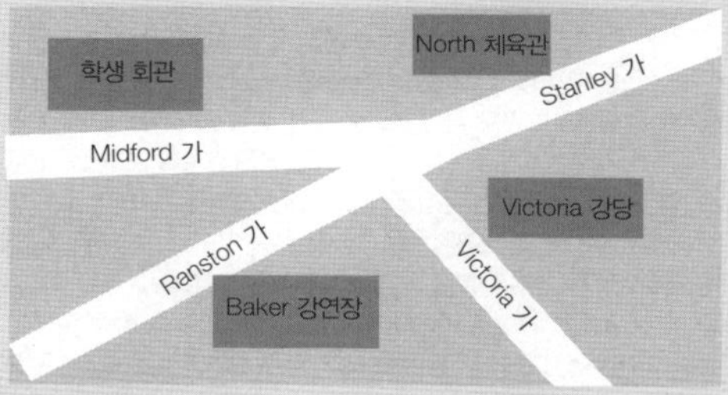

남 안녕하세요. 제가 다음 달부터 여기 Karachi 교육 센터에 일자리를 제안받았는데, 업무를 시작하기 전에 시설을 둘러보고 싶습니다. 가능할까요?

여 죄송하지만 바로 안내해 드릴 수 있는 분이 아무도 없습니다. 약속을 잡으시고 다른 날 다시 오시는 것이 좋겠는데요.

남 음, 하지만 제가 이 지역에 살고 있지 않고, 이번 달에 또 언제 올 수 있을지 알 수가 없거든요.

여 그렇다면, 제가 이 지도를 드리면 어떨까요? 길을 쉽게 찾으실 수 있을 거예요. 이 고객 방문증을 소지하는 것을 잊지 마세요. 그리고 Ranston 가로 가는 것은 의미가 없습니다. 그곳에 하나 있는 건물은 수리 때문에 닫혀 있거든요.

어휘 take a look around 주위를 둘러보다 facility 설비, 시설 available 구할 수 있는, 이용할 수 있는, 가능한 recommend 추천하다, 권하다 no point ~해 봐야 소용없다 renovation 보수, 수리

65 What does the man ask the woman to do?
(A) Take a map
(B) Make an appointment
(C) Arrange a tour
(D) Apply for a position

남자가 여자에게 요청하는 것은 무엇인가?
(A) 지도를 가지고 가는 것
(B) 약속을 잡는 것
(C) 견학을 주선해 주는 것
(D) 업무에 지원하는 것

해설 〈구체적 정보 파악 – 요청 관련〉
남자가 요청하는 것이므로 남자의 대사에서 근거를 찾아야 한다. 남자가 첫 대사에서 이곳을 둘러보고 싶은데 가능한지 묻고 있으므로 정답은 (C)이다.

66 What most likely is the problem?
(A) An interview has been postponed.
(B) Some people do not like a tour.
(C) A guide is not available.
(D) There will not be another meeting.

무엇이 문제인가?
(A) 면접이 연기되었다.
(B) 일부 사람들은 견학을 좋아하지 않는다.
(C) 가이드를 이용할 수 없다.
(D) 다른 회의가 없을 것이다.

해설 〈구체적 정보 파악 – 특정 사항〉
65번에서 남자가 교육 센터 견학을 요청하자 여자가 오늘은 안내해 줄 사람이 없다고 대답하고 있으므로 정답은 (C)이다.

67 Look at the graphic. Which building is under construction today?
(A) North Gym
(B) Student Union Center
(C) Baker Lecture Hall
(D) Victoria Hall

시각 자료를 보시오. 어떤 건물이 오늘 공사 중인가?
(A) North 체육관
(B) 학생 회관
(C) Baker 강연장
(D) Victoria 강당

해설 〈구체적 정보 파악 – 시각 자료 연계〉
지도의 건물 이름들이 제시되어 있으므로 대화에서는 도로명이 단서로 언급될 것을 예측하고 들어야 한다. 또한 공사하고 있는 곳을 묻고 있으므로 under construction을 키워드로 잡고 그 주변에서 단서가 제시될 것도 함께 생각해야 한다. 여자가 마지막에 Ranston 가를 언급하며 그곳의 건물은 수리로 인해 문을 닫았으니 가지 말라고 안내하고 있으므로 Ranston 가에 있는 Baker 강연장이 공사 중임을 알 수 있다. 따라서 정답은 (C)이다.

패러프레이징 renovation (건물의) 보수, 개조
→ under construction 공사 중

Questions 68-70 refer to the following conversation and list. (영M) (미W)

Items for repair		
Item	Quantity	Time
Fax machines	2	1:00 P.M.
Photocopiers	2	2:00 P.M.
Scanners	3	3:00 P.M.
Color printers	4	4:30 P.M.

M Good afternoon. ⓺⓼ I'm here to perform some maintenance work for your department. Mr. Rodriguez dispatched me here as soon as he received your list. Apparently, there's quite a bit of work to be done.
W That's right. Thanks for coming so quickly. I sent him an e-mail with the things that should be fixed. Do you have a copy as well?
M Yes, and I'll get started right away. ⓺⓽ I've already prepared the right equipment, so it shouldn't take me long to finish.
W Wonderful! We'd like to make one slight change, though. ⓻⓪ Is it possible for you to switch the times of the first and last items on the list? That way, we can start using the most important ones more quickly.

수리 물품		
물품	수량	시간
팩스 기기	2	오후 1시
복사기	2	오후 2시
스캐너	3	오후 3시
컬러 프린터	4	오후 4시 30분

남 안녕하세요. 여기 부서에 보수 작업을 하러 왔습니다. Rodriguez 씨가 당신의 리스트를 받자마자 저를 보내셨어요. 할 일이 많다고 들었습니다.
여 맞아요. 이렇게 빨리 와 주셔서 감사합니다. 꼭 고쳐야 하는 것들을 제가 이메일로 보냈거든요. 리스트를 가지고 계신가요?
남 네. 바로 시작하겠습니다. 제가 이미 알맞은 장비들을 준비해 왔기 때문에 끝내는 데 오래 걸리지 않을 겁니다.
여 훌륭하네요! 약간 변경하고 싶은 부분이 있는데요. 리스트에서 처음 물품과 마지막 물품의 수리 시간을 바꿀 수 있을까요? 그렇게 하면, 가장 중요한 것을 더 빠르게 사용할 수 있거든요.

어휘 perform 행하다, 수행하다 maintenance work 보수 업무, 정비 작업 dispatch 보내다, 발송하다 apparently 듣자 하니, 보아 하니 quite a bit of 많은 equipment 장비, 용품 slight 약간의, 조금의, 경미한

68 Who most likely is Mr. Rodriguez?
(A) A client
(B) An accountant
(C) An assistant
(D) A supervisor

Rodriguez 씨는 누구인가?
(A) 고객
(B) 회계사
(C) 보조
(D) 관리자

해설 〈구체적 정보 파악 – 특정 사항〉
Mr. Rodriguez를 핵심 키워드로 잡고 문제를 풀어야 한다. 남자가 첫 대사에서 Mr. Rodriguez가 보내서 보수 작업을 하러 왔다고 방문 목적을 말하고 있다. 따라서 남자는 Mr. Rodriguez의 지시를 받고 일하러 왔다는 것을 알 수 있으므로 정답은 (D)이다.

69 What does the man say he has already done?
(A) Sent some tools
(B) Brought items for repair
(C) Purchased new equipment
(D) Contacted a manager

남자가 이미 한 것은 무엇인가?
(A) 기구를 보내는 것
(B) 수리를 위한 물건들을 가져온 것

(C) 새로운 기기를 구매하는 것
(D) 매니저에게 연락하는 것

해설 〈구체적 정보 파악 – 특정 사항〉
남자의 대사에서 키워드인 already가 언급될 때 집중해야 한다. 남자가 대화 중반에 이미 필요한 장비를 준비해 왔기 때문에 작업 시간이 오래 걸리지 않을 것이라고 설명하고 있으므로 (B)가 정답이다.

70 Look at the graphic. What items will be repaired first?
(A) Fax machines
(B) Photocopiers
(C) Scanners
(D) Color printers
시각 자료를 보시오. 어떤 물품이 먼저 수리될 것인가?
(A) 팩스 기기
(B) 복사기
(C) 스캐너
(D) 컬러 프린터

해설 〈구체적 정보 파악 – 시각 자료 연계〉
선택지와 시각 자료 관계부터 파악해야 한다. 물품이 선택지로 제시되어 있으므로 대화 속 정답의 단서는 시간이나 수량이 언급된다는 것을 예측하고 들어야 한다. 대화 마지막에 여자가 리스트에서 처음 물품과 마지막 물품의 수리 시간을 바꿀 수 있는지 물어보고 있다. 따라서 제시된 수리 목록 표의 첫 번째인 팩스와 마지막으로 예정된 컬러 프린터가 서로 바뀌게 되므로 가장 먼저 수리되는 것은 (D) 컬러 프린터임을 알 수 있다.

Questions 71-73 refer to the following talk. (영W)

Thank you all for joining us this afternoon. ⑪ We're conducting this session to get consumer reviews on various aspects of our new mobile device. Feedback from previous groups has already helped us to improve the product. ⑫ We've made it even easier to use its basic features and built-in apps. Today, we're going to concentrate on topics related to the eventual marketing of the product. ⑬ We'll start by looking over some preliminary ideas for the package design. After that, we'll show you some sample layouts and different versions of copy for commercial advertisements, and then we'll go over a few survey questions.

오늘 오후 이렇게 저희와 함께해 주신 여러분께 감사드립니다. 저희는 새로운 무선 단말기의 다양한 특징에 대한 고객의 평가를 받기 위해 이 시간을 갖게 되었습니다. 이전 그룹들의 피드백은 이미 제품 향상에 많은 도움을 주었습니다. 저희는 기본 기능과 탑재된 어플들의 사용을 더욱 쉽게 만들었습니다. 오늘, 우리는 제품의 최종 마케팅에 대한 주제에 집중하려고 합니다. 우선 포장 디자인에 대한 사전 아이디어 몇 가지를 살펴보는 것으로 시작하겠습니다. 그 후에는, 몇 가지 샘플 레이아웃과 여러 가지의 광고 문구를 보여드릴 것입니다. 그런 후에 설문지의 질문들을 검토하도록 하겠습니다.

어휘 conduct 하다, 지휘하다 various 여러 가지의, 각양각색의 aspect 관점, 양상 previous 이전의 improve 개선되다, 나아지다, 향상시키다 built-in 탑재된 concentrate 집중하다, 집중시키다 related to ~와 관련 있는 eventual 최종적인 preliminary 예비의 commercial advertisements 광고 survey 조사, 설문 조사 evaluate 평가하다

71 What is the purpose of today's session?
(A) To evaluate staff performance
(B) To conduct an interview
(C) To gather opinions
(D) To explain a company regulation
오늘 세션의 목적은 무엇인가?
(A) 직원 수행 능력을 평가하기 위해
(B) 면접을 진행하기 위해
(C) 의견을 모으기 위해
(D) 회사의 규정을 설명하기 위해

해설 〈기본 정보 파악 – 목적〉
목적을 묻는 문제의 단서는 담화 초반에 언급된다. 화자가 인사 후에 소비자의 평가를 받기 위해 이 세션을 실시한다고 말하고 있으므로 정답은 (C)이다.

패러프레이징 get reviews 평가 받기 → gather opinions 의견 모으기

72 According to the speaker, how has the new device been improved?
(A) It performs more easily.
(B) It is light-weight.
(C) It is faster to use.
(D) It is a cost-effective product.
화자에 의하면, 새 단말기는 어떻게 개선되었는가?
(A) 더 쉽게 작동한다.
(B) 무게가 가볍다.
(C) 사용이 더 빠르다.
(D) 가성비가 좋은 제품이다.

해설 〈구체적 정보 파악 – 특정 사항〉
문제의 키워드인 improve가 언급된 후 바로 다음 문장에서 기본 기능과 탑재된 어플들의 사용을 더욱 쉽게 만들었다고 설명하고 있으므로 정답은 (A)이다.

73 What will the listeners probably do next?
(A) Ask questions
(B) View package designs
(C) Create the advertisement
(D) Call a client's office
화자들은 다음에 무엇을 할 것인가?
(A) 질문을 한다.
(B) 포장 디자인을 본다.
(C) 광고를 만든다.
(D) 고객 사무실에 전화한다.

해설 〈구체적 정보 파악 – 미래〉
청자들이 다음에 할 일은 담화 후반에 언급된다. 화자가 후반부에 포장 디자인에 대한 사전 아이디어 몇 가지를 살펴보는 것으로 시작하겠다고 언급하고 있으므로 정답은 (B)이다.

Questions 74-76 refer to the following speech. 미W

(75) Thanks to the University of St. Andrew for hosting tonight's event. (74) It's my great privilege to accept the Edger Prize on behalf of Edinburgh Institute, where (76) I've had the opportunity to collaborate with some of the most gifted linguists in the country. They are certainly in a class of their own. Special thanks go to the Research Foundation, which provides the majority of the funding for our study, and, of course, the panel of judges for selecting the Edinburgh Institute for this honor.

오늘 밤 행사를 개최해 주신 St. Andrew 대학에 감사드립니다. 전국에서 가장 재능 있는 언어학자들과 함께 작업할 수 있는 기회를 준 Edinburgh Institute을 대표하여 Edger 상을 받게 되어 큰 영광입니다. 그들은 타의 추종을 불허할 만큼 뛰어난 분들입니다. 저희 연구 대부분의 자금을 지원해 주신 Research Foundation에게도 특별히 감사를 전합니다. 그리고 물론, Edinburgh Institute을 선택해 주신 심사위원단에게도 감사드립니다.

어휘 host (행사를) 주최하다 privilege 특전, 특혜, 영광 accept 수락하다, 받아들이다 on behalf of ~을 대표하여 opportunity 기회 collaborate with ~와 협력하다, 협동하다 gifted 재능이 있는 linguist 언어학자 certainly 틀림없이, 확실히 in a class of one's own 타의 추종을 불허한, 뛰어난 majority 가장 많은 수, 다수 funding 자금, 자금 제공, 재정 지원 the panel of judges 심사위원단 arena 경기장 exclude 제외하다 exceptional 우수한

74 What is the purpose of the speech?
(A) To request funding
(B) To report research findings
(C) To accept an award
(D) To welcome guests

이 연설의 목적은 무엇인가?
(A) 모금을 요청하기 위해
(B) 연구 결과를 보고하기 위해
(C) 상을 받기 위해
(D) 손님을 환영하기 위해

해설 〈기본 정보 파악 – 목적〉
담화 목적의 단서는 지문의 초반에 언급된다. 화자는 인사말을 한 후 Edger 상을 받게 되어 큰 영광이라고 소감을 밝히고 있으므로 정답은 (A)이다.

75 Where is the speech probably taking place?
(A) At a university
(B) At a firm's auditorium
(C) At a city's arena
(D) At a town center

연설을 하는 곳은 어디인가?
(A) 대학
(B) 회사 강당
(C) 도심 경기장
(D) 마을 회관

해설 〈기본 정보 파악 – 장소〉
목적에 이어 장소에 대한 언급도 담화의 초반에 등장한다. 첫 문장에서 오늘 밤의 행사를 개최한 St. Andrew 대학에 감사한다는 인사말을 하는 것으로 보아 정답은 (A)이다. 74번 목적 문제와 75번 장소 문제의 단서 모두 초반에 언급되기 때문에 첫 부분을 듣고 두 문제를 모두 풀어야 한다는 것을 미리 예측하고 들어야 한다.

76 What does the speaker mean when she says, "They are certainly in a class of their own"?
(A) Some of the researchers are excluded.
(B) Several of the colleagues are exceptional.
(C) Some of the instructors teach only one class.
(D) Several students contributed their ideas.

화자가 "그들은 타의 추종을 불허할 만큼 뛰어나다"라고 말한 의미는 무엇인가?
(A) 몇 명의 연구원들이 제외되었다.
(B) 여러 동료들이 매우 우수하다.
(C) 몇 명의 강사들은 하나의 수업만 가르친다.
(D) 몇 명의 학생들은 아이디어를 주었다.

해설 〈구체적 정보 파악 – 화자 의도〉
문제에 언급된 문장의 앞뒤 문맥을 종합하여 화자의 의도를 파악해야 한다. 문제에서 주어진 문장이 언급되기 바로 직전에 전국에서 가장 재능 있는 언어학자들과 함께 작업했다고 말하고 있으므로 그들이 우수하다는 것을 암시하고 있다. 따라서 정답은 (B)이다.

Questions 77-79 refer to the following advertisement. 호M

After more than ten happy years at its location in Lambeth, (77) Skin Clear & Beauty Clinic is happy to announce it is relocating to new premises in the heart of Westminster. (78) Our beautiful modern clinic opens tomorrow on the corner of Vincent Street and Grosvenor Avenue. (79) Skin Clear & Beauty Clinic utilizes cutting-edge technology to help treat a variety of skin conditions caused by aging, sun damage and allergies. To celebrate our move, (79) all customers who visit before the end of February will receive 30 percent off any treatment. To take advantage of this offer, or to make an appointment, call us at 934-555-0381.

10년 이상 동안 Lambeth에서의 행복을 뒤로하고, Skin Clear & Beauty가 Westminster 중심의 새로운 건물로 이전한다는 기쁜 소식을 알려드립니다. 우리의 아름답고 현대적인 클리닉은 Vincent 거리와 Grosvenor 가의 코너에서 내일 문을 엽니다. Skin Clear & Beauty Clinic은 노화, 자외선, 알레르기로 인해 발생하는 다양한 피부 상태의 치료를 돕기 위해 최첨단의 기술을 활용합니다. 이전을 기념하기 위해 2월 말까지 방문하는 모든 고객들은 어떤 치료에나 30% 할인을 받으실 수 있습니다. 이 행사를 이용하시거나 예약하고 싶으시면, 934-555-0381로 전화주세요.

어휘 announce 발표하다, 알리다 relocate 이전하다, 이동하다 premise (건물이 딸린) 부지, 구내 utilize 이용하다 cutting-edge technology 최첨단 기술 treat 다루다, 치료하다, 처리하다 a variety of 여러 가지의 advantage 이점, 장점 cosmetic 화장품 consultation 상담

77 What type of business is being advertised?
(A) A beauty clinic
(B) A cosmetic company
(C) A stationery store
(D) A fitness center

어떤 종류의 사업이 광고되고 있는가?
(A) 미용 클리닉
(B) 화장품 회사
(C) 문구점
(D) 피트니스 센터

해설 〈기본 정보 파악 – 주제〉
피부 클리닉의 광고문이다. 초반에 업체명이 나오고 중반부에서 피부 치료를 돕는다는 내용이 나오므로 정답은 (A)이다.

78 What will happen tomorrow?
(A) A new product will be launched.
(B) A special offer will end.
(C) A consultation will begin.
(D) New premises will open.

내일 무슨 일이 있을 것인가?
(A) 새로운 제품이 출시될 것이다.
(B) 특별한 행사가 종료될 것이다.
(C) 상담이 시작될 것이다.
(D) 새로운 부지가 열릴 것이다.

해설 〈구체적 정보 파악 – 특정 사항〉
Tomorrow를 문제의 키워드로 잡고 들어야 한다. 초반부에 새로운 부지로의 이전을 알리며 내일 오픈한다는 안내가 이어지고 있으므로 정답은 (D)이다.

79 What is offered at a 30 percent discount?
(A) A consultation
(B) Any treatment
(C) A training session
(D) All products

30% 할인되는 것은 무엇인가?
(A) 상담
(B) 모든 치료
(C) 교육 세션
(D) 모든 제품

해설 〈구체적 정보 파악 – 특정 사항〉
광고문에서 할인 정보에 관한 단서는 주로 후반부에 등장한다. 문제의 30 percent discount가 정답의 단서가 되며 지문의 후반부에 2월 말까지 방문하는 모든 고객들은 어떤 치료든지 30% 할인을 받을 수 있다고 광고하고 있다. 따라서 정답은(B)이다.

Questions 80-82 refer to the following news report. (영M)

In business news today, (80) Advanced Electronics has announced its acquisition of Lunar Printer. The decision to sell Lunar, best known for its popular line of color printers, (81) comes only three months following the retirement of the company's founder, Glen Lunar. Reportedly, negotiations have been taking place throughout the week and a deal was finalized on Wednesday, when Lunar directors agreed to an improved offer from Advanced Electronics. When asked to comment, Mr. Lunar supported the move, (82) saying Advanced Electronics' wide distribution network would help introduce Lunar products to new customers.

오늘의 비즈니스 뉴스입니다. Advanced Electronics가 Lunar Printer의 인수를 발표했습니다. 컬러 프린터로 유명한 Lunar의 판매 결정은, 회사의 창립자인 Glen Lunar 씨의 은퇴 후 3개월 만에 나온 것입니다. 전하는 바에 따르면, 협상은 일주일 내내 진행되었고, 협상은 Lunar의 이사진들이 Advanced Electronics의 개선안에 동의한 수요일에 마무리되었다고 합니다. 견해를 묻자, Lunar 씨는 Advanced Electronics의 광범위한 유통망이 신규 고객들에게 Lunar 제품을 소개하는 데 도움이 될 것이라며, 이번 조치를 지지한다고 밝혔습니다.

어휘 announce 발표하다, 알리다 acquisition (기업) 인수, 매입 popular 인기 있는 retirement 은퇴 founder 설립자, 창설자 reportedly 전하는 바에 따르면 negotiation 협상, 교섭 throughout ~ 동안 죽, 내내 finalize 마무리 짓다, 완결하다 comment 견해를 밝히다 take-over 인수 distribution 분배, 분포

80 What is being reported?
(A) A stock offering
(B) A retirement event
(C) A construction project
(D) A business take-over

무엇이 보도되고 있는가?
(A) 주식 공모
(B) 은퇴 행사
(C) 건설 프로젝트
(D) 기업 인수

해설 〈기본 정보 파악 – 주제〉
주제는 담화의 초반에 등장한다. 화자가 첫 부분에서 Advanced Electronics가 Lunar Printer의 인수를 발표했다고 보도하고 있으므로 정답은 (D)이다.

패러프레이징 acquisition (기업) 인수 → take-over (사업 등의) 인계

81 What did Glen Lunar do three months ago?
(A) He founded a new company.
(B) He opened a new store.
(C) He retired from his career.
(D) He launched a new line of products.

Glen Lunar는 3개월 전에 무엇을 했는가?
(A) 새로운 회사를 세웠다.
(B) 새로운 상점을 열었다.
(C) 직장에서 은퇴했다.
(D) 새로운 제품 라인을 출시했다.

해설 〈구체적 정보 파악 – 특정 사항〉
문제 안의 Glen Lunar과 three months가 키워드이므로 해당 표현이 언급되는 문장에 주목한다. 회사 창립자인 Glen Lunar 씨의 은퇴 후 3개월 만에 인수 결정이 나온 것이라고 언급한 부분에서 정답이 (C)임을 알 수 있다.

82 What does the speaker mean when he says, "Mr. Lunar supported the move"?
(A) Mr. Lunar approved of a decision.
(B) Mr. Lunar wanted to relocate the headquarters.
(C) Mr. Lunar provided financial assistance.
(D) Mr. Lunar rejected the offer.

화자가 "Lunar 씨는 이번 조치를 지지한다"라고 말한 의미는 무엇인가?
(A) Lunar 씨는 결정에 찬성한다.
(B) Lunar 씨는 본사의 이전을 원했다.
(C) Lunar 씨는 금융 지원을 제공했다.
(D) Lunar 씨는 제안을 거절했다.

해설 〈구체적 정보 파악 – 화자 의도〉
언급된 문장의 주변 문맥을 통해 정답을 유추해야 한다. 이번 문제는 언급된 문장 직후의 설명을 통해 정답을 알 수 있는데 Lunar 씨는 Advanced Electronics의 광범위한 유통망이 Lunar 제품을 신규 고객들에게 소개하는 데 도움이 될 것으로 보고 이번 조치를 지지한다고 설명하고 있다. 따라서 정답은 (A)이다.

Questions 83-85 refer to the following announcement. 미M

Good afternoon, everyone. As you all know, 83 84 we are relocating to a new facility next week, and working there will be much more efficient with the state-of-the-art production equipment that has been installed. So, put all your belongings into boxes. Take as many boxes as you need from the supply room. And remember, the company will be closed for Monday and Tuesday, 85 but if you need to work on those days please consult with your managers so that we can assign you to a temporary workstation in the new building.

안녕하세요, 여러분. 여러분 모두 아시다시피, 우리는 다음 주에 새로운 시설로 이전하여 그곳에 설치된 최신 생산 장비로 훨씬 더 효율적인 작업을 하게 될 것입니다. 그러므로 여러분의 모든 물건들을 상자 안에 넣어 주세요. 필요한 상자는 비품실에서 얼마든지 가져가셔도 됩니다. 그리고 기억하실 것은 월요일과 화요일에 회사를 닫는다는 것입니다. 그러나 이 날 작업을 하셔야 한다면 새로운 건물에 임시 작업 공간을 지정받을 수 있도록 여러분의 매니저에게 알려주시기 바랍니다.

어휘 relocate 이전하다, 이전시키다 facility 시설, 기관 efficient 효율적인, 능률적인 state-of-the-art 최신의, 최신 기술의 equipment 장비, 용품, 설비 install 설치하다, 설비하다 belonging 소지품, 소유물 supply room 비품실 consult 상담하다, 상의하다 assign 맡기다, 배정하다 temporary 임시의, 일시적인 workstation 작업실

83 Who most likely are the listeners?
(A) Department heads
(B) Fitness instructors
(C) Marketing representatives
(D) Factory workers

청자들은 누구이겠는가?
(A) 부서 책임자
(B) 피트니스 강사
(C) 마케팅 담당자
(D) 공장 근로자

해설 〈기본 정보 파악 – 청자〉
청자에 관한 정보는 담화의 첫 부분에 근거가 제시된다. 담화 초반에 화자가 다음 주에 새로운 시설로 이전하여 그곳에 설치된 최신 생산 장비로 효율적인 작업을 하게 될 것이라며 생산 시설에 대해 언급하고 있다. 따라서 정답은 (D)이다.

84 What will happen next week?
(A) The company will move to a new building.
(B) Some employees will be recruited.
(C) The budget will be shortened.
(D) New tasks will be assigned.

다음 주에는 무슨 일이 있을 것인가?
(A) 회사가 새로운 건물로 이전할 것이다.
(B) 직원들이 채용될 것이다.
(C) 예산이 삭감될 것이다.
(D) 새로운 업무가 할당될 것이다.

해설 〈구체적 정보 파악 – 특정 사항〉
키워드인 next week가 언급되는 부분에서 정답을 찾아야 한다. 초반에 다음 주에 새로운 시설로 이전한다고 알리고 있으므로 정답은 (A)이다. 83번과 84번 모두 초반에 정답의 단서가 제시되고 있다. 비교적 단순한 '시점'이나 '장소'가 키워드인 문제들이 주로 한꺼번에 정답의 단서가 제시되는 경향이 있으므로 주의해야 한다.

85 What are some listeners requested to do?
(A) Contact their supervisors
(B) Put in extra hours
(C) Submit their report
(D) Assign a task

청자들이 요청받는 것은 무엇인가?
(A) 관리자에게 연락하는 것
(B) 추가 근무를 하는 것
(C) 보고서를 제출하는 것
(D) 업무를 지정하는 것

해설 〈구체적 정보 파악 – 요청 관련〉
요청 관련 문제의 정답 단서는 담화의 후반부에 제시되는 경우가 대부분이다. 담화의 후반부에서 특정한 날 작업하기를 원하면 매니저에게 이야기하라고 설명하고 있으므로 정답은 (A)이다.

패러프레이징 consult with your managers 매니저와 상의하다
→ contact their supervisors 관리자에게 연락하다

Questions 86-88 refer to the following excerpt from a meeting. 호M

86 In today's meeting we're going to look at how we can improve our service performance as hotel receptionists. We know that many guests, whether overseas tourists, company CEOs, or married couples, feel tired when they arrive to check in. They may be suffering jet lag from a long international flight, or may have been on the road for several hours. 87 In your folder, you'll find our hotel's employee handbook and a questionnaire that I will ask you to complete later today. Now I'm going to play a short video clip. 88 I'd like you to make some notes about the things our employees did well, and the things that you feel they should have done differently. After the video is finished, I'd like you to share your ideas, and then we'll take a short break.

오늘 회의에서는 호텔 접수 담당자로서 우리의 서비스 수준을 향상시킬 수 있는 방법에 대해 검토할 예정입니다. 우리의 많은 고객들, 그들이 해외 관광객이거나 회사의 CEO이거나 또는 결혼한 커플들이거나 모두 체크인을 하러 도착했을 때 피곤하다는 것을 알고 있습니다. 그들은 긴 국제 비행의 시차로 인해 불편을 겪을 수도 있고, 또는 몇 시간 동안 도로 위에 있었을 수도 있습니다. 여러분의 폴더 안에 우리 호텔의 직원 안내서와 잠시 후에 작성해 주실 설문지가 들어 있습니다. 이제 제가 짧은 비디오 영상을 보여드릴 예정입니다. 여러분께서는 우리 직원들이 잘했던 것들과 다르게 했어야 한다고 느끼는 것들에 대해 메모해 주시길 바랍니다. 비디오가 끝난 후, 여러분의 생각을 공유하고 짧은 휴식을 가질 것입니다.

어휘 improve 개선되다, 나아지다, 향상시키다 receptionist 접수 담당자 overseas 해외 suffer 시달리다, 고통받다, 겪다 jet lag 시차로 인한 피로 international 국제적인 questionnaire 설문지 wage slip 월급 명세서

86 Who is the announcement intended for?
(A) Restaurant servers
(B) Hotel employees
(A) Married couples
(D) Overseas tourists

이 안내는 누구를 위해 의도된 것인가?
(A) 레스토랑 종업원들
(B) 호텔 직원들
(C) 결혼한 커플들
(D) 해외 관광객들

해설 〈기본 정보 파악 – 청자〉
청자를 묻는 문제이므로 담화의 초반에서 단서를 찾아야 한다. 첫 문장에서 화자가 호텔 접수 담당자로서 서비스 수준을 향상시킬 수 있는 방법에 대해 검토할 것이라고 설명하고 있으므로 청자들이 호텔 접수원임을 알 수 있다. 따라서 정답은 (B)이다.

87 According to the speaker, what is contained in the folder?
(A) An employee ID card
(B) A floor plan
(C) An employee manual
(D) A wage slip

화자에 의하면, 폴더 안에는 무엇이 들어 있는가?
(A) 직원 ID 카드
(B) 평면도
(C) 직원 안내서
(D) 월급 명세서

해설 〈구체적 정보 파악 – 특정 사항〉
in the folder를 키워드로 잡고 문제의 단서를 찾아야 한다. 화자가 중반부에 폴더 안에 호텔 직원 안내서와 설문지가 들어 있다고 언급하고 있으므로 (C)가 정답이다.

패러프레이징 employee handbook 직원 안내서
→ employee manual 직원 안내서

88 What does the speaker ask listeners to do next?
(A) Evaluate staff members
(B) Take a short break
(C) Work in groups
(D) Complete a questionnaire

화자는 청자에게 다음에 무엇을 하라고 요청하는가?
(A) 직원들을 평가하는 것
(B) 휴식을 갖는 것
(C) 그룹으로 일하는 것
(D) 설문지를 작성하는 것

해설 〈구체적 정보 파악 – 요청 관련〉
요청 관련 문제이므로 정답은 지문의 후반부에 제시될 것을 예측하고 들어야 한다. 화자가 후반부에 청자들에게 직원들이 잘했던 것들과 다르게 했어야 한다고 느끼는 것들에 대해 메모해 달라고 요청하고 있다. 따라서 이를 바꾸어 표현한 (A)가 정답이다.

Questions 89-91 refer to the following telephone message. (영M)

Hello, Ms. Gray. This is Frank from Cleveland Services. I'm calling to confirm that my team members and I will be getting to your house between 10:00 and 11:00 A.M. tomorrow with ⑧⑨ the refrigerator that you ordered from us. We'll place the new unit in the same wall where your old refrigerator is now. ⑨⓪ We can take that one away and dispose of it for you if you'd like. Also, I got your message asking if you needed to pull the sofa and table away from the window. Don't worry about it. ⑨① We'll move them ourselves tomorrow morning. See you then.

안녕하세요, Gray 씨. Cleveland Services의 Frank입니다. 저의 팀과 제가 주문하신 냉장고를 가지고 내일 오전 10시에서 11시 사이에 댁에 방문할 예정임을 확인 드리려고 전화했습니다. 새 냉장고는 지금 쓰시는 냉장고와 같은 자리에 두려고 합니다. 원하신다면 쓰시던 냉장고는 저희가 가지고 가서 처리해 드리겠습니다. 소파와 테이블을 창문에서 치워야 하는지 문의주신 것을 봤습니다만 그것은 걱정하지 마십시오. 저희가 내일 아침에 옮기겠습니다. 그때 뵙겠습니다.

어휘 confirm 확인해 주다, 확정하다 refrigerator 냉장고 take away 가지고 가다 dispose of 없애다, 처리하다

89 What type of company does the speaker probably work for?
(A) A moving company
(B) A real estate agency
(C) An appliance dealer
(D) A cleaning service

화자가 근무하는 곳은 어떤 종류의 회사인가?
(A) 이삿짐 회사
(B) 부동산 중개업소
(C) 가전제품 판매소
(D) 청소 서비스

해설 〈기본 정보 파악 – 화자 근무처〉
화자가 일하는 장소에 관한 문제는 담화의 초반에 단서가 제시된다. 화자가 인사말을 한 후 내일 청자가 주문한 냉장고를 가지고 특정 시간에 방문하겠다고 알리고 있으므로 (C)가 정답이다.

90 What does the speaker offer to do tomorrow?
(A) Dispose of old equipment
(B) Repair a product
(C) Give a brochure
(D) Call before his arrival

화자는 내일 무엇을 하겠다고 제안하는가?
(A) 오래된 장비를 처리하는 것
(B) 제품을 수리하는 것
(C) 안내 책자를 주는 것
(D) 도착 전에 전화하는 것

해설 〈구체적 정보 파악 – 특정 사항〉
문제의 키워드인 tomorrow와 관련해서는 89번의 정답 단서에서 내일이 방문하는 날이라는 것을 알 수 있다. 그러므로 그 이후의 문장에서 청자가 원하면 냉장고를 가지고 가서 처리하겠다고 제안하고 있으므로 정답은 (A)이다.

91 What does the speaker imply when he says, "Don't worry about it"?
(A) His staff will not damage anything.
(B) His team will take care of a task.
(C) He will be able to sell the furniture.
(D) He will get an estimate.

화자가 "걱정하지 마세요"라고 말할 때 암시하는 것은 무엇인가?
(A) 그의 직원들은 어떤 것에도 손상을 주지 않을 것이다.
(B) 그의 팀이 일을 처리할 것이다.
(C) 그가 가구를 판매할 수 있을 것이다.
(D) 그는 견적을 받을 것이다.

해설 〈구체적 정보 파악 – 화자 의도〉
문제에 언급된 문장을 주변 문맥과 함께 종합하여 화자의 의도를 파악해야 한다. 이 문장이 언급되기 직전에 화자는 청자가 문의한 사항에 대해 걱정 말라고 하며 내일 직접 처리하겠다고 설명하고 있다. 따라서 필요한 일을 화자가 처리하겠다는 의미이므로 정답은 (B)이다.

Questions 92-94 refer to the following radio announcement. (영W)

⑨② Milkyway Cereal has issued a recall for its "Coco Oatmeal" brand cereal, after it was reported yesterday that some of the cartons did not contain their 450 gram capacity. ⑨③ Researchers of the production quality indicated a packing equipment failure, which has since been corrected. Affected batch numbers are from CP243 to CP390. These numbers appear on the carton label. ⑨④ If you have one of these cartons, you can exchange it for a free new box at any participating retailer. Milkyway offers its sincere apologies for any inconvenience this may have caused.

Milkyway Cereal은 어제 일부 포장 용기에 450그램의 용량이 들어 있지 않다는 보도 이후에 "Coco Oatmeal" 상표 시리얼의 리콜을 발표했습니다. 생산 품질 조사원들은 포장 기기의 고장을 지적했으며, 그 후로 그 부분은 현재 수리되었습니다. 영향을 받는 생산 번호는 CP243부터 CP390까지이며, 이 번호들은 상품 라벨에 표시되어 있습니다. 이 상품을 가지고 계시다면, 지정된 소매점 어디서나 새로운 상품으로 무료 교환을 받을 수 있습니다. Milkyway는 이번 일로 불편을 끼친 점에 대해 진심으로 사과했습니다.

어휘 issue 발표하다, 공표하다 recall 회수, 리콜 carton 통, 상자 contain ~이 들어있다 capacity 용량, 수용력 indicate 가리키다, 지적하다 correct 바로잡다, 정정하다 affect ~에 영향을 미치다, 작용하다 batch 묶음 appear 나타나다, 나오다 exchange 교환하다 participate 참가하다, 참여하다 inconvenience 불편한 complimentary 무료의

92 What is the problem?
(A) Some cereal cartons have wrong information.
(B) Some products have been mislabeled.
(C) Some cereal cartons are not full.
(D) Some products are of poor quality.

무엇이 문제인가?
(A) 일부 시리얼 상자의 정보가 잘못되어 있다.
(B) 일부 제품의 라벨이 잘못 붙여져 있다.
(C) 일부 시리얼 상자가 가득 차 있지 않다.
(D) 일부 제품의 품질이 나쁘다.

해설 〈구체적 정보 파악 – 문제점〉
첫 문제로 등장하는 문제점은 담화의 주제와 동일한 경우가 대부분으로 정답의 단서 또한 담화의 초반에 언급된다. 특정 회사가 시리얼의 내용물 미달로 리콜을 발표했다는 설명으로 지문이 시작되고 있으므로 정답은 (C)이다.

93 What is mentioned about the packing equipment?
(A) It is no longer malfunctioning.
(B) It will be replaced next month.
(C) It had been repaired before the incident.
(D) It will be inspected regularly.

포장 기기에 대해 무엇이라고 언급하는가?
(A) 더 이상 오작동되지 않는다.
(B) 다음 달에 교체될 것이다.
(C) 사건 전에 수리되었다.
(D) 규칙적인 점검을 받을 것이다.

해설 〈구체적 정보 파악 – 언급〉
문제의 키워드인 packing equipment가 언급되는 부분에서 정답을 찾아야 한다. 담화 중반에 생산 품질 조사원들이 포장 기기의 고장을 지적했으며 그것은 현재 수리되었다고 설명하고 있다. 따라서 정답은 (A)이다.

94 What will customers who return cartons receive?
(A) A new box of cereal
(B) A refund
(C) A complimentary gift
(D) A discount coupon

상품을 반납하는 고객은 무엇을 받게 되는가?
(A) 새 시리얼 상품
(B) 환불
(C) 무료 선물
(D) 할인 쿠폰

해설 〈구체적 정보 파악 – 특정 사항〉
화자가 후반부에서 이 상품을 가지고 있다면, 지정된 소매점 어디서나 새로운 상품으로 무료 교환을 받을 수 있다고 언급하고 있다. 따라서 정답은 (A)이다.

Questions 95-97 refer to the following announcement and graph. 미W

Customer Rating by Flavor

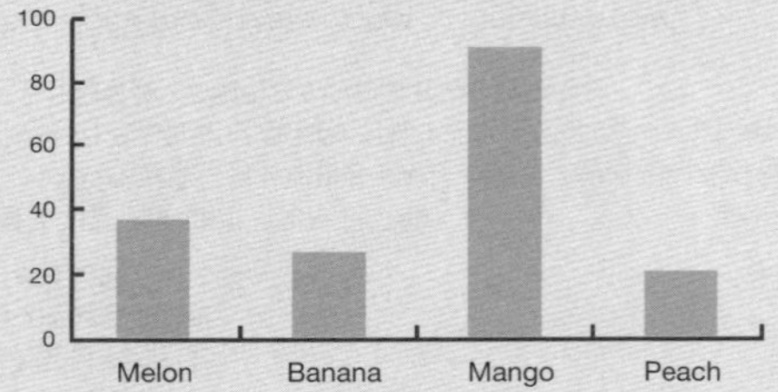

I have one last thing to announce before we wrap up the meeting. As we all know, at the end of the last quarter, ⑮ we asked our customers to send us their feedback on the new flavors they would like to add to our ice cream range. We narrowed down these proposals to four different flavors that would appeal to the widest range of consumers. ⑯ We carried out nationwide taste tests last week and, overall, the melon flavors we produced were popular across the country. However, ⑰ mango taste was people's favorite in Florida and banana was the best flavor in California.

고객 맛 평가

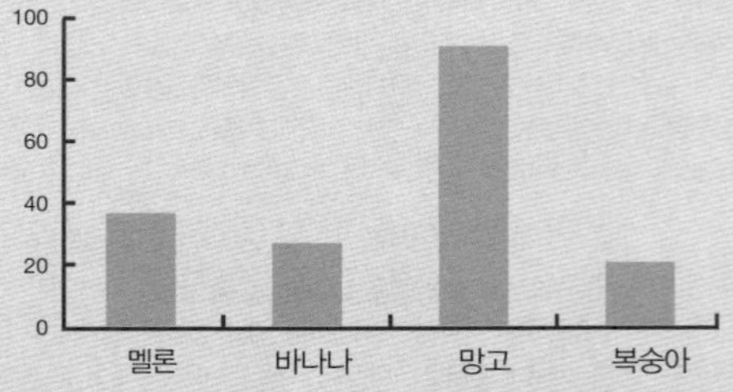

회의를 마무리하기 전에 한 가지 더 알려드릴 것이 있습니다. 모두 아시다시피, 지난 분기 말에 우리는 고객들에게 우리 아이스크림 제품군에 추가해 넣고 싶은 새로운 맛에 대한 의견을 보내달라고 요청했습니다. 우리는 이러한 제안들을 가장 광범위한 소비자들에게 어필할 수 있는 네 가지 다른 맛으로 좁혔습니다. 우리는 지난주에 전국적으로 맛 테스트를 실시했고, 전반적으로 우리가 만들어 낸 멜론 맛이 전국적으로 인기가 있었습니다. 하지만 망고 맛은 플로리다 사람들이 가장 좋아하는 맛이었고, 바나나는 캘리포니아에서 최고의 맛이었습니다.

어휘 wrap up (회의, 합의 등을) 마무리 짓다 feedback 피드백, 개선의 위한 의견 또는 정보 flavor 풍미, 맛 조경사 narrow down 좁히다, 줄이다 wide range 광범위한 carry out 이행하다, 수행하다 nationwide 전국적인

95 What does the speaker's company produce?
(A) Canned fruit
(B) Milk
(C) Bottled drinks
(D) Ice cream

화자의 회사가 생산하는 제품은 무엇인가?
(A) 통조림 과일
(B) 우유
(C) 병에 든 음료
(D) 아이스크림

해설 〈구체적 정보 파악 – 특정 사항〉
화자의 회사가 생산하는 제품은 주로 회사명에 함께 제시되는 경우가 많으나 이 경우는 회사 이름이 따로 언급되지 않으므로 구체적인 상품을 제시하는 문장에 집중해야 한다. 담화의 초반에 화자가 고객들에게 추가하고 싶은 아이스크림 맛에 대한 의견을 요청을 했다고 언급하므로 정답은 (D)이다.

96 According to the speaker, what did the company do last week?
(A) Conducted product trials
(B) Added a new facility
(C) Reduced a product price
(D) Launched an advertising campaign

화자에 따르면, 회사는 지난주에 무엇을 했나?
(A) 제품의 시험
(B) 새 시설 추가
(C) 제품의 가격 인하
(D) 광고 캠페인 시작

해설 〈구체적 정보 파악 – 특정 사항〉
문제의 키워드인 last week가 언급되는 부분에서 정답을 찾아야 한다. 담화 중반에 지난주에 전국적으로 시식회를 실시했다고 설명하고 있으므로 정답은 (A)이다.

패러프레이징 carry out taste tests 맛 평가를 실시하다
→ conduct product trials 제품을 시험하다

97 Look at the graphic. Where most likely is the result of this graph relevant?
(A) California
(B) Florida
(C) Texas
(D) Colorado

시각 자료를 보시오. 이 그래프의 결과로 가장 적절한 곳은 어디인가?
(A) 캘리포니아
(B) 플로리다
(C) 텍사스

해설 〈구체적 정보 파악 – 시각 정보 연계〉
선택지와 시각 자료의 관계를 먼저 파악하는 것이 중요하나 이 문제의 경우는 선택지의 지역들이 시각 자료에 나타나 있지 않으므로 선택지의 지역명과 함께 그래프의 가로축도 함께 집중해서 들어야 한다. 담화 후반에 화자가 망고 맛은 플로리다 사람들이 가장 좋아하고 바나나는 캘리포니아에서 좋아한다고 언급하고 있으므로 문제의 그래프는 망고 맛을 가장 좋아하는 플로리다의 결과임을 알 수 있다. 따라서 정답은 (B)이다.

Questions 98-100 refer to the following speech and table. 호M

The Future Conference Center		
Friday, June 18		
Hall Name	**Event**	**Time**
Apollo Hall	Employee Workshop	6:00 P.M.-9:00 P.M.
Dominion Hall	Product Launching Event	7:30 P.M.-10:00 P.M.
Empire Hall	Retirement Party	6:30 P.M.-9:30 P.M.
Warner Hall	Award Ceremony	8:00 P.M.-11:00 P.M.

Before we enjoy this lovely meal, 98 100 let's remember that we're here to honor Henry Williamson and his two decades of amazing service to M&T Developer. When Mark and I founded this company in 1998, Henry was our very first employee. 99 We were two landscapers who knew a lot about plants but not much about the industry, and Henry had good communications with people. He answered the phones, negotiated contracts, and dealt with all of our clients. As we grew, he grew too, eventually becoming our general manger and overseeing the more than 50 employees who work 100 for M&T today. We couldn't have become what we are today without him, and although we're sad that he's retiring, we wish him nothing but the best in the future. Let's raise our glasses to Henry Williamson, everyone!

The Future Conference Center		
6월 18일 금요일		
회의실 이름	**행사**	**일정**
Apollo 홀	직원 워크숍	오후 6:00-오후 9:00
Dominion 홀	제품 출시 행사	오후 7:30-오후 10:00
Empire 홀	은퇴 행사	오후 6:30-오후 9:30
Warner 홀	시상식	오후 8:00-오후 11:00

이 훌륭한 식사를 즐기기 전에, Henry Williamson과 그가 M&T Developer를 위해 열심히 근무한 20년에 경의를 표하기 위해 이곳에 있음을 기억합시다. 1998년에 Mark와 제가 이 회사를 설립했을 때, Henry는 우리의 첫 번째 직원이었습니다. 우리는 식물에 대해 많이 알고는 있지만 업계에 대해서는 잘 모르는 두 명의 조경사였고, Henry는 사람들과 의사소통을 잘 해주었습니다. 그는 전화를 받고, 계약을 협상하고, 우리의 모든 고객들과 거래를 했습니다. 우리가 성장하면서 그도 성장했으며 결국엔 우리의 총 관리자가 되었고, 오늘날 M&T에서 근무하는 50명 이상의 직원들을 감독하게 되었습니다. 그가 없었다면 오늘날의 우리도 없었을 겁니다. 비록 그의 은퇴는 슬프지만, 우리는 그에게 최고의 미래만을 바랍니다. 모두 Henry Williamson를 위해 잔을 듭시다!

어휘 decade 10년 found 설립하다, 세우다 landscaper 정원사, 조경사 industry 산업, 공업, 업계 negotiate 협상하다, 성사시키다 deal with ~을 다루다, ~을 대하다 eventually 결국, 마침내 oversee 감독하다 raise 들어 올리다, 들다 celebrity 유명 인사

98 Why is the speaker delivering this speech?
(A) To introduce a celebrity
(B) To celebrate a company's anniversary
(C) To introduce a new employee
(D) To recognize an employee's service

화자가 연설을 하는 이유는 무엇인가?
(A) 유명 인사를 소개하기 위해서
(B) 회사의 기념일을 축하하기 위해서
(C) 새로운 직원을 소개하기 위해서
(D) 직원의 공로를 인정하기 위해서

해설 〈기본 정보 파악 – 주제〉
담화의 주제는 처음에 제시된다. 화자가 첫 문장에서 Henry Williamson이 M&T Developer를 위해 열심히 근무한 20년에 경의를 표하기 위해 이곳에 있음을 기억하자고 설명하고 있다. 따라서 특정인의 공로를 인정하기 위한 자리이므로 정답은 (D)이다.

99 What kind of services does M&T provide?
(A) Landscaping
(B) Product development
(C) Accounting
(D) Retail management

M&T가 제공하는 서비스는 어떤 종류인가?
(A) 조경
(B) 제품 개발
(C) 회계
(D) 소매업 관리

해설 〈구체적 정보 파악 – 특정 사항〉
어떤 일을 하는 회사인지는 주로 회사명에서 단서가 제시되는 경우가 대부분이나 M&T Developer는 회사 이름에서 예측하기 불가능하므로 지문에서 다른 단서를 찾아야 한다. 화자가 중반부에 회사 설립 당시를 소개하며 본인과 사업 파트너(Mark)를 조경사라고 소개하고 있으므로 정답은 (A)이다.

100 Look at the graphic. Where is the event taking place?
(A) Apollo Hall
(B) Dominion Hall
(C) Empire Hall
(D) Warner Hall

시각 자료를 보시오. 행사가 열리는 곳은 어디인가?
(A) Apollo 홀
(B) Dominion 홀
(C) Empire 홀
(D) Warner 홀

해설 〈구체적 정보 파악 – 시각 자료 연계〉
선택지와 시각 자료의 관계를 파악하고 들어야 한다. 표에서 행사가 열리는 장소가 선택지로 제시되어 있으므로 지문 속 단서는 행사와 일정에 관련해서 언급된다는 것을 예측하고 들어야 한다. 행사가 직원의 은퇴를 기념하는 것이므로 표에서 은퇴 행사가 Empire Hall에서 열린다는 것을 알 수 있다. 따라서 정답은 (C)이다.

PART 5

101 해석 Casper 항공사 소유주가 새로운 비행기를 구매하기 위해 Super Jet과 거래를 협상 중이라고 공지했다.
해설 that절 안에 주어 자리가 비었으므로 정답은 주격 (B)이다. 재귀대명사는 주어 자리에 사용할 수 없으므로 (D)는 오답이다.
어휘 negotiate a deal 거래를 협상하다

102 해석 지난 10년 동안 Madison City의 인구가 약 30% 성장했다.
해설 빈칸은 전치사 자리로, 기간 앞에 쓰이고 있으므로 (C)가 정답이다.
어휘 population 인구

103 해석 모든 시설 입장이 Grand Plaza 호텔 숙박 비용에 포함되어 있다.
해설 빈칸은 주어 자리이므로 명사가 와야 하며 access는 불가산명사이므로 (A)가 정답이다.
어휘 facility 시설 access 접근 accessible 접근할 수 있는

104 해석 Chalmers 씨가 최종 원고를 도울 것이므로 당신 혼자서 전부 편집할 필요는 없을 것입니다.
해설 by oneself는 '혼자서'의 의미를 갖는 재귀대명사 관용어구이므로 정답은 (D)이다.
어휘 final draft 최종 원고 editing 편집하기

105 해석 습도가 철을 손상시킬 수 있으므로, 재료 보관실의 기후는 조절되어야만 한다.
해설 빈칸은 조동사 can 뒤의 일반동사 자리이므로 동사원형 (A)가 정답이다.
어휘 humidity 습도 climate 기후

106 해석 업데이트가 필요한지 알아보기 위해 Bukowski 씨가 훈련 지침서를 검토할 것이다.
해설 빈칸은 if절의 동사 자리로서 목적어가 없는 형태이므로 수동형인 (C)가 정답이다.
어휘 manual 지침서, 안내서

107 해석 프랑스에서 10년 동안 일한 후에 Georgina Garcia는 고급 식당을 열기 위해 Madrid로 돌아왔다.
해설 has 뒤의 과거분사 자리이다. 전치사 to와 함께 쓰이는 자동사이고 뒤에 Madird라는 장소가 등장했으므로 (B)가 정답이다.
어휘 fancy 화려한, 고급의 occur (to) ~에게 떠오르다

108 해석 도시 위원회는 도로 개선 프로젝트의 자금 지원을 인상하는 청원서를 승인했다.
해설 자금이 지원되어야 하는 것은 (D) project가 적절하다.
어휘 bill 청원서 funding 자금 지원 improvement 개선 statement 성명, 진술 permission 허가

109 해석 Finch 씨를 직접 인터뷰한 후에 회사 사장은 그를 부사장으로 고용하고자 하는 위원회의 결정을 승인했다.
해설 목적어 decision과 어울리는 동사가 빈칸에 들어가야 하므로 (A)가 정답이다.
어휘 host ~의 사회를 보다

110 해석 일단 가장 최근의 업데이트가 설치되고 나면 태블릿 플랫폼은 더 이상 이 소프트웨어를 지원하지 않는다.
해설 no longer는 '더는 ~하지 않는'의 뜻으로 쓰이므로 정답은 (C)이다.

111 해석 각 판매 팀은 이달 말까지 연간 판매 보고서의 결과를 제출해야 한다.
해설 빈칸은 동사 자리이고 result를 목적어로 받는 자리이므로 (A)가 정답이다.
어휘 match ~와 어울리다 earn 벌다

112 해석 South Central School의 지역 매니저들은 다양한 업계에서 풍부한 전문성을 갖고 있는 은퇴한 중역들입니다.
해설 expertise(전문성)는 a wealth of expertise 형태로 '풍부한 전문성'이라는 뜻으로 사용될 수 있으므로 (D)가 정답이다.
어휘 height 높이 labor 노동 wealth 부, 풍부함

113 해석 공항 건설의 첫 번째 단계는 중간 크기의 상업용 비행기를 처리할 용량이 가능한 활주로를 건설하는 것이다.
해설 전치사 of 뒤의 자리로서 빈칸 뒤의 midsize commercial airplanes를 목적어로 취할 수 있어야 하므로 동명사형인 (A)가 정답이다.
어휘 runway 활주로 capable of ~할 수 있는 handle 처리하다

114 해석 Sonja Pakov는 음반 판매에서는 Wright Band의 바로 뒤에 있는 남미에서 가장 인기 있는 음악가 중 한 명이다.
해설 빈칸은 전치사 자리로서 Wright Band와 비교하는 것이므로 순위를 나타낼 수 있는 (D)가 정답이다. behind only는 뒤에 나오는 것만 빼고라는 의미로 바로 다음이라는 뜻이다.
어휘 toward ~방향으로 except ~을 제외한, ~가 없는

115 해석 쉽게 참고할 수 있도록 운영 지침은 복사기 위에 게시되어 있다.
해설 refer to를 강조하는 부사이므로 문맥상 (D)가 정답이다.
어휘 consequently 결과적으로 standardly 평범하게 namely 즉 easily 쉽게

116 해석 Narumi Skincare의 마케팅 계획에 대한 팀의 기여는 매우 우호적으로 인정받았다.
해설 부사 very와 분사 acknowledged 사이의 위치이므로 부사형 (B)가 정답이다.
어휘 contribution to ~에 대한 기여 acknowledge ~을 인정하다, 승인하다 favor 호의, 부탁 favorably 우호적으로, 순조롭게

117 해석 지난주에 우리가 받은 수치는 아직 디지털 자료로 입력되어야 한다.
해설 need to를 수식하는 부사 자리로서 '여전히, 아직도'라는 의미의 (D)가 정답이다.
어휘 lately 최근에 evenly 균등하게

118 해석 최소 14일 전에 서면으로 공지가 이루어진다면 계약자들은 아무 때나 계약을 종료할 수 있다.
해설 빈칸 이하에 동사 is가 있으므로 절을 만들 수 있는 접속사 (C)가 정답이다. 나머지 선택지는 모두 뒤에 절이 올 수 없다.
어휘 terminate 종료시키다 at any time 아무 때나 notification 공지 in writing 서면으로 at least 적어도, 최소 along with ~와 함께 provided that 만약 ~라면 regardless of ~와 상관없이

119 해석 컴퓨터 바이러스 제거에 대한 최고의 해결 방법을 선택하는 것은 간단하지 않으므로 전문가 의견을 구하는 것이 중요하다.
해설 빈칸은 콤마 앞뒤의 절을 연결할 수 있는 등위접속사 자리이므로 정답은 (D)이다. 접속사 nor는 뒤의 절이 도치되어야 하므로 오답이다.
어휘 elimination 제거 rarely 거의 ~하지 않는 seek 구하다 expert 전문가

120 해석 Samuel Jenkins의 원래 원고는 Sylvon 출판사가 그의 가족들의 허락을 구한 후에 작년에 출판되었다.
해설 동사 obtain의 목적어 자리로서 '가족들의 허가를 구했다'는 것이 문맥상 어울리므로 정답은 (A)이다.
어휘 manuscript 원고 permission 허가 comparison 비교 registration 등록

121 해석 Lai 씨의 Sientech Industries의 새 임무 성명서의 초안은 회사의 목표를 정확하게 표현한다.
해설 빈칸 앞 전체 문장의 구성이 완전하므로 정답은 부사인 (D)이다.
어휘 precise 정확한 precisely 정확하게

122 해석 우수한 텔레비전 콘텐츠의 공급업자인 Yoon Station은 서비스를 개선하기 위한 구체적인 아이디어를 환영합니다.
해설 명사 idea를 수식하는 형용사형이 필요하므로 정답은 (C)이다.
어휘 provider 공급업자, 회사 content 내용 specifics 세부 사항, 내용 specific 구체적인 specify 구체화하다

123 해석 Jarman Food Company는 최근에 소비자들에게 받은 인기를 새로운 포장보다는 요리법의 변화 덕분이라고 하였다.
해설 빈칸 앞의 recipe와 뒤의 packaging을 대조할 수 있는 어휘인 (C)가 정답이다.
어휘 attribute A to B A는 B에 기인하다 recent 최근의 popularity 인기 recipe 요리법 packaging 포장 rather than ~보다는 다소 after all 결국에는

124 해석 조립 라인은 긴급한 관심을 필요로 하는 문제가 없다면 계속 운영될 것이다.

해설 명사 attention을 수식하는 형용사 어휘이므로 (D)가 정답이다.

어휘 assembly 조립 fluent 유창한 gentle 부드러운 urgent 긴급한

125 해석 Charat Properties와의 임대 계약이 곧 끝나기로 되어 있으므로 이용 가능한 사무 공간이 광고될 것입니다.

해설 be set to는 '~하기로 정해져 있다'는 뜻으로 쓰이므로 to부정사 (B)가 정답이다.

어휘 lease agreement 임대 계약 office space 사무 공간

126 해석 11월 한 달 내내 Green Company에서 구매되는 어떤 가구라도 영업일 기준 5일 이내로 배달될 것입니다.

해설 '5일'이라는 기간 앞에 쓸 수 있는 전치사이므로 정답은 (C)이다.

어휘 throughout 내내

127 해석 Chung & Cho 자동차 정비소는 정비공들에게 벨트 가장자리에 마모의 징후를 인지하면 감독자에게 즉시 연락하라고 요구한다.

해설 빈칸은 부사 자리로서 동사 contact를 수식할 수 있는 (D)가 정답이다. finally와 somewhat은 동사나 형용사 앞에서 사용하며 절의 마지막 자리에서 사용하지 않는다.

어휘 auto shop 자동차 수리소 mechanic 정비공 notice 인지하다 signs of wear 마모의 흔적, 징후 somewhat 다소, 약간 right away 즉시

128 해석 First Carey 은행의 주차장은 이제 대중에게 개방되긴 했지만, 한 구역은 은행의 VIP 고객들에게만 배정되어 있다.

해설 부사절 접속사 자리로서 부사절과 주절의 의미가 양보절로 이루어져야 하므로 정답은 (A)이다.

129 해석 Ricci 주상복합 건물 프로젝트 계약은 가장 에너지 효율적인 디자인을 제출하는 어떤 건설 회사에라도 주어질 것입니다.

해설 전치사 to 이하의 명사절을 이끄는 접속사 자리이므로 복합관계형용사인 (B)가 정답이다.

어휘 award 주다, 수여하다

130 해석 Cresson 씨의 지불 기록과 대출을 받은 금액 둘 다 재융자 신청에서 고려될 것입니다.

해설 amount를 뒤에서 수식하는 과거분사 어휘를 골라야 한다. 문맥상 뒤에 his loan이 있고 '대출받은 금액'이라는 뜻이 적절하므로 (B)가 정답이다.

어휘 refinancing 재융자 owe 빚지다

[131-134]

수신: jhewittt@mailday.co.uk
발신: customerservice@powerprotection.com
날짜: 10월 10일
주제: 제품 후기

Hewitt 씨에게,

최근 131 구매에 대해 감사드립니다. Power Protection 소프트웨어 사용을 즐기시기를 바랍니다. 혹시라도 어떤 문제를 132 겪으신다면, 034-555-3746번인 고객 서비스로 전화해 주시기 바랍니다. 우리 기술자들이 24시간 내내 도와드릴 준비가 되어 있습니다.

제품에 만족하셨다면, www.powerprotection.com/yourvoice를 방문하셔서 온라인 후기를 작성하시는 것을 고려해 주세요. 133 그런 후기는 여러 면에 있어서 감사할 만한 것입니다. 그것은 134 잠재적 고객들에게 정보를 주고 우리 사업이 번창할 수 있도록 도움이 되어 고품질 소프트웨어 제품 라인을 확장하도록 도움이 될 수 있습니다.

어휘 be ready to ~할 준비가 되어 있다 expand 확장하다

131 해설 뒤의 내용에서 소프트웨어를 이미 구매한 소비자에게 보내는 이메일인 것을 알 수 있으므로 정답은 (B)이다.

132 해설 in the unlikely event that ~ 구문으로 미래의 일을 가정하고 있으나 부사절 안의 동사 사용이므로 현재시제인 (A)가 정답이다.

133 (A) 월별 자원 봉사 프로젝트에 대해서 다시 한 번 상기시켜 드리고 싶습니다.
(B) 모든 제품 할인을 제공하면서 행사가 방금 시작되었습니다.
(C) 일정대로 공사는 약 3개월 후에 시작될 것입니다.
(D) 그런 후기는 여러 면에 있어서 감사할 만한 것입니다.

해설 앞 문장에서 'online review'를 언급하고 있으므로 연결되는 Such review가 나오는 (D)가 정답이다.

어휘 as scheduled 일정대로

134 해설 customers를 수식하는 문맥이고 '잠재적 고객'이라는 의미가 적합하므로 정답은 (C)이다.

어휘 selective 선택적인 required 필수적인 beneficial 유익한

[135-138]

발신: Jane Fisherman
수신: 전 직원
날짜: 5월 1일
주제: 새로운 제품 작명 지침
첨부: pdf 서류

이 이메일에는 새로운 로고, 폰트, 색상 목록을 포함한 기업 제품 작명 지침서의 축약본이 135 첨부되었습니다. 이 지침은 지금부터 136 유효하며 내부 직원 웹사이트에도 또한 게시되어 있습니다.

새로운 기준을 반영하는 프린트물과 전자상의 홍보물은 아직 작업 중입니다. 137 이달 말까지는 이 과정이 마무리되기를 바랍니다. 이러한 변화를 반영하는 전체 양식이 138 배포될 것입니다.

문제점이나 염려하시는 점이 있다면 알려 주시기 바랍니다.

어휘 abbreviated 축약된 corporate 기업의 branding 제품 작명 including ~을 포함하여 internal 내부의 work on ~에 대해 작업하다 publicity 홍보 standard 기준 reflect 반영하다

135 해설 문장의 주어는 'an abbreviated version'이며 수동태의 분사 구문이 문장 앞으로 도치된 것이므로 정답은 (B)이다.

136 해설 These guidelines를 수식하는 형용사절 안의 보어 자리로 '효력을 발생하는 지침'이라는 뜻이 되어야 하므로 정답은 (B)이다.

어휘 out of date 구식인, 낡은 beside the point 요점을 벗어난 on purpose 고의로

137 (A) 지원금 신청이 허가되었다는 것을 기쁘게 알려 드립니다.
(B) 프로그램에 참여하시려면 매니저에게 이야기하세요.
(C) 이달 말까지는 이 과정이 마무리되기를 바랍니다.
(D) 현대적인 외관을 위해서 지점 중 한 곳을 수리할 것입니다.

해설 앞 문장에서 still working(아직도 작업 중)이라고 언급했으므로 끝내고 싶다는 (C)가 문맥에 적합하다.

어휘 grant 지원금

138 해설 문장의 동사 자리로서 distribute 동사 뒤로 목적어가 없으므로 수동태인 (D)가 정답이다.

어휘 distribute 분배하다, 유통시키다

[139-142]

중요! (139) 새로운 세탁기를 작동하기 전에 설명서를 잘 읽어주시기 바랍니다. 여러분의 새로운 Power Tech 340 세탁기는 내용물이 가득 찼을 때 무게를 지탱할 수 있을 만큼 (140) 충분히 튼튼한 기초 위에 설치해 주시기 바랍니다. 소음과 진동을 막기 위해서 이 제품은 수평으로 놓여져야 합니다. 기계의 바닥 구석에 있는 작은 발의 높이를 (141) 조정하셔서 하실 수 있습니다. 반드시 기계 뒤쪽에 있는 수로 공급 호스를 냉온수 물 밸브에 (142) 안전하게 연결하십시오.

어휘 washing machine 세탁기 foundation 기초, 설립 support 지지하다, 받치다 fully 완전히 loaded 짐을 실은 prevent 예방하다 vibration 진동 level 수평으로 하다 be sure to 반드시 ~하다 attach A to B A를 B에 첨부하다

139 (A) 기술이 우리 고객들의 경험을 개선시키는 데 기여할 것이라고 믿습니다.
(B) 우리는 빠르고 효율적인 과정으로 유명합니다.
(C) 정확하게 몇 명이 나타날지 알 수 없습니다.
(D) 새 세탁기를 작동하기 전에 설명서를 잘 읽어 주시기 바랍니다.
해설 설명서의 첫 번째 문장이므로 주의 깊게 읽어야 할 것을 강조하는 내용의 (D)가 정답이다.
어휘 contribute to ~에 기여하다 be famous for ~에 유명하다 speedy 신속한 efficient 능률적인 turn up 나타나다, 등장하다

140 해설 빈칸 뒤의 to부정사와 함께 사용하여 strong을 수식하는 어휘이므로 부사 (A)가 정답이다.

141 해설 앞뒤 문맥을 살펴보면 기계는 수평이 되도록 설치해야 하는데, 이는 발 높이를 '조절해서' 할 수 있는 것이므로 정답은 (A)이다.
어휘 adjust ~을 조절하다

142 해설 빈칸 뒤의 전치사 to 이하를 수식할 수 있는 부사 (B)가 정답이다.
어휘 secure 안전하게 하다, 확보하다 security 보안

[143-146]

독감의 계절이 다시 (143) 다가옴에 따라 사람들은 끔찍한 바이러스에 감염되는 것을 피할 수 있는 방법을 궁금해 합니다. 예방 접종을 받는 것이 가장 좋은 해결책이지만 다른 여러 (144) 예방책들도 있습니다!

손을 자주 그리고 잘 씻어야 하는 것을 기억하세요. (145) 비타민 C를 많이 섭취하여 면역 체계를 튼튼하게 유지하세요. 아프면 영웅이 되려 하지 마세요 – 집에 가서 쉬세요! 아직 몸이 많이 아프지는 (146) 않더라도, 종종 질병 초기여서 독감을 퍼뜨릴 수 있습니다.

어휘 flu 독감 wonder 의아해 하다, 궁금해 하다 keep from ~를 막다 contract 감염되다 get vaccinated 예방 접종을 받다 rest 쉬다 stage 단계 spread 퍼뜨리다 illness 질병

143 해설 주절의 wonders와 시제를 일치하여 현재시제와 3인칭 단수형을 사용한 (B)가 정답이다.

144 해설 빈칸이 있는 문장은 첫 문장에 제시된 바이러스 감염 예방책을 소개하는 내용이다. 문맥상 '예방책'을 의미하는 precautions가 적절하므로 정답은 (C)이다.
어휘 warning 경고 symptom 증상 precaution 예방책

145 (A) 직원들에게 최대 10일까지 병가를 줍니다.
(B) 독감이 그 지역에서 국경을 넘어서 퍼지고 있습니다.
(C) 비타민 C를 많이 섭취하여 면역 체계를 튼튼하게 유지하세요.
(D) 어떤 사람들은 몇 년 동안 증상 없이 있습니다.
해설 독감 바이러스 예방법을 나열하고 있으므로 정답은 (C)이다.
어휘 up to 최대 ~까지 sick leave 병가 across borders 국경을 넘어서 immune system 면역 체계 symptom-free 증상이 없는

146 해설 문맥상 '아직 몸이 많이 아프진 않더라도 그것이 초기 단계일 수도 있다'는 뜻으로 부사절과 주절을 연결하는 접속사로서 양보의 뜻을 갖는 (A)가 정답이다.
어휘 as if 마치 ~인 것처럼 in case of ~하는 경우에 rather than ~보다는, 다소

[147-148]

Seattle 영화 클럽

(147) Seattle 영화 클럽이 첫 번째 인도 영화 축제를 진행하게 되어서 자랑스럽습니다. 9월 18일부터 11월 6일까지, 인도 영화 제작자들의 최근 및 고전 영화 8편이 Lloyd Mall 가까이에 있는 Coleman 극장에서 상영됩니다. 이 무료 영화는 스페인어와 영어 자막이 있으며 매주 토요일 오후 7시에 시작합니다. (148) 전체 프로그램을 보시려면 웹 사이트 seattlemovieclub.org를 방문해 주세요.

어휘 contemporary 동시대의

147 무엇이 공지되고 있는가?
(A) 영화제 개막
(B) 인도 영화배우의 인터뷰
(C) 영화 제작
(D) 영화 시리즈
해설 초반에 'The Seattle Movie Club is proud to present our first Bollywood Festival'이라고 했으므로 정답은 (A)이다.

148 전단지에 따르면 Seattle 영화 클럽 웹 사이트에서 알 수 있는 것은?
(A) 새로운 영화 무료 입장권
(B) Coleman 극장으로 가는 길 안내
(C) 행사 일정
(D) 영화감독의 전기
해설 마지막 문장에서 'To view the complete program, please visit our Web site at seattlemovieclub.org'라고 한 것으로 정답이 (C)인 것을 알 수 있다.
어휘 direction 안내 biography 전기

[149-150]

Gold 항공

(150) Gold 항공은 3시간 이상 비행 시에는 무료로 특별 식사를 제공합니다. (149) Gold 항공이나 다른 공인된 여행사를 통해서 비행기를 예약하셨다면, 특별 식사 요청을 하시기 위해 예정된 항공기가 출발하기 적어도 24시간 전에 고객 서비스 직통 번호 121-555-0987로 전화해 주세요. 식사 제한이나 걱정이 있으신 여행자는 직통 전화로 연락해 주시기 바랍니다. (150) 식사 제공 직원들은 당신의 필요를 수용하기 위해 최선을 다할 것입니다. 특별 식사, 시식, 공통 재료 목록을 보시려면 www.airgold.com을 방문해 주세요.

어휘 free of charge 무료로 authorized 공인된 catering 식사 서비스 do one's utmost 최선을 다하다 accommodate 수용하다 ingredient 재료

149 이 광고는 누구를 대상으로 하는가?
(A) 여행 가이드
(B) 여행사 직원
(C) 비행기 승객
(D) 비행기 승무원

해설 지문에서 'Whether you reserved your flight with Air Gold'라고 했으므로 정답은 (C)이다.

150 공지의 목적은 무엇인가?
(A) 회원제 프로그램의 혜택을 홍보하기 위해서
(B) 식사 선택에 대한 정보를 주기 위해서
(C) 비행기 조종사 고용을 공지하기 위해서
(D) 건강한 식습관 지침을 제안하기 위해서

해설 글 전반에 걸쳐서 식사 서비스에 대해 언급하고 있고 'Our catering staff will do its utmost to accommodate your needs'라고 나와 있으므로 정답은 (B)이다.

어휘 benefit 혜택 eating 식습관

[151-153]

개장 기념 축하 행사!
Ashland Brothers Company
54 Thompson Plaza (Kathryn 제과점 옆)
San Diego, CA 94789
512-555-0090

(151) 개장 특별 행사:
모든 책상과 의자 30% 할인
소파 (가죽 한정) 25% 할인
모든 식탁 15% 할인

행사는 7월 3일부터 8월 3일까지 진행됩니다.
(Thompson Plaza 매장에서만 30달러 이상 구매 시 청소 도구 무료 증정)
영업 시간: 오전 8시-오후 8시

Ashland Brothers Company 회원제를 신청해 주세요 – 1년에 단 25달러로 온라인뿐만 아니라 (152) Thompson Plaza와 Alina Mall 가게 지점에서 구매하시는 모든 제품에 대해 10퍼센트 추가 할인을 받으실 수 있습니다!

웹 사이트 www.ashlandbrotherscompany.com으로 방문해 주세요.

(153) 이번 주 한정, 온라인으로 책장 주문 시 40% 할인!

어휘 good 유효한 sign up for ~에 신청하다

151 Ashland Brothers Company에서 판매하는 것은 어떤 상품인가?
(A) 전자제품
(B) 사무용품
(C) 의류
(D) 가구

해설 '30% off all desks and chairs, 25% off sofa (leather only), 15% off any dining tables'에서 가구점임을 알 수 있으므로 (D)가 정답이다.

어휘 clothing 의류

152 Ashland Brothers Company에 대해서 알 수 있는 것은?
(A) 개장 기념행사가 일주일 동안이다.
(B) 8월 3일에는 오후 10시까지 문을 연다.
(C) 판매원들은 훈련을 잘 받았다.
(D) 한 곳 이상의 지점이 있다.

해설 지문 중간에 'both our Thompson Plaza and Alina Mall store locations'라고 한 것으로 정답은 (D)임을 알 수 있다.

어휘 highly 매우

153 온라인으로 구매 했을 경우에만 할인 받을 수 있는 제품은?
(A) 제빵류
(B) 청소용품
(C) 책장
(D) 가죽 물품

해설 지문 마지막 문장에서 'This week only, order any bookcase online and get 40% off!'라고 하였으므로 정답은 (C)이다.

[154-155]

Sally Kleinman 오전 11시 36분
Ali, 주문 번호 A 321이 발송되었는지 확인해 주시겠어요? (154) 고객이 방금 ZDS12를 추가하고 싶다고 요청했어요.

Ali Griffin 오전 11시 39분
고객 맞춤 운동화 맞죠? 새기는 작업자들이 고객 메시지를 추가하는 데 적어도 3일은 필요해요.

Sally Kleinman 오전 11시 39분
(155) 빨리 해 주시겠어요? 고객이 되도록 빨리 필요하다고 해요.

Ali Griffin 오전 11시 41분
얼마나 빨리 필요해요? (155) 내일이면 될까요?

Sally Kleinman 오전 11시 44분
네, 되겠어요. 도와줘서 고마워요!

어휘 customized 고객 맞춤인 engraver 새기는 사람 rush job 급한 일

154 고객이 원하는 것은?
(A) 주문에 물품 추가
(B) 제품 교환
(C) 환불받기
(D) 할인 코드 사용

해설 Kleinman 씨가 오전 11시 36분에 'The customer has just asked us to add item ZDS12'라고 한 것으로 (A)가 정답임을 알 수 있다.

155 오전 11시 44분에, Kleinman 씨가 "되겠어요"라고 쓴 것은 어떤 뜻인가?
(A) 회의에서 슬라이드 발표를 할 것이다.
(B) 장비가 수리되었다고 전달받았다.
(C) 물건이 내일 준비되면 고객이 만족할 것이다.
(D) 배송 회사가 오늘 내로 물건을 배송할 것이다.

해설 오전 11시 39분에 Kleinmna 씨가 'Can you do a rush job? The customer needs it as soon as possible'이라고 물은 것에 대해 Griffin 씨가 오전 11시 41분에 'How soon do you need it? Is tomorrow okay?'라고 한 것에 대한 대답이므로 정답은 (C)이다.

[156-157]

전기 비용을 줄이기 위한 현명한 생각들

높은 사무실 사용 비용에 대한 몇 가지 도움이 될 만한 제안들이 있습니다.

환경: 156 더 많은 자연광이 들어오도록 가능하면 커튼과 블라인드는 걷어 두세요. 더 많은 자연광을 반사하도록 밝은 벽지를 사용하세요.

조명: 백열등을 형광등 전구로 교체하시면 조명 시설을 교체하지 않고서도 똑같은 밝기로 적은 에너지를 사용하게 됩니다. 창고나 옷장처럼 조명이 지속적으로 사용되지 않는 일하지 않는 장소에서는 전기 사용을 줄이기 위해서 모션 센서를 사용하세요.

사무 장비: 사용하지 않을 때 프린터와 복사기를 끄세요. 157-C 멀티탭을 사용하세요. 스위치 한 번으로 모든 사무 장비를 끄는 것이 편리합니다. 157-B 화면 보호기는 에너지 절약이 아닙니다. 사무실을 나갈 때는 모니터를 끄세요. 157-D 사무실에 아무도 없을 때는 전기를 끄기 위해 자동 타이머를 사용하세요.

어휘 electricity 전기 office utility 사무실 공공 비용 pull up 올리다, 걷다 shade 블라인드, 커튼 reflect 반사하다 incandescent 백열등 florescent 형광등의 usage 사용 constantly 지속적으로 flip 뒤집음 occupied 차지한, 사람이 있는

156 정보에 따르면 직장에서 조명은 어떻게 최대화될 수 있는가?
(A) 조명을 이동시킴으로써
(B) 일하는 곳에 모션 센서를 설치함으로써
(C) 더 밝은 전등을 사용함으로써
(D) 방에 더 많은 햇빛이 들도록 해서

해설 두 번째 단락에서 'Pull up the shades and blinds for more natural light, whenever possible'이라고 했으므로 (D)가 정답임을 알 수 있다.

어휘 light fixture 조명물

157 에너지 소비를 제한하는 방법으로 언급된 것이 아닌 것은?
(A) 사무 장비를 더 효율적인 것으로 교체하는 것
(B) 화면 보호기 대신에 모니터를 끄는 것
(C) 여러 개의 장비를 끄기 위해서 멀티탭을 사용하는 것
(D) 자동 시간 장치를 설치하는 것

해설 네 번째 단락에서 'Use a power strip. It will be very convenient to turn off all office equipment with the flip of the switch'에서 (C)가 언급되었고 'A screen saver is not an energy saver. Please turn off your monitor when you leave the office'에서 (B)가 언급되었고, 'Use an auto timer to turn off electricity when the office is not occupied'에서 (D)가 언급되었다. 언급되지 않은 (A)가 정답이다.

어휘 energy consumption 에너지 소비 limit 제한하다 replace A with B A를 B로 교체하다 efficient 효율적인

[158-160]

수신: Julie Chan
발신: Daniel Rhee
날짜: 3월 14일
주제: Oakland 컨퍼런스

158 3월 28일 Oakland 조경 학회 참가 신청서가 부사장에 의해서 승인되었습니다. 160 회사 출장 정책에 따라, 비행기표, 렌터카, 호텔이 회사에 의해 사전에 지불될 예정입니다. -[1]-. 160 돌아와서 식사, 주유, 그리고 다른 업무 관련 비용의 영수증을 제출해 주세요. 회사 정책은 오락 비용은 환급해 드리지 않는다는 것을 기억해 주세요. -[2]-.

사전 일정표에 의해서 오전 6시 28분 출발하는 3월 28일 Super Jet 263편을 예약하였습니다. 159-C 돌아오는 항공편은 3월 30일 오후 3시 5분에 Oakland를 출발하는 319편입니다. -[3]-. 159-A 159-D 공항의 Patel Autos에 소형 차량이 예약되어 있습니다. 도착하시면 그곳에서 차를 찾으시면 됩니다. San Andreas 거리에 있는 Plaza Fisher 호텔에서 숙박하게 될 것입니다. 이러한 모든 예약 사항들이 당신의 동의를 얻기를 바랍니다. -[4]-. 모든 세부 사항이 최종 승인될 수 있도록 내일 오전 9시 15분에서 오후 4시 30분 사이에 내선번호 2326으로 저에게 전화해 주시기 바랍니다. 이번 주 말까지 공식적인 일정표를 이메일로 보내 드리겠습니다.

감사합니다.

Daniel Rhee
행정 지원 사무실

어휘 landscaping 조경 approve 승인하다 in keeping with ~을 준수하여 in advance 사전에 reimbursable 환급 가능한 preliminary 사전의 itinerary 여행 일정(표) compact vehicle 소형차 arrangement 예약 meet with approval 동의를 얻다 extension 내선번호 finalize 최종 승인하다 formal 공식적인 administrative 행정의

158 출장 요청에 대해 알 수 있는 것은?
(A) 여행 일정에 대한 세부 사항이 있어야 한다.
(B) 프로젝트 제안서를 포함해야만 한다.
(C) 식사 비용의 견적을 내야만 한다.
(D) 중역에 의해 승인되어야 한다.

해설 초반에 'Your request to attend the environmental law seminar in Oakland on March 28 has been approved by the vice president'라고 한 것으로 정답이 (D)인 것을 알 수 있다.

어휘 estimate 견적을 내다 authorize 승인하다

159 Patel Autos에 대해서 언급되지 않은 것은?
(A) 예약을 받는다.
(B) San Andreas 거리에 위치해 있다.
(C) Oakland에 지점이 있다.
(D) 소형차를 대여한다.

해설 지문의 'A compact vehicle has been reserved at Patel Autos at the airport'에서 (A)와 (D)가 언급되었으며 차량을 예약한 곳은 Oakland이므로 (C)도 맞는 내용이다. San Andreas 거리에 있는 것은 호텔이고 Patel Autos는 공항에 있으므로 (B)가 정답이다.

160 [1], [2], [3], [4]로 표시된 위치들 중 다음 문장이 들어가기 적절한 곳은?
"Oakland에 있는 동안 발생하는 추가 비용은 환급될 것입니다."
(A) [1]
(B) [2]
(C) [3]
(D) [4]

해설 [1] 뒤 문장에서 'Please plan to turn in receipts for meals, gasoline, and any other business-related expenses on your return'로 추가 환급 방법을 제시하고 있으므로 (A)가 정답이다.

[161-164]

발신: Jane Kovar, 대표 이사
수신: Bartel Financial Group 본사 전 직원
날짜: 2월 3일
주제: Ellen Ortiz

Bartel 이사회가 심사숙고 후에 현재 투자 홍보부 담당인 161 Ellen Ortiz가 다음 달 Andres Hildebrand가 은퇴한 후에 유럽 지역 매니저를 맡게 되었다는 것을 기쁘게 공지합니다. Ortiz 씨의 승진은 국제 시장에 중요도가 증가한 이때에 함께 왔습니다. 로마 사무실에서 일한 후에 그녀는 Italy에서의 Bartel 성장과 독일과 서남부 유럽으로 Bartel이 확장해 나가는 것을 감독할 것입니다.

Ortiz 씨와 함께 일해 보신 분들은 그녀가 이 일에 훌륭한 선택이라는 것을 아실 것입니다. Dublin의 Kingston 대학을 졸업한 후에, 20년 전 Bartel에 입사하기 전에 Italy에 있는 Ostrava Finance에서 수년 동안 일했습니다. 162 그녀는 이태리어가 모국어일 뿐만 아니라 몇 가지 다른 언어들에도 능숙합니다. Bartel에 있었던 처음 몇 년 동안, Paris 사무실로 전근 가기 전에는 Brussels에서 일했었고, 마침내 이곳 164 London 본사로 오게 되었습니다. 투자 홍보부에서의 그녀의 놀라운 지도력은 지난 10년 동안 고객 저변이 20%가 넘게 성장하는 것을 도왔습니다.

마침내, 163 164 Bartel에서 Hildebrand 씨가 있는 동안 이루었던 많은 업적을 기리기 위해서, 2월 28일 오후 6시에서 8시까지 회사 본사 가까이에 있는 Prost 카페에서 송별회를 계획했습니다. 이 행사에 대해서 더 많은 것을 알고 싶으시면 내선번호 1259로 제 비서인 Stan Milton에게 연락해 주시기 바랍니다. 이번 직원 교체에 대한 질문은 인사부 담당자인 Bill Belmore에게 내선 1286으로 문의하시기 바랍니다.

어휘 deliberation 심사숙고 take over 이어받다, 계승하다 emphasis 강조 oversea 감독하다 expansion 확장 join 입사하다, 합류하다 fluent 유창한 transfer 전근 가다 finally 마침내 headquarters 본사 outstanding 뛰어난, 놀라운 client base 고객 저변 commemorate 기념하다 accomplishment 업적 farewell gathering 송별회

161 현재 Hildebrand 씨의 직책은?
(A) 최고 경영자
(B) 투자 홍보 매니저

(D) 유럽 지역 매니저

해설 첫 번째 지문에서 'Ellen Ortiz will take over as European Regional Manager when Andres Hildebrand retires next month'라고 한 것으로 정답이 (D)임을 알 수 있다

162 Ortiz 씨에 대해서 나타나 있는 것은?
(A) 20년이 넘게 Brussel에서 살았다.
(B) 몇 개 국어를 할 수 있다.
(C) 국제 사업에 학위를 갖고 있다.
(D) 독일 회사에서 일하기 위해 Bartel을 그만둘 것이다.

해설 두 번째 단락에서 'She is a native Italian speaker and is fluent in several other languages'라고 했으므로 정답은 (B)이다.

163 2월 28일 행사의 목적은 무엇인가?
(A) Hildebrand 씨를 대신할 가능성 있는 사람을 논의하기 위해서
(B) 미래 고객과 투자 의견을 나누기 위해서
(C) 경쟁 업체와의 합병 계획을 공지하기 위해서
(D) Bartel에 대한 Hildebrand 씨의 헌신을 인정하기 위해서

해설 마지막 단락에서 'to commemorate Mr. Hildebrand's many accomplishments during his years with Bartel, we have planned a farewell gathering for Friday, February 28'라고 한 것으로 정답은 (D)이다.

어휘 potential 잠재적인 replacement 후임자, 교체 prospective 전망 있는 merger 합병 recognize 인정하다 contribution 공헌

164 이 행사는 어느 도시에서 열릴 것 같은가?
(A) Brussels
(B) Paris
(C) London
(D) Rome

해설 마지막 단락에서 'at the Prost Café near company headquarters'라고 하였으므로 본사가 있는 London인 것을 알 수 있다.

[165-167]

http://easyservicestation.com

EASY SERVICE STATION

165 Easy Service Station은 Wisconsin 전역에서 대규모 체인의 트럭 휴게소와 운행 센터를 보유하고 있고 이를 운영하고 있습니다. 우리 센터는 대부분의 주요 고속도로에 편리한 위치에 있으며 1년 365일 24시간 개방되어 있습니다.

Easy Service Station 센터는 주유소, 편의점, 모든 서비스를 제공하는 식당, 장거리 여행을 좀 더 편안하게 할 수 있는 편의 시설 등을 갖추고 있습니다.

- 자동 현금 인출기가 24시간 내내 이용 가능합니다.
- 오전 8시부터 오후 4시까지, 월요일부터 금요일까지 수표 현금화와 이체 서비스가 가능합니다.

- 모든 지점에는 세탁실이 있습니다; 166 몇몇 지점에는 샤워실이 있습니다.
- 각 지점에는 케이블 TV와 무선 인터넷이 제공되는 실내 휴게소가 있습니다.
- 뜨거운 식사는 식당에서 이용 가능하고 커피와 제빵류는 편의점에서 구매하실 수 있습니다.

167 Easy Service Station 센터의 전체 목록은 아래 링크를 클릭해 주세요.

www.easyservicestation.com/list

어휘 operate 운영하다 be equipped with ~로 갖춰져 있다 fueling station 주유소 convenience store 편의점 amenity 편의 시설 teller machine 현금 지급기 laundry 세탁소

165 웹 페이지에서 설명하는 것은?
(A) 도로변 시설
(B) 자동차 영업소
(C) 이전 지원
(D) 할인된 호텔

해설 첫 번째 단락의 'Easy Service Station owns and operates a large chain of truck stops and travel centers throughout Wisconsin. Our centers are conveniently located along most major highways'에서 고속도로 휴게소 안내문인 것을 알 수 있으므로 정답은 (A)이다.

166 몇몇 지점에서만 제공되는 것은?
(A) 샤워실
(B) 휴게실
(C) 따뜻한 식사
(D) 세탁실

해설 지문에서 'some have public showers'라고 언급하였으므로 정답은 (A)이다.

167 제공된 링크를 클릭하면 어떤 정보가 제공될 것 같은가?
(A) 객실 요금
(B) 서비스 요금
(C) 위치 정보
(D) 예약 세부 사항

해설 마지막 문장에서 'For a full list of Easy Service Station centers, click the link below'라고 한 것으로 정답은 (C)임을 알 수 있다.

[168-171]

Munich (3월 22일) – Munich에 근거지를 둔 Steinmeier가 화요일에 두 번째 가공 시설을 건설하겠다는 계획을 발표했다. 현재, 이 회사의 유일한 시설은 Munich 본사에서 약 480킬로미터 떨어진 Frankfurt 근처에 위치해 있다. 3천만 유로 이상의 비용이 예상되는 새로운 시설은 해외 시장으로 확장하는 것으로 이익을 증진시키고자 하는 기업 전략의 일부이다.

중역들은 168 중국 Shanghai로의 이 야심 찬 확장이 회사가 중국 시장에서 중요한 경쟁 업체가 되는 것을 돕기를 바라고 있다. 일단 완공되면, 이 두 곳의 처리 공장은 중국과 유럽 시장 두 곳의 수요를 충족할 만한 용량을 갖게 될 것이다. –[1]–. "추가되는 장점은 두 시설물 중 한 곳이 관리 작업이나 수리 때문에 임시로 중단되는 경우에 두 시장을 위한 필수 생산은 유지할 수 있을 것이라는 것입니다." 라고 회사 사장인 Daniel Hoffman이 말했다.

171 Hoffman 씨의 아버지 Jeremy Hoffman 씨는 Beijing에서 경영 대학원을 졸업한 후에 1979년에 Steinmeier를 설립했다. –[2]–. 171 사업 첫 해에 꽤 큰 이익을 냈고 그 다음 해에 47% 더 성장했다. 오늘 날 Steinmeier는 전 유럽 30개 국가에서 유통되는 국제적으로 알려진 음료 상표이다. 그러나 169 거대한 성장에도 불구하고 시장 점유율이 하락하면서 최근 판매량도 속도가 느려졌다. 그래서 Hoffman 씨가 주도하는 새로운 경영팀은 회사를 호전시키기 위해 적극적으로 노력하고 있다. –[3]–.

지역 판매 매니저 Amy Garrett에 따르면, Steinmeier의 현재 전체 음료 제품은 올 여름이 끝날 때까지는 중국의 20개 도시에서 구할 수 있을 것이다. –[4]–. Garrett 씨는 회사의 현재 제품 라인을 보충하기 위해서 170 과일을 기반으로 한 과자와 케이크 같은 제과제빵류 라인도 출시할 것을 구상하고 있다. "우리의 희망은 우리가 계속해서 발전해 나가고 고객들이 사랑하는 새로운 제품을 개발하는 것입니다."라고 그녀는 말했다.

어휘 processing facility 가공 시설 sole 유일한 upward 상향세로 corporate 기업의 headquarters 본사 strategy 전략 boost 증진시키다 expand into ~로 확장하다 overseas 해외의 executive 중역 ambitious 야망의 expansion 확장 capacity 능력, 수용량 meet the demand 요구를 충족시키다 benefit 혜택 maintain 유지하다 essential 필수적인 in the event that ~하는 경우에 temporarily 임시로 found 설립하다 sizable 상당한, 규모가 큰 recognized 인정받는 distribute 분배하다 enormous 거대한 market share 시장 점유율 drop 떨어지다 aggressively 공격적으로, 적극적으로 turn around 쇄신하다, 호전시키다 full range 전체 범위 envision 구상하다 complement ~을 보충하다

168 새로운 시설은 어디에 위치하는가?
(A) Munich
(B) Frankfurt
(C) Shanghai
(D) Beijing

해설 두 번째 지문에서 'the ambitious expansion to Shanghai in China'라고 한 것으로 (C)가 정답이다.

169 Steinmeier에 대해서 언급된 것은?
(A) 경쟁 업체가 Steinmeier보다 더 적은 제품을 판매한다.
(B) 뮌헨에서만 제품을 판매한다.
(C) 제품 판매가 최근에 하락했다.
(D) 새로운 이사회 회원 모집을 계획 중이다.

해설 세 번째 지문에서 'sales have slowed recently as market share has dropped'라고 언급하였으므로 (C)가 정답이다.

어휘 competitor 경쟁업체 decline 하락하다

170 Steinmeier는 어떤 종류의 제품을 개발할 계획인가?
(A) 디저트
(B) 화장품
(C) 식기류
(D) 음료수

해설 네 번째 지문에서 'Ms. Garrett envisions launching a line of fruit-based baked goods such as cookies and cakes to complement the company's current product line'이라고 하였으므로 (A)가 정답이다.

171 [1], [2], [3], [4]로 표시된 위치 중 다음 문장이 들어가기 적절한 곳은?
"독일 북부 지역으로 돌아온 후에, 지역 전체에서 신선한 과일 주스를 식당과 슈퍼마켓에 판매하기 시작했다."
(A) [1]
(B) [2]
(C) [3]
(D) [4]

해설 'Mr. Hoffman's father, Jeremy Hoffman, founded Steinmeier in 1979 after graduating from business school in Beijing'에서 귀국 전 내용이 언급되었고 'In its first year of business, the company managed to turn a sizeable profit, which grew by 47% the following year'에서 귀국 후의 사업에 대해 설명하고 있기 때문에 (B)가 정답이다.

어휘 fresh-squeezed 신선하게 착즙한

[172-175]

Almed Abedi	오후 4시 30분
172 우리가 현재 비타민 보충제를 광고하는 방법을 다시 점검하고 싶어요.	
Saori Iwamoto	오후 4시 31분
173 Marina, 당신이 우리 회사에 처음이니 몇 가지 배경 정보를 드릴게요. 판매량을 늘리기 위해서 우리는 여성 전용 비타민 보충제 제작을 시작했어요.	
Almed Abedi	오후 4시 32분
1년 전에 이 보충제 판매를 시작했고 홍보하기 위해서 광고에 상당한 예산을 들였어요.	
173 Marina Jordan	오후 4시 33분
자세한 설명 감사드립니다. TV에서 광고를 본 것 같아요. 길 한쪽에 있는 광고판을 운전하다가 지나간 적도 있고요. 분명히 판매량에 많은 도움이 되었을 거예요.	
Almed Abedi	오후 4시 34분
맞아요. 판매량을 분석했어요. 결과가 우리가 예상했던 것보다 20퍼센트나 높았어요.	
Saori Iwamoto	오후 4시 35분
판매량이 높기 때문에 이제는 광고에 그렇게 많이 투자하는 것을 그만둘 때가 된 것 같아요. 더 이상 그렇게 큰 광고를 계속 할 필요가 없어요.	
Almed Abedi	오후 4시 36분
동의해요. 광고 없이도 할 수 있어요. 분명히 이 상품은 시장의 필요에 응답한 거예요. 174 고객들은 우리가 광고를 덜 해도 이 보충제를 계속해서 구매할 거라고 생각해요.	
Marina Jordan	오후 4시 37분
맞아요. 이제 다음 제품을 위한 광고 계획을 시작해야 한다고 생각해요.	
Saori Iwamoto	오후 4시 38분
175 노인들을 위한 새로운 비타민 보충제를 뜻하는 건가요?	
Marina Jordan	오후 4시 39분
맞아요. 약 3개월 후에 판매하기 시작할 거예요.	

어휘 re-examine 재점검하다 supplement 보충 background 배경 allocate 할당하다 substantial 상당한 commercial 광고 billboard 전광판 project 예상하다 respond 반응하다

172 논의의 목적은 무엇인가?
(A) 특정 임무를 할당하기 위해서
(B) 직원 생산성을 향상하기 위해서
(C) 예산 제안서를 작성하기 위해서
(D) 홍보 전략을 수정하기 위해서

해설 오후 4시 30분에 Abedi가 'I'd like to re-examine the way we are currently advertising our line of vitamin supplements'라고 하였으므로 정답은 (D)이다.

어휘 assign 할당하다 specific 구체적인 modify 수정하다

173 Jordan 씨에 대해서 알 수 있는 것은?
(A) 발표를 진행할 것이다.
(B) 인사부 담당이다.
(C) 보고서 판매 자료를 분석했다.
(D) 이 회사에서 일을 막 시작했다.

해설 오후 4시 31분에 Iwamoto 씨가 'Marina, since you are new to our company'라고 한 것으로 (D)가 정답임을 알 수 있다.

어휘 in charge of ~을 책임지고 있는

174 오후 4시 37분에 Jordan 씨가 "맞아요"라고 쓴 뜻은 무엇인가?
(A) 여성을 위한 신제품을 개발하여야 한다는 것에 동의한다.
(B) 광고를 줄여도 제품이 잘 팔릴 것이라고 생각한다.
(C) 비타민이 여자와 아이들 모두에게 필요하다고 생각한다.
(D) 온라인과 오프라인 광고를 시작해야 한다고 제안한다.

해설 오후 4시 36분 Almedi 씨가 'I think customers will continue to buy these supplements even if we do less marketing'이라고 한 말에 대한 동의이므로 정답은 (B)이다.

어휘 essential 필수적인

175 신제품에 대해 사실인 것은?
(A) 특히 여성을 위해 고안되었다.
(B) 복용하기 쉽다.
(C) 나이 많은 사람을 위해 개발되었다.
(D) 반드시 음식과 함께 섭취해야 한다.

해설 오후 4시 38분에 Iwamoto 씨가 'Do you mean our newest line of vitamin supplements intended for seniors?'라고 했으므로 정답이 (C)임을 알 수 있다. 여성을 위해 고안된 제품은 현재 홍보 중인 제품이므로 (A)는 오답이다.

어휘 specifically 특히 consume 소비하다

[176-180]

http://www.citizenfirstbank.com

CITIZEN FIRST BANK

공지	나의 계좌	자금 이체	고용

(176) Special Savings Starting을 소개합니다!

Citizen First 은행은 이제 Special Savings Starting이라는 새로운 계좌를 소개합니다! 이 계좌는 유리한 이자율, 지금 이체의 다양한 방법을 포함해서 우리의 Choice Savings 계좌보다 몇 가지 장점을 제공합니다.

(179) 일정 기간 동안, 우리는 고객들께 일반적인 계좌 전환 수수료 없이 Choice Savings 계좌에서 Special Savings Starting 계좌로 이동하실 것을 권해드립니다. 추가로, (177) 변경하시는 고객들은 처음 12개월 동안은 한 달에 단 5달러의 특별 운영 비용을 누리실 수 있습니다. 12개월 후에 이 비용은 월 8.25달러의 정상 Special Savings Starting 운영비로 오를 것입니다.

더 궁금하신 사항이 있거나 이 제안을 이용하시려면 800-555-0111로 전화하셔서 우리의 계좌 상담원과 이야기해 보세요.

수신: customerservice@citizenfirstbank.com
발신: jtownsend@blakeleyryecable.com
주제: 새로운 저축 계좌
날짜: 4월 2일

(179) 최근에 Special Savings Starting 계좌를 개설했습니다. 그리고 저는 제 Choice Savings 계좌의 잔고가 새로운 계좌로 자동으로 이체되는 것으로 이해했습니다. 그러나 (178) 온라인 은행 목록으로 접속하니 이용 가능한 잔고가 0달러로 기재되어 있습니다. 자금이 새로운 계좌로 언제 이체될 것인지 말씀해 주시겠습니까?

도와주셔서 감사합니다.

Jessica Townsend

어휘 including ~을 포함하여 favorable 우호적인, 유리한 interest rates 이자율 transfer 이체하다 funds 자금 limited 제한된 convert A into B A를 B로 전환하다 conversion 전환, 변경 in addition 게다가, 추가로 operation fee 운영 수수료 take advantage of ~을 이용하다 representative 대표, 상담원 savings account 저축 계좌 understanding 이해 balance 은행 잔고 automatically 자동으로

176 웹 페이지 정보의 목적은 무엇인가?
(A) 고객들에게 지불을 요청하기 위해서
(B) 새로운 유형의 은행 서비스를 홍보하기 위해서
(C) 온라인 은행 업무 절차를 점검하기 위해서
(D) 두 은행의 합병을 알리기 위해서

해설 웹 페이지의 첫 부분 'Introducing Special Savings Starting!'에서 새로운 은행 상품을 소개하는 글임을 알 수 있으므로 (B)가 정답이다.

어휘 procedure 절차 merger 합병

177 운영 비용에 대해서 알 수 있는 것은?
(A) 고객들은 할부로 지불할 수 있다.
(B) 처음에는 할인되어 제공된다.
(C) 다른 은행보다 저렴하다.
(D) 고객들은 마감 날짜를 협상할 수 있다.

해설 웹 페이지 두 번째 단락에서 'a special maintenance fee of only $5 per month for the first 12 months'라고 한 것으로 (B)가 정답임을 알 수 있다.

어휘 in installments 할부로 initially 처음에는 due date 만기 날짜

178 Townsend 씨가 염려하는 이유는?
(A) 새 계좌로 돈이 아직 이체되지 않아서
(B) 운영비가 너무 많이 청구되어서
(C) 은행 거래를 업데이트할 수가 없어서
(D) 그녀 계좌가 그녀 허가 없이 접속되어서

해설 이메일에서 'when I log in to my online banking profile, I see that available funds listed are $0 for the Special Savings Starting account'라고 한 것으로 (A)가 정답임을 알 수 있다.

어휘 overcharge 너무 많이 청구하다 transaction 거래 access 접속하다 permission 허가, 허락

179 Townsend 씨에 대해서 사실인 것 같은 것은?
(A) 불편함으로 인해 계좌를 닫을 것이다.
(B) 그녀의 운영 비용이 증가했다.
(C) 계좌 변경으로 인한 수수료를 부과받지 않을 것이다.
(D) Citizen First 은행의 신규 고객이다.

해설 연계 지문 문제이다. 이메일에서 'I recently opened a Special Savings Starting account, and it was my understanding that the balance of my Choice Savings account would be transferred into the new account automatically'라고 한 것으로 계좌 변경을 한 것을 알 수 있고 웹 페이지에서 'we are inviting our customers to convert their Choice Savings accounts into Special Savings Starting accounts without our usual account conversion fees'라고 하였으므로 정답은 (C)이다.

180 이메일의 첫 번째 단락, 세 번째 줄의 profile과 뜻이 가장 가까운 것은?
(A) 목록
(B) 평등
(C) 평균
(D) 안정성

해설 'my online banking profile'에서 profile은 계좌 개요나 목록이라는 뜻이므로 (A)가 정답이다.

[181-185]

International Business Reconstruction Association (IBRA)

정보 획득 기회

(181) IBRA가 여러분들을 "기업 자금 모금 전략"이라는 제목의 라이브 온라인 세미나에 참가할 것을 권합니다. 이 세미나는 여러분의 기업이 지역과 국제 기업에서 금전적 혹은 다른 형태의 지원을 보장할 지원금 제안서에 반드시 포함시켜야 할 필수 정보에 집중하고 있습니다.

(184) 이 행사는 Rosario Foundation의 개발 이사인 Michelle Conner가 제공하는 것입니다. (181) (182) (183) 7월 22일 표준 시간 오후 1시 30분에서 3시까지 진행될 이 행사는 텔레비전 프로그램 World Business Reports의 기자인 Virginia Ross가 사회를 맡을 것입니다. 등록은 6월 30일까지입니다. 비용과 추가 세부 사항에 대한 정보는 www.ibra.org.uk/seminar0722를 방문해 주십시오.

등록할 때, Conner 씨에게 질문을 제출할 기회가 주어질 것입니다. 이 세미나 동안에 제한된 수의 질문에 답변을 할 수 있을 것입니다. 그러나 참가자들이 제출한 모든 관련 문제에 대한 그녀의 답변은 8월 1일에 게시될 것입니다.

발신: mconner@rosariofoundation.org
수신: keikomatusi@ibra.org.uk
참조: swinkley@rosariofoundation.org
주제: 세미나
날짜: 6월 24일

Matusi 씨에게

제가 더 이상 당신 기관에 대한 약속을 이행하지 못하게 되었다는 것을 알려 드리게 되어서 매우 죄송합니다. (183) 당신 행사를 안내하기로 한 바로 그날에 예상치 못하게 Barcelona로 출장을 가게 되었습니다. (184) 부개발국장인 Simth Winkley에게 7월 31일 화상 회의에 참여하는 것뿐만 아니라 저를 대신해서 세미나를 주최할 것을 요청했습니다. 그가 이 변경 사항에 대해서 곧 당신에게 이메일로 연락할 것입니다.

Winkley 씨는 25년간 다국적 기금 모금 홍보를 기획하고 감독해 왔습니다. 게다가, (185) 그는 현재 우리 기관에서 온라인 교육과 현장 연수 프로그램 시행을 담당하고 있습니다. 그러니 세미나 참가자들이 능력 있는 분과 함께할 것이니 안심하시기 바랍니다.

저의 취소 때문에 생기는 모든 불편함에 대해 다시 한 번 사과드립니다.

Michelle Conner

어휘 entitled 제목이 있는 raise funds 기금을 모금하다 focus on ~에 집중하다 grant proposal 지원금 제안서 ensure ~을 보장하다 organization 기관, 단체 present 제공하다, 사회를 보다 take place 일어나다, 발생하다 moderate 조정하다, 사회를 보다 registration 등록 respond to ~에 응답하다 relevant 관련 있는 participant 참가자 post 게시하다 no longer 더 이상 ~하지 못하다 fulfill 이행하다 commitment 약속, 전념 headline 진행하다 unexpectedly 예상치 못하게 on business 사업차 on one's behalf ~를 대신하여 as well as ~뿐만 아니라 shortly 곧 regarding ~에 관하여 supervise 관리하다, 감독하다 fundraising 기금 모금 campaign 행사, 광고 currently 현재 in-person 현장에 참석한 training session 연수, 교육 rest assured that ~에 대해 안심하다 capable hands 능력 있는 사람 cancellation 취소

181 7월 22일의 행사에 대해 알 수 있는 것은?
(A) 자선 단체의 지원금으로 운영되어 왔다.
(B) 외국인 학생들을 대상으로 한다.
(C) 다국적 기업 입사에 대한 조언을 할 것이다.
(D) 방송국이 실황 중개할 것이다.

해설 공지글 첫 번째 단락에서 'a live, online seminar'와 두 번째 단락에서 'The seminar, which will take place on July 22 from 1:30 P.M. to 3:00 P.M. GMT, will be moderated by Virginia Ross, a reporter for the television program World Business Reports'라고 한 것으로 정답은 (D)임을 알 수 있다.

어휘 charity organization 자선 단체 be intended for ~를 대상으로 하다

182 세미나 참가자들에 대해 알 수 있는 것은?
(A) 전문 개발 자격증을 받게 될 것이다.
(B) 질문을 Ross 씨에게 보내야 한다.
(C) IBRA의 회원이어야 한다.
(D) 사전에 행사 참가 신청을 해야 한다.

해설 공지에서 'The seminar, which will take place on July 22'와 'Registration is required by June 30'에서 사전 등록이 필요하다는 것을 알 수 있으므로 (D)가 정답이다.

어휘 certificate 자격증 direct A to B A를 B로 보내다 sign up for 신청하다

183 Conner 씨가 출장 가는 것은 어느 날인가?
(A) 6월 24일
(B) 7월 22일
(C) 7월 31일
(D) 8월 1일

해설 연계 지문 문제이다. 공지에서 'The seminar, which will take place on July 22'로 세미나 날짜는 7월 22일이며 이메일에서 'On the day I am scheduled to headline your event, I now, quite unexpectedly, need to travel to Barcelona on business'라고 하였으므로 같은 날 출장을 가는 것을 알 수 있으므로 정답은 (B)이다.

어휘 go on a business trip 출장 가다

184 Conner 씨가 행사를 위해 무엇을 준비했는가?
(A) 재정 지원이 IBRA로 보내지는 것
(B) Barcelona에서 Matusi 씨를 만나는 것
(C) 발표 영상을 녹화하는 것
(D) 동료가 대신하도록 하는 것

해설 이메일에서 'I have asked Smith Winkley, Associate Development Director, to present the seminar on my behalf'라고 한 것으로 정답은 (D)이다.

어휘 substitute for ~을 대신하다

185 Rosario Foundation에 대해서 알 수 있는 것은?
(A) 온라인으로 교육 프로그램을 제공한다.
(B) 새로운 개발 이사를 구하고 있다.
(C) 업계에 25년 동안 있어 왔다.
(D) World Business Reports에 정기적으로 등장한다.

해설 연계 지문 문제이다. 공지문에서 Conner 씨가 Rosario Foundation의 개발 이사인 것을 알 수 있다. 이어 Conner 씨의 이메일에서 'our organization's online and in-person training sessions'라고 언급한 것으로 (A)가 정답임을 알 수 있다.

어휘 feature 등장하다, 있다

[186-190]

Madison Autos에서 꿈의 자동차를 구하세요!

멋진 자동차를 원하지만, 많은 돈을 쓰고 싶지는 않으시다면 Madison Autos로 오세요. (186) 우리는 중고 차량을 사고팔고 있습니다. 우리 자동차는 신제품은 아니지만 아주 훌륭한 상태인 것을 보장해 드릴 수 있습니다. 모든 차량은 우리 주차장에 도착하면 바로 점검을 받은 후 1년의 보증 기간과 함께 판매됩니다. (189) 우리는 8,000달러 이상을 구매하시면 2년의 연장 보증 기간을 제공해 드립니다. 우리는 또한 바로 이곳 주차장에서 수리도 하고 부품 교체 주문도 하고 있습니다.

가격은 조정 가능하니 Madison Autos로 오셔서 당신의 자동차를 찾아보세요! 우리 주소는 1807 Pine 거리, Twin City, MN 00987입니다.

수신: Marco Colombo <marcocolombo@madisonautos.com>
발신: Sydney Payton <sidneypayton@gmail.net>
날짜: 3월 21일
주제: 자동차 구매

Colombo 씨에게

(190) 동료 중 한 명이 당신의 서비스를 제게 추천하여 연락드립니다. 분명히 당신은 친절하고 인내심이 있는 판매원으로 명성이 있는 듯합니다. (188) 제 자동차가 요즘 계속 고장 나서 자동차를 구매하려고 보고 있는 중입니다. 조금 더 신형으로 바꾸고 싶습니다. (187) 제게 적합한 제품을 찾아 줄 수 있을 것이라고 기대하고 있습니다.

그러나 예산이 적어서 중고 자동차에 만 달러 이상은 쓰고 싶지 않습니다. 제가 최근에 본 광고에 따르면, 당신 회사가 적당한 것을 몇 대 갖고 있는 것 같습니다. (187) 당신과 만날 시간을 정하고 싶습니다. 조금 더 제게 알려주실 수 있을 겁니다.

Sydney Payton

MADISON AUTOS
1807 Pine 거리, Twin City, MN 00987
555-7465

청구 번호: 123098
판매 날짜: 3월 30일

구매자 정보

이름:	Sydney Payton
주소:	8912 South Hill Dr., Twin City, MN 00989
전화번호:	555-1423
면허증 번호:	K500-2507-0902-00

자동차 정보:

자동차:	Prius Hybrid Z12
등록번호:	J87F09876SS
마일리지:	82,000
자동차 연식:	2013
판매 가격:	(189) 9,700달러
보증기간:	(189) 연장
지불 방법:	_√_ 수표 ___ 현금 ___ 신용 카드
판매자 서명:	Marco Colombo
구매자 서명:	Sydney Payton

어휘 used vehicle 중고 차량 brand-new 신제품의 in great condition 훌륭한 상태인 extended 연장된 replacement parts 교체 부품 apparently 명백히, 분명히 patient 참을성이 있는 break down 고장 나다 suitable 적절한 on a tight budget 예산이 적은 recently 최근에

186 Madison Autos의 자동차에 대해 알 수 있는 것은?
(A) 구매 직후에 무료로 서비스를 받는다.
(B) 금융 지원 상품을 통해 지불될 수 있다.
(C) 이전에 소유된 적이 있다.
(D) 가장 인기 있는 기능들을 갖고 있다.

해설 광고에서 'We are in the business of buying and selling used vehicles'라고 언급하였으므로 정답은 (C)이다.

어휘 previously 이전에, 사전에 features 기능

187 이메일의 목적은 무엇인가?
(A) 자동차 디자인을 돕기 위해서
(B) 정보를 나누기 위해서
(C) 절차를 설명하기 위해서
(D) 상담을 요청하기 위해서

해설 이메일 전반적으로 차 구매에 대해 관심을 보이는 내용이며 첫 번째 단락에서 'I was hoping that you would be able to help me find something suitable'라고 언급하고 마지막 문장에서 'I'd like to schedule a time for me to meet with you'라고 하였으므로 (D)가 정답이다.

어휘 consultation 상담

188 Payton 씨의 현재 차량에 대해 알 수 있는 것은?
(A) 10년 전에 구매했다.
(B) 4개의 문이 있는 차량이다.
(C) 동료에게 팔고 싶어 한다.
(D) 완벽히 작동되는 것은 아니다.

해설 이메일에서 'mine keeps breaking down these days'라고 한 것으로 (D)가 정답이다.

어휘 in working order 작동되는

189 Payton 씨가 보증 기간 연장을 받은 이유는?
(A) 특정 금액 이상을 지불했기 때문에
(B) 단골 고객이기 때문에
(C) 회원 프로그램에 가입해서
(D) Madison Autos가 특별 행사 중이므로

해설 연계 지문 문제이다. 광고에서 'We offer an extended two-year warranty with a purchase over $8,000'라고 하였고 청구서에서 차 가격이 9,700달러인 것이 확인되므로 (A)가 정답이다.

190 Payton 씨에 대해서 알 수 있는 것은?
(A) 차량을 현금으로 지급했다.
(B) 동료가 Colombo 씨에게서 차량을 구매했다.
(C) 두 사람이 앉을 수 있는 차량을 선택했다.
(D) SUV 차량을 구매했다.

해설 이메일에서 'one of my colleagues recommended your services'라고 언급한 것으로 (B)가 정답임을 알 수 있다.

어휘 seat ~을 앉히다

[191-195]

Fragment Master

오래된 전자 제품을 버리는 데 어려움을 겪고 있다면, Fragment Master가 여러분께 갑니다.

(191) 우리는 이 지역에서 가장 규모가 큰 전자 부품 재활용 업체입니다. 전자 제품을 버리실 때는, 적합한 장소에 물건을 넣어 주세요.

A 상자: 외부 장비, 잡동사니
B 상자: 모니터, 스피커, 노트북, PC
C 상자: 키보드, 액세서리, 다른 장비

특정 희귀 금속에 대한 현재 시장은 아주 원활합니다. 그러므로 한동안 핸드폰, 태블릿, 손으로 잡는 비디오 게임기를 포함한 작은 장비들은 10월 18일까지는 계속 받습니다.

우리는 여러분을 돕기 위해 있습니다. 창구에서 도움 요청하는 것을 주저하지 마세요.

수신: dwerner@haverlyelectronics.com
발신: Lgrove@fragmentmaster.org
날짜: 9월 5일
주제: 10월 약속

Werner 씨에게

Fragment Master 대표, Matt Lovito가 10월 19일 아침에 Haverly Electronics를 방문한다는 것을 다시 한 번 상기시켜드립니다. 평가 과정을 신속히 하기 위해 전자 제품 조각들을 분류해 두시기를 부탁드립니다. 그때 가격을 협상할 수 있도록 준비해 두세요.

아시다시피 제공하는 가격은 매일 시장 상황에 따라 달라질 수 있습니다. 현재 겪는 상황에 대해서 조금 알려 드리겠습니다. 재수습된 플라스틱 가격은 하양세인 경향입니다. 유사하게, 구리와 은의 공급이 현재 높기 때문에 재활용 자원에 대한 가격 하락 압박이 있습니다. 그러나 타이타니움 수요가 선례가 없는 정도인 것을 아시면 기쁠 것입니다. 가격은 이미 올해에 2배가 되었습니다. (193) 싱가포르에 있는 Baxon 주식회사라는 제조 업체가 당분간은 우리가 제공하는 모든 물건을 기꺼이 구입하고 있습니다.

당신과 계속 거래하는 것은 기쁜 일입니다.

진심으로,

Lucia Grove
Fragment Master

싱가포르 (11월 1일) – (194) Baxon 주식회사는 오늘 최신 노트북 컴퓨터 Moonlight X10의 초기 출시를 선언했습니다. 이 신제품은 동급에서 가장 빠르고 가장 가벼운 노트북이 될 것입니다. 이러한 고성능 품질은 새롭게 디자인된 희귀 금속 콘덴서의 사용으로 가능하게 되었습니다. (193) Moonlight X10은 또한 50% 이상이 구형 모델의 소비자 전자 제품에서 다시 살아난 재활용 재료를 포함하는 첫 번째 대량 생산되는 노트북 중의 하나입니다. 한정 수량의 Moonlight X10가 싱가포르에 위치한 싱가포르 회사의 주력 상점에 등장할 것입니다. (195) 국제 고객들은 11월 30일까지는 기다려야 하지만 Baxon은 11월 10까지 싱가포르 전역 아울렛으로 이 장비 배송을 시작할 계획입니다.

어휘 fragment 조각 have trouble -ing ~에 어려움을 겪다 component 부품 drop off 맡기다, 떨구다 proper 적절한 external 외부의 miscellaneous 잡동사니 rare 드문 for the time being 한동안 held-held 손으로 잡는 representative 대표 scrap 조각 sort 분류하다 expedite 신속히 하다 negotiate 협상하다 at that time 한번에 aware 인지하는 be subject to ~에 영향을 받다 fill in 정보를 주다 currently 현재 reclaimed 다시 수집된, 소환된 downward 하향인 similarly 유사하게 pressure 압력, 압박 copper 구리 demand 수요 unprecedented 선례가 없는 double 두 배가 되다 be willing to 기꺼이 ~하다 in the short term 단기적으로 initial 초기의, 처음의 light 가벼운 high-performance 고성능 capacitor 콘덴서, 축전기 mass-produced 대량 생산되는 salvage 구조된 out-modeled 구식이 된, 낡은 flagship store 주력 상점

191 Grove 씨가 하는 일은 무엇인 것 같은가?
(A) 판매를 위해 골동품 수집
(B) 컴퓨터 액세서리 판매
(C) 소프트웨어 프로그램 개발
(D) 재활용 시설 운영

해설 이메일에서 Grove 씨가 Fragment Master에서 일하고 있는 것을 알 수 있고 공지에서 Fragment Master가 'the region's largest recycler of electronic components'이므로 정답은 (D)이다.

어휘 antique 골동품

192 공지에서 네 번째 문단, 첫 번째 줄의 'strong'과 가장 의미가 가까운 것은?
(A) 명석한
(B) 운동하는
(C) 밝은
(D) 활동적인

해설 'The current market for certain rare metals is strong'에서 시장 상황이 원활하다라는 문맥이므로 (D)가 정답이다

193 Baxon 주식회사에 대해 사실인 것은?
(A) 재활용 센터를 직접 운영한다.
(B) 외장 하드 장치를 주로 만든다.
(C) Fragment Master의 가장 큰 고객이다.
(D) 최신 노트북의 일부 부품이 Fragment Master의 제품이다.

해설 이메일에서 'A manufacturer called Baxon Ltd. in Singapore has been willing to buy all we can provide in the short term'이라고 했고, 기사에서 'The Moonlight X10 is also one of the first mass-produced laptops containing more than 50 percent recycled material, much of it salvaged from out-modeled consumer electronics'라고 했으므로 최신 노트북의 일부 부품이 Fragment Master의 재활용 부품임을 알 수 있다. 따라서 (D)가 정답이다.

어휘 effective 효력을 발휘하는

194 기사의 주요 목적은?
(A) 제품 제작 비용을 설명하기 위해서
(B) 제품 개발에 있어서 변화에 질문을 하기 위해서
(C) 전자 업계의 새로운 제품을 소개하기 위해서
(D) 제품 오작동을 보도하기 위해서

해설 기사는 'Baxon Ltd. today announced the initial release of its newest model laptop computer, the Moonlight X10'로 시작하여 전체 내용이 제품을 소개하고 있으므로 정답은 (C)이다.

어휘 malfunction 오작동

195 Moonlight X10에 대해서 알 수 있는 것은?
(A) 경쟁 업체 제품보다 많은 기능을 갖고 있다.
(B) 한동안 싱가포르 밖에서는 팔리지 않을 것이다.
(C) 시장에 나온 제품 중에서 가장 가볍다.
(D) 재활용 재료들로만 만들어졌다.

해설 기사에서 'international customers must wait until November 30'라고 언급하였으므로 (B)가 정답이다. 경쟁 업체는 언급되지 않았으므로 (A)는 오답이고 'The new product will be the fastest and lightest laptop in its class'라고 한 것으로 전 제품을 언급한 것은 아니므로 (C)도 해당되지 않고 'containing more than 50 percent recycled material'이므로 재활용 재료들로만 만들어졌다는 (D)도 오답이다.

어휘 compared to ~와 비교하여 competitor 경쟁업체 for some time 한동안

[196-200]

발신: Scott Han <shan@dyscomventures.org>
수신: Dyscom Ventures 전 직원 <allstaff@dyscomventures.org>
날짜: 1월 9일
주제: 업데이트
첨부: 마감 일정.pdf

동료 여러분,

지난 우리 회사 사보는 IT 업계의 발전과 그것이 어떻게 우리 회사에 영향을 끼치는가에만 집중되어 있었습니다. 196 197 올해부터는 매 호에 우리 직원들에 대한 정보를 포함시키고 싶습니다. 저는 두 가지 특징을 생각하고 있습니다.

197 첫 번째는 전문적인 업적 성취에 대한 공지입니다. 예를 들어 학회에서 논문을 발표하거나, 상을 받거나 학위 프로그램을 이수하게 되면, 업적을 40자 이내로 설명한 것과 이름, 부서를 함께 제게 이메일로 보내 주세요.

두 번째 특징의 목적은 지역 사회에서 자원봉사하는 직원들을 인정하고 지역 사회에 관여할 기회에 대한 관심을 불러일으키기 위한 것입니다. 도움이 필요한 단체의 회원이라면, 자선 골프 대회 같은 일회성 행사인지 아니면 지역 학교에서의 봉사처럼 빈번한 행사인지 관계없이, 관련 서비스와 활동 유형의 빈도에 관한 정보를 제게 보내 주세요. 첨부한 것은 마감 날짜와 출판 일정에 대한 전체 리스트입니다.

Scott Han
내부 관계 부서 담당자

DYSCOM VENTURES 회사 사보

자료	마감 날짜	출판
사진, 삽화 기사, 에세이	199 2월 8일	3월
사진, 삽화 기사, 에세이	5월 8일	199 6월
사진, 삽화 기사, 에세이	8월 8일	9월
사진, 삽화 기사, 에세이	11월 8일	12월

199 마감 날짜 이후에 받은 제출은 그 다음 호에 출판됩니다. 질문이 있으면 Scott Han에게 shan@dyscomventures.org로 문의해 주세요.

발신: David Greenberg <dgreenberg@dyscomventures.org>
수신: Scott Han <shan@dyscomventures.org>
199 날짜: 2월 28일
제목: 곧 있을 행사
첨부: 사진.jpg

안녕하세요, Scott,

더 일찍 연락 못해서 미안해요.

200 Zuengler Library가 현재 7월 8일 오전 10시부터 오후 4시까지 열릴 연간 책 판매 행사를 위한 중고 서적 기부를 받고 있습니다. 그 전날 책을 정리할 자원 봉사자 인력을 구성하고 있어요. 198 책으로 가득 찬 큰 상자들을 많이 받기 때문에 몇 개 분야로 나누어 정리해서 판매하는 동안에 고객들이 찾고 있는 것이 어떤 종류이든 간에 쉽게 찾을 수 있게 할 거예요. 일이 많아서 도움이 많이 필요합니다.

199 회사 사보를 위해 작년도 제가 나온 행사 사진을 보냅니다. 이 사진이 이 멋진 행사의 인지도를 높일 수 있기를 바랍니다. 정보가 더 필요하시면 알려 주세요.

감사합니다.

David Greenberg
연구 개발 부서

어휘 edition 판, 호 affect 영향을 끼치다 issue (잡지의) 호, 판 have in mind 생각하다, 염두에 두다 achievement 업적, 성취 present a paper 논문을 발표하다 win an award 상을 받다 description 설명 accomplishment 업적, 공적 recognize 인정하다, 상을 주다 perform 수행하다 bring to attention 관심을 불러 일으키다 frequency 횟수 involved 관련한, 참여한 illustration 삽화 publication 출판 submission 제출 following 다음의 gently 가볍게 used books 중고 서적 coordinate 기획하다 effort 노력 organize 기획하다, 구성하다 tend to ~하는 경향이 있다 sort into ~로 분류하다 raise awareness 인지도를 높이다

196 첫 번째 이메일의 목적은?
(A) Dyscom 직원에게 컨퍼런스 논문 제출을 권장하기 위해서
(B) 연구 부서의 공식을 공지하기 위해서
(C) 학위 프로그램 절차를 설명하기 위해서
(D) Dyscom 직원들의 정보를 요청하기 위해서

해설 첫 번째 이메일에서 'This year I'd like to start including information about our employees in every issue'라고 언급하고 있으므로 정답은 (D)이다.

197 공지에 대해서 언급되지 않은 것은?
(A) 회사 사보에 새롭게 추가되는 사항이다.
(B) 부서 담당자들에 의해서 제출되어야만 한다.
(C) 상을 받은 사람들은 예우한다.
(D) 최대 40자로 구성될 수 있다.

해설 첫 번째 이메일의 첫 번째 단락 'This year I'd like to start including'이라고 언급한 것에서 (A)를 알 수 있고 두 번째 단락 'The first will be announcements of professional achievements에서 (C)를, 'your name and department and a description of your accomplishments in 40 words or less'라고 한 것에서 (D)를 알 수 있다. 언급되지 않은 (B)가 정답이다.

어휘 addition 추가, 첨가 recipient 수상자 contain 포함하다

198 책 판매에 대해서 알 수 있는 것은 ?

(A) 지역 커뮤니티 센터의 도서관에서 열린다.
(B) 새 책과 중고 서적 모두 다룬다.
(C) 사람들이 많은 책을 기부한다.
(D) 수익금은 어린이 자선 단체에 기부될 것이다.

해설 두 번째 이메일에서 'We tend to receive large boxes full of books'라고 했으므로 정답은 (C)이다.

어휘 proceeds 수익금 charity 자선 단체

199 Greenberg 씨의 사진은 회사 사보에 언제 등장할 것 같은가?

(A) 3월
(B) 6월
(C) 7월
(D) 9월

해설 연계 지문 문제이다. 두 번째 이메일에서 작년 행사 사진을 보낸다고 했는데 발송 날짜가 2월 28일이므로 일정표에 따르면 6월에 출간될 것을 알 수 있으므로 (B)가 정답이다.

200 Greenberg 씨가 7월 7일에 계획하고 있는 일은?

(A) Zuengler 도서관이 받은 물건들을 정리하는 것
(B) 운동 대회에 참석하는 것
(C) Zuengler 도서관에서 작가의 강의에 출석하는 것
(D) IT 업계에 대한 기사를 쓰는 것

해설 두 번째 이메일에 따르면 'book sales that will be held on July 8'라고 하였고 'I will be coordinating volunteer efforts to organize the books the day before'에서 행사 전날인 7월 7일에 할 일은 도서관이 받은 물건들은 정리하는 것이므로 (A)가 정답이다.

어휘 organize 기획하다 competition 대회 author 작가

Actual Test 05

Listening Comprehension

본책 P182

PART 1

1 (A)	2 (C)	3 (C)	4 (B)	5 (C)	6 (C)

PART 2

7 (C)	8 (A)	9 (C)	10 (B)	11 (C)	12 (C)	13 (C)	14 (A)	15 (B)	16 (A)
17 (A)	18 (B)	19 (C)	20 (C)	21 (A)	22 (C)	23 (B)	24 (C)	25 (C)	26 (A)
27 (A)	28 (B)	29 (C)	30 (B)	31 (A)					

PART 3

32 (A)	33 (C)	34 (C)	35 (B)	36 (A)	37 (D)	38 (A)	39 (B)	40 (B)	41 (A)
42 (D)	43 (C)	44 (C)	45 (D)	46 (D)	47 (A)	48 (A)	49 (C)	50 (B)	51 (C)
52 (C)	53 (C)	54 (C)	55 (D)	56 (C)	57 (B)	58 (A)	59 (C)	60 (C)	61 (B)
62 (B)	63 (C)	64 (D)	65 (B)	66 (D)	67 (C)	68 (B)	69 (C)	70 (A)	

PART 4

71 (B)	72 (C)	73 (A)	74 (A)	75 (C)	76 (B)	77 (D)	78 (C)	79 (C)	80 (D)
81 (A)	82 (C)	83 (D)	84 (A)	85 (C)	86 (C)	87 (C)	88 (A)	89 (C)	90 (A)
91 (B)	92 (B)	93 (A)	94 (A)	95 (D)	96 (B)	97 (C)	98 (B)	99 (B)	100 (D)

Reading Comprehension

본책 P194

PART 5

101 (A)	102 (B)	103 (C)	104 (A)	105 (A)	106 (D)	107 (D)	108 (D)	109 (A)	110 (B)
111 (D)	112 (B)	113 (B)	114 (A)	115 (B)	116 (C)	117 (B)	118 (B)	119 (B)	120 (C)
121 (A)	122 (A)	123 (D)	124 (A)	125 (A)	126 (D)	127 (B)	128 (A)	129 (D)	130 (C)

PART 6

131 (B)	132 (C)	133 (A)	134 (D)	135 (C)	136 (B)	137 (B)	138 (A)	139 (D)	140 (C)
141 (B)	142 (C)	143 (C)	144 (B)	145 (C)	146 (D)				

PART 7

147 (B)	148 (D)	149 (D)	150 (C)	151 (D)	152 (A)	153 (B)	154 (C)	155 (B)	156 (B)
157 (D)	158 (C)	159 (D)	160 (B)	161 (B)	162 (C)	163 (A)	164 (D)	165 (B)	166 (C)
167 (B)	168 (C)	169 (D)	170 (A)	171 (C)	172 (D)	173 (B)	174 (A)	175 (D)	176 (A)
177 (D)	178 (B)	179 (B)	180 (C)	181 (D)	182 (C)	183 (B)	184 (A)	185 (C)	186 (D)
187 (A)	188 (B)	189 (D)	190 (C)	191 (A)	192 (D)	193 (C)	194 (A)	195 (A)	196 (B)
197 (A)	198 (C)	199 (B)	200 (D)						

PART 1

P182

1 (A) **A woman is gesturing at a white board.**
미M (B) A woman is handing out some papers.
(C) A woman is holding a cup.
(D) A woman is writing on a board.

(A) 여자가 화이트보드에서 손짓을 하고 있다.
(B) 여자가 종이를 나누어 주고 있다.
(C) 여자가 컵을 들고 있다.
(D) 여자가 보드에 글을 쓰고 있다.

해설 사진에 여러 명이 있으나 선택지의 주어(woman)가 모두 동일하므로 서 있는 여자의 동작에 주목하며 들어야 한다. 여자가 손동작을 하며 발표하고 있는 모습을 가장 적절히 묘사한 (A)가 정답이다. 나머지 선택지에서 언급한 종이, 컵, 보드 모두 사진에 등장하지만 여자의 행동과 상관없는 묘사이므로 정답이 될 수 없다.

어휘 gesture 손짓을 하다 hand out 나누어 주다

2 (A) Street performers are setting up their instruments.
미W (B) Equipment is being loaded into a van.
(C) Pedestrians are watching a performance.
(D) People are performing in an auditorium.

(A) 길거리 공연자들이 악기를 설치하고 있다.
(B) 장비가 승합차에 실리고 있다.
(C) 보행자들이 공연을 보고 있다.
(D) 사람들이 강당에서 공연하고 있다.

해설 다수의 인물이 혼재된 야외 사진으로 각 인물의 행동 묘사에 주목해야 한다. 거리 공연을 하는 남자가 있고 사람들이 이를 구경하는 모습이 확인되므로 (C)가 정답이다. (A)는 공연하는 사람은 있으나 동작 묘사가 잘못되었으며, (C)는 사진에서 승합차가 확인되지 않으므로 오답이다. (D)는 사진의 장소와 무관하다.

어휘 instrument 장비, 악기 load 싣다, 태우다, 실리다. pedestrian 보행자 performance 연주, 공연 auditorium 객석, 강당

3 (A) A clipboard is being placed on a desk.
영M (B) The doors of the cabinet have been left open.
(C) Flowers have been put in a vase.
(D) Some cups of coffee are being served.

(A) 클립보드가 책상 위에 놓여지고 있다.
(B) 캐비닛의 문이 열린 채로 있다.
(C) 꽃들이 꽃병에 놓여 있다.
(D) 커피 몇 잔이 제공되고 있다.

해설 사람이 등장하지 않는 실내 사진으로 각 사물의 명칭을 집중해서 들어야 한다. 꽃이 있는 꽃병을 가장 적절히 묘사한 (C)가 정답이다. (A)와 (D)는 사람이 없는 사진에서 사물을 주어로 하는 수동태 진행형(be being p.p.)을 사용한 오답이며, (B)는 사진의 캐비닛은 닫혀 있으므로 적절하지 않다.

어휘 leave (어떤 장소에) 있게 만들다, 그대로 두다

4 (A) A walkway runs along the beach.
미W **(B) Two women are standing near one another.**
(C) Railings line both sides of the path.
(D) A vendor is selling goods to the beachgoers.

(A) 산책로가 해변을 따라 나 있다.
(B) 여자 두 명이 서로의 가까이에 서 있다.
(C) 난간이 길 양쪽에 있다.
(D) 상인들이 해수욕하는 사람들에게 물건을 팔고 있다.

해설 두 여자가 서로 가까이 서 있는 모습을 가장 적절히 묘사한 (B)가 정답이다. (A)는 길이 해변을 따라 있는 것이 보이지 않으며, (C)는 사진의 난간이 길의 한쪽에서만 확인되고 있으므로 답이 될 수 없다. (D)는 사진에서 볼 수 없는 상인의 행동을 묘사하고 있으므로 오답이다.

어휘 walkway 산책길, 보도 along ~을 따라, 앞으로 one another 서로 railing 난간, 울타리 path 길, 방향 vendor 상인, 노점상 beachgoer 해수욕하는 사람

5 (A) Some people are standing near an intersection.
미M (B) Some vans are parked on the street corner.
(C) Some trolley tracks run alongside a street.
(D) Some pedestrians are crossing the road.

(A) 몇몇 사람들이 교차로 근처에 서 있다.
(B) 승합차들이 길모퉁이에 주차되어 있다.
(C) 전차의 선로들이 길을 따라 이어져 있다.
(D) 몇몇 보행자들이 길을 건너고 있다.

해설 사진에서 확인되는 전차 선로의 모습을 가장 적절히 묘사한 (C)가 정답이다. 사람이 없는 야외 배경 사진이므로 사람을 주어로 동작을 묘사한 (A)와 (D)는 답이 될 수 없으며, 길모퉁이에 주차된 승합차는 보이지 않으므로 (B)도 오답이다.

어휘 intersection 교차로, 교차 지점 trolley 전차, 손수레 track 기차선로 run (한 곳에서 다른 곳으로) 이어지다, 연결하다 alongside 옆에, 나란히 pedestrian 보행자

6 (A) The umbrella has been folded up.
영M (B) The chairs are being placed around the table.
(C) The shadow of the umbrella is being cast on a patio.
(D) Some bushes are being trimmed.

(A) 우산이 접혀 있다.
(B) 의자들이 테이블 주위에 놓여지고 있다.
(C) 파라솔 그늘이 테라스에 드리워지고 있다.
(D) 관목들이 다듬어지고 있다.

해설 파라솔이 있는 테라스의 풍경을 묘사한 (C)가 가장 적절한 답이다. 접힌 우산은 사진에 보이지 않으므로 (A)는 오답이며, (B)와 (D)는 사람이 없는 사진에서 사물을 주어로 하는 수동태 진행형(be being p.p.)을 사용한 오답이다.

어휘 umbrella 우산, 파라솔 fold up 접다 cast (그림자를) 드리우다. patio 뜰, 테라스 bush 관목, 덤불 trim 다듬다, 손질하다

PART 2

P186

7 Who's recording the meeting minutes today?
미M (A) She came in five minutes ago.
미W (B) It belongs to Ms. Wallace.
(C) Our assistant will.

오늘 회의록은 누가 기록하나요?
(A) 그녀는 5분 전에 도착했어요.
(B) Wallace 씨 소유입니다.
(C) 저희 비서가 할 겁니다.

해설 회의록 작성자를 묻는 Who 의문사에 적절한 직책을 언급하며 그 사람이 할 것이라고 대답한 (C)가 정답이다. (A)는 도착한 시점을 말하고 있으므로 When 의문사에 어울리는 답변이며, (B)는 제3자의 이름을 언급하여 Who 의문사에 알맞은 답인 것처럼 혼동을 유도하고 있으나 질문과 무관한 답변이다.

어휘 meeting minutes 회의록 belong to ~에 속하다

8 What will be the price to ship this package to Seattle?
영M **(A) I have to know how much it weighs.**
미W (B) Two hundred fifty dollars for a round-trip ticket.
(C) About a week or so.

Seattle로 이 소포를 발송하는 데 비용이 얼마인가요?
(A) 무게가 얼마인지 알아야 합니다.
(B) 왕복 티켓은 250달러예요.
(C) 일주일 내외입니다.

해설 비용을 묻는 What 의문사에 무게에 따라 다르다고 우회적인 표현을 한 (A)가 정답이다. (B)는 비용을 언급하며 혼동을 유도하고 있으나 소포 발송 비용과 무관하며, (C)는 기간에 대한 답변이므로 질문과 상관없다.

어휘 weigh 무게(체중)가 ~이다, 무게를 달다 round trip 왕복 여행

9 Would you like to serve sandwiches at the reception?
미W (A) Everything was delicious.
미M (B) In Victoria Hall at 2.
(C) Cheese and crackers would be easier.

연회에서 샌드위치를 제공하시겠어요?
(A) 모든 것이 맛있었어요.
(B) 2시에 Victoria 홀에서요.
(C) 치즈와 크래커가 더 쉬울 것 같아요.

해설 샌드위치를 제공할 것인지 묻는 질문에 다른 종류의 다과를 제공하겠다며 거절의 의미로 답하는 (C)가 정답이다. (A)는 질문의 sandwiches에서 연상 가능한 delicious와 (B)는 reception에서 연상 가능한 연회 장소 Victoria Hall을 언급하여 혼동을 유도한 오답이다.

어휘 serve 제공하다, 차려주다 reception (환영, 축하) 연회, 접수처

10 미W Which location are you being transferred to?
영M (A) I'll get him on the line.
(B) I'm being sent to Montreux.
(C) The one next to the mirror.

당신이 전근 가는 곳이 어느 지역인가요?
(A) 제가 그분께 (전화를) 바꿔드릴게요.
(B) 저는 Montreux로 가요.
(C) 거울 옆에 있는 그것이요.

해설 어느 곳으로 전근 가는지 묻는 Which 의문사에 장소로 적절히 대답하는 (B)가 정답이다. (A)는 질문의 transfer에서 연상이 가능한 전화를 연결해 주겠다는 의미의 문장으로 혼동을 유도하고 있으며, (C)는 전근 가는 장소와 상관없는 단순한 사물의 위치에 대한 정보이므로 답이 될 수 없다.

어휘 transfer 옮기다, 이동하다

11 영M I heard that Paul Martinez won the employee of the year award.
미M (A) That's great, I should do that.
(B) I heard that sound, too.
(C) I thought it was William Sanchez.

Paul Martinez가 올해의 직원상을 받았다고 들었어요.
(A) 좋네요, 그렇게 해야겠어요.
(B) 저도 그 소리를 들었어요.
(C) 저는 William Sanchez라고 생각했어요.

해설 특정인이 상을 받았다는 정보를 듣고 다른 사람으로 잘못 알고 있었다고 대답한 (C)가 적절한 답이다. (A)는 That's great라고 대답하면 수상 소식을 기뻐하는 의미로는 연결이 되나 부연 설명이 질문과 무관하다. (B) I heard that을 반복 사용하여 혼동을 주고 있으며, 또한 sound는 어떤 일에 대한 '소식'이 아닌 자연스럽게 들리는 '소리'를 의미한다.

어휘 the employee of the year award 올해의 직원상

12 미M How much do you think we should budget for the project?
미W (A) That sounds like a good amount.
(B) I definitely think we should.
(C) It's hard to say at this point.

그 프로젝트에 예산을 얼마로 해야 한다고 생각하세요?
(A) 좋은 금액인 것 같아요.
(B) 저는 틀림없이 우리가 해야 한다고 생각해요.
(C) 지금 시점에서는 말하기 어렵네요.

해설 예산 금액을 묻는 How much 질문에 말하기 어렵다는 회피성 답변을 하는 (C)가 정답이다. (A)는 금액을 묻는 질문에 연상이 가능한 amount를 이용하여 혼동을 유도하고 있으며, (B)는 질문의 think를 반복 사용한 오답이다.

어휘 budget 예산 definitely 분명히, 틀림없이 at this point 이쯤에서, 현 시점에서

13 영M Do you know when your train is due to arrive?
미W (A) From Oxford to New Castle.
(B) Yes, I will.
(C) Let me look at my ticket.

언제 기차가 도착하는지 아세요?
(A) Oxford에서 New Castle로요.
(B) 네, 제가 할 거예요.
(C) 제가 표를 확인해 볼게요.

해설 기차의 도착 시점을 묻는 간접의문문에 확인해 보겠다며 회피성 답변을 하는 (C)가 가장 적절한 답이다. (A)는 장소로 대답하고 있으므로 답이 될 수 없으며, (C)는 Yes로 대답하면 알고 있다는 의미로는 연결이 되나 시점에 대한 부연 설명이 없으므로 적절하지 않다.

어휘 due ~하기로 되어 있는, 예정된

14 미W Are these the applications that we received today?
미M **(A) No, those are yesterday's.**
(B) Don't leave it behind.
(C) Mr. Miller sent them.

이 신청서들이 우리가 오늘 받은 건가요?
(A) 아니요, 어제 것들입니다.
(B) 두고 가지 마세요.
(C) Miller 씨가 보냈어요.

해설 오늘 받은 신청서들인지 묻는 질문에 부정으로 답하며 부연 설명하고 있는 (A)가 적절한 답이다. (B)는 질문의 received와 발음이 유사한 leave를 사용하여 혼동을 유도하고 있으나 질문과 무관한 답변이며, (C)는 신청서들이 누가 보낸 것인지 묻는 질문이 아니므로 제3자가 보냈다고 언급한 답변은 적절하지 않다.

어휘 application 지원서, 신청서

15 미W Where will this afternoon's workshop be held?
영M (A) I'm sorry I can't make it.
(B) It's been put off until Friday.
(C) It's usually in the cabinet.

오후 워크숍은 어디에서 열리나요?
(A) 죄송하지만, 전 못 갈 것 같아요.
(B) 금요일까지 연기되었어요.
(C) 보통 캐비닛 안에 있어요.

해설 워크숍의 개최 장소를 묻는 Where 의문문에 연기되었다고 답하며 대화가 자연스럽게 이어지는 (B)가 가장 적절한 답이다. (A)는 참석 제안에 대한 완곡한 거절의 표현으로 의문사 의문문에 정답이 될 수 없으며, (C)는 물건이 위치한 장소로 대답하여 혼동을 유도하고 있으나 질문에서 묻는 워크숍의 장소와 무관하다.

어휘 be held 열리다 make it 시간 맞춰 가다, 참석하다 usually 보통, 대개 put off (시간, 날짜를) 미루다, 연기하다

16 미M Did you hear that Mr. Banks is planning to retire this month?
영M **(A) I knew he was going to step down soon.**
(B) I think he will be perfect for the job.
(C) He went out this morning.

Banks 씨가 이번 달에 은퇴할 계획이라는 것을 들었나요?
(A) 그가 곧 그만둘 예정이라는 것을 알고 있었어요.
(B) 그가 그 일에 꼭 맞는다고 생각해요.
(C) 그는 오늘 아침에 나갔어요.

해설 제3자의 은퇴 소식을 들었는지 묻는 조동사 의문문에 긍정적인 표현으로 답변을 하는 (A)가 정답이다. (B)와 (C) 모두 질문과 연관성이 없는 답변을 하고 있으므로 오답이다.

어휘 retire 은퇴하다 step down (요직 등에서) 물러나다, 사직하다

17 미M How far have you progressed on your assignment?
미W **(A) I'm nearly halfway through.**
(B) About a ten-minute drive.
(C) No, I must have missed the sign.

업무를 어느 정도 진행하셨어요?
(A) 거의 반쯤이에요.
(B) 차로 약 10분쯤이요.
(C) 아니요, 제가 표지판을 못 본 것이 틀림없어요.

해설 업무의 진행 정도를 묻는 How far 의문문에 반 정도 완성했다고 대답한 (A)가 가장 알맞은 답이다. (B)는 10분 정도 떨어져 있다는 답변으로 거리가 얼마나 먼지 묻는 How far 의문문에 알맞은 답인 것처럼 혼동을 유도하고 있으며, (C)는 의문사 의문문에 Yes/No로 대답할 수 없으므로 오답이다.

어휘 how far (거리, 정도가) 어디까지, 어느 정도까지 progress 진행하다 assignment 과제, 임무, 배정 nearly 거의 halfway 중간에, 가운데쯤에

18 영M Would you rather have Mr. Cabrera or Ms. Hernandez assist you?
미W (A) She is a very good assistant.
(B) I think I can do it on my own.
(C) He's right over there.

Cabrera 씨나 Hernandez 씨가 당신을 도와주는 것이 나을까요?
(A) 그녀는 아주 좋은 보조인입니다.
(B) 저 혼자 할 수 있을 것 같아요.
(C) 그는 바로 저기 있어요.

해설 보조가 필요한지 묻는 질문에 스스로 하겠다며 완곡한 거절의 의미로 답하는 (B)가 가장 알맞은 답이다. (A)는 질문의 assist와 발음이 유사한 assistant를 사용하여 혼동을 유도하고 있으며, (C)는 질문과 무관한 답변을 하고 있다.

어휘 rather 꽤, 약간, 좀 assist 돕다, 도움이 되다 on one's own 혼자서, 자력으로

19 How would you describe the new financial adviser?
미W (A) Please explain in detail.
미M (B) By calling the adviser.
(C) Quite friendly, I think.

새로운 재정 고문을 어떻게 묘사하시겠어요?
(A) 좀 더 자세히 설명해 주세요.
(B) 고문에게 전화해서요.
(C) 꽤 친절한 것 같아요.

해설 어떤 사람인지 의견을 묻는 How 의문문에 친절하다고 대답한 (C)가 정답이다. (A)와 (B) 모두 방법을 묻는 How에 어울리는 답변이므로 주어진 문제에 적절하지 않으며, (B)는 또한 질문의 adviser를 반복 사용한 오답이다.

어휘 describe 말하다, 묘사하다 financial adviser 재정 고문 friendly 친절한, 상냥한

20 These end-of-the-year sales performances are incredible.
미W (A) On the calendar.
영M (B) No, I don't work in sales.
(C) Yes, aren't they?

연말 판매 실적이 정말 놀랍네요.
(A) 달력에요.
(B) 아니요, 저는 영업부에서 일하지 않아요.
(C) 맞아요, 그렇지 않나요?

해설 판매 실적을 긍정적으로 평가하는 평서문에 동의하며 되묻고 있는 (C)가 가장 적절한 답이다. (B)는 질문의 end-of-the-year에서 연상이 가능한 calendar를 사용한 오답이며, (C)는 질문의 sales를 반복 사용한 오답이다.

어휘 end-of-the-year 연말 performance 공연, 실적, 성과, 수행 incredible 믿을 수 없는, 믿기 힘든

21 When will the shipment of bulbs get here?
영M **(A) They're sitting in my office as we speak.**
미M (B) About this time last year.
(C) To the new branch office.

전구 배송이 언제 도착하나요?
(A) 지금 제 사무실에 있어요.
(B) 작년 이맘때요.
(C) 새로운 지점 사무실로요.

해설 도착 시점을 묻는 When 의문문에 이미 도착해서 사무실에 있다고 우회적인 답을 하는 (A)가 가장 알맞은 답이다. (B)는 시점으로 대답하여 혼동을 유도하고 있지만 시제 불일치 오답이며, (C)는 Where 의문사에 어울리는 답이므로 질문과 무관하다.

어휘 bulb 전구 sit (어떤 곳에) 있다 branch office 지점, 지사

22 The contents of this package are very fragile.
미M (A) About three hundred dollars.
미W (B) I think my schedule is flexible.
(C) I'll handle it carefully, then.

이 소포 내용물은 깨지기 쉽습니다.
(A) 약 3백 달러예요.
(B) 제 일정은 유동적인 것 같아요.
(C) 그럼 제가 조심히 다룰게요.

해설 내용물이 깨지기 쉬운 물건이라는 정보를 전달하는 평서문에 조심하겠다며 적절히 대화를 이어가는 (C)가 정답이다. (A)는 금액을 언급하고 있으므로 질문과 무관한 답변이며, (B)는 질문의 fragile과 발음이 유사한 flexible을 사용하여 혼동을 유도하고 있는 발음 오답 유형이다.

어휘 contents 내용물 fragile 부서지기 쉬운, 취약한 flexible 유연한, 융통성 있는

23 Whose marketing proposal was chosen for this week?
영M (A) Brian says it'll begin soon.
미W **(B) Mr. Lansing's was, I think.**
(C) Yes, I went there last week.

이번 주는 누구의 마케팅 제안이 선택되었나요?
(A) Brain 씨가 곧 시작할 거라고 했어요.
(B) Lansing 씨 것 같아요.
(C) 네, 지난주에 갔었어요.

해설 누구의 제안이 채택되었는지 묻는 Whose 의문문에 제3자의 것임을 언급하며 답하는 (B)가 정답이다. (A)는 사람 이름을 언급하며 혼동을 유도하고 있으나 질문과 무관한 답변이며, (C)는 의문사 의문문에 Yes/No로 대답할 수 없다.

어휘 proposal 제안, 제의

24 Haven't the tires for Mr. Sergio's car arrived yet?
미W (A) I'm not that tired.
미M (B) He's the head of marketing.
(C) You mean the ones for that sedan?

Sergio 씨의 차 타이어가 아직 도착하지 않았나요?
(A) 저는 그렇게 피곤하지 않아요.
(B) 그가 마케팅 부장이에요.
(C) 저 승용차 타이어 말씀이신가요?

해설 타이어 도착 여부를 확인하는 부정의문문에 특정 자동차를 언급하며 되묻고 있는 (C)가 가장 알맞은 답이다. (A)는 질문의 tires와 발음이 비슷한 tired을 사용하여 혼동을 유도하는 오답이며, (B)는 직급을 설명하고 있으므로 질문과 무관한 대답이다.

어휘 arrive 도착하다, 배달되다

25 Why weren't this year's profits as high as last year's?
미W (A) To meet important clients.
영M (B) Yes, it was profitable.
(C) Costs have increased.

왜 올해 수익이 지난해만큼 높지 않은 건가요?
(A) 중요한 고객을 만나기 위해서요.
(B) 네, 수익이 있었어요.
(C) 비용이 증가했어요.

해설 이익이 작년보다 낮은 이유를 묻는 Why 의문문에 비용이 증가했다며 원인을 설명한 (C)가 정답이다. (A)는 Why 의문사의 정답 유형으로 자주 출제되는 to부정사를 이용하여 혼동을 유도하고 있으나 질문과 무관한 답변이며, (C)는 의문사 의문문에 Yes/No로 대답할 수 없다.

어휘 profit 이익, 수익, 이윤 profitable 수익성이 있는, 유익한 increase 증가하다, 인상되다

26 Will you be working overtime this weekend?
미M **(A) Yes, both days in fact.**
영M (B) After lunch on Friday.
(C) He worked hard.

이번 주말에 야근을 하실 건가요?
(A) 네, 사실 양일 모두요.
(B) 금요일 점심 후에요.
(C) 그는 열심히 일했어요.

해설 주말 추가 근무 여부를 묻는 조동사 의문문에 긍정적으로 답하며 토요일, 일요일 모두 일한다고 부연 설명하는 (A)가 적절한 답이다. (B)는 시점을 언급하고 있으므로 질문과 무관하며, (C)는 질문의 work를 반복 사용한 오답이다.

어휘 overtime 초과 근무, 야근

27 You are working on your report, aren't you?
미M **(A) Actually, I haven't even started.**
미W (B) That's what Liam said.
(C) Nobody is working here.

보고서를 작성하는 중이죠, 그렇지 않나요?
(A) 사실, 시작도 못 했어요.
(B) 그것이 Liam 씨가 말한 거예요.
(C) 아무도 여기서 일하지 않아요.

해설 보고서를 작성하는 중인지 확인하는 부가의문문에 시작도 안 했다고 부정적인 답변을 하는 (A)가 가장 알맞은 답이다. (B)는 질문과 무관한 제3자를 언급하고 있으며, (C)는 질문의 working을 반복 사용한 오답이다.

어휘 work on ~에 애쓰다, 착수하다

28 Why don't you come to my office to go over this proposal?
영M (A) Sorry, I forgot to do it.
미W **(B) Let me finish writing this e-mail first.**
(C) Next year's budget proposal.

제 사무실로 와서 제안서를 검토하는 것이 어떨까요?
(A) 죄송합니다, 제가 하는 것을 잊었어요.
(B) 이 이메일 작성을 먼저 끝내고요.
(C) 내년의 예산안이에요.

해설 제안서를 사무실에서 검토하자는 제안의문문에 다른 일을 마친 후에 하자는 (B)가 가장 적절한 답이다. (A)는 Sorry로 답하면 정중한 거절의 의미로는 이해할 수 있으나 부연 설명이 질문과 무관하며, (C)는 질문의 proposal을 반복 사용한 오답이다.

어휘 go over ~을 검토하다 proposal 제안, 제의 budget 예산, 비용

29 There's been a steady rise in demand for our products.
미W (A) I heard it's being held in Sydney this year.
미M (B) Let's check to see if he's available.
(C) Then we'll need to increase our production.

우리 제품의 수요가 꾸준히 상승했어요.
(A) 올해는 Sydney에서 열린다고 들었어요.
(B) 그가 가능한지 확인해 봅시다.
(C) 그렇다면 우리의 생산을 증가시킬 필요가 있겠네요.

해설 제품 수요가 상승한다는 정보를 전달하는 평서문에 그럼 생산을 증가시킬 필요가 있다는 (C)가 정답이다. (A)는 행사 장소를 언급하며 질문과 상관없는 답변을 하고 있으며, (B)는 Let's check로 답하면 질문의 정보를 확인해 보겠다는 의미로 이해할 수 있지만, 이어지는 부연설명이 질문과 무관하다.

어휘 steady 꾸준한, 고정적인 demand 수요, 요구 available 시간이 있는, 여유가 있는

30 Where can I buy something to drink during the break?
미W (A) Yes, they break very easily.
영M **(B) Complimentary beverages will be provided.**
(C) I didn't bring one.

쉬는 시간 동안에 마실 것을 어디서 살 수 있나요?
(A) 네, 그것들은 아주 쉽게 고장 나요.
(B) 무료 음료가 제공될 거예요.
(C) 저는 가져오지 않았어요.

해설 음료를 구입할 장소를 묻는 Where 의문문에 무료 음료가 제공되므로 구입할 필요가 없다고 알려주는 (B)가 정답이다. (A)는 의문사 의문문에 Yes/No로 대답할 수 없고, (C)는 무엇인가 가지고 오지 않았다고 말하며 질문과 전혀 무관한 답변을 하고 있다.

어휘 complimentary 무료의

31 Should we post the updates to the schedule on the Intranet?
영M **(A) Not until they've been approved.**
미M (B) I've already sent it by e-mail.
(C) I'm not sure he does.

인트라넷에 업데이트 일정을 공지해야 할까요?
(A) 승인받은 다음에요.
(B) 저는 이미 이메일로 보냈어요.
(C) 그가 할지 모르겠네요.

해설 일정의 공지 여부를 묻는 조동사 의문문에 승인을 받는 것이 먼저라고 언급하며 거절의 의미로 답변한 (A)가 가장 알맞은 답이다. (B)는 질문의 Intranet에서 연상이 가능한 e-mail을 사용한 오답이며, (C)는 회피성 답변을(I'm not sure) 이용하여 혼동을 유도하고 있으나 질문과 무관한 내용이 이어지고 있다.

PART 3

Questions 32-34 refer to the following conversation. 미W 영M

W Hi, Gabriel. (32) I'd like to discuss the plans for the exterior work of Memphis House. Do you have a moment?
M I'm sorry, not today. (33) I'm taking a client to look at some apartments in West End area this afternoon.
W I see, but we have to talk about this soon. I hope you're not planning on driving to West End. There's huge traffic congestion due to road repair work. (34) You'd better take the subway.
M Thanks for your advice, but I'll be okay. I'm going to leave an hour early, just in case.

여 안녕하세요, Gabriel. Memphis House의 외부 공사 계획을 논의하고 싶은데요. 시간 있으세요?
남 미안하지만, 오늘은 안 되겠는데요. 제가 오늘 오후에 고객을 모시고 West End 지역에 있는 아파트를 보러 가야 해요.
여 알겠어요. 하지만 곧 이것에 대해 우리가 얘기해야 할 거예요. West End에 운전해서 가지 않는 것이 좋겠어요. 도로 공사 작업 때문에 교통 체증이 엄청나거든요. 지하철을 타는 것이 나을 거예요.
남 조언은 고맙지만 괜찮아요. 만약을 위해서, 1시간 일찍 떠나려고 하거든요.

어휘 discuss 상의하다, 의논하다 exterior (특히 건물의) 외부, 외면 traffic congestion 교통 혼잡

32 What does the woman want to discuss with the man?
(A) A remodeling project
(B) An advertising strategy
(C) An event plan
(D) A traffic problem

여자는 남자와 함께 무엇을 의논하길 원하는가?
(A) 리모델링 프로젝트
(B) 광고 전략
(C) 행사 계획
(D) 교통 문제

해설 〈기본 정보 파악 – 주제〉
대화의 주제는 주로 첫 부분에 근거가 제시되는데 여자가 첫 대사에서 Memphis House의 외부 공사에 대한 계획을 논의하자고 말하고 있으므로 정답은 (A)이다.

패러프레이징 exterior work 건물 외부 공사 → remodeling 리모델링, 주택 개보수

33 Where does the man say he is taking a client?
(A) To a manufacturing facility
(B) To a construction site
(C) To some properties
(D) To a client's office

남자는 고객을 어디로 데려간다고 말하는가?
(A) 생산 시설로
(B) 공사 현장으로
(C) 몇몇 건물로
(D) 고객 사무실로

해설 〈구체적 정보 파악 – 특정 사항〉
taking a client를 키워드로 잡고 남자의 대사에서 언급되는 부분을 들어야 한다. 남자가 오후에 고객과 아파트를 보러 가야 한다고 말하고 있으므로 정답은 (C)이다.

패러프레이징 some apartments 몇몇 아파트
→ some properties 몇몇 건물

34 What does the woman suggest?
(A) Calling a client
(B) Checking the schedule
(C) Taking public transportation
(D) Submitting a list

여자가 권하는 것은 무엇인가?
(A) 고객에게 전화하는 것
(B) 일정을 확인하는 것
(C) 대중교통을 이용하는 것
(D) 리스트를 제출하는 것

해설 〈구체적 정보 파악 – 제안 관련〉
여자의 제안 사항을 묻는 문제이므로 여자의 말에서 정답을 찾아야 한다. 여자가 남자에게 교통 정체가 심하니 지하철을 타라고 제안하고 있으므로 정답은 (C)이다.

패러프레이징 take the subway 지하철을 타다
→ take public transportation 대중교통을 이용하다

Questions 35-37 refer to the following conversation. (미W) (미M)

W Ryan, do you know if the new projector in Conference Room 203 is functioning? We're scheduled to have a meeting there next week.

M Oh, ㉟ Maintenance said they'll have it ready by Tuesday, including the new screen. Is that too late?

W Well, ㊱ I'm just worried I won't have enough time to try out the new projector beforehand. The presentation is on Wednesday morning, and I'd like to make sure I can operate it smoothly.

M Well, ㊲ I suppose we still have enough time to reschedule the presentation to Conference Room 201. It has an older projector and it's on the 5th floor. But on the other hand, the room is bigger and it's near the staff lounge.

여 Ryan, 203호 회의실에 있는 새 프로젝터가 제대로 작동되는지 알고 있나요? 다음 주에 그곳에서 회의하기로 일정이 잡혀 있거든요.

남 오, 시설 관리부가 새 스크린을 포함해서 화요일까지 준비될 거라고 했어요. 너무 늦을까요?

여 새 프로젝터를 미리 테스트해 볼 수 있는 시간이 충분하지 않아서 걱정이 돼요. 프레젠테이션이 수요일 오전이라 원활하게 작동하는지 확인하고 싶어요.

남 제 생각에는 발표 일정을 201호 회의실로 조정할 시간은 아직 충분한 것 같은데요. 더 오래된 프로젝터고 5층에 있지만 반면에 회의실도 더 크고 직원 휴게실도 가까워요.

어휘 function (제대로) 작동하다 schedule 일정을 잡다, 예정하다 maintenance 유지, 보수 try out ~을 테스트해 보다, 시험적으로 사용해 보다 beforehand 사전에, 미리 operate 작동되다, 조작하다 suppose 생각하다, 추측하다 reschedule 일정을 변경하다 on the other hand 반면에

35 What are maintenance workers going to do by next Tuesday?
(A) Introduce the new system
(B) Install new equipment
(C) Clean the Conference Room
(D) Submit the form

관리부 직원은 다음 주 화요일까지 무엇을 할 예정인가?
(A) 새로운 시스템을 소개한다.
(B) 새로운 장비를 설치한다.
(C) 회의실을 청소한다.
(D) 양식을 제출한다.

해설 〈구체적 정보 파악 – 특정 사항〉
maintenance workers가 언급되는 부분에서 정답의 근거를 찾아야 한다. 남자가 여자에게 관리부가 프로젝터를 화요일까지 설치한다고 말하고 있으므로 이를 바꾸어 표현한 (B)가 정답이다.

36 What is the woman concerned about?
(A) Testing a new device
(B) Meeting the deadline
(C) Using old equipment
(D) Rescheduling a presentation

여자는 무엇에 대해 걱정하는가?
(A) 새로운 기기를 테스트해 보는 것
(B) 마감일을 맞추는 것
(C) 오래된 기기를 이용하는 것
(D) 발표 일정을 바꾸는 것

해설 〈구체적 정보 파악 – 특정 사항〉
여자의 대사에서 문제점이나 걱정거리를 언급할 때 답의 근거를 찾아야 한다. 대화 초반에 여자가 회의를 해야 한다며 중반에서 새 프로젝터를 미리 테스트해 볼 수 있는 시간이 충분하지 않은 것에 대한 걱정을 하고 있으므로 정답은 (A)이다.

패러프레이징 try out the projector 프로젝터 시험해 보기
→ test a device 장비 테스트해 보기

37 What does the man suggest the woman do?
(A) Send an e-mail
(B) Try a bigger screen
(C) Go to the staff lounge
(D) Use another place

남자는 여자에게 무엇을 하라고 제안하는가?
(A) 이메일 보내기
(B) 더 큰 화면 사용하기
(C) 직원 휴게실에 가기
(D) 다른 장소 이용하기

해설 〈구체적 정보 파악 – 제안 관련〉
남자가 제안하는 것이므로 남자의 말에 주목해야 한다. 대화 후반에 남자가 201호 회의실로 장소를 조정하는 것을 제안하고 있으므로 정답은 (D)이다.

Questions 38-40 refer to the following conversation. (영M) (미W)

M Hi. ㊳ I'd like to return this tie that I bought here three days ago.

W Certainly, sir. ㊴ Do you have your receipt?

M Yes, here it is.

W Thanks. Can you tell me the reason for the return? Is there any problem?

M No, the design is good and I really like it. But I got it as a gift for my coworker, and it turns out he already owns the exact same one. In fact, he bought it here.

W It is a popular one. Would you like to have the money refunded to your card, or would you like a store credit instead?

M I'll take the store credit. ㊵ I shop here all the time.

남 안녕하세요. 제가 3일 전에 여기서 산 이 넥타이를 반품하고 싶은데요.

여 알겠습니다, 손님. 영수증 가지고 계시나요?

남 네, 여기 있어요.

여 감사합니다. 반품 이유를 말씀해 주실 수 있으신가요? 무슨 문제라도 있나요?

남 아니요, 디자인도 좋고, 마음에 들어요. 그런데 동료 선물로 구입한 건데, 그가 이미 동일한 것을 가지고 있더라고요. 사실 그 사람도 여기서 샀어요.

여 인기 있는 제품이라서요. 카드로 환불하시겠어요? 아니면 대신 적립금으로 드릴까요?

남 적립금으로 받고 싶어요. 저는 항상 여기서 쇼핑하거든요.

어휘 return 돌려보내다, 반납하다, 돌아가다 receipt 영수증 exact 정확한, 정밀한 popular 인기 있는 refund 환불, 환불하다 store credit 물건 값을 상점의 채무로 처리하는 것

38 Why has the man come into the store?
(A) To bring back an item
(B) To get a gift
(C) To apply for a job
(D) To make a complaint

남자가 상점에 온 이유는 무엇인가?
(A) 제품을 반납하기 위해
(B) 선물을 구입하기 위해
(C) 직업에 지원하기 위해
(D) 항의하기 위해

해설 〈구체적 정보 파악 – 특정 사항〉
남자가 상점에 온 이유는 대화의 주제와 밀접한 관계가 있으므로 앞부분에 집중해야 한다. 첫 대사에서 남자가 3일 전에 이 상점에서 구입한 넥타이를 반품하고 싶다고 말하고 있으므로 (A)가 정답이다.

39 What does the woman ask the man to provide?
(A) Personal information
(B) Proof of purchase
(C) A gift voucher
(D) A store credit

여자는 남자에게 무엇을 요청하는가?
(A) 개인 정보
(B) 구매 증거
(C) 상품권
(D) 적립금

해설 〈구체적 정보 파악 – 특정 사항〉
물건의 반품을 원하는 남자에게 여자는 영수증이 있는지 묻고 있으므로 정답은 (B)이다.

패러프레이징 receipt 영수증 → proof of purchase 구매 증거

40 What does the man let the woman know?
(A) He doesn't like the item.
(B) He is a regular customer.
(C) He came with his coworker.
(D) He lives near the store.

남자는 여자에게 무엇을 알려주는가?
(A) 남자는 물건을 좋아하지 않는다.
(B) 남자는 단골손님이다.
(C) 남자는 그의 동료와 함께 왔다.
(D) 남자는 상점 근처에 산다.

해설 〈구체적 정보 파악 – 특정 사항〉
마지막 대사에서 남자가 항상 이곳에서 쇼핑한다고 말하고 있으므로 남자는 이 상점에 자주 오는 단골손님임을 알 수 있다. 따라서 정답은 (B)이다.

Questions 41-43 refer to the following conversation. 미W 미M

W I was listening to the radio in the car and ㊶ I heard that the tunnel construction in Midtown has finally been done.
M Yes, I read that in the newspaper. The project was far behind schedule. I've been waiting for them to finish it since I moved here. ㊷ The traffic down to Kingston Avenue should be much smoother from now on.
W Absolutely! But it's going to cost us.
M I know. ㊸ It'll be free during August, but from September onward it's going to be $5 per vehicle.

여 제가 차에서 라디오를 들었는데 Midtown의 터널 공사가 드디어 끝났답니다.
남 그래요, 저도 신문에서 읽었어요. 그 프로젝트는 일정이 많이 늦어졌어요. 제가 이곳으로 이사 온 이후부터 공사가 끝나는 것을 기다려 왔거든요. 이제부터는 Kingston 가로 내려가는 교통이 훨씬 원활해질 거예요.
여 당연하죠! 그렇지만 비용이 들어요.
남 알아요. 8월 동안은 무료지만 9월 이후로는 차량당 5달러예요.

어휘 construction 건설, 공사 behind schedule 예정보다 늦게 absolutely 틀림없이, 전적으로 onward 앞으로 (계속 이어서) 나아가는 commencement 시작 restoration 복원

41 What are the speakers discussing?
(A) The completion of a project
(B) The commencement of the fiscal year
(C) The construction of a street
(D) The restoration of a bridge

화자들이 논의하는 것은 무엇인가?
(A) 프로젝트 완료
(B) 회계 연도 시작
(C) 도로 공사
(D) 다리 복원

해설 〈기본 정보 파악 – 주제〉
대화의 주제는 첫 대사를 주목해야 한다. 첫 대사에서 여자가 남자에게 Midtown의 터널 공사가 끝났다는 소식을 알리고 있으므로 정답은 (A)이다.

42 What does the woman mean when she says, "Absolutely"?
(A) The tunnel should be renovated again.
(B) The transportation expenses will be increased.
(C) Kingston Avenue will be closed in September.
(D) There will be less traffic congestion.

여자가 "당연하죠!"라고 말한 의미는 무엇인가?
(A) 터널은 다시 보수되어야 한다.
(B) 교통비가 증가할 것이다.
(C) Kingston 가는 9월에 폐쇄될 것이다.
(D) 교통 체증이 줄어들 것이다.

해설 〈구체적 정보 파악 – 화자 의도〉
화자 의도 문제는 주어진 표현의 앞뒤 상황을 파악해야 한다. 남자가 터널 공사가 끝난 후 특정 도로로 가는 구간의 교통이 훨씬 원활해질 것이라고 말하자 여자가 강한 동의의 뜻을 나타내고 있다. 따라서 정답은 (D)이다.

43 According to the man, what will be offered in August?
(A) Discount fare
(B) New bus routes
(C) Free usage
(D) A travel card

남자에 의하면, 8월에 제공되는 것은 무엇인가?
(A) 할인 요금
(B) 새로운 버스 노선
(C) 무료 사용
(D) 여행 카드

해설 〈구체적 정보 파악 – 특정 사항〉
키워드인 in August가 나오는 남자의 대사에 집중해야 한다. 남자가 마지막 문장에서 8월 동안 터널 이용 요금은 무료라고 언급하고 있으므로 정답은 (C)이다.

Questions 44-46 refer to the following conversation. 미W 영M

W Hey, Andy.
M Good morning, Ms. Walters. ⓸⓸ The new shipment of women's summer clothing arrived this morning. Should I restock the section now?
W ⓸⓹ No, Daniel called in sick, so I need you to fill in for him on register until Jasmine comes at noon.
M Is Daniel okay? I remember he had a terrible headache yesterday.
W I hope he gets well soon. You can get to the clothing this afternoon.
M Sure. ⓸⓺ I did notice that we only have a couple of purses left on the shelf. We'd better put out some more.
W That's a good idea. Do that right away while there aren't any customers in the store.

여 안녕하세요, Andy.
남 안녕하세요, Walters 씨. 여름 여성 의류 배송이 오늘 아침에 도착했어요. 그쪽 구역을 지금 채울까요?
여 아니요, Daniel이 병가를 냈어요. 오늘 당신이 그를 대신해서 Jasmine이 도착하는 정오까지 계산대를 맡아야 해요.
남 Daniel은 괜찮은가요? 어제 머리가 심하게 아프다고 한 걸 기억하고 있거든요.
여 그가 빨리 나아지길 바라야죠. 옷은 오후에 정리하면 돼요.
남 알겠습니다. 선반에 지갑이 두어 개만 있는 걸 봤어요. 몇 개 더 꺼내 놓는 것이 좋겠습니다.
여 좋은 생각이에요. 고객이 없는 동안 그렇게 해 주세요.

어휘 restock 다시 채우다, 보충하다 call in sick 전화로 병가를 내다 fill in for ~를 대신(대리)하다 headache 두통, 머리가 아픔 get to 일에 착수하다 notice 의식하다, 알다 put out 내다 놓다, 내놓다

44 Where do the speakers most likely work?
(A) At a restaurant
(B) At a travel agency
(C) At a retail store
(D) At a hospital

화자들이 일하는 곳은 어디인가?
(A) 식당
(B) 여행사
(C) 소매점
(D) 병원

해설 〈기본 정보 파악 – 장소〉
화자들이 일하는 장소를 묻는 문제는 대화 첫 부분에서 단서를 찾아야 한다. 화자들이 서로 인사를 나눈 후 의류의 배송이 도착했다는 소식으로 대화가 시작되므로 의류와 관련된 곳이 화자들의 근무처임을 알 수 있다. 따라서 가장 적절한 답은 (C)이다.

45 What can be inferred about Daniel?
(A) He will handle the clothes.
(B) He is caught in traffic.
(C) He is out of town.
(D) He works as a cashier.

Daniel에 대해 유추할 수 있는 것은 무엇인가?
(A) 그는 의류를 다룰 것이다.
(B) 그는 교통 체증에 걸렸다.
(C) 그는 도시를 떠나 있다.
(D) 그는 계산원으로 일한다.

해설 〈구체적 정보 파악 – 특정 사항〉
키워드인 Daniel이 언급되는 부분에서 정답을 유추해야 한다. 여자가 남자에게 병가를 낸 Daniel 대신 계산대에서 일해 달라는 요청을 하고 있으므로 정답은 (D)이다.

46 What will the man probably do next?
(A) Talk to Jasmine
(B) Restock some clothing
(C) Leave the office
(D) Put out some items

남자는 다음에 무엇을 하겠는가?
(A) Jasmine에게 이야기한다.
(B) 의류를 채운다.
(C) 사무실을 떠난다.
(D) 물건들을 꺼내 놓는다.

해설 〈구체적 정보 파악 – 미래〉
남자의 다음 행동에 관한 문제는 대화의 후반부에서 정답의 근거를 찾을 수 있다. 남자가 선반에 지갑을 몇 개 더 꺼내 놓는 것이 좋겠다고 제안하자, 여자가 동의했으므로 남자는 판매를 위해 물건을 꺼내 놓을 것임을 알 수 있다. 따라서 정답은 (D)이다.

Questions 47-49 refer to the following conversation. 미W 미M

W ⓸⓻ Ian, did you hear that the marketing director decided to go ahead with his plan to open a branch in Brussels next month?
M That's right. An analysis of market research conducted in Belgium last month revealed a high potential demand for our services there. ⓸⓼ At the moment, there aren't many Belgian companies in our industry now.
W ⓸⓼ Then the marketing director's decision makes a lot of sense. We should quickly settle down there when the competition isn't fierce. I'd like to see the market survey you told me about. Is there any way I can have a look?
M I am not the right person to answer that. ⓸⓽ You need to talk to someone in marketing about it.

여 Ian, 마케팅 이사님이 다음 달에 Brussels에 지사를 설립하려는 계획을 추진하기로 결정했다는 소식을 들었나요?
남 맞아요. 지난달에 벨기에에서 실시한 시장 조사를 분석한 결과, 그곳이 우리 서비스를 위한 많은 잠재적 수요가 있다고 나타났어요. 현재 우리 업계에는 벨기에 회사가 많지 않아요.
여 그렇다면, 마케팅 이사님의 결정에 일리가 있네요. 경쟁이 치열하지 않을 때 우리가 빨리 그곳에 정착해야 해요. 말씀하신 시장 조사를 보고 싶은데, 제가 그것을 볼 수 있는 방법이 있을까요?
남 제가 대답할 수 있는 사항은 아닌 것 같아요. 그 점에 대해서는 마케팅부 사람과 상의해 보셔야 할 겁니다

어휘 branch 지사, 분점 analysis 분석 reveal 드러내다, 밝히다 potential 잠재적인 demand 수요 Belgian 벨기에의, 벨기에 사람 make sense 의미가 통하다, 이해가 되다 settle down 정착하다 competition 경쟁 fierce 거센, 심한 acquire 인수하다

47 According to the woman, what will happen next month?
(A) A regional office will open.
(B) A Belgian firm will be acquired.
(C) An analysis will be conducted.
(D) A decision will be made.

여자에 따르면, 다음 달에 무슨 일이 생기는가?
(A) 지역 사무소가 문을 열 것이다.
(B) 벨기에 회사가 인수될 것이다.
(C) 분석이 실시될 것이다.
(D) 결정이 내려질 것이다.

해설 〈구체적 정보 파악 – 특정 사항〉
문제의 키워드인 next month를 언급하는 부분에 집중한다. 대화 초반, Brussels에 지사를 설립하려는 계획을 다음 달에 추진하기로 결정했다는 소식에 대해 이야기하고 있으므로 정답은 (A)이다.
패러프레이징 branch 지점, 지사 → regional office 지역 사무실

48 What was the reason for the marketing director's decision?
(A) A lack of competition
(B) A certain industry regulation
(C) A shortage of hands
(D) An increase in efficiency

마케팅 이사가 이런 결정을 한 이유는 무엇인가?
(A) 경쟁의 부족
(B) 특정 산업 규정
(C) 인원 부족
(D) 효율성 증가

해설 〈구체적 정보 파악 – 특정 사항〉
marketing director's decision이 언급되는 대사에 집중해야 한다. 대화 중반에 여자가 경쟁이 치열하지 않을 때 빨리 그곳에 정착해야 한다며 이사님의 결정을 긍정적으로 이야기하고 있으므로 정답은 (A)이다.

패러프레이징 The competition isn't fierce 경쟁이 심하지 않다
→ A lack of competition 경쟁의 부족 .

49 What does the man mean when he says, "I am not the right person to answer that"?
(A) He is unable to contact the CEO.
(B) He does not know the survey result.
(C) He is unable to answer the particular question.
(D) He is not in charge of the report.

남자가 "제가 대답할 수 있는 사항은 아닌 것 같아요"라고 말한 의미는 무엇인가?
(A) 그는 최고 경영자에게 연락할 수 없다.
(B) 그는 조사의 결과를 모른다.
(C) 그는 특정 질문에 대답할 수 없다.
(D) 그는 보고서를 담당하고 있지 않다.

해설 〈구체적 정보 파악 – 화자 의도〉
화자 의도 문제는 주어진 표현의 앞뒤 상황을 파악해야 한다. 여자가 남자에게 직접 결과를 검토할 수 있는 방법을 묻자 남자가 해당 표현을 언급한 후, 그 부분은 마케팅부 사람과 상의해 보라고 조언하고 있다. 따라서 정답은 (C)이다.

Questions 50-52 refer to the following conversation with three speakers. (미W) (영M) (영W)

W1 Isaac, do you have a minute? I was off on a business trip on Tuesday and Wednesday, and I'm behind schedule on the Rebecca Fashion ad campaign. ⑩ Is there any way I can submit my work next Monday?
M I'm sorry, Zoe, but it's not possible. ⑫ I also have to send the copy to Rebecca by Friday evening. If you need help, I can assign part of it to someone else in your department.
W1 OK. Maybe I should ask someone else to join me.
W2 Sorry to interrupt, Zoe, but I just overheard what you were saying to Isaac. ⑪ I could help out, if you like. I've worked with Rebecca before and I know her preferences.
W1 That's perfect, Sophia! Your help is needed.
W2 Is that okay with you, Isaac? If we work together, I'm sure we can complete it on time.
M Why not? Go ahead. Let me know if you need anything.

여1 Isaac, 잠깐 시간 있으신가요? 제가 화요일과 수요일에 출장으로 자리를 비워서 Rebecca 패션 광고 캠페인이 일정보다 늦어졌어요. 제 작업을 다음 주 월요일에 제출할 방법이 있을까요?
남 미안해요, Zoe, 그건 불가능해요. 저도 금요일 저녁까지 Rebecca에게 사본을 보내야 하거든요. 만약 도움이 필요하면, 당신 부서의 다른 누군가에게 일부를 맡길 수는 있어요.
여1 알겠습니다. 다른 사람에게 같이 하자고 부탁해야겠네요.
여2 방해해서 미안하지만 Zoe, 제가 우연히 Isaac 씨와 이야기하는 것을 들었어요. 원하시면 제가 도와 드릴 수 있습니다. 제가 전에 Rebecca 씨와 같이 일한 적이 있어서 그녀가 좋아하는 것들을 알거든요.
여1 완벽하네요, Sophia! 당신의 도움이 필요해요.
여2 Isaac 씨도 괜찮으신 거죠? 우리가 같이 작업하면 제시간에 끝낼 수 있을 겁니다.
남 그럼요, 같이 하세요. 필요한 것이 있으면 무엇이든 알려 주세요.

어휘 behind schedule 예정보다 늦은 interrupt 방해하다, 중단시키다 overhear 우연히 듣다 preference 선호도, 선호

50 What does Zoe ask of Isaac?
(A) If he can let her leave early
(B) If he can extend a deadline
(C) If he can give her a day off
(D) If he can buy her some new clothes

Zoe가 Isaac에게 요청하는 것은 무엇인가?
(A) 여자를 일찍 퇴근시켜 줄 수 있는지
(B) 마감일을 연장해줄 수 있는지
(C) 휴가를 줄 수 있는지
(D) 새 옷들을 사줄 수 있는지

해설 〈구체적 정보 파악 – 요청 관련〉
여자1과 남자가 대화 초반에 이름을 부르며 인사하는 부분에서 남자가 Issac, 여자1이 Zoe임을 알 수 있다. 여자1이 남자에게 다음 주 월요일에 작업을 제출해도 되는지 묻고 있으므로 정답은 (B)이다. 3인 대화에서는 여러 명의 이름이 언급되는 경우가 많다. 그러므로 문제의 키워드가 이름일 경우, 해당 이름이 대화를 나누는 등장인물 중 한 명인지 아니면 제3의 인물인지 반드시 확인해야 한다.

51 What does Sophia tell Zoe?
(A) She will take some time off.
(B) She can ask someone to help.
(C) She knows Rebecca.
(D) She knows Zoe's preferences.

Sophia는 Zoe에게 무엇이라고 말하는가?
(A) 그녀는 휴식을 가질 것이다.
(B) 그녀는 누군가에게 도움을 요청할 수 있다.
(C) 그녀는 Rebecca를 알고 있다.
(D) 그녀는 Zoe의 선호도를 알고 있다.

해설 〈구체적 정보 파악 – 특정 사항〉
문제에서 제시된 이름들이 언급되는 부분을 잘 들어야 한다. 여자1이 여자2에게 Shopia라고 부르며 동의하고 있으므로 여자2가 Shopia임을 알 수 있다. 여자2는 여자1을 도와주겠다고 말하며 Rebecca와 과거에 일한 경험이 있음을 언급한다. 따라서 정답은 (C)이다.

52 By when must the work be finished?
(A) Monday
(B) Wednesday
(C) Friday
(D) Sunday

작업은 언제까지 끝내야 하는가?
(A) 월요일
(B) 수요일
(C) 금요일
(D) 일요일

해설 〈구체적 정보 파악 – 특정 사항〉
여자1이 남자에게 마감일을 월요일로 연기해 달라고 하자 남자는 금요일 저녁까지 Rebecca에게 보내야 한다고 설명하고 있으므로 늦어도 금요일까지는 일이 끝나야 함을 알 수 있다. 따라서 정답은 (C)이다.

Questions 53-55 refer to the following conversation. (미M) (미W)

M Okay, that's all I have to ask you. ⑬ Do you have any questions about the job before we wrap up?
W Thanks to your lucid explanation, ⑭ if I was hired as a researcher, I would understand what to do. I have a question about the institution itself, though.
M Feel free to ask me anything you'd like to know.
W I was curious to know how your organization is funded. Is it mostly through government subsidy?
M Partially, but not mainly. ⑮ Personal donations are the highest percentage of our total funds. We also receive substantial contributions from corporate donors and various charities.

남 좋아요. 제가 드릴 질문은 여기까지입니다. 마무리 짓기 전에 이 직책에 대해 물어보고 싶은 게 있으신가요?
여 당신의 명료한 설명 덕분에 제가 만약 연구원으로 고용된다면 제가 무엇을 해야 하는지 이해할 수 있었습니다. 하지만 이 기관 자체에 관해서는 궁금한 것이 있습니다.
남 알고 싶은 것이 있으시면 무엇이든 물어보세요.
여 귀사의 자금이 어떻게 조달이 되고 있는지 알고 싶습니다. 주로 정부 보조금을 통해서입니까?
남 부분적으로는요. 하지만 주로 그렇지 않아요. 개인 기부금이 우리의 전체 자금 중 가장 높은 비율을 차지합니다. 우리는 또한 기업 기부자들과 여러 자선 단체들로부터 상당한 기부금을 받습니다.

어휘 wrap up (회의 등을) 마무리 짓다 lucid 명쾌한, 명료한 explanation 설명 institution 기관, 시설 feel free to 마음껏 ~해도 괜찮다 subsidy (국가, 기관이 제공하는) 보조금 partially 부분적으로, 불완전하게 donation 기부금 substantial (양, 가치 등이) 상당한

53 Who most likely is the woman?
(A) A charity organizer
(B) An office administrator
(C) A job candidate
(D) A research manager
여자는 누구인가?
(A) 자선 단체 주최자
(B) 사무실 관리자
(C) 입사 지원자
(D) 연구 관리자

해설 〈기본 정보 파악 – 정체〉
남자가 첫 대사에서 이 직책에 관해 알고 싶은 것이 있는지 묻고 여자가 고용되는 것을 전제로 대화를 이어가고 있으므로 여자는 면접을 보러 왔음을 알 수 있다. 따라서 (C)가 가장 적절한 답이다.

54 Where does the conversation most likely take place?
(A) In a marketing office
(B) In an educational institution
(C) At a research institute
(D) At a fundraising event
대화가 일어나는 장소는 어디인가?
(A) 마케팅 사무실
(B) 교육 기관
(C) 연구소
(D) 기금 모금 행사

해설 〈기본 정보 파악 – 장소〉
입사 지원자인 여자가 남자의 설명 덕분에 연구원으로 고용된다면 무엇을 해야 하는지 알겠다고 말하고 있으므로 여자가 연구원 직책에 지원했음을 알 수 있다. 따라서 정답은 (C)이다.
패러프레이징 informative 유용한 → helpful 도움이 되는

55 According to the man, which group provides the most funding?
(A) Charitable organizations
(B) The government
(C) Corporations
(D) Private donors
남자에 따르면, 어떤 그룹이 가장 많은 자금을 제공하는가?
(A) 자선 기관들
(B) 정부
(C) 기업들
(D) 개인 기부자들

해설 〈구체적 정보 파악 – 특정 사항〉
남자가 키워드인 funding과 관련된 내용을 언급하는 대사에서 정답을 찾아야 한다. 남자가 마지막 대사에서 개인 기부금이 전체 자금 중 가장 높은 비율을 차지한다고 설명하고 있으므로 정답은 (D)이다.
패러프레이징 personal donations 개인 기부금
→ private donors 개인 기부자들

Questions 56-58 refer to the following conversation with three speakers. (미W) (영M) (미M)

W Hi, guys. ⑯ How's the layout of the advertisement for GS7 Automobiles coming along? Are you making any progress?
M1 Hi, Stephanie. We're running behind schedule. I doubt if we'll be able to finish on time. The clients have requested to have it done by next week.
M2 That's right. I have told them enough about the possibility of extending the deadline, but they didn't change their mind.
W Well, they did. You're not going to believe this. ⑰ They've just decided to push the due date back until the middle of October.
M1 Really? That's a relief. That will greatly reduce the pressure on us.
W Yeah. ⑱ As a matter of fact, they're having problems with their budget and cannot go ahead as planned.
M2 Thank you for the good news.

여 안녕하세요, 여러분. GS7 자동차 광고의 레이아웃 작업이 어떻게 되고 있나요? 진전이 좀 있나요?
남1 안녕하세요, Stephanie. 일정이 늦어지고 있습니다. 제시간에 끝낼 수 있을지 모르겠어요. 고객들은 다음 주까지 꼭 끝내 달라고 했거든요.
남2 맞아요, 마감 시한을 연장할 수도 있다는 가능성에 대해 그들에게 충분히 이야기했지만, 그들은 마음을 바꾸지 않았어요.
여 그랬었죠. 당신들은 믿지 못할 거예요. 그들이 마감일을 10월 중순으로 연기하기로 막 결정했거든요.
남1 정말이에요? 그거 다행이네요. 그렇게 되면 우리에게 가해지는 압박이 크게 줄어들 것입니다.
여 네, 사실 그들이 예산에 문제가 생겨서 계획대로 진행할 수가 없게 되었답니다.
남2 좋은 소식 알려주셔서 감사합니다.

어휘 layout (책, 건물 등의) 레이아웃, 배치 coming along 되어 가다 behind schedule 예정보다 늦은 doubt 의심하다, 확신하지 못하다 push back (시간, 날짜 등을) 뒤로 미루다 pressure 압력, 압박 as a matter of fact 사실은 go ahead 진행하다

56 What type of business do the speakers probably work for?
(A) An automobile company
(B) A financial firm
(C) An advertising agency
(D) An electronic manufacturer
화자들은 어떤 종류의 사업체에서 일하고 있는가?
(A) 자동차 회사

(B) 금융 회사
(C) 광고 회사
(D) 전자제품 제조사

해설 〈기본 정보 파악 – 장소〉
화자들이 일하는 장소에 대한 정답은 대화 초반에 근거가 제시된다. 여자가 첫 대사에서 GS7 자동차 광고의 레이아웃 작업에 대해 언급하고 있으므로 정답은 (C)이다.

57 Why does the woman say, "You're not going to believe this"?
(A) A project has made much progress.
(B) An unexpected decision has been made.
(C) An advertising campaign was very successful.
(D) The deadline will be moved forward.

여자는 왜 "믿기 힘들 겁니다"라고 말하는가?
(A) 프로젝트의 진행이 많이 진전되었다.
(B) 뜻밖의 결정이 내려졌다.
(C) 광고 캠페인은 매우 성공적이었다.
(D) 마감일이 앞으로 당겨질 것이다.

해설 〈구체적 정보 파악 – 화자 의도〉
주변 문맥과 종합하여 여자의 의도를 파악해야 한다. 남자가 고객에게 마감 시한의 연장 가능성에 대해 알렸지만 그들은 마감일을 맞춰 달라며 마음을 바꾸지 않았다고 하자, 여자가 해당 표현을 언급하며 고객이 마감일을 연기하기로 결정했다는 소식을 알리고 있다. 따라서 정답은 (B)이다.

58 What does the woman say about the clients?
(A) They are suffering from a lack of funds.
(B) They recently started their business.
(C) They are having difficulty exporting.
(D) They recently hired a new manager.

여자는 고객들에 대해 무엇이라고 말하는가?
(A) 그들은 자금 부족을 겪고 있다.
(B) 그들은 최근에 사업을 시작했다.
(C) 그들은 수출에 어려움을 겪고 있다.
(D) 그들은 최근에 새 매니저를 고용했다.

해설 〈구체적 정보 파악 – 특정 사항〉
여자가 고객에 대해 언급하는 부분에 집중해야 한다. 대화 후반에 여자가 고객 예산에 문제가 생겨 계획대로 진행할 수 없게 되었다고 말하고 있으므로 정답은 (A)이다.

패러프레이징 have problems with the budget 예산에 문제가 있다
→ suffer from a lack of funds 자금 부족으로 고생하다

Questions 59-61 refer to the following conversation. 미W 영M

W Good morning, Scott. ⑲ Do you need any help putting together the data for the presentation on our car sales tomorrow?
M I'm almost done, thanks, but there is something you could do for me. I still need to make some graphics to show last quarter's sales by branch. You're much better at using those chart programs than I am.
W Sure, no problem. ⑳ Actually, I made a very similar chart myself the other day. It'll be much faster if I update that with the new sales figures. Send me the data and I can do it right now.
W That'd be a great help. ㉑ Now I can finish up the sales projection, and we'll be ready by 6 o'clock.

여 안녕하세요, Scott. 내일 자동차 판매 실적 발표를 위한 데이터 준비에 도움이 필요한가요?
남 거의 다 했어요, 감사합니다. 그런데 저를 위해 해 주셨으면 하는 것이 있어요. 제가 지점별로 지난 분기의 판매 실적을 보여줄 도표를 만들어야 하는데요. 당신이 저보다 이 차트 프로그램을 더 잘 사용하시잖아요.
여 그럼요, 문제없어요. 사실 지난번에 제가 아주 비슷한 차트를 직접 만들었거든요. 새로운 판매 수치로 갱신하면 훨씬 더 빠를 거예요. 데이터를 보내주시면 바로 해 드릴게요.
남 큰 도움이 되겠어요. 이제 매출 추정치를 끝낼 수 있으니 6시까지는 준비할 수 있겠어요.

어휘 put together 모으다, 준비하다 quarter 분기 similar 비슷한, 유사한 figure 수치, 숫자 projection 예상, 추정 estimate 추정, 추산

59 What is the topic of the conversation?
(A) A meeting plan
(B) A retirement event
(C) A sales presentation
(D) The latest car model

이 대화의 주제는 무엇인가?
(A) 회의 계획
(B) 은퇴 행사
(C) 판매 실적 발표
(D) 최신 자동차 모델

해설 〈기본 정보 파악 – 주제〉
주제의 단서는 대화의 초반에 정답의 근거가 제시된다. 첫 대사에서 여자가 자동차 판매 실적 발표를 위한 데이터 준비에 도움이 필요한지 묻고 있으므로 이들이 발표 준비를 하고 있음을 알 수 있다. 따라서 (C)가 가장 적절한 답이다.

60 What has the woman recently done?
(A) Designed a car
(B) Updated the figures
(C) Created a chart
(D) Attended a meeting

여자가 최근에 한 것은 무엇인가?
(A) 자동차 디자인
(B) 수치 갱신
(C) 차트 생성
(D) 회의 참석

해설 〈구체적 정보 파악 – 특정 사항〉
여자가 이미 한 행동에 대해 말하는 부분에 주목해야 한다. 대화 중반에 남자가 여자에게 차트 프로그램 사용에 대해 도움을 청하자 여자가 비슷한 차트를 직접 만든 적이 있다고 말한다. 그러므로 정답은 (C)이다.

61 What will the man do next?
(A) Contact a client
(B) Work on an estimate
(C) Revise data
(D) Attend a meeting

남자는 다음에 무엇을 할 것인가?
(A) 고객에게 연락한다.
(B) 추산 작업을 한다.
(C) 데이터를 수정한다.
(D) 회의에 참석한다.

해설 〈구체적 정보 파악 – 미래〉
미래에 할 일과 연관된 문제는 마지막 대사에서 단서가 제시된다. 대화 후반에 남자가 매출 추정치를 끝내겠다고 말하고 있으므로 정답은 (B)이다.

Questions 62-64 refer to the following conversation and directory. 미W 미M

Department Manager Directory		
Dept.	Manager	Extension No.
Advertising	Nicole Martinez	210
Human Resources	Erica Lopez	324
Maintenance	Ethan Cabrera	420
Accounting	Lewis Moore	518

W Douglas, (62) I've just finished reviewing your report, and I've found some things that you need to change before you submit it to Mr. Moore. Some of the data you used is not accurate.

M What do you mean? Do I have to start it over again? I've spent the whole week working on it.

W No, you don't have to start over. You only need to revise the information regarding last year's second quarter. Somehow you entered the information from 2016 instead of 2017. It won't be difficult to correct the figures.

M That's a relief. I think I can handle it then. (63) (64) Thanks for catching that for me. Mr. Moore would have been annoyed if I'd given him the report with faulty data.

부서 매니저 명단		
부서	매니저	내선
광고부	Nicole Martinez	210
인사부	Erica Lopez	324
관리부	Ethan Cabrera	420
회계부	Lewis Moore	518

여 Douglas, 제가 방금 당신의 보고서 검토를 끝냈는데 Moore 씨에게 제출하기 전에 몇 가지 변경이 필요한 것들을 발견했어요. 사용한 데이터의 일부가 정확하지 않네요.

남 무슨 말씀이세요? 처음부터 다시 해야 한다는 건가요? 그것을 작업하는 데 일주일 걸렸어요.

여 아니요, 처음부터 할 필요는 없어요. 작년 2분기에 대한 정보만 수정하면 됩니다. 왜 그런지 모르겠지만 당신이 2017년 대신 2016년의 정보를 입력했어요. 수치를 수정하는 것은 어렵지 않을 거예요.

남 다행이네요. 그럼 제가 처리할 수 있을 것 같아요. 발견해 줘서 고마워요. Moore 씨에게 잘못된 데이터가 담긴 보고서를 제출했다면 Moore 씨가 화가 났을 겁니다.

어휘 review 검토하다, 확인하다 submit 제출하다 accurate 정확한, 정밀한 start over 다시 시작하다 revise 변경하다, 수정하다 regarding ~에 관하여, 대하여 somehow 왜 그런지 모르겠지만, 왠지 handle 다루다, 처리하다 annoy 짜증나게 하다, 귀찮게 하다 adjustment 수정

62 What is the main topic of the conversation?
(A) Plans for a seminar
(B) Adjustment of a document
(C) Ideas for a presentation
(D) Budgets for a project

이 대화의 주제는 무엇인가?
(A) 세미나를 위한 계획
(B) 문서 수정
(C) 프레젠테이션을 위한 아이디어
(D) 프로젝트 예산

해설 〈기본 정보 파악 – 주제〉
주제를 묻는 문제는 대화 초반에 집중해야 한다. 첫 대사에서 여자가 남자의 보고서를 검토했다고 말하며 상사에게 제출하기 전에 수정이 필요하다고 지적하고 있으므로 정답은 (B)이다.

63 Why does the man thank the woman?
(A) She gathered some information.
(B) She gave him a ride.
(C) She noticed some errors.
(D) She sent an e-mail.

남자는 여자에게 왜 감사하는가?
(A) 여자가 정보를 모았다.
(B) 여자가 남자에게 차를 태워주었다.
(C) 여자가 오류를 인지했다.
(D) 여자가 이메일을 보냈다.

해설 〈구체적 정보 파악 – 특정 사항〉
thank를 키워드로 잡고 남자가 여자에게 감사를 표하는 부분에 집중해야 한다. 대화 후반에 남자가 여자에게 실수를 발견한 것에 대해 고맙다고 말하고 있으므로 정답은 (C)이다.

64 Look at the graphic. In which department do the speakers most likely work?
(A) Advertising
(B) Human Resources
(C) Maintenance
(D) Accounting

시각 자료를 보시오. 화자들은 어떤 부서에서 근무하겠는가?
(A) 광고부
(B) 인사부
(C) 관리부
(D) 회계부

해설 〈구체적 정보 파악 – 시각 정보 연계〉
선택지에 부서가 제시되어 있으므로 대화에서는 매니저 이름이나 내선번호가 언급될 것을 미리 예측하고 이 부분을 주목해야 한다. 남자가 오류를 지적한 여자에게 감사하며, 수정 없이 보고서를 제출했다면 Moore 씨가 화냈을 것이라고 했으므로 그가 남자의 상사이며 화자들은 Moore 씨와 같은 부서에서 일하고 있음을 알 수 있다. 따라서 (D)가 정답이다.

Questions 65-67 refer to the following conversation and chart.
미W 영M

Oscar Electronics

Air Purifiers Efficiency Rating

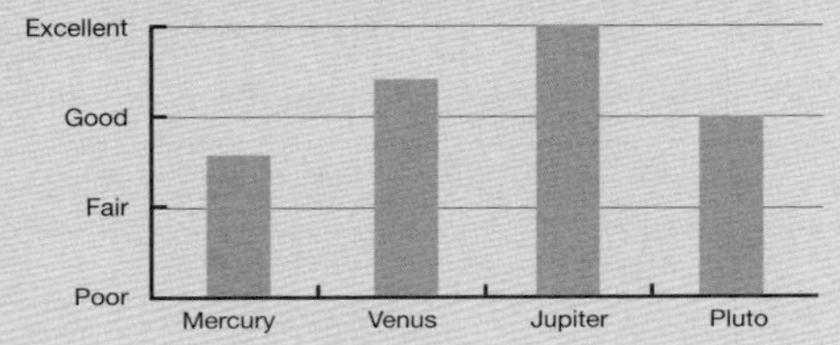

W Excuse me. ⑮ I saw your ad in the newspaper that all of your air purifiers are on sale for 20% off this week, so I came to have a look.

M You are at the right place. ⑯ Are you interested in a high-capacity model for industrial use, or something for the home?

W For family use only. And I'd like something made by Oscar Electronics.

M Great choice. Oscar Electronics makes excellent machines.

W I'd like to see whichever model is most efficient in terms of energy consumption.

M Okay. Let me explain to you some details. ⑰ The one with the highest efficiency rating is their most expensive model, but at the same time it's their best selling model.

Oscar 전자

공기 청정기 효율 등급

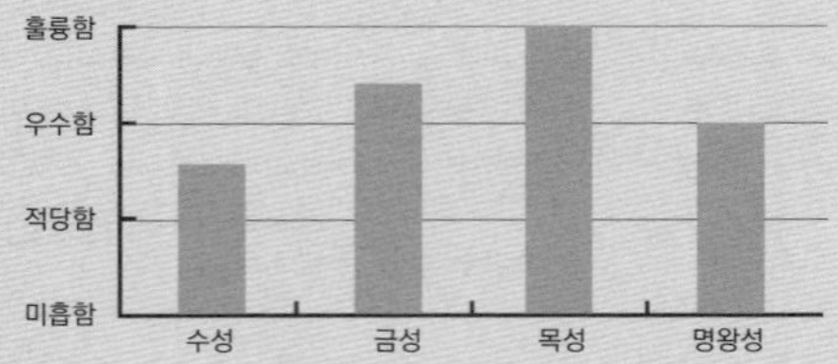

여 실례합니다. 이번 주에 모든 공기 청정기가 20% 할인된다는 신문 광고를 보고 왔습니다.

남 잘 찾아 오셨습니다. 산업용으로 쓰실 고성능 제품을 원하시나요, 아니면 집에서 쓰실 것을 찾으시나요?

여 가정용으로요. 그리고 Oscar 전자에서 만든 것이었으면 좋겠습니다.

남 좋은 선택이십니다. Oscar 전자가 제품들을 잘 만들죠.

여 어떤 모델이든 에너지 소비면에서 가장 효율적인 것으로 봤으면 좋겠어요.

남 알겠습니다. 제가 자세한 사항들을 설명해 드리겠습니다. 가장 높은 효율 등급을 가진 이 제품이 가장 비싼 모델이지만 동시에 가장 잘 팔리는 모델입니다.

어휘 air purifier 공기 청정기 capacity 용량, 능력, 수용력 industrial 산업, 공업의, 공업용의 whichever 어느 쪽이든 efficient 능률적인, 효율적인 energy consumption 에너지 소비 efficiency rating 효율 등급

65 According to the woman, how was the sale advertised?

(A) On the Web site
(B) In the newspaper
(C) On the television
(D) On the radio

여자에 의하면, 할인은 어떻게 광고되었는가?

(A) 웹 사이트에
(B) 신문에
(C) 텔레비전에
(D) 라디오에

해설 〈구체적 정보 파악 – 특정 사항〉
sale를 키워드로 잡고 여자의 말에 집중해야 한다. 여자가 첫 대사에서 신문 광고를 보고 왔다고 언급하고 있으므로 정답은 (B)이다.

66 What does the man ask about?

(A) Where the item is displayed
(B) When a shipment will be made
(C) Whether a discount coupon is valid
(D) How a product will be used

남자는 무엇에 대해 묻고 있는가?

(A) 제품이 어디에 진열될 것인지
(B) 배송이 언제 이루어질 것인지
(C) 할인 쿠폰이 유효한지 아닌지
(D) 제품이 어떻게 이용될 것인지

해설 〈구체적 정보 파악 – 특정 사항〉
남자가 여자에게 질문하는 부분에서 정답의 단서를 찾아야 한다. 제품을 구입하러 온 여자에게 남자가 산업용인지 집에서 사용할 것인지 묻고 있으므로 정답은 (D)이다.

67 Look at the graphic. Which model does the man say is the most expensive?

(A) The Mercury
(B) The Venus
(C) The Jupiter
(D) The Pluto

시각 자료를 보시오. 남자는 어떤 제품 모델이 가장 비싸다고 말하는가?

(A) 수성
(B) 금성
(C) 목성
(D) 명왕성

해설 〈구체적 정보 파악 – 시각 정보 연계〉
문제의 선택지로 그래프의 가로축인 제품들의 이름이 제시되어 있다. 따라서 정답의 단서는 그래프의 세로축인 성능이나 또는 그래프의 높낮이가 정답의 단서로 언급될 것이므로 이에 집중해야 한다. 남자가 마지막 대사에서 가장 높은 효율 등급을 가진 제품이 가장 비싼 모델이라고 했으므로 가장 높은 등급의 (C)가 정답이다.

Questions 68-70 refer to the following conversation and layout. 미W 영M

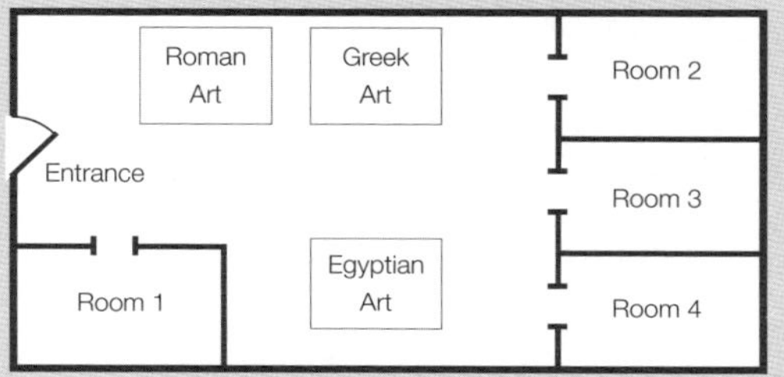

W Thanks for coming in today, Mr. Jonson. 68 You had a meeting with the mayor last night, didn't you? How did it go?

M It went well. 69 I was asking her to promote our museum more on the city's Web site and she gave me positive answers. Anyway, what was it you wanted to discuss?

W You know, I don't think the collection of statues should be kept in Room 2. All of the exhibits on that side of the museum are related to Greek art. I think the statues are more related to Egyptian art.

M That makes sense. 70 Let's move them to the room near the entrance beside the Egyptian art.

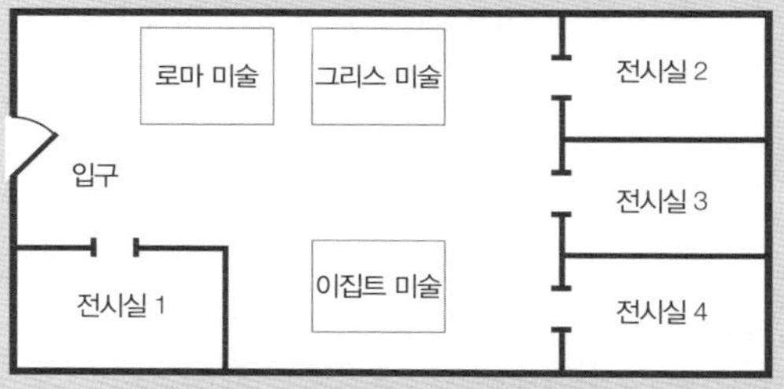

여 Jonson 씨, 오늘 와 주셔서 감사합니다. 어젯밤에 시장님과 회의하셨잖아요, 그렇죠? 어떻게 되었나요?

남 잘 되었습니다. 제가 시의 웹 사이트에 우리 박물관을 더 홍보해 달라고 요청했고, 그녀도 저에게 긍정적인 답변을 주었어요. 그건 그렇고, 의논하고 싶으신 것이 무엇인가요?

여 아시겠지만, 저는 조각상의 컬렉션을 2번 전시실에 보관해야 한다고 생각하지 않아요. 그쪽에 있는 모든 전시물들은 그리스 미술과 관련이 있잖아요. 저는 조각상들이 이집트 미술과 더 관련이 있다고 생각해요.

남 옳은 말씀이네요. 그럼 이집트 미술 옆, 정문 근처 방으로 옮기도록 하죠.

어휘 promote 촉진하다, 홍보하다 positive 긍정적인 statue 조각상 exhibit 전시품, 전시하다 relate to 와 관련되다, ~와 관계가 있다

68 Who did the man meet yesterday?
(A) A museum director
(B) A town official
(C) A tour guide
(D) A department manager

남자는 어제 누구를 만났는가?
(A) 박물관 관장
(B) 시 공무원
(C) 여행 가이드
(D) 부서 매니저

해설 〈구체적 정보 파악 – 특정 사항〉
키워드인 yesterday를 언급하는 부분에 집중해야 한다. 여자가 남자에게 어젯밤 시장님과 한 회의가 어땠는지 묻고 있으므로 남자는 어제 시장님을 만났음을 알 수 있다. 따라서 이를 바꾸어 표현한 (B)가 정답이다.

패러프레이징 mayor 시장 → town official 시 공무원

69 How would the man like to promote the museum?
(A) In a newspaper
(B) On the television
(C) On the Web site
(D) On a street banner

남자는 박물관을 어떻게 홍보하고 싶어 하는가?
(A) 신문으로
(B) 텔레비전으로
(C) 웹 사이트로
(D) 길거리 현수막으로

해설 〈구체적 정보 파악 – 특정 사항〉
남자가 키워드인 promote를 언급하는 부분에서 정답의 근거를 찾아야 한다. 남자가 회의에서 시의 웹 사이트에 박물관의 홍보를 요청했다고 말하고 있다. 따라서 정답은 (C)이다.

70 Look at the graphic. Where will the collection of statues most likely be placed?
(A) In Room 1
(B) In Room 2
(C) In Room 3
(D) In Room 4

시각 자료를 보시오. 조각상 컬렉션 전시는 어디에서 열릴 것인가?
(A) 1전시실에서
(B) 2전시실에서
(C) 3전시실에서
(D) 4전시실에서

해설 〈구체적 정보 파악 – 시각 정보 연계〉
평면도의 전시실이 선택지로 제시되어 있으므로 대화에서는 평면도에서의 나머지 정보 즉 Roman Art, Greek Art, Egyptian Art가 단서로 언급될 것을 예측하고 들어야 한다. 여자가 키워드인 collection of statues를 언급하며 전시 장소 변경을 제안하자 남자가 이집트 예술 옆 정문 근처 방으로 옮기자고 동의한다. 따라서 정답은 (A)이다.

Questions 71-73 refer to the following talk. 영W

Thank you for joining the tour of our food processing facility. I'm Melissa Grey, your guide today. Natural Catering has been providing ingredients for Auckland restaurants for ten years now. We're currently the main suppliers of vegetables to more than 20 percent of the eateries in Auckland. 72 We're starting the tour here in the storage facility because I'd like to show you the fresh vegetables being delivered and taken directly to our processing area. 71 We start preparing the vegetables minutes after they arrive to ensure that they're fresh when they reach your restaurants. 73 At the end of the tour, I'd like to offer each of you an apron with the Natural Catering logo on it. I hope you will all like them. Let's get started.

우리의 음식 가공 시설 견학에 함께해 주셔서 감사합니다. 저는 오늘의 가이드 Melissa Grey입니다. Natural Catering은 Auckland의 레스토랑들에게 지금까지 10년 동안 재료를 공급해 오고 있습니다. 현재 우리는 Auckland의 20%가 넘는 식당의 주요 채소 공급업체입니다. 신선한 야채들이 배달된 후 직접 가공 시설로 이동되는 것을 여러분께 보여드리기 위해 이곳 저장 시설에서 견학을 시작하겠습니다. 저희는 채소가 여러분의 식당에 신선한 상태로 도착할 수 있도록 채소들이 도착한 직후 바로 준비하기 시작합니다. 견학의 마지막에는, Natural Catering 로고가 새겨진 앞치마를 여러분께 드리도록 하겠습니다. 마음에 드셨으면 좋겠습니다. 시작합시다.

어휘 food processing 식품 가공 처리, 조리 ingredient 재료, 성분 currently 현재, 지금 supplier 공급 회사 eatery 음식점, 식당 storage facility 저장 설비, 저장 시설 prepare 준비하다 ensure 반드시 ~ 하게 하다, 보장하다

71 Who most likely are the tour participants?
(A) Natural Park tourists
(B) Restaurant owners
(C) New interns
(D) Local residents

견학 참가자들은 누구인가?
(A) 야생 공원 관광객들
(B) 레스토랑 운영자들
(C) 새로운 인턴들
(D) 지역 주민들

해설 〈기본 정보 파악 – 청자〉
담화에서 청자에 대한 정보는 초반에 답의 단서가 언급되는 것이 대부분이다. 앞부분에서 catering과 restaurant에 대한 언급이 있은 후, 중반에 화자가 여러분의 식당에 채소가 신선한 상태로 도착할 수 있도록 준비한다고 안내하고 있다. 따라서 정답은 (B)이다.

72 Where will the tour begin?
(A) At the main entrance
(B) In the manufacturing facility
(C) In the warehouse
(D) In the marketing office

견학은 어디에서 시작하는가?
(A) 정문
(B) 제조 시설
(C) 창고
(D) 마케팅 사무실

해설 〈구체적 정보 파악 – 특정 사항〉
tour begin을 키워드로 잡고 이 부분에 집중한다. 담화 중반에 화자가 이곳 저장 시설에서 견학을 시작한다고 언급하고 있으므로 정답은 (C)이다.

패러프레이징 storage facility 저장 시설 → warehouse 창고

73 What will participants receive at the end of the tour?
(A) An item of clothing
(B) Food samples
(C) A carrier bag
(D) A booklet

참가자들은 견학 마지막에 무엇을 받을 것인가?
(A) 의류 제품
(B) 음식 샘플
(C) 쇼핑백
(D) 안내 책자

해설 〈구체적 정보 파악 – 특정 사항〉
키워드인 end of the tour가 언급되는 부분에서 답을 찾아야 한다. 담화의 후반에 견학 마지막에 회사 로고가 새겨진 앞치마를 증정한다고 말하고 있으므로 정답은 (A)이다.

Questions 74-76 refer to the following news report. (호M)

And for today's local news, ⓻⓸ Finsbury City Council announced yesterday that it has approved the construction of the proposed Square One multiplex cinema and shopping mall complex located in the northwest of Bedford County. The project will cost an estimated two million dollars and is expected to take three years to complete. ⓻⓹ Controversy has swirled around the project, as many citizens wanted the land to remain protected open space. ⓻⓺ However, the Mayor of Finsbury argued that once completed, the complex will bring in millions of dollars in revenue for the city every year. "This development will be a boon to our city," he said. The groundbreaking ceremony for the complex will take place next Tuesday at 11 A.M.

이어서 오늘의 지역 뉴스입니다. Finsbury 시 의회는 어제 Bedford County의 북서쪽에 위치한 멀티플렉스 영화관과 복합 쇼핑몰인 Square One의 건설 제안을 승인했다고 밝혔습니다. 이 프로젝트는 2백만 달러의 비용이 들 것이며, 완공되는 데 3년이 걸릴 것으로 예상됩니다. 많은 시민들은 그 땅이 공공용지로 남아 있기를 원했기 때문에 이 프로젝트를 둘러싸고 논란이 일고 있습니다. 그렇지만 Finsbury 시장은 복합몰의 공사가 완성되면 매년 도시에 수백만 달러의 수익을 가져올 것이라고 주장하며 "이 개발은 우리 도시에 큰 혜택이 될 것이다"라고 말했습니다. 기공식은 다음 주 화요일 오전 11시에 진행될 예정입니다.

어휘 announce 발표하다 approve 승인하다 construction 건설, 공사 controversy 논란 swirl 소용돌이치다, 빙빙 돌다 open space 공공용지 revenue 수익 boon 혜택, 은혜 groundbreaking ceremony 기공식, 착공식 tear down ~을 허물다

74 What was announced yesterday?
(A) A proposal has been approved.
(B) A protest is going to be held.
(C) A new business has opened.
(D) A construction project has been completed.

어제 발표된 것은 무엇인가?
(A) 제안이 승인되었다.
(B) 시위가 열릴 것이다.
(C) 새로운 사업이 시작된다.
(D) 공사 프로젝트가 완료되었다.

해설 〈구체적 정보 파악 – 특정 사항〉
키워드인 yesterday가 언급되는 부분에서 답을 찾아야 한다. Finsbury 시 의회가 어제 Bedford County의 북서쪽에 위치한 복합 쇼핑몰의 건설 제안을 승인했다고 보도하고 있다. 따라서 정답은 (A)이다.

75 What can be understood from the report?
(A) Construction has already started.
(B) The shopping mall will be torn down.
(C) Many residents are against the project.
(D) The tax will be increased next month.

이 보도를 통해 알 수 있는 것은 무엇인가?
(A) 공사가 이미 시작되었다.
(B) 쇼핑몰을 허물 것이다.
(C) 많은 주민들이 프로젝트에 반대한다.
(D) 다음 달에 세금이 인상될 것이다.

해설 〈구체적 정보 파악 – 특정 사항〉
특정한 키워드가 제시되지 않았기 때문에 담화에서 각 선택지의 내용이 언급되는 부분에 집중해야 한다. 담화 중반에 많은 시민들이 건설 부지가 공공용지로 남아 있기를 원하고 있기 때문에 이 프로젝트를 둘러싸고 논란이 일고 있다고 보도하고 있다. 따라서 정답은 (C)이다.

76 What did the Mayor of Finsbury mean when he said, "This development will be a boon to our city"?
(A) The tax increase will be worth it.
(B) The project will generate more income.
(C) The land should remain as open space.
(D) The construction will cost a lot of money.

Finsbury의 시장이 말한 "이 개발은 우리 도시에 큰 혜택이 될 것이다"가 의미하는 것은 무엇인가?
(A) 세금 인상은 가치가 있을 것이다.
(B) 프로젝트는 더 많은 수입을 발생시킬 것이다.
(C) 그 땅은 공공용지로 남아 있을 것이다.
(D) 공사에 많은 비용이 들 것이다.

해설 〈구체적 정보 파악 – 화자 의도〉
문제에 언급된 문장의 앞뒤 문맥을 종합하여 화자의 의도를 파악해야 한다. Finsbury 시장이 공사가 완성되면 매년 수백만 달러의 수익을 가져올 것이라고 주장하며 해당 표현을 말하고 있으므로 정답은 (B)이다.

Questions 77-79 refer to the following excerpt from a meeting. 미W

Let me introduce myself. (77) I'm Jade Larkin, and I'm in charge of the accounting department here at JAC recruitment. In a few minutes, (78) I'll address how to get your business travel costs reimbursed, but first, did you all get the workshop pamphlet? (79) Let's look at the front page. There you'll see a list of expense guidelines as well as price limits. For example, receipts are not required for meals or public transportation reimbursement unless the prices exceed the stated cost limits. Please use this information as a general planning guide when scheduling your travel. The second page includes a form to record your travel expenses. Now let's move on to page three, which details the official reimbursement procedure.

제 소개를 하겠습니다. 저는 Jade Larkin이고 이곳 JAC recruitment의 회계팀을 맡고 있습니다. 잠시 후에 출장 비용을 환불 받을 수 있는 방법에 대해 말씀 드리겠습니다. 하지만 먼저, 모두 워크숍 소책자를 받으셨나요? 그 책자의 첫 페이지를 봅시다. 거기에는 비용에 대한 가이드라인과 가격 한도를 볼 수 있습니다. 예를 들어, 영수증은 가격이 명시된 비용 한도를 초과하지 않는 한 식사나 대중교통 비용 보상에 필요하지 않습니다. 여행 일정을 잡을 때 이 정보를 일반적인 계획 가이드로 사용하시기 바랍니다. 두 번째 페이지에는 여행 경비를 기록하기 위한 양식이 포함되어 있습니다. 이제 공식 보상 절차를 자세히 설명하는 세 번째 페이지로 넘어가겠습니다.

어휘 in charge of ~을 맡아서, 담당해서 address 연설하다 reimburse 변상, 변제하다 receipt 영수증 public transportation 대중교통 exceed 넘다, 초과하다 state (문서에) 명시하다 record 기록하다

77 Who most likely is the speaker?
(A) A travel expert
(B) A personnel manager
(C) A recruitment officer
(D) A department head

화자는 누구인가?
(A) 여행 전문가
(B) 인사 부장
(C) 채용 모집관
(D) 부서 책임자

해설 〈기본 정보 파악 - 화자〉
화자의 정체는 담화의 초반에 언급된다. 화자가 앞부분에서 자기소개를 하며 JAC recruitment의 회계부를 담당하고 있다고 말하므로 정답은 (D)이다. 담화에서 언급된 회사명(JAC recruitment)을 듣고 화자의 정체를 채용 모집관인 (C)로 혼동하지 않도록 주의한다.

78 What is the talk mainly about?
(A) Employee benefits
(B) Paid vacations
(C) Business travel expenses
(D) Travel schedules

담화는 무엇에 대한 내용인가?
(A) 직원 수당
(B) 유급 휴가
(C) 출장 비용
(D) 여행 일정

해설 〈기본 정보 파악 - 주제〉
담화의 주제는 초반에 단서를 찾아야 하는데, 화자가 초반에 출장 비용의 환불 방법에 대해 말하겠다고 언급한다. 따라서 정답은 (C)이다.

79 What is on the first page of the booklet?
(A) A hiring contract
(B) An accounting report
(C) A set of rules
(D) A dress code

소책자의 첫 번째 페이지에는 무엇이 있는가?
(A) 채용 계약서
(B) 회계 보고서
(C) 일련의 규칙들
(D) 복장 규정

해설 〈구체적 정보 파악 - 특정 사항〉
화자가 키워드인 first page를 언급할 때 집중해야 한다. 책자의 첫 페이지(front page)에 비용에 대한 가이드라인과 가격 한도에 대한 내용이 있다고 설명하고 있으므로 정답은 (C)이다.

패러프레이징 a list of expense guidelines 비용에 대한 가이드라인
→ a set of rules 일련의 규칙들

Questions 80-82 refer to the following announcement. 미M

Good food costs less at Freshisland! We always offer you the best deals. (80) Today's specials include our food and beverage department; get three liters of fresh-squeezed orange juice for only ten dollars! Our meat department is featuring the best quality beef for just a dollar nineteen per 100 grams. Look for a host of yellow-marked items throughout the store. (81) And don't forget our delicatessen. Our soups and made-to-order sandwiches are perfect for a fresh, hot lunch on the go. (82) This week, our chicken sandwich and vegetable soup set is an amazing half off. Remember, you can always find the best deals here at Freshisland.

Freshisland에서는 좋은 음식의 가격이 저렴합니다! 우리는 항상 여러분께 최고의 가격을 제공해 드리고 있습니다. 오늘의 특가 상품은 음식과 음료 코너가 포함됩니다. 3리터의 신선한 착즙 오렌지 주스를 단 10달러에 가져 가세요! 정육 코너에서는 최고 품질의 쇠고기를 100그램당 19달러에 드리고 있습니다. 상점 여기저기에서 노란색 마크가 붙어 있는 여러 상품들을 찾아보세요. 그리고 저희 조리식품 판매점을 잊지 마세요. 스프와 주문 제작 샌드위치는 바쁜 시간에도 신선하고 따뜻한 점심 식사로 안성맞춤입니다. 이번 주에는 치킨 샌드위치와 채소 스프 세트가 놀랍게도 반값입니다. 기억하세요! 이곳 Freshisland에서는 항상 최고의 제품을 찾으실 수 있습니다.

어휘 squeeze 짜내다, 짜다 a host of 다수의 delicatessen 델리카트슨, 조리된 육류, 채소, 치즈, 샌드위치 등을 파는 가게 on the go 정신없이 바쁜

80 What does the speaker imply when he says, "Look for a host of yellow-marked items throughout the store"?
(A) Expiry dates are organized by color.
(B) Shoppers must go to the service desk.
(C) The store will be renovated soon.
(D) There are many bargain items.

화자가 "상점 여기저기에서 노란색 마크가 붙어 있는 여러 상품들을 찾아보세요"라고 말한 의미는 무엇인가?
(A) 유통 기한이 색상별로 정리되어 있다.
(B) 쇼핑객들은 서비스 데스크에 가야 한다.
(C) 상점은 곧 수리될 것이다.
(D) 할인 제품들이 많이 있다.

해설 〈구체적 정보 파악 - 화자 의도〉
언급된 문장의 주변 문맥을 통해 정답을 유추해야 한다. 언급된 문장 주변에서 화자는 여러 상품들의 저렴한 가격을 안내하고 있으므로 정답은 (D)이다.

81 Where can shoppers get lunch?

(A) In the deli department
(B) In the vegetables and fruit section
(C) In the food and beverage department
(D) In the meat and fish section

쇼핑객들은 점심을 어디에서 살 수 있는가?

(A) 조리 식품부
(B) 채소와 과일부
(C) 음식과 음료부
(D) 정육과 생선부

해설 〈구체적 정보 파악 – 특정 사항〉
키워드인 lunch가 언급되는 부분에 집중해야 한다. 화자는 조리식품 판매점의 스프와 샌드위치는 바쁜 점심시간에도 안성맞춤이라고 말하고 있으므로 정답은 (A)이다.

82 What item is fifty percent off?

(A) Beef
(B) Today's fish
(C) Lunch set
(D) Orange juice

50% 할인하는 제품은 무엇인가?

(A) 쇠고기
(B) 오늘의 생선
(C) 점심 세트
(D) 오렌지 주스

해설 〈구체적 정보 파악 – 특정 사항〉
화자가 키워드인 fifty percent off을 언급하는 부분에서 정답을 찾아야 한다. 담화의 후반에 점심식사로 적당한 치킨 샌드위치와 야채 스프 세트가 이번 주에는 반값이라고 안내하고 있으므로 정답은 (C)이다.

패러프레이징 half off 반값 → fifty percent off 50% 할인

Questions 83-85 refer to the following telephone message. 호M

Hello, Ms. Blair. This is Will Mackenzie. 84 I've almost got your tax return ready; it looks like you'll be getting a healthy refund this year. Congratulations! 83 I need a few more things though, to complete your file. For the work you completed at your apartment, we'll deduct Internet fees, phone bills, and even a portion of your rent from your taxes. If you could scan and send me copies of those three bills today, that would be very helpful. 85 I also need you to sign a couple of documents. I'll be in Liverpool on Monday from 10 A.M. to 6 P.M., so I could either stop by your place or we could meet at a coffee shop. You can reach me on my mobile at 805-555-0307 and let me know which you'd prefer.

안녕하세요, Blair 씨. Will Mackenzie입니다. 당신의 소득 신고서 준비가 거의 끝났습니다. 당신은 올해 환급을 많이 받게 될 것 같습니다. 축하 드려요! 다만 이 일을 완성하는 데 몇 가지가 더 필요합니다. 당신의 자택에서 끝낸 작업에 대해서는 인터넷 요금, 전화 요금 그리고 심지어 임대료 일부분을 세금에서 공제할 것입니다. 오늘 이 세 가지 영수증의 사본을 스캔한 후 저에게 보내주실 수 있다면 아주 유용할 것입니다. 또한 서류 두어 개에 당신의 서명이 필요합니다. 제가 월요일 오전 10시부터 오후 6시까지는 Liverpool에 있을 것이므로 제가 댁에 들르거나 아니면 커피숍에서 만날 수도 있습니다. 제 휴대폰 805-555-0307로 연락해 주셔서 어떤 것을 더 선호하는지 알려 주세요.

어휘 tax return 소득 신고서 healthy (양이) 많은 deduct 공제하다, 제하다 a portion of 약간의 stop by 잠시 들르다

83 Why has the speaker made the call?

(A) To arrange an interview
(B) To find out when taxes are due
(C) To share work assignment
(D) To obtain more information

화자가 전화한 이유는 무엇인가?

(A) 면접을 잡기 위해
(B) 세금 납부 기한을 알아보기 위해
(C) 업무를 공유하기 위해
(D) 더 많은 정보를 얻기 위해

해설 〈기본 정보 파악 – 목적〉
담화의 초반에 환급을 많이 받게 될 거라고 말하며 이를 위해 몇 가지가 더 필요하다고 했으므로 정답은 (D)이다.

84 Who most likely is the speaker?

(A) An accountant
(B) A customer service representative
(C) A secretary
(D) A store clerk

화자는 누구인가?

(A) 회계사
(B) 고객 서비스 담당자
(C) 비서
(D) 가게 점원

해설 〈기본 정보 파악 – 화자〉
화자의 정체는 담화의 초반에 제시된다. 초반에 청자의 소득 신고서 준비가 모두 끝나 간다고 말하고 있으므로 화자는 소득 신고와 관련된 일을 하는 사람임을 알 수 있다. 따라서 정답은 (A)이다.

85 What does the speaker let the listener know?

(A) His taxes are completed.
(B) He lives in Liverpool.
(C) He needs her signature.
(D) He owns a coffee shop.

화자는 청자에게 무엇을 알려주는가?

(A) 그의 세금 납부가 완료되었다.
(B) 그는 Liverpool에 산다.
(C) 그는 여자의 서명이 필요하다.
(D) 그는 커피숍을 소유하고 있다.

해설 〈구체적 정보 파악 – 특정 사항〉
특정한 키워드가 주어지지 않았으므로 선택지 내용이 언급될 때마다 집중해야 한다. 화자가 담화의 후반에 청자의 서명이 필요하다고 말하고 있으므로 (C)가 가장 적절한 답이다.

Questions 86-88 refer to the following talk. 영W

This year marks the 10th anniversary for us, and the celebration banquet begins in three hours. ⓼⓺ We have a lot of preparation to do, so we need all hands on deck. First, we don't have enough seats in the hall to accommodate the 300 guests we're expecting, but Ravensdale Publishing next door has agreed to loan us some chairs. 87 88 We've already got 150 in place, so we need to carry the other half from their building to ours. 88 Dave and Nathan, I'll assign that task to you. Amy and Daniel, could you please go to the fifth floor, get the printed programs, and bring them down here? While you're doing that, Charles and I will get started on arranging the place settings on the banquet tables. The caterers are expected to arrive at half past six.

올해는 우리의 10주년을 기념하는 해이며 축하 연회는 3시간 뒤에 시작합니다. 준비해야 할 일이 많은 관계로, 모두 힘을 합쳐 도와야 합니다. 우선 홀에는 우리가 예상한 300명의 손님을 수용해야 할 좌석이 충분하지 않습니다. 하지만 옆 건물의 Ravensdale 출판사에서 의자를 빌려주기로 했습니다. 홀에는 이미 150개가 있으니 그들의 건물에서 우리 건물로 나머지 반을 옮겨 와야 합니다. Dave와 Nathan 두 분에게 이 일을 맡길게요. Amy과 Daniel은 5층에서 인쇄된 프로그램들을 받아서 여기로 가지고 내려와 주시겠어요? 여러분이 그 일을 하는 동안 Charles와 저는 연회 테이블을 놓고 정리를 시작하겠습니다. 출장 요리는 6시 반에 도착할 예정입니다.

어휘 mark 표시하다, 기념하다 banquet 만찬, 연회 preparation 준비, 대비 all hands on deck 모두 힘을 합쳐서 accommodate 공간을 제공하다, 수용하다 loan 빌려주다 arrange 마련하다, 처리하다, 정리하다

86 What does the speaker mean when she says, "we need all hands on deck"?
(A) The listeners should applaud now.
(B) The event will be held on the ship.
(C) Everyone should work together.
(D) The listeners should submit the reports.

화자가 말한 "모두 힘을 합쳐 도와야 합니다"의 의미는 무엇인가?
(A) 청자들이 지금 박수를 쳐야 한다.
(B) 행사가 선상에서 진행될 것이다.
(C) 모두 함께 일해야 한다.
(D) 화자들이 보고서를 제출해야 한다.

해설 〈구체적 정보 파악 – 화자 의도〉
문제에 언급된 문장의 앞뒤 문맥을 종합하여 화자의 의도를 파악해야 한다. 화자가 준비해야 할 일이 많다고 말 한 후 해당 문장을 언급하고 있으므로 정답은 (C)이다.

87 How many more chairs should the employees carry?
(A) 50
(B) 100
(C) 150
(D) 300

직원들은 얼마나 많은 의자를 추가로 옮겨야 하는가?
(A) 50
(B) 100
(C) 150
(D) 300

해설 〈구체적 정보 파악 – 특정 사항〉
화자가 의자의 숫자를 언급할 때 집중해야 한다. 홀에는 이미 150개가 있고 다른 건물에서 나머지 반을 옮겨 와야 한다고 말하고 있으므로 정답은 (C)이다.

88 According to the speaker, what task will Nathan take on?
(A) Moving the chairs
(B) Printing the programs
(C) Preparing the tables
(D) Greeting the guests

화자에 의하면, Nathan은 어떤 업무를 받을 것인가?
(A) 의자를 옮기는 것
(B) 프로그램을 인쇄하는 것
(C) 테이블을 준비하는 것
(D) 손님을 맞이하는 것

해설 〈구체적 정보 파악 – 특정 사항〉
Nathan을 키워드로 잡고 앞뒤를 집중해서 들어야 한다. 의자를 옮겨야 한다고 말한 후, Dave와 Nathan에게 이 일을 맡기겠다고 말하고 있다. 따라서 정답은 (A)이다.

Questions 89-91 refer to the following advertisement. 미W

89 Are you seeking fast, effective relief from your seasonal allergies? Allegra has been used for years to treat allergy symptoms from sneezing and nasal congestion to itchy throat. A single dose of Allegra relieves symptoms for 24 hours. 90 It comes in both a capsule, and a child-friendly liquid in two different flavors: orange, and strawberry. It has never been easier to get your kids to take their medicine! 91 Allegra also produces none of the unpleasant side effects that many other allergy medications do, such as drowsiness, dry throat, or a cough. Get Allegra to help manage your health. It can make a huge difference in your life.

계절성 알레르기로부터 빠르고, 효과적인 해결책을 찾고 계시나요? Allegra는 재채기, 코막힘, 목의 가려움까지 알레르기 증상들을 치료하는 데 수년 동안 사용되어 왔습니다. Allegra의 1회 복용으로 24시간 동안 증상이 완화됩니다. 이 제품은 알약과 어린아이를 위한 오렌지와 딸기 두 가지 다른 맛의 물약으로 출시됩니다. 아이들에게 약을 먹게 하는 것이 이보다 더 쉬운 적이 없었습니다. Allegra는 또한 다른 많은 알레르기 약들처럼 졸음, 목이 건조해지거나 기침과 같은 불편한 부작용이 전혀 없습니다. 여러분의 건강 관리를 위해 Allegra를 구매하세요. 여러분의 일상을 매우 다르게 만들 수 있습니다.

어휘 seek 찾다, 구하다 seasonal 계절적인 symptom 증상, 징후 nasal congestion 코막힘 itchy 가려운, 가렵게 하는 dose 복용 relieves 없애주다, 덜어주다, 완화하다 produce 생산하다 unpleasant 불쾌한, 불편한 side effect 부작용 drowsiness 졸음 cough 기침하다

89 What is Allegra's intended use?
(A) To treat back pain
(B) To stop coughing
(C) To ease allergy symptoms
(D) To help with sleeping problems

Allegra의 용도는 무엇인가?
(A) 요통을 치료하는 것
(B) 기침을 멈추게 하는 것
(C) 알레르기 증상을 완화시키는 것
(D) 수면 문제에 도움을 주는 것

해설 〈구체적 정보 파악 – 특정 사항〉
키워드인 Allegra가 언급되는 부분에 집중해야 한다. 광고의 첫 부분에서 알레르기의 효과적인 해결책으로 Allegra를 추천하고 있으므로 정답은 (C)이다.

90 What is true of the medication?

(A) It is available in two flavors.
(B) It is not for children.
(C) It only comes in capsules.
(D) It has been discontinued.

약품에 대한 설명으로 옳은 것은 무엇인가?
(A) 두 가지 맛으로 이용 가능하다.
(B) 아이들을 위한 것은 아니다.
(C) 알약으로만 나온다.
(D) 생산이 중단되었다.

해설 〈구체적 정보 파악 – 특정 사항〉
문제에서 특정한 키워드가 주어지지 않았으므로 선택지의 내용이 언급될 때마다 집중해야 한다. 담화의 중반에 제품은 알약과 어린 아이를 위한 두 가지 다른 맛의 물약으로 출시된다고 말하고 있으므로 (A)가 가장 적절한 답이다.

91 What does the speaker say about Allegra?

(A) It will be available soon.
(B) It causes no side effects.
(C) It is good for long-term use.
(D) It should be taken three times a day.

화자는 Allegra에 대해 무엇이라고 말하는가?
(A) 곧 이용 가능할 것이다.
(B) 부작용을 일으키지 않는다.
(C) 장기 복용에 좋다.
(D) 하루에 세 번 복용해야 한다.

해설 〈구체적 정보 파악 – 특정 사항〉
담화의 후반에 Allegra는 부작용이 전혀 없다고 말하고 있다. 따라서 정답은 (B)이다.

Questions 92-94 refer to the following talk. (영W)

92 Congratulations on joining us at Telpod Network. We're glad to have you all in our team. 93 The first thing you should know is that due to the sensitivity of our clients' information, we have very strict safety measures in place. All of you will be expected to show your employee badge every time you enter or exit the premises. This rule applies at all times, for every employee. 94 If for some reason you don't have your badge and need to come in or leave, you should get help from the guards. They will verify your identity and sign you in or out. At the end of this orientation session you'll each be issued your own badge. Keep the badge in a very safe place when it is not being worn as you will need to pay a fee of $100 to replace your badge if it somehow becomes lost.

Telpod 네트워크에 합류하신 것을 환영합니다. 여러분을 우리 팀에 모실 수 있어서 기쁩니다. 여러분이 알아야 할 첫 번째는 고객 정보의 민감성 때문에 우리는 아주 엄격한 안전 수칙을 가지고 있다는 것입니다. 여러분 모두는 건물을 들어오고 나갈 때마다 직원 배지를 보여 달라는 요청을 받을 것입니다. 이 규칙은 항상, 모든 직원에게 적용됩니다. 어떤 이유로든 배지를 소지하고 있지 않은 상태로 들어오거나 나가야 할 필요가 있을 때는 경비 요원의 도움을 받아야 합니다. 그들이 여러분의 신분을 확인하고, 여러분의 출입을 기록할 겁니다. 이 오리엔테이션의 마지막에, 여러분은 각자 배지를 발급받을 것입니다. 배지를 착용하지 않을 경우에는 아주 안전한 장소에 보관해 주십시오. 만약 배지를 분실할 경우 재발급을 위해 100달러를 지불해야 합니다.

어휘 sensitivity 세심함, 민감함 strict 엄격한, 엄한 safety measures 안전장치, 안전 대책 in place 가동 중인 premises 부지, 구내 verify 확인하다, 입증하다 replace 대신하다, 대체하다 generous 후한

92 Who most likely are the listeners?

(A) Security guards
(B) New employees
(C) Department heads
(D) Visitors

청중들은 누구일 것 같은가?
(A) 보안 경비 요원들
(B) 신입 직원들
(C) 부서장들
(D) 방문객들

해설 〈기본 정보 파악 – 청자〉
청자들의 정체에 대한 단서는 담화의 앞부분에 언급되는 경우가 많다. 담화의 처음에 회사에 합류한 것을 축하하며, 함께 일하게 되어 기쁘다고 말하고 있다. 따라서 정답은 (B)이다.

93 What aspect of the firm does the speaker emphasize?

(A) Its strong security
(B) Its generous pay
(C) Its friendly managers
(D) Its talented workers

화자는 회사의 어떤 면을 강조하는가?
(A) 강력한 보안 정책
(B) 후한 임금
(C) 친절한 관리자들
(D) 재능 있는 직원들

해설 〈구체적 정보 파악 – 특정 사항〉
화자가 신입 직원들에게 강조하는 내용에 집중해야 한다. 담화 초반에 청자들이 알아야 할 첫 번째로 회사의 엄격한 안전 수칙을 언급하고 있다. 따라서 정답은 (A)이다.

패러프레이징 strict safety measures 엄격한 안전 수칙
→ strong security 강력한 보안

94 What should listeners do if they temporarily misplace their badge?

(A) Call a guard
(B) Pay a fine
(C) Use a main entrance
(D) Request a receipt

화자들이 일시적으로 배지가 없을 경우, 어떻게 해야 하는가?
(A) 경비 요원을 부른다.
(B) 벌금을 낸다.
(C) 정문을 이용한다.
(D) 영수증을 요청한다.

해설 〈구체적 정보 파악 – 특정 사항〉
temporarily misplace their badge를 키워드로 잡고 앞뒤를 집중해서 들어야 한다. 담화 중반에 어떤 이유로든 배지를 소지하고 있지 않은 상태로 들어오거나 나가야 할 필요가 있을 때는 경비 요원의 도움을 받아야 한다고 설명하고 있다. 따라서 정답은 (A)이다. 담화 후반에 배지를 잃어버리면 재발급 비용이 든다고 언급한다. 재발급 비용과 벌금 지불을 혼동하지 않도록 주의해야 한다.

Questions 95-97 refer to the following advertisement and schedule. 영M

Hotel Montana – Event Bookings

Event Date(s)	Venue
September 1-4	The Euros Room
September 2-4	The Zepiros Room
September 5&6	The Notos Room
September 6	The Boreas Room

I have one last thing to tell you. We are planning a seminar by Chloe Adams, one of the most successful marketing entrepreneurs in our country. ⑮ When she was a university student, she started her first business and turned it into a multi-million-dollar company within a few short years. Now, Chloe devotes her time to helping others follow in her footsteps. ⑯ Her two-day seminar will show you how to analyze markets, identify opportunities, and think strategically so that you too can establish and develop a successful business. ⑰ Chloe will be leading her two-day seminar here in Zurich the first weekend in September at the Hotel Montana. So please visit her Web site at chloeadamsevent.com and register today.

호텔 몬타나 – 이벤트 예약

이벤트 날짜	장소
9월 1일-4일	Euros 룸
9월 2일-4일	Zepiros 룸
9월 5일&6일	Notos 룸
9월 6일	Boreas 룸

마지막으로 알려드릴 사항이 있습니다. 우리는 우리 나라에서 가장 성공적인 마케팅 기업가 중 한 명인 Chloe Adams의 세미나를 계획하고 있습니다. 그녀는 대학생일 때, 첫 번째 사업을 시작했고 몇 년 안에 수백만 달러짜리 회사로 바꾸어 놓았습니다. 이제, Chloe는 다른 사람들이 자신의 발자취를 따르도록 돕는 데 시간을 바치고 있습니다. 그녀는 이틀 간 열리는 이번 세미나에서 여러분도 성공적인 비즈니스를 구축하고 개발할 수 있도록 시장을 분석하고 기회를 식별하며 전략적으로 생각하는 방법에 대해 설명할 것입니다. Chloe는 9월 첫 주말에 이곳 Zurich의 Hotel Montana에서 이틀간 세미나를 열 것입니다. 그녀의 웹 사이트인 chloeadamsevent.com을 방문하여 지금 바로 등록하시기 바랍니다.

어휘 entrepreneurs 기업가 devote (시간, 돈, 노력) 바치다 footstep 발자국 identify (신원 등을) 확인하다, 알아보다 strategically 전략적으로 establish 설립하다, 수립하다

95 What did Chloe Adams do when she was a university student?
(A) She married an entrepreneur.
(B) She studied abroad.
(C) She created a software program.
(D) She founded a company.

Chloe Adams가 대학생일 때 무엇을 했나?
(A) 그녀는 기업가와 결혼했다.
(B) 그녀는 해외에서 공부했다.
(C) 그녀는 소프트웨어 프로그램을 만들었다.
(D) 그녀는 회사를 설립했다.

해설 〈구체적 정보 파악 – 특정 사항〉
문제의 키워드인 university student 가 들리는 주변에 집중한다. 담화 초반에 그녀가 대학생일 때, 첫 번째 사업을 시작했다고 소개하고 있으므로 정답은 (D)이다.

96 What skill does Chloe Adams teach at her seminar?
(A) Software development
(B) Strategic thinking
(C) Decision making
(D) Risk analysis

Chloe Adams가 세미나에서 가르칠 기술은 무엇인가?
(A) 소프트웨어 개발
(B) 전략적 사고
(C) 의사 결정
(D) 위험 분석

해설 〈구체적 정보 파악 – 특정 사항〉
담화 중반에 이번 세미나에서 성공적인 비즈니스의 구축과 개발, 시장 분석, 기회를 식별하며 전략적으로 생각하는 방법에 대해 설명할 것이라고 안내하고 있다. 따라서 정답은 (B)이다.

97 Look at the graphic. In which venue will Chloe Adams' seminar probably be held?
(A) The Euros Room
(B) The Zepiros Room
(C) The Notos Room
(D) The Boreas Room

시각 자료를 보시오. Chloe Adams의 세미나는 어느 장소에서 열릴 것인가?
(A) 유로 룸
(B) 제피러스 룸
(C) 노토스 룸
(D) 보리아스 룸

해설 〈구체적 정보 파악 – 시각 정보 연계〉
예약 리스트의 장소가 선택지로 제시되어 있으므로 담화에서는 각 장소에 예약된 이벤트 날짜를 단서로 언급될 것을 예측하고 들어야 한다. 담화 후반에 9월 첫 주말에 이틀간 세미나를 열 것이라고 언급하고 있으므로 5일과 6일 이틀에 걸쳐 예약이 잡힌 (C)가 정답이다.

Questions 98-100 refer to the following announcement and map. 호M

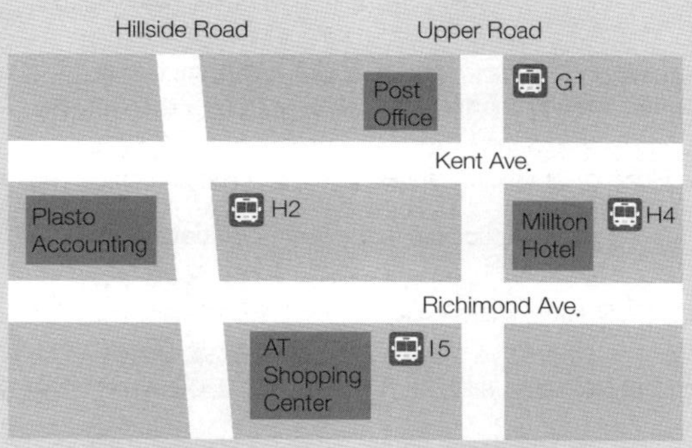

⑱ Employees of Plasto Accounting who make use of the Number 46 bus to come to work will no longer be able to get off the bus at the bus stop across from the office. ⑲ We have been informed that beginning Wednesday next week, the bus will be stopping at the newly renovated Millton Hotel instead. We have decided to provide a shuttle bus from the hotel once in the morning and once in the evening. ⑳ The departure times will be decided based on a survey of employees to be conducted on Thursday afternoon.

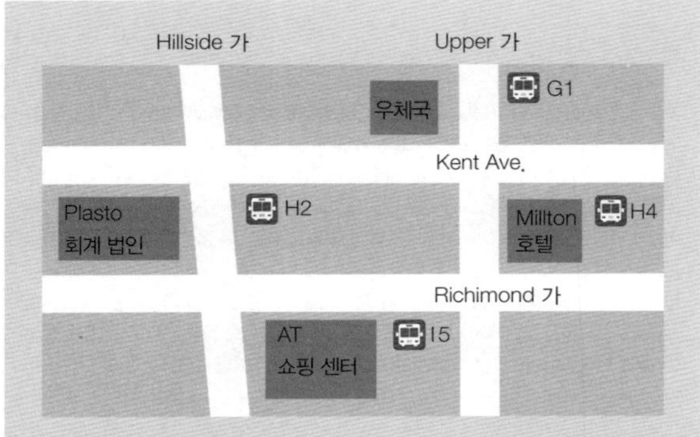

46번 버스를 이용하여 출근하는 Plasto 회계 사무실의 직원들은 더 이상 사무실 반대편의 버스 정류장에서 내릴 수 없게 되었습니다. 버스가 다음 주 수요일부터 최근 보수 공사가 끝난 Millton 호텔에서 정차한다는 것을 알려 왔습니다. 우리는 호텔에서 회사까지 아침과 저녁에 한 번씩 셔틀 버스를 제공하기로 결정했습니다. 출발 시간은 목요일 오후에 진행되는 직원 설문 조사를 바탕으로 결정될 예정입니다.

어휘 no longer 더 이상 ~ 아닌 newly 최근에, 새로 respectively 각각 departure 출발, 떠남 base on ~에 근거를 두다, 기초를 두다 survey 설문 조사 conduct (특정 활동을) 하다, 지휘하다 hand out 나누어 주다 renew 갱신하다

98 Look at the graphic. Which bus stop will no longer be available?
(A) G1
(B) H2
(C) H4
(D) I5
시각 자료를 보시오. 어떤 버스 정류장이 더 이상 이용할 수 없게 되는가?
(A) G1
(B) H2
(C) H4
(D) I5

해설 〈구체적 정보 파악 – 시각 정보 연계〉
대화를 듣기 전에 문제와 시각 자료를 보고 단서를 예측할 수 있어야 하는데, 지도 관련 문제이므로 위치 묘사를 통해 단서가 제시될 가능성이 높다. 담화 초반에 화자가 Plasto 회계 법인 직원들에게 더 이상 사무실 반대편의 버스 정류장을 이용할 수 없다고 안내하고 있으므로 정답은 Plasto Accounting의 반대편 정류장임을 알 수 있다. 따라서 정답은 (B)이다.

99 When is the change scheduled to occur?
(A) On Tuesday
(B) On Wednesday
(C) On Thursday
(D) On Friday
일정 변경은 언제 일어나는가?
(A) 화요일
(B) 수요일
(C) 목요일
(D) 금요일

해설 〈구체적 정보 파악 – 특정 사항〉
담화의 중반에 버스가 다음 주 수요일부터 다른 곳에 정차한다고 안내하고 있으므로 정답은 (B)이다.

100 What are employees asked to do?
(A) Hand out some forms
(B) Renew their contracts
(C) Attend a conference
(D) Give their opinions
직원들은 무엇을 하라고 요청받는가?
(A) 양식들을 나누어 주는 것
(B) 계약을 갱신하는 것
(C) 회의에 참석하는 것
(D) 의견을 주는 것

해설 〈구체적 정보 파악 – 요청 관련〉
담화의 후반에 셔틀 버스의 출발 시간을 결정하는 직원 설문 조사가 진행될 것임을 알리고 있다. 따라서 직원들은 설문 조사 참여 요청을 받고 있는 것이므로 정답은 (D)이다.

101 해석 회사 계약서를 이메일에 첨부할 때 보호하는 암호로 이 서류들의 보안을 유지하세요.
해설 keep 동사의 목적격보어 자리로서 목적어 documents를 보충하는 형용사 (A)가 정답이다.
어휘 attach A to B A를 B에 첨부하다 secure 안전한 securely 안전하게

102 해석 나라 전역에서 컴퓨터 판매 증가의 원인은 완전히 분명하지는 않다.
해설 '완전히 확실하지는 않다'는 문맥으로 clear를 수식하는 적절한 부사인 (B)가 정답이다.
어휘 throughout ~에 걸쳐서 smoothly 순조롭게 entirely 완전히 justly 정당하게 tightly 단단히

103 해석 Sherman 씨가 회사 연회를 기획하고 있으므로 참석할 수 있으면 그에게 알려 주세요.
해설 let 동사의 목적어 자리이고 Mr. Sherman을 지칭하고 있으므로 (C) him이 정답이다.
어휘 organize 기획하다 banquet 연회

104 해석 새로운 카펫을 깔기 전에 그 아래 표면이 완전히 평평한지 확인하세요.
해설 빈칸은 be동사의 보어 자리로 부사 completely의 수식을 받고 있으므로 형용사 (A)가 정답이다.
어휘 lay a carpet 카펫을 깔다 surface 표면 beneath ~의 바로 아래 flat 평평한 flatly 단호하게 flatten ~을 납작하게 하다

105 해석 소비자 상담원은 음성 메시지를 남기는 전화한 사람들에게 2시간 이내에 응답할 것으로 예상됩니다.
해설 명사 callers와 동사 leave 사이의 빈칸이므로 주어와 접속사 역할을 할 수 있는 주격 관계대명사 (A)가 정답이다.
어휘 service representative 상담원 respond 응답하다

106 해석 Oldbrook 마을의 연간 패션 박람회는 주민들이 즐기는 동안에 현재 트렌드를 알 수 있게 도와준다.
해설 빈칸은 부사 자리로서 주절의 'learn about current trends'와 'having fun'이 같이 일어나는 일이므로 '또한'이라는 의미의 (D)가 정답이다.
어휘 formerly 이전에 lastly 마지막으로 also 또한

107 해석 Copper 주식회사에서는 경력상의 승진에 대한 많은 기회가 있다.
해설 빈칸은 opportunities를 수식하는 수량 형용사이므로 복수 명사와 사용할 수 있는 (D)가 정답이다. plenty는 of와 함께 쓰이며 each와 every는 단수 명사와 사용해야 한다.
어휘 advancement 승진

108 해석 Norman Printing Services는 경쟁업체보다 더 높은 품질의 종이를 사용한다.

해설 빈칸 앞에 비교급(higher)이 있으므로 (D)가 정답이다.

어휘 competitor 경쟁업체

109 해석 좋지 않은 날씨 때문에 페인트 칠하는 사람들은 건물의 북쪽면을 끝내지 못했다.

해설 be finished with는 '~을 끝내다'라는 뜻으로 쓰이므로 정답은 (A)이다.

어휘 unfavorable 좋지 않은

110 해석 환자들은 의료 기록이 새로운 보험 회사로 전달되기 전에 승인 양식에 서명해야만 합니다.

해설 빈칸 이하에 동사 can이 있으므로 접속사가 필요한 문장으로 문맥상 (B)가 정답이다. instead와 rather는 부사이다.

어휘 authorization 승인 medical record 의료 기록 insurance provider 보험 회사 except ~은 제외하고 rather 다소

111 해석 보안상의 이유로 Green Bay 과학 기술 연구소 방문객들은 항상 다른 사람과 함께 있어야 한다.

해설 선택지는 be동사 뒤의 과거 분사 자리이므로 수동태 문장의 동사 어휘를 판단하는 문제인 것을 알 수 있다. 주어인 visitors와 문맥이 맞는 동사는 (D) escorted이다. display와 estimate는 visitor를 목적어로 사용하기에 문맥이 어색하며, confer는 with와 함께 사용하는 자동사이므로 수동태의 분사 자리에 적합하지 않다.

어휘 security 보안 visitor 방문객 at all times 항상 estimate 견적을 내다 confer 상담하다

112 해석 실험실 안내 책자는 가능한 한 안전하게 재료를 다루는 절차를 자세하게 설명하고 있다.

해설 as ~ as 동등 비교 표현으로 빈칸에는 형용사나 부사 원급만 가능하다. 빈칸은 handling materials를 수식하는 부사가 적절하므로 정답은 (B)이다.

어휘 detail 자세하게 설명하다 procedure 절차

113 해석 Bukowski 씨가 없을 때는 교대 근무 책임자가 식당을 책임지고 있습니다.

해설 in one's absence는 '~의 부재 시에'라는 뜻으로 쓰이므로 (B)가 정답이다.

어휘 shift 교대 근무 in charge of ~을 책임지는, 담당하는

114 해석 전화상으로 즉각적인 가격 견적을 받으시려면 Perrybridge 사무 가구 담당자에게 전화하세요.

해설 Call로 시작하는 명령문으로 접속사가 없으므로 준동사를 사용하여 목적을 뜻하는 부사적 용법의 to부정사가 적합하므로 정답은 (A)이다.

어휘 immediate 즉시의 cost estimate 가격 견적

115 해석 이메일이나 전화로 당신의 리모델링 요구에 대해 자세하게 이야기하게 되어 기쁩니다.

해설 be delighted to는 '~해서 기쁘다'라는 뜻으로 쓰이므로 (B)가 정답이다.

어휘 in detail 자세하게 via ~을 통해서

116 해석 Kerton 시 의회는 정기적으로 프로젝트 제안을 받으니 지원자들은 결정을 몇 개월 동안 기다리는 것을 예상해야 한다.

해설 빈칸은 동사 receives를 수식하는 부사 자리로 현재 시제가 사용되었고 '정기적으로 받는다'는 뜻이 적절하므로 (C)가 정답이다. (B) recently는 단순 현재 시제와 사용하지 않는 부사이다.

어휘 expect 예상하다 recently 최근에 regularly 늘, 항상 similarly 유사하게

117 해석 Jung's Burger가 새로운 프랜차이즈를 개점했을 때, 처음 100명의 고객들은 무료 음료를 받았다.

해설 빈칸은 부사절 접속사 자리이며 문맥상 시간을 나타내는 (B)가 정답이다. Now와 After all은 부사이고 As if는 가정법에 주로 사용된다.

어휘 after all 결국

118 해석 소비자 서비스 부서와의 모든 편지에 제품 일련번호를 포함시키세요.

해설 빈칸은 any 뒤의 명사 자리이고 편지를 뜻하는 것이므로 (B)가 정답이다.

어휘 serial number 일련번호 correspond 일치하다, 상응하다 correspondingly 부응하여, 서로 맞게 correspondence 서신, 편지 correspondent 통신원, 특파원

119 해석 Fisher & Phillips 보험 회사는 Barcelona의 주거와 상업 건물 소유주들에게 보험을 제공한다.

해설 등위접속사 and로 commercial과 연결되는 표현이므로 (B)가 적절하다.

어휘 coverage 보급 범위 property 부동산, 건물 habitual 습관적인 residential 주거지의 settled 안정적인

120 해석 Heike 건설 회사는 적어도 2년의 관련 경험이 있는 중장비 운영자를 구하고 있다.

해설 빈칸 이전 불가산명사 equipment 앞에 관사 a가 있으므로 빈칸은 가산명사 단수 자리임을 알 수 있으므로 정답은 (C)이다.

어휘 at least 적어도 related 관련된 operational 운영의 operator 운영자

121 해석 파란색 상표는 엑스트라 버진 올리브 오일을 포함하고 있다는 것을 나타내는 반면, 녹색 상표는 발사믹 식초를 포함하고 있다는 것을 나타낸다.

해설 빈칸은 앞뒤의 절을 연결하는 부사절 접속사 자리로서 문맥상 대조의 뜻을 이루는 (A)가 정답이다.

어휘 indicate 나타내다 contain 포함하다 whereas ~하는 반면에

122 해석 Vogel 마라톤이 취소된다면, 등록비를 먼저 지불한 사람들은 전액 환불받을 것이다.

해설 빈칸 뒤 주격 관계대명사 who의 선행사로 불특정 다수를 지칭할 수 있는 대명사 (A)가 정답이다.

어휘 prepay 먼저 지불하다 registration fee 등록 수수료 full refund 전액 환불

123 해석 Orangedale 출판사의 본부장은 절차가 정확하게 실행되고 있는지 확인하기 위해서 정기적으로 직원들과 만나고 있다.

해설 빈칸은 that절의 동사 자리로 perform 동사가 목적어 없이 사용되고 있으므로 수동태인 (C)와 (D) 중에서 주절의 동사 meets와 시제가 맞아야 하므로 (D)가 정답이다.

어휘 chief of staff 본부장 ensure that ~를 보장하다 procedure 절차 correctly 정확하게, 제대로

124 해석 기술자들은 건물의 정전을 야기한 것이 정확히 무엇인지 알아내기 위해 노력하고 있다.

해설 동사 determine의 목적어 자리로 뒤에 동사 caused가 있는 것으로 접속사와 명사의 역할도 같이 할 수 있는 명사절을 이끄는 의문사 (A)가 정답이다.

어휘 determine 알아내다 power failure 정전

125 해석 새로운 무선 스피커의 인기 때문에 생산량은 내년에 5배로 늘어날 것이다.

해설 빈칸은 명사구 앞의 전치사 자리로 의미상 주절의 원인이 되고 있으므로 정답은 (A)이다

어휘 popularity 인기 fivefold 5배의 as a result of ~의 결과로 on behalf of ~ 대신에 moreover 더욱이 assuming that ~을 가정하여

126 해석 지역 공무원들의 지지를 받았음에도 불구하고 Highbrook 도서관 개조 프로젝트는 많은 차질을 겪었다.

해설 빈칸 뒤에 동명사구가 있으므로 정답은 전치사 (D)이다.

어휘 official 공무원 numerous 많은, 다양한 setback 저지, 차질 conversely 역으로, 거꾸로 otherwise 달리, 그렇지 않으면

127 해석 Blakeley 건축가 회사는 커뮤니티 센터가 최대한의 이용성을 위해서 1층 건물로 남아 있어야 한다고 언급했다.

해설 that절 안의 동사 자리이므로 정답은 (B)이다.

어휘 note 주목하다, 언급하다 one-story 1층의

128 해석 Nelson Groth 학원은 학생들의 수요에 맞는 일련의 전문적인 서비스를 제공한다.

해설 an array of는 '일련의'라는 뜻으로 쓰이므로 (A)가 정답이다.

어휘 entity 독립체

129 해석 올해 2분기와 3분기에 예상하지 못한 일이 일어나서 이익이 원래 예상과 상당히 빗나갔다.

해설 events를 수식하는 형용사로 원래 예상과 다르다는 문맥과 어울리는 (D)가 정답이다.

어휘 cause 야기하다 differ from ~과 다르다 significantly 상당히 projection 예상 marginal 미비한, 중요하지 않은 unforeseen 예

상하지 못한

130 **해석** Hendley 씨는 비상시에 가장 신임하는 직원들에게 권한을 이임했다.

해설 delegate authority to는 '~에게 위임하다'라는 뜻으로 정답은 (C)이다.

어휘 trusted 신임 받는 align ~을 조정하다, 나란히 하다 exercise 실행하다, 행사하다 nominate 임명하다

PART 6

P197

[131-134]

Household Superstore에서 우리는 최고 브랜드의 전자제품을 판매합니다. 우리는 이 지역에서 유일하게 모든 전자제품의 교체 부품이 있는 가게입니다. 부품은 전화번호 032-555-2938이나 온라인으로 (131) 주문할 수 있습니다. 등록은 온라인 주문 시에 반드시 (132) 필요한 것은 아닙니다. 그러나 다음 번 구매하실 때 절차를 조금 더 빠르게 할 것입니다. (133) 주문 배송을 신속히 하기 위하여 부품은 각각 다른 공급업자에게서 직접 배송됩니다. 결과적으로, 당신의 주문은 몇 개의 배송으로 도착할 수도 있습니다. (134) 이것이 배송비를 오르게 할 것입니다.

어휘 replacement part 교체 부품 registration 등록

131 **해설** 동사 자리로 빈칸 뒤로 목적어가 없으므로 수동형이 와야 하고 앞으로의 가능성을 이야기하는 것이므로 (B)가 정답이다.

132 **해설** 뒤 문장에서 However, it will make the process faster the next time you shop with us로 연결되고 있으므로 문맥상 반드시 필수는 아니라는 의미가 될 수 있는 (C)가 정답이다.

어휘 advisable 권장할 만한 renewable 갱신할 수 있는

133 (A) **주문 배송을 신속히 하기 위하여 부품은 각각 다른 공급업자에게서 직접 배송됩니다.**
(B) 회사는 현재 그 직책 지원자들을 인터뷰하고 있습니다.
(C) 행사 준비를 위해 필요한 모든 부품을 제공합니다.
(D) 비행기에서 허락된다면 안내 데스크에 문의하세요.

해설 뒤 문장에서 결과적으로 여러 차례 배송될 것(in several shipments)이라고 언급하고 있으므로, 여러 배송업체(different suppliers)의 내용이 나오는 (A)가 정답이다.

어휘 expedite 신속히 하다 inquire 문의하다

134 **해설** 앞 문장의 상황을 지칭하는 것이므로 (D)가 정답이다.

[135-138]

수신: Karen Karl
발신: Liz Steinhauer
제목: 특별 프로젝트
날짜: 4월 2일

안녕하세요, Karl 씨.

저에게는 완수해야 할 특별 프로젝트 목록이 있어요. 그래서 당신에게 안내 책자 목록을 (135) 업데이트하는 작업을 맡기고 싶어요. 이 책자는 정기적으로 수정되고 (136) 최신 판만이 도서관 고객들이 이용할 수 있기 때문에 이 일은 앞으로 계속해야 할 업무가 될 거예요.

(137) 도서관 입구와 대출 데스크에 있는 안내 진열대를 확인하세요. 올해 2월 이전 날짜인 것은 모두 수정된 자료로 교체되어야 하고, 이 자료는 도서관 내부 웹페이지에서 인쇄할 수 있어요. 많은 책자가 날짜가 이미 지났기 때문에 (138) 신속히 이 일을 마무리해주기 바랍니다.

고마워요.

Liz Steinhauer
수석 사서

어휘 assign 할당하다 ongoing 지속적인 periodically 정기적으로 patron 고객, 후원자 be replaced with ~와 교체되다 internal 내부의 outdated 낡은 librarian 사서

135 **해설** 빈칸 뒤 문장에서 revised periodically라고 언급하였기 때문에 빈칸의 목적어인 our collection과 어울리는 것은 (C)이다.

136 **해설** 빈칸은 versions를 수식하는 형용사로서 앞 문장에서 revised periodically라고 언급하였으므로 이용 가능한 것은 현재의 것이므로 정답은 (B)이다.

어휘 initial 처음의 current 현재의 duplicate 복사의 draft 초안의

137 (A) 도서관 회원이 되어 주셔서 감사합니다.
(B) **도서관 입구와 대출 데스크에 있는 안내 진열대를 확인하세요.**
(C) 수리된 사무실은 일정대로 4월에 문을 열기로 되어 있습니다.
(D) 당신의 지지는 우리가 사무 제품을 개선할 수 있게 해 왔습니다.

해설 빈칸 뒤로 날짜가 지난 오래된 것들은 교체해야 한다고 했으므로 이를 확인해야 한다는 (B)가 정답이다.

어휘 entrance 입구 checkout desk 대출 데스크 be due to ~하기로 예정되다 enable 가능하게 하다

138 **해설** 동사 complete를 수식하는 부사 자리이므로 정답은 (A)이다.

어휘 promptly 즉시

[139-142]

Windom Pharmacy가 고객들의 처방전 주문을 더 쉽게 만듭니다.

Daniel Banaszek

Seattle(7월 12일) - Windom Pharmacy가 기술에 잘 적응하는 고객들을 위해 생활을 더 편리하게 만들려고 합니다. (139) 인기 있는 약국 체인점이 곧 처방전 주문을 모바일로 알리는 것을 제공할 것입니다. 고객들은 처방전이 준비되었을 (140) 때 문자 메시지를 받게 될 것입니다. 이전 공지 체계는 약국 직원이 시간이 낭비되는 전화를 해야 했습니다.

"이전 시스템은 정말 (141) 효율적이지 않았어요"라고 회장인 Jessica Windom이 언론 발표에서 말했습니다.

"사람들이 항상 시간에 딱 맞게 음성 메시지를 듣지는 않습니다. 문자 공지는 7월 15일에 시작할 거예요. (142) 하지만 전화를 더 좋아하는 고객들은 아직 선택권이 있어요"라고 Windom 씨가 덧붙였습니다.

어휘 pharmacy 약국, 제약업체 prescription 처방전 be about to 막 ~하려 하다 tech-savvy 기술에 잘 적응하는 pickup 물건 찾기 notification 공지 time-consuming 시간이 소요되는, 시간이 낭비되는 press release 언론 보도 in a timely manner 시기적절하게 note 언급하다, 덧붙이다

139 (A) 우리가 지금 꽤 바쁘지만 직원들이 그 일을 잘 할 수 있습니다.
(B) 친구들에게 이 서비스에 대해서 이야기했다는 것을 당신에게 알려 주기 위해서 이 편지를 씁니다.
(C) 이것들 중 하나는 새로운 여성용 비타민 보충제 제품을 만들고 있어요.
(D) **인기 있는 약국 체인점이 곧 처방전 주문을 모바일로 알리는 것을 제공할 것입니다.**

해설 빈칸 뒤 문장에 'to receive a text message'라는 내용이 있으므로 문자 서비스에 관련된 이야기가 언급된 (D)가 정답이다.

어휘 workload 작업량 alert 알림

140 **해설** 빈칸은 앞뒤 문장을 연결하는 부사절 접속사 자리로 문맥상 시간을 뜻하는 (C)가 정답이다.

141 **해설** 문자 서비스 이전의 서비스를 뜻하는 형용사이고 not과 함께 쓰여야 하므로 효율적이지 않았다는 문맥을 이어주는 (B)가 정답이다.

어휘 profitable 이익이 나는 clarifying 명백히 하는

142 **해설** 앞뒤의 내용이 반대로 이루어져 있으므로 (C)가 문맥상 적절하다.

어휘 therefore 그러므로 likewise 이처럼

수신: 모든 회원
발신: Vanessa Kwan
날짜: 8월 21일
제목: 좋은 소식

Durian 아트 센터의 Balmer 극장은 시즌 정기 이용자와 좋은 소식을 나누게 되어 기쁩니다. 중앙 건물의 별관 공사가 거의 마무리되었고 9월 20일에 개장할 준비가 될 것입니다.

지난 가을, Durian 아트 센터는 극장 건물에 스튜디오를 추가하기로 143 결정하여 이제 극장은 드라마 제작을 위한 배경을 만들 수 있습니다. 이 새로운 144 공간은 극장이 모든 관객들에게 현재의 행사를 확장할 수 있도록 합니다. 145 또한, 수업과 여름 캠프의 근거지가 될 것입니다. 146 우리는 여러분의 지지에 감사드리며 여러분에게 우리의 새로운 시설물을 보여드릴 기대에 차 있습니다.

Vanessa Kwan
예술 감독, Balmer 극장

어휘 be pleased to 기쁘게 ~하다 share A with B A를 B와 나누다 subscriber 정기 구독, 정기 이용자 annex 별관 auditorium 강당 set 배경

143 해설 빈칸은 동사 자리로 Last fall로부터 과거 시제임을 알 수 있으므로 정답은 (C)이다.

144 해설 앞 문장의 studio를 지칭하는 말로 공간이 넓어졌다는 의미가 되어야 하므로 (B)가 정답이다.

어휘 donor 기증자

145 해설 앞 문장에 더해지는 추가의 내용이므로 (C)가 정답이다.

어휘 in spite of ~에도 불구하고 on the contrary 반대로 additionally 추가로 nevertheless 그럼에도 불구하고

146 (A) 올해 무역 박람회에서 일어날 행사 목록을 첨부했습니다.
(B) 복잡한 시내에서 1시간 거리라서 이상적인 목적지가 될 것입니다.
(C) 웹 사이트에서 공석을 검토하고 더 필요한 정보가 있으면 제게 연락해 주세요.
(D) 우리는 여러분의 지지에 감사드리며 여러분에게 우리의 새로운 시설물을 보여드릴 기대에 차 있습니다.

해설 이메일의 주요 내용이 새로운 시설물을 알리는 것이므로 마지막 문장으로 (D)가 적절하다.

어휘 take place 일어나다 ideal 이상적인 destination 목적지

[147-148]

이것은 아래를 증명하고 있습니다.

147 148 Jennifer Lloyd는 5월 25일 Lamnan 직업 개발 센터에서 이루어진 "온라인 뉴스 보도의 문제: 정치와 경제 기사의 중립성"이라는 제목의 세 차례 연수를 마쳤습니다.

그녀의 연수 과정은 수업 참가자들에 의해 아주 우수함으로 평가되었습니다.

Mark Linksky, 연수 감독
Lamnan 직업 개발 센터

어휘 certify 증명하다 complete 마치다 entitle ~라고 제목을 달다 neutrality 중립성

147 Lloyd 씨는 5월 25일에 무엇을 했는가?
(A) 강의를 했다.
(B) 훈련을 받았다.
(C) 신문에 등장했다.
(D) 기술적인 문제를 보고했다.

해설 지문에서 'completed a series of three training sessions entitled "Issues of Online News Reporting: Neutrality in Economic and Political Stories" on May 25'라고 하였으므로 정답은 (B)이다.

어휘 deliver a lecture 강의를 하다 undergo training 훈련을 받다

148 Lloyd 씨는 누구인 것 같은가?
(A) 웹 디자이너
(B) 프로그램 개발자
(C) 개발 센터 감독
(D) 기자

해설 수업의 제목이 'Issues of Online News Reporting: Neutrality in Economic and Political Stories'인 것으로 Lloyd는 기자임을 알 수 있으므로 정답은 (D)이다.

[149-150]

Quentin Power Tools 주식회사
보증서 카드

Quentin Power Tools 주식회사는 지정된 기간 안에는 어떤 결점이 있는 제품이라도 무료로 수리해 드립니다. 이 보증은 제품의 원래 구매자에게 해당되며 구매일로부터 최대 3주까지 지속됩니다. 만약 수리가 불가능하다면 유사한 제품으로 교체해 드릴 수 있습니다.

이 보증서는 소비자 부주의나 사고 손상은 보상하지 않습니다. 또한 Quentin 직원 이외의 사람이 제품을 수리할 때 발생하는 부품 고장도 보상하지 않습니다.

150 수리나 교체로 물품을 보내실 때, 다시 배송 시에 우리에게 도움이 될 여러분의 이름, 주소, 전화번호를 반드시 포함시켜 주십시오. 물건을 사용할 때 생긴 문제를 설명하는 쪽지를 포함시켜 주시는 것을 추천 드립니다. (의무 사항은 아닙니다)

149 저희가 당신의 배송품을 받으면 저희가 응답할 때까지 영업일 기준으로 14일에서 21일 정도가 걸립니다.

제품 보증이나 수리 정보에 대해서 더 궁금한 질문이 있으시면 보증 정보 전화번호인 1-800-555-4455로 전화해 주십시오.

11월 10일 수정됨

어휘 power tool 전동 공구 at no cost 무료로 defective 결함이 있는 designated 지정된 extend to ~까지 미치다 up to 최대 ~까지 comparable 필적할 만한, 유사한 cover 보상하다 negligence 부주의 accidental 우연한, 사고의 attempt to ~을 시도하다 replacement 교체 enclose 포함시키다, 동봉하다 normally 보통

149 보증서에 언급된 정보는 무엇인가?
(A) 교체 부품을 제공하는 거래업자의 이름
(B) 배상하는 공구 목록
(C) 특정 수리 유형의 비용
(D) 수리를 끝내는 데 필요한 시간의 추정

해설 'Once we receive your shipment, it normally takes 14 to 21 business days until we respond'에서 (D)가 언급되었음을 알 수 있다.

어휘 dealer 거래업자 cover 포함하다, 지불하다 specific 특정한 estimation 추정

150 보증서에 따르면 수리 서비스 신청과 함께 반드시 포함시켜야 할 것은?
(A) 보증서 복사본
(B) 제품 사진
(C) 배송 주소
(D) 문제 설명 쪽지

해설 지문의 'you must include your name, street address and phone number for us to assist in returning shipment'에서 (C)가 정답임을 알 수 있다. 문제를 설명하는 쪽지는 의무 사항은 아니라고 했으므로 (D)는 오답이다.

[151-153]

지역 업체가 인정받다

Walter Vine

Milwaukee — 12월 호에서, 〈Adventure Wilderness Magazine〉은 152-B Milwaukee에 근거지를 둔 Quest Out 여행사를 다가올 해에 최고 10개의 여행사 중에서 7위로 평가했습니다.

〈Adventure Wilderness Magazine〉에 따르면 151 Quest Out은 여행 참가자들에게 보람 있고 기억에 남을 만한 경험을 주는 데 많은 기여를 해서 순위에 이름을 올렸습니다. 152-C 카누와 하이킹부터 크로스컨트리 스키, 새 관찰, 고래 관찰, 개 썰매 등의 경험들이 있습니다. Quest Out은 즐거움이 가득한 야외 모험의 여러 가지 유형들을 개발해 왔습니다.

152-D Quest Out의 소유주인 Campbell Hargrove는 회사가 순위에 오른 것을 알고 기뻐했습니다. 회사가 어제 발표한 성명서에서 153 그는 "우리보다 에코 어드벤처 업계에 훨씬 오랫동안 있었던 Igloo Ice Explorer나 Eco-World Travel Company 같은 인기 있는 회사와 함께 나란히 탁월한 여행사 중의 하나로 인정받은 것은 너무나 영광스럽습니다"라고 말했습니다.

어휘 issue (잡지, 책) 호, 판　rate 평가하다, 등급을 주다　make the list 목록에 오르다, 순위에 오르다　demonstrate 보여주다, 시연하다　commitment 헌신, 전념　rewarding 보람 있는　memorable 기억에 남을 만한　whale-watching 고래 보기　sledding 썰매 끌기　fun-filled 즐거움이 가득한　be delighted to ~하게 되어 기쁘다　statement 성명, 언급　release 발표하다　be honored to ~하게 되어 영광이다　preeminent 탁월한　alongside ~와 함께, 나란히

151 Quest Out 여행사가 〈Adventure Wilderness Magazine〉에 의해 선택된 이유는 무엇인가?
(A) 지역에서 가장 인기 있는 여행사 중의 하나이다.
(B) 경쟁업체보다 환경에 좀 더 헌신한다.
(C) 다른 여행사보다 더 많은 야외 활동을 제공한다.
(D) 오래 기억에 남을 여행을 기획한다.

해설 두 번째 단락에서 'offering tour participants a rewarding and memorable experience'라고 언급하고 있으므로 (D)가 정답이다.

어휘 select 선택하다　be committed to ~에 전념하다　competitor 경쟁업체　be likely to ~하는 것 같다

152 Quest Out 여행사에 대해서 언급되지 않은 것은?
(A) 여행 비용이 많이 든다.
(B) Milwaukee에 근거를 두고 있다.
(C) 여행자들을 스키 여행에 참여시킨다.
(D) 소유주는 Campbell Hargrove이다.

해설 'Milwaukee-based Quest Out Tour Agency'에서 (B)가 언급되었고 'They range from canoeing, hiking, and cross-country skiing, to bird-watching, whale-watching, and dog sledding'에서 (C)가 언급되었고, 'The owner of Quest Out, Campbell Hargrove'에서 (D)도 언급되었다. 언급되지 않은

153 Eco-World Travel Company에 대해 알 수 있는 것은?
(A) 여행자들을 외국으로 데려간다.
(B) 업계에 상당히 오래 있었다.
(C) 야외 활동을 제공하지 않는다.
(D) Quest Out 여행사만큼 인기 있지 않다.

해설 마지막 문장에서 'Eco-World Travel Company, which have been in the eco-adventure business much longer than we have'라고 언급하였으므로 정답은 (B)이다.

어휘 destination 목적지　quite a while 한동안

[154-155]

Sean Renault [오후 2시 30분]	154 이사회 회의 때문에 회의실에 장비 설치 중이에요. 그런데 노트북 선을 찾을 수가 없어요.
Natalie Albright [오후 2시 32분]	어떤 선을 이야기 하는지 잘 모르겠어요.
Sean Renault [오후 2시 35분]	컴퓨터를 프로젝터에 연결하는 거요. 없어진 것 같아요.
Natalie Albright [오후 2시 37분]	전에도 그런 적이 있어요. 155 금방 하나 가지고 갈게요. 다른 것은요?
Sean Renault [오후 2시 39분]	프로젝터 리모컨도 있을 텐데요. 그것도 찾을 수가 없네요.
Natalie Albright [오후 2시 43분]	그것도 가져갈게요.
Sean Renault [오후 2시 45분]	고마워요.

어휘 set up 설치하다　board meeting 이사회 회의　hook up 연결하다　missing 분실된　in a few minutes 곧, 금방　remote 리모컨　grab 쥐다, 갖다　as well 또한

154 Renault 씨가 Albright 씨에게 연락한 이유는?
(A) 이사 회의 날짜를 확인하기 위해서
(B) 회의 안건을 토의하기 위해서
(C) 장비에 대한 도움을 요청하기 위해서
(D) 행사 장소를 확인하기 위해서

해설 오후 2시 30분에 Renault 씨가 'I'm setting up the conference room for the board meeting, but can't find the cable for the laptop'이라고 한 것으로 (C)가 정답임을 알 수 있다.

어휘 verify 확인하다　venue 행사 장소

155 오후 2시 37분에 Albright 씨가 "전에도 그랬어요"라고 한 것은 어떤 의미인가?
(A) 장비가 왜 교체 되었는지 알고 있다.
(B) Renault 씨가 어떤 케이블이 필요한지 알고 있다.
(C) 컴퓨터가 고장이라고 생각한다.
(D) 그녀의 실수를 인정한다.

해설 'I'll bring one down in a few minutes'라고 이어서 말한 것으로 정답이 (B)임을 알 수 있다.

어휘 out of order 고장난　acknowledge 인정하다

[156-157]

수신: Sandy Baxter (001-555-0129)
발신: Marco Connelly (002-555-9801)
날짜: 7월 23일 오전 10시 1분

안녕, Sandy. 우연히 사무실에 일정표를 두고 왔어요. Chester Systems 주소가 거기 있어요. 156 나에게 그 주소를 보내주겠어요? 오늘 오후에 거기서 사장님을 만나기로 했어요. 157 또한 Rogers and Master Express 주식회사의 계약서를 당신 책상에 두었어요. Paul Rogers에게 정오 전에 배달 부탁해요. 고마워요!

Marco

어휘 accidentally 우연히　planner 일정표, 다이어리

156 메시지를 쓴 목적은 무엇인가?
(A) 회의를 취소하기 위해
(B) 정보를 요청하기 위해
(C) 새로운 일정표를 요청하기 위해
(D) 약속을 잡기 위해

해설 'Could you send me the address?'라고 썼으므로 (B)가 정답임을 알 수 있다.

157 Baxter 씨가 해야 하는 것은?
(A) 고객에게 메시지를 전하는 것
(B) Chester Systems 사무실로 가는 것
(C) Rogers 씨를 위해 계약서를 작성하는 것
(D) 서류를 전달하는 것

해설 'Please deliver the contract to Paul Rogers'라고 썼으므로 정답은 (D)이다.

[158-160]

수신: 모든 직원들
발신: Linda Meyerson, Meyerson Lighting Company 회장
주제: 사무실 이전
날짜: 4월 30일

158 Meyerson Lighting Company는 지난 2년 동안 경이적인 성장을 경험해 왔고, 그것은 사업에는 좋은 일이지만 또한 우리가 이곳 역사적인 Creston Building의 공간을 넘어서 성장해 왔다는 것을 뜻합니다. -[1]-. 3월 29일 회사 회의에서 토의했듯이, 우리는 최근에 수리된 Barnet Building을 구매하기 위해 협상 중이었습니다. 4월 14일에 우리는 판매자와 합의에 도달했다는 것을 기쁘게 알려드립니다. 160 Barnet Building 시설은 추가 사무실, 회의실, 몹시 필요했던 제조 공간까지 제공하며 현재 위치의 거의 2배의 크기입니다. -[2]-.

Barnet Building은 우리의 현재 위치에서 단지 2킬로미터 떨어져 있습니다. 5월 16일 목요일, 이사 시에 우리를 도와줄 Kalamar & Murray 전문 이사업체와 계약을 했습니다. -[3]-. 159 다음 주에 우리는 각각 개인이 책임져야 할 짐 싸기, 이사하는 주의 전체적인 일정 설명이 포함되어 있는 이사에 대한 정보가 있는 특별 꾸러미를 모든 직원들에게 제공할 것입니다. -[4]-. 159 사무실, 회의실, 제작 공간의 배치를 보여주는 Barnet Building의 요약도와 새로운 사무실 배정도 또한 제공될 것입니다. 5월 13일에는 모든 직원들이 실내에 익숙해지기 위해서 새로운 건물을 방문하는 것을 환영합니다. 우리의 목표는 가능한 한 빨리 업무를 재개하는 것입니다.

새로운 시설에서 여러분을 만나기를 기대하고 있습니다.

어휘 phenomenal 경이로운, 감탄스러운 outgrow 넘치게 성장하다 historic 역사적인 as discussed 토의했듯이 negotiation 협상 be happy to 기쁘게 ~하다 reach an agreement 합의에 도달하다 much-needed 몹시 필요한 present 현재의 contract 계약하다 mover 이삿짐 회사 provide A with B A에게 B를 제공하다 containing ~을 포함하는 move 이사 description 설명 be responsible for ~에 대해 책임지다 packing 짐 싸기 comprehensive 종합적인 timeline 시간에 따른 일정 layout 배치 become acquainted with ~에 익숙하게 되다 resume 재개하다 look forward to ~을 기대하다

158 Creston Building에 대해서 알 수 있는 것은?
(A) 더 넓은 공간을 갖기 위해 수리되었다.
(B) 4월에 다른 조명 회사에 판매되었다.
(C) Meyerson Lighting Company가 처음으로 사업을 시작한 곳이다.
(D) 원래 Meyerson Lighting Company의 창고로 사용하려던 곳이다.

해설 첫 번째 단락에서 'we have outgrown our original space here in the historic Creston Building'이라고 언급했으므로 (C)가 정답임을 알 수 있다.

어휘 intend to ~로 의도되다 storage 보관, 창고

159 직원들이 받게 될 묶음에 포함되는 것으로 언급된 것이 아닌 것은?
(A) 짐 싸기 안내
(B) 자세한 일정
(C) 건물 도표
(D) 새 위치로 가는 길안내

해설 'what each person will be responsible for packing and a comprehensive timeline for the week of the move'에서 (A), (B)가 언급되었고 'sketches of the Barnet Building that show the layout of offices'에서 (C)도 언급되었으나 (D)는 언급되지 않았으므로 (D)가 정답이다.

어휘 packing 짐 싸기 diagram 도표

160 [1], [2], [3], [4]로 표시된 위치 중 다음 문장이 들어가기 적절한 곳은?
"우리는 이제 빠르게 증가하는 고객 맞춤 조명 수요를 충족시키기 위해서 생산량을 증가할 수 있을 것입니다."
(A) [1]
(B) [2]
(C) [3]
(D) [4]

해설 [2] 앞에서 'The Barnet Building facility is almost double the size of our current location, providing additional offices, conference rooms, and much-needed manufacturing space'라며 기존의 시설 규모를 설명하는 내용은 이제 수요를 맞출 수 있다는 제시문의 내용과 연결되므로 정답은 (B)이다.

어휘 meet the demand 수요를 충족시키다 rapidly 빠르게 growing 증가하는 custom-designed 고객 맞춤의

[161-164]

수신: altongilman@carroltonbusinesspost.com
발신: agonzalez@endayafoundation.org
주제: 오늘의 기사
날짜: 6월 12일

Gilman 씨에게

162 Carrolton Business Post의 오늘 자 신문에 난 기사에 감사드립니다. 저희 단체는 우리의 다음 번 기금 모금 행사에 대해서 아주 자세하게 써 주셔서 기뻐하고 있으며 신문사 사진작가가 찍은 우리 건물 사진도 마음에 듭니다. 저희는 기사가 가져올 홍보 효과를 기대하고 있습니다. 161 그러나 한 가지를 명확히 하고 싶습니다. 우리 연사의 이름은 기사에 쓰여진 대로 "Ferriz"가 아니라 Milo Ferris입니다.

당신이 매일 마감의 압박을 163 직면하고 있다는 것을 알고 있지만 161 162 내일 자 호에 작은 정정 공지를 내는 것이 너무 늦지 않았기를 바랍니다. 혹시 다른 기자가 당신 기사를 참고해서 Ferris 씨의 이름을 잘못 작성하는 상황을 피하고 싶습니다. 164 추가로, 만약 원래 판을 업데이트할 수 있으면 수정이 된 후에 그것을 저희에게 이메일로 보내 주시면 감사하겠습니다. 우리는 다른 뉴스 단체가 이용할 수 있는 저희의 온라인 미디어 세트의 일부로 기사를 이용하고 싶습니다.

감사합니다.

Alicia Gonzalez
Ben Knight

어휘 issue (잡지, 신문) 호, 판 organization 조직, 단체 be pleased that ~에 기뻐하다 upcoming 다음의 fundraising 기금 모금 행사 in detail 자세하게 publicity 홍보 clarify 확실히 하다 realize 깨닫다 face 직면하다 pressure 압력, 압박 correction 수정, 정정 notice 공지 reference 참고하다 inaccurately 부정확하게 accessible 이용할 수 있는

161 이메일의 목적은 무엇인가?
(A) 구독을 취소하기 위해서
(B) 수정을 요청하기 위해서
(C) 다음 행사를 홍보하기 위해서
(D) 새로운 단체 회원을 추천하기 위해서

해설 지문의 첫 번째 단락에서 'I do, however, want to clarify one point. Our speaker's name is Milo Ferris, and not "Ferriz," as written in the article'이라고 언급하며 두 번째 단락에서 'I'm hoping that it is not too late to print a small correction notice in tomorrow's issue'라고 하였으므로 정답은 (B)이다.

162 Carrolton Business Post에 대해 사실로 추정되는 것은?
(A) 독자 칼럼이 있다.
(B) 최근에 자선 행사에 자금을 지원했다.
(C) 매일 출판된다.
(D) 비즈니스 행사 정보를 공개한다.

해설 첫 번째 문장에서 'your article in today's issue'와 두 번째 단락에서 'Tomorrow's issue'라고 언급한 것으로 (C)가 정답임을 알 수 있다.

어휘 charity 자선 모금 행사

163 두 번째 단락, 첫 번째 줄의 "face"와 뜻이 가장 가까운 것은?
(A) 직면하다
(B) 특징으로 하다
(C) 반대하다
(D) 간과하다

해설 'you face deadline pressure every day'에서 face의 의미는 '마감일을 만나다, 직면하다'로 사용되므로 정답은 (A)이다.

164 Gonzalez 씨가 이메일로 요청한 것은?
(A) 출판 지침 수정본
(B) 미디어 단체 목록
(C) 추천서
(D) 기사 사본

해설 두 번째 단락에서 'I would appreciate if you could please update the original version and email it to us once the change has been made'라고 언급한 것으로 기사를 이메일로 보내 달라는 것을 알 수 있다. 따라서 (D)가 정답이다.

[165-167]

Drayton 음악 축제

다양한 멋진 음악을 즐기면서 당신의 시간을 기부하는 데 관심이 있으신가요? 그렇다면 매년 열리는 제15회 Drayton 음악 축제에 자원하세요! 올해 행사는 10월 25일부터 31일까지 Drayton 축제 마당에서 운영되며 지역의 인기 있는 165 Starroad Pop Band, Jazz Heroes, Jackson 현악 4중주단을 포함하여 50개 이상의 재능 있는 단체들의 음악이 있습니다.

자원 봉사자들은 아래의 일에 필요합니다.
- 홍보 돕기 – 167-D 전단지 디자인과 게시, 언론 발표 보내기 – 10월 시작
- 음악가들을 맞이하고 그들이 10월 23일부터 29일까지 주거 배정지를 찾는 것을 돕기. 166 모든 외부 음악가들은 이 지역 가족들의 집에 머뭅니다.
- 167-A 167-B 매표소 운영, 축제 동안 손님을 주차장으로 안내하고 일반적인 정보 제공하기

감사의 표시로 각 봉사자들은 한정판 Drayton 음악 축제 티셔츠와 4장의 무료 티켓을 받게 됩니다.

자원 봉사 지원에 관심 있으시면, 9월 17일까지 Justin Brown에게 justinbrown@draytonmusicfest.org로 연락 바랍니다.

어휘 volunteer 자원 봉사하다 annual 매년의 run 운영하다 fairground 축제 마당 talented 재능 있는 string quartet 현악 4중주 publicity 홍보 post 게시하다 press release 언론 발표 greet 인사하다 locate 찾다, 위치를 확인하다 housing 주거 out-of-town 외부 지역의 operate 운영하다 direct A to B A를 B로 안내하다 in appreciation 감사하여, 감사의 뜻으로 limited 한정된 complimentary 무료의

165 행사에 대해 나타나 있는 것은?
(A) 10월 1일에 진행될 것이다.
(B) 다양한 음악 유형이 있다.
(C) 전문 음악인에 의해 운영된다.
(D) 비 때문에 일정이 다시 조정될 수 있다.

해설 지문의 첫 번째 단락에서 'features music from more than 50 talented groups, including local favorites Starroad Pop Band, Jazz Heroes, and Jackson's String Quartet'라고 언급하고 있으므로 정답은 (B)이다.

어휘 take place 발생하다 feature ~가 (특징으로) 있다 a variety of 다양한 run 운영하다

166 공연자에 대해서 알 수 있는 것은?
(A) 중고 악기를 기부할 것이다.
(B) 행사에 자금을 제공할 것이다.
(C) Drayton의 집에서 머무를 것이다.
(D) 행사에서 중요한 상을 받을 것이다.

해설 지문에서 자원 봉사자들이 할 업무를 언급하면서 'All out-of-town musicians will be hosted by area families'를 언급하고 있으므로 정답은 (C)이다.

어휘 used instruments 중고 악기 major 중요한

167 자원 봉사자가 할 업무가 아닌 것은?
(A) 행사 공연 표 판매
(B) 음악가들을 공연 마당으로 이동시키기
(C) 관객들에게 주차장으로 가는 길 안내하기
(D) 홍보 자료 배포하기

해설 자원 봉사자의 업무로 언급된 것 중에서 'operate the ticket booth'로 (A)가 언급되었고, 'direct guests to the parking areas during the festival'에서 (C)도 언급되었으며, 'designing and posting a flyer and sending press release'에서 (D)가 언급되었으므로 언급되지 않은 (B)가 정답이다.

[168-171]

Miranda Keo 안녕, Lucy. 본사에 있나요?	오전 10시 30분
Lucy White 아직 아니에요. 지금 가는 중인데요. 왜요?	오전 10시 31분
Miranda Keo 168 170 여기 Oakwood 거리의 보도 작업 벽돌이 다 떨어지고 있어요. 창고에 남은 게 있나요? 아니라면, Hampton Plaza 창고에서 가져와야 해요.	오전 10시 33분
Lucy White Patrick이 사무실에 있어요. 지금 그를 대화에 초대할게요. 169 몇 상자가 필요한가요?	오전 10시 34분
Miranda Keo 169 12개면 될 거 같아요.	오전 10시 35분
Patrick Adams 있습니다!	오전 10시 36분
Miranda Keo 좋아요. 오늘 정오까지 필요해요. 제가 가서 가져올게요.	오전 10시 40분
Lucy White 사실, 지금 차를 세우는 중이고 Calvin 대로와 Garner 길에 있는 집의 측면 공사 작업 때문에 트럭에 짐을 실을 거예요. 벽돌도 트럭에 맞을 거예요. 다 실으면, 170 먼저 당신에게 갈게요.	오전 10시 41분
Miranda Keo 고마워요, Lucy. 그리고 Patrick, 171 일지에 제 이름과 상자 숫자를 추가해 주시겠어요?	오전 10시 42분
Patrick Adams 알겠어요.	오전 10시 43분

어휘 headquarters 본사 head ~로 가다 run out of ~이 부족하다 brick 벽돌 walkway 보도 storehouse 창고 pull in 차를 세우다 load 싣다 house-siding 주택 측면 fit 맞다 log sheet 일지

168 아마도 Keo 씨가 일하는 곳은?
(A) 건축 회사
(B) 배송 서비스
(C) 건설 업체
(D) 주택 개조 가게

해설 오전 10시 33분에 Keo 씨가 'We are running out of bricks for the walkway job'이라고 한 것으로 정답은 (C)임을 알 수 있다.

169 오전 10시 36분에 Adams 씨가 "You got it!"이라고 한 것은 어떤 의미인가?
(A) 교통이 원활하다.
(B) 정오에 도울 수 있다.
(C) White 씨가 필요로 하는 트럭이 이용 가능하다.
(D) 작업에 충분한 재료가 있다.

해설 오전 10시 34분에 White 씨가 'How many boxes do you need?'라고 질문한 후 오전 10시 35분에 Keo 씨가 'Twelve should cover it'이라고 대답한 것에 대한 반응이므로 12개가 있다는 것이다. 따라서 (D)가 정답이다.

어휘 smoothly 원활히, 부드럽게

170 White 씨는 어디로 갈 것이라고 말하는가?
(A) Oakwood 거리
(B) Hampton Plaza
(C) Calvin 대로
(D) Garner 길

해설 오전 10시 41분에 White 씨가 'When I'm done loading it, I'll come to you first'라고 Keo 씨에게 알리고 있으며 Keo 씨는 오전 10시 33분 메시지에서 Oakwood 거리에 있음을 알 수 있으므로 정답은 (A)이다.

171 Keo 씨가 Adams 씨에게 요청한 일은?
(A) White 씨에게 길을 설명하기
(B) 휴가 신청서 제출하기
(C) 물품을 정확히 기록하기
(D) 고객에게 청구할 금액 계산하기

해설 오전 10시 42분에 Adams 씨에게 'could you add my name and the number of boxes to the log sheet?'라고 한 것으로 정답은 (C)이다.

어휘 time off 휴가 accurate 정확한 keep a record of ~을 기록하다 calculate 계산하다 bill 청구하다

[172-175]

MAYHEN 은행을 보내야 할 시간

Dublin (7월 1일) – Dublin의 중앙 상업 지구에서 얼마 떨어지지 않은 Broadstone에 위치한 Mayhen 은행이 8월 31일 50년이 넘는 영업을 마치고 문을 닫을 것입니다. –[1]–.

Mayhen 은행은 개점 이후로 수천 명의 고객들을 위한 제1의 주요 재정 기관으로 역할을 해 왔습니다. –[2]–. 그러나 173 약 10년 전, 많은 사람들이 더 많은 지점과 서비스를 제공하는 지역 대형 기관들을 선호하여 지점이 하나인 기관을 떠나면서 고객 수가 급격히 하락하기 시작했습니다.

172 그러나 Mayhen 은행은 다양한 개인과 기업 은행 서비스를 제공하는 다도시 기업인 Ireland's First 은행과 성공적으로 합병을 협상함으로써 영원히 사라지는 것은 아닙니다. "우리는 모든 Mayhen Bank 고객들에게 긍정적인 은행 경험을 제공할 것을 기대하며 그들을 고객으로 맞게 되어서 기쁩니다"라고 Ireland's First 은행의 운영 담당 책임자인 Adam Petrovich가 말했습니다. –[3]–.

175 이전 Mayhen 은행 고객들은 은행 계좌와 대출에 대한 더 넓어진 선택 사항을 포함해서, 합병 이후에 몇몇 새로운 상품과 서비스를 이용할 수 있게 될 것입니다. –[4]–. 172 174 합병은 Mayhen 은행의 남아 있는 500명의 고객이 원하는 Ireland's First 은행 지점으로 옮겨 가는 다음 달 말에 완료될 것입니다.

어휘 short distance 짧은 거리 business district 상업 지구 close a door 폐점하다 serve as ~로 일하다 primary 주요한, 제1의 financial 재정의 institution 기관, 조직 significant 상당한, 큰 decline 쇠퇴, 감소 in favor of ~을 더 좋아하는 for good 영원히 multicity 다도시 corporation 기업 commercial 상업의 operating officer 업무 담당자 former 이전의 expanded 확장된, 넓어진 remaining 남아 있는 switch ~로 전환하다, 바꾸다

172 기사의 목적은 무엇인가?
(A) 은행의 개점을 공지하기 위해서
(B) 지역 업체에 대한 고객 후기를 요청하기 위해서
(C) 고객들에게 영향을 주는 새로운 정책을 보고하기 위해서
(D) 두 업체의 합병을 알리기 위해서

해설 기사의 대부분이 Mayhen 은행의 합병 과정에 대해 설명하고 있고 기사 마지막 부분에서 'The merger will be completed at the end of next month'라고 했으므로 정답은 (D)이다.

어휘 affect ~에 영향을 끼치다 publicize 공표하다, 알리다 merger 합병

173 Mayhen 은행이 많은 고객을 잃은 이유는?
(A) 너무 많은 수수료를 청구했기 때문에
(B) 지점이 너무 적었기 때문에
(C) 직원들이 훈련이 잘 되지 않았기 때문에
(D) 주중에 너무 일찍 문을 닫았기 때문에

해설 두 번째 단락에서 'many left the single-branch institution in favor of larger ones in the area that offered more branch locations and services'를 언급한 것으로 정답은 (B)이다.

어휘 well trained 훈련이 잘 된 weekdays 주중

174 Mayhen 은행에 대해 언급된 것은?
(A) 약 500명의 고객이 있다.
(B) 10년 전에 문을 열었다.
(C) 사장이 곧 사직할 것이다.
(D) 이전에 Ireland's First 은행이라고 불렸다.

해설 마지막 문장에서 'Mayhen Bank's 500 remaining customers'라고 하였으므로 (A)가 정답이다. 첫 번째 단락에서 'over 50 years of being in business'라고 했으므로 (B)는 오답이며 (C)와 (D)는 언급되지 않았다.

어휘 resign 사직하다 formerly 이전에

175 [1], [2], [3], [4]로 표시된 위치 중 다음 문장이 들어가기 적절한 곳은?
"추가로, 모든 Mayhen 고객들은 계좌가 전환되면 곧 Ireland's First 은행으로부터 환영의 선물로 40달러의 무료 상품권을 받게 될 것입니다."
(A) [1]
(B) [2]
(C) [3]
(D) [4]

해설 제시문에 'Additionally'가 있으므로 추가된 사항임을 알 수 있으므로 혜택을 설명하고 있는 'Former Mayhen Bank customers will have the availability of several new products and services after the merger, including expanded options for banking accounts and loans' 뒤에 위치하는 것이 문맥상 자연스러우므로 정답은 (D)이다.

어휘 additionally 추가로 complimentary 무료의 transfer 전환하다

[176-180]

수신: Parker 보험사 직원 여러분
발신: Aoto Kintoshita, 인사부
날짜: 9월 1일
주제: NWMS 제휴

176 직원 감사 프로그램의 일환으로 Parker 보험사는 직원들에게 할인된 휴대폰 요금을 제공하기 위해 New Way Mobile Service(NWMS)와 제휴하였습니다. 179 NWMS에서 개인이나 가족 서비스 상품 개설로 전환하는 직원들은 사용 첫 달에 각각 휴대폰 요금을 20%(개인)나 25%(가족)를 절약하실 수 있습니다. 177 추가로 계정 서비스 요금은 면제될 것입니다. 월 사용 상품은 1년 동안이며 취소하지 않는다면 1년 더 자동으로 연장될 것입니다.

이 제안을 이용하고 싶은 직원들은 321-555-0123번으로 NWMS 소비자 서비스 부서로 연락해 주십시오. 신청은 www.nwms.com/corpsaving에서 온라인으로도 접수됩니다. 월 사용 과정을 시작하기 위해서, 178 직원들은 직장 이메일 주소와 직원 번호를 제공하여야 합니다. 추가로, 면허증이나 여권처럼 고유 ID 번호가 있는 정부 기관 발급의 증명서뿐만 아니라 유효한 신용 카드 번호를 제출할 준비를 해 주세요.

NWMS 소비자 불만 사항 양식

고객 세부 사항

이름: Edward Boulanger

계좌 번호: BA834-1

날짜: 12월 3일

이메일 주소: eboulanger@parkerinsurance.com

불만 세부 사항

지난 10월에 Parker 보험사 직원 대상 특별 할인에 대해서 알고 나서 휴대폰 상품을 개설했습니다. 회사에서 받은 홍보 자료에 따르면 서비스를 시작하기 위한 계정 서비스 비용이 청구되지 않았어야 합니다. 신청할 때 저와 전화상으로 이야기했던 NWMS 직원도 이것을 확인해 주었습니다. 그럼에도 불구하고 11월 30일 자 저의 첫 번째 청구서에 서비스 수수료가 청구되었습니다. (180) 청구서에서 문제가 있는 금액을 제외하고 수정된 것을 다시 보내 주세요. (179) 물론 새 청구서는 전화 요금 25% 할인도 적용해야만 합니다.

감사합니다.

어휘 partnership 제휴 appreciation 감사 partner with ~와 제휴하다 individual 개인 respectively 각각 waive 면제하다 subscription 구독, 월 사용 automatically 자동으로 renew 갱신하다 take advantage of ~을 이용하다 application 신청 electronically 전자상으로, 온라인으로 be ready to ~할 준비를 하다 valid 유효한 carry 갖고 있다 unique 독특한, 고유한 customer complaint 소비자 불만 사항 special offer 특별 행사, 할인 promotional 홍보용의 distribute 배포하다 representative 직원 sign up 신청하다 confirm 확인하다 nevertheless 그럼에도 불구하고 erroneous 문제가 있는, 실수한 amended 수정된, 정정된 reflect 반영하다

176 메모는 무엇에 관한 것인가?
(A) 직원 복지 혜택의 추가
(B) 업무용 회사 전화 사용
(C) 휴대전화 서비스 이용 갱신
(D) 직원들의 NWMS 등록 의무

해설 메모의 첫 문장에서 'As a part of its employee appreciation program'이라고 한 것으로 직원 복지 프로그램인 것을 알 수 있고 'Parker Insurance Agency has partnered with New Way Mobile Service (NWMS) to offer employees discounted mobile phone service'라고 하였으므로 정답은 (A)이다.

어휘 benefit 복지(혜택) renewal 갱신 register 등록하다

177 계정 서비스 요금에 대해 알 수 있는 것은?
(A) 할부로 지불할 수 있다.
(B) 계정이 취소되면 환불된다.
(C) 보통 25달러이다.
(D) 무료이다.

해설 메모에서 'the account service charge will be waived'라고 하였으므로 (D)가 정답이다.

어휘 in installments 할부로, 분할로 complimentary 무료인

178 NWMS 신청에 필요한 것이 아닌 것은?
(A) 직원 번호
(B) 우편 번호
(C) 신용 카드 번호
(D) 이메일 주소

해설 메모의 마지막 문장 'employees must provide a work e-mail address and employee number'와 'be ready to submit a valid credit card number as well as a government-issued document, such as a driver's license or passport, that carries a unique identification number'에서 (A), (C) (D)는 언급되었다. 언급되지 않은 (B)가 정답이다.

179 Boulanger 씨에 대해서 알 수 있는 것은?
(A) Kintoshita 씨의 부서에서 일한다.
(B) 가족 통합 상품을 이용한다.
(C) Parker 웹 사이트에서 계정을 개설했다.
(D) NWMS에 대해서 가족에게서 들었다.

해설 연계 지문 문제이다. 메모에서 'Staff members who change to open either an individual or family service plan with NWMS will save 20% and 25%, respectively, off telephone charges'라고 한 것과 양식의 'the new bill should continue to reflect a 25% discount on phone charges'라고 언급한 것에서 정답이 (B)임을 알 수 있다.

180 Boulanger 씨가 NWMS에 요청하는 것은?
(A) 월 상품 이용 취소
(B) 수정된 회사 정책 변화
(C) 정정된 청구서 발송
(D) 할인을 친구들에게도 적용

해설 양식에서 'Please remove the erroneous fee from the bill and send me an amended version'이라고 하였으므로 정답은 (C)이다.

어휘 revised 수정된 corrected 정정된 billing statement 청구서 extend 연장하다

[181-185]

(181) Connelly Publishing House가 Randy Carmichael의 〈The Art of Daydreaming〉 전국 도서 투어를 진행합니다.
남서부 지역 – 5월 일정

(184) 5월 10일 목요일 오후 6시
Jessie's Book Haven – 500 Oak Terrace, Tucson, AZ 02116
Carmichael 씨와의 인사회가 오후 5시에 초대받으신 분들에 한해 열립니다. 낭독회는 6시에 시작이며 일반 대중에게 공개됩니다.

5월 12일 토요일, 오후 5시
Barnes and Nomads – 218 Maynard 거리, Austin, TX 78704
책 낭독회는 5시에 시작하며 바로 다음 6시에 책 사인회를 진행합니다. 일정 문제로 이번 행사에서는 질문을 받을 수 없을 것입니다.

5월 16일 수요일, 오후 6시
(182) Café Reynolds – 685 Cherry Tree 가, Houston, TX 19103
좌석이 제한되어 있습니다. www.cafereynolds.com을 방문하셔서 행사에 등록해 주세요. (182) 미리 구매 시, 표 값은 5달러입니다. 현장에서 표는 8달러에 판매됩니다.

5월 21일 월요일, 오후 6시
Jefferson Public Library – 400 Jefferson 가, New Orleans, LA 21202
참석자들은 질문할 기회를 가질 것입니다.
이후에, 모든 참가자들에게 저녁 식사 환영회가 도서관 컨퍼런스 센터에서 열릴 것입니다.

추가 사항:
- 모든 날짜, 시간, 장소는 변경될 수 있습니다.
- 다른 언급이 없다면, 매 등장마다 Carmichael 씨는 〈The Art of Daydreaming〉의 일부 낭독, 책 사인회, 독자들의 질문에 답변할 것입니다.
- 모든 행사 장소에서 〈The Art of Daydreaming〉 구매가 가능할 것입니다.
- 6월 1일에, 이후 투어 날짜와 도시가 출판사 웹 사이트와 지역 신문에 게시될 것입니다.

작가의 등장을 요청하시려면, chaywood@connellypublishing.com으로 Cecilia Haywood에게 연락해 주세요.

수신: Cecilia Haywood ⟨chaywood@connellypublishing.com⟩
발신: Jason King (185) ⟨jasonking@tucsonuniversity.com⟩
날짜: 5월 25일
주제: Carmichael 씨의 도서 투어
첨부: 질문.doc

Haywood 씨께

(184) Carmichael 씨를 Tucson으로 모시고 온 것과, 저를 공개 행사 이전 개인 환영회에 초대해 주셔서 Connelly Publishing에게 감사하고 싶습니다. 좋아하는 작가 중 한 분을 직접 만나서 이야기를 나누는 기회를 가진 것은 제게는 영광이었습니다. (185) ⟨The Art of Daydreaming⟩을 입문 심리학 수업에서 사용할 계획이어서 질문이 몇 가지 있었습니다. 그것에 대해 이야기할 시간이 충분하지 않았기 때문에 그가 질문을 당신에게 보내 달라고 제안하셨습니다. (첨부 파일을 봐 주세요.) 그리고 또 (183) Carmichael 씨를 수업에 초대해서 학생들과 이야기할 수 있는지 이야기하고 싶습니다. 매 학기마다 한 명의 초청 연사를 모시는 데 Carmichael 씨가 적임자라고 생각됩니다. 곧 소식 전해 주시기를 바랍니다.

Jason King

어휘 present 제공하다 appearance 등장 meet-and-greet 인사회 invitation 초대 book signing 책 사인회 scheduling conflict 일정이 겹침 advance 먼저, 사전 afterward 이후에 be subject to ~할 가능성이 있다 otherwise 달리, 다르게 excerpt 요약 precede 먼저 하다, 선행하다 in person 직접 introductory 입문의 psychology 심리학 forward 보내다 semester 학기

181 도서 투어에 대해서 알 수 있는 것은?
(A) 모든 행사 장소는 100명이 넘는 좌석 수용량이 있다.
(B) 초청 게스트들은 Carmichael 씨의 책을 받을 것이다.
(C) 5월 25일에 종료된다.
(D) Connelly Publishing이 기획했다.

해설 일정표의 제목에서 'Connelly Publishing House Presents Randy Carmichael's *The Art of Daydreaming* National Book Tour'로 명시하고 있으므로 (D)가 정답이다.

어휘 venue 행사 장소 seating capacity 좌석 수용 conclude 끝나다 organize 기획하다

182 입장료가 필요한 장소는 어느 곳인가?
(A) Jessie's Book Haven
(B) Barnes and Nomads
(C) Café Reynolds
(D) Jefferson Public Library

해설 일정에서 'There is a $5 advance ticket fee. Tickets sold at the door will be $8'라고 언급하였으므로 정답은 (C)이다.

183 이메일의 목적은 무엇인가?
(A) 책 출판에 대한 설명을 하기 위해서
(B) 약속 잡는 것에 도움을 요청하기 위해서
(C) 심리학 수업 정보를 주기 위해서
(D) 다른 작가들의 투어에 대해 문의하기 위해서

해설 이메일에서 'I also want to speak with you about the possibility of having Mr. Carmichael visit my class to talk to my students'라고 하였으므로 정답은 (B)이다.

어휘 instruction 설명 make an arrangement 일정을 잡다 inquire about ~에 대해 문의하다 author 작가

184 King 씨가 Carmichael 씨를 만난 날짜는?
(A) 5월 10일
(B) 5월 12일
(C) 5월 16일
(D) 5월 21일

해설 연계 지문 문제이다. 이메일 첫 문장에서 'I want to thank Connelly Publishing for bringing Mr. Carmichael to Tucson and for inviting me to the private reception that preceded the public event'라고 한 것으로 Tuscon에서 열린 도서 투어에서 만난 것을 알 수 있으므로 일정에 나와 있는 날짜인 (A)가 정답이다.

185 King 씨는 누구인 것 같은가?
(A) 교재 출판 업자
(B) 서점 주인
(C) 대학 교수
(D) 신문사 통신원

해설 이메일에서 'I am planning to use *The Art of Daydreaming* in my introductory psychology class'라고 하였고 King 씨의 이메일 주소가 'jasonking@tucsonuniversity.com'이므로 (C)가 정답임을 알 수 있다.

[186-190]

수신: 모든 Multiflex Gym 전문가들
발신: Donald Warren
날짜: 4월 22일
주제: 홍보

여러분도 알다시피, (189) 많은 Dover 대학 학생들은 여름 동안 도시에 머무릅니다. 그래서 우리는 6월의 처음 2주 동안에 등록하는 학생들에게는 여름 할인으로 1년에 30% 할인을 제공할 것입니다. 그러나 Multiflex Gym은 다가오는 여름 시즌(6월 1일-8월 1일) 동안에 신규와 지속 회원들에게 2가지 특별 할인을 제공할 것을 또한 고려 중입니다.

(186) 2가지 가능한 제안 중에서 최종 결정하기 전에 직원들로부터 이야기를 듣고 싶습니다. 첫 번째는 가족 할인을 제공하는 것입니다. 이것은 현재 회원이 가족 구성원(16세 이상)을 현재 회원 멤버십에 추가하면 (187) 일반 회원 요금보다 20% 할인해 주는 것을 뜻합니다.

두 번째는 (189) 골드 회원들이 매주 화요일과 수요일에 오전 6시부터 오후 4시까지 친구를 무료로 동반하게 하는 것입니다. 친구들은 요가실을 포함해서 전체 체육관을 다 이용할 수 있습니다. 그러나 (188) 현재 회원들이 이용하기 위해서 이미 기다리고 있는 것보다 더 대기하지 않도록 실내 골프 연습실은 출입할 수 없습니다.

회원들에게 가장 혜택을 주는 행사가 무엇이라고 생각하는지 5월 3일까지 답장 주세요.

결정 내리는 데 도와주셔서 감사합니다.

Dover College 학생들만을 위한 특별 행사를 놓치지 마세요!

6월 1일부터 8월 1일 사이에 등록하여 모든 레벨의 여름 회원 가에서 30% 할인 받으시고 개인 물병도 무료로 받으세요.

매주 화요일과 수요일에는 친구를 데려오세요:
(189) 6월 1일부터, 모든 골드와 플래티넘 레벨 회원들은 화요일과 수요일 피트니스를 방문할 때 친구를 데려올 수 있습니다. 우리 시설을 이용하기 위해서 친구들은 이름을 적고 접수원에게 유효한 신분증을 보여주어야 합니다.

Multiflex Gym

수신: Kevin Diego ⟨ksukel@bvgfitness.com⟩
발신: Bill Pullman ⟨avelez@bvgfitness.com⟩
날짜: 8월 2일
제목: 답장: 수치

Kevin,

평소처럼, 보고서 보내줘서 고마워요. (189) 골드와 플래티넘 회원이 여름 행사 시작 이후로 각각 18%가 증가한 것을 보고 짜릿했어요.

골드 레벨 회원으로 등록한 Dover 대학 학생들의 수가 많은 것이 가을에 수업이 시작할 때에도 학생 할인을 제공할 것을 고려하게 만들었어요. (190) 학교의 피트니스 시설이 내년에 다시 정비된다고 들었고 그렇게 되면 학생들은 대안을 찾게 될 거예요. 더 좋은 것은, 우리의 주 경쟁업체가 학교에서 10킬로미터 더 멀리 있다는 거예요. 그래서 우리는 학생들이 체육관을 오고 갈 때 셔틀 버스를 이용할 수 있도록 학교와 협업하는 방법을 찾고 있어요. 이것이 더 많은 학생들이 Multiflex Gym을 선택하도록 만들기를 바랍니다.

계속 공지할게요.

Bill Pullman, 영업 매니저
Multiflex Gym 회사 사무실

어휘 enroll 등록하다 continuing 지속하는 upcoming 다가오는, 곧 있을 household 식구, 가구 have access to ~에 접근 가능하다, 이용할 수 있다 driving range 골프 연습장 ensure that ~을 보장하다 reply 응답하다 beneficial 혜택이 되는 miss out 놓치다 sign up 등록하다 personalized 개인용의 for free 무료로 be thrilled to ~하게 되어 짜릿하다, 전율이 느껴지다 alternative 대체의, 대안의 competitor 경쟁업체 farther 거리가 더 먼 collaborate 협업하다 to and from 오고 가는 keep posted 계속 공지하다 corporate 기업의

186 메모의 목적은 무엇인가?
(A) 새로운 강사 고용을 공지하기 위해서
(B) 체육관 회원들에게 휴무 날짜를 알리기 위해서
(C) 직원들에게 감사하기 위해서
(D) 직원들에게 의견을 구하기 위해서

해설 메모의 두 번째 단락에서 We would like to hear from our staff before making a final decision about the two possible offers'라고 언급하였으므로 정답은 (D)이다.

187 메모의 두 번째 단락, 네 번째 줄의 normal과 뜻이 가장 가까운 것은?
(A) 일반의
(B) 평균의
(C) 자연스러운
(D) 특이한

해설 normal membership fee는 '일반 요금'이라는 뜻이므로 정답은 (A)이다.

188 골프 연습장에 대해서 알 수 있는 것은?
(A) 요가실로 전환될 것이다.
(B) 인기 있는 부분이 있다.
(C) 다른 건물에 위치해 있다.
(D) 여름 동안은 임시로 이용할 수 없다.

해설 메모에서 'the driving range for golfers would be off limits to ensure that our members do not have to wait longer than they already do for their availability'라고 하였으므로 현재 회원들이 사용을 위해 기다린다는 말은 골프 연습장이 인기 있다는 뜻이다. 따라서 (B)가 정답이다.

어휘 convert 전환하다 separate 별개의 temporarily 임시로

189 Multiflex Gym에 대해 알 수 있는 것은?
(A) 화요일과 수요일에는 무료 간식을 제공한다.
(B) 모든 가족 회원은 할인을 받을 수 있다.
(C) 플래티넘 회원들은 신청하면 티셔츠를 받는다.
(D) 많은 학생들이 여름에 친구들을 데리고 왔다.

해설 연계 지문 문제이다. 이메일에서 'I was thrilled to see that the numbers of Gold- and Platinum-level members have each increased by 18 percent since the start of the summer promotion'이라고 하였고 여기서 'summer promotion'은 광고에서 언급한 'all Gold- and Platinum-level members can bring a friend for free during their fitness visits on Tuesdays and Wednesdays'이므로 (D)가 정답임을 알 수 있다.

190 Dover 대학에서 일어날 것 같은 것은?
(A) 운동 대회가 여름에 시작될 것이다.
(B) 피트니스 전문가가 고용될 것이다.
(C) 피트니스 시설이 개선될 것이다.
(D) 피트니스 수업이 지역 사회에 제공될 것이다.

해설 이메일에서 'I have also heard that the fitness facility of the college is going to be remodeled over the next school year'라고 언급하였으므로 정답은 (C)이다.

[191-195]

Carolina 아파트 오픈 하우스 행사에 오세요!

(195) Carolina 아파트는 이번 주 금요일과 토요일, 3월 1일과 2일에 오픈 하우스 행사를 합니다. (193-B) 2년간의 공사 후에, Carolina 아파트는 거의 완성되었습니다. 그래서 사람들은 5월 초에 이사 올 수 있을 것입니다. 아직 구매나 임대 가능한 아파트가 100채 이상 있습니다. 침실 2개, 3개, 4개의 아파트 포함입니다. 가구가 갖춰진 아파트와 그렇지 않은 아파트 모두 있습니다. 하지만 가구가 있는 아파트는 임대만 가능합니다. Carolina 아파트의 시설은 최고이며, 이 주상복합 건물은 London의 (193-A) 뛰어난 학교와 주요 쇼핑 지역 가까이에 위치하고 있습니다. 누구나 오픈 하우스 행사에 참여하는 것은 환영입니다. (191) 가능한 아파트 투어가 있으며 방문객들은 전체 건물 주변도 둘러보실 것입니다. 더 많은 정보와 오픈 하우스로 오시는 길 안내는 023-555-4321로 전화해 주세요.

수신: inquiries@krausrealestate.com
발신: teresawalters@gmail.net
제목: Carolina 아파트
날짜: 3월 6일

담당자께,

(195) 지난 토요일에 Carolina 아파트의 오픈 하우스 행사에 참석했습니다. 아들들과 저는 본 것에 좋은 인상을 받았고 그곳에서 살고 싶다는 의견에 동의했습니다. 우리는 6월에 London으로 이사를 가고 앞으로 3년 동안 살 생각입니다. 그후에, 저는 회사 본사가 있는 Manchester로 이동하게 됩니다. 그것이 제가 아파트 구매에 관심을 갖지 않고 대신에 임대하는 것을 더 선호하는 이유입니다. 저는 아들들이 각자 방을 가지게 하기 위해 3개의 침실이 있는 아파트를 임대하고 싶습니다.

저는 현재 Edinburgh에 있습니다만 제가 계약서에 서명할 때는 언제나 London으로 갈 계획입니다. 아파트의 임대 가능 여부를 제게 알려 주세요.

추신: (193-D) 3개의 침실이 있는 아파트가 월 1,200파운드라고 들었습니다. 아직도 (192) 유효한가요?

Teresa Walters

수신: teresawalters@gmail.net
발신: lindakraus@krausrealestate.com
날짜: 3월 7일
주제: 답장: Carolina 아파트

Walters 씨에게,

Carolina 아파트에 대해 문의 주셔서 감사합니다. 당신처럼 많은 사람들이 이 아파트 외관을 매우 좋아하고 그래서 이 지역에서 가장 인기 있는 건물 중의 하나입니다. 이 사실 때문에 더 이상 침실 3개 아파트는 이용 가능하지 않습니다. 마지막 침실 3개 아파트가 오늘 아침에 판매되었습니다. 결과적으로 몇 개의 침실 4개의 아파트만 임대 가능합니다. 물론, 이 아파트의 임대료는 약간 더 높습니다. (193-D) 침실 3개의 아파트를 임대하는 것보다 한 달에 600파운드가 더 듭니다. 아직 관심 있으시다면, 즉시 알려 주시고, (194) 제가 환불이 불가한 보증금 100파운드를 받으면 이곳으로 오셔서 계약서에 서명할 때까지 한 채를 예약해 놓을 수 있습니다. 더 이상 Carolina 아파트에 관심이 없다면, 당신이 분명히 인정할 만한 같은 이웃에 있는 다른 몇 개의 부동산들을 소개해 드릴 수 있습니다.

Linda Kraus
Kraus 부동산 중개 업소

어휘 unit (아파트) 호, 채 furnished 가구가 갖춰진 outstanding 훌륭한 top-notch 최고의, 뛰어난 as well 또한 be impressed with ~에 감명받다, 인상을 받다 intend 의도하다, 뜻하다 headquarters 본사 prefer 선호하다 arrange ~를 계획하다 in place 유효한, 가능한 inquire about ~에 대해 문의하다 be pleased with ~에 만족하다, 좋아하다 property 건물, 부동산 no longer 더 이상 ~하지 않다 as a result 결과적으로 a bit 약간 nonrefundable 환불 불가의 neighborhood 이웃 approve of 승인하다 real estate 부동산

191 광고에 따르면 행사에서는 어떤 일이 있을 것인가?
(A) 방문객들은 둘러보게 된다.
(B) 영화가 상영될 것이다.
(C) 계약서에 서명할 것이다.
(D) 협상이 시작될 것이다.

해설 광고에서 'Tours of the available apartments will be given'이라고 했으므로 정답은 (A)이다.

192 첫 번째 이메일의 추신에서 in place와 가장 가까운 의미는?
(A) 적절한
(B) 유효하지 않은
(C) 능률적인
(D) 유효한

해설 'Is it still in place?'에서 it은 앞 문장의 rent를 가리키는 것으로 그 가격이 아직도 유효하냐는 뜻이므로 정답은 (D)이다. 형용사 'good'은 계약, 조건 등과 함께 '유효한'의 의미를 갖는다.

193 Carolina 아파트에 대해서 언급되지 않은 것은?
(A) 학교에서 편리한 곳에 있다.
(B) 현재 공사가 진행 중이다.
(C) 20층 건물이다.
(D) 침실 4개 아파트의 임대료는 1,800파운드이다.

해설 광고에서 'the complex is located near outstanding schools'와 'After two years of construction, Carolina Apartments are almost complete'를 언급하였으므로 (A)와 (B)는 언급되었다. 첫 번째 이메일의 'the rent on a three-bedroom unit is £1,200 a month'와 두 번째 이메일의 'It costs £600 more a month to rent a four-bedroom unit than it does to rent a three-bedroom unit'에서 침실이 4개인 아파트는 임대료가 1,800파운드임을 알 수 있다. 정답은 언급되지 않은 (C)이다.

어휘 story (건물이) ~층인

194 Kraus 씨가 Walters 씨에게 제안한 것은?
(A) 아파트를 구하는 것을 보장할 비용을 내는 것
(B) 이번 주말에 London으로 가는 것
(C) 임대하는 것보다 구매하는 것을 고려하는 것
(D) 더 낮은 가격의 더 작은 아파트를 구하는 것

해설 두 번째 이메일에서 'once I receive a nonrefundable payment of £100, I can reserve one for you until you are able to fly here to sign a contract'라고 언급하였으므로 정답은 (A)이다.

195 Walters 씨에 대해서 암시된 것은?
(A) 3월 2일에 오픈 하우스를 방문했다.
(B) Kraus 씨에게 이미 집세를 보냈다.
(C) 다음 달에 방 3개짜리 아파트로 이사 간다.
(D) 2년 후에 Manchester로 옮긴다.

해설 연계 지문 문제이다. 광고에서 'Carolina Apartments are having an open house this Friday and Saturday, March 1 and 2'라고 하였고 이메일에서 'I attended the open house at the Carolina Apartments last Saturday'라고 하였으므로 정답은 (A)이다.

[196-200]

Stewart Dance Company를 후원해 주세요.

Stewart Dance Company는 지난 40년 동안 호주 댄스계의 선두에 있었습니다. 우리는 공연 목록에 (197) 다양성을 제공하고 연간 100회가 넘는 공연을 제공합니다. 우리가 계속해서 이러한 일들을 할 수 있도록 여러분의 도움이 필요합니다. (196) 여러분의 재정적인 지원이 우리들로 하여금 티켓 가격을 낮게 유지하고 댄스 공연이 모두에게 다가갈 수 있도록 할 것입니다.

여러분들이 Stewart Dance Company에게 주시면, 우리는 여러분들에게 되돌려 드립니다. 여러분들이 더 많이 주실수록 우리는 더 많이 되돌려 드립니다. 회원제 프로그램 전체 목록을 보시기 위해서 웹 사이트 www.stewartdancecompany.com을 방문해 주세요. 또한 올해 공연 목록도 보실 수 있습니다.

www.stewartdancecompany.com

이력	일정	**회원 프로그램**	연락하기

실버: 49달러
혜택: 한 달에 한 번 주말 낮 공연 티켓과 댄스 잡지 (200) 〈Movement〉(연 4회 출간) 1년 정기 구독권을 받습니다.

(199) **골드: 99달러**
혜택: 한 달에 한 번 주말 낮 공연 티켓, 주중 저녁 공연 20% 할인 혜택과 댄스 잡지 〈Movement〉 1년 정기 구독권을 받습니다.

(199) **플래티넘: 199달러**
혜택: 골드 레벨 혜택, 특별 지정 좌석, (199) 저녁 오프닝 공연 티켓, 저명한 안무가이자 수상 경력의 댄스 공연 〈Dubliners〉를 감독한 Tom Roman과 (198) 연례 Stewart Dance Company 연회에서 함께 식사할 기회를 드립니다.

여러분의 기부금을 기금 모금 매니저인 Elena Gibson 앞으로 Stewart Dance Company, 199 Chestnut 거리, Sydney로 보내 주시기 바랍니다.

199 Chestnut 거리, Sydney

Gibson 씨께,

항상 그렇듯이, 올해도 Stewart Dance Company를 후원하는 기회를 갖는 것은 기쁜 일입니다. 199 200-C 작년과 같은 금액인 199달러의 기부금을 동봉했습니다.

199 200-A 200-C 우리 여행사에서 직원으로 일하고 있는 제 동료인 Karen Myers와 Justin Copperfield가 Stewart Dance Company를 후원하는 데 관심을 보였습니다. 그들은 조만간 당신에게 연락할 것이고 당신은 그들에게서 99달러의 후원금을 받게 될 거예요.

200-B 작년 행사에 참여해서 멋진 시간을 보냈으므로 올해 Stewart Dance Company 연회에도 반드시 참석할 것입니다. 멋진 공연의 또 다른 시즌을 기대하고 있습니다.

Amy Hollister
Hollister Travel
187 Howell St, Birmingham, Sydney

어휘 forefront 선두 repertoire 공연 목록 present 제공하다 annually 매년 enable ~을 가능하게 하다 keep up 유지하다 financial 재정적인 maintain 유지하다 accessible 다가갈 수 있는, 익숙한 view 보다 matinee 낮 공연 subscription 정기 구독 reserved 지정된, 예약된 dine 식사하다 choreographer 안무가 direct 감독하다, 지휘하다 award-winning 수상 경력의 fund-raising 기금 모금 as always 항상 그렇듯이 enclose 동봉하다 colleague 동료 currently 현재 in the near future 조만간 definitely 확실히, 분명히

196 전단지의 주요 목적은?
(A) 사람들에게 댄스 공연에 가는 것을 권장하기 위해서
(B) 대중들에게 기부를 요청하기 위해서
(C) 새로운 댄스 잡지의 출간을 알리기 위해서
(D) 사람들을 시상식에 초대하기 위해서

해설 전단지의 첫 번째 단락에서 'Your financial support will allow us to maintain low ticket prices and keep dance performances accessible to everyone'이라고 언급하였으므로 정답은 (B)이다.

197 전단지의 첫 번째 단락, 두 번째 줄의 variety와 뜻이 가장 가까운 것은?
(A) 다양성
(B) 차이
(C) 오락
(D) 변화

해설 offer great variety in은 '~에 다양성을 보여 주었다'라는 뜻이므로 정답은 (A)이다.

198 Stewart Dance Company에 대해서 알 수 있는 것은?
(A) 하루에 2번 댄스 공연을 운영한다.
(B) 최근에 안무가 Tom Roman을 고용했다.
(C) 매년 연회를 개최한다.
(D) 기금을 모금하기 위해서 공연을 열 것이다.

해설 웹 페이지의 'the annual Stewart Dance Company banquet'에서 (C)가 정답임을 알 수 있다.

어휘 banquet 연회 raise funds 기금을 모금하다

199 Myers 씨가 받지 못하는 Hollister 씨의 혜택은?
(A) 입장료 할인
(B) 저녁 오프닝 공연 무료 티켓
(C) 잡지 정기 구독
(D) 주말 낮 공연 티켓

해설 연계 지문 문제이다. 편지에서 'I have enclosed a donation in the same amount of $199 as last year'라고 하였으므로 Hollister 씨는 플래티넘 회원임을 알 수 있고 'They will contact you in the near future and you will be receiving donations of $99 from both of them'이라고 한 것으로 Myers 씨는 골드 회원임을 알 수 있다. 웹 페이지에서 골드 회원과 플래티넘 회원을 비교해 보면 잡지 정기 구독과 주말 낮 공연 티켓은 공통되는 혜택이지만 저녁 오프닝 공연 티켓은 플래티넘 회원만을 위한 혜택이므로 (B)가 정답이다.

200 Hollister 씨에 대해 사실이 아닌 것은?
(A) Myers 씨와 함께 일하고 있다.
(B) Stewart Dance Company 연회에 이전에 참여한 적이 있다.
(C) Copperfield 씨보다 많은 돈을 기부한다.
(D) 매달 〈Movement〉 잡지를 받을 것이다.

해설 편지에서 'My colleagues, Karen Myers and Justin Copperfield'라고 하였으므로 (A)는 사실이고 'since I had a great time in joining last year's event'에서 (B)도 사실인 것을 알 수 있으며 'I have enclosed a donation in the same amount of $199 as last year'와 'you will be receiving donations of $99 from both of them'에서 (C)도 사실임을 알 수 있다. 웹 페이지에서 〈Movement〉는 연 4회 발행되므로 정답은 (D)이다.

MEMO

MEMO

나혼자 끝내는 新 토익

FINAL 실전 모의고사

LC+RC 5회

- 최신 출제 경향을 완벽 반영한 실전 모의고사 5회분 수록
- 문제집과 해설집이 한 권으로 구성된 LC+RC 합본 실전서
- 정답/오답 이유, 패러프레이징, 문제의 키워드를 단숨에 파악하는 핵심 강의 해설집 수록
- 전문 성우의 발음을 통한 미국식, 영국식, 호주식 발음 완벽 대비
- 실전용·복습용·고사장 버전의 3종 MP3 무료 다운로드
- 까다로운 호주, 영국 발음 대비 추가 MP3 제공
- 청취력 향상 및 핵심 구문을 복습하는 받아쓰기 테스트 제공
- 정답만 입력하면 점수를 바로 확인할 수 있는 자동 채점 시스템 제공

} QR코드 & 홈페이지

- 신토익 빈출 어휘 리스트 & 테스트지 제공 ▶www.nexusbook.com